C0-CEW-069

Information Analysis in
Management Accounting

**Wiley Series in
Accounting, and Information Systems**

Consulting Editor   John W. Buckley

Buckley and Buckley
The Accounting Profession

Buckley, Nagaraj, Sharp, and Schenk
Management Problem-Solving with APL

DeCoster, Ramanathan, and Sundem
Accounting for Managerial Decision Making, 2nd

Estes
Accounting and Society

Estes
Corporate Social Accounting

Hill
Information Processing and Computer Programming: An Introduction

Kircher and Mason
Introduction to Enterprise: A Systems Approach

Largay and Livingstone
Accounting for Changing Prices

McCullers and Schroeder
Accounting Theory: Text and Readings

McCullers and Van Daniker
Introduction to Financial Accounting

McCullers and Van Daniker
Contemporary Business Environment: Readings in Financial Accounting

Mock and Vasarhelyi
APL for Management

Patz and Rowe
Management Control and Decision Systems

Seidler
Social Accounting: Theory, Issues, and Cases

Seidler, Andrews, and Epstein
The Equity Funding Papers: The Anatomy of a Fraud

Sethi
The Unstable Ground: Corporate Social Policy in a Dynamic Society

Vazsonyi
Finite Mathematics/Quantitative Analysis for Management

Information Analysis in Management Accounting

Donald L. Anderson
California State University, Northridge

Donald L. Raun
California State University, Northridge

JOHN WILEY & SONS, New York • Chichester • Brisbane • Toronto

List of Authors

American Accounting Association Committee on Managerial Decision Models; Committee on Information Systems

Donald L. Anderson, *California State University, Northridge*

Henry R. Anderson, *California State University, Fullerton*

F. A. Bailey, *University of Manchester (England)*

George J. Benston, *University of Rochester*

Harold Bierman, Jr., *Cornell University*

P. F. Bourke, *Associate of Royal Melbourne Institute of Technology*

Richard S. Bower, *Dartmouth College*

William J. Bruns, Jr., *Harvard University*

Edwin A. Bump, *Eastern Washington State College*

Howard B. Burdeau, *Management Consultant*

Richard M. Burton, *Duke University*

Roger Clayden, *Management Consultant*

A. Wayne Corcoran, *University of Massachusetts*

Joel S. Demski, *Stanford University*

Peter Dohrn, *Commonwealth Development Finance Company, Ltd., (London)*

William L. Ferrara, *The Pennsylvania State University*

Lawrence E. Fouraker, *Harvard University*

Horace R. Givens, *West Virginia University*

Richard A. Grosse, *Xavier University*

Jack C. Hayya, *The Pennsylvania State University*

Frank C. Herringer, *Bay Area Rapid Transit District*

David B. Hertz, *McKinsey and Company, Inc.*

Richard F. Hespos, *Dun & Bradstreet, Inc.*

H. Peter Holzer, *University of Illinois at Urbana-Champaign*

William C. House, *University of Arkansas*

V. Bruce Irvine, *University of Saskatchewan*

Robert K. Jaedicke, *Stanford University*

Patrick S. Kemp, *Oregon State University*

John M. Kohlmeier, *Arthur Anderson & Co.*

Donald A. Krueger, *(deceased) Arthur Andersen & Co.*

Yow-Min R. Lee, *California State University, Northridge*

Robert D. Neimeyer, *Haskins & Sells*

Mohamed Onsi, *Syracuse University*

George G. C. Parker, *Stanford University*

Donald L. Raun, *California State University, Northridge*

Alexander A. Robichek, *Stanford University*

W. R. Ross, *The University of Texas at Arlington*

C. Stevenson Rowley, *Arizona State University*

Edilberto L. Segura, *International Bank for Reconstruction and Development*

Paul A. Strassman, *Xerox Corporation*

Robert J. Thierauf, *Xavier University*

Richard E. Trueman, *California State University, Northridge*

J. Peter Williamson, *Dartmouth College*

James D. Willson, *formerly with Tidewater Oil Company, Los Angeles*

This book was set in Melior by Graphic Typesetting Service and printed and bound by Halliday Lithograph. It was designed by Bernice Glenn, copyedited by Ruth Glushanok and illustrated by Graphics Two. The cover was designed by Jack Schwartz and production was supervised by Chuck Pendergast.

Library of Congress Cataloging in Publication Data

Main entry under title:

Information analysis in management accounting.

    1. Managerial accounting—Addresses, essays, lectures. I. Anderson, Donald L. II. Raun, Donald L.

HF5635.I45   658.1'513   77-14938

ISBN 0-471-02815-0

Printed in the United States of America

10 9 8 7 6 5 4

About the Editors

Donald L. Anderson, Ph.D., is Professor and Coordinator of Accounting Graduate Studies at California State University, Northridge. He has received the Distinguished Professor Award from the University and the Outstanding Accounting Professor Award from the University's Accounting Association. He holds the M.A. in Economics and the Ph.D. in Business Administration (major field, accounting) from the University of Minnesota. He has public accounting experience with Peat, Marwick, Mitchell & Co., and while studying for the doctorate, taught at the University of Minnesota. Professor Anderson is a member of the American Accounting Association, American Institute for Decision Sciences and the National Association of Accountants. During his term as Director of Manuscripts for the San Fernando Valley Chapter of the NAA, the Chapter placed first in the nation in the manuscript category; for his work with the Chapter, he has received the Manuscript and Most Valuable Member awards. Professors Anderson and Raun are the co-authors of other accounting works including a previous book, prepared for use in the management accounting and information systems courses.

Donald L. Raun, M.B.A., CPA, is Professor of Accounting and Information Systems at California State University, Northridge. He served as the first Chairman of the Division of Business and was instrumental in the development of the University Computer Center and the School of Business Administration and Economics. His degrees are from Stanford University. Professor Raun is a member of the American Accounting Association and has received the National Association of Accountants Certificate of Merit for manuscript writing. His articles about management accounting and information system subjects have appeared in the *Accounting Review* and *Management Accounting* and a number of the articles appear in readings collections. He is the author of four textbooks.

PREFACE

Management accountants have a responsibility to provide management with something more than data. They have a responsibility to provide analyzed data or useful information for specific purposes. The purpose of management accounting is to aid management in:

a. The evaluation of the overall results of management decisions—the measurement of income for management evaluation;
b. Analyzing alternative decision problems;
c. Planning—including long-range planning and preparing plans and budgets for a coming period;
d. Control and performance evaluation of enterprise activities.

Because management accounting systems should provide information that is most useful to the various levels of management of an enterprise, management accounting education requires considerable emphasis upon the understanding of the following aids to management decisions, planning, control, and evaluation:

a. Model building. A model is a tool used to summarize the effects and relationships of relevant factors of a specific problem. In this sense a model may be a method of analysis, or more commonly, a system of measuring the relevant factors for a business decision and summarizing the results of varying the relevant factors or variables.

b. Mathematical and statistical tools. These tools are used for constructing and testing models.

c. Computers for analysis. The computer can make it feasible for management to use mathematical and statistical tools and a major importance of the computer rests with its application in the area of model building.

For solving management problems, the "scientific management" method of investigation, analysis and decision is aided by the application of quantitative techniques and computers. This book includes introductory and advanced articles concerned with behavioral, mathematical, statistical, and computer applications for the solution of management accounting problems in decision making, planning, and control.

It can be used in advanced courses and has been successfully used by the editors for an accounting course concerned with planning and decision making where students were not required to have a background other than an introductory course in financial accounting, and where they had not necessarily completed courses in statistics, quantitative analysis, and/or computers. Introductory text materials and problems are provided to meet the needs of students who have little or no background in quantitative methods or computers. Advanced text materials and problems are included to enable instructors to provide the depth they desire for their courses. Selected CPA and CMA application questions are included in Appendix B. The application questions were not an afterthought; rather, the collection of articles was chosen to aid the reader in understanding the topics and in solving the application problems.

The articles in the book about quantitative techniques acquaint the readers with basic mathematical and statistical tools for solving management accounting problems, and aid them in selecting and applying appropriate tools of analysis for specific problems. A computer can accomplish mathematical and statistical analyses automatically, and a user of a computer program that is designed to accomplish a mathematical or statistical analysis needs to be able to interpret the results of a computer printout solution; the use of a computer for analysis is integrated with the discussions in the different sections of the book. It is very important, however, that a user of quantitative tools should understand the limitations and pitfalls in the application of specific techniques, and additional courses in quantitative analysis and statistics are appropriate for this purpose. These courses also acquaint students with additional useful methods of analysis.

If properly programmed, a computer can aid managers in making an analysis and can quickly perform required computations for the analysis. Computers have created an era in which it is now feasible to apply mathematical and statistical techniques to many types of management accounting problems as aids to decision making, planning, and control; only a few years ago, without computers, the application of these analytical tools was completely impractical or impossible.

The editors thank the authors and copyright holders for permissions given to reprint their material. We thank the American Accounting Association, the American Institute of Certified Public Accountants and the National Association of Accountants for their kind responses to our numerous requests. We thank our colleagues, Yow-Min R. Lee and Albert W. Wright, for their suggestions and cooperation in the development of this book, and we thank John W. Buckley, University of California, Los Angeles, John T. Crain, Wiley/Hamilton, Santa Barbara, and Don T. DeCoster, University of Washington, Seattle, for their constructive recommendations.

Donald L. Anderson
Donald L. Raun

Los Angeles, California

Contents

ONE
Project Profit Planning

ALTERNATIVE DECISION PROBLEMS

QUANTITATIVE AND COMPUTER APPLICATIONS
FOR ALTERNATIVE DECISION ANALYSIS

DECISION MAKING AND BEHAVIORAL
CONSIDERATIONS

Period profit planning (budgeting—the subject of Part II of this book) cannot be completed without the solution of project or alternative decision problems, such as whether to make or buy products or parts, sell or process products further, add or drop product lines or departments, the price to charge for additional orders (the subjects of Part I), and equipment replacement decisions (the subject of Part III, Capital Budgeting). Quantitative decision models can be used to aid management in making these decisions.

Various relevant factors used in quantitative decision models may be expressed in cost terms. The cost figures needed for decision purposes are estimated future costs since the decisions are being made for a future period. The past or historical costs may be analyzed by management in an attempt to determine possible relationships for use in developing the future cost estimates (see Part IV, Forecasting), but the past costs are not the relevant decision-making costs.

Article 1, "What Does It Cost?" provides an introduction for Part I, the project-planning section of the book. The article emphasizes the concept of relevancy, i.e., that management requires different cost information to meet different needs, and discusses relevant data for income measurement, cost control, profit planning and tailor-making cost data for various decision-making purposes (i.e., alternative decision problems). For the latter, the article gives examples of special order, sell or process further, and replacement of machine problems. The make or buy decision and a drop decision about a product line are listed in the special decisions section but are not discussed in the article. The make or buy decision is covered in Article 3 and the drop decision is covered in Article 2, "Contribution Margin Analysis by Company Segments—Three Uses." Article 2 also provides complementary information for the performance evaluation discussion in Article 1 and Part V of this book (Performance Evaluation and Control).

For internal reporting purposes, statements that emphasize the contribution approach and relevant costs can be used for decision making and to reflect the plans and performance of product lines, departments, sales territories, and other segments of an organization. For example, statements can be prepared to show relevant information such as sales minus controllable costs (this can be used to focus attention on cost control), incremental revenue minus incremental cost (this can be used for decisions such as adding orders or processing products further), lost sales or decremental revenue minus avoidable costs (this can be used for decisions such as dropping products or departments), and income statements can be prepared that show a contribution margin.

Under the contribution margin approach, income statements are prepared that separate costs into fixed and variable components. This form of statement emphasizes the importance of cost behavior patterns for planning and control purposes. For example, contribution margin information is used in breakeven analysis. The contribution margin can be determined as sales minus the variable cost of goods sold (direct material, direct labor, and variable overhead) and the variable selling and administrative costs of earning revenue (see Article 1). Thus, the contribution margin or *marginal income* is the excess of sales price over variable costs. The contribution margin may be expressed as a total, on a per-unit basis, or as a ratio. Variable costs can be identified as those that vary in total and in direct proportion (the latter is the case where straight-line cost functions are used for relevant ranges) with some measure of activity or volume. A relevant range is the band of activity over which cost and revenue relationships remain valid. A variable cost fluctuates in total but is constant per unit over the relevant range of activity. In contrast, fixed costs do not change in total for a given period of time and range of activity, but on a per-unit basis vary inversely with changes in volume.

For project decision problems, such as to add products, drop products, sell or process further, make or buy products or components, the costs that are relevant are those that change with the decision, and differential costs (i.e., incremental or decremental costs) are compared with the change in sales revenue. Differential costs may be the same as variable costs, but they may not involve all costs that are classified as variable and they may include some costs that are usually classified as fixed but that have to be added for the particular decision alternative.

Articles 3 through 6 involve mathematical and statistical applications, computer applications and behavioral considerations in alternative decision problems.[1]

Article 3, "To Buy or To Make," includes the traditional cost accounting approach for this decision analysis. However, the make or buy decision can be a complex problem that involves many variables; the authors of the article apply linear programming for an analysis involving two products and two production facilities. If background information about linear programming is needed by the reader as an aid to understanding this application, see Article 30.

Article 4, "Lease Evaluation," presents a discussion of different considerations involved in leasing and includes a flow chart for translating a quantitative method of lease evaluation into operating instructions for making a decision. The method is applied to a sample problem and a time-sharing computer system is used for the step-by-step calculations. The article includes sensitivity analysis where the effect of changes in problem parameters is shown for the comparison of the lease with the purchase

---

[1]An article by Michael S. Morton and Andrew M. McCosh, "Terminal Costing for Better Decisions," *Harvard Business Review*, May–June 1968, pp. 147–156, is concerned with the applicability of computer time-sharing for such purposes as pricing, make or buy, return on investment, and short-term sales emphasis decisions. This article explains the use of time-sharing and includes computer printouts for an illustrative problem.

For an article that analyzes the decision process, considers behavior on the part of the decision maker, and incorporates utility, probability, and the concepts of personalistic and impersonalistic control as these relate to the decision process, see Samuel Eilon, "What Is a Decision?" *Management Science*, December 1969, pp. B-172–B-189.

alternative; the characteristics of the computer system applied for the problem facilitate sensitivity analysis.

Since the future costs and revenues included in decision models need to be estimated, these models do not necessarily have the precision that a quantitative answer may imply. Because of uncertainty as to the future, managers may include probabilities in decision models. The determination of an expected value for alternatives is presented in Article 5, "Illustration of Model of Cost and Value of Information." The article includes decision trees and along with "Cost-Volume-Profit Analysis Under Conditions of Uncertainty," an article in Part II, provides background information for another Part II article, "Toward Probabilistic Profit Budgets."

The topic of behavioral considerations in decision making is discussed in Article 6. The importance of behavioral considerations for management accounting analyses is indicated by the following quotation from "The Report of Committee on Managerial Decision Models," contained in *The Accounting Review Supplement to Vol. XLIV,* pp. 46–47:

> ... , the *Statement* [*A Statement of Basic Accounting Theory*—AAA] assertion that "accounting information could usefully be expressed in probabilistic terms" (p. 55) contains the implicit assumption that the user will be more likely to make "better" decisions with probabilistic rather than with deterministic information. Certainly a more complete decision model may be specified using probabilities, but do users deal with probabilities in a consistent, "rational" way, as every good "economic man" should? The information specialist should know the answers to such questions before giving unqualified support to any particular timing, summarization, format, or configuration of information.
>
> The increasing use of mathematical decision models has some intriguing behavioral ramifications. Dehumanization of specific planning and controlling functions occurs when mathematical models and computers are used. Therefore, at least for the specific activities being analyzed, the human problem disappears as activities are finely programmed and computerized. But there are still many behavioral problems. How does the use of more rules and models affect the organization as a whole and the managers who determine the inputs to the models?

Article 6, "Accounting Information and Decision-Making: Some Behavioral Hypotheses," emphasizes that if accounting information is perceived as relevant to a decision maker, it may affect decisions. In the article, decision makers are classified for the purpose of providing insight into how they might judge the relevance of accounting information for their decision models. A manager's perception of the significance of accounting information for decisions is affected by the relevance of information that may be available from sources other than the accounting information system. In addition to Article 6, behavioral articles are included in Parts II and V, and references for additional behavioral articles are included in the Part V introductory discussion.

1.
WHAT DOES IT COST?*

P. F. Bourke

It is generally accepted that the purpose of cost accounting is to provide data (incorporating costs and income) to enable product costing for inventory valuation and profit determination, and for planning and control. Cost accounting is a highly developed quantitative device for helping managers select and reach their objectives. It is a means to an end, the end being decision making.

So the above points are really sub-objectives, as the justification for the management accountant's existence is the aid he gives management in making decisions. The decision maker requires from the management accountant relevant information in the right form at the right time. I stress the word *relevant*.

COST TERMINOLOGY

A multitude of terms has arisen to describe different types of costs. One wonders whether the variety of terms is not more confusing than illuminating, particularly when a good proportion of them have no uniform and precise definition, and their meaning often varies from enterprise to enterprise and accountant to accountant.

All these terms qualify the concept of cost in an endeavour to make the meaning of the particular cost known, or rather, to describe a particular concept of cost.

---

*From the *Australian Accountant*, April 1969, pp. 176–182. Reprinted by permission.

THE CONCEPT OF COST

Two definitions of "cost" are given below:

(a) "Cost means economic sacrifice measured in terms of the standard monetary unit incurred, or potentially to be incurred, as a consequence of business decision."[1]

(b) "Cost is a general term for a measured amount of value purposefully released or to be released in the acquisition or creation of economic resources, either tangible or intangible."[2]

All costs are not measurable in monetary terms as these definitions imply. However, in a business situation as many factors as possible must be quantified, for quantitative factors are the bases on which the manager makes his decision.

The definitions quoted above are broad because of the complexity of the nature of cost. The term requires specific qualification to make its meaning clear, as the items to be included in a particular concept of cost depend on the conditions under which the costs are required to be measured and the purpose for which the measurement is required. That is, there is no single concept of cost that is applicable in all situations.

THE CONCEPT OF RELEVANCY

Different costs for different purposes or different cost concepts for different situations, I would term "the concept of cost relevancy." If this concept is not observed by the management accountant, the data he provides is valueless for the question at hand. It would be interesting to analyse and trace decisions, both good and bad, back to the cost data on which they were based.

It is likely that a good many decisions which have had undesirable results could be traced to cost data prepared without the understanding, or application, of the concept of cost relevancy.

MANAGERIAL NEEDS

Management requires different cost information to meet different needs in different situations. What are these situations and what are their needs? There are four distinct business needs, in the managerial sense, i.e.:

[1]*Handbook of Modern Accounting Theory*, Morton Backer.
[2]Executive Committee of the American Accounting Association, *The Nature of Business Cost—General Concepts*.

1.   Income measurement
2.   Cost control
3.   Profit planning
4.   Special situations requiring special decisions.

It is important that the data provided for these needs be relevant because there are different ways of handling the same cost data for the same purpose, but with different results. This is highlighted by the direct costing controversy.

DIRECT COSTING AND ABSORPTION COSTING

Probably the easiest way to define each of these approaches to cost accounting is to describe the difference between them.

The philosophy of direct costing holds that only variable production costs are "inventoriable," as they are the only costs that are created because of the manufacture of a product unit. These are often called product costs.

Fixed factory or production costs are related to capacity to produce and thus to time. They are not generated by the production of a specific product unit, and generally they are not varied by fluctuations in the level of production. These are sometimes called period costs.

The absorption costing view is that inventories should carry a fixed cost component, because both fixed and variable costs are necessary to produce. Therefore both of these costs should be attached to products and inventoried regardless of the difference in their behavioural patterns.

It seems relevant to ask: Do either of these approaches provide the framework from which any of the multitude of cost concepts can be extracted to meet the concept of cost relevancy?

A modern cost system is surely based on standards, irrespective of whether it employs direct or absorption costing techniques, or whether the nature of its business requires the use of job or process costing methods. Such a cost system will equally as surely separate fixed from variable cost components and have established behavioural patterns for those costs.

Therefore, the real issue between the two approaches relates to periodic income determination through inventory valuation.

THE MEASUREMENT OF
INCOME—INVENTORY VALUATION

Both direct costing and absorption costing approaches seem illogical in one way or another. If we accept the point that fixed factory costs should be assigned to products and inventoried, is that as far as we should go?

Why should fixed costs other than factory costs not be included in inventory: for example, administrative costs? Substantial administrative costs are generated by the same factors as fixed factory costs: for example, certain senior executive salaries, the Accounts Section, the Supply Department, Stock Records and Costing. Surely a good proportion of these costs are applicable to products on the same basis as are factory costs. What logical reason is there for drawing an imaginary line, on one side of which fixed costs are added to products and find their way into inventories, while on the other side, fixed costs are written off against the period in which they were incurred, irrespective of the reason for their incurrence?

The only explanation appears to be one of practical expediency. It seems the accountant has enough problems in allocating fixed factory costs to products on the basis of some predetermined notion of capacity, without having to do the same thing with other fixed costs.

The theory of direct costing is equally illogical. Are variable production costs the only true product costs? If this view is accepted, a rather ridiculous situation can arise. For example, a product manufactured on an operator-controlled machine is subsequently converted to an automated process involving high cost machinery, with no variation in material costs or variable manufacturing costs per unit, and the direct labour costs become part of the fixed cost associated with the machine. The result, therefore, is that the inventory cost would be reduced from direct materials, plus direct labour, plus variable manufacturing expenses to direct materials, plus variable manufacturing expenses only, simply because of a change in the method of manufacture.

The principal argument that the benefits of fixed costs expire with the passage of time and therefore must be absorbed by the revenues of the period to which they relate, ignores the point that the facilities represented by those costs are value creating.

The time period certainly receives the standby benefit of the facilities but actual production receives the usage benefit. The product cannot be manufactured without these facilities. They add value to the product, and the value is normally recovered in the selling price. It is therefore illogical that the unit of product does not carry the cost of facilities used.

So much for the lack of logic in these approaches. We now come to the question of relevance. To determine what costs are relevant in terms of inventory, we must first establish what inventory is. Inventory is universally accepted as an asset, and an asset could be defined as "an economic resource devoted to business purposes within a specific accounting entity. It is an aggregate of service potential available for or beneficial to future operations." Therefore, we could say that:

> Any cost is an asset if it will have a favourable economic effect on future costs or revenue.
> If a given cost will not influence either total future revenue or total future costs, it is not an asset.

Since this is so:

Variable costs are relevant and inventoriable, because they have been incurred and the necessity to incur them again has been obviated.

Fixed costs are inventoriable only when utilisation of these costs will have a favourable economic effect on the future. That is, when failure to produce now will lead to additional costs or loss of revenue in the future.

Inventories are designed *solely* for future economic benefit. Goods are retained in inventories for the purpose of being available for sale in the future, whether it be tomorrow, next week or next month. Therefore, fixed costs are relevant and inventoriable, and it is suggested that relevant fixed costs in this concept include fixed costs other than those classified as manufacturing expense.

COST CONCEPTS FOR CONTROL

Cost data is required by management so that responsibility for cost incurrence can be identified. This requires a system of accounting which ensures that costs are accumulated by levels of responsibility within the organisation structure—and that each supervisor may be held accountable for the costs over which he has control, and the authority to incur.

For control purposes, other cost concepts, e.g., those used in product costing, are irrelevant. Only those costs directly controllable by a given level of managerial authority within a given time period are relevant. Controllable costs are not synonymous with variable costs nor are non-controllable costs synonymous with fixed costs.

Cost controllability is a matter of degree and is determined by (a) the managerial area of responsibility involved, and (b) the time period under review.

For example, a factory manager may have authority to purchase specified raw materials, in which case the raw material price may be controllable by him because he can influence it. On the other hand, the foreman responsible to the factory manager may have a strong influence on the usage of that raw material, but no influence on its price. So raw material usage is controllable by the foreman. If the factory manager entered into a set price contract, say for six months, then price is non-controllable by him for any period less than six months, but possibly controllable beyond that period.

It is important to remember that it is often the physical cost generator which is the relevant factor for control. The monetary unit is merely attached to the physical unit and simply follows the usage fluctuations of that physical unit.

An allocated (indirect) cost item, whether fixed or variable, is irrelevant, as is any direct fixed cost over which the respective supervisor has no con-

A Relevant Periodic Income Statement

	COMPANY $000		DIVISION A		SEGMENTS DIVISION B		DIVISION C	
	B	A	B	A	B	A	B	A
Net Sales	$3,200	$3,000	$1,800	$1,500	$1,000	$1,000	$400	$500
Less Standard Variable Manufacturing Cost of Sales	1,560	1,500	720	600	600	600	240	300
Standard Manufacturing Margin	$1,640	$1,500	1,080	900	400	400	160	200
Less Standard Cost Variance	—	20	—	6	—	4	—	10
Actual Manufacturing Margin	$1,640	$1,480	1,080	894	400	396	160	190
Less Variable Selling and Administrative Costs	492	440	360	300	100	100	32	40
Contribution Margin	$1,148	$1,040	720	594	300	296	128	150
Less Direct Controllable Fixed Costs	385	380	210	200	100	100	75	80
Performance Margin	$763	$660	510	394	200	196	53	70
Less Direct Non-Controllable Fixed Costs	140	140	80	80	20	20	40	40
Segment Margin	$623	$520	430	314	180	176	13	30
Less Joint Costs	270	270	—	—	Not Allocated		—	—
Net Unadjusted Profit	$353	$250						
Add (Deduct) Standard Fixed Cost Content of Inventory Variation	(3)	5	—	10	—	—	(3)	(5)
ADJUSTED NET PROFIT	$350	$255	430	324	180	176	10	25
Standard Fixed Costs Content of Inventory Variation								
Standard Fixed Costs in Opening Inventory	$56,000	$50,000	$26,000	$20,000	$20,000	$20,000	$10,000	$10,000
Standard Fixed Costs in Closing Inventory	53,000	55,000	26,000	30,000	20,000	20,000	7,000	5,000
ADJUSTMENT	$(3,000)	$5,000	—	$10,000	—	—	$(3,000)	$(5,000)
Standard Fixed Cost Absorption								
Actual Fixed Cost	$405,000	$400,000	$227,000	$220,000	$100,000	$100,000	$78,000	$80,000
Allocated as S.C. to Production	390,000	380,000	210,000	200,000	100,000	100,000	80,000	80,000
UNABSORBED & INCLUDED IN ABOVE FIGURES	$15,000	$20,000	$17,000	$20,000	—	—	$(2,000)	—

Exhibit 1

trol. Only direct variable costs (which should be measured in both quantity and price if possible) and direct fixed costs which the given manager can influence within the time period under review, are relevant.

THE INCOME STATEMENT

The conventional income statement, produced by either direct costing or absorption costing, often fails to distinguish between fixed and variable costs, controllable and non-controllable costs, direct and indirect costs, and joint (common) and separable costs. These distinctions are vital for judging performance and for various marketing, manufacturing and financial decisions.

The direct costing controversy is an excellent illustration of the need for accountants to realise that no single version of inventory cost or income will be a valid guide to interpretation and action under all circumstances.

The income statement should be designed to facilitate its multi-purpose use. It should be designed to focus on the appropriate data for appraisals of performance. It should not aim to produce one income figure, because the singular concept of income is obsolete. It should be relevant to the multipurpose requirements of modern management.

An income statement (see Exhibit 1) provides basic overall data which can be used for the following purposes:

> Performance appraisal
> Disclosing the effect of changes in cost, price and/or volume on
> profit
> Disclosing the effect of fluctuating inventory levels on profit
> Determining the impact on profits of two or more contemplated
> courses of action.

The income statement is only relevant if it reflects the effect on profit of all of the activities of the business. Fluctuations in the level of production can only be shown through sales and/or inventory variations. In Exhibit 1, the effect of inventory fluctuations on periodic profit is highlighted by separating the standard fixed cost content of that inventory variation.

In addition to highlighting the effects of inventory build-up (or reduction) on profit, Exhibit 1 has other features:

> (a) The contribution margin for the business and for segments is shown. This figure is important for decision making in particular. However, its use must always be considered in the light of the limiting factor, e.g. machine capacity, labour hours, etc.

> (b) The performance margin is particularly helpful in judging performance by segment managers, particularly when used in conjunction with the contribution margin. Direct controllable fixed costs are sometimes termed programmed costs, that is, they are relatively fixed costs arising from managerial policy decisions.

Whilst they have no particular relation to any base of activity, they are controllable at least when they are planned. Such costs include advertising, sales promotion, engineering, research, management consulting and supervision costs.

(c) The segment margin is computed after deducting direct fixed costs which are generally non-controllable in the short run, for example, depreciation, insurances, certain executive salaries, rates and taxes, etc. This figure is helpful as an indicator to long-run segment profitability but should not influence appraisals of current performance. A segment is any line of activity of the business for which cost and income data is required. In Exhibit 1, they have been called divisions, but they can be products, branches, departments, territories, customers, order sizes, distribution channels, etc.

(d) The effect on profit of alternative courses of action can be easily seen; e.g. increase or decrease in volume, price variations, changes in product mix, etc. Through variations of the contribution margin, the effect of such alternatives is disclosed on the net unadjusted profit figure.

(e) Joint costs are not allocated to segments as such allocation serves no useful purpose. These costs include those which have no clear relationship to segments and cannot be separated in any meaningful manner. However, attempts should be made to ensure that joint costs are really joint or common before giving up the attempt to identify them with particular segments.

PROFIT PLANNING

Profit planning is nothing more than a series of decisions between alternative courses of action. The sum total of such decisions is the optimum plan of operations, having regard to operating conditions, financial limitations and long-term objectives.

Planning involves answering questions such as: "What would happen if the sales mix were changed this way or that? If we reduced the selling price of product X? If we increased advertising by X amount of dollars? If we changed our distribution methods to such and such? If we installed an automated machine process instead of the manual controlled machine process?" and so on.

Planning deals with the future and the alternatives considered are alternatives of the future. So, future costs are relevant costs in the planning function. However, all future costs are not necessarily relevant: only those future costs which will be different under each of the alternatives considered are relevant. For example, a company is considering rearranging its finishing plant facilities with the aim of reducing direct labour costs per

	Finishing Plant	
	UNCHANGED	REARRANGED
Direct material per unit	$10	$10
Direct labour per unit	$5	$4
Variable overhead cost per unit	$3	$3
Total fixed costs per month	$1,000	$1,100
Production level per month	400 units	400 units
Cost of rearrangement	—	$500

Figure 1

unit of product. This rearrangement will generate additional fixed costs for the department concerned, will reduce direct labour costs per unit by 20% and is estimated to cost $500 (see Figure 1).

All of the costs shown in Figure 1 (although based on historical costs, which are irrelevant) are expected future costs. But the relevant costs are direct labour per unit, total fixed costs and rearrangement costs, for they are the only ones which are different.

Whatever costs are used within whatever framework, such as cost-volume-profit analysis, must be future costs to be relevant.

PRICING

Few businesses are in a position where costs are the only factor in determination of pricing policy. It is my experience that accountants and businessmen think costs influence pricing decisions, but their actions show that customer demand and competitor behaviour are the prime factors in determining pricing policy.

Price levels, in the main, are set in the market-place, and are subject to three main influences: customers, competitors and costs.

A businessman must examine his pricing problems through the eyes of his customer. The customer cannot be forced to buy a company's product. He can reject it and turn to competitors' or substitute products, for any of a variety of reasons.

Rivals' reactions, or lack of reactions, will also influence pricing decisions. Knowledge of the competitors' costs is important. Knowledge of his plant size, technologies and operating policies, help in estimating his costs, for it is often his costs that are relevant, not your own.

In the long run, all costs must be recovered through selling prices, otherwise the business will fail. In the short run, the minimum price should never be below the variable costs of accepting the order. Costs may determine the minimum price, but have no bearing on the maximum price, for the maximum price is the one which will not drive the customer away.

Where a company has discretion in price setting, customer demand at various price levels determines the sales volume. In this situation, cost-volume-profit analysis is useful in pricing decisions within the framework of market conditions, elasticity of demand, production capacity and competitors' reaction. When such is not the case, a company ordinarily accepts the price range that competition has set, and selects the level of production and sales which maximise profit.

An understanding of the interplay of price, cost and volume is a key factor in pricing. The cost-plus formula, often stated to be the most popular method, is in most situations the wrong approach, for several reasons:

It ignores demand. What the market will pay bears no necessary relationship to the cost incurred by the manufacturer.

It involves circular reasoning. Unit cost depends on volume which depends on price.

It fails to adequately reflect competition. That is, what competitors' prices are and what alternative products are available and their price.

Finally, and most important, the costs are often irrelevant. Not current costs or past costs but future costs are required. Relevant costs are future costs, whether they be unit variable, total variable or total fixed costs.

Often the relationship of cost to price is inverted. That is, costs are tailored to fit selling prices. An excellent example is in the case of timber components for metal windows. The market volume is known, as is the market price range, and estimates of volume can be determined for given price levels. Having determined the price, costs are determined as follows:

Predetermined acceptable market price	$14
Less Desired contribution margin	$4
Unit variable cost	$10
Less Variable manufacturing, selling and distribution costs (including direct labour)	$2
Unit material costs	$8

Materials are sought which will produce an acceptable quality article at a cost not exceeding that determined by the above. If none can be found, then either the contribution margin and/or the price would have to be varied within the framework of the effect of such variations on volume and profit.

The study of pricing policy is complex because of the variety of influences all of which are interrelating. No one concept of cost is relevant in all pricing situations. However, two are common to all: the concept of cost variability, and the concept that relevant costs are future costs.

SPECIAL DECISIONS

Special decisions which face management are many and varied and involve choosing between alternative courses of action. Such decisions take many forms, some of which are:

> The special order.
> Make or buy.
> Sell or process further.
> Drop a product line.
> Replacement of a machine.

Let us examine examples of three of the above; the special order, sell or process further, and replacement of machine. Relevant costs in every special decision are future costs that are different under each of the alternatives considered.

The Special Order

The question is whether or not an order for 1,000 units of product at a price of $5 per unit should be accepted. The order could be fulfilled as capacity is available, and its acceptance is not likely to adversely affect the company's market (see Figure 2).

Obviously, the order should be accepted because its acceptance will contribute an extra $350 to profit. Note that the relevant costs in this example are the variable costs. Fixed costs are the same under either alternative and could be completely disregarded. The relevant figures in the example are revenue and variable costs.

Sell or Process Further

This is a fairly frequent question, whether to sell a given item at a given stage of completion or to process it further for sale at a higher price. The question in this example is whether Product B can be sold as such or processed further to make Product C. Figures involved are:

Costs of carrying on the joint process:	$36,000
PRODUCT A	
Output 10,000 lb. at $3 per lb. Sales Value:	= $30,000
PRODUCT B	
Output 10,000 lb. at $1.50 per lb. Sales Value:	= $15,000
10,000 lbs. of Product B plus $16,000 of additional processing will yield 8,000 lbs. of Product C which can be sold for a unit selling price of $4 per lb.	

Anticipated Month's Results

	WITHOUT SPECIAL ORDER	DIFFERENCE		WITH SPECIAL ORDER
SALES (20,000 units)	$140,000	1,000 @ $5 =	5,000	$145,000
FACTORY COSTS		1,000 @ $4.60 =		
Variable	92,000		4,600	96,600
Fixed	18,000		—	18,000
	110,000			114,600
GROSS MARGIN:	30,000		400	30,400
SELLING & ADMINISTRATIVE COSTS		1% $5,000		
Variable	1,400		50	1,450
Fixed	20,000		—	20,000
	21,400			21,450
NET PROFIT:	$8,600		$350	$8,950

Figure 2

If the joint costs are allocated on any basis, different and irrelevant answers will be obtained, for cost allocation and past costs are irrelevant. The relevant costs are:

a)	Lost selling price of Product B:	$15,000
b)	Additional cost of producing Product C:	$16,000
c)	The revenue from the sale of Product C:	$32,000

The calculation is as follows:

The cost of not selling Product B:	$15,000
Add additional cost of processing to Product C:	$16,000
	$31,000
Revenue from Product C (8,000 × $4.00)	32,000
Net Gain:	$1,000

The data that is relevant must include the revenue foregone by not selling the product. Costs to that point are irrelevant unless they are altered by the decision to process further. Incidentally, the same approach could be used even if Product A did not exist.

Replacement of Machine

All historical costs are irrelevant in decision making, and this includes the book value of fixed assets. On the question whether an asset should be replaced or not, the only relevant factor in relation to the asset is its disposal value, if any, and then only if the value is different under available alternatives. For example:

> We have a machine, original cost $125,000, with a disposal value of $10,000 now or $5,000 in four years' time.
> The machine has a book value of $45,000 and a remaining useful life of four years.
> A new machine is available that will cost $60,000 with a zero disposal value at the end of its four year life.
> This new machine will reduce total variable operating costs from $80,000 per annum to $56,000 per annum.
> The annual revenue of $125,000 will not be changed irrespective of the decision.
> Annual other fixed costs of $100,000 will also be unchanged irrespective of the decision.

Many accountants and managers would not replace the old machine because it would entail recognising a $35,000 loss on disposal. The calculation in Figure 3 shows that this is faulty thinking because the $35,000 loss is not relevant.

Replacement of Machine (Four Years Added Together)

	RETAIN	DIFFERENCE	REPLACE
Net sales	$500,000	—	$500,000
Variable expenses	$320,000	− 96,000	$224,000
Depreciation/write-off old machine	45,000		45,000
Proceeds from disposal	− 5,000	− 5,000	− 10,000
New machine		+ 60,000	+ 60,000
Other fixed cost	100,000		100,000
Total expenses	460,000	− 41,000	419,000
Net profit	$ 40,000	+ $41,000	$ 81,000

Net added average annual income: $\dfrac{41,000}{4} = \$10,250$

Net added initial investment: $\$60,000 - 10,000 = \$50,000$

Rate of return on added initial investment: $\dfrac{10,250}{50,000} = 20.5\%$

Figure 3

Note that the relevant figures in Figure 3 are variable expenses, disposal values of the old machine, and the cost of the new machine. The book value of the old machine is the same under each alternative and thus irrelevant.

Here the accounting method of evaluation of return on investment is used, but the more intricate compound interest technique of discounted cash flow can be used. However, for this purpose, the emphasis is on the isolation and measurement of relevant revenue and cost items.

CONCLUSION

No single concept of cost is valid under all circumstances. We need different cost constructions and income concepts for different purposes. Costs take on a useful meaning only in relation to the specific objective for which they are accumulated. Whether for income determination, planning, control, or special decisions, the cost data must be relevant.

It is the responsibility of the management accountant to learn the uses that are to be made of his data and to ensure that the data is relevant to the purposes for which it is to be used. Only then can an adequate answer be given to the question, "What does it cost?"

The ability to discard the irrelevant and dwell on the relevant is a leading characteristic of outstanding executives and should be a prerequisite for management accountants.

Do we have this ability? Or more important, do we use it?

REFERENCES

Cost Accounting a Managerial Emphasis, C. T. Horngren.

Tailormaking Cost Data for Specific Uses, W. J. Vatter.

Cost Factors in Price Making, H. C. Greer.

"Costs Included in Inventories," *N.A.A. Research Bulletin* No. 10. *N.A.A. Research Bulletin on Direct Costing* Nos. 23 and 37.

2.

CONTRIBUTION MARGIN ANALYSIS BY
COMPANY SEGMENTS—THREE USES*

Patrick S. Kemp

One of the more important tasks of modern business management is the evaluation of the performance of various segments of the business. While operating performance may be measured and reported in many different ways, the manager invariably turns to accounting data for at least part of his evaluation.

There are several types of managerial decisions which require evaluation of performance as a prerequisite. The manager may, for example, be interested in a routine examination of the month-by-month operations of the various organizational divisions of his company, both in order to control cost incurrence by responsible individuals within the organization and, possibly, to reward or penalize these lower-level managers for their operating performances. In quite a different context, he may be concerned with deciding whether or not to keep or eliminate a particular product line, department, or sales territory. Or, still differently, his decision may involve determining which products or product lines should be emphasized in the company's sales effort and which should receive less attention. In all of these cases, the business manager requires reliable, meaningful accounting data to help him in making his decision.

The word "meaningful" is a key here. Despite a good deal of accounting literature casting doubt on the results, the general inclination of businessmen, and indeed of many accountants, is still to accumulate information in such a way that each segment evaluated shows a net profit or net loss for the accounting period or periods under consideration. In other words, the approach is one of assigning to operating segments, in some reasonable and equitable manner, all costs even remotely related to them.

*From *NAA Bulletin*, November 1962, pp. 29–37. Copyrighted 1962 by National Association of Accountants. Reprinted by permission.

This approach, of course, is easily recognized by any accountant as cost allocation. While the allocation process certainly has its place in product cost determination for income measurement, it can result in misleading, and often meaningless, information for the purpose of performance evaluation. By general admission, cost allocation is never entirely accurate. At best, it can only be said to be reasonable.

Such allocation is frequently necessary for product costing purposes, but for performance evaluation two objections to it appear. First, the fact that allocation is to some degree inaccurate frequently leads to contentions that it is unfair. Second, and more important, is the theoretical objection that it is illogical to assume that it is possible for company segments to earn a profit or sustain a loss, since they are, after all, not independent operating units but merely parts of an overall enterprise. Thus, if one thinks the situation through, he frequently comes to the conclusion that the best that can be done to represent segment performance is to reflect a positive or negative contribution made to cover the overall costs and the net income of the business as a whole. This is the contribution margin approach, presentation of which forms the substance of this article.

A SIMPLE EXAMPLE OF DIFFERENTIAL ANALYSIS

Economists are frequently concerned with the inadvisability of business operations beyond the optimum level of operation. As an analytical tool in determining this optimum level, they use a concept of marginal costs and revenue to examine the profit effects of changes in volume of operations. Simply stated, the marginal cost of production is the addition to total cost incurred in producing one additional unit of product, while the marginal revenue is the addition to total revenue attributable to the sale of one additional unit. The optimum level of operations, then, is the point at which marginal cost and marginal revenue are exactly equal, since at that point total revenue will exceed total cost by the widest possible margin and total profits will be maximized. Any production and sales beyond that point will cause total profits to decline. The businessman (and, hence, the accountant), on the other hand, is seldom concerned with the result of production and sale of one additional unit. He is often concerned, however, with the results obtained through the production and sale of blocks or groups of additional units.

Thus, a tool has been developed to serve his needs in this respect. It is usually referred to as the concept of differential costs and revenue. Under this approach, differential costs are the costs associated with the production of additional blocks of units. Much more meaningful results can be obtained through the use of this technique than can be obtained by thinking simply in terms of average costs and revenues, with the averages extended to cover the additional units under consideration.

An example may serve to illustrate the use of differential analysis. Assume that a company has the following structure of costs and revenue at its current operating level of 100,000 units:

Fixed costs	$55,000
Variable costs	$2.00 per unit
Selling price	$3.00 per unit

Assume further that this company receives a request to produce and sell 10,000 additional units at a price of $2.25 per unit. To simplify the example, we will ignore the effects of inventory fluctuations. We will also assume that the cost structure will remain the same if the proposed order is accepted (that the company will be able to produce the additional units by using existing facilities and manpower) and that this order can be sold at $2.25 per unit without affecting the selling price of other units.

One's natural inclination might be to approach the problem from an average cost standpoint, resulting in the analysis shown in the top portion of Exhibit 1.

The obvious conclusion, if this is regarded as correct, is to refuse the order because it appears to result in a loss of $2,500. But this conclusion is a false and misleading one, since actually the order will result in an increase in the company's net income of $2,500, rather than a "loss" of the same amount. The differential cost analysis shown in the lower portion of Exhibit 1 gives the true results to be expected.

Using this approach, we see that the proposed order will contribute $2,500 toward covering the company-wide costs producing net income. We have already assumed that the proposed order will cause no change in the cost structure of the company. This means that the fixed costs will remain the same in total and the variable costs will remain the same per unit. We have also assumed that the selling price of other units will not be affected. If these conditions do not exist, of course, the analysis will have to be mod-

---

Average Cost Analysis for 10,000 Unit Order

Revenue ($2.25 × 10,000)		$22,500
Fixed costs ($.50 × 10,000)	$ 5,000	
Variable costs ($2.00 × 10,000)	20,000	
Total costs		25,000
Net loss		$ (2,500)

Differential Cost Analysis for 10,000 Unit Order

Differential revenue ($2.25 × 10,000)	$22,500
Differential costs ($2.00 × 10,000)	20,000
Contribution margin	$ 2,500

Exhibit 1

ified to include expected changes in the cost structure or selling price. Note also that the accuracy of the analysis depends upon the accuracy of the predictions of cost behavior. The superiority of the differential analysis over the average analysis is that the differential approach recognizes the facts of the situation rather than hiding them in totals. No new fixed costs will be incurred in filling the proposed order. Hence the analysis concentrates on a comparison of the additional (differential) revenue and the additional (differential) variable cost, yielding the differential contribution to net income.

Proof of the truthfulness of the differential approach may be obtained through a tabulation comparing the results of operations at the current level and at the new level including the proposed order. The differential analysis is repeated to furnish a link between the two levels of operations. This comparison is presented in Exhibit 2.

Once the order is accepted, of course, the 10,000 units would simply be merged for accounting purposes with all other units produced and sold by the company, with only the income statement at the 110,000 unit level to show the results of operations for the year. In other words, the company's accountants would very likely return to an average costing approach for income determination purposes, which indeed they should. Once the order is accepted, it is no different from any other order. No one is likely to suppose that the production and sale of any one order alone would result in profit or loss. Rather, each order merely makes a contribution to the net income of the entire company. This is the essence of the differential analysis concept. By comparing only differential revenues and differential costs of the order in question, we are able to view clearly the expected results.

THE DERIVED CONCEPT OF CONTRIBUTION MARGIN

In a limited sense, the proposed order in the previous example represents a segment of business operation. The same general technique will now be applied to other situations which may be more accurately described as op-

Comparative Income Statements

	CURRENT LEVEL (100,000 UNITS)	DIFFERENTIAL (10,000 UNITS)	NEW LEVEL (110,000 UNITS)
Revenues	$300,000	$22,500	$322,500
Variable costs	200,000	20,000	220,000
Contribution margin	$100,000	$ 2,500	$102,500
Fixed costs	55,000		55,000
Net income	$ 45,000		$ 47,500

Exhibit 2

erational segments of a business. Since the application of the technique to these situations varies somewhat from the economist's concept of marginal analysis and the accountant's adaptation of it as differential analysis, a new title seems in order. Due to the concentration on the contribution to net income made by the segments, the name "contribution margin analysis" appears to be descriptive and is used throughout the remainder of this article.

The primary use of the contribution margin analysis appears in situations in which the natural tendency is to attempt to allocate to segments of the business costs incurred by the business as a whole. These cost allocations are often criticized on grounds of difficulty and inaccuracy, but the most important point against their use is often overlooked. The allocation implies, theoretically, that segments of a business are capable of earning a profit or sustaining a loss on their own. But to assume that they are capable of doing so would be to assume that they are independent operating units, an assumption which simply is not true. The basic approach of contribution margin analysis is to assign to operations of these segments only those revenues and costs which are directly associated with them and to treat as costs of the entire business those costs which are actually incurred for the benefit of the entire business.

CONVENTIONAL DEPARTMENTAL
INCOME STATEMENT

In order to illustrate the use of the contribution margin approach, it is first necessary to present an illustrative situation which will embrace the assumed data necessary for further analysis. Assume that the ABC Company has three selling departments: Department A, Department B, and Department C. A conventional departmentalized income statement for this company appears in Exhibit 3.

Notice that several expenses have been allocated to the departments on arbitrary bases, while others were incurred directly by the departments. On the basis of this statement, it appears that Department C is easily the most profitable of the three departments, while Department B is sustaining a loss of $20,000. Thus it would seem that the manager of Department C should be praised for his good performance and the manager of Department B reprimanded for his poor showing. From another point of view it might seem advisable to discontinue Department B, certainly as far as profitability is concerned. Both of these conclusions are false, however, as will be shown in the following sections.

CONTRIBUTION TO COMPANY-WIDE
EXPENSES AND NET INCOME

First, let us consider a routine sort of evaluation of performance of the departments. The store manager is interested in an overall view of the profitability of the company, both by departments and in total, in order to ad-

ABC Company
Departmentalized Income Statement
Period Ended December 31, 19_1
(in thousands of dollars)

	DEPT. A	DEPT. B	DEPT. C	TOTAL
Sales	$450	$1,200	$1,450	$3,100
Cost of sales[5]	300	900	900	2,100
Gross profit	150	300	550	1,000
Advertising[1]	15	40	45	100
Administrative expense[2]	30	120	50	200
Rent[3]	15	30	15	60
Departmental wages[5]	45	100	115	260
Insurance and taxes[3]	10	20	10	40
Utilities[5]	5	10	5	20
Total expenses	120	320	240	680
Net income (loss) before taxes	30	(20)	310	320
Income taxes[4]	14		146	160
Net income (loss) after taxes	$ 16	(20)	$ 164	$ 160

[1] Allocated on the basis of sales volume.
[2] Allocated on the basis of number of employees.
[3] Allocated on the basis of floor space.
[4] Allocated on the basis of relative net income before taxes, ignoring the net loss in Department B.
[5] Incurred directly by the departments.

Exhibit 3

minister adequately the affairs of the enterprise. While the conventional income statement presented in Exhibit 3 presents a valid picture of the results of operations of the company as a whole, it misrepresents the results of operations of each of the three departments. This misrepresentation is caused by the allocation of company-wide expenses to the departments. Since the departments are not independent operating units, but simply segments of the overall operation, the executive needs some measure of performance other than profit or loss if he is to get a clear picture of departmental operations. Such a measure is the contribution margin. Exhibit 4 recasts the conventional departmentalized income statement in terms of the contribution margin.

The focus of this statement is on expenses which are direct as to the departments versus expenses incurred by the company as a whole. Thus, the contribution margin reflects a contribution made by each department to the company-wide expenses and to net income of the company. This presentation reflects acceptance of the idea that the departments are incapable of making a profit or sustaining a loss, as discussed above. Not only are the troublesome and sometimes indefensible allocations eliminated, but the statement compares operations of the three departments on a sound and reasonable basis.

ABC Company
Departmentalized Income Statement
Period Ended December 31, 19_1
(in thousands of dollars)

	DEPT. A	DEPT. B	DEPT. C	TOTAL
Sales	$450	$1,200	$1,450	$3,100
Direct departmental expenses:				
Cost of sales	300	900	900	2,100
Departmental wages	45	100	115	260
Utilities	5	10	5	20
Total direct expenses	350	1,010	1,020	2,380
Contribution margin	$100	$ 190	$ 430	$ 720
Company-wide expenses:				
Advertising				100
Administrative expenses				200
Rent				60
Insurance & taxes				40
Income taxes				160
Total company-wide expenses				560
Net income				$ 160

Exhibit 4

In appraising the results of operations of the departments, the executive finds that Department B, which appeared to sustain a net loss of $20,000 on the conventional income statement, actually makes a contribution to company-wide expenses and net income of $190,000 or about 26 percent of the total contribution. Obviously, a department (or other segment) is less likely to show a negative contribution margin under this approach to evaluation than to show a net loss under the conventional method. This does not preclude disclosure—and management evaluation—of weak segments, however, as one might conclude at first glance.

Many approaches to isolation of weak segments are possible, one being to develop standard or expected contribution margins, perhaps in terms of percentages of sales or return on investment. This might be done either uniformly for all segments, if the segments are sufficiently similar, or individually according to expectations of what constitutes satisfactory performance for each segment. Thus, if Department B were expected to produce a 15 percent contribution margin on sales, the evaluation for this period would be that this department has met the standard, since it shows a 15.8 percent margin. Department C, on the other hand, might be expected to attain a 35 percent margin. Since it shows only a 29.6 percent contribution margin, it would be judged to have fallen short of the standard for this period, even though its contribution is approximately 60 percent of the total contribution margin.

Operating departments are not the only organizational segments to which this technique is applicable. Contribution margin statements can replace conventional income statements just as effectively for sales territories, branch offices, divisions, or any other segments of a business enterprise. In fact, in any situation in which cost allocation is a problem, the use of contribution margin analysis should be investigated. Although the kinds of expenses involved may be different and the task of distinguishing between direct and indirect expenses may vary in difficulty, the basic technique is applicable.

Contribution margin analysis is frequently useful, also, in evaluating the performance of non-organizational segments. For example, management may need to decide, on a recurring, periodic basis, the product lines upon which the greatest sales effort should be placed. The basis for this decision may be relative profitability. It is clearly fallacious to assume that individual product lines can earn a profit or sustain a loss, yet this is the assumption frequently followed in product line analysis. The contribution margin approach, on the other hand, provides profitability data that are not only reliable, but also more meaningful, since only the revenues produced by the particular product line and the expenses directly associated with that line are considered.

CONTRIBUTIONS TO
NON-CONTROLLABLE COSTS AND INCOME

If the focus of executive attention were on cost control in the operating departments, rather than on overall performance evaluation, the contribution margin approach would have to be modified somewhat in order to furnish useful data to management. In this situation, the statements would be constructed so as to distinguish between expenses that are under the control of the departmental managers and those which can be controlled only at a higher level in the enterprise. In other words, we would be concerned with controllable versus uncontrollable expenses at the department level rather than with direct versus indirect expenses at that level. Thus the contribution margins would reflect departmental contributions to company-wide *controllable* expenses and net income. Comparison of incurred departmentally controllable expenses with budgetary standards would assist management in controlling the incurrence of these expenses. This controllable versus uncontrollable expense distinction would also be appropriate if the contribution margins are to be used as the basis of bonuses or other financial rewards to departmental managers. Here again, contribution margin statements would replace conventional departmentalized income statements as regularly prepared internal reports.

CONTRIBUTION TO UNAVOIDABLE COSTS AND INCOME

Looking back to Exhibit 3, we see that Department B appears to have sustained a net loss of $20,000. If similar results had occurred in the past and could reasonably be expected to occur in the future, then, based on profit and loss considerations alone, it would appear that Department B should be discontinued. A decision to discontinue the department, however, would significantly reduce the overall net income of the company, as can easily be demonstrated through contribution margin analysis.

In shifting to contribution margin analysis for this purpose, our concern is not with direct departmental expenses versus company-wide expenses, as it was in the periodic performance analysis presented in the previous section. Rather, this time we must be concerned with avoidable versus unavoidable expenses. In other words, we must determine which expenses will be eliminated if Department B is dropped, and exclude these from the computation of contribution margin for that department. Thus, the contribution margin becomes a contribution made by this department to unavoidable expenses and net income, rather than to company-wide expenses and net income.

For purposes of illustration, assume that the following results could be expected if Department B were discontinued. The cost of sales for this department, of course, would be avoided. Only part of the departmental wages would be eliminated, however, since employees earning a total of $50,000 would be shifted to other departments. None of the utilities expense would be avoided, since the other departments would expand to occupy the store space now occupied by Department B. In addition, part of the income tax expense would be avoided due to the reduction in overall net income which would occur. Based on these assumptions, a contribution margin analysis schedule for Department B can be constructed. This schedule is presented in Exhibit 5.

Department B
Contribution Margin Analysis
Period Ended December 31, 19_1
(in thousands of dollars)

Sales		$1,200
Avoidable expenses:		
Cost of sales	$900	
Department wages	50	
Income taxes	125	1,075
Contribution margin		$ 125

Exhibit 5

The contribution margin of $125,000 indicates that net income for the company as a whole could be expected to be reduced by $125,000 if Department B were eliminated. In other words, the elimination of this department would eliminate $1,200,000 in sales, but would avoid only $1,075,000 in expenses. The decision indicated is now quite different—the company cannot afford to eliminate Department B. The above result is corroborated by an income statement comparing operations of the company including Department B and projected operations without that department, with the Department B contribution margin analysis interposed as a connecting link. Exhibit 6 presents such a statement.

This type of contribution margin analysis (contribution to unavoidable expenses and net income) can be used as well in connection with decisions to drop or continue product lines, sales territories, or any other segments of a business enterprise. In addition, it may be used to aid management in decisions such as whether to produce a certain part or to buy it from an outside source, to sell a semifinished product or to process it further and then sell, etc.

The difference between this use of contribution margin analysis and that presented in Exhibit 4 should be noted. Exhibit 4 is a departmental contribution margin statement which can be used to replace the conventional departmentalized income statement as shown in Exhibit 3. Thus, this type of statement becomes a regularly prepared internal report rendered to top management for its periodic evaluation of the performances of segments of

ABC Company
Comparative Income Statements
Period Ended December 31, 19_1
(in thousands of dollars)

	WITH DEPT. B	DEPT. B	WITHOUT DEPT. B
Sales	$3,100	$1,200	$1,900
Expenses:			
Cost of sales	2,100	900	1,200
Advertising	100		100
Administrative expenses	200		200
Rent	60		60
Departmental wages	260	50	210
Insurance and taxes	40		40
Utilities	20		20
Income taxes	160	125	35
Total expenses	2,940	1,075	1,865
Net Income	$ 160	$ 125	$ 35

Exhibit 6

the business. The contribution margin statements presented in Exhibits 5 and 6, on the other hand, represent special reports prepared to aid management in arriving at particular decisions. Thus, one would not expect to find this type of report being prepared at regular intervals, but only as the need for such analysis arises.

OBJECTIVE: ANALYSIS TO FIT THE SITUATION

Based upon the economic technique of marginal analysis and its accounting derivative, differential analysis, contribution margin analysis represents a useful and logical tool for evaluating the performances of segments of the business enterprise. As a substitute for conventional profit and loss analysis by segments, the contribution margin approach not only eliminates the practical difficulty of cost allocation, but also removes the theoretical objection to the idea that segments of a business can earn a profit or sustain a loss individually.

The essence of contribution margin analysis lies in distinguishing between expenses that are relevant and irrelevant to the managerial purpose at hand. If the task of management is to appraise the results of operations generally, a distinction must be made between expenses incurred directly by the segments under examination and expenses incurred by the company as a whole. If the object is control of expense incurrence, the relevant distinction is between controllable and uncontrollable expenses at the segment level. An analysis of the advisability of eliminating or continuing a particular segment requires a distinction between avoidable and unavoidable expenses.

In all cases, the expenses relevant to the managerial decisions are compared with the revenues assignable to the segment in arriving at the contribution margin. It is important in each instance to identify the residual expenses plus net income to which the contribution margin applies.

In conclusion, the development of contribution margin analysis reflects a trend in the thinking of accountants—an increasing awareness of the opportunities and responsibilities of accountants to assist management in the decision-making process. To be sure, the accountant's task is basically one of furnishing data to be used in formulating managerial decisions, and attention must be given to adapting traditional methods of data presentation to meet the needs of modern management.

3.
TO BUY OR TO MAKE?*

Richard M. Burton
and
H. Peter Holzer

The term "make or buy analysis" is commonly used to describe special studies designed for the evaluation of alternatives involving the manufacture or purchase of products and parts. The alternatives available to a firm within this framework can be classified as follows:[1]

> 1. Make or buy a product (or a component) the firm is not currently making.
>
> 2. Continue to make or begin purchasing a product the firm is currently making.
>
> 3. Make more or less (or buy more or less) of a product the firm is currently making.

The first class of make or buy alternatives will usually involve the commitment of long-term funds; thus, it is essentially a capital budgeting problem. The second class of alternatives may or may not require long-term commitments. If no capital outlays are required and the make or buy decision involves only one product, an incremental cost analysis will usually provide sufficient quantitative data for both the second and third class of alternatives.[2] We are not suggesting that qualitative factors such as quality of the product, reliability of the vendor, etc., are not important consid-

---

*From *Management Services* (*Management Adviser*), July–August 1968, pp. 26–31. Copyright © 1968 by the American Institute of Certified Public Accountants, Inc. Reprinted by permission.

[1]See H. Bierman, Jr., *Topics in Cost Accounting and Decisions*, McGraw-Hill Book Company, Inc., New York, 1963, p. 163.
[2]Gordon Shillinglaw, *Cost Accounting Analysis and Control*, Revised Edition, Richard D. Irwin, Inc., Homewood, Illinois, 1967, p. 639.

31

erations. But we shall assume that these factors do not affect the choice between external supply and internal manufacture.[3]

In this article we consider a short-run case which might be classified under both the second and third classes of alternatives. We are considering a firm which has the capabilities and the capacity to manufacture all products internally but also has the opportunity to purchase the same products from an outside vendor. We will not consider any possibility of changing plant and equipment; thus the capital budgeting aspects of the make or buy alternatives can be disregarded. The question is whether the firm should buy the products from a vendor, make them internally, or use some combination of make and buy.

The analysis suggested in this article is quite general and may be extended to more complex situations;[4] we use a special example, however, to carry the argument and make the link between the suggested approach and the more familiar cost accounting approach. We begin by presenting the problem, then consider the cost accounting approach, and finally make the link to a linear programing model.

THE PROBLEM

Consider a small firm with two departments. In each department the normal operating time is 40 hours per week. Department 1 has fifteen machines with a normal operating time of 600 (15 × 40) machine hours per week. Department 2 has eight machines, or 320 (8 × 40) available machine hours per week.

The firm has a certain demand for its two products, each of which it can make or buy. For the present planning period, there is a certain weekly demand for 5,000 units of the first product and 4,000 units of the second product. For the firm's own facilities, the required usage coefficients (machine hours required for each unit of output) are given as follows:

	Machine Hours Per Unit	
Product	Dept. 1	Dept. 2
1	.1	.2
2	.3	.2

The firm would like to produce and purchase in a manner enabling it to meet the demand for the products at the least cost. It is assumed that the capital requirements for the alternatives to be considered do not differ significantly and can be ignored.

---

[3]For a good listing of relevant qualitative considerations see: R. I. Dickey, Editor, *Accountant's Cost Handbook*, Ronald Press Company, New York, 1960, pp. 19/14–15 or Harry Gross, *Make or Buy*, Prentice-Hall, Inc., Englewood Cliffs, N.J., 1966.

[4]We comment on generalizations later.

The cost accounting section of the firm has made available the following cost estimates:

	Variable Cost Per Machine Hour	Regular Time	Overtime
Department 1	$10.00	$15.00
Department 2	$12.00	$18.00

The raw materials costs for Products 1 and 2 are $10 per unit and $5 per unit, respectively. An outside vendor has offered to supply the firm with any quantity of Products 1 and 2 at $18.00 per unit and $12.00 per unit, respectively.

Before considering the cost accounting approach to the problem, let us indicate the decision alternatives of the problem. The firm can manufacture varying quantities of Products 1 and 2; hence there are two decision variables. Varying hours of overtime can be used in the two departments, which gives us two additional decision variables. Finally, the firm can purchase varying quantities of Products 1 and 2 from the outside vendor. Thus, there are six decision variables in the problem as given; any solution to the problem must specify these six quantities. We begin by indicating how a cost accountant may obtain a solution of the problem.

COST ACCOUNTING APPROACH

The cost accounting approach to this problem would require a careful comparative analysis of incremental costs relevant to all available alternatives. Such an analysis may well follow the format shown in Table 1 below.

	PRODUCT 1	PRODUCT 2
Dept. 1	.1 × $10.00 = $ 1.00	.3 × $10.00 = $ 3.00
Dept. 2	.2 × $12.00 = $ 2.40	.2 × $12.00 = $ 2.40
Raw Material	$10.00	$ 5.00
Total Per Unit	$13.40	$10.40

PRODUCT 1		PRODUCT 2	
Purchase Price	$18.00	Purchase Price	$12.00

Table 1. Variable Manufacturing Costs Per Unit During Regular Operating Time

Making the products is clearly the better alternative if output during regular operating time were sufficient to meet demand. A brief investigation will reveal that the capacity available during normal operating hours is not sufficient (see Table 2 on the next page).

	DEPT. 1	DEPT. 2
Product 1	500	1,000
Product 2	1,200	800
Total	1,700	1,800
Normal Operating Capacity	600	320
Required Overtime Hours	1,100	1,480

Table 2. Analysis of Machine Hour Requirements

Thus, if no outside purchases are made, overtime is required in both departments to meet the given demand. Since overtime use of the firm's facilities is an available alternative, variable costs per unit produced on overtime must be established, as shown in Table 3.

	PRODUCT 1	PRODUCT 2
Dept. 1	.1 × $15.00 = $ 1.50	.3 × $15.00 = $ 4.50
Dept. 2	.2 × $18.00 = $ 3.60	.2 × $18.00 = $ 3.60
Raw Material	$10.00	$ 5.00
	$15.10	$13.10

Table 3. Variable Manufacturing Costs Per Unit During Overtime

Table 3 would indicate that it is advantageous to buy all units of Product 2 that must be produced on overtime in both departments. To obtain the cost data for all the possible alternatives we still have to consider the combination of units produced on overtime in one department and regular time in the other (see Tables 4 and 5 below).

	PRODUCT 1	PRODUCT 2
Dept. 1	.1 × $10.00 = $ 1.00	.3 × $10.00 = $ 3.00
Dept. 2	.2 × $18.00 = $ 3.60	.2 × $18.00 = $ 3.60
Raw Material	$10.00	$ 5.00
	$14.60	$11.60

Table 4. Variable Manufacturing Costs Per Unit—Regular Time in Dept. 1, Overtime in Dept. 2

	PRODUCT 1	PRODUCT 2
Dept. 1	.1 × $15.00 = $ 1.50	.3 × $15.00 = $ 4.50
Dept. 2	.2 × $12.00 = $ 2.40	.2 × $12.00 = $ 2.40
Raw Material	$10.00	$ 5.00
	$13.90	$11.90

Table 5. Variable Manufacturing Costs Per Unit—Overtime in Dept. 1, Regular Time in Dept. 2

Thus, any combination of overtime in one and regular time in the other department yields production costs which are lower than the purchase price.

Having obtained the relevant cost data, a cost accountant would now proceed to search for the least cost combination of making and buying.

As a first step we consider the alternative of making all the demanded products with the firm's facilities. Table 3 shows, however, that all units of Product 2 produced on overtime have a unit cost ($13.10) that exceeds the purchase price ($12.00). Obviously we could reduce costs by buying some units of Product 2. As a first step we would probably buy enough units of Product 2 to eliminate its production on overtime in one department (see Table 6 below).

	DEPT. 1	DEPT. 2
Overtime Used	1,100	1,480
Per Unit Requirements of Product 2	.3	.2
Corresponding Units of Product 2	3,667	7,400

Table 6

By buying 3,667 units of Product 2 we would eliminate all overtime in Department 1; the remaining 333 units of Product 2 would be made during regular operating hours. The results of this decision can now be summarized as follows:

Make: 5,000 units of Product 1
                     333 units of Product 2
Buy: 3,667 units of Product 2
Overtime:
    Dept. 1   zero
    Dept. 2   .2 × 5,000 + .2 × 333 − 320 = 747 hours

Now we should find out whether this solution could be improved by buying additional quantities of Product 1 or Product 2. In our simple example we refer to tables 3, 4, and 5. Here we find that:

> 1. The total cost of Product 1 cannot be reduced by buying, since all combinations of manufacturing costs are less than the purchase price.

> 2. Buying additional quantities of Product 2 would mean cutting down its production at a unit cost which is less than the purchase price. We have therefore arrived at a minimum cost solution.[5]

We have shown that the intuitive yet systematic approach of what one might call traditional incremental cost analysis leads to an optimal solution of our relatively simple problem. It should be apparent, however, that the approach is rather laborious even under our simple assumptions of only two departments and two products. The number of alternatives to be analyzed would, of course, be vastly greater if we assume a more complex situation, and practical limitations would soon make the traditional approach impractical.

LINEAR PROGRAMING

The simple illustrative problem permits us to make an interesting observation. Our cost accounting approach is actually an intuitive application of the simplex algorithm for linear programs. Carefully consider each step in our analysis:

> 1. We assumed internal production of total demand requirements for both products. This required overtime in both departments. That is, of our six decision variables four are positive, i.e., production of both products and overtime in both departments, and two are zero, i.e., the purchase levels for both products. Refer to Tables 1 and 2. In the terminology of linear programing, this is a basic solution.[6]

> 2. We asked if it is less costly to change from this basic solution. In our case the alternatives were to buy one (or more) unit(s) of either

---

[5] We have only shown here that the solution is a local minimum and not necessarily a global minimum. However, for the linear programing formulation, this minimum solution can be shown to be global also.

[6] A basic solution is defined as one which contains as many nonzero variable values as there are constraints. See for example: W. J. Baumol, *Economic Theory & Operations Analysis*, Prentice-Hall, Inc., Englewood Cliffs, N.J., 1963, pp. 73 and 77. In this problem, there are four constraints: two production constraints, i.e., one for each department, and two demand requirements, i.e., one for each four variables with a positive level.

Product 1 or Product 2. In either case, this permitted the firm to make one unit less of either Product 1 or Product 2, respectively. The evaluation was to consider the manufacturing cost of each product (at the current basis) and compare it with the purchase cost. For Product 2, the internal manufacturing cost was $13.10 (refer to Table 3), and the purchase price was $12.00 per unit. Thus, it was less costly to buy one unit of Product 2 and make one unit less. Our procedure is equivalent to the optimality test of the simplex method.[7]

3. Now we want to know how many units of Product 2 should be purchased. So long as overtime is required in both departments (i.e., the basic solution above), it would be less costly to buy an additional unit of Product 2 and manufacture one unit less. We must, therefore, determine the number of units to be bought in order to eliminate overtime in both departments. In Table 6, we found that it was necessary to buy 3,667 units of Product 2 before overtime was eliminated in the first department. (Overtime is still required in Department 2.) We have now found another basic solution. (Note that we still have four positive variable values for our six variables.) In linear programing terminology, we found an adjacent basic feasible solution to the problem. This new basic solution called for:

Make:	Product 1	5,000 units
	Product 2	333 units
Buy:	Product 2	3,667 units
Overtime:		
	Department 2	747 hours

4. With this basic solution, we try to find a less costly solution. No simplex evaluation indicates a decrease in costs. E.g., to buy Product 1 costs $18 per unit, and the internal manufacture cost is $14.60 per unit (refer to Table 4). Thus, it is not profitable to buy any of Product 1. We have found the optimal solution of our problem.

FORMALIZED LINEAR PROGRAM

Previously, we indicated that there are six decision variables for this illustrative problem and four constraints. The variables are as follows:

X_1 The amount of internal production of Product 1
X_2 The amount of internal production of Product 2
O_1 The amount of overtime in Department 1
O_2 The amount of overtime in Department 2
Y_1 The amount of Product 1 bought externally
Y_2 The amount of Product 2 bought externally

[7]Ibid., p. 78.

The four constraints (stated in terms of the variables) are:

Demand Requirement Constraint:
$$X_1 + Y_1 \geqslant 5,000$$
$$X_2 + Y_2 \geqslant 4,000$$

The first constraint says that the amount made of Product 1 plus the amount bought must be at least equal to the amount required. A similar statement is appropriate for the second constraint for Product 2.

Production Constraints:
$$.1\, X_1 + .3\, X_2 \leqslant 600 + O_1$$
$$.2\, X_1 + .2\, X_2 \leqslant 320 + O_2$$

The first production constraint says that for Department 1 the production of X_1 and X_2 made must not require more than the time available on regular time (600 machine hours) plus the amount on overtime (O_1 machine hours).

Specifically, each unit of Product 1 uses .1 machine hours in Department 1, and Product 2 uses .3 machine hours per unit. A similar statement is appropriate for the second production constraint for Department 2. The above statements constitute a complete statement of the constraints for the problem. Now we consider an objective function.

Our goal is to minimize total cost. Each of the six decision variables has an associated variable cost per unit of measure. Namely, the variable costs for X_1 and X_2 are the raw material cost of $10.00 and $5.00 per unit, respectively; the variable overtime costs for O_1 of $15.00 and O_2 of $18.00; and finally, the purchase costs for Y_1 and Y_2 at $18.00 and $12.00 per unit, respectively. Thus the objective function becomes:

Minimize $10X_1 + 5X_2 + 18Y_1$
$+ 12Y_2 + 15O_1 + 18O_2$, the cost
equation for our problem.[8]

Of course, we require:

$$X_1 \geqslant 0,\ X_2 \geqslant 0,\ O_1 \geqslant 0,\ O_2 \geqslant 0,$$
$$Y_1 \geqslant 0,\ Y_2 \geqslant 0.$$

One advantage in formulating the problem as a linear program is that we can simply state what is feasible (i.e., what is possible in terms of our production constraints in algebraic terms). Also, we can state in algebraic terms our demand requirements. These two sets of algebraic statements together state what is possible and what is required. Then, we state our objective, here to minimize the total cost of overtime, purchases, and materials.

---

[8]The objective function stated here does not include the cost of operating both departments on regular time, which is considered fixed in our formulation of the problem. When using the objective function for calculating the total cost of the firm one would have to add $9,840, the cost of operating the two departments during regular time.

Once the linear program is stated, it is a mechanical process to find a solution for the linear program. This solution process is referred to as the simplex method (or simplex algorithm).

Although it is beyond the scope of this article to describe the simplex method in detail, it should be mentioned that the simplex method is discussed in very lucid terms by Baumol in his *Economic Theory and Operations Analysis.*[9] Also, there are numerous other introductory texts in operations research, mathematics for business applications, and modern accounting which develop the technique in straightforward terms. For purposes of this article, it is sufficient to indicate that the simplex method is a general technique for solving a linear objective function with an arbitrary number of variables subject to an arbitrary number of linear constraints. That is, the simplex method is not dependent upon the size of the problem. For example, the simplex method could just as easily handle the problem with twenty products and thirty departments as the problem discussed in this paper. However, this is not true of the cost accounting approach.

Consider again the cost accounting approach to the problem. For two departments and two products, there were only a few possible solutions to the problem, namely, (1) make all of both products and incur overtime in both departments; (2) buy some of one product (both products were considered in turn) and make the rest of this product and all of the other product internally, thus incurring overtime in only one department; and, (3) buy some of both products and make the remaining amount required of both products internally, incurring no overtime.

We carefully (and laboriously) considered, one by one, all of these possibilities and chose the best alternative.

ALL SOLUTIONS UNNECESSARY

For the linear programing formulation, we do not have to enumerate all the possible solutions; the simplex method selects the best solution without requiring us to think about all the possible solutions. That is, once we have the formulation as a linear program, the simplex method is a systematic method to select the best solution of all the feasible solutions. In our cost accounting approach we could easily overlook one of the possibilities, and it might be the best one. The possibility of overlooking a possible solution for our small problem is not serious, but consider the problem with twenty products and thirty departments.

To enumerate all of them would be an impossible task. But with the linear programing formulation, we can find a solution in a few minutes with the aid of a digital computer. For the small problem here, the solution was obtained on a relatively slow computer[10] in less than thirty seconds,

---

[9]Ibid.
[10]The IBM 1620.

and this reason is a primary reason for using the linear programing formulation. The optimal solution to the linear program as we formulated the problem is:

$$
\begin{aligned}
X_1 &= 5{,}000 \\
X_2 &= 333.33 \\
Y_1 &= 0 \\
Y_2 &= 3{,}666.67 \\
O_1 &= 0 \\
O_2 &= 746.67
\end{aligned}
$$

Computer programs for the simplex method are readily available on the market today. Practically all computer manufacturers who will sell you a computer will also sell you a computer program for the simplex method for the particular computer.[11]

The significance of the above discussion is that 1) the cost accounting approach is correct but unworkable for large problems; and 2) computer programs are readily available to solve linear programing problems. The advantage of the linear programing approach is not that the simplex method is more easily explained than the cost accounting approach, but that we can reasonably consider larger problems and solve them by using the digital computer in a reasonable amount of time.

CONCLUSIONS

Although not stated explicitly, it is implicit in the foregoing analysis that the linear programing approach to make or buy analysis can be extended to more than two products and more than two departments. Also, if this extension is made, the simplex algorithm can readily provide the optimal solution.

Traditional Approach Laborious

However, the more complex situation just suggested would create a rather laborious task if the traditional cost accounting approach is undertaken. The multiperiod solution adds a considerable number of variables which can be handled by linear programing but would increase considerably the computational burdens of the cost accounting approach. Likewise, variables in workforce level could be considered where there are trade-offs between hiring workers for many periods and employing these workers on regular time rather than requiring overtime for the present workforce.

In comparing the two approaches to the problem, we should keep in mind that the assumptions for both approaches are the same. Although it is more obvious for the linear programing formulation, both models assume linearity in the production processes and linearity of the cost terms.

---

[11]One example is the MPS program for the IBM 360 computer series.

Furthermore, both models assume that fixed costs and variable costs are segregated in like manner—namely, the fixed costs involve operations on regular time and the variable costs involve purchasing costs and overtime costs. One advantage of the linear programing formulation is that it is more obvious that we are making these assumptions than it is with the more traditional cost accounting approach.

Throughout this paper we have referred to the firm as the basic organizational unit. However, this type of model is equally applicable (and, perhaps more useful) for a division within a larger decentralized firm.

Not infrequently, a division is given the task of supplying the firm with a given amount (i.e., a demand requirement) of parts or subassemblies which may be made or bought at a minimum total cost.

4.
LEASE EVALUATION*

Richard S. Bower,
Frank C. Herringer,
and
J. Peter Williamson

For some years, users of industrial equipment have been offered the choice of leasing or purchasing. Estimates are that, in the decade of the 1950's equipment leasing increased 30% a year and real estate leasing 15% a year.[1] This growth record suggests there is often a genuine advantage in leasing rather than in owning equipment.

This advantage is difficult to evaluate. On the one hand many lessors claim that leasing provides "free" financing, that is, it makes equipment available without the appearance of any debt on a company's balance sheet and hence leaves the company free to borrow for other purposes. On the other hand, a growing number of financial analysts claim that leasing is in

---

*From *The Accounting Review,* April 1966, pp. 257–265. Reprinted by permission of the authors and the American Accounting Association.

[1]Data on leasing are very poor and any estimate of growth is bound to be suspect. In spite of this, there seems to be consensus that growth has been very rapid but is now slowing. The estimate for equipment leasing in the text is reported by Eugene F. Brigham, "The Impact of Bank Entry on Market Conditions in the Equipment Leasing Industry," *The National Banking Review,* September 1964, pp. 11–26. Brigham's estimate for 1960–1964 is 15% per annum. J. Fred Weston and Rupert Craig, "Understanding Lease Financing," *California Management Review,* Winter 1960, pp. 67–75, estimate growth of equipment leasing during the 1950's at 25% per annum. The estimate for real estate leasing was based on the holdings of commercial property by life insurance companies reported in *Life Insurance Fact Book,* 1964, New York: Institute of Life Insurance, 1964. This is in keeping with the source-use estimates of the Federal Reserve Board and of David Meiselman and Eli Shapiro, *The Measurement of Corporate Sources and Uses of Funds,* Technical Paper 18, New York: National Bureau of Economic Research, 1964. In making this estimate, as Meiselman and Shapiro observe, p. 59, "it is assumed that such property has been built by corporations and subsequently sold to and simultaneously leased back from life insurance companies." Since this method of estimation neglects all other real estate lessors, it must understate leasing in any one year and probably understates growth.

no sense "free" because a company's borrowing capacity is used up just as much by leasing as by ordinary debt.[2]

The purpose of this paper is to propose a new method of making the lease-loan choice.[3] This should be of interest to accountants since methods of lease evaluation have important implications for accounting. Much of the disagreement referred to in the preceding paragraph relates to the "proper" treatment of lease obligations in financial statements. Just as these statements and the judgment of accountants that lies behind them are important determinants of the attitudes of lenders and analysts towards leasing, so also the financial aspects of leasing have implications for proper accounting treatment.

LEASE ADVANTAGES

Various advantages have been attributed to leasing by lessors and financial analysts.[4] These advantages can be classified into three groups, though there is some overlap:

1. Advantages pertaining to basic cash flows (that is, after-tax inflows from operations before deduction of financing charges).[5] These could also be termed operating advantages. Examples are:

---

[2]The opposing arguments have been expressed in the *Harvard Business Review*: see, for example, Donald R. Gant, "Illusion in Lease Financing," *Harvard Business Review*, March–April 1959, and the letters of comment on this article in the May–June 1959 and July–August 1959 issues of the *Harvard Business Review*.

[3]The research leading to the development of this method was supported by grants from the Sloan Foundation and the Tuck Associates.

[4]Among the sources used to compile this list were works cited in other footnotes as well as the following: Joel Dean, "The Economics of Equipment Leasing," *University of Illinois Law Forum*, Equipment Leasing Volume, 1962; Alvin Zises, *Equipment Leasing: Its Place in the Corporate Financial Design*, a paper presented at the Graduate School of Business Administration, Harvard University, May 2, 1962; W. Bernard Thulin, "Own or Lease? Underlying Financial Theory," *Financial Executive*, April 1964; George Terborgh, *Lease-Purchase Alternatives*, Studies in the Analysis of Investment Projects, No. 5, Machinery and Allied Products Institute: Washington, 1961; Alexander P. Celia, *Financing Industrial Equipment Leases*, Credit Research Foundation, Inc.: New York, 1961; A. Tom Nielson, *The Impact of Leases on Financial Analysis*, Occasional Paper No. 10, Bureau of Business and Economic Research, Graduate School of Business Administration, Michigan State University: East Lansing, 1963; The Foundation for Management Research, *The Pros and Cons of Leasing*, The Foundation for Management Research: Chicago, 1959; various pieces of promotional material from Rochester Capital Leasing Corporation, Boothe Leasing Corporation and Cars Rental System of the World; Frank K. Griesinger, "Pros and Cons of Leasing Equipment," *Harvard Business Review*, March–April 1955; and Richard F. Vancil and Robert N. Anthony, "The Financial Community Looks at Leasing," *Harvard Business Review*, November–December 1959.

[5]An example may help to describe "basic cash flow": A firm with a $100,000 income before depreciation, interest and taxes, with $50,000 chargeable depreciation, $10,000 interest expense and a 48% tax rate would have a basic cash flow of $76,000. This is $100,000 less the tax that would be paid in the absence of any debt financing, $100,000 (1 − .48) or $52,000, plus the tax saving from depreciation, $50,000 (.48) or $24,000.

Leasing provides tax advantages through acceleration of
deductions.

Leasing permits firms that are unable to use the investment tax
credit to benefit through lower rental payments from the
lessor's ability to use the credit.

Leasing reduces accounting and maintenance costs, property
taxes, and insurance, and eases problems of asset disposal.

Leasing may permit higher charges on government contracts.

Leasing conserves cash and working capital.

2. Advantages pertaining to the uncertainties of basic cash flows
which can be called risk advantages. Among these are:

Leasing reduces risk of obsolescence and passes the risk in
residual value to the lessor.

Leasing provides uninterrupted service, avoiding down time.

Leasing permits rapid changes in equipment and simplifies
renegotiation.

3. Advantages pertaining to prior claims on the basic cash flows,
which we can also describe as financial advantages. Examples are:

Leasing permits 100% financing.

Leasing leads to junior claims, does not add debt on a balance
sheet, and is ignored by financial analysts, hence it adds to
borrowing capacity.

This classification of advantages reveals important characteristics of a
lease. It also suggests why leases are sometimes classified as either operating or financial. A firm's monthly rental of trucks is an operating lease
arrangement, while the New York Yankees' arrangement for occupying
Yankee Stadium represents a financial lease. Richard Vancil, in drawing
this distinction, describes the financial lease as one that is non-cancelable,
committing the lessee to payments which in total equal or exceed the purchase price of the property leased. The operating lease he defines as one
that is cancelable or that terminates before the lease payments have repaid
the purchase price.[6]

This distinction may be a useful one, because a lease is usually characterized by features included in only one of our three classifications. But it
may also be diverting. Almost all lease arrangements will have some financial, operating, and risk characteristics. The non-cancelable lease on
equipment will not only commit the lessee to a system of prior claims and a
series of payments which vary from those for a purchase arrangement. It
will also change the basic cash flows from the equipment and the risk of
investing in it: the timing of tax payments will change, maintenance outlays may vary, flows at the time of equipment retirement will alter, and the

---

[6]Richard F. Vancil, "Lease or Borrow—New Method of Analysis," *Harvard Business Review*, September–October 1961; "Lease or Borrow—Steps in Negotiation," *Harvard Business Review*, November–December 1961; *Leasing of Industrial Equipment*, McGraw-Hill: New York, 1963.

uncertainty of the flows may change. Similarly, a short-term rental arrangement for office space will not only affect basic cash flows. It will also involve some future commitment, even if for only a few months or years. Lease arrangements form a continuum. They all have some financial, operating, and risk characteristics. In a particular lease one may be dominant, but this does not allow us to ignore the others in making an evaluation.

To evaluate a lease properly, we must determine how cash flows and risk affect the value of the corporation, and how fixed financing charges affect the market value of the prior claims they represent and hence the market value of the owners' equity.

METHOD OF LEASE EVALUATION

The decision to enter a leasing arrangement, if it is to be rational, must be made with reference to a firm's objectives. If the principal objective is to maximize the wealth of stockholders, then our method of evaluation provides all the information necessary to make the lease-loan choice. If there are other important objectives, our method should still be helpful since it provides an estimate of the effect leasing will have on the market value of the owners' equity.

The market value of the owners' equity equals the market value of the firm less the market value of the firm's debt. The market value of the firm depends upon the stream of payments expected to be available from the firm, its basic cash flows, and the rate of discount the market applies to this stream. The market value of the firm's debt depends on the prior claims of, or payments promised to, lenders and the rate of discount.

Disagreements exist about the stream and the discount rate to be used in explaining the firm's market value, but most analysts concur that there is some mix of debt and equity which will place this value at a maximum. If a firm tends to maintain a given debt-equity structure, whether it is optimal or not, it is possible to determine the discount rate which equates market value with basic cash flows. This rate, which we label k, is a weighted average of the interest rate and the rate of return that stockholders expect, and it can be applied to basic cash flows associated with leasing to discover how the market value of the firm will be affected by the lease choice. This measures the operating advantage or disadvantage of the lease.

The non-cancelable claims included in the lease agreement can be capitalized at the rate that applies to debt—this is the interest rate designated r—to determine the market value of the lease. The difference between the market value of the lease and the loan that could replace it measures the financial advantage or disadvantage of the lease.

The rates k and r and the optimal mix of debt and equity are related to the risk in the firm's flows. If leasing changes this risk, or if reporting differences or other factors cause the market to act as if leasing changes this risk, then lease and loan alternatives can be evaluated using different rates.

When the firm's total market value and the market value of its debt taken alone are calculated in this way for the lease and loan alternatives, an estimate of the effect on owner's equity results which reflects operating, financial, and risk advantages of the lease.

This estimate is very greatly affected by the loan that is assumed to be alternative to the lease. It seems clear that the limit on debt that can be advantageously incorporated in the firm's structure is set by the expected value and uncertainty of basic cash flows in future years. With the uncertainty or risk effect of a lease's being handled by adjusting r and k as described above, the proper assumption is that a lease payment schedule of any configuration can be matched by a loan or series of loans with the same configuration. Therefore, the loan we take to be alternative to or equivalent to the lease has payments proportional to the lease payments in each period; the proportion is equal to the purchase price of the asset (the loan required) divided by the capitalized value of the lease.

FLOW CHART AND EXAMPLE

The flow chart of our method, Figure 2, and the information which must be given, Figure 1, are for a situation in which the risk of the enterprise is not affected by the lease-loan choice and in which the lease payments are noncancelable claims. The charts translate our ideas on leasing into operating instructions for making a decision. These operating instructions are next applied to a specific example.

GIVEN
LEASE PAYMENTS
$(LEPA_1, LEPA_2, \ldots LEPA_i \ldots LEPA_N)$

and
PURCHASE PRICE (PR_0)

and
LOAN RATE (r)

and
AVERAGE COST OF CAPITAL (k)

and
DEPRECIATION FOR TAX PURPOSES
$(DEP_1, DEP_2 \ldots DEP_i \ldots DEP_N)$

and
TAX RATE (TAX %)

and
OPERATING FLOW DIFFERENCE
ASSOCIATED WITH LEASING
including loss of salvage
$(\Delta OP_1, \Delta OP_2 \ldots \Delta OP_i \ldots \Delta OP_N)$

Figure 1. "Givens" in Lease Evaluation

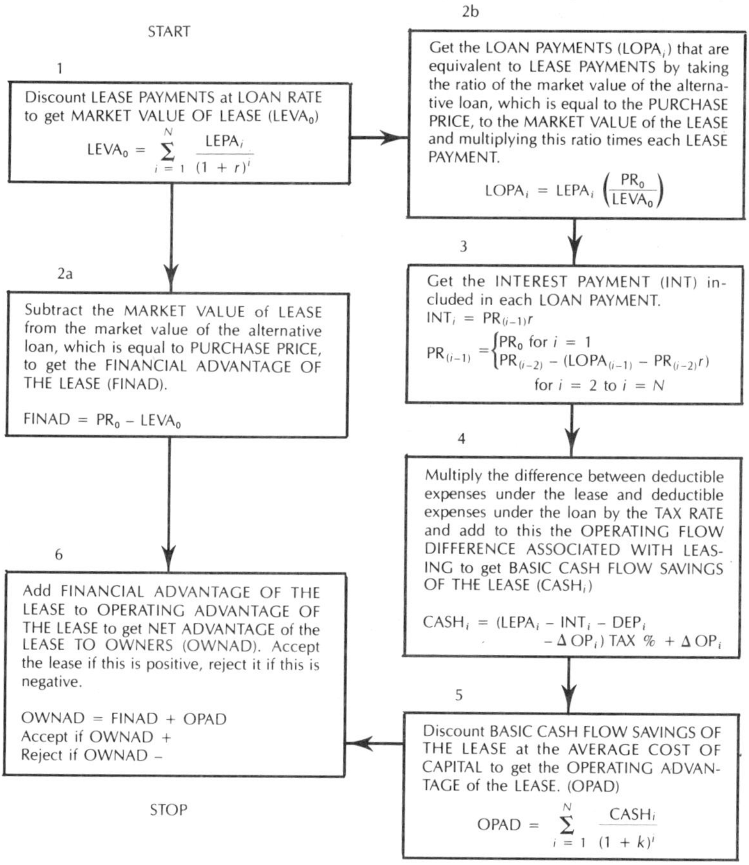

Figure 2. Flow Chart for Lease Evaluation

The flow chart boxes contain:

START

Box 1: Discount LEASE PAYMENTS at LOAN RATE to get MARKET VALUE OF LEASE (LEVA$_0$)

$$LEVA_0 = \sum_{i=1}^{N} \frac{LEPA_i}{(1+r)^i}$$

Box 2b: Get the LOAN PAYMENTS (LOPA$_i$) that are equivalent to LEASE PAYMENTS by taking the ratio of the market value of the alternative loan, which is equal to the PURCHASE PRICE, to the MARKET VALUE of the LEASE and multiplying this ratio times each LEASE PAYMENT.

$$LOPA_i = LEPA_i \left(\frac{PR_0}{LEVA_0}\right)$$

Box 2a: Subtract the MARKET VALUE of LEASE from the market value of the alternative loan, which is equal to PURCHASE PRICE, to get the FINANCIAL ADVANTAGE OF THE LEASE (FINAD).

FINAD = PR_0 − $LEVA_0$

Box 3: Get the INTEREST PAYMENT (INT) included in each LOAN PAYMENT.

$INT_i = PR_{(i-1)}r$

$$PR_{(i-1)} = \begin{cases} PR_0 \text{ for } i = 1 \\ PR_{(i-2)} - (LOPA_{(i-1)} - PR_{(i-2)}r) \\ \text{for } i = 2 \text{ to } i = N \end{cases}$$

Box 4: Multiply the difference between deductible expenses under the lease and deductible expenses under the loan by the TAX RATE and add to this the OPERATING FLOW DIFFERENCE ASSOCIATED WITH LEASING to get BASIC CASH FLOW SAVINGS OF THE LEASE (CASH$_i$)

$CASH_i = (LEPA_i - INT_i - DEP_i - \Delta OP_i) \text{ TAX } \% + \Delta OP_i$

Box 5: Discount BASIC CASH FLOW SAVINGS OF THE LEASE at the AVERAGE COST OF CAPITAL to get the OPERATING ADVANTAGE of the Lease. (OPAD)

$$OPAD = \sum_{i=1}^{N} \frac{CASH_i}{(1+k)^i}$$

Box 6: Add FINANCIAL ADVANTAGE OF THE LEASE to OPERATING ADVANTAGE OF THE LEASE to get NET ADVANTAGE OF THE LEASE TO OWNERS (OWNAD). Accept the lease if this is positive, reject it if this is negative.

OWNAD = FINAD + OPAD
Accept if OWNAD +
Reject if OWNAD −

STOP

A piece of equipment with a purchase price of $28,350 may be leased under a contract that calls for a $10,000 payment in the first and second years, and $4,000 payment in the third, fourth, fifth, and sixth years. Under the contract, which is renewable for six more years at the $4,000 rate, insurance and maintenance are to be provided by the lessor and the investment tax credit is to be passed on to the lessee. The firm offered this contract expects maintenance and insurance to be $1,000 a year if the equipment is purchased. It also expects that the equipment will be used only six years and that its net salvage value at the end of six years will be $3,000. In spite of the salvage estimate, the equipment, if purchased, would be completely depreciated over the six years using sum-of-the-year-digits. The firm's tax rate is 48%, its loan interest rate is 5%, and its average cost of capital is 10%. Should the firm accept the lease contract? The "givens" are summarized in Figure 3.

The first calculation, Box 1 in Figure 2, determines the market value of the lease. This is the value the market assigns to these claims on the company in determining the value of the owner's shares. Discounting the lease payments (LEPA), at the loan rate (r) of 5%, gives the market value of the

Purchase Price $(PR_0) = \$28{,}350$
Tax Rate $(TAX\%) = .48$
Loan Rate $(r) = .05$
Average Cost of Capital $(k) = .10$

YEAR	LEASE PAYMENTS (LEPA)	DEPRECIATION (DEP)	OPERATING FLOW DIFFERENCE ASSOCIATED WITH LEASING (ΔOP)
1	$10,000	$8,100	$1,000
2	10,000	6,750	1,000
3	4,000	5,400	1,000
4	4,000	4,050	1,000
5	4,000	2,700	1,000
6	4,000	1,350	−2,000

Figure 3. The "Givens" in the Example

lease $(LEVA_0)$ as \$31,459. This is then subtracted (Box 2a of the flow chart) from the market value of the alternative loan, which is equal to the purchase price, to get the financial advantage of the lease:

PURCHASE PRICE (PR_0)	$28,350
MARKET VALUE OF LEASE $(LEVA_0)$	31,459
FINANCIAL ADVANTAGE OF THE LEASE (FINAD)	$−3,109

Thus, the lease has a financial disadvantage. Whether the operating advantage of the lease (OPAD) more than offsets this has to be determined.

The equivalent loan and interest components of each loan payment must be calculated (Boxes 2b and 3 of the flow chart). This is done in Figure 4.

$$\frac{PR_0}{LEVA_0} = \frac{28{,}350}{31{,}459} = .9012$$

YEAR	LEASE PAYMENTS (LEPA)	LOAN OUTSTANDING (PR)	LOAN PAYMENTS LEPA × .9012	INTEREST PAYMENTS $(PR_{(i-1)}r)$	LOAN REPAYMENTS (LOPA − INT)
0		$28,350			
1	$10,000	20,756	9,012	1,418	$7,594
2	10,000	12,782	9,012	1,038	7,974
3	4,000	9,816	3,605	639	2,966
4	4,000	6,702	3,605	491	3,114
5	4,000	3,432	3,605	335	3,270
6	4,000	0	3,605	173	3,432

Figure 4. Calculation of Loan Payments and Their Interest Component

Now we have all the information needed to figure out the effect of the lease choice on basic cash flows—the cash available in each period for distribution to residual and prior claimants. This is the operation described in Box 4 of the flow chart. In this case the choice of the lease affects both pre-tax flows and tax payments. The basic cash flow savings of the lease (CASH) and its components are shown in Figure 5.

YEAR	LEASE PAYMENT (LEPA)	DEPRECIATION (DEP)	LOAN INTEREST (INT)	OPERATING FLOW DIFFERENCES ASSOCIATED WITH LEASE (ΔOP)	DECREASE IN TAX PAYMENTS WITH LEASE*	BASIC CASH FLOW SAVINGS OF THE LEASE (CASH)**
1	$10,000	$8,100	$1,418	$1,000	$– 248	$ 752
2	10,000	6,750	1,038	1,000	582	1,582
3	4,000	5,400	639	1,000	–1,459	– 459
4	4,000	4,050	491	1,000	– 740	260
5	4,000	2,700	335	1,000	– 17	983
6	4,000	1,350	173	–2,000	2,148	150

*This equals (LEPA – DEP – INT – ΔOP) (TAX %).
**CASH = (LEPA – DEP – INT – ΔOP) (TAX %) + OP.

Figure 5. Basic Cash Flow Savings of the Lease

The basic cash flow savings of the lease displayed in the last column of Figure 5 are flows which the market recognizes in valuing the firm. Discounting these flows at the average cost of capital (k) of 10% (Box 5 of the flow chart), we get the operating advantage of the lease:

Basic Cash Flow Savings of the Lease (CASH)	Basic Cash Flow Savings Discounted @ 10%
$ 752	$ 683
1,582	1,307
– 459	– 345
260	178
983	610
150	84
Operating Advantage of the Lease (OPAD)	$2,517

Since the operating advantage is less than the financial disadvantage of the lease in this case, the sum of advantages (calculated in accordance with Box 6) is negative and the lease contract fails to meet our objective. If it is to be accepted, this must be for reasons related to other objectives.

COMPUTER CALCULATIONS

It has probably occurred to the reader that the example we chose to illustrate our method of analysis is a very simple one, easily handled by a desk calculator. But actual choices faced by businessmen may involve many time periods, greater variations in rentals, additional expense items, renewal options, termination arrangements, and the possibility of altering any of these through negotiation. The problem may quickly grow beyond the capacity of a desk calculator, at least if the calculations are to be done in a reasonable time. All of these complexities can be handled by the method we have described, and all can be handled easily on a computer.

PURCHASE PRICE $28350   LOAN INT RATE 5 PERCENT

TAX RATE 48 PERCENT   AVG COST OF CAP. 10 PERCENT

YEAR	LEASE PAYMENT	DEPREC'N	LOAN INTEREST	OP'G FLO DIFF'CE WITH LEASE	BASIC CASH FLO SAVING WITH LEASE	BASIC CASH FLOW DISC. AT 10 PERCENT
1	10000	8100	1417.5	1000	751.6	683.273
2	10000	6750	1037.79	1000	1581.86	1307.32
3	4000	5400	639.098	1000	−458.767	−344.679
4	4000	4050	490.82	1000	260.406	177.861
5	4000	2700	335.128	1000	983.139	610.452
6	4000	1350	171.651	−2000	149.608	84.4496

FINANCIAL ADVANTAGE OF LEASE −3109.23

OPERATING ADVANTAGE OF LEASE 2518.68

NET ADVANTAGE OF LEASE −590.552

TIME: 2 SECS.

Figure 6. Comparison of Lease with Purchase

Figure 6 is the output of a program run at the Tuck School on Dartmouth's GE 235 time-sharing computer, duplicating the step-by-step calculations above. The output summarizes the given information, shows the derivation of the operating advantage of the lease, and prints the results. Figure 6 is an exact copy of the output of a remote teletype station.

The computer system we have used has the advantages of a simple language, easy and rapid access, quick calculations, and immediate delivery of results. The notation at the bottom of the output in Figure 6 records two seconds of computation time to solve our problem. The time involved from sitting down at the teletype to insert the given data until the answers are printed is three or four minutes.

The characteristics of the computer system make sensitivity analysis particularly easy. Figure 7 shows the output from an analysis to determine the effect of a change in the loan rate on the advantage of a lease, for our example. We find that at about 6.3%, other givens held constant, the lease replaces the loan as the more advantageous financial arrangement. In similar fashion, the effects of varying any of the givens can be determined.

PURCHASE PRICE $28350   TAX RATE   48 PERCENT
AVG COST OF CAP. 10 PERCENT
TEST SENSITIVITY TO LOAN INT RATE

ADVANTAGE OF LEASE OVER PURCHASE

INT RATE	FIN'L	OP'G	NET
.05	−3109.23	2518.68	−590.552
.052	−2948.48	2455.00	−493.479
.054	−2789.16	2391.26	−397.908
.056	−2631.27	2327.44	−303.822
.058	−2474.77	2263.56	−211.203
.06	−2319.65	2199.62	−120.035
.062	−2165.91	2135.61	−30.2995
.064	−2013.51	2071.53	58.0197
.066	−1862.45	2007.39	144.939
.068	−1712.71	1943.18	230.474
.07	−1564.27	1878.91	314.642

TIME: 2 SECS.

Figure 7. Comparison of Lease with Purchase: Sensitivity Analysis

CONCLUSION

We have progressed from a discussion of the nature of leasing to the explanation of a method of lease evaluation which recognizes the nature of leasing. We have fashioned a set of operating instructions that apply this method to lease situations of a particular type. And we have applied these instructions in a sample calculation showing also how a computer may be used. Still, the problems of leasing have not all been settled nor have all the questions associated with our method been answered. There are still questions about estimating the loan rate and the average cost of capital, determining whether the lease choice has a risk effect, applying our method when there is a risk effect, and about the investment decision to take the equipment even in its more advantageous (lease or loan) form. Some of these questions can be answered easily enough by the reader. Others require demanding analysis and are part of our continuing research on leasing. Here we are content to introduce a method of lease evaluation which we feel is both more general and more reasonable than other methods that have been proposed.

5.

ILLUSTRATION OF MODEL OF COST AND VALUE OF INFORMATION* [DECISION TREES AND EXPECTED VALUE]

American Accounting Association—
Committee on Managerial Decision Models

The accountant should assist the decision maker in assessing the expected value of information. Consider a simplified example of the measurement of the value of information. An oil-well wildcatter is considering investing $50,000 in an oil well lease and contract drilling. He has estimated the probability of finding a producing well to be .4, which would result in a net gain of $100,000 ($150,000 revenue − $50,000 cost). There is a .6 probability of a $50,000 loss.

His present situation can be depicted by the decision tree shown in Exhibit I.

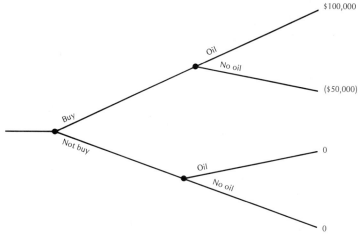

Exhibit 1. Decision Tree

* From *The Accounting Review,* Supplement to Vol. XLIV, pp. 61–64. Reprinted by permission of the American Accounting Association.

The tree in Exhibit 1 describes the possible outcomes: he either buys or does not buy the lease and he either does or does not find oil. The expected value of the alternative acts, given the particular cost and probability estimates, can be calculated as shown in Exhibit 2.

		ACT			
		BUY		DO NOT BUY	
Event	(1) Probability of Event	(2) Conditional Value	(1) × (2) Expected Value	(3) Conditional Value	(1) × (3) Expected Value
Oil	.4	$100,000	$40,000	$0	$0
No oil	.6	(50,000)	(30,000)	0	0
Net expected value with existing information			$10,000		$0

Exhibit 2. The Values of Alternative Acts Under Uncertainty

Because the net expected value of the decision to buy is $10,000 greater than that of not buying, the best act, *based on the information available*, is to buy and drill. However, notice that the outcome has a 60% chance of being unfavorable, which will result in a loss of $50,000. This is referred to as a "conditional value" of ($50,000).

The wildcatter would desire more information because of the large amount of uncertainty involved in this situation and the sizeable costs of making a wrong decision (an unrecoverable $50,000 out-of-pocket cost if no oil is found; a $100,000 opportunity cost if he does not buy and the oil is really there). Ideally, he would want *perfect* information, which would permit him to predict with absolute certainty whether oil is present. The net expected value of making the correct decision in the given circumstances (the optimal decision) is calculated in Exhibit 3. Note that he will *only* drill *if* there is oil. That is why the conditional value is "O" for "No oil."

With perfect information the maximum expected profit would be $40,000 because there is a probability of .4 that the perfect information will disclose that oil exists, and the investment leading to a profit would therefore be made. The most he would be willing to pay for the perfect information would be the difference between the expected value with perfect information and the expected value with existing information: $40,000 − $10,000 = $30,000. The $30,000 difference is called the expected value of perfect information (EVPI).[1]

---

[1]The EVPI is also equal to the $50,000 loss multiplied by a .6 probability that is avoided by acquiring the information.

Event (E)	Probability of Event P (E)	OPTIMAL DECISION		
		Decision	Conditional Value	Expected Value
Oil	.4	Buy	$100,000	$40,000
No oil	.6	Do not buy	0	0
	Net expected value			$40,000

Exhibit 3. The Value of Decisions Based on a Perfect Predictor

The EVPI is important because it indicates the maximum amount which a "rational" decision maker[2] would pay for *perfect* information. Although information is virtually never perfect, the EVPI is very useful as an upper boundary in assessing the probable value of additional information in a particular situation.

Although perfect information is usually unobtainable, some additional information is likely to be available at some price. In our example, the wildcatter might consider a geological test of the subsurface. His decision tree would then appear as shown in Exhibit 4.

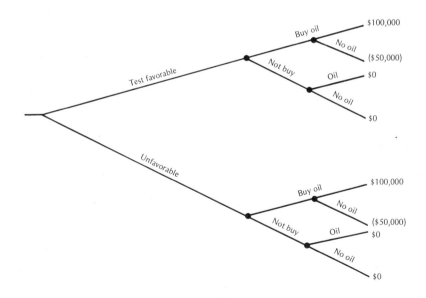

Exhibit 4. Possible Outcomes and Conditional Value

[2] A "rational" decision maker is defined for our purposes as a being willing to make decisions using expected monetary value and having no preference or aversion for risk.

The geological testing company might advise the wildcatter that if there is oil on the land, the test results will be favorable (positive) three-quarters of the time and unfavorable (negative) one-quarter of the time. In other words, the test is not perfect. Similarly, if there is no oil, the test will give unfavorable results two-thirds of the time, but will be (falsely) favorable one-third of the time. (These probabilities will be referred to as conditional probabilities.)

The wildcatter wants to know the probability of finding oil *given* the result of the test. These revised conditional probabilities are found by weighing the prior subjective probabilities by the appropriate likelihoods as shown in Exhibit 5.

EVENT (E)	(1) PRIOR P (E)	(2) CONDITIONAL PROBABILITIES OF FAVORABLE TEST	(1) × (2) PROBABILITIES OF TEST OUTCOME AND EVENT	PROBABILITIES OF EVENTS GIVEN THE TEST OUTCOMES
If the test is favorable:				
Oil	.4	¾	.3	.3 ÷ .5 = .6
No oil	.6	⅓	.2	.2 ÷ .5 = .4
Probability of favorable test			.5	1.0
If the test is unfavorable:				
Oil	.4	¼	.1	.1 ÷ .5 = .2
No oil	.6	⅔	.4	.4 ÷ .5 = .8
Probability of unfavorable test			.5	1.0

Exhibit 5. Probabilities of States, Given a Favorable or Unfavorable Test Result

The computations of conditional probabilities show that the probability of finding oil is .6, given a *favorable* test. However, if the test is unfavorable, the probability of finding oil is only .2. With this knowledge, a pay-off table can now be constructed for the wildcatter (Exhibit 6).

Exhibit 5 showed that probabilities of favorable and unfavorable test results were each .5, based upon the prior probability of oil and the likelihood of correct and incorrect results. Exhibit 6 shows that we can maximize expected value (E.V.) by buying if results are favorable but by not buying if results are unfavorable. Taken together, these facts allow us to compute our expected pay-off from testing (and buying only if favorable results are received) to be:

$$(.5) (\$40,000) + (.5) (\$0) = \$20,000$$

To determine the maximum amount which the wildcatter should pay for the test, we compare his E.V. with and without the test. With the test the

If the test is favorable:

		ACT			
		BUY		DO NOT BUY	
Event	Conditional Probability	Conditional Value	Expected Value	Conditional Value	Expected Value
Oil	.6	$100,000	$60,000	$0	$0
No oil	.4	(50,000)	(20,000)	0	0
Net Expected Value			$40,000		$0
If the test is unfavorable:					
Oil	.2	$100,000	$20,000	$0	$0
No oil	.8	(50,000)	(40,000)	0	0
Net Expected Value			($20,000)		$0

Exhibit 6. The Values of Alternative Acts after Test Results

E.V. is $20,000, (as computed above). Without the test the E.V. of the best act (buying and drilling) is only $10,000 (as shown in Exhibit 2). Therefore, he should be willing to pay up to $10,000 for the test, and $10,000 is the expected value of the information resulting from the test.

6.

ACCOUNTING INFORMATION AND DECISION-MAKING: SOME BEHAVIORAL HYPOTHESES*

William J. Bruns, Jr.

Consider the following statements:

> 1. If accounting information is not considered relevant by a decision-maker to a decision under consideration, a change in the accounting information will not affect his decision.

> 2. The conception of accounting information held by a decision-maker—his opinion on how well the accountant and accounting system measures significant attributes and characteristics of factors affecting and affected by a decision—will affect the weight given to accounting information in the decision process when other information is available.

> 3. The availability of other information will be an important determinant of the weight assigned by a decision-maker to accounting information in the decision process.

Each of these statements has many characteristics of a truism. Many more like them, each concerned with the relationship between accounting systems, accounting information, decision-makers, and decision-making could be easily constructed. Though behavioral relationships on which such statements rest are potentially important to the development of accounting theory and the design of information-decision systems, the study of those relationships is in the earliest stages.

*From *The Accounting Review*, July 1968, pp. 469–480. Reprinted by permission of the author and the American Accounting Association. Part of this work was completed while the author was a Faculty Fellow in the New York Office of Price Waterhouse & Co. However, the statements, opinions, and conclusions in this paper are solely those of the author.

Relatively little is known about the way in which information is used in decision-making, and without such knowledge it is difficult to predict the diverse effects which different accounting systems or information will have on decisions. A model developed below explicitly identifies and relates some factors which may determine when decisions are affected by accounting systems and information. The hypotheses on which this model is based are intended to stimulate and direct part of the study of accounting and decision-making. While the model is not tested here, some implications of the hypothesized relationships for both accounting theory and accounting systems are discussed.

RATIONALES FOR RESEARCH ON DECISION-MAKING AND BEHAVIOR BY ACCOUNTANTS

The problems that demand new research in behavioral aspects of accounting are familiar to almost all who have studied economics and accounting. The relationship between available information and decisions is basic to economic theories of decision-making. Knowledge about costs, prices, and competitors is assumed in almost all traditional theory, and much effort has been directed toward developing models of decision-making for use when information about one or more of these factors is unknown. As these models have been explored and modified, and as new procedures for analysis of alternative courses of action have been developed, new attention has been given to the role of data as determinants of decisions.

Accounting systems of firms are important sources of information for business decision-making. The information which systems provide for decision-making can be grouped in three classes: financial statements, quantitative reports on selected aspects of operations, and special analyses. Information from each class can be grouped with information from another or with information from sources outside the accounting system in the set of information used by a decision-maker.

Almost all accounting information is affected by the body of rules and procedures called generally accepted accounting principles. Efforts to develop and improve generally accepted accounting principles have been underway since the 1930's, and since 1960 these efforts have found vigorous support from the accounting profession. Thus far, these efforts have not been notably successful, for there are few, if any, bases on which all accountants can agree to select among alternative general principles.

It is possible that much of the effort directed toward resolution of controversy about generally accepted accounting principles has been premature or misdirected. Accounting is a service activity carried out to provide information for decisions within and about business firms. Analyses of alternative sets of generally accepted accounting principles have often been based on the assumption that the relationship between an accounting report or information contained therein and each decision is direct. But this assumption has not been tested, and alternative hypotheses abound. When these have been tested and efforts to develop generally accepted accounting principles can be based upon knowledge of the manner in which accounting affects decisions about business activity, new and important criteria for selecting among alternative methods and alternative systems will be available.[1]

DEFINING ACCOUNTING SYSTEMS AND INFORMATION

One complication in the task of relating accounting information to decision-making is the fact that "accounting systems" are diverse and "accounting information" describes many different sets of data and information. For purposes of this paper, an "accounting system" will refer to the methods by which financial data about a firm or its activity are collected, processed, stored and/or distributed to members of the firm or other interested parties. It is possible to consider that any data or information which are obtained from or created in the accounting system of a firm are accounting information, whether contained in a financial statement, a special report, or verbal statement. However, for our immediate purposes, that interpretation is too broad to be useful. Hereafter, "accounting information" will refer to written information of the type that might be contained in a complete or partial financial report—balance sheet, income statement, or funds flow statement—though in many cases this limitation is not critical to the discussion.

THE RELEVANCE OF ACCOUNTING INFORMATION FOR DECISION-MAKING

By definition, decisions affect future events, for future actions are determined as a decision is made. In the case of management decisions, decisions may affect only a single event or they may affect all events subsequent to the decision. But no event which has been completed can be altered by a decision.[2] Furthermore, accounting information, in the sense

---

[1]This call for attention to the relationships between accounting, decision-makers, and decisions is not new. See for example Carl T. Devine, "Research Methodology and Accounting Theory Formation," The Accounting Review (July 1960), pp. 387–399; Myron J. Gordon, "Scope and Method of Theory and Research in the Measurement of Income and Wealth," The Accounting Review (October 1960), pp. 603–618; and the more recent Statement of Basic Accounting Theory (American Accounting Association, 1966), especially Chapter 5.

[2]Here we approach an interesting point about which more will be said later. Decisions about the accounting methods to be used can alter the reports of events which have occurred in the past. It is the effect of these reports which is the principal topic of interest here.

that we are using that term here, focuses on past events.[3] Accounting cannot change events or their effects unless it is through the decision process where future events and their effects are determined. Decision-making and accounting information focus on different time periods except to the extent that the decision process employs accounting information. An important question then is, when is accounting information relevant for decision-making?

In a recent paper, Ijiri, Jaedicke, and Knight have provided a framework which is extremely useful as a basis for discussing the relationship of accounting information and decision processes.[4] They represent a decision process as a function that relates a set of decision inputs to a unique set of decisions. Symbolically,

$$(z_1, z_2, \ldots, z_n) = h(x_1, x_2, \ldots, x_n).$$

Here $z_1, z_2, \ldots, z_n$ are a set of decisions based upon inputs, $x_1, x_2, \ldots, x_n$, according to a decision rule, h. Each set Z and X, must contain at least one element, but there is no requirement that the number of inputs be equal to the number of decisions.

Selection of a particular decision rule by a decision-maker is affected by many factors, among them his analytical capabilities and objectives. The rule associates inputs with decisions, and selection of a decision rule establishes the degree to which objectives will be met by the expected effects of a particular set of decisions. The decision-maker explores the relationships between decisions and objectives prior to the selection of a rule by analysis and through evaluation of the effects of past events similar to those contemplated in the future.

If accounting information affects decisions, it does so through a decision rule which relates decisions to inputs, which include accounting information. The decision-maker uses or selects a decision rule which relates inputs to decisions in a manner consistent with his experience, perceptions, and his objectives. Suppose we let x_1 represent consistent accounting information, one element of a set of all decision inputs available at the time a set of decisions is to be made. The decision rule weights each decision input, which determines each decision in the set Z, and the weight assigned to x_1 will determine what effect, if any, accounting information has on decisions affecting future events. All other decision inputs, x_2 through x_m, are also weighted by the decision rule, and each affects the resulting set of decisions. These inputs may provide nonfinancial information essential

---

[3]In many cases assumptions about future events affect reports of past events. Depreciation accounting is a good example of this; an asset may be assumed to have value in future events, and therefore, its cost is not charged only against events which occur in the period of acquisition.

[4]Yuji Ijiri, Robert K. Jaedicke, and Kenneth E. Knight, "The Effects of Accounting Alternatives on Management Decisions," *Research in Accounting Measurement*, (American Accounting Association, 1966), pp. 186–199.

to decisions, and in some cases their weights will overwhelm any possible effects of accounting information.

In selecting a decision rule, the decision-maker must consider all inputs available and their relevance to the set of decisions to be made. It is the decision-maker who decides whether any input is relevant or not. The perceived relevance of the decision inputs to the decisions at hand determine whether the decision rule selected will apply a weight different from zero to accounting information. If a weight different from zero is applied, accounting information may affect decisions; if not, decisions will not be affected by accounting information. Therefore, we hypothesize: *if accounting information is perceived as irrelevant for the set of decisions to be made, accounting information will not affect decisions; if accounting information is perceived as relevant to the set of decisions to be made, it may affect decisions.*

THE ROLE OF THE DECISION-MAKER'S CONCEPTION OF ACCOUNTING

Accounting is a systematic process of providing information about wealth and the effects of economic events. The methods, rules, and procedures that comprise accounting are here assumed to be familiar to the reader. However, there are reasons to believe that accounting is different things to different participants in economic events, and if so, the conceptions of accounting held by individuals or organizations may influence the impact of accounting information on behavior.

Away from reality, accounting can be regarded as a perfect measure. A perfect measure can be defined as a measure where there is a zero probability that the true measurement of an attribute differs from the reported measurement. We can assume that identifiable objects and legal rights have value and that these values are enhanced or destroyed as economic events occur, and we can assume that these values and effects are measurable. To many persons, accounting practice, carried out by trained observers applying consistent and objective methods of measurement and attested to by independent agents, holds the image of a perfect measure applied by professionals. There is an aura of authenticity that surrounds accounting data, and to the untrained user of information, accounting may appear to be a perfect source. We must recognize, however, that few, if any, of the persons who have processed or reviewed the data and the procedures that have converted it to information would consider it perfect.

More realistically, accounting can be considered as a process by which the value or effects of events is reported as accurately as possible but without pretense of being a perfect measure. Here, this conception of accounting will be referred to as an "imperfect measure." Such a measure is defined when the probability that the true value differs from the reported value is greater than zero. This conception is probably closest to that held by most practicing accountants. Errors and inaccuracy in the process of measuring, counting, and reporting are inevitable, and most persons who are familiar with accounting measures and procedures are familiar with these problems. This notion may cause accounting to have a different impact on behavior than the "perfect measure" notion. It allows for a "margin of disbelief" that may in some cases affect the kind of action taken as accounting information is used in decision processes.

A third conception of accounting is fundamentally different from the "perfect measure" or "imperfect measure" notions advanced above. Accounting information may be a goal for actors in economic events. When a businessman seeks profit, he does so for many reasons. For some purposes, the profit reported by accounting is far more important to the businessman or manager than the "true" or "perfectly measured" profit. Modern business organization has given this conception of accounting wide significance, and the implications of this notion for accounting warrant close examination.

Accounting becomes a goal when rewards or satisfactions accrue to a decision-maker as a result of accounting information, and the relationship of the true measure to the reported measure is unimportant. For example, if a manager hopes to advance and feels he will be promoted if he can effect cost reductions, and if accounting information will provide the basis for determining whether costs have been reduced, then it is the accounting information which shows reduced costs that becomes the goal. Likewise, where management is rewarded by stockholders with salary and prerequisites on the basis of reported earnings or growth, the reports which result in these rewards may become more important—the goal of management decision-makers—than the long-run earnings or healthy growth which the stockholders really intend to reward.

While not exclusive, this brief recognition of diverse conceptions of accounting seems essential to understanding the effects of accounting information on behavior and decision-making. Below it will be assumed that any individual in a decision situation conceives accounting information either as a goal or at a point on a continuum on which accounting varies from a perfect measure to an imperfect one. This assumption is necessary to state a second set of hypotheses relating accounting information and decisions: *the conception of accounting held by a decision-maker will affect his selection of a decision rule to be used in reaching a set of decisions.* This hypothesis can be further specified by stating it in two parts:

> 1. If accounting information is both a decision input and an objective (goal) sought by a decision-maker, accounting information will affect decisions.

> 2. The more a decision-maker conceives accounting as being a perfect source of information, the more likely the decision-maker will select decision rules that weight accounting heavily, and the more likely accounting information will affect decisions.

CLASSIFYING DECISIONS-MAKERS

Because accounting information can be conceived as a goal, and because accounting information is determined in part by an accounting system, a classification of decision-makers provides insight into a final effect which accounting information may have on the set of decisions selected by the decision-makers. Three classes are suggested; first, decision-makers within the firm who make decisions both about operations and about the accounting system used to prepare reports; second, decision-makers within the firm who can make operating decisions but who cannot affect the methods used to prepare reports; and third, those outside of the firm who make decisions about the firm which may affect its environment and operations but who have no direct control over the operation of the firm or any activities in which it is engaged. The reasons for separating the first two classes of decision-makers, both of which are internal to the firm, will later become more obvious.

The first class of decision-makers is comprised of top management. Financial reports are the reports of this group and they are responsible for their preparation and presentation. If a choice must be made between accounting methods, this group is responsible for making that decision. This means that the set of possible decisions available to this class of decision-makers includes modification of the accounting system.[5]

The second class of decision-makers is distinguished from the first only in one important way. Their position in the organization precludes their determining the information included in accounting reports by modifying the accounting system. However, they make decisions about the activities of the firm and we can assume that accounting information enters into their decision processes. They can, of course, influence the content of accounting information by their decisions about activities, in which case accounting information may be affecting decisions.

The distinction between top management, who may affect accounting information, and internal decision-makers who cannot, is most critical where accounting information is conceived as a goal.[6] The decision function for such managers may contain important options between operating decisions and decisions to change the methods by which accounting information is prepared. In any event, decisions are affected, but predicting directions of the effects is much more complicated than it is for decision-makers who do

---

[5]There are, of course, limits to the modifications of the accounting system which can be effected. For example, requirements for consistency prevent selection of different inventory valuation or depreciation methods each year. However, methods used for new acquisitions can be selected, and questions about expense vs capitalization arise frequently and can be answered uniquely as they arise.

[6]An example of this would arise where management wished to report a particular amount for earnings per share.

not have authority to modify accounting methods or procedures. Requirements for independent audits and certification of consistency in methods between accounting periods reduces the significance of the two levels of management, though few would argue that this requirement is such that the effects of top management's discretion in accounting can be ignored.

The third class of decision-makers consists of several sets of interested outsiders. Investors, legally the owners of the firm but in fact usually somewhat removed from it, are ostensibly the group for which accounting information in published form is prepared. Creditors, in some cases merely another class of investors, usually seek the same information. A third major set of outsiders consists of government agencies who seek bases for taxation, regulation, and economic analysis. Each of these sets of outsiders makes decisions that may affect the firm and its operations, and to the extent that accounting information is utilized as part of their decision processes, it will affect these decisions. However, the goals of the decision-makers external to the firm presumably may differ from the objectives of the firm or objectives which concern decision-makers within the firm. This possibility (as well as the obvious diversity of goals in the sets of outsiders) makes analysis of effects of accounting information on decisions of this class of decision-makers very difficult.

Nevertheless, the classification of decision-makers yields an important hypothesis: *if a decision-maker can affect the accounting system as well as the activities of the firm, and if he conceives accounting information as a goal, accounting information will affect decisions about either or both the accounting system and operations.*

NON-ACCOUNTING INFORMATION

The final hypothesis to be introduced in this model concerns the role played by information which is not a product of the accounting system in determining the impact of accounting information on decisions. Above, accounting information was defined as information of the type that might be contained in a conventional financial report. In many respects, the effects of non-accounting information on decisions can be analyzed in the same framework as accounting information. However, the importance of non-accounting information here is that it may determine the effects of accounting information on decisions.

If non-accounting information becomes a goal or is perceived as having special relevance for decisions undergoing evaluation, the impact of accounting information will be reduced. If non-accounting information is not relevant to decisions, the effects of relevant accounting information will be enhanced. Therefore, we hypothesize: *the impact of accounting information on decisions is affected by the perceived relevance of other information also available to the decision-maker.*

A MODEL FOR ANALYZING THE EFFECTS OF ACCOUNTING INFORMATION ON DECISIONS

The hypotheses developed above are all summarized and their interrelationships are made clear in Figure 1. Rather than restate all hypotheses or describe the model in detail, a summary of hypotheses which lead to the principal outcomes predicted by the model will be used to reveal the interrelationships within it.

I.　*Accounting information will either affect decisions or affect decisions about the accounting system if:*

　　(a)　accounting information is relevant to decisions;
　　　(b)　the decision-maker conceives accounting as a goal;
and　　　　(c)　the decision-maker is a member of the firm who can control the selection and operation of the accounting system.

II.　*Accounting information will affect decisions if:*

　　(a)　accounting information is relevant to decisions;
　　　(b_l)　the decision-maker conceives accounting as a goal;
and　　　　(c_l)　the decision-maker is a member of the firm who cannot control the selection and operation of the accounting system;
or　　　　(c_2)　the decision-maker is external to the firm;
or　　　(b_2)　the decision-maker conceives accounting as a perfect measure;
and　　　　(c)　non-accounting information is not relevant to the decision.

III.　*Accounting information may affect decisions if:*

　　(a)　accounting information is relevant to decisions;
　　　(b_l)　the decision-maker conceives accounting as a perfect measure;
and　　　　(c)　non-accounting information is relevant to the decision;
　　　(b_2)　the decision-maker conceives accounting as an imperfect measure;
but　　　　(c)　non-accounting information is not relevant to the decision.

IV.　*Accounting information will not affect decisions if:*

　　(a_l)　accounting information is not relevant to decisions;
or　　(a_2)　accounting information is relevant to the decision;

but	(b) the decision-maker conceives accounting information as an imperfect measure;[7]
and	(c) non-accounting information is relevant to the decision.

SOME FURTHER EXPLORATION OF THE MODEL

The flow chart format used in Figure 1 is extremely demanding and, possibly, too restrictive. This format demands that we state precisely what will happen at each branch of the model. Yet there appear to be some situations in which it would be more satisfactory to think in terms of effects along a continuum.

Examine, for example, the lower right-hand portion of Figure 1, where the model predicts the impact of other information when accounting has been perceived as relevant and when the decision-maker perceives accounting information as being either perfect or imperfect. The model predicts that accounting information perceived as perfect may have some effect on decisions. However, when the decision-maker perceives accounting information as being something less than perfect (for example, recognizes that errors or biases may have been introduced into the measurements reported), the impact of other information becomes less certain. The degree of conceived imperfection and the amount and quality of other information are important variables in such cases. Likewise, even in cases where accounting information is perfect, and other information is relevant, the decision might be affected, but not altered, by accounting information. Similar questions can be raised at other points and simply reinforce conclusions about the need for testing the hypotheses on which this model is based.

While these uncertain conclusions beg for clarification and discriminating research, they are perhaps the least interesting. In cases where decisions may be little affected by accounting information, the choice of a particular accounting system, or particular accounting methods used in that system, may be of little importance. It is at the other extreme, where the model predicts that accounting information will affect decisions that the choice of accounting systems and methods becomes critical.

INTERACTION WITHIN THE MODEL

Further complications in interpreting or using the model stem from possible interaction between the method of accounting used and/or the accounting system developed and the perceived relevance of accounting for

---

[7]The degree of conceived imperfection is important for this conclusion. If accounting information is conceived as being so imperfect it is of no use, it will not affect decisions in this case. If, however, the degree of imperfection conceived is not great enough to preclude the use of accounting information in the decision process, accounting information may or may not affect decisions.

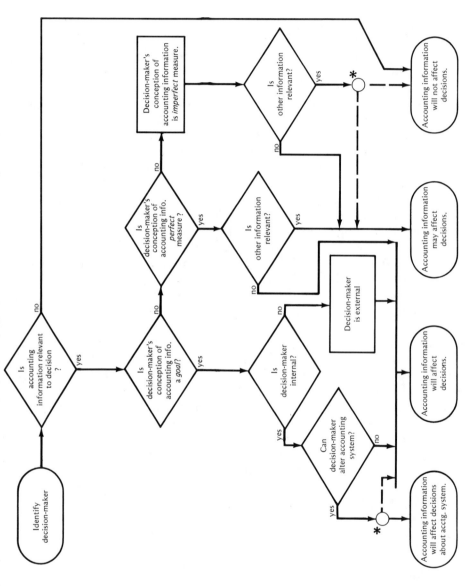

*Dotted lines indicate that effects depend on particular decision rule selected.

Figure 1. Accounting Information and Decisions

decision-making purposes. If the decision-maker feels that a particular method or system of accounting is inappropriate as a basis for measurements relating to a particular problem, he will be led to a position where the effective accounting information will be reduced. Unless we know something about the particular class of decision-makers and their perceptions of accounting methods, it is difficult to predict whether any examination of the conception of accounting held by the decision-maker will be of importance. Likewise, if the method chosen, or the process of selecting a method, affects the conception of accounting held by the decision-maker, then this will affect the relationship between a particular method and decisions.

A DIGRESSION: THE MEANING OF RELEVANCE

The proposal made here to recognize relevance as a primary determinant of the effect of accounting on decision-making is not new. The degree of relevance has frequently been suggested as a basis for choosing between alternative accounting methods and forms of accounting information. This has been particularly true in the literature relating to accounting within the firm, where it is frequently asserted that those methods that result in revelation of cost-volume-profit relationships are most appropriate. Likewise, in the recent *Statement of Basic Accounting Theory*, formulated by a committee of the American Accounting Association, relevance is proposed as a primary standard for selecting among alternative forms of accounting information.[8]

However, the meaning of relevance appropriate for its use as a criterion in the development of accounting methodology and theory is not clear. While users are frequently the point of reference in analyses employing "relevance," the determination of "relevant information" is left to the accountant, who uses some standard, generally accepted model for decision-making as the criterion in determining what should be reported. In the formulation which has been presented above, relevance is determined by the user of the information, and the effect of this choice creates several problems which require careful consideration before this criterion is employed.

If the user determines relevance, we should expect that, in some cases, what the user feels is relevant would not be relevant in those standard, accepted models with which we are familiar, such as those drawn from economics. Suppose the accountant knows the objectives of the firm and those objectives correspond to those in an accepted model of decision-making, but the decision-maker feels the relevant information is different

---

[8]*A Statement of Basic Accounting Theory* (American Accounting Association, 1966), especially Chapter 2.

from that called for by the model. The accountant may be placed in a position of second guessing the user, in order to provide the data that will allow him to make a correct decision, because the user's idea of what information is relevant is wrong from the standpoint of the decision models. This is a position in which I believe most accountants would feel somewhat uncomfortable.

We must also be concerned with the possibility that the conception of accounting held by the decision-maker affects the perception of relevance to a significant degree. The more a decision-maker conceives of accounting as being perfect, the more relevant accounting information is likely to be for decision-making purposes, and the more importance can be attached to the part that accounting systems and methods will play in the decision-making process. In so far as this writer is aware, this relationship has seldom been considered, and never carefully explored.

If the hypotheses developed in this paper are valid, then it is clear that relevance alone cannot serve as a primary standard for the development of accounting theory and methods. If accounting is to serve users of accounting information then something besides whether or not the data is relevant must be known. These hypotheses would lead us to believe that critical variables are the conception of accounting held by a decision-maker and the perceived relevance of other kinds of information to the problems under examination at the time the user chooses to employ or not to employ accounting information.

SOME EXAMPLES OF THE USE OF RELEVANCE AND THE CONCEPTION OF ACCOUNTING AS BASES FOR ACCOUNTING SYSTEMS DEVELOPMENT

Suppose that research fails to lead to rejection of the hypotheses presented above, and consider a case in which we are concerned with designing an appropriate accounting system to facilitate effective decision-making. Imagine that the organization in question is a business firm. Among the products of an accounting system are financial statements issued at regular intervals. These intervals may vary in length from very short periods to relatively longer periods; that is, financial statements may be prepared for internal use as frequently as daily or weekly, or they may be issued less often, perhaps annually, to employees of the firm. It is possible to hypothesize that the more frequently financial reports are issued and attention is drawn to the financial condition of the firm, the more relevant accounting information will appear to people within the firm who are making decisions about prices, promotion policies, and production quantities.[9] Yet, for

---

[9] An attempt to test whether decisions might be affected by varying the time periods between accounting reports is reported in William J. Bruns, Jr., "The Accounting Period Concept and Its Effect on Management Decisions," in *Empirical Research in Accounting: Selected Studies, 1966* (The Institute of Professional Accounting, University of Chicago, 1967), pp. 1–14.

many decisions of this type, we might argue that other information would be more important and relevant. Therefore, we might be led to a situation in which we wish to reduce the perceived relevance of accounting information by reducing the frequency of reports, so that decision-makers within the firm would rely more heavily on other information which would allow their decisions to be more appropriate for the conditions under which the firm was operating.

Consider pricing decisions. In general, economists and other analysts would agree that the financial condition of the firm is not necessarily an appropriate basis for choosing a price strategy and selecting terms of sale. However, if financial statements are issued very frequently, thus enhancing their perceived relevance, and the conception of accounting held by decision-makers is such that we might expect accounting information to have some effect, then favorable or adverse profit information and/or other financial information might affect decisions with respect to price. It is possible, then, that by developing an accounting system in which the frequency of reporting reduces the perceived relevance of accounting information we could improve pricing decisions in the firm.

In other cases, we might come to an opposite conclusion. In decision-making related to the acquisition and management of working capital, the availability of frequent information on the status of assets and liabilities of the firm may be very important, and we might choose to issue reports to persons concerned with these matters very frequently in hopes of increasing the efficiency of such decisions.

The point of these examples is that changes in the accounting system may affect perceived relevance of accounting information and may determine the effect of accounting information on decisions, and furthermore, that the interactions between relevance and conceptions of accounting which we have considered above may be important also. In designing an accounting system, relying on cliches like ". . . the more information, the better . . ." may lead to surprising results.

Consider another example, in which we are concerned with a choice between alternative accounting methods for reporting on a particular class of assets or liabilities. For sake of illustration, let us consider a choice between two alternative inventory valuation methods—LIFO and FIFO. Assuming that the reader is familiar with the characteristics of these methods, we can quickly conclude that in cases where prices are changing frequently that LIFO will reveal through the income statement the effects of these changes on the profitability of the firm more rapidly than FIFO. To the extent that this is important for the types of decisions being made, this model might provide us with the basis for preferring one method of accounting for inventories over another.

Let us assume that the prices of raw materials for the production process or the price of goods to be resold is rising. From the standpoint of decision-makers within the firm, this is important information, and information which we would expect to be important for decision-making purposes within the firm. To the extent that the decision-maker felt accounting information was relevant to his decisions, a conception of accounting as perfect information would make the choice of LIFO more important than if the decision-maker's conception of accounting information was that it was an imperfect measure. If accounting information is not perceived as relevant, or if the decision-maker feels accounting measures are imperfect and other information is also relevant for decision-making, the choice of inventory valuation methods is unlikely to affect decisions.

Here also we can consider the possible usefulness of this model for evaluating the selection of a method for reporting to external users. Assume that external users feel accounting information is relevant for their decisions. The more perfect their conception of accounting, the more likely that the choice between methods of accounting will affect their decisions. If the current performance of the firm is important to external users because they wish to use it as a basis for decisions, then LIFO may be more appropriate than FIFO for inventory valuation purposes.

In either of these last two cases, if accounting information were perceived as being irrelevant and/or if accounting information were conceived as being so imperfect a measure that it is not weighted heavily by the decision rule, then a decision on an inventory valuation method might not be very important. Such would be the case in any choice between accounting systems or methods. The implication of this is, I believe, quite clear: until we know more about the conditions that affect perceived relevance of accounting information for decision-making and until we know more about the conceptions of accounting held by users we do not have adequate bases on which to reduce diversity in accounting or to increase it selectively.

IMPLICATIONS FOR FURTHER RESEARCH

It is clear that a great deal more research about behavioral relationships between accounting and decision-making is required. The hypotheses which comprise the model presented here demand that we learn more about the factors that influence a decision-maker's perception of the relevance of accounting information. We need to know more about the conceptions of accounting held by individuals, both within business enterprises and external to them, and it would be useful also to know more about the magnitudes of difference required before perceptions of relevance and conceptions would be affected.

One way of finding data about these variables would be to go into the field and do field research about the perceived relevance of accounting for various decision problems. Some attempts have been made in this direction, and while the results are still inconclusive, they provide a basis for the design of further studies.[10] It is also necessary that something be

[10]See, for example, James L. Gibson and W. Warren Haynes, *Accounting in Small Business Decisions* (University of Kentucky Press, 1963). Results of this study were summarized in James L. Gibson, "Accounting in the Decision-Making Process," *The*

learned about the conceptions of accounting held by users. Is it true that the majority of users feel accounting is a valid and good source of information? Or do most experienced users of accounting information conceive of accounting as being imperfect in the sense that the term is used here, and hence, the types of decisions made about accounting systems and accounting methods are relatively unimportant?

Another approach to this type of problem is the experimental approach, where in a laboratory or a simulated environment, we place people in alternative conditions in hopes of comparing their behavior under the conditions we have created. This, in my opinion, provides a most promising avenue for testing some of the hypotheses we have created in this study.

Consider, for example, an experiment to determine if the relevance of accounting information is a determinant of the effect of that information on decision-making. We could, for example, take a sample group and partition it to obtain a control section and an experimental section. The experimental section could be instructed as to the types of situations in which, given generally accepted models of decision-making, accounting information is relevant. Having provided this background, this group could then take part in a simulated exercise—a business game—in which accounting information and other information are controlled. The control group would receive no instructions about the role of accounting. The decisions of the groups could be compared, and if there were differences, there might be reasons to believe that when accounting information is perceived as being relevant, it will have an effect and that relevance, then, is something that can be affected through educational experiences.

In like manner, it should be possible to explore in the laboratory the effect of conception of accounting. After determining through tests or interviews the conception of accounting held by subjects, we could partition the group in such a way that those having one conception of accounting are used for a control group, while those having another conception of accounting serve as an experimental group.

Experiments of the type proposed above would have to be replicated many times before we could employ the findings with confidence. Nevertheless, the "obvious" character of the hypotheses developed here gives hope that they may provide keys to new criteria for use in the design of accounting systems and reports.

SUMMARY

Relationships between accounting methods, accounting information, and business decision-making are largely unexplored. Hypotheses developed here relate the user of accounting information, the relevance of accounting

Accounting Review (July 1963), pp. 492–500. The faculty of the Ohio State University conducted two seminars in early 1966 during which users of accounting information discussed prepared papers on their work and the effects of accounting. See Thomas J. Burns, *The Use of Accounting Data in Decision Making* (College of Commerce and Administration, The Ohio State University, 1967).

information for decisions, the decision-maker's conception of accounting, and other information available, to the effect of accounting information on decisions. No tests of the hypotheses have been made and additional research is warranted.

TWO
Period Profit Planning

FINANCIAL MODELING AND BUDGETING

PROFIT PLANNING AND COST-VOLUME-PROFIT
   ANALYSIS

PROBABILISTIC PROFIT BUDGETS

A period profit plan or budget for the firm as a whole, integrated with the budgets for the subdivisions or departments, is a formalized plan expressed in quantitative terms (money, units, hours, etc.) for the various phases of the future operations of the business. It is the estimate of operations that management has adopted for a future time period and can be used as a plan of action and for the purpose of control over future operations.

For control purposes, the actual results are compared with the budget, and variations are determined and analyzed. The control function involves action by management so that the company plans can be realized. Variations that are controllable should be identified and reported to the responsible management level for attention. A computer can be used to aid the control process by being programmed to print out only those variances that are significantly different from budget (i.e., that are beyond a control range); this is the concept of management by exception. Articles concerned with performance evaluation and control, and models for the investigation of variances from budget and standard are included in Part V of this book.

The profit-planning function involves a number of factors, which can include (1) the establishment of long-range company objectives; (2) the setting up of an organizational structure and functional areas of responsibility to accomplish the company objectives; (3) the analysis of operations to determine the behavior of the costs of production and expenses with regard to changes in the level of activity or volume for a given business environment. Information about cost behavior can be used in the development of period profit plans (budgets) and for project planning problems (alternative decision problems—make or buy, sell or process further, etc.; see Part I) that enter into the period profit plans, and where some or all of the variable costs are relevant for a decision.

Article 7, "Financial Modeling and 'What If' Budgeting," provides an introduction for the budgeting section. It includes a discussion of long-range planning and interrelationships of components that are used in planning models. If the projection for one of the components in a planning model is changed, several other elements in the model are likely to be affected. The article emphasizes the usefulness of a computer in preparing alternative projections based on "what if" questions. For example, what if raw material prices change by a certain percentage, what if we drop a product line, etc.?[1]

As indicated by the article, a budgetary system can include an operating budget for the planning and control of operating activities (costs, output, transactions) of a future period, a cash budget (discussed in Article 10) for the planning and control of receipts and disbursements of cash and to indicate when borrowing may be necessary, and a capital budget concerned

---

[1]For an article that shows the application of a computer for preparing "what if" planning models, see Daniel J. McCarthy and Charles A. Morrissey, "Using the Systems Analyst in Preparing Corporate Financial Models," *Financial Executive*, June 1972, pp. 40–52.

with proposed capital additions (discussed in Part III of this book and Article 4 in Part I). The different budgets affect the projected balance sheet and income statement for a future period.

The operating budget can be subdivided into such budgets as sales, production, purchases of raw material, labor, overhead, selling and administrative expenses. Where the operating programs of the company (for example, the plan for the product lines) are broken down in terms of areas of responsibility, the budget can be used as a plan of action and for the evaluation and control of the performance of departments, foremen, etc.

A budgetary process that results in establishing plans and objectives in quantitative terms and by areas of responsibility can be an important motivating factor, so that the various levels of management are concerned with the function of planning and use the adopted company budget and the specific goals set for areas of responsibility as a basis for future operations. Note that budgets for the various segments of a business should be integrated with the plan for operations of the company as a whole; this is important so that the segments are coordinated and operate to achieve a common objective for the company. A discussion of the motivational aspects of budgets and accounting system reports is presented in Article 8, "Budgeting: Functional Analysis and Behavioral Implications," and in a Part V article, "The Role of the Firm's Accounting System for Motivation."

Because of uncertainty about factors that can affect future sales, such as the action of competitors, general economic conditions and consumer demand, it is difficult to estimate accurately the future sales volume to use for budgetary planning purposes. A flexible budget model requires a knowledge of cost behavior, and this allows management to prepare budgets associated with different possible volumes of sales. The flexible budget is discussed in Article 9, "Variable Budgets and Direct Costing." This article applies techniques (high-low method, scatter diagram, and least-squares method) for separating mixed costs into fixed and variable components. A flexible or variable budget system is useful for control purposes because actual results can be compared with a budget computed for the actual volume of sales. Actual results could be compared with a target budget (i.e., the plan adopted for the period), but the target budget, unlike the flexible budget, may be based on a different volume than actually attained and the volume difference enters into the reported variances.

The article includes breakeven analysis, or the more comprehensive term cost-volume-profit analysis. This technique requires the separation of costs into fixed and variable components. The article includes a discussion of the technique, indicates it can add to the understanding and usefulness of budget procedures and forecasts, and provides information for many types of decisions. Direct (variable) costing is also part of the article discussion. The author states: "Direct costing is concerned with integrating and incorporating into the accounts a group of related techniques which include the variable budget, breakeven chart, and contribution margin analysis."

As part of the analysis of operations for profit planning and flexible budgeting purposes, a study may be made of the costs actually incurred at various volumes. Techniques for determining cost and sales volume functions include the methods of least squares and multiple regression analysis; these techniques are discussed in Part IV about forecasting. Article 9, "Variable Budgets and Direct Costing," provides useful background information for the concepts discussed in Part IV, Article 20, "The Limitations of Profit Graphs, Breakeven Analysis and Budgets," which is concerned with correlation and regression analysis, and emphasizes the importance of multiple regression analysis. Article 9 shows the application of the least-squares method for separating mixed costs into fixed and variable components. Article 20 discusses tests of the resulting equation that show the "goodness of fit" of a straight line to observed data. Depending on the outcome of the tests and whether or not future operating conditions will approximate those of the past, the resulting equation for a straight line, with fixed and variable elements developed by the least-squares method, could be used in forecasting costs for various sales volumes as required for flexible budgeting. In profit planning, we are concerned with the effects of decisions upon costs, volume and profits; therefore, a knowledge of cost behavior patterns or functions is important for planning and decision making.

Article 10, "Computer-Assisted Cash Budgeting and Sensitivity Analysis," shows how to prepare a cash budget and then explains the use of a computer program (CASHB) for cash forecasting and sensitivity analysis purposes. The article includes the FORTRAN IV computer program that can be used with a time-sharing computer system to facilitate the preparation of cash forecasts and projected income statements, and for performing sensitivity analysis.

Breakeven analysis along with the charts and graphs for presenting the profits and losses at different sales volumes is used for profit-planning purposes.[2] A master plan for the coming period may well include the cost-volume-profit information by graph and/or by formula. Article 11,

---

[2] Charles D. Mecimore, in the article, "Flexible Break-Even Analysis," *Managerial Planning*, January/February 1970, pp. 22–25, proposes the application of nomographs in breakeven analysis. A nomograph is useful in solving equations of 3 or more variables and therefore breakeven analysis would not be restricted by constraints on the number of variables employed if the proposed method is applied. The proposal for a flexible breakeven analysis could aid managers in preparing breakeven models that incorporate changes in fixed costs or changes in variable costs as a percentage of sales.

For a discussion of the expansion of the traditional form of breakeven analysis, see Rene Manes, "A New Dimension to Breakeven Analysis," *The Journal of Accounting Research*, Spring 1966, pp. 87–100. The article shows how to give effect to the time value of money, taxes, and inflation in calculating the breakeven point. Also see Ted F. Anthony and Hugh J. Watson, "Probabilistic Breakeven Analysis," *Managerial Planning*, November/December 1976, pp. 12–19, 37.

"Practical Applications of Cost-Volume-Profit Analysis," which is concerned with profit planning and breakeven analysis, and Article 20, concerned with determining cost functions and with the possible weaknesses or limitations of breakeven analysis, both include breakeven graphs showing straight lines for the cost and revenue functions. Because the accountant draws the graph with straight lines, it should be used only for a relevant range or band over which the linear cost and revenue relationships are valid. Within a range, a straight line can be a close approximation to a curve. The relevant range must be considered because once the breakeven point is passed on the accountant's graph, the greater the volume, the greater will be the profit, and this would indicate that production should continue to increase indefinitely.

The economist shows total cost and total revenue as curved lines that bend toward each other. The slope of a line tangent to the economist's total revenue curve describes the marginal revenue, and the slope of a line tangent to the total cost curve describes the marginal cost. A line tangent to the total revenue curve, and a line tangent to the total cost curve at the volume where the total cost and total revenue curves are farthest apart, will each have the same slope. This means marginal revenue and marginal cost are equal, and provides the basis for the statement in economics that where marginal cost equals marginal revenue, profit is at a maximum.

For project decisions, the manager may use the comparison of marginal cost and marginal revenue as a guide to decisions, but in actual practice may compare incremental cost and incremental revenue rather than marginal cost and marginal revenue, as the latter terms are used in economics. Remember that incremental revenue is not necessarily the same as marginal revenue nor is incremental cost necessarily the same as marginal cost. Marginal revenue is the increment in total revenue from adding one more unit, and marginal cost is the cost of one additional unit. However, in practice, a company may not be able to add just one more unit, but will rather add a block of units. Nevertheless, the guide provided by MC = MR can be useful for decision making.

The manager is seldom certain about future events and must make decisions and budgetary plans in an environment of uncertainty. Article 12, "Cost-Volume-Profit Analysis Under Conditions of Uncertainty," written by Professors Jaedicke and Robichek, introduced risk into the C-V-P model. Cost-volume-profit analysis is used in planning (see Article 11), but the traditional analysis ignores the problem of uncertainty.[3] Article 12 shows the application of probabilities resulting in an expected value model for planning purposes. Expected value models and decision trees are discussed in Article 5 of Part I about project decisions. Articles 12 and 5 provide

---

[3]The Jaedicke-Robichek article assumes a normal distribution for the problem parameters and the profit that results. For an article that discusses this assumption, see William L. Ferrara, Jack C. Hayya, and David A. Nachman, "Normalcy of Profit in the Jaedicke-Robichek Model," *The Accounting Review*, April 1972, pp. 299–307.

useful background information for the discussion in Article 13, "Toward Probabilistic Profit Budgets."

Article 13 is concerned with applications of probability concepts to develop probabilistic planning models that help management deal with the problem of uncertainty. The article integrates three probabilistic techniques, suggested in the literature, with profit budgets. "The PERT-like and probability-tree approaches [used in the article] emphasize most likely and mean values as well as measures of variability for each item in the income statement. Monte Carlo is used to simulate probability intervals for complex distributions that are too difficult to treat analytically."

7.
FINANCIAL MODELING AND "WHAT IF" BUDGETING*

Donald A. Krueger
and
John M. Kohlmeier

Many business managers are finding it increasingly productive, if not imperative, to devote more of their time and energy to planning future activities and programs. More and more, the executives responsible for directing the organization are placing increased emphasis on business strategy and the quantification of alternatives. This has all been made possible by the increased use of the computer. After years of merely processing clerical transactions, it now appears that the computer has progressed to the point where it provides management with useful tools for the planning process. Two of the most powerful tools available are financial modeling and "what if" budgeting. To place these tools in perspective, it is desirable to review the management planning process and then to define the underlying concepts of financial modeling and "what if" budgeting and describe how they are similar and how they are different.

MANAGEMENT PLANNING PROCESS

Management initiates the planning process by first establishing goals or objectives. The next step is to develop the policies and programs which will best achieve these objectives. At the top level, both the goals and the related policies and programs are likely to be broad in nature. For example, some companies state their top-level goal in terms of a desired growth rate of earnings per share. Their top-level programs identify the major businesses they want to be in and whether to achieve their objective through internal growth or through acquisition.

---

*From *Management Accounting*, May 1972, pp. 25–30. Copyrighted 1972 by National Association of Accountants. Reprinted by permission.

At the operational levels in the organization there is a narrowing of the scope of concern and greater emphasis on timing. For example, goals at this level are expressed in terms of a time phased, desired market-share penetration. The programs embrace the introduction of specific new products or services and the related promotional campaigns. To develop these programs and policies, management would:

1.   Determine the market potential and the competitive climate,
2.   Assess the strengths and weaknesses of their own organization,
3.   Define alternative courses of action,
4.   Evaluate the alternatives, and
5.   Select the best program to follow.

As a starting point, historical data relating to markets and competition, costs, technology and financial results often provide the first clues about the future. When this data is properly manipulated, it often suggests relationships and trends useful in projecting the future. But the past does not always repeat itself, and a key ingredient in planning is management's expectations as to how future conditions will differ from those of the past.

The planning process may encompass many different time horizons. Logically, top-level, longer-range plans would precede the development of more detailed shorter-range plans. The horizon of the long-range planning process is determined by the time necessary to change the business such as building a new plant, introducing a new product, developing a new market, or acquiring raw materials.

The first output should be a long-range plan. This overall plan might include a marketing plan, research and development plan, an operating plan, a capital expenditure plan, a cash-flow plan and a profit plan. Obviously, these individual plans should be consistent and well coordinated.

Although in some instances the word "plan" may have a rigid, frozen, monolithic connotation, a plan should be a flexible, dynamic set of guidelines for action. As such, a plan is subject to review and revision by management at any time.

In addition to long-range plans, a well-managed company requires a short-range plan or budget. This plan would contain many of the same elements as the long-range plan and should logically be coordinated with it. A common failure of the planning activities of many companies today is a lack of proper coordination between the current-year plan and the long-range plan.

Current-year plans typically encompass considerably more detail than the long-range plan because the freedom to change things is much less in the short run.

LONG-RANGE PLANNING PROBLEMS

In many companies, there is a failure to quantify plans and to perform adequate quantitative analysis of alternatives. This is unfortunate because the process of putting numbers on concepts and ideas provides a realistic hard-headed approach to planning. The failure to carry out this function can be attributed to the amount of detail involved and the need to recognize many business interrelationships. Those companies that do put numbers on their plans typically find the process slow and time consuming. It is not unusual to wait weeks or even months for the development of an overall plan. Because of this slowness and consequent expense, many companies limit the number of alternatives considered and curtail the scope of their analysis.

Now, however, through the use of the computer and the technique of financial modeling, these problems of long-range planning can be overcome. Our experience has shown that using these tools, it is possible to:

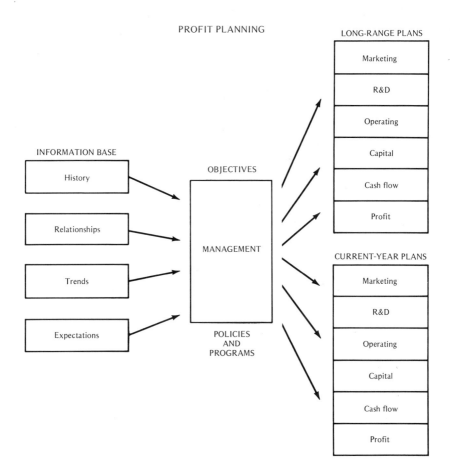

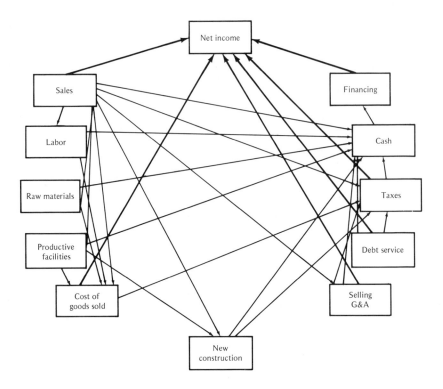

1. Recognize the significant interrelationships,
2. Consider all the reasonable alternatives,
3. Determine the full financial effect of each alternative, and
4. Do all of these at computer speed.

In order to understand the use of a model in the planning process it is necessary to review and illustrate the steps involved in developing a comprehensive long-range plan.

PLANNING INTERRELATIONSHIPS

Consider the problem of developing a long-range financial projection for a manufacturing company. The starting point is, of course, a sales forecast. This projection would be derived from a study of:

1. Past trends,
2. Expected changes, and
3. Knowledge of the markets involved.

Based on the sales forecast, projections of the labor, raw materials, and productive facilities required are made. Usually, these projections would reflect the activity levels implied by the sales forecast and the cost rates expected to prevail. These projections of labor, raw materials and overhead would then lead to a determination of the cost of sales.

Next, new construction of plant and equipment must be considered. Plant expenditure decisions logically depend on expected sales volumes, the development of new markets or products, and the relative efficiency of existing plant facilities.

Finally, general and administrative expenses and debt interest costs must be projected, and all the tax consequences must be considered. The changes in sales, cost of goods sold, new construction, selling, general and administrative expenses, and debt interest directly affect the amount of taxes to which the company would be subject, including both federal and state income taxes and local taxes as well. At this point we begin to see some of the complexities of these interrelationships.

These interrelationships become graphically more apparent when the effect of all these changes on available cash and the requirements for cash are considered. Additional sales will generate more cash but these funds will be offset by expenditures incurred for:

1. Labor,
2. Raw materials,
3. New construction,
4. Selling, general and administrative costs,
5. Debt interest, and
6. Taxes.

This in turn leads to a consideration of financing which plays such a crucial role in business planning today. Logically, financing plans are developed after giving consideration to all cash requirements and the amount of cash generated internally to meet such needs. And, of course, no consideration of financing is possible today without first considering mergers and acquisitions and their impact on the financial structure of the company. And, finally, the objective of all these interrelated calculations is reached which is a projection of net income and earnings per share.

The significance of these interrelationships is that when one component of the projection is changed, several other components are likely to be affected. And, changing components of the projection is exactly what an alert management and planning group want to do. No sooner is a projection completed than a wide range of questions arise; questions such as:

What if raw material prices increase 10 percent?
What if we drop a product line?
What if we close a plant?
What if we acquire another company?

To answer each of these questions would require a complete re-analysis which, using conventional manual methods, would be slow and time consuming. This is the place where the use of financial models and the computer is advantageous.

FINANCIAL PLANNING MODELS

A financial planning model is a representation of a company based on a set of assumed conditions. The model is capable of generating pro forma or projected operating and financial statements. Use of the model facilitates answering "what if" type questions.

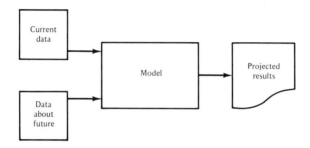

In operation, a model requires data representing the current status of the company. This type of data is routinely produced by a good information reporting and control system. In addition to current status data, a model requires data describing the future; these are management's planning assumptions. The model itself is a set of logical business relationships and the output is a set of projected results.

Models basically provide two types of services: data management functions, and projection power. Data management includes: the definition and establishment of a data base, facility to update this data base, provision for access to the data for use in projections, capability to compare and summarize the data, facility to display or print the data, and the ability to retain the data for future use.

Projection power is the capability of a model to perform computations and make projections. The goal of projection power is to transfer the routine clerical computational aspects of planning from the planner to the computer. This frees the planner to concentrate on the more important creative aspects of planning.

To illustrate this concept, consider the problem of projecting sales over a five-year period. One approach would require the user to input a sales figure for each year. This approach involves no projection power and such a model would be little more than a typewriter.

Another approach, however, might use a relationship to project sales whereby sales this year are set equal to sales last year increased by a growth factor. This approach involves the use of projection power. A truly flexible model would provide for either use of the relationship or user input.

A more complex illustration of projection power is the set of relationships shown below which might be used to project cost of sales.

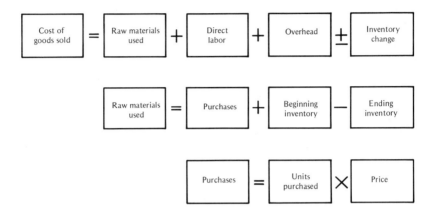

Notice that these relationships are basically simple and arithmetic in nature and would be understandable to most businessmen. These are the type of relationships contained in most financial planning models.

Turning to the design of a model, an important consideration is the proper balance between complexity and simplicity. All models are abstractions and, as such, represent a compromise between complexity and simplicity.

By adding details and relationships to a model and thereby increasing complexity, the model builder provides greater realism and the ability to explain more phenomena. Complexity, however, reduces our ability to understand the model and its relevance to the real world, and extraneous detail often clouds the real issues. Furthermore, complexity results in higher cost and greater difficulty in operating a model.

A satisfactory balance between complexity and simplicity is one of the most important considerations in the use of models.

Some of the important contributions of the modeling approach to planning are as follows:

First, the process of developing an overall model of a company forces everyone to take a top-level, overall viewpoint. Second, since a model must be capable of evaluating alternatives, the major thrust of the effort is to discover and use relationships between key factors, which leads to a better understanding of the business itself. Executive participation in a model building project can result in an unparalleled learning experience. Third, a model projects over several time periods and forces consideration of lead/lag precedent relationships which can be lost in a single period analysis. Furthermore, it forces consideration of whether important sectors are growing or declining.

ANNUAL PROFIT PLANNING

During the long-range planning process, management must develop a strategy for the future, and by examining alternative programs, must identify those that appear to be superior. Further, from this process a valid starting point will be developed for current-year action. The current-year budget is then, in some respects, the first year of the longer-range plan. This is the first difference between financial modeling and budgeting—the time horizon used.

Functional and department budget guidelines are developed by executive management from the planning process in order that the task of coordination and involvement of key supervisors can result in specific action plans for their departments. These guidelines are distributed to the organization for detailed development of specific plans as well as the development of the revenue and cost data associated with the plan. The interpretation which flows back up level by level, is the budget. In this manner, another difference between modeling and budgeting can be loosely described as a top-down versus bottom-up approach.

In a common timing sequence, the steps involved in preparation of the annual profit planning budget include development of the market plan, the research and development budget (and related projects), the sales item forecast and the marketing expense budget. After allowing for changes in inventory levels, an inventory and production plan, a manufacturing budget for labor, material, and expense are developed, and then the general

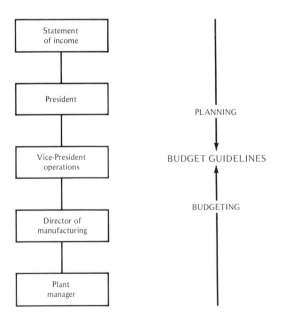

ANNUAL PROFIT PLANNING OVERVIEW

Capital expenditures budgeting

R&D budget

Market plan → Sales item forecast → Inventory & production plan → Manufacturing budget (labor & materials) → Balance sheet, cash flow, profit plan

Expense budget —marketing → Expense budget —manufacturing → Expense budget —G&A

and administrative expense budget. All of these must be coordinated with the capital expenditures budget in order to prepare the balance sheet, cash flow, and final profit plan.

TYPICAL BUDGETING PROBLEMS

In far too many instances, the budgeting process is hampered because it starts with an inadequate determination of the ground rules and assumptions under which the budget will be prepared. In practice, too, the benefits resulting from budgeting have frequently been minimized, if not negated, by some apparently chronic budgeting problems, such as:

1. The budgeting process is time consuming both in executive and clerical effort and also in elapsed time. Many companies start a calendar year budget in summer and end six or seven months later—exhausted.
2. The budget process is prone to clerical error because the mass of detail involved almost automatically precludes supervisory review.
3. Few companies have an adequate historical record that can be examined in order to exclude nonrecurring activity and provide a proper base to project new programs.
4. The clerical effort involved discourages analysis. As a result, very few of these alternatives are ever really examined in depth.

5.   Finally, the end budget is frequently changed by executive management when the return on investment and earnings per share are not up to expectations. Insufficient time remains to correct the underlying budgets with the result that departmental plans do not support the overall corporate plan.

"WHAT IF" BUDGETING

The use of the computer in budgeting not only provides the ability to perform the normal planning process and develop a basis for evaluating performance in terms of actual activity compared to planned activity but, in addition, such systems enhance the budget preparation process by:

1.   Providing the ability to retrieve historic data for analysis,
2.   Requiring minimal clerical effort through the use of turnaround documents and computer processing for computations and summaries; and
3.   Making possible a budget cycle that could start in the fall and conclude prior to the start of the calendar year—a significant reduction in the budget time cycle.

Such a budget system could be processed on the computer in about four hours for a medium-sized company. Thus the computer budgeting system encourages a rigorous analysis of alternatives and facilitates the preparation of departmental and corporate plans on a coordinated basis. Further,

an integrated budgeting system enables management to track current and projected performance against the original target for the full year and obtain better information regarding the results for the full year.

An overview of the data base required is useful to explain the specific, detailed data used in "what if" budgeting as compared to an average relationship used in modeling.

The system (through programmed instructions and a detailed data base of lead times, desired inventory levels, production capacities, standard data and standard costs) develops preliminary operating plans that would include the sales forecast, production plan, responsibility reporting budgets, standard costs, and profit plan. Budgets may be on either a fixed or variable basis.

Typical of the reports produced during this process would be a sales profitability forecast—summarized by key product, key customer and by district. The production plan would include reports as to manpower and material requirements. And the responsibility reporting modules would provide departmental and summary reports which would include the latest estimates for the current year for purposes of review and evaluation. Illustrative of this is the quarterly budget summary of expense for the manufacturing manager. Illustrative of the completion of the initial budgeting process is the quarterly profit plan compared to the latest estimate for the current year.

ANALYSIS OF ALTERNATIVES

Now the company executives must decide whether the annual plans developed by the management team, in response to the budget guidelines, are satisfactory in view of the company's long-range objectives. Net profit, earnings per share, cash and inventory positions are only a few of the items management will screen during this review period. Some or many of these elements may appear undesirable and management may then start to examine alternatives such as:

> What if unit sales increase 15 percent through changed marketing programs?
>
> What if we add a second shift to accommodate a revised marketing program?
>
> What if wage rates increase 5 percent because of pending union negotiations?
>
> What if selected expenses are cut 10 percent to improve earnings per share?

Typically, these questions are narrower in scope than those suggested during the long-range planning process and represent more a fine tuning

PROFIT PLAN

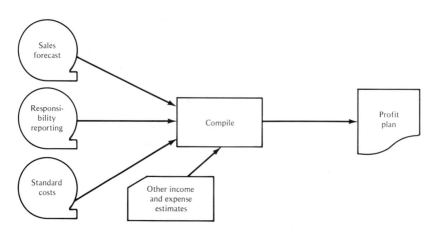

and balancing process. As a result of this reexamination phase, new profit plans are developed. Any factor which is changed will be discussed with the responsible supervisor for review and comment.

This process will continue until the management team has settled on an agreeable plan. At this point, it can be finalized as the formal operating and profit plan for the year which can be characterized as a type of contract between executive and operating and supervisory management for the coming year.

THE BUDGET IN USE

During the year, the budget is used as a standard of performance. Usually, the question arises each month as to what the full year will look like. Rather than do a straight-line projection, the computer budgeting system permits a rapid, supportable answer to that question and is capable of responding to changed business conditions. Note the columns "current estimate" and "original target" which illustrate how comparisons can be developed during the year of projected activity while maintaining the base checkpoint of the original budget.

"WHAT IF" BUDGETING SUMMARY

Having now briefly defined "what if" budgeting, and illustrated certain of its features, the key benefits of this approach can be summarized as:

First, the process facilitates the preparation of the preliminary budget by providing a coordinated basis for each supervisor to begin the budgeting process, by permitting the work of preparing the budget to take place

INCOME STATEMENT

(000 OMITTED)

| | --------YEAR TO DATE-------- | | --------TOTAL YEAR-------- | |
	AMOUNT	UNDER OVER-U BUDGET	CURRENT ESTIMATE	ORIGINAL TARGET
NET SALES	$3,977	$25	$12,050	$11,965
COST OF SALES	2,874	24	8,705	8,610
GROSS PROFIT	1,103	1	3,345	3,355
EXPENSES—				
GENERAL AND ADMINISTRATIVE	206	3	613	625
SALES	288	15U	867	837
RESEARCH AND ENGINEERING	46	1	141	145
TOTAL EXPENSES	540	11U	1,621	1,607
OPERATING PROFIT	563	12	1,724	1,748
PROVISION FOR INCOME TAXES	309	5	942	954
NET PROFIT	$ 254	$ 7	$ 782	$ 794
EARNINGS PER SHARE			2.61	2.65

nearer in time to the period being planned and by minimizing the clerical effort while improving accuracy through an integrated approach.

Second, "what if" budgeting facilitates analysis through a fast, comprehensive response that encourages management to consider new alternatives with the realization they can in fact receive an answer capable of being reviewed in a short period of time. These analyses can be performed with the assurance that departmental goals are properly related to overall corporate plans because of the comprehensive and integrated processing of the computer budgeting system. This consideration of alternatives greatly improves the validity and reliability of the final budget.

Third, a "what if" budgeting system not only provides the traditional budget basis for performance measurement but also provides the ability during the year to project and compare revised plans with the original plan.

CONCLUSION

Management today is becoming increasingly aware of the practical tools available to assist it in areas that are uniquely its responsibility. These tools may be implemented on either in-house or service bureau facilities, and accordingly, company size is no barrier to their use. Rather, the main limitation would be management philosophy about the future.

8.

BUDGETING: FUNCTIONAL ANALYSIS AND BEHAVIORAL IMPLICATIONS*

V. Bruce Irvine

The budget can be a powerful tool for motivating people to achieve the organization's objectives or it can be a positive hindrance. This article analyzes the effects of budgeting on people and shows how it can lead to either bad or good consequences according to the way it is applied in various types of organization.

Many of those who have written about budgets have emphasized the problems resulting from typical budgeting systems. Little enthusiasm has been voiced for the practical effectiveness of budgets as a means of obtaining the optimal benefits of which such a device is capable.

A more positive approach might result from a consideration of the control and motivational effects of budgets on the behavior of people. But an analysis of the reactions of these people (supervisors, foremen, laborers) to control devices (such as budgets) has received little attention as a specific subject in the literature of the past decade. The studies reported have usually concentrated attention on improving the usefulness of budgets from a top management viewpoint and have de-emphasized the subordinate positions. Also, many of the studies have been conducted by behavioral scientists and have not been incorporated into accounting and management thought and teaching. Consequently, although accountants and management are aware that their actions have behavioral implications, they have not thoroughly understood what these are. The result is uncertainty, confusion and indecision when human problems do arise.

The purpose of this article will be to make a functional analysis of budgeting towards the goal of maximizing long-run profits (considered to be the present value of the owner's net worth). An analysis of reactions of the employees on whom budgets are primarily exercised, rather than a purely management viewpoint analysis, will be used to develop basic propositions. Human behavioral aspects of budgets, therefore, become a very relevant factor in this approach. After investigation of why employees react as they do, the usefulness of budgets in view of such reactions and the

*From *Cost and Management*, March–April 1970, pp. 6–16. Reprinted by permission of the publisher.

implications of suggestions for making budgets more successful and acceptable can be considered within particular situations facing modern-day business.

DEFINITIONAL AND TECHNICAL CONSIDERATIONS

A functional analysis considers the various consequences of a particular activity and determines whether or not these consequences aid in the achievement of the organization's objective. According to Merton,[1] the consequences of an activity are functional if they increase the ability of a given system to achieve a desired goal. A consequence is dysfunctional if it hinders the achievement of the goal. Consequences of an activity may also be classified as manifest (recognized and intended by the participants in the system) or latent (neither intended nor recognized). Decisions based only on manifest consequences may often be incorrect because of latent consequences.

A budget is a device intended to provide greater effectiveness in achieving organizational efficiency. To be effective, however, the functional aspects must outweigh the dysfunctional aspects. Whether or not this will be true will depend upon many factors which will be discussed and summarized in a model of the elements of budgeting.

First, it is necessary to understand what a budget is. Although formal definitions of a budget exist, a definition is not always the most relevant aspect of understanding a concept.

Amitai Etzioni distinguishes between two types of models in organizational analysis.[2] The survival system consists of activities which, if fulfilled, allow a system to exist. Budgets are not part of such a system. Organizations in the past have functioned and in the future will function without the help of budgets. Budgets can be classified within an effectiveness system. These "define a pattern of interactions among the elements of the system which would make it more effective in the service of a given goal."[3]

A budget, as a formal set of figures written on a piece of paper, is in itself merely a quantified plan for future activities. However, when budgets are used for control, planning and motivation, they become instruments which cause functional and dysfunctional consequences both manifest and latent which determine how successful the tool will be.

Budgets mean different things to different people according to their different points of view. Accountants see them from the preparation aspect,

---

[1]Merton, R. "A Paradigm for Functional Analysis in Sociology," in *Sociological Theory: A Book of Readings*, by L. Coser and B. Rosenberg, New York, Macmillan, 1957, pp. 458–467.

[2]Etzioni, Amitai, "Two Approaches to Organizational Analysis: A Critique and a Suggestion," in Bobbs-Merrill Reprint Series in the Social Sciences 8–80. Reprinted by permission of *Administrative Science Quarterly*, Vol. 5 (September 1960), pp. 257–278.

[3]Ibid., p. 272.

managers from the implementation aspect, and behavioral scientists from the human implication aspect. All of these viewpoints must be melded together if budgets are to obtain the best functional results.

There are many types of budgets. The major purpose for having budgets, the type of organization using a budget, the personalities of people handling the budget, the personal characteristics of people subject to budget direction, the leadership style of the organization, and the method of preparing a budget are all factors accounting for budget type and style.

The technical procedures involved in the preparation and use of budget figures are similar for most organizations. People make estimates (standards) of what they expect should reflect future events. These estimates are then compared to what actually happened and the differences (variances) are studied.

THE FUNCTIONAL ASPECTS OF BUDGET SYSTEMS

In what specific way do budgets make management action more efficient and effective in maximizing the present value of the owners' worth?

Basically, a budget system enables management more effectively to plan, coordinate, control and evaluate the activities of the business. These are functional, manifest consequences in terms of their desirability.

Planning means establishing objectives in advance so that members of the organization will have specific, activity-directed goals to guide their actions. Budgets are quantitative plans for action. As such, they force management to examine the available resources and to determine how these can be used efficiently.

The point that budgets require this clarification and concrete quantification of ideas is not usually recognized directly by budgeting people as a benefit. As such, it could be considered functional and latent.

The planning aspect of budgeting has other latent functions. Planning requires that the plans be communicated to those involved in carrying them out. Communication is enhanced by distributing the budget to those responsible for various parts of it.

A budget makes lower level managers more aware of where they fit into an organization. Their budget indicates what is expected of them and that they have a goal towards which their activities are to be directed.

With a budget, junior (new) members of an organization have a better idea of where the company is going and are made to feel that the business is concerned about their future. This can affect both their own future plans and the company's recruitment policy and turnover problems.

When a person is given an objective, he is more likely to feel that he is part of the organization and that the upper echelons are interested in his work. Conversely, top management is likely to become more interested in, and aware of, the activities of lower level employees.

These latent, functional consequences of budgets create interest and, possibly, enthusiasm which increases morale and could result in greater efficiency and initiative.

Planning of departmental activities must be coordinated so that bottlenecks do not occur and interdepartmental strife can be limited. A budget system can assist in this coordination. By basing organizationl activity on the limiting factor (such as sales, production, working capital), a comprehensive budget coordinating all of the firm's activities can be approved by top management and the controller. Such a budget permits these people to bring together their overall knowledge of the firm's abilities and limitations. By using budgets to coordinate activities, the organization is more likely to operate at an optimal level, given the constraints on its resources.

The control consequences are among the more important aspects of budgeting. Because a budget plan exists, decisions are not merely spontaneous reactions to stimuli in an environment of unclarified goals. The budget provides relevant information to a decision maker at the time he must choose between alternatives. Therefore, a budget implicitly incorporates control at the point of the decision. However, provision for taking advantage of unforeseen situations should certainly be allowed even though a budget is violated.

A second type of control can be derived from budgets. A comparison of actual with budgeted performance after decisions have been made reveals to management the performance of the organization as a whole and of the individual responsible members.

A comparison merely reveals discrepancies. The action which is taken as a result of variances is in the hands of management. But the investigation of why there are variances, whether or not they are controllable, and the resulting control procedures is stimulated by the budgeting process. The result is the discovery of methods to save costs, improvement in the firm's efficiency, and better future planning.

Control of both types is important to top management because it cannot maintain personal contact with those in the lower management ranks. Devices such as budgets, employment contracts, job descriptions and rules are therefore necessary to direct subordinate behavior. In general, control is based on the assumption that individuals are motivated by their own security needs to fulfil the plans and obey the rules. To the extent that this is true, the benefits to be derived from the control aspects of budgeting can be deemed functional and manifest.

These benefits could be obtained only in the ideal situation where budgets work as they are intended to work. The theoretical benefits make budgets very appealing devices, but the practical problems of implementing and using them greatly affect their usefulness. Most of the problems arise from the difficulty of convincing people to accept and use a budget. Mechanical problems also exist. These difficulties create many possibilities for dysfunctional consequences to occur with the result that some functional consequences become difficult, if not impossible, to attain.

DYSFUNCTIONAL ASPECTS OF BUDGET SYSTEMS

Any system which involves motivation and control of individuals has dysfunctional aspects, simply because human behavior cannot be predicted or controlled with certainty. Frequently, activities by management to obtain desired functional results will actually lead to dysfunctional consequences. Management must understand why such a reversal can occur so that existing problems can be solved or an environment created which prevents problems arising.

This section will indicate how results of a budget system can be dysfunctional in nature. The basic approach will be to analyze the deterrents to achieving particular functional results. Within a particular organization, the dysfunctional aspects must be considered in relation to the functional aspects in order to evaluate the worthiness of a budget system. Obviously, if the dysfunctional consequences of an action outweigh the functional aspects, management should delete the activity. Because each business is unique, no attempt can be made to state that certain activities will be dysfunctional or functional in every situation.

Because factors which can lead to dysfunctional consequences are complex, each will be analyzed separately although it is realized they are usually interrelated.

A. The Term "Budget"

The first dysfunctional consequence of a budget system results from the name itself. Traditionally, budgets have carried a negative connotation for many:

> . . . some of the words historically associated with the term budget are; imposed, dictated by the top, authorized. And what are the original purposes of control—to reduce, to eliminate, to increase productivity, to secure conformance, to assure compliance, to inform about deviation. An historical meaning of budget is to husband resources—to be niggardly, tight, Scrooge-like.[4]

If attitudes expressing such beliefs are not eliminated at the start, the budget will never get off the ground. One method of eliminating this problem is to refrain from calling the activity "budgeting."

B. Organizational Arrangements of Authority and Responsibility

If a budget system is to be used to control and evaluate personnel, the persons involved must possess responsibility and authority over what is being assigned to them. Consequently a large and/or decentralized organi-

---

[4]Green, Jr., David, "Budgeting and Accounting: The Inseparable Siamese Twins," *Budgeting*, November 1965, p. 11.

zation would probably have a greater potential use for budgeting than would a small, highly centralized business.

Centralized organizations may simply use budgets to plan and coordinate future activities. Because responsibility, control and authority rest with the top executives in such a business, any attempt to reward, punish or hold lower level employees responsible for variances would achieve nothing beneficial and would probably cause resentment. Any negative feelings on the part of those who follow directives in carrying out operations would likely lead to less than optimal achievement of organizational objectives. Therefore, even though budgets can be used to improve planning and coordination, assignment of control responsibilities where there is no power to carry out those responsibilities could easily create dysfunctional, latent consequences.

On the other hand, overemphasis on departmentalization can also have dysfunctional, latent effects:

> Budget records, as administered, foster a narrow viewpoint on the part of the user. The budget records serve as a constant reminder that the important aspect to consider is one's own department and not one's own plant.[5]

Overemphasis on one's own department can lead to considerable cost in man hours, money and interpersonal relations when responsibility for variances, particularly large ones, is being determined. The result is a weakening of cooperation and coordination between departments.

C. Role-Conflict Aspects of Budgeting

Status differences, or more accurately role-conflict between staff and line personnel, are an important source of dysfunctional consequences. The problems created affect budget usefulness directly and also indirectly through their effect on communication, motivation and participation. The basic difficulties arise because of differences in the way budget staff people and line personnel understand the budgeting system and each other.

From Figure 1,[6] it can be seen how important budgets and the budget staff are in the supervisors' or foremen's working world. Ninety-nine percent of the supervisors and foremen questioned in four companies stated that the budget department was either first or second in importance of impact on the performance of their activity.

---

[5] Argyris, Chris, *The Impact of Budgets on People*, Ithaca, N.Y. Prepared for the Controllership Foundation, Inc. at Cornell University, 1952, p. 23.
[6] The source of this figure and study is Argyris, C., op. cit., a summary of comments and statements, pp. 10–12.

	MOST AFFECT	2ND MOST AFFECT	TOTAL
Production Control	55%		
Budget Department	45%	54%	99%

Figure 1. Responses to the Request "Name the departments affecting your actions most"—Asked of Supervisors and Foremen Individually in Four Firms

From the supervisors' and foremen's follow-up comments, it was readily apparent that the budget department's influence was not only significant, it was usually considered troublesome as well. Why should this be so? Some suggested reasons are:

1. Line employees see budgets as providing results only and not the reasons for those results. Any explanations of variances by the financial staff, such as failure to meet expected production or inadequate use of materials, prove grossly insufficient. Causes behind these explanations still have to be determined before the supervisors and foremen could consider budget reports as being useful to them or presenting a fair appraisal of their activities to top management.

2. Budgets are seen as emphasizing past performance and as a device for predicting the future. Supervisors and foremen are basically concerned with the present and with handling immediate problems. Budget figures would often be ignored in order to solve present difficulties.

3. Supervisors and foremen apparently see budgets as being too rigid. In some cases, budget standards have not been changed for two or three years. Even if they now met such a budget, they often would not be performing efficiently. Budget people would then adjust the budget. In such cases, those working under a budget would not really know what was expected of them until after they had submitted their cost reports and had received a control report.

4. Supervisors and foremen would also resent the opposite treatment of constantly changing a budget in the belief that increased efficiency would result. Such a procedure would lead them to believe, and often justly so, that budgets were unrealistically set. Budget men would be seen as individuals who could never be satisfied as they would raise the budget if a person made or came close to his previous budget. This would only result in frustration for the supervisor or foreman. The feeling that the company executives did not believe in the supervisor's own desire to do a good job could easily be implied when budgets are continually changing.

5. Thoughts about budgets are further aggravated when foremen and supervisors receive budget reports on their performance in a complicated format with an analysis that is incomprehensible to them. Supervisors felt that the job of budget people was to be critical and that the use of jargon and specialized formats enabled them to justify their criticism of others without too much debate.

Whether or not these criticisms are logical and rational is not important. The point is that such feelings can and do exist. If the budget is regarded as merely emphasizing history, being too rigid, unrealistic, unattainable and unclear and if budget people are seen as overconcerned with figures, unconcerned with line problems and cut off by a language of their own, there can be no doubt that the effectiveness of a budget system would deteriorate.

The problems are compounded if the budget personnel's attitude is unconducive to overcoming these opinions. Budget people should see their jobs as examining, analyzing and looking for new ways to improve plant efficiency. They should also think of a budget as an objective that should fairly challenge factory personnel. Since it cannot be assumed that line personnel subscribe to or even recognize these ideas, the ideas should be impressed upon them directly through adequate budget introduction and education. Moreover, the effective use of budgets cannot be forced upon supervisors and foremen; it must be accepted by them. This can only be accomplished if budget people try to work constructively with line people as compatriots rather than commanders. This accord is usually very difficult to bring about. Often budget people will not even attempt it or simply give up on it because of lack of success. They conclude, correctly or incorrectly, that the line personnel's unsatisfactory use of budgets is due to their lack of education, understanding and interest.

Given this unwillingness to buck line opposition by the budget personnel and the line's viewpoint of budgeting as a hindrance to their performance, a classic role conflict is created. The optimal benefits possible from budgeting cannot be obtained in such an environment.

Argyris also determined how foremen and supervisors felt the potential dysfunctional results of budgeting could be overcome. Suggestions dealt mainly with improving the outlook of budget men. According to the line personnel, budgeting people should be taught that budgets are merely opinions, not the "be-all and end-all." They should also be taught, it was felt, that line employees are not inherently lazy, that budget men should learn to look at a problem from another's point of view, and that they are not superior to supervisory people. Also suggested were the use of timely and understandable reports to foremen and supervisors, the practice of conferring with people who have variances so that the budget report indicates the real cause to top management, and the setting of realistic budgets.

The problems arising are not, however, entirely the fault of the budget staff. Supervisors and foremen must put more effort into understanding the budget figures, they must not be continually suspicious of budgets, and they should use budgets in performing their duties. Most important, they should alter their outlook toward budgeting. Budgets must be realistic and fair, but also foremen and supervisors should realize that the budget is designed to help them achieve the standards management expects of them.

How can these requirements be achieved? An educational program involving foremen, supervisors, middle and upper management, and budget personnel could help to clarify the different viewpoints and promote understanding of each other's objectives and difficulties. Such a program should precede the introduction of a budgeting system and continue after the system has been introduced.

D. Budgets and Non-Management People

The involvement of laborers (non-management personnel) in the budgeting process presents both functional and dysfunctional possibilities. Often, front-line supervisors who have a budget to meet do not use it as a device to spur their subordinates. According to the comments reported by Argyris, they fear that workers would look upon such action unfavorably and that no benefit would be received.

The proposition that workers would not respond to budgetary pressures is challenged by W. F. Whyte:

> "How do workers see budgets? They often recognize that management people are worried about costs, but with the foremen afraid to put the cost situation to them, they remain uninvolved in the struggle."[7]

Since workers generally have not been directly involved in budgetary systems, the question of whether or not such involvement would be functional is unresolved.

E. Motivational Aspects of Budgeting

The most controversial area of budgeting concerns its motivational implications.

The budget makes information available for comparison of expected with actual performance. When such an evaluation of performance is known to result in rewards and punishments, people are expected to be motivated to do their best. Let us examine this assumption and its possible functional or dysfunctional consequences.

Argyris states that budgets are principal instruments for creating pressure which motivates individuals.[8] Budgets can also be seen as creating more pressure than they actually do. This "pressure illusion" is due to the

---

[7]Whyte, W. F., Men at Work, Richard D. Irwin, Inc. and The Dorsey Press, Inc., Homewood, Ill., 1961, p. 495.

[8]Op. cit., Argyris.

fact that the budget is a concrete, quantitative instrument and managers and supervisors, feeling pressure from more abstract sources, place the blame for it on the concrete budget.

Factors directly related to budget pressures are budget "pep" talks (A), red circles around poor showings (B), production and sales drives using budgets (C), threats of reprimand (D), and feelings of failure if budgets are not met (E). These can all be considered as functional and manifest in terms of their motivational intent.

There are, however, counteracting effects which can be dysfunctional and latent in terms of budget effectiveness. These factors include informal agreements among managers and/or supervisors (V), fear of loss of job if efficiency increases but cannot be maintained (W), union agreements against speedups (X), performance abilities of individual employees (Y), and abilities of work teams as a whole (Z).

Equilibrium is attained when:

$$A + B + C + D + E = V + W + X + Y + Z$$

Management, by increasing one or more of the components on the left hand side of the relationship or by adding additional ones, can increase productivity. This increase is matched by an increase in tension, uneasiness, resentment and suspicion on the part of the employees. This pressure increase is absorbed by joining groups which are strongly cohesive against top management and budget people. Again equilibrium is attained but each time pressures are increased by top management, they must become more intense as resistance is higher.

When and if management feels that the pressures are detrimental to the organization, it may attempt to reduce the causes on the left hand side of the equation. This does not result in decreased anti-management feeling because the groups have developed into relatively permanent social units and the individuals feel the pressures may occur again. Therefore, in the long run, increasing pressures may be very dysfunctional because of these latent features.

The rational way for management to approach this problem would be to concentrate its activities on reducing the forces that decrease efficiency rather than on increasing the factors that tend to increase efficiency.

Other dysfunctional ways of relieving motivational pressure could easily exist:

1. Interdepartmental strife could occur. A manager, supervisor or foreman could try to blame the variances on someone else. This would result in concentrated effort by individuals to promote only the cause of their own departments. The personal rivalries thus caused and the lack of cooperation among departments could mean decreased efficiency for the company in achieving its overall goals.

2. Another type of strife develops when the line employees blame the staff employees for their predicaments and absolve themselves

of the responsibility for the variances. Budget people become scapegoats for problems and salesmen are blamed for incorrect predictions or orders that make the production process unstable.

3. An individual may internalize the personal pressure he feels. By not outwardly showing his problems, he would build up tension within himself. Eventually, frustration would develop and he would perform less efficiently in the long run.

4. If internal means of relieving pressure are used, manipulation of activities may result. Reporting sizable variances when one knows he will be over his budget may allow him to shift his costs so that he will easily make his budget in the next period. Saving easy jobs until just before the end of a budget period may enable a person to achieve the stipulated goal.

The point is that, in the short run, increasing motivational pressure through budgets may be functional but, in the long run, it may also be very dysfunctional.

Andrew C. Stedry postulates additional concepts concerning motivation through budgeting.[9] Through experiment, Stedry developed the findings shown in Figure 2.

The level of costs for which a person will strive (aspired costs) will be conceived by the individual in relation to past experience, confidence in his personal skills, expectation of future difficulties, and his feelings about the budget costs. Aspired and budget costs do not necessarily (or usually) coincide. The aspired costs are what the individual sets for himself. The

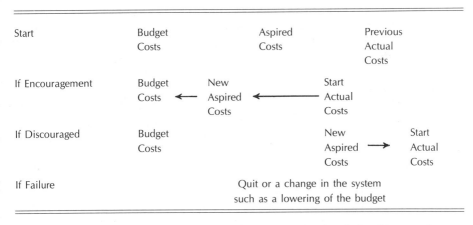

Figure 2. Simplified Model of Stedry's Motivational Relationships Involving Aspirations

[9] Stedry, Andrew C., *Budget Control and Cost Behavior*, Englewood Cliffs, N.J., Prentice-Hall, Inc., 1960.

budget costs are set by top management. When actual costs are compared to these two costs, the reaction of the employees depends on the discrepancies involved:

1. Other things being equal, aspiration levels will move relative to the actual costs depending on the degree of discrepancy.

2. A person will be encouraged if the discrepancy between actual costs and aspired costs is not greater than an amount known as the discouragement point. Aspirations would be set higher on the next period of performance measurement.

3. A person will be discouraged if the discrepancy is greater than the discouragement point but less than a failure point. In this case, aspirations would move downward.

4. If the discrepancy is greater than the failure point, the system would cease to exist or a new one would be needed. Otherwise the individual concerned would resign.

Stedry concludes that management should set high, unattainable budgets to motivate individuals to achieve the greatest efficiency. "Unattainable" would have to mean that the discrepancy between aspired costs, formulated after the high budget was presented, and actual costs could not exceed the discouragement point. Such a policy would mean that individuals receiving separate budgets would be manipulated in accordance with the variances in the size of their discouragement points.

This may sound all right in theory but in practice the reactions of employees could make this a dangerous proposition for long-run efficiency. If individuals found out that they were the subjects of outright manipulation, they could become rebellious and ignore future budgets whether they were fair or not. Other management control devices would probably be considered with unwarranted suspicion. Moreover, how is management going to determine the aspiration level and discouragement point of each individual, a necessary requirement for setting "personal" budgets? The use of individual budget standards would also have to be kept confidential. Otherwise, the resentment that employees would feel might lead them to resist all budgeting attempts and even to leave the organization.

Stedry's study suggests that participation in budget preparation is not as beneficial as having management set the budget. He points out, however, that participation may be desirable where low budgets are given as managers, supervisors and foremen would likely feel that they are capable of achieving greater efficiency and would say so.

Stedry's study is limited in that long-run results were not extensively examined. Also, the nature of his "laboratory" data leads to serious questions as to whether "real business world" conditions were reproduced.[10]

---

[10]Becker, Selwyn and Green, Jr., David, "Budgeting and Employee Behavior," in *Journal of Business*, Vol. 35 (1962). These are among the authors who debate the practical application of Stedry's conclusions.

However, his research on the reactions of lower level management to budgets does help to explain the behavior of these people. The study also indicates how management can improve a budgeting process where budgets are being ignored or causing personnel problems, because it shows why such situations exist.

Another consequence of budgetary motivation which has received little emphasis involves "a fear of failure" on the part of the individual. The failure to meet a budget or at least come close to it when it is accepted and fairly determined and when other members of a person's reference group are successful, represents a potential loss of status both within the group and the organization. A person's self-concept is also deflated in such circumstances.

The fear of such a loss may be a stronger motivating factor for a person to achieve his budget than any of the other pressures mentioned. "Fear of failure" then is a very powerful functional consequence of budgeting systems and, quite likely, is latent.

One of the major benefits of budgeting is motivation, explicitly incorporated in the use of standards. Budgets should reflect a goal which people can strive towards and achieve. To provide maximum motivation for employees, management should judge failure to achieve an objective in the context of the situation causing failure and not merely in terms of a figure circled in red. All members of the organization must be aware of this basic principle.

F. Participation in Budgeting

In a participatory system of budgeting, preparation of budget schedules would start at the lower levels of the hierarchy and move upward. As it moved upward, various people would make additional suggestions and some eliminations until the schedules reached the controller and top management. These people would analyze it and see that it was a coordinated plan in accordance with organizational goals before final approval would be given. Movement up and down the hierarchy could be made if drastic changes were necessary. By reciprocal communications, people would know why changes were justified and could constructively criticize them if they desired.

Behavioral scientists and accountants generally believe that such a system would be an improvement on imposed budgets. The functional, manifest results claimed for this system are:

1. It would have a healthful effect on interest, initiative, morale and enthusiasm.

2. It would result in a better plan because the knowledge of many individuals is combined.

3. It would make all levels of management more aware of how their particular functions fit into the total operational picture.

4. It would increase interdepartmental cooperation.

5. As a result of their direct involvement in the planning function, it would make junior management more aware of the future with respect to objectives, problems and other considerations.

It is possible to achieve these benefits through successful participation. There are, however, factors that have a significant impact on whether or not participation can lead to successful results.

One essential requirement is that participation be legitimate. If participation is allowed but top management continually changes the budgeted figures resulting from participation, legitimate participation does not exist. This might better be described as a form of "pseudo-participation." The supposed "participants" would likely resent such a policy and the consequences would be dysfunctional. This is borne out by the studies of V. H. Vroom who found that productivity was higher when participation was viewed as legitimate, but lower when it was viewed as not legitimate.[11]

Other factors limiting the usefulness of budget participation are:

1. Personality differences of managers as reflected in their leadership style are important. Aggressive managers can put forth their demands more strongly than meek ones. Subordinates would view the latter as not looking out for their interests and antagonism between subordinates and their superiors, and managers themselves, could easily develop.

2. An autocratic, centralized organization would have little use for a participation policy whereas a democratic, decentralized organization would likely benefit from, and almost require, a participation policy.

3. Those allowed participation rights must be positively oriented towards the objectives of the firm. Only if the group is cohesive in thought and desire toward and understands the plan can participation policy be functional.

4. The cultural setting of an organization and the background of employees should be considered. People in rural areas or with a rural background are more inclined to accept assigned tasks. In such an atmosphere, a participation policy would probably meet with little response.

---

[11] Stedry, Andrew C., "Budgeting and Employee Behavior: A Reply," in *The Journal of Business*, Vol. 37 (April 1964), p. 198.

Studies have been carried out showing that participation in any situation is not necessarily useful for increasing efficiency.[12] Other studies have reported that when a non-participative group became participative and was compared with an existing non-participative or participative group, the former never caught up in terms of performance with the latter two groups. These studies imply that the introduction of a participation policy for a formerly non-participative group would not likely lead to increased efficiency and may even result in decreased efficiency. If this conclusion is accepted, a group should be endowed with the right to participate only when the group is created or the budget system is being implemented and not after either has previously been directed through decisions made by superiors.

The most severe criticism offered against participation is that the increased morale which supposedly results does not necessarily result in increased efficiency. Is high morale a cause of increased efficiency or is greater efficiency a cause of high morale, or is there some intervening variable which must be present if a true causal relationship is to exist? Group cohesiveness seems to be the most significant of possible variables that have been examined although other variables are obviously involved. Figure 3 shows postulated relationships that could develop using group cohesiveness with regard to subordinate thoughts toward management.

As those participating in a budget (foremen and up) would be management-oriented, at least to some extent, they would probably have a positive approach to management activities and objectives. The previous

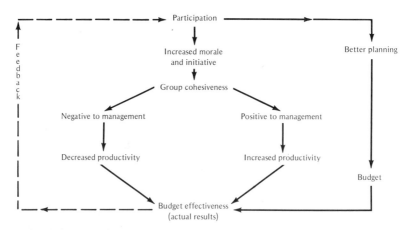

Figure 3. Participation and Budgets

[12] See Stedry, ibid., p. 196; also Morse, Nancy and Reimer, E., "The Experimental Change of a Major Organizational Variable," in *Journal of Abnormal and Social Psychology*, Vol. LII (1956), pp. 120–129; and French, Jr., J. R. P., Kay, E. and Meyer, H. H., *A Study of Threat and Participation in a Performance Appraisal Situation*, New York, General Electric Co., 1962.

discussion on role-conflict situations shows, however, that negative attitudes towards budgeting are quite possible.

If the group is anti-management or anti-budget, a participation policy would be of little use. Supervisors may even propose ridiculously low standards and upper management would be forced to revise them. Pseudo-participation would exist and likely result in the increase of negative attitudes toward management or budgeting.

If the atmosphere is favorable for allowing participation, group cohesiveness toward management and budgeting should be maintained and enhanced if possible. Group discussions led by an able management man to inform *and* listen to supervisors, foremen and other management people could probably aid in implementing the budget. By listening to and taking action on suggestions made by the group, he would be able to indicate his and top management's sincerity in gaining successful participation in the budgeting system.

Undoubtedly, the evidence on the effectiveness of participation in budgeting is mixed. Supporters of participation readily admit that it is by no means a panacea for achieving the full motivational potential of the budget. The fact is that participation is not a segregated aspect of management but embraces several technical and behavioral concepts which make it more or less useful in different organizations. The organization's particular situation with regard to the development of these concepts must be recognized and thoughtfully considered when contemplating or evaluating a participation policy.

It should be noted that, even if productivity does not increase directly through participation, better planning and increased morale and initiative may, of themselves, justify such a policy.

G. Communication Aspects of Budgeting

Researchers on control and motivation generally agree that information on planned and actual results should be communicated to the employee whose performance is being measured.

Nevertheless, many budget departments merely communicate the results to management with the result that the employee does not know how he has done until he is called up to discuss his performance report. Consequently, the individual may ignore the budget and perform without a guide, hoping for the best.

When results are communicated as rapidly as possible, an employee's mistakes can be associated with his recent actions and he is likely to learn more from the experience than if reports are received long after the action has been taken. This learning would likely result in improved performance on future budgets.

When reports given to management employees are timely, reasonably accurate and understandable, functional consequences are more likely to occur than if the opposite exists. Figure 4 summarizes the effect of the communication system on the behavior of line people.

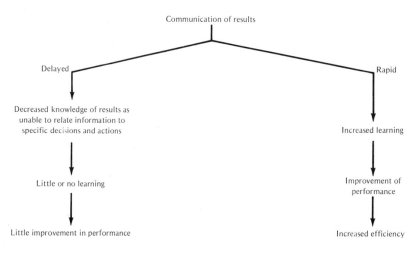

Figure 4. The Importance of the Communication Factor When Using Budgets to Control and Motivate Employees

H. Employee Group Behavior and its Effects on Budgeting

Peter Blau's study on the use of statistical measures in evaluating employee performance has implications for evaluating and understanding budgeting.[13] The study examined the effect of group cohesiveness, in the sense of willingness to cooperate among members, and the resulting productivity in different situations.

His findings showed that the group which cooperated was more productive than the group which did not cooperate but competed individually among themselves. He also discovered that highly competitive individuals in the latter group were more productive than any individual in the cooperative group. Blau's hypothesis was that a paradox existed:

> The resulting paradox is that competitiveness and productivity are inversely related for groups but directly related for individuals in the competitive group.[14]

In terms of the achievement of organizational objectives, the implication is that cooperative cohesiveness among group members assigned a particular task is most desirable. When this is achieved, cooperation will result in each member helping others in the group even though it may result in a decrease in the performance record of the assisting individual.

---

[13] Blau, Peter M., "Cooperation and Competition in a Bureaucracy" in Bobbs-Merrill Reprint Series in the Social Sciences, S-28. Reprinted by the permission of *The American Journal of Sociology*, Vol. LIX, May 1964.

[14] Ibid., p. 530.

Applying this to budgeting, the suggestion is that individual perform-ance should not be the ultimate objective in the eyes of top management or employees. Rewards and punishments should not be based entirely on an individual's performance as compared to the plan. The budget reports should be only one of many factors used for evaluation and superiors should recognize this fact. The result would be a decline in individual competition and greater cooperation towards the achievement of a goal. This environment could eliminate possible dysfunctional consequences. Group cohesiveness will be affected greatly by the leadership style of the group's superior. Whether he believes in rigidity or flexibility, whether he is authoritative or democratic, and the freedom granted him by the organi-zational structure and policies, will influence the way he controls his subordinates.

I. Mechanical Considerations of Budgeting

Dysfunctional consequences can arise from the mechanical aspects of budgeting.

Budgeting systems cost money to install and continue. These costs must always be considered in evaluating the worthiness of a system.

It must also be remembered that budgets are merely estimates or predic-tions. As such, they could be incorrect or inappropriate because of eco-nomic, technical and environmental changes. The estimating procedure itself may be inappropriate. If budgets are thought of as a goal rather than a means of reaching the goal, the emphasis on budgets cannot help but carry dysfunctional consequences, particularly when the estimates have been incorrectly computed.

A final mechanical problem involves the assignment of costs to the person deemed responsible for them. There is always a strong possibil-ity that costs assigned to one person may have been caused by another. The subsequent bickering and ill-feeling would obviously be dysfunc-tional.

Budgets must be capable of flexibility. This is fundamentally the result of management attitudes and not inherent in the budget itself. Management must recognize that forced adherence to a plan could cause decisions to be made that are not in the long-run interest of the business. Unfore-seen opportunities may arise which were not planned. A decision result-ing in a significant, unfavorable variance on the short-range plan may be the best alternative in terms of long-range profitability. Failure to take ad-vantage of such situations may result in adherence to the budget but also in dysfunctional consequences in terms of achieving the objectives of budgeting.

Alternatively, failure to adhere to budget figures when they are correct, merely to protect the individuals involved or their superiors, must also be avoided. Such an attitude would destroy one of the corner-stones of a successful budgeting system.

- Interpreted meaning of word "Budget"
- Personality and leadership expression of person subject to a budget or using a budget
- Role conflict involving line and budget staff personnel
- Involvement of workers
- Mechanical considerations:—monetary cost
  —Substitution of budget as goal rather than as means to a goal
  —Realistic standards

Organization Structure: Overemphasis on department rather than whole organization

Participation: More knowledge about limiting factors and human capabilities is gained and departments will have greater respect for each other and what they are doing

Motivation: If budgets are primarily used as motivating devices for individuals, a loss of overall co-ordination occurs

Mechanical Considerations: Possibility of incorrect estimates
- assignment of costs to persons deemed responsible for them

Participation:
- draws toegether knowledge diffused among participants
- results depend on feelings of individuals and group toward management

Organization Structure and Leadership:
- authoritative or democratic
- centralized or decentralized

Motivation:
- the determination of how the budget is to affect motivation has direct influence on the way it is planned

Mechanical Considerations:
- possibility of incorrect estimates
- assignment of costs to persons deemed responsible for them

Planning:
- objectives established in advance
- clarifies ideas
- improved communication
- increased interest and enthusiasm by lower management
- awareness of lower management activities by top management

Coordination:
- unifies departmental efforts
- a means to limit strife between departments

BUDGET

Evaluating Performance:
- assign budget costs to those controlling them
- comparison of planned with actual means evaluation of individuals which yields motivation

Control:
- quickly reveals discrepancies in quantitative terms
- stimulates investigation
- useful for development of decision rules for enabling management by exception
- savings on controlable costs

Organization Structure:
- centralized or decentralized
- personality and leadership expression of individual using the budget
- status differences and conflicting opinions on budget by budget and line personnel

Motivations:
- variances for particular individuals rather than for operations destroy the ability to use budgets for control unless a separate, realistic budget is also used

Communication:
- timely, accurate, understandable

Mechanical Considerations:
- possibility of incorrect estimates
- assignment of costs to persons deemed responsible for them

Organization Structure: Centralized or decentralized
- status differences and conflicting opinions on budget by budget and line personnel

Participation: Results in better morale and initiative depending on direction of feelings toward top management of those participating

Motivation: High performance can be gained by using budgets as individual motivational devices but the risk of losing other benefits is high
- motivation can be attained by setting realistic, acceptable and understandable budgets without using them primarily for motivation

Communication: Timely, accurate, understandable

Mechanical Considerations: Possibility of incorrect estimates
- assignment of costs to persons deemed responsible for them

Effectiveness in increasing organizational efficiency in achieving its goal of maximizing the present value of the owner's wealth

Figure 5. General Model of the Factors to Consider When Determining the Functional and Dysfunctional Aspects of Introducing and Using a Budgeting System

GENERAL MODEL OF THE CONSEQUENCES
OF A BUDGETING SYSTEM

Figure 5 summarizes the factors which must be considered when determining the functional and dysfunctional consequences possible from a budgeting system.

The square immediately outside the BUDGET square indicates the potential benefits to be derived from a successful budgeting system. These benefits are functional to the more efficient achievement of an organization's goal of making profit. The next surrounding square indicates many of the factors which can aid or prevent the achievement of the desired benefits. The descriptive model is arranged so that the effects of various environmental circumstances and managerial policies (participation, motivational intentions, organization structure, etc.) can be immediately related to a particular benefit (planning). The square at the top of the diagram includes factors which are not specifically related to any one particular benefit but which have an important influence on the success or failure of the overall budget system.

The points mentioned in the peripheral square and the top square cannot be clearly identified as either functional or dysfunctional. The relationship of these points to the benefits of budgeting depends upon the particular circumstances.

CONCLUSION

The model which has been developed to point out the functional possibilities of budgeting and to identify the sources of possible dysfunctional consequences represents a summary of relevant findings and statements by behavioral scientists, accountants and managers.

Budgeting is only one type of control technique used by top management. Many of the propositions developed are equally applicable to other types of quantitatively oriented control techniques.

The points developed in this paper should be considered by any organization using or contemplating the introduction of a budgeting process. The importance of each point will vary, however, according to the particular organization, its strategy, history, organizational structure, reasons for using the system, the personalities involved, the leadership style of individuals in responsible positions, the general attitudes of employees toward the organization and control devices, the cohesiveness of reference groups working on and with the budget, and the personal attitudes of employees regarding the justification of, and methods of achieving, organizational goals.

The major proposition suggested is that a budgeting system designed to accomplish the designated benefits is something more than a series of figures. Its origination, implementation, and degree of success are significantly related to the behaviorally oriented problems that can easily arise. Management methods for solving these problems cannot be generalized into a specific set of rules. Definite rules can seldom cover the particular developments of unique situations. Therefore, only general aspects of budgeting systems with emphasis on behavioral topics have been considered.

The only absolute conclusion that can be proposed is that the human factors involved are generally more difficult to identify and deal with and more serious in nature than the development of quantifying and figure determination techniques. Accountants and managers must recognize this fact if they expect to perform their functions adequately.

9.
VARIABLE BUDGETS AND DIRECT COSTING*

Howard B. Burdeau

The term "annual operating budget" can best be described as the "action plan of management." Budgeting is not a new technique, for it has been used for many years as a management practice of major importance in some companies, while it may merely be a routine clerical process in others.

In recent years, with the great improvement in management information systems (total systems), communications, electronic data processing, quantitative management techniques, budgeting is fast becoming the focal point for more effective management processes. Therefore, the integrated budgetary system is the most effective method to help accomplish the overall objectives of management.

The growth of large and complex industrial organizations and the decentralizing of management has led the individual manager of the various divisions to optimize his individual operations. The different objectives of the various divisions of a concern are often inconsistent with each other and frequently come into direct conflict.

The vast sums spent on product research in recent years has led to the development of many new products which have to be manufactured, sold, and the entire operation financed. This has led to major decisions concerning plant capacity, production processes, marketing strategy, and foreseeing the action of competitors. In planning we must identify the various conditions of uncertainty we find, study the potential impact of these rapidly changing conditions and we must develop our proposed reactions to these conditions. Our company must be able to react quickly to a changing business environment.

*From *Managerial Planning*, January/February 1971, pp. 4–11. Reprinted by permission of the author and the publisher.

The budget is management's answer to the query whether it has the capacity to handle and respond to change. Planning is the action by top management and supervisory personnel at all levels to decide on objectives, to identify the market areas in which to sell, and to react to the current business conditions. This plan of action is a quantitative technique that results in specific programs for the future growth of the business. The operating plan, once developed, is not static, but must be flexible (variable), so that it will change with the ever-changing business conditions.

To review briefly the mechanics of the budget process, we first start with the sales budget, which has a relation to the advertising, promotion, and research budgets. As the sales budget sets the contemplative activity level of the company, it is used to some extent to develop the selling, distribution, and administrative expense budgets. The sales budget provides information to establish the finished goods inventory budget, which also takes into account the optimum inventory levels as adjusted for production requirements. The finished goods requirements are used to establish the production budget. The production budget leads to the development of the purchase budget for direct materials, and also to the development of direct labor requirements. The manufacturing overhead budgets for both the production and service departments are developed by the responsible managers with assistance from the budget officers staff. After these various individual budgets are summarized, reviewed, and finally approved by top management, we have our plan (the operating budget).

Management control is the effort to follow the budget plan so that organizational requirements are met and the ultimate goals of our organization accomplished. Management control utilizes the feedback of information so that the manager can compare the actual results of his department with what should have been attained under the actual operating conditions. These performance reports are sent to the line manager responsible for a particular operation and they highlight the differences between the actual results and the desired results that should have been realized if expected levels of efficiency were achieved in internal operation. The manager responds to the unfavorable variances by attempting to correct the underlying cause, and, in some instances, sends higher echelon a report of what actions are to be taken to correct the situation requiring attention.

After this brief review of planning and control, let us turn our attention to variable budgeting to control overhead expenses. Variable budgets are schedules of costs that indicate for each subdivision of the company, how each expense should change with volume, output, or activity. They express short-term costs—volume relationship within the narrow relevant range of volume. We are dealing with the concept of cost variability which holds that cost can be related to output or activity. Costs then are primarily the result of two factors (1) passage of time and (2) activity.

Our first task in developing the variable budget is to analyze cost behavior. Under proper control, every cost will follow some definite pattern of behavior—although this pattern may not always be the expected one. Assumptions on cost behavior can be dangerous.

It cannot be presumed that certain costs will fluctuate with volume in some definite manner or remain constant because of their nature. Only through scientific analysis, drawing upon the skills of the industrial engineer, mathematician, statistician, economist, and production personnel can the answer be found.

To simplify our examination of cost behavior patterns, let us classify cost in accordance with the concept of cost variability into the three categories as (1) nonvariable, (2) variable, and (3) semi-variable.

1. Nonvariable costs, or fixed costs, are those items of cost which do not vary with volume or productive activity—they remain constant in amount regardless of the production activity within the relevant range of activity. Nonvariable costs can be classified as (a) committed costs, which are related to the provision of a capacity to do business; and (b) programmed, or managed costs, which are related to the utilization of the capacity provided. The amount of fixed costs remains the same over the relevant range of activity, but the unit cost varies inversely with activity. Step-fixed costs are those which remain constant only for a limited range of activities. The average step-fixed cost will decrease as production increases within the range. It may actually increase on a per unit basis as the next range of activity is reached, but usually only a portion of the new range, and then decrease as production activity is increased within that range. An example of a step-fixed cost is that one lead man can control fifteen (15) employees. As the number of employees increases to sixteen (16) and up to thirty (30) employees, a second lead man is required.

2. Variable costs are those items of cost that vary directly with volume or productive capacity. For if there is no productive activity, the variable cost is zero. If the activity increases fifty percent, the variable cost increases the same percentage. The variable cost is variable in amount, but the cost per unit remains the same.

3. Semi-variable, or mixed costs, are those items of cost that increase or decrease as volume or activity increase, but not in proportion thereto. These costs possess some of the characteristics of both fixed and variable costs. As the level of activity changes, the amounts incurred will change but not in direct proportion to activity changes. With an increase in activity, the average cost will decrease because the variable portion remains constant on a per unit basis, while the fixed portion will decrease on a per unit basis. Therefore, we are faced with a fixed element which represents the minimum cost of supplying the service and a variable portion which is influenced by changes in activity.

There are various methods of determining cost variability with the majority of the methods involving an analysis of historical costs. First, we would carefully study each expense account in a department and isolate those expenses which can be identified as either fixed or variable. The mixed cost

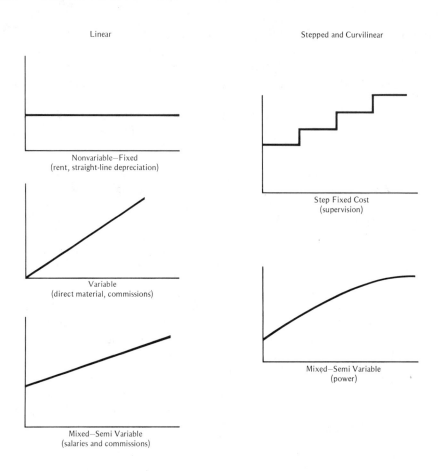

Exhibit A. Basic Cost Behavior Patterns

must be further studied to identify the fixed and variable components of cost.

To understand how an expense varies for different activity levels, we can draw a graph, with the Y axis indicating the expense and the X axis indicating a measure of activity (which can be units produced, direct labor hours, direct machine hours). Exhibit A presents graphs of basic cost behavior patterns. By changing the measure of activity, a recognizable pattern of cost behavior may become apparent on the graph.

Basically there are three methods of determining cost variability for the mixed expenses, which can be described as (1) direct estimate method, (2) arithmetic approach, and (3) statistical correlation methods.

The direct estimate method is not normally used for routine expenses, and is utilized for particular cost problem areas. One technique of this method is industrial engineering studies, which utilizes engineering studies based on analysis and direct observations of the manufacturing operations and often provide the most reliable cost estimates of certain expenses. Also engineering studies should be undertaken to check the results obtained from historical cost data. Such studies provide rates of material consumption, labor requirements, waste and spoilage allowances among others. The engineering approach to cost analysis is one of the more preferable techniques, but the expense of using it for all expenses year after year can be prohibitive for a concern. A National Association of Accountants Research Report dealing with industrial engineering describes some of the uses of engineering studies.

The information used to explain the arithmetic approach is shown in Exhibit B. Here we have a tabulation by months of a mixed expense, (indirect material cost) and the activity index (units produced).

MONTH	INDIRECT MATERIAL COST (y Value)	PRODUCTION ACTIVITY (UNITS) (x Value)
January	$ 1,250	100
February	1,500	150
March	1,680	200
April	1,750	250
May	1,900	300
June	1,375	125
July	1,600	180
August	1,680	200
September	1,750	250
October	1,700	225
November	1,650	200
December	1,260	100
	$19,095	2,280

Exhibit B. Tabulation by Months of Indirect Material Cost and Units Produced

The high and low method basically develops, for each item of expense, two budget allowances at two different levels of activity. The fixed and variable components are simply computed on an arithmetic basis assuming a straight line relationship. The calculations to employ this method are shown in Exhibit C. After the computations are made we have separated the mixed expense into its variable and fixed components and can express the results as a budget formula as follows:

	Fixed	Variable	
Indirect Material Cost	925	3.25	per unit of production

1. Select the HIGH and LOW activity months for the relevant range of activity and list.

	MAXIMUM	MINIMUM	DIFFERENCE
Budget Allowance	$ 1,900	$ 1,250	$ 650
Volume (units)	300	100	200

2. Compute the rate of variability.

$$\frac{\text{Difference in Allowance}}{\text{Difference in Volume (activity)}} \quad \frac{650}{200} = \$3.25 \text{ per production unit}$$

3. Compute the fixed cost.

Total cost at volume level of 300 units	$1,900
Variable expense (300 units x $3.25)	975
FIXED COST	$ 925

4. Express the results as a variable budget formula.

Cost	Fixed	Variable per production Unit
Indirect Material	$925	$3.25 per unit of production

Exhibit C. High and Low Method for Determining the Budget Formula for Mixed Expenses Using Data from Exhibit B

Correlation and statistical methods are widely used in the analysis of costs. These methods use historical data to determine how costs have varied in the past to estimate how costs should vary in the future. An example of this method is the use of scatter charts. This method involves the use of scatter graphs in order to determine visually the fixed and variable components of cost. The data from Exhibit B is plotted on a graph, Exhibit D, with the cost on the vertical scale (Y axis) and volume on the horizontal scale (X axis).

A visual trend line is drawn through the plotted points, and the point at which the trend line intersects the vertical scale (zero volume) indicates the fixed element while the slope of the trend line represents the variable rate. The variable component can be found by subtracting the nonvariable component from the total cost at any volume.

For example, the total cost of 300 units is $1,900; the variable cost then is $975, or $3.25 per unit, determined as follows:

Total cost of 300 units	$1,900
Less nonvariable component	925
	$ 975

Variable cost per unit—$975 divided by 300 units = $3.25. Exhibit D gives an example of this method.

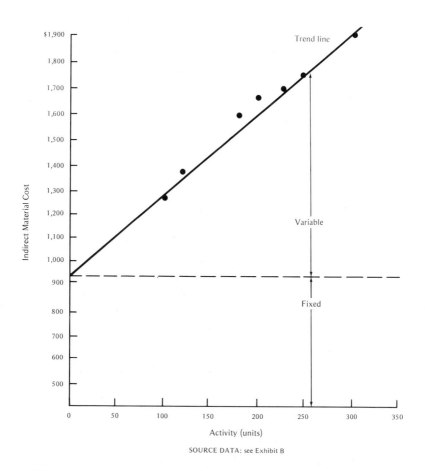

SOURCE DATA: see Exhibit B

Exhibit D. Scattergraph Separating Variable and Nonvariable Components of a Mixed Cost Trend Line Fitted by Inspection (Source Data: See Exhibit B)

This procedure provides a simple comprehensible look at the interrelationships. It can be criticized in that no two individuals would draw the same trend line through the points, but the margin of error is usually within acceptable limits.

The statistical method of least squares is a technique that is used for computing the trend line. This method is based on the formula for a straight line, $y = a + bx$, where y represents the dependent variable, a the constant factor, b the slope of the trend line, and x the independent variable. Simply, a expresses the fixed portion of the line and b the slope of the trend line. Exhibit E shows the computations required for fitting a regression line to the data previously used.

After having examined our cost behavior and decided which expenses are nonvariable, variable, and mixed, we can now develop our variable

MONTH	INDIRECT MATERIAL COST (y Value)	PRODUCTION ACTIVITY (UNITS) (x Value)	x^2	xy
J	$ 1,250	100	10,000	125,000
F	1,500	150	22,500	225,000
M	1,680	200	40,000	336,000
A	1,750	250	62,500	437,500
M	1,900	300	90,000	570,000
J	1,375	125	15,625	171,875
J	1,600	180	32,400	288,000
A	1,680	200	40,000	336,000
S	1,750	250	62,500	437,500
O	1,700	225	50,625	382,500
N	1,650	200	40,000	330,000
D	1,260	100	10,000	176,000
	Σ y $19,095	Σ x 2,280	Σ x^2 476,150	Σ xy 3,765,375

1. Convert the formula for a straight line (y = a + bx) into two simultaneous equations which are the same as those developed by using the method of least squares:

$\Sigma y = Na + b\Sigma x$ (N is the number of items in the listing)

$\Sigma(xy) = a\Sigma x + b\Sigma x^2$

2. Substitute the values into the equations.

$19,095 = 12a + 2,280b$

$3,765,375 = 2,280a + 476,150b$

3. Solve for a (fixed portion) and for b (variable portion), resulting in the following:

Fixed portion= a = 984

Variable portion= b = 3.20

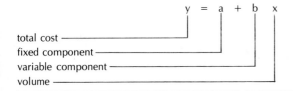

```
              y  =  a  +  b   x
                    │     │   │
total cost ─────────┘     │   │
fixed component ──────────┘   │
variable component ───────────┘
volume ───────────────────────
```

Exhibit E. Computations Required for Fitting a Regression Line—Statistical Method of Least Squares

budget for our service and production departments. An example of a variable (flexible) budget formula for a production department is shown in Exhibit F, part A.

Part A. Budget Formula

	FIXED	VARIABLE (per 100 direct machine hour)
Supervisory salaries	$ 9,000	$ 0
Indirect labor	6,000	15.00
Maintenance parts	500	1.00
Depreciation	1,000	
Insurance and taxes	200	
Miscellaneous	300	2.00
	$17,000	$18.00

Part B. Variable Budget for Month of January
(10,000 direct machine hours were actually incurred in January)

	FIXED	VARIABLE CALC.		TOTAL
Supervisory salaries	$ 9,000	0		$ 9,000
Indirect Labor	6,000	15 x 100 =	$1,500	7,500
Maintenance parts	500	1 x 100 =	100	600
Depreciation	1,000			1,000
Insurance and taxes	200			200
Miscellaneous	300	2 x 100 =	200	500
TOTAL	$17,000		$1,800	$18,800

Exhibit F. Variable Budget for Production Dept. 1

Now let us assume that for the month of January, 10,000 direct machine hours were actually incurred. The variable budget for the month of January is computed in part B of Exhibit F.

After the variable budget is computed for a month based on actual activity (in this case, direct labor hours), it is compared with actual costs and a performance report prepared by the Accounting Department and sent to the manager responsible for Production Department One. Exhibit G shows the performance report for Department One.

Performance reports of this type for internal use constitute an important part of a comprehensive budget system. Every firm should design for itself an integrated cost report system constructed around (a) the organizational structure, (b) the budget objective, and (c) the exception principle. It must be remembered that the control reports must be suited to the individual user, for the different levels of management have different responsibilities and these frequently call for different kinds of information. We find a detailed report, similar to our performance report (Exhibit G), going to the lower levels of management (supervisors and foremen) to facilitate the

THE MUNCIE MANUFACTURING COMPANY
PERFORMANCE REPORT
JANUARY 19_1

Department: *Production Dept. #1*   Supervisor *J. Smith*

	ACTUAL	BUDGET	VARIANCE (over) or under budget
Supervisory salaries	$ 9,000	$ 9,000	$ —
Indirect labor	8,000	7,500	(500) Unfavorable
Maintenance parts	550	600	50 Favorable
Depreciation	1,000	1,000	—
Insurance and taxes	200	200	—
Miscellaneous	575	500	(75) Unfavorable
TOTAL	$19,325	$18,800	($525) Unfavorable

Note: *The activity level for the month was 10,000 direct machine hours.*

Exhibit G. Performance Report for Production Dept. 1

control of current operations. Budget reports for middle and top management would be summary in nature. If the variation is significant, it should result in an investigation to determine the underlying causes, because the cause rather than the result provides the basis for corrective action.

Although an adequate budget program can be developed without using cost-volume-profit techniques, these techniques can add to the understanding and usefulness of budget procedures and forecasts, as well as providing us with information for many types of managerial decisions.

This technique can be used, of course, with historical data, but can make a greater contribution to management planning when used for future estimates based on the budget. The use of this technique depends upon the valid identification of cost variability with volume. That is the identification of cost as nonvariable and variable, which we have previously discussed.

In our discussion concerning cost-volume-profit analysis, we will take a simplified presentation of a complex subject and, it must be remembered that this concept must be used with care. It is a static representation of a dynamic set of data and its application is restricted by the assumption on which it is based. These assumptions are valid for limited periods of time and only within a limited relevant range of activity. Cost-volume-profit analysis has proven itself in practice.

What management questions can be answered by this technique? Just a few of these questions are:

1. What is the breakeven point?
2. What profit can be expected on a given sales volume?
3. What sales volume is required to produce a desired profit?

4. How would a change in capacity affect the profit potential?
5. What additional sales volume would be required to cover the increase in wages that the labor union is demanding?
6. What effect would a change in selling prices have on profits?

The profit of a business is dependent on three basic factors:

1. Selling Price of the product
2. Cost of Manufacturing and Distributing the product
3. Volume of sales.

No one factor is independent of the others because cost determines the selling price to arrive at a desired rate of profit. The selling price affects the volume of sales, and the volume of sales directly influences the volume of production. The volume of production, in turn, influences the cost. The cost-volume-profit relationship is influenced by five factors, or a combination of them. They are:

1. Selling price
2. Volume of sales
3. Product mix
4. Variable cost per unit
5. Total fixed cost.

To permit effective profit planning, management must foresee the part that each of these factors plays, or will play, in changing the net income, the breakeven point, and the return on investment for the firm. To illustrate this technique, let us assume the following budget figures for our firm as shown on Exhibit H.

Management is interested in the sales volume to which the company breaks even; that is, the point at which sales revenue equals the cost to make and sell the product and no profit or loss is reported. Cost-volume-profit analysis lends itself to graphic representation on a breakeven chart, as shown in Exhibit H, part B. Sales volume is plotted along the X axis; cost and revenue related to this volume are plotted along the Y axis. The nonvariable line was drawn first, $25,000 at all volumes. The variable cost line was drawn next, starting at $25,000 and moving upward uniformly with volume at the rate of 60% of sales. Finally the sales revenue line was plotted. The intersection of the total cost line with the sales revenue line is the breakeven point. The wedge to the right of the breakeven point represents the profit potential; the wedge to the left represents losses.

An examination of this chart will reveal that a company with a high fixed cost and low contribution margin (P/V ratio) will have a very high breakeven point. The breakeven point of a company with low fixed costs and high contribution margin will be low. The company with the higher contribution margin has the higher profit potential. We can compute the breakeven point

Exhibit H
Cost—Volume—Profit

A. BASIC INFORMATION

MUNCIE MANUFACTURING COMPANY
BUDGETED INCOME STATEMENT
YEAR ENDED DECEMBER 31, 19_1

SALES		$ 100,000	100%
VARIABLE COSTS TO MANUFACTURE AND SELL			
Material-Direct	$ 10,000		
Direct Labor	25,000		
Indirect Manufacturing Expenses	15,000		
Selling and Administrative Expenses	10,000	60,000	
CONTRIBUTION MARGIN (P/V RATIO)		$ 40,000	40%
NONVARIABLE (FIXED COSTS)			
Indirect Manufacturing Expenses	$ 5,000		
Selling and Administrative Expenses	20,000	25,000	
NET INCOME BEFORE TAXES		$ 15,000	

B. BREAKEVEN CHART

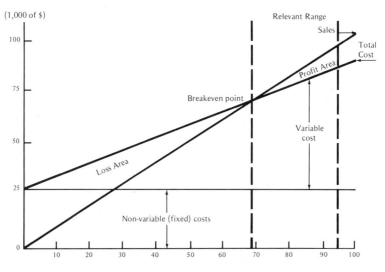

Sales Volume (thousands of dollars)

Exhibit H
Schedule 1
Breakeven Computations

1. Breakeven formula:

$$\frac{\text{Nonvariable Cost + Desired Net Income}}{\text{P/V RATIO (Contribution Margin \%)}} = \text{B.E. SALES IN DOLLARS}$$

2. Breakeven Point for the Muncie Manufacturing Company (EXHIBIT I)

$$\frac{\$25,000}{.40} = \$62,500$$

3. What sales are required to make a net income of $11,000?

$$\frac{\$25,000 + \$11,000}{.40} = \$90,000 \text{ Sales}$$

4. For our company, variable expenses increase to $80,000 (80%) due to rising material and increased wage rates. The nonvariable expenses remain the same. The P/V RATIO IS NOW 20%

$$\text{B.E.} = \frac{\$25,000}{.20} = \$125,000$$

5. We plan a plant expansion which will increase production capacity 30% which will increase nonvariable costs to $60,000. The variable costs will not change, and therefore the P/V RATIO remains at 40%.

$$\text{B.E.} = \frac{\$60,000}{.40} = \$150,000$$

6. Our sales manager requests an advertising campaign which will cost $3,000 per year. How much additional sales must be generated to cover this expenditure?

$$\text{Sales Required} = \frac{\$3,000}{.40} = \$7,500$$

(just a few of the applications for breakeven analysis)

mathematically by using the formula as shown on Exhibit H, Schedule 1. Also on this schedule is shown the answers to certain questions management might ask.

It can be seen where cost-volume-profit analysis can be developed with a reasonable degree of accuracy that can be of considerable value as a managerial tool. It is a technique that provides insight into the economic characteristic of a firm and can be used as we have seen to determine the approximate effect of various alternatives. Although the results we obtain from this analysis are not precise, it is a "slide rule" approach that can be used to develop and test, with a minimum of effort, the appropriate effect on costs and profits of several types of managerial decisions.

As we have reviewed variable budgets, the nature of cost-volume-profit relationships and breakeven analysis, we can see the usefulness of this type of data for profit planning, cost control, and decision making.

Direct costing is concerned with integrating and incorporating into the accounts a group of related techniques which include the variable budget, breakeven chart, and contribution margin analysis.

Under the conventional (absorption) costing, all factory costs are treated as product costs. Factory overhead which includes variable and fixed costs is applied to items produced. Income is not affected by fixed factory overhead until the products are sold.

The essential difference between direct costing and conventional costing relates to the treatment of fixed factory overhead. Under direct costing, fixed factory overhead costs are treated as period costs rather than product costs. They are written off during the period in which they are incurred.

Therefore, under direct costing, fixed factory overhead is excluded from inventories of work in process and finished goods. Under direct costing, all variable costs, including selling and manufacturing, are deducted from the selling price, resulting in the contribution margin toward fixed costs and profits.

Exhibit I presents a partial income statement comparing conventional (absorption) and direct costing. On the conventional income statement the Cost of Goods Sold is deducted from the Sales to obtain the Gross Profit. You will notice that all manufacturing expenses are deducted, which include the fixed and variable overhead. The inventory is costed out at the Total Manufacturing Cost which includes fixed overhead. In the direct costing statement all variable costs, which include manufacturing, selling, and administrative expenses, are deducted from the Sales to obtain the contribution margin. The inventory is costed out at the total variable manufacturing expenses.

Exhibit J gives a comparative effect on income and inventories under conventional and direct costing. The income statement under direct costing is rearranged to emphasize the contribution margin, that is, the excess of sales revenue over variable production, selling, and administrative costs. All the fixed costs are deducted in full as period costs. A study of these two costing methods shows that the income varies substantially under the two

PARTIAL INCOME STATEMENTS
CONVENTIONAL COSTING

Selling Price (per unit)		$ 90
Factory Cost		
Direct Material	$ 13	
Direct Labor	19	
Variable Factory Overhead	18	
Fixed Factory Overhead		
$400,000/20,000 units	20	
Cost to Make		70
Gross Profit before Selling and Admin. Expenses		$ 20

DIRECT (VARIABLE) COSTING

Selling Price (per unit)		$ 90
Total Variable Costs		
Direct Material	$ 13	
Direct Labor	19	
Variable Factory Overhead	18	
Variable Cost to Manufacture	50	
Variable Selling and Admin. Expenses	5	
Total Variable		55
CONTRIBUTION MARGIN		$ 35

Exhibit I. Comparison of Conventional (Absorbtion) And Direct Costing

methods. What caused this difference? It is due to costing the inventories under conventional costing at their full factory cost of $70.00, while under direct costing, inventories are costs of $50.00.

Income will always be lower under direct costing when sales lag behind production and the company has accumulated a larger inventory at the end of the period than at the beginning of the period. Under direct costing, profits vary more directly with sales, while under conventional costing, profits are dependent on the level of production as well as sales.

Although direct costing has its shortcomings it is far better suited to the needs of management than conventional costing. Management requires a knowledge of cost behavior patterns under various operating conditions. Planning and control are more concerned with nonvariable and variable costs than with full costing under the conventional method. Under direct costing, the cost data needed for profit planning and decision making are readily available from the accounting records and statements. Cost-volume-profit relationships and the effect of changes in sales volume on net income can be readily computed from the direct costing income statement. Profits and losses reported under direct costing bear a relationship with

January activity data:

Production (normal activity 20,000)	20,000
Sales units	21,000
Opening Finished Goods Inventory (units)	3,000
Closing Finished Goods Inventory (units)	2,000

CONVENTIONAL COSTING

Sales 21,000 at $ 90	$ 1,890,000
Cost of Sales 21,000 at $ 70	1,470,000
Gross Profit	420,000
Selling and Administrative Expenses	165,000
Net Income	$ 255,000

DIRECT COSTING

Sales	21,000 at $ 90			$ 1,890,000
Variable Costs				
Direct Material	21,000 at	13	$ 273,000	
Direct Labor	21,000 at	19	399,000	
Variable				
Factory Ohd.	21,000 at	18	378,000	
Selling & Admin.	21,000 at	5	105,000	
Total Variable				1,155,000
Contribution Margin				$ 735,000
Period (Fixed) Costs				
Fixed Factory Overhead			$ 400,000	
Fixed Selling and Admin.			60,000	460,000
Net Income				$ 275,000

INVENTORY VALUATION

	CONVENTIONAL	DIRECT
Opening Inventory	$210,000	$150,000
Closing Inventory	140,000	100,000

Reconciliation of Difference in Net Income

Net Income Direct Costing	$ 275,000
Net Income Conventional Costing	255,000
Difference	$ 20,000

Difference between ending and beginning inventories (1,000)
Times fixed factory overhead unit cost ($20) = $20,000.

Exhibit J. Comparative Effect on Income and Inventories under Conventional and Direct Costing

sales revenue and are not affected by inventory or production variations. The full impact of nonvariable costs on net income is brought to the fore by the presentation of costs on an income statement prepared under direct costing.

Direct costing is preferred over conventional costing in analysis of relative profitability of products, territories, and other segments of a business. Direct costing concentrates on the contribution that each segment is making to the recovery of nonvariable costs which will not be altered by decisions to make and sell.

Direct costing provides valuable data for short-term decision making— for in the short run, period costs are not relevant. Direct cost data are also useful in capital investment and make or buy decisions which depend on direct cost data. A few examples of decision making which utilize the direct costing information are:

1.   Selection among alternative uses of production facilities
2.   Selling versus additional processing of manufactured items
3.   Optimizing the production mix
4.   Determining the inventory levels
5.   Selective selling decisions.

I have briefly discussed the concept of direct costing and I do not want to get into the controversy between the adherents of conventional and direct costing. Simply stated, direct costing has its merits, and for internal reporting with its separation of nonvariable and variable costs, it is better adapted to managerial uses in profit planning and decision making. Direct costing should be judged solely on its merits.

10.

COMPUTER-ASSISTED CASH BUDGETING AND SENSITIVITY ANALYSIS*

Donald L. Raun
and
Donald L. Anderson

INTRODUCTION

In this paper we will first show the preparation of a forecasted income statement and cash budget for an illustrative problem; we will list possible purposes for sensitivity analysis; and then show the use of a computer program (CASHB) to prepare income statements and cash budgets, and to aid management in sensitivity analysis. We also include the computer program (a FORTRAN IV program) that is used for preparation of the statements and alternative income statements and cash budgets for sensitivity analysis purposes. Sensitivity analysis studies can be used in planning and budgeting; they can be designed to determine such things as the possible effect that changes in cost relationships, business environment, policies, or activities can have on the future profits and cash requirements of the business.

FORECASTED INCOME STATEMENT

A factor of major importance for budgeting is the sales estimate or forecast. Sales may be forecast by such procedures as using the past relationship of sales to some independent factor, or by using a relationship of sales to such multiple determining factors as sales price, advertising, salaries and/or commissions of sales personnel, credit policy, and product research expenditures, or by obtaining the opinions of managers and/or salesmen.

---

*Printed by permission of the authors.

In discussing sales forecasting, Richard J. Tersine in "Forecasting: Prelude to Managerial Planning," *Managerial Planning*, July/August, 1975, (p. 11) states:

> Top-down forecasting and bottom-up forecasting are general forecasting patterns used for predicting product demand. Top-down forecasting begins with a forecast of general economic activity (GNP, national income, etc.) for the geopolitical unit where the organization resides. Industry forecasts are developed from the general economic activity forecast. The organization's share-of-the-market forecast is predicted from the industry forecast and specific product group forecasts are developed from it.
>   Bottom-up forecasting begins at the product level. Forecasts are made for each product or product group and the forecasts are summed to obtain the aggregate organizational forecast. The aggregate forecast can be modified in relation to the general business outlook and the competitive situation. Advertising and promotion might necessitate an additional forecast revision.

He also lists basic sales forecasting techniques (p. 12).

> There are four basic sales forecasting techniques—soliciting opinions, economic indicators, time series analysis, and econometric models. These techniques are short-range forecasting devices and their value diminishes as the time horizon increases. Many of the techniques are based on extrapolation into the future of trends that have existed in the past.

See the introduction for Part IV of this book for a brief discussion of these methods, and see the sales forecasting discussion in Article 21, "How to Get a Better Forecast,"

The adopted sales budget is the plan for the forthcoming period and it reflects, not just a sales forecast based upon a past relationship(s), but in addition, the plans of action by management for the purpose of influencing the future sales. These plans may include changes in the design of the product, changes in sales territory emphasis, changes in advertising, media mix, etc.

If some method can be employed to forecast sales reasonably well, many of the other items can be forecast by employing their relationships to sales in the past and, if necessary, adjusted by management's knowledge of changes in the relationships or possible trends in the future. Adjustments may be made for inflation, new labor contracts, etc.

As an example for the preparation of a forecasted income statement, we will assume that the sales for January are forecast as $20,000, and that in the past the cost of goods sold has been 40 percent of sales, sales discounts 0 percent, purchase discounts 2 percent, selling expenses 35 percent, variable general and administrative expense 10 percent and that the fixed general and administrative expense has been $100. A forecasted income state-

Exhibit 1. Forecast Income Statement: January

			PERCENTAGE OF SALES
Sales	$20,000		
Less sales discount	00		
Net sales		$20,000	100 %
Cost of goods sold	8,000		40 %
($20,000 × 40%)			
Less purchase discounts	40		.2%
($8,000 × .25 × .02)[1]			
Net cost of goods sold		7,960	39.8%
Gross profit on sales		12,040	60.2%
Variable selling expense	7,000		35 %
($20,000 × 35%)			
Variable general and			
administrative expense	2,000		10 %
($20,000 × 10%)			
Total variable expense		9,000	45 %
Contribution margin		3,040	15.2%
(Margin over variable expense)			
Fixed selling expense	00		
Fixed general and administrative expenses	100	100	.5%
Net Income		$ 2,940	14.7%

[1] The problem assumes purchases for a month equal cost of goods sold, or $20,000 of sales × .40 = $8,000. The cash discount on purchases is 2% with 25% of the purchases being paid within the discount period. The purchase discount is $8,000 × .25 × .02 = $40. See Exhibit 3 for the problem information.

Note that sound financial management policy would be to take all the discounts. Using the terms of purchase of 2/10, n/30, the annual rate of interest for not taking the discount is approximately 36%. The firm gives up a 2% discount to allow the liability to run 20 days more (30 days – 10 days = 20 days) and in a 365-day year there are eighteen 20-day periods; 2% × 18 = 36% interest. Preparing a cash forecast and asking a bank for a credit line based on the forecast can help the firm pay its open accounts within the discount period and avoid such a heavy financial charge.

ment for January based on this information might appear as presented in Exhibit 1.

THE PROFIT PLAN

An integrated profit plan or budget will consist of forecasted or planned revenues and costs for each department, product, etc., integrated with the total company budgeted revenue and expense statement. As we progress through the year of operations, the detailed profit plans or budgets should be altered as the business environment changes, assumptions are proven to be incorrect, or additional commitments effecting cost (such as changes in labor contracts) are realized.

The primary purpose of the planned detailed costs and revenues (or ranges for costs and revenues which is another alternative) for the different segments of a business is to provide goals which, if realized, will result in the planned profit. *Management by exception* means that executive attention is directed to the actual costs and revenues that have significant variances from the budgeted or planned costs and revenues. If unfavorable variances occur, they are investigated by management to determine what action can be taken to lower costs to their expected levels or raise revenues to their expected or planned levels. On the other hand, significant favorable variances are investigated to determine if there are increased efficiencies that might be applied to other activities to improve their efficiency.

Thus, as part of the function of planning for profit, management prepares the detailed profit plan. As part of the control function, management determines important deviations from budget and directs action where it is needed.

THE CASH BUDGET

Even though a firm has the potential to be profitable, it may be forced into bankruptcy by the creditors if management has not thoroughly anticipated the short-term and long-term cash requirements. Without adequate cash forecasts, the company may not have an opportunity to remain in business long enough to realize its profits.

The cash budget is a forecast of the cash flowing into and out of the business for a specific period of time. Generally, if the sales revenue and expenses can be forecast, the cash requirements or cash surplus also can be forecast, employing the same or similar methods. Exhibit 2 presents an example of a cash forecast. Exhibit 3 contains the problem information used for preparing the income statement for January in Exhibit 1 and the cash forecast for January in Exhibit 2. The Exhibit 3 problem also is used for the subsequent discussion of the cash budget computer program application (Exhibits 4 and 5).

SENSITIVITY ANALYSIS

Sensitivity analysis involves a study to determine the effect of changes or errors in problem parameters on the results of an analysis or decision model. For example, sensitivity analysis enables management to answer a question such as: What will be the effect on cash requirements if the cost of goods sold relationship of Exhibit 3 changes to 50 percent and only 20 percent of sales are collected in the month of sale? Sensitivity analysis may be accomplished by recalculating the cash forecast, as presented in Exhibit 2, and the forecasted income statement, as presented in Exhibit 1, for a

Exhibit 2. Cash Forecast: January[1]

Cash balance—beginning			$ 2,000
Add: Collection of accounts receivable			17,500
Sales Dec. $15,000 × .50 =	$ 7,500		
Sales Jan. $20,000 × .50 =	10,000		
	$17,500		
Total cash available			$19,500
Less: Cash to be paid out			
Payments on accounts payable		$6,460	
Payments for January purchases[2]			
$20,000 × .40 × .25 =	$2,000		
less cash discount			
$2,000 × .02 =	40		
	$1,960		
Payments for December purchases			
$15,000 × .40 × .75 =	4,500		
	$6,460		
Payments for selling expenses		7,000	
($20,000 × .35)			
Payments for general and			
administrative expenses		2,100	
$20,000 × .10 =	$2,000		
plus fixed expense =	100		
	$2,100		
Capital and loan payments		00	
Income tax payments		00	
Total cash to be paid out			15,560
Cash balance—ending			$3,940
Target balance (Cash balance required for the beginning of next month)			2,000
Cash surplus (Cash available for investment or for			$1,940
payment of short-term loans)			

[1] See Exhibit 3 for the problem information.
[2] The problem assumes purchases for a month equal cost of goods sold, or $20,000 of sales × .40 = $8,000. Twenty-five percent of purchases are paid in the month of purchase. $8,000 × .25 = $2,000 payment for January purchases.

whole series of alternatives, varying the parameters or cost relationships and studying the results. As part of Exhibit 4, we include the computer printouts for requirements A and B of the Exhibit 3 sample problem. Requirement B gives parameter changes for sensitivity analysis. Sensitivity analysis may be used for the following purposes:

Exhibit 3. A Sample Problem: Company Relationships and Forecasts

The following information was obtained from company past records and current forecasts of relationships.

1. The percentage of sales collected in month of sale is 50%.
2. The percentage of sales collected in the next month is 50%.
3. The percentage of sales collected in the third month is 0%.
4. The cash discount on sales is 0%.
5. The cost of goods sold is 40% of gross sales. Purchases equal cost of goods sold.
6. The purchases paid for in the month of purchase are 25%.
7. The purchases paid for in the next month are 75%.
8. The cash discount on purchases is 2% if paid for in month of purchase.
9. The variable selling expense is 35%.
10. The variable general and administrative expenses are 10%.
11. The tax rate is 50% paid quarterly in April, June, September and December.
12. The lead time for purchases is zero.
13. The target for cash on hand is $2,000.
14. The fixed selling expenses are zero.
15. The fixed general and administrative expense is $100.
16. The purchases paid for in the third month are zero.
17. The cash discount on sales after the month of sale is zero.
18. The cash discount on purchases after the month of purchase is zero.
19. The capital and loan payments are zero.
20. The sales for November and December were $15,000 each. The forecasted sales for the next twelve months are $20,000, $20,000, $21,000, $21,000, $22,000, $22,000, $23,000, $23,000, $24,000, $24,000, $25,000, and $25,000.

Required:

A.   Prepare a cash forecast for twelve months, January through December.   Prepare a forecasted income statement for twelve months.

B.   Repeat A above changing the parameters as follows:
       Cost of goods sold % = .50 of gross sales
       % of sales collected in month of sale = .20
       % of sales collected within the next month = .30
       % of sales collected within the third month = .45
       Note: .20 + .30 + .45 = 95% and, therefore, .05 of sales are bad debts.

1. To forecast the effect of any changes in cost and volume relationships upon cash requirements and profits.

2. To provide an understanding of the activities that have the greatest influence upon cash balances and profits.

3. To test alternatives.

4. To emphasize the importance of controlling or maintaining cost relationships.

5. To prepare alternative cash forecasts (possibly with probabilities of occurrence) and thus determine a probable range of cash requirements rather than a single cash forecast.

6. To prepare alternative profit plans or budgets, and thus determine a probable range of planned revenue, expense and profit.

Management can perform sensitivity analysis by manual calculations to a very limited extent at a cost of say $100 to $200, but the computer can accomplish the task in a matter of minutes at a cost of $5 to $20 depending upon the computer system employed. The computer is a tool of analysis for management which frequently provides the least-cost solution. The computer application can be accomplished on a time-sharing system, mini-computer system, or a batch processing system. We used a time-sharing system for the printouts included in this paper.

INTRODUCTION FOR EXHIBITS 4, 5, and 6

Exhibit 4 is prepared from a computer printout that shows the procedure for obtaining the cash forecasts and income statements for the Exhibit 3 problem using a computer to prepare the statements. Note that the printout asks the users to enter data for their particular problems and provides instructions to perform this task. The underlined portions of the printout represent the response of a user. All other items are the response of the computer.

The computer application shown below stores all variable data (such as report headings and problem parameters) in a data file. Therefore, a data file must be created in the computer system before the program is run. Exhibit 5 describes the method by which the data file is established in the computer system on a disc storage device. The same method is employed to store the computer program in the computer system. After this standard data file has been established, any number of users may change the data file indefinitely for as many problems as may be desired. In Exhibit 4, after the printout for requirement A of the problem example, we include the printout that shows how the data file can be changed to agree with information for other problems. This procedure allows the user to make changes for other problems but does not permanently replace the information we originally entered into the data file.

Exhibit 6 presents the FORTRAN IV computer program used for preparing the cash forecasts and income statements. The program provides the opportunity for sensitivity analysis computations because it allows the program user to change problem parameters and to receive alternative outputs.

How to Run the Cash Budget and Sensitivity
Analysis Program (Exhibit 4)

The problem information of Exhibit 3 and report headings may be stored in a computer data file by the procedure shown in Exhibit 5. The data file is read by the computer following the 1029IR13 CASHDATA user response in Exhibit 4 (the underlined portions of the printout represent the response of the program user). The problem data, except for report headings, may be directly entered without first being stored in a data file. The data file information that was read after the appropriate user response can be replaced by information that is entered after answering yes to the Exhibit 4 question: *"Do you wish to change all of the parameters?"* The information is then entered by the user for each of the parameters. In the printout, we are asked if parameters are to be changed, but after answering yes, we then enter the same information that we stored in the data file for the Exhibit 3 problem; the information is directly entered to show how this can be done without first storing it in a data file.

The Exhibit 5 data file is necessary for storing the headings for the cash forecast and income statement even if the problem information is not stored in the file. By storing the headings in a data file, a user of the cash budget program can change such things as the company name and date without having to change the CASHB program. This can facilitate applying the program to different companies and cash budget problems.

Note that 1029IR13 is the job number we used in storing the Exhibit 3 information for a cash forecast and forecasted income statement problem in the California State University's Time-Sharing System. CASHDATA is the name of the data file set up for the Exhibit 3 problem information, and CASHB is the name given to the FORTRAN IV program (Exhibit 6) that was prepared and then stored in the time-sharing system to solve an Exhibit 3 problem.

After showing how to enter the problem information (immediately below), we include the printout resulting from requirement A of the Exhibit 3 problem. We then show how to change parameters using the requirement B information for the changes, and we include the printout resulting from the change in problem parameters.

Exhibit 4. Running the Program: Requirement A of Exhibit 3

WHAT SYSTEM? EXFOR

NEW OR OLD--RERUN
BINARY FILE NAME: 1029IR13 CASHB
ENTER DATA FILE NAME

OPEN FILE 2 INPUT: 1029IR13 CASHDATA
DO YOU WANT OUTPUT ON TERMINAL? ANS = 1, or FILE? ANS = 3
1
DO YOU WISH TO CHANGE PARAMETERS? ANS: YES,NO,END
YES
DO YOU WANT A DEFINITION OF THE PARAMETERS? ANS: YES
YES
1. C1 = % OF SALES COLLECTED IN MONTH OF SALE
2. C2 = % OF SALES COLLECTED WITHIN THE NEXT MONTH
3. C3 = % OF SALES COLLECTED WITHIN THE THIRD MONTH
4. D1 = % OF CASH DISCOUNT ON CASH SALES
5. X = % OF COST OF GOODS SOLD
6. P1 = % OF PURCHASES PAID FOR IN MONTH OF BUY
7. P2 = % OF PURCHASES PAID FOR NEXT MONTH
8. D2 = % OF CASH DISCOUNT ON PURCHASES
9. Y = % OF VARIABLE SELLING EXPENSE
10. Z = % OF VARIABLE GENERAL AND ADMINISTRATIVE EXPENSE
11. TAXR= TAX RATE
12. NN= LEAD TIME FOR PURCHASES
13. TARG= CASH ON HAND GOAL
14. FSE= FIXED SELLING EXPENSE
15. FGAE= FIXED GENERAL AND ADMINISTRATIVE EXPENSE
16. P3 = % OF PURCHASES PAID FOR IN THIRD MONTH
17. D3 = % OF CASH DISC ON SALES COLLECTED IN NEXT MONTH
18. D4 = % OF CASH DISC ON PURCHASES PAID FOR IN NEXT MONTH
DO YOU WISH TO CHANGE ALL OF THE PARAMETERS?(YES)
YES
ENTER THE PARAMETERS AS FOLLOWS:
C1,C2,C3,D1,X,P1,P2,D2,Y,Z,TAXR,NN,TARG,FSE,FGAE,P3,D3,D4
.50,.50,0,0,.40,.25,.75,.02,.35,.10,.50,0,2000,0,100,0,0,0
IS THE INPUT LINE CORRECT? (YES OR NO)
YES
DO YOU WISH TO CHANGE THE LOAN PAYMENTS
YES
ENTER THE CAPITAL EXPENDITURES AND LOAN PAYMENTS
FOR EACH OF 12 MONTHS. — ENTER DATA AS FOLLOWS:
90000,60000,0,0,0,0,0,0,0,0,0,0
0,0,0,0,0,0,0,0,0,0,0,0
DO YOU WISH TO CHANGE THE SALES EST.? ANS: YES OR NO
YES
ENTER THE EST. SALES AS FOLLOWS: NOV,DEC,JAN, ... DEC
15000,15000,20000,20000,21000,21000,22000,22000,23000,23000
24000,24000,25000,25000

**Cash Forecasts and Income Statements
(reproduced from the computer printout solution
for requirement A of the Exhibit 3 problem)**

THE STANDARD COMPANY
CASH FORECAST
FOR THE YEAR 19_2

	JAN	FEB	MAR	APR	MAY	JUN
CASH BAL-BEGINNING	2000	2000	2000	2000	2000	2000
ADD:COLLECT OF A/R	17500	20000	20500	21000	21500	22000
TOTAL CASH AVAILABLE	19500	22000	22500	23000	23500	24000
LESS: PAY ON A/P	6460	7960	8058	8358	8456	8756
SELLING EXPENSE	7000	7000	7350	7350	7700	7700
GEN AND ADM EXP.	2100	2100	2200	2200	2300	2300
INCOME TAXES	0	0	0	4980	0	4980
CAPITAL & LOAN PAYM	0	0	0	0	0	0
CASH BAL-ENDING	3940	4940	4892	112	5044	264
TARGET BALANCE	2000	2000	2000	2000	2000	2000
CASH SURPLUS (+)	1940	2940	2892	−1888	3044	−1736

	JUL	AUG	SEP	OCT	NOV	DEC
CASH BAL-BEGINNING	2000	2000	2000	2000	2000	2000
ADD:COLLECT OF A/R	22500	23000	23500	24000	24500	25000
TOTAL CASH AVAILABLE	24500	25000	25500	26000	26500	27000
LESS: PAY ON A/P	8854	9154	9252	9552	9650	9950
SELLING EXPENSE	8050	8050	8400	8400	8750	8750
GEN AND ADM EXP.	2400	2400	2500	2500	2600	2600
INCOME TAXES	0	0	4980	0	0	4980
CAPITAL & LOAN PAYM	0	0	0	0	0	0
CASH BAL-ENDING	5196	5396	368	5548	5500	720
TARGET BALANCE	2000	2000	2000	2000	2000	2000
CASH SURPLUS (+)	3196	3396	−1632	3548	3500	−1280

ESTIMATED NET INCOME IS	39840.00
TOTAL CASH REQUIRED IS	−17920.00

DO YOU WANT INCOME AND EXPENSE STATEMENTS? ANS=YES
YES

THE STANDARD COMPANY

ESTIMATED	JAN	FEB	MAR	APR	MAY	JUNE
SALES LESS BAD DEBT	20000	20000	21000	21000	22000	22000
LESS SALES DISCOUNT	0	0	0	0	0	0
NET SALES	20000	20000	21000	21000	22000	22000
COST OF GOODS SOLD	8000	8000	8400	8400	8800	8800
LESS PURCHASE DISC	40	40	42	42	44	44
NET COST OF GDS SOLD	7960	7960	8358	8358	8756	8756
VARIABLE SELLING EXP	7000	7000	7350	7350	7700	7700
VARIABLE GEN & ADM EXP	2000	2000	2100	2100	2200	2200
MARGIN OVER VARIABLE COSTS	3040	3040	3192	3192	3344	3344
FIXED SELLING EXP	0	0	0	0	0	0
FIXED GEN & ADM EXP	100	100	100	100	100	100
NET INCOME	2940	2940	3092	3092	3244	3244

THE STANDARD COMPANY

ESTIMATED	JUL	AUG	SEP	OCT	NOV	DEC
SALES LESS BAD DEBT	23000	23000	24000	24000	25000	25000
LESS SALES DISCOUNT	0	0	0	0	0	0
NET SALES	23000	23000	24000	24000	25000	25000
COST OF GOODS SOLD	9200	9200	9600	9600	10000	10000
LESS PURCHASES DISC	46	46	48	48	50	50
NET COST OF GDS SOLD	9154	9154	9552	9552	9950	9950
VARIABLE SELLING EXP	8050	8050	8400	8400	8750	8750
VARIABLE GEN & ADM EXP	2300	2300	2400	2400	2500	2500
MARGIN OVER VARIABLE COSTS	3496	3496	3648	3648	3800	3800
FIXED SELLING EXP	0	0	0	0	0	0
FIXED GEN & ADM EXP	100	100	100	100	100	100
NET INCOME	3396	3396	3548	3548	3700	3700

Data Changes for Requirement B of Exhibit 3

Note that the following questions allow the user to change the input data used for the above forecasts in order to obtain new forecasts. For sensitivity analysis, a comparison can be made between the new forecasts and the previous ones to show the effect of changes in problem parameters.

DO YOU WISH TO CHANGE THE PARAMETERS? ANS: YES,NO,END
YES
DO YOU WANT A DEFINITION OF THE PARAMETERS? ANS: YES
NO
DO YOU WISH TO CHANGE ALL OF THE PARAMETERS?(YES)
NO
HOW MANY PARAMETERS DO YOU WISH TO CHANGE?
4
ENTER WHICH PARAMETER YOU WISH TO CHANGE: 1,2 . . . 18
5
ENTER THE VALUE OF THIS PARAMETER
.50
ENTER WHICH PARAMETER YOU WISH TO CHANGE: 1,2 . . .18
1
ENTER THE VALUE OF THIS PARAMETER
.20
ENTER WHICH PARAMETER YOU WISH TO CHANGE: 1,2 . . . 18
2
ENTER THE VALUE OF THIS PARAMETER
.30
ENTER WHICH PARAMETER YOU WISH TO CHANGE: 1,2 . . . 18
3
ENTER THE VALUE OF THIS PARAMETER
.45
DO YOU WISH ANOTHER CHANGE ANS: YES OR NO
NO
DO YOU WISH TO CHANGE THE LOAN PAYMENTS
NO
DO YOU WISH TO CHANGE THE SALES EST.? ANS: YES OR NO
NO

Cash Forecasts and Income Statements
(reproduced from the computer printout solution
for requirement B of the Exhibit 3 problem)

THE STANDARD COMPANY
CASH FORECAST
FOR THE YEAR 19_2

	JAN	FEB	MAR	APR	MAY	JUN
CASH BAL-BEGINNING	2000	2000	2000	2000	2000	2000
ADD: COLLECT OF A/R	15250	16750	19200	19500	20150	20450
TOTAL CASH AVAILABLE	17250	18750	21200	21500	22150	22450
LESS: PAY ON A/P	8075	9950	10072	10447	10570	10945
SELLING EXPENSE	7000	7000	7350	7350	7700	7700
GEN AND ADM EXP.	2100	2100	2200	2200	2300	2300
INCOME TAXES	0	0	0	1621	0	1621
CAPITAL & LOAN PAYM	0	0	0	0	0	0
CASH BAL-ENDING	75	−300	1577	−119	1580	−116
TARGET BALANCE	2000	2000	2000	2000	2000	2000
CASH SURPLUS (+)	−1925	−2300	−422	−2119	−420	−2116

	JUL	AUG	SEP	OCT	NOV	DEC
CASH BAL-BEGINNING	2000	2000	2000	2000	2000	2000
ADD: COLLECT OF A/R	21100	21400	22050	22350	23000	23300
TOTAL CASH AVAILABLE	23100	23400	24050	24350	25000	25300
LESS: PAY ON A/P	11067	11442	11565	11940	12062	12437
SELLING EXPENSE	8050	8050	8400	8400	8750	8750
GEN AND ADM EXP.	2400	2400	2500	2500	2600	2600
INCOME TAXES	0	0	1621	0	0	1621
CAPITAL & LOAN PAYM	0	0	0	0	0	0
CASH BAL-ENDING	1582	1507	−36	1510	1587	−109
TARGET BALANCE	2000	2000	2000	2000	2000	2000
CASH SURPLUS (+)	−417	−492	−2036	−490	−412	−2109

ESTIMATED NET INCOME IS	12975.00
TOTAL CASH REQUIRED IS	15262.50

DO YOU WANT INCOME AND EXPENSE STATEMENTS? ANS=YES
YES

THE STANDARD COMPANY

ESTIMATED	JAN	FEB	MAR	APR	MAY	JUN
SALES LESS BAD DEBT	19000	19000	19950	19950	20900	20900
LESS SALES DISCOUNT	0	0	0	0	0	0
NET SALES	19000	19000	19950	19950	20900	20900
COST OF GOODS SOLD	10000	10000	10500	10500	11000	11000
LESS PURCHASES DISC	50	50	52	52	55	55
NET COST OF GDS SOLD	9950	9950	10447	10447	10945	10945
VARIABLE SELLING EXP	6650	6650	6982	6982	7315	7315
VARIABLE GEN & ADM EXP	1900	1900	1995	1995	2090	2090
MARGIN OVER VARIABLE COSTS	500	500	525	525	550	550
FIXED SELLING EXP	0	0	0	0	0	0
FIXED GEN & ADM EXP	100	100	100	100	100	100
NET INCOME	400	400	425	425	450	450

THE STANDARD COMPANY

ESTIMATED	JUL	AUG	SEP	OCT	NOV	DEC
SALES LESS BAD DEBT	21850	21850	22800	22800	23750	23750
LESS SALES DISCOUNT	0	0	0	0	0	0
NET SALES	21850	21850	22800	22800	23750	23750
COST OF GOODS SOLD	11500	11500	12000	12000	12500	12500
LESS PURCHASES DISC	57	57	60	60	62	62
NET COST OF GDS SOLD	11442	11442	11940	11940	12437	12437
VARIABLE SELLING EXP	7647	7647	7980	7980	8312	8312
VARIABLE GEN & ADM EXP	2185	2185	2280	2280	2375	2375
MARGIN OVER VARIABLE COSTS	575	575	600	600	625	625
FIXED SELLING EXP	0	0	0	0	0	0
FIXED GEN & ADM EXP	100	100	100	100	100	100
NET INCOME	475	475	500	500	525	525

DO YOU WISH TO CHANGE THE PARAMETERS? ANS: YES,NO,END
END

Exhibit 5. How to Prepare the Data File

This shows how to store the Exhibit 3 problem information and report headings in a computer data file. Once the file is established, input data can be changed by following the Exhibit 4 procedure and a cash forecast and income statement based on the new | information can be prepared.

WHAT SYSTEM? EXFOR
EXFOR
NEW
NEW FILE NAME: CASHDATA
READY

40 .50,.50,.00,.00,.40,.25,.75,.02,.35,.10,.50,0,2000,0,100,0,0,0
50 0,0,0,0,0,0,0,0,0,0,0,0
60 15000,15000,20000,20000,21000,21000,22000,22000,23000
61 23000,24000,24000,25000,25000
70 THE STANDARD COMPANY
71   CASH FORECAST
72   FOR THE YEAR 19_2
80 CASH BAL-BEGINNING
81 ADD:COLLECT OF A/R
82 TOTAL CASH AVAILABLE
83 LESS: PAY ON A/P
84   SELLING EXPENSE
85   GEN AND ADM EXP.
86   INCOME TAXES
87   CAPITAL & LOAN PAYMENTS
88 CASH BAL-ENDING
89 TARGET BALANCE
90 CASH SURPLUS (+)
110   ESTIMATED
120 SALES
130 LESS SALES DISCOUNTS
140 NET SALES
150 COST OF GOODS SOLD
160 LESS PURCHASES DISC
170 NET COST OF GDS SOLD
190 VARIABLE SELLING EXP
200 VARIABLE GEN & ADM EXP
220 MARGIN OVER VARIABLE COSTS
230 FIXED SELLING EXP
240 FIXED GEN & ADM EXP
260 NET INCOME
300 JAN FEB MAR APR MAY JUN JUL AUG SEP OCT NOV DEC

SAVE

Exhibit 6. The FORTRAN IV Computer Program

This program along with the data file allows the user to obtain printouts for cash forecasts and income statements. It also allows the user to change parameters and thereby obtain a printout based on the change in information; this is useful for the purposes of sensitivity analysis.

```
LIST
5C                          SENSITIVITY ANALYSIS PROGRAM

10 DIMENSION MON(12),SA(20),COMM(25,5),ARR(25,12),HEAD(6,5),S(20)
20 DIMENSION DASH(6),IARR(25,12),P(18)
21 INTEGER COMM
22 WRITE (1,791)
23 791 FORMAT ("ENTER DATA FILE NAME")
24 REAL MON
30 2   OPEN (2) INPUT
40 READ(2,0)L,P
41 INC=1
42 GO TO 909
50 1770 READ(2,0)L,(ARR(8,I),I=1,12)
60 READ (2,0) L,(SA(I), I = 1,9)
61 READ (2,0) L,(SA(I), I=10,14)
62 DO 63 I=1,20
63 63 S(I)=SA(I)
65 4 FORMAT (3X, 5A6)
66 DO 3 K = 1,3
70 3   READ (2,4) (HEAD(K,I),I = 1,5)
80 DO 10 J=1,24
90 10 READ (2,5) (COMM(J,I),I=1,5)
100 5 FORMAT (3X,5A4)
101 WRITE(1,0) "DO YOU WANT OUTPUT ON TERMINAL? ANS=1, OR FILE? ANS=3"
102 READ(0,0)N
103 IF(N-3)701,800,701
110 701 READ(2,6) (MON(I),I=1,12)
112 700 WRITE(1,0)"DO YOU WISH TO CHANGE THE PARAMETERS?ANS:YES,NO,END"
113 READ(0,900)IANS
114 IF(IANS-3HEND)899,2000,899
115 899 IF(IANS-3HYES)901,950,901
116 901 WRITE(1,0)"DO YOU WISH TO CHANGE THE SALES EST.? ANS: YES OR NO"
117 READ(0,900) IANS
118 IF(IANS-3HYES)967,975,967
120 6 FORMAT (3X,12A5)
122 900 FORMAT (A3)
124 902 SALE = 0.0
125 DO 20 I=1,12
130 20   SALE = SALE + SA(I+2)
140 TINC=SALE-SALE*C1*D1-SALE*C2*D3-SALE*(X+Y+Z)+SALE*X*P1*D2
141 + + SALE*X*P2*D4 -12*(FSE+FGAE)
142 TAX= TINC*TAXR
150 IF(TAX)30,30,40
160 30   TAX=0.0
170 GO TO 50
180 40   TAX=TAX/4.0
190 50   DO 41 K=1,6
200 41 DASH(K)= 6H------
210 DO 60 I=1,12
220 ARR(1,I)=TARG
```

```
230 ARR(10,I) = TARG
240 ARR(2,I) = SA(I + 2)*(C1-C1*D1) + SA(I + 1)*(C2-C2*D3) + SA(I)*C3
250 ARR(3,I) = ARR(1,I) + ARR(2,I)
257 NNNN = I + NN
258 KKK = I + 1 + NN
259 NNN = I + 2 + NN
260 ARR(4,I) = SA(NNN)*X*(P1-P1*D2) + SA(KKK)*X*(P2-P2*D4) + SA(NNNN)*X*P3
270 ARR(5,I) = FSE + SA(I + 2)*Y
280 ARR(6,I) = FGAE + SA(I + 2)*Z
290 IF(I-4)80,70,71
300 71   IF(I-6)80,70,72
310 72   IF(I-9)80,70,73
320 73   IF(I-12)80,70,80
330 80   ARR(7,I) = 0.0
340 GO TO 74
350 70 ARR(7,I) = TAX
360 74 ARR(9,I) = ARR(3,I)-ARR(4,I)-ARR(5,I)-ARR(6,I)-ARR(7,I)-ARR(8,I)
370 ARR(11,I) = ARR(9,I)-ARR(10,I)
380 60   CONTINUE
390 DO 61 I = 1,11
400 DO 61 K = 1,12
410 61   IARR(I,K) = ARR(I,K)
415 WRITE(N,130)
420 DO 90 K = 1,3
430 90   WRITE(N,100) (HEAD(K,I),I = 1,5)
440 100 FORMAT (20X,5A6)
450 KKK = 1
460 M = 6
470 97      WRITE(N,1)
480 1   Format (/)
490 WRITE(N,101)(MON(I),I = KKK,M)
500 101   FORMAT (26X,6(2X,A5))
510 DO 110 I = 1, 11
520 IF(I-3)115,111,112
530 112 IF(I-4)115,111,113
540 113   IF(I-9)115,111,114
550 114   IF(I-10)115,111,115
560 111 WRITE(N,131)(DASH(J),J = 1,6)
580 131 FORMAT (24X,6(A6,2X))
590 115 CONTINUE
610 200   FORMAT (//)
620 WRITE(N,120)(COMM(I,K),K = 1,5),(IARR(I,J),J = KKK,M)
630 120   FORMAT (5A4,2X,6I8)
640 110   CONTINUE
650 IF(M-12)140,150,150
660 140   M = 12
670 KKK = 7
675 WRITE(N,131)(DASH(I),I = 1,6)
676 WRITE(N,130)
680 GO TO 97
690 150   WRITE(N,131)(DASH(I),I = 1,6)
700 WRITE(N,1)
702 WRITE(N,707)TINC
703 707 FORMAT("ESTIMATED NET INCOME IS ",F12.2)
704 TOT = 0.0
705 DO 600 J = 1,12
706 600 TOT = ARR(11,J) + TOT
707 TOT = TOT*(-1)
708 WRITE(N,601)TOT
709 601 FORMAT ("TOTAL CASH REQUIRED IS ",F12.2)
710 WRITE(N,130)
720 130 FORMAT (/////)
```

```
722 WRITE(1,0)"DO YOU WANT INCOME AND EXPENSE STATEMENTS? ANS=YES"
723 READ(0,900)IANS
724 IF(IANS-3HYES)700,1200,700
750 950 WRITE(1,0)"DO YOU WANT A DEFINITION OF THE PARAMETERS? ANS: YES"
752 READ(0,900) IANS
753 IF (IANS-3HYES)959,1000,959
754 951 WRITE(1,0)"ENTER THE PARAMETERS AS FOLLOWS:"
755 WRITE(1,0)"C1,C2,C3,D1,X,P1,P2,D2,Y,Z,TAXR,NN,TARG,FSE,FGAE,P3,D3,D4"
756 READ(0,0)P
757 WRITE(1,0)"IS THE INPUT LINE CORRECT? (YES OR NO)"
758 READ (0,900)IANS
759 IF (IANS-3HYES)951,909,951
960 975 WRITE(1,0)"ENTER THE EST. SALES AS FOLLOWS: NOV,DEC,JAN, . . . . DEC"
965 READ(0,0)(SA(I),I=1,14)
966 967 C9=C1+C2+C3
967 DO 966 I=1,14
968 966 S(I)=SA(I)
969 IF (C9-1.00)902,902,990
970 999 WRITE(1,0)"ENTER THE CAPITAL EXPENDITURES AND LOAN PAYMENTS"
971 WRITE(1,0)"FOR EACH OF 12 MONTHS. ENTER DATA AS FOLLOWS:"
972 WRITE(1,0)"90000,60000,0,0,0,0,0,0,0,0,0,0"
973 READ(0,0) (ARR(8,I),I=1,12)
974 GO TO 901
990 990 WRITE(1,0)"ERROR C1+C2+C3 > 1.00, CORRECT PARAMETERS"
991 GO TO 1550
1000 1000 WRITE (1,0)" 1.  C1=%OF SALES COLLECTED IN MONTH OF SALE"
1010 WRITE (1,0)" 2.  C2=% OF SALES COLLECTED WITHIN THE NEXT MONTH"
1020 WRITE (1,0)" 3.  C3=% OF SALES COLLECTED WITHIN THE THIRD MONTH"
1030 WRITE (1,0)" 4.  D1=% OF CASH DISCOUNT ON CASH SALES"
1040 WRITE (1,0)" 5.  X=% OF COST OF GOODS SOLD"
1050 WRITE (1,0)" 6.  P1=% OF PURCHASES PAID FOR IN MONTH OF BUY"
1060 WRITE (1,0)" 7.  P2=% OF PURCHASES PAID FOR NEXT MONTH"
1070 WRITE (1,0)" 8.  D2=% OF CASH DISCOUNT ON PURCHASES"
1080 WRITE (1,0)" 9.  Y=% OF VARIABLE SELLING EXPENSE"
1090 WRITE (1,0)"10.  Z=% OF VARIABLE GENERAL AND ADMINISTRATIVE EXPENSE"
1100 WRITE (1,0)"11.  TAXR= TAX RATE"
1110 WRITE (1,0)"12.  NN= LEAD TIME FOR PURCHASES"
1120 WRITE (1,0)"13.  TARG= CASH ON HAND GOAL"
1130 WRITE (1,0)"14.  FSE= FIXED SELLING EXPENSE"
1140 WRITE (1,0)"15.  FGAE= FIXED GENERAL AND ADMINISTRATIVE EXPENSE"
1141 WRITE (1,0)"16.  P3 = % OF PURCHASES PAID FOR IN THIRD MONTH"
1143 WRITE (1,0)"17.  D3 = % OF CASH DISC ON SALES COLLECTED IN NEXT MONTH"
1145 WRITE (1,0)"18.  D4=% OF CASH DISC ON PURCHASES PAID FOR IN NEXT MO"
1150 GO TO 959
1175 959 WRITE(1,0)"DO YOU WISH TO CHANGE ALL OF THE PARAMETERS?(YES)"
1176 READ(0,900)IANS
1177 INC=2
1180 IF(IANS-3HYES)1550,951,1550
1210 1200 DO 31 I=1,12
1211 SA(I+2)=SA(I+2)*C9
1215 ARR(12,I) = SA(I+2)
1220 ARR(13,I) = SA(I+2)*C1*D1+SA(I+2)*C2*D3
1230 ARR(14,I) = SA(I+2)- ARR(13,I)
1240 ARR(15,I) = S(I+2)*X
1250 ARR(16,I) = S(I+2) * X * P1*D2 + S(I+2) * X *P2 * D4
1260 ARR(17,I) = ARR(15,I)-ARR(16,I)
1270 ARR(18,I) = SA(I+2) * Y
1280 ARR(19,I) = SA(I+2) * Z
1290 ARR(20,I) = ARR(14,I) -ARR(17,I) -ARR(18,I)-ARR(19,I)
1300 ARR(21,I) = FSE
1310 ARR(22,I) = FGAE
1320 ARR(23,I) = ARR(20,I)- FSE - FGAE
```

```
1325 SA(I+2)=S(I+2)
1330 31 CONTINUE
1340 KKK=1
1350 M=6
1360 DO 32 J=12,23
1370 DO 32 I=1,12
1380 32 IARR(J,I) = ARR(J,I)
1400 1411 WRITE(N,100) (HEAD(1,I),I=1,5)
1410 WRITE(N,197)(COMM(12,K),K=1,5)
1411 197 FORMAT (5A4)
1420 WRITE(N,101) (MON(I),I=KKK,M)
1430 DO 301 I=12,23
1440 II=I+1
1450 301 WRITE(N,120)(COMM(II,K),K=1,5),(IARR(I,J),J=KKK,M)
1460 IF (M-12)1400,1500,1500
1470 1400 M=12
1480 KKK=7
1490 WRITE(N,130)
1500 GO TO 1411
1510 1500 WRITE(N,130)
1520 GO TO 700
1530 800 WRITE(1,0)"ENTER NAME OF OUTPUT REPORT FILE"
1540 OPEN (3) OUTPUT
1545 GO TO 701
1546 1550 WRITE(1,0)"HOW MANY PARAMETERS DO YOU WISH TO CHANGE?"
1547 READ (0,0)J
1548 DO 1590 I=1,J
1550 WRITE(1,0)"ENTER WHICH PARAMETER YOU WISH TO CHANGE: 1,2 . . . 18"
1560 READ(0,0)IN
1570 WRITE(1,0)"ENTER THE VALUE OF THIS PARAMETER"
1580 READ(0,0)A
1590 1590 P(IN)=A
1600 WRITE(1,0)"DO YOU WISH ANOTHER CHANGE ANS: YES OR NO"
1610 READ(0,1551)NY
1620 1551 FORMAT (A1)
1630 IF(NY-1HY)909,1550,909
1640 909 C1=P(1)
1650 C2=P(2)
1660 C3=P(3)
1670 D1=P(4)
1680 X=P(5)
1690 P1=P(6)
1700 P2=P(7)
1710 D2=P(8)
1720 Y=P(9)
1730 Z=P(10)
1740 TAXR=P(11)
1750 NN=P(12)
1760 TARG=P(13)
1770 FSE=P(14)
1780 FGAE=P(15)
1790 P3=P(16)
1800 D3=P(17)
1810 D4=P(18)
1820 IF(INC-1)1770,1770,1780
1830 1780 WRITE(1,0)"DO YOU WISH TO CHANGE THE LOAN PAYMENTS"
1840 READ(0,900)IANS
1850 IF(IANS-3HYES)901,999,901
1900 2000 WRITE (1,130)
1910 CLOSE
2000 END
READY
```

11.
PRACTICAL APPLICATIONS OF
COST-VOLUME-PROFIT ANALYSIS*

James D. Willson

The success of a top business executive today depends in large part on his ability to deal effectively with probable conditions of tomorrow. In such a task he needs knowledge of the economic characteristics or structure of the business he manages, which the accountant can provide him. The principal accounting official should constantly make available to the chief executive such information, in readily understandable reports, to enable him to evaluate the hazards and recognize the potentials in the various business alternatives available.

This entire field of "profit planning" has become associated with the break-even analysis, or the cost-volume-profit interrelationship. We will not concern ourselves here with the usual preparation of such planning or control devices as variable budgets or forecasts. It is assumed that the reader has a reasonable knowledge of the principles related to these areas of planning and control. Our starting point is in a more sophisticated area—the application of the break-even analysis and related data in profit planning techniques. Let us consider the forecast, for instance. What purpose does it serve? Is it satisfactory? How do we know? If your company is typical, there are many useful ways of putting cost-volume-profit analysis to work. Such a technique is not merely a means of determining at what point income equals outgo and the business "breaks even." The dynamic company of today wants more than just to break even. Profits or the expectation of profits must be in the picture, or the incentive under the free enterprise system is gone.

The significance of this type of thinking may be illustrated by some of the questions which management is prone to ask and which accounting

---

executives should be ready to answer, or assist in development of the answer, by the use of break-even analysis:

1. Does the forecast represent a reasonable profit objective? (More particularly for this purpose, are costs and expenses in proper relationship to income?)

2. What will be the operating profit or loss at X sales volume?

3. What profit will result from a fifteen percent increase in sales volume?

4. What additional sales volume is necessary to produce X dollars of operating profit?

5. What additional sales volume is necessary to offset a ten percent reduction in selling price?

6. If the company can reduce fixed costs by X dollars and achieve a five percent reduction in material costs, what will be the effect on income?

7. What is the required sales volume to meet the additional fixed charges from the proposed plant expansion?

8. What sales volume is needed to provide for all costs in Territory Y?

Can you give an intelligent answer to intelligent questions of this nature as applied to your company? If you cannot, take heart. The techniques to develop answers to these questions are essentially quite simple.

BASIC ASSUMPTIONS IN COST-VOLUME-PROFIT ANALYSIS

Before discussing some adaptations of the cost-volume-profit analysis to planning and control, a review of a few simple fundamentals might be helpful. The effectiveness of our application depends in large part on proper assumptions relating to costs and profits. The economic structure of a company may be portrayed in the more simple break-even chart to depict merely the profit or loss effect of an increase in volume of sales as related to a ratable increase in variable costs, with a sales income line, a fixed cost line, and a line of variable costs. It may also be portrayed in a more refined but complex presentation, as in Exhibit 1, setting forth the relationships to sales volume of various costs and expenses. Regardless of the degree of complexity of the analysis, the principal assumptions on which such a study is based are:

1. Unit selling prices will not change with volume.

2. Costs and expenses can be segregated with reasonable accuracy into their fixed and variable components.

3. Fixed or standby costs will remain constant in the aggregate within the limits of the study.

4. Variable costs will vary generally in a constant ratio, i.e., in direct proportion to volume.

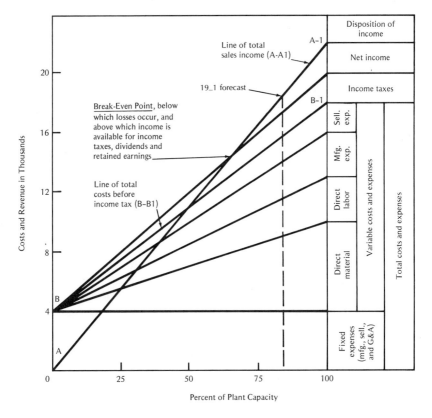

Exhibit 1. The Presentation Company Profit Structure Chart (Showing Major Segments of Costs)

5. Where several products are involved, the mix will remain constant.

When the proper cost segregations are known, income, costs, and the break-even point may be determined, with or without a chart. Whether or not it is decided to use the formalized chart in the determinations, the mathematical equation is:

$$\text{Break-even point} = \frac{\text{Aggregate fixed expense}}{1 - \dfrac{\text{Variable costs}}{\text{Sales}}}$$

The denominator, which is equal to the ratio of variable income to sales (marginal income ratio), represents that share of the sales dollar which is available to contribute to fixed costs and, if adequate, to income. It is a highly significant ratio. In analyzing economic behavior, this relationship becomes a much more useful concept than the break-even point itself.

USING BREAK-EVEN ANALYSIS TO TEST THE FORECAST

For illustrative purposes, we will consider the Sample Company with an economic structure such as that shown in Exhibit 2. It is to be observed that not only have fixed and variable costs been segregated but also the variable costs for each major function or cost segment have been translated into their applicable percentages of the net sales dollar. This information can now be applied in an evaluation of the reasonableness of the forecast. Typically, a projection is compared with some past year, usually the immediately preceding year, to determine whether or not it appears satisfactory. Such a comparison has value. It may be a gauge as to the adequacy of the sales volume and, in a general way, it may raise questions about cost or expense levels. However, such a comparison is not as sharp a tool as is available. Most of the time, the sales level and product mix in the forecast year will not be identical with that of the past year. Therefore, it may be difficult to measure more precisely the propriety of the costs and expenses in relationship to sales volume. To further complicate the problem, management, when looking at a higher sales volume and a net income which appears more favorable, tends to be less critical. In most instances, if net income expressed as a percent of sales is greater than the preceding year, the forecast is gleefully pronounced satisfactory.

Why not use a superior tool which permits a more effective evaluation of the volume factor? Once management has agreed upon a reasonable sales objective, a volume for the year under forecast, then it becomes practical to measure the proposed forecast against the break-even structure, i.e., to apply the break-even economic structure of the company to the projected

The Sample Company
Profit Structure

Description	Fixed Costs	VARIABLE COSTS Total	% Net Sales	Combined
Net Sales				$10,000,000
Costs and expenses:				
Direct material	$	$4,000,000	40.00%	
Direct labor		1,000,000	10.00	
Manufacturing expenses	500,000	1,000,000	10.00	
Selling expenses	400,000	100,000	1.00	
Research and development expenses	250,000	50,000	.50	
General and administrative expenses	150,000	50,000	.50	
	$1,300,000	$6,200,000	62.00%	7,500,000
Profit before income taxes				$ 2,500,000

Exhibit 2

sales volume. Essentially, we are saying that management should decide upon reasonable cost-profit-volume relationships and that this standard should be used as a measure of the forecast. The results of the application of the break-even factors, as shown in Exhibit 2, to a projected sales volume (standard profit structure) and the comparison of such results with the aggregate costs and expenses as set forth in an illustrative forecast, are shown in Exhibit 3. It is to be noted that percentage relationships are developed to aid in detecting out-of-line conditions. The exhibit portrays one of the basic considerations in the preparation of forecasts, i.e., that the company must not be allowed to develop or assume a less favorable cost structure. Hence, it is necessary to apply some overall tests quite distinct, for example, from individual departmental budget performance.

The greatest dollar increase and relative increase is in prime material costs. This 5 percent or $250,000 increase must be analyzed to determine whether the cost increase results from changes in product mix or from cost increases in any given product line. The initial break-even application has isolated this apparently excessive cost relationship. Now it should be analyzed in more depth and a decision made as to an acceptable plan. Perhaps the product mix is not the optimum believed to be attainable in the forecast year. Perhaps action can be taken on cost increases to reduce or eliminate them. The next largest relative increase, amounting to $60,000, is in direct labor. A similar analysis should be made to localize the cause and seek an improvement in the plan.

The Sample Company
Break-Even Analysis of Forecast

Fiscal 19_1

DESCRIPTION		APPLICATION OF STANDARD PROFIT STRUCTURE	TENTATIVE FORECAST	FORECAST OVER (UNDER) STANDARD	
				AMOUNT	%
Net sales		$12,500,000	$12,500,000	$	
Cost of sales:					
Direct material		$ 5,000,000	$ 5,250,000	$250,000	5.00%
Direct labor		1,250,000	1,310,000	60,000	4.80
Manufacturing expenses		1,750,000	1,820,000	70,000	4.00
	Total	$ 8,000,000	$ 8,380,000	$380,000	4.75%
Gross margin		$ 4,500,000	$ 4,120,000	($380,000)	(8.44%)
Operating expenses:					
Selling		$ 525,000	$ 540,000	$ 15,000	2.86%
Research and development		312,500	310,000	(2,500)	(.80)
General and administrative		212,500	190,000	(22,500)	(10.59)
	Total	$ 1,050,000	$ 1,040,000	($ 10,000)	(.95%)
Profit before taxes		$ 3,450,000	$ 3,080,000	$370,000	(10.72%)
Other data:					
Break-even point		$ 3,421,050	$ 3,714,290	$293,240	8.6%
Marginal income ratio		.38	.35		

Exhibit 3

Next, manufacturing expenses have increased by 4 percent or $70,000. Departmental budgets should be reviewed to determine the areas of greatest increase and causes should be determined. Management must then decide what corrective action need be taken. If, for example, the increase is in maintenance expense, is it sound to defer projects? What is the best approach when considering the longer term interests of the business? Similar analyses should be made of the other expense areas. If expenses are under the standard, the accountant should ascertain that no omissions have been made erroneously.

It is to be observed that the break-even point has risen by 8.6 percent to $3,714,290. Perhaps a better way to state the case is that the forecast is based on a somewhat changed cost structure. This change may be shown graphically as in Exhibit 4. The solid lines indicate the acceptable cost-volume-profit structure and the dotted lines reveal the condition as planned in the forecast. Incidentally, any change in these relationships can be

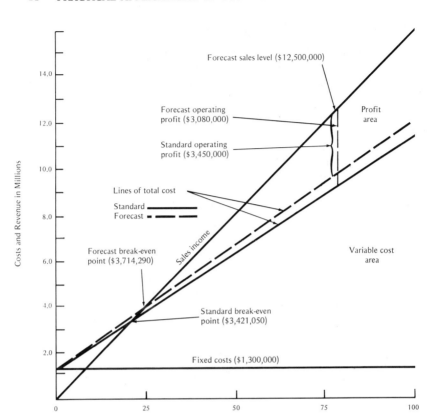

Exhibit 4. The Sample Company Profit Graph: Standard and Forecast

readily shown on the graph, whether they appear in sales, variable costs or fixed expense.

In poor economic weather, a reasonable margin of safety is necessary. Accordingly, in the Sample Company, if management agrees that the standard profit structure must be maintained, every element should be analyzed and explored by the accountant so that the final business plan for the ensuing year retains the characteristics of this structure. As an alternative, once the most satisfactory cost-volume-profit relationship is determined, including the proper product mix, then the possibility of securing additional sales volume to offset cost increases is to be considered.

OTHER USES OF COST-VOLUME-PROFIT DATA

A knowledge of the economic structure of the business, together with the related analysis, can identify areas of cost increases and, as illustrated, permit an evaluation of the forecast. In addition, such information can provide answers to other typical questions. The value of the cost-volume-profit concept is inherently in the facility with which volume can be treated as a variable factor. Because of considerations relating to the market or to expansion, management many times desires information concerning the results of a contemplated action, such as what the operating profit would be at X dollars sales volume or what the effect on operating profit would be if X percentage increase in sales volume were realized, etc. The marginal income ratio and the related segergation of fixed expense simplify the solution of such problems.

Operating profit at any given sales volume.   Using the Sample Company's profit structure, what would be the operating profit at an annual sales level of $13,000,000? The operating profit will be the marginal contribution (amount of sales income less all variable costs and expenses) less the fixed expense:

Contribution margin	=	$13,000,000 × .38
	=	$ 4,940,000
Less fixed expense		1,300,000
Equals operating profit of		$ 3,640,000

Effect on operating profit of a given percent increase in sales volume.   In setting the sales objective each year or for several years, management typically likes to know the profit result at any number of sales levels expressed as amounts or percentages of increase. The answer may be determined easily from a reading of a cost-volume-profit graph as shown in Exhibit 4. This increased flexibility is a tremendous advantage of the chart approach. However, results from each requested percentage increase also can be individually calculated. If the present sales volume is $10,500,000, with our marginal income ratio of .38, the computation of a 15 percent increase in sales is as follows:

Sales increase = $10,500,000 × 15% = $1,575,000
At marginal income ratio of .38
Produces an increase in operating profit of $598,500

In such an instance, with no change in fixed expense, the operating profit is simply the sales increase multiplied by the marginal income ratio.

Sales volume required to produce X dollars of operating profit.   In planning, management quite often decides that, for financial or other considerations, a given profit must be attained. The question then will naturally arise as to the sales volume necessary to produce it. In a calculation of this type, the desired operating profit becomes, in effect, the equivalent of fixed expense. If the desired operating profit of the Sample Company is $4,200,000, then the simple computation and result are as follows:

$$\text{Required sales volume} = \frac{\text{Fixed expense} + \text{Desired operating profit}}{\text{Marginal income ratio}}$$

$$= \frac{\$\ 1,300,000 + \$4,200,000}{.38}$$

$$= \$14,473,700$$

Additional sales volume needed to offset a reduction in selling price. The sales department may insist that the present low sales volume is due to prices which are out of line with competition. It may advise a reduction of 10 percent in these prices. We will assume that the company has a sales volume of $10,500,000, with fixed expenses of $1,300,000, and a marginal income ratio of .38. With a 10 percent reduction in selling prices, what sales volume is needed just to maintain present operating results? Our initial step is to calculate the present operating income as follows:

Marginal income	=	$10,500,000 × .38
	=	$ 3,990,000
Deduct fixed expense		1,300,000
Present operating income		$ 2,690,000

Next, we must adjust to the changed marginal income ratio (or the variable cost ratio).

$$\text{Sales volume to offset reduced selling price} = \frac{\text{Desired profit} + \text{Fixed expense}}{1 - \left(\dfrac{\text{Present variable cost ratio}}{1 - \text{Proposed \% reduction in selling price}}\right)}$$

$$= \frac{\$2,690,000 + \$1,300,000}{1 - \left(\dfrac{.62}{1 - .10}\right)} = \frac{\$3,990,000}{.3112} = \$12,821,000$$

The required sales volume of $12,821,000 represents an increase of about 22 percent over the present level. The ability to secure such an increase should be explored in terms of both sales potential and plant capacity.

Effect of changes in fixed expense and variable cost ratios. Since the objective of business management should be the earning of the maximum return on invested capital, consistent with proper social objectives, there is often a continuous search for reduced costs. In the case of the Sample Company, assume that management, after some study, feels the "normal" or standard profit structure may be improved. As an example, it may be concluded that direct material costs may be reduced 10 percent through certain substitutions and that fixed expenses may be lowered by $250,000 annually. Then the question may be asked, "What would the probable operating profit be at a sales level of $12,000,000 annually?" The answer could be calculated using the profit-structure shown in Exhibit 2:

The new variable cost ratio   =   Present variable cost of material less
10% plus other variable costs
=   (.40 less 10%) + .22 = .58

The new marginal income ratio =   1 − variable cost ratio = 1 − .58 = .42

Now operating results may be quickly determined as follows:

Marginal income   = Sales volume × marginal income ratio
= $12,000,000 × .42 = $5,040,000

The $5,040,000 marginal income less the revised fixed expense of $1,050,000 ($1,300,000 − $250,000) will produce a more favorable operating income of $3,990,000. If preferred, a more detailed comparison of the present operation and the $12,000,000 sales level may be made as follows:

Description	Present		Higher level	
	Amount	% Net sales	Amount	% Net sales
Net sales	$10,000,000	100.00	$12,000,000	100.00
Variable costs	6,200,000	62.00	6,960,000	58.00
Marginal income	$ 3,800,000	38.00	$ 5,040,000	42.00
Fixed expense	1,300,000	13.00	1,050,000	8.75
Operating income	$ 2,500,000	25.00	$ 3,990,000	33.25

Advisability of plant expansion.   Sooner or later most progressive businesses are faced with a problem of plant expansion. This solution should not rest merely on available funds. Rather, management should have a full realization of the economic questions involved and here, again, cost-volume-profit analysis can be helpful. The chief executive might find break-even analysis valuable in providing information needed in a critical review of the proposed commitment, answering such points as:

1.   Relative break-even points.
2.   Sales volume required to earn the present level of profits.
3.   Sales volume necessary to earn the same rate of profit on the proposed facility as on the existing one.
4.   Maximum profit potential.

The development of these criteria is simply the application of the basic formula already discussed. There are simply more aspects to the problem and perhaps more sales attainment levels to consider before making an intelligent commitment of long-term funds.

Planning for adequate facilities preferably should take place sufficiently ahead of the date when the plant and equipment are needed for operations. In our example, the Sample Company, the sales forecast is already at the $12,500,000 level. However, management is of the opinion that the full plant capacity of $15,000,000 will be required within the next eighteen months. Therefore, assume these facts, using the profit structure (Exhibit 2) of the company:

Maximum annual earnings of the company with present facilities:

Net sales	$15,000,000
Costs and expenses:	
Variable (62% of net sales)	9,300,000
Fixed	1,300,000
Total	$10,600,000
Income before taxes	$ 4,400,000
Federal income tax (50%)	2,200,000
Net income	$ 2,200,000
Annual fixed expense of new plant	$ 700,000
Desired annual income (net) on new investment	$ 140,000
Maximum sales volume of new plant	$ 8,600,000

On the basis of this information, these determinations can be made:

BREAK-EVEN POINTS

$$\text{Present facilities} = \frac{\text{Fixed costs}}{\text{Marginal income ratio}} = \frac{\$1,300,000}{.38}$$

$$= \$3,421,050 \text{ sales volume.}$$

$$\text{Proposed facilities} = \frac{\text{Present} + \text{Additional fixed expense}}{\text{Marginal income ratio}}$$

$$= \frac{\$1,300,000 + \$700,000}{.38} = \$5,263,200 \text{ sales volume.}$$

SALES VOLUME REQUIRED

To earn existing income =

$$\frac{\text{Present fixed expense} + \text{Additional fixed expense} + \text{Existing income}}{\text{Marginal income ratio}}$$

$$= \frac{\$1,300,000 + \$700,000 + \$3,450,000}{.38} = \$14,340,000 \text{ sales volume.}$$

To earn a given return on investment =

$$\frac{\text{Present fixed expense} + \text{Added fixed expense} + \text{Present return on investment} + \text{Return (before taxes) on new investment}}{\text{Marginal income ratio}}$$

$$= \frac{\$1,300,000 + \$700,000 + \$3,450,000 + \$280,000}{.38} = \frac{\$5,730,000}{.38}$$

$$= \$15,000,000 \text{ sales volume.}$$

MINIMUM EARNINGS POTENTIAL WITH NEW PLANT

Net sales (capacity)		$23,600,000
Costs and expenses		
Variable (62% of net sales)	$14,632,000	
Fixed or continuing expenses	$ 2,000,000	$16,632,000
Profit before income taxes		$ 6,968,000
Federal income taxes (50%)		3,484,000
Net income—potential		$ 3,484,000

These determinations may be summarized for management somewhat in this fashion:

Description	Present facilities	Prospective facilities	Increase
Annual break-even sales volume	$ 3,421,050	$ 5,263,200	$1,842,150
Annual sales volume to earn existing income	12,500,000	14,340,000	1,840,000
Annual sales volume to earn desired return on new facility	12,500,000	15,100,000	2,600,000
Maximum sales volume	15,000,000	23,600,000	8,600,000
Maximum profit potential	2,200,000	3,484,000	1,284,000

A prudent management will consider carefully its ability to secure and maintain, at the assumed prices, an additional sales volume of at least $2,600,000. Moreover, because of a very favorable marginal income ratio and the consequent relatively small increase in sales needed to provide an adequate return, further thought should be given to:

1. Possible or probable competitive action and the need for price changes to discourage competition.
2. The prospects of achieving a more substantial increase in sales to utilize the new facilities and realize more of the profit potential.

USES OF COST-VOLUME-PROFIT ANALYSIS FOR PART OF THE BUSINESS

Previous illustrations have dealt with the use of cost-volume-profit analysis for the business as a whole. Yet, the same approach may be applied to problems relative to individual product lines, territories, methods of sale, channels of distribution, or any particular segment of the business which is under scrutiny. In all of these decisions, the significant factors are the marginal income ratio and the fixed expense or cost. Where both direct and allocated costs are involved, several different break-even points may be determined. For example, suppose these conditions exist in a sales territory:

Direct and continuing territory selling expense	$310,000
Marginal income ratio	.25
Allocable share of home office (fixed) expense	$130,000

The sales volume required merely to cover the direct territorial fixed expense would be:

$$\frac{\text{Direct fixed expenses}}{\text{Marginal income ratio}} = \frac{\$310,000}{.25} = \$1,240,000 \text{ sales volume.}$$

The annual sales volume sufficient to cover the direct expenses and allocated home office fixed expense would be:

$$\frac{\text{Direct expense} + \text{allocated expense}}{\text{Marginal income ratio}} = \frac{\$310,000 + \$130,000}{.25} = \frac{\$1,760,000}{\text{sales volume.}}$$

... AND IN CONTROL

The preceding discussion has related principally to the planning phase of business, that is, to showing what must be done to achieve a given objective. Once the best plan has been selected and the goal has thus been defined, the same cost-volume-profit analysis can be used for control purposes. Charts may be helpful in such an approach. One such application is a sales control chart as shown in Exhibit 5. This chart shows three important factors cumulatively: actual sales volume, sales forecast, and sales volume required to break-even. Based on existing sales plans, the chart shows that eight months of sales are required just to meet all costs and

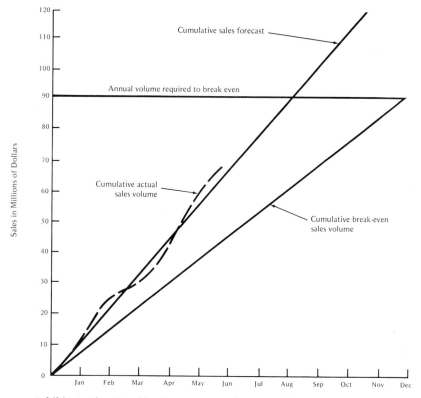

Exhibit 5. The Graphic Company Break-Even Sales Control Chart

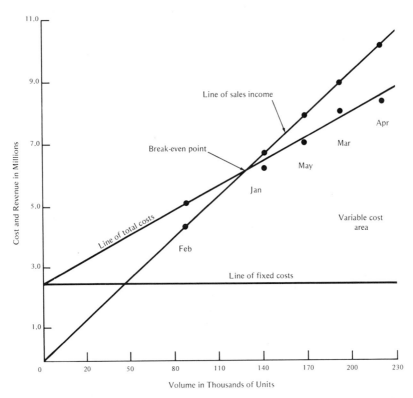

Exhibit 6. The Illustrative Company Break-Even Control Chart (monthly)

expenses and that profits will be realized for the year only after the cumulative sales level has been attained.

Another chart designed to show progress—or lack of progress—in keeping with the acceptable cost-volume-profit structure is illustrated in Exhibit 6. In this application, monthly costs are charted against the corresponding sales level to detect out-of-line trends.

A MAJOR HELP IN ANSWERING MANY QUESTIONS

The applications of the cost-volume-profit relationship, illustrated in this article, are suggestive only. Further refinements and modifications may be found necessary, desirable, and useful in your particular business. Moreover, as conditions change, the desired profit structure must be adjusted. Nevertheless, there are a great many questions that the cost-volume-profit relationship may help to answer. It is one facet of putting facts and figures to work for management and it is one of the more interesting aspects of accounting planning and control.

12.

COST-VOLUME-PROFIT ANALYSIS
UNDER CONDITIONS OF UNCERTAINTY*

*Robert K. Jaedicke
and
Alexander A. Robichek*

Cost-volume-profit analysis is frequently used by management as a basis for choosing among alternatives. Such decisions as: (1) the sales volume required to attain a given level of profits; and (2) the most profitable combination of products to produce and sell are examples of decision problems where C-V-P analysis is useful. However, the fact that traditional C-V-P analysis does not include adjustments for risk and uncertainty may, in any given instance, severely limit its usefulness. Some of the limitations can be seen from the following example.

Assume that the firm is considering the introduction of two new products, either of which can be produced by using present facilities. Both products require an increase in annual fixed cost of the same amount, say $400,000. Each product has the same selling price and variable cost per unit, say $10 and $8 respectively, and each requires the same amount of capacity. Using these data, the breakeven point of either product is 200,000 units. C-V-P analysis helps to establish the breakeven volume of each product, but this analysis does not distinguish the relative desirability of the two products for at least two reasons.

The first piece of missing information is the *expected* sales volume of each product. Obviously, if the annual sales of A are expected to be 300,000 units and of B are expected to be 350,000 units, then B is clearly preferred to A so far as the sales expectation is concerned.

However, assume that the expected annual sales of each product is the same—say 300,000 units. Is it right to conclude that management should be indifferent as far as a choice between A and B is concerned? The answer is *no, unless* each sales expectation is certain. If both sales estimates are

*From *The Accounting Review*, October 1964, pp. 917–926. Reprinted by permission of the authors and the American Accounting Association.

subject to uncertainty, the decision process will be improved if the relative risk associated with each product can somehow be brought into the analysis. The discussion which follows suggests some changes which might be made in traditional C-V-P analysis so as to make it a more useful tool in analyzing decision problems under uncertainty.

SOME PROBABILITY CONCEPTS RELATED TO C-V-P ANALYSIS

In the previous section, it was pointed out that the *expected* volume of the annual sales is an important decision variable. Some concepts of probability will be discussed using the example posed earlier.

The four fundamental relationships used in the example were: (1) the selling price per unit; (2) the variable cost per unit; (3) the total fixed cost; and (4) the expected sales volume of each product. In any given decision problem, all four of these factors can be uncertain. However, it may be that, *relative to* the expected sales quantity, the costs and selling prices are quite certain. That is, for analytical purposes, the decision maker may be justified in treating several factors as certainty equivalents. Such a procedure simplifies the analysis and will be followed here as a first approximation. In this section of the paper, sales volume will be treated as the only uncertain quantity. Later, all decision factors in the above example will be treated under conditions of uncertainty.

In the example, sales volume is treated as a *random variable*. A random variable can be thought of as an *unknown quantity*. In this case, the best decision hinges on the value of the random variable, sales volume of each product. One decision approach which allows for uncertainty is to estimate, for each random variable, the likelihood that the random variable will take on various possible values. Such an estimate is called a subjective probability distribution. The decision would then be made by choosing that course of action which has the highest *expected monetary value*. This approach is illustrated in Table 1.

EVENTS (UNITS DEMANDED)	PROBABILITY DISTRIBUTION— (PRODUCT A)	PROBABILITY DISTRIBUTION— (PRODUCT B)
50,000	—	.1
100,000	.1	.1
200,000	.2	.1
300,000	.4	.2
400,000	.2	.4
500,000	.1	.1
	1.00	1.00

Table 1. Probability Distribution for Products A and B

The expected value of the random variables, sales demand for each product, is calculated by weighting the possible conditional values by their respective probabilities. In other words, the expected value is a weighted average. The calculation is given in Table 2.

(1) EVENT	(2) P(A)	(1 × 2)	(3) P(B)	(1 × 3)
50,000	—	—	.1	5,000
100,000	.1	10,000	.1	10,000
200,000	.2	40,000	.1	20,000
300,000	.4	120,000	.2	60,000
400,000	.2	80,000	.4	160,000
500,000	.1	50,000	.1	50,000
	1.00		1.00	
Expected Value		300,000 units		305,000 units

Table 2. Expected Value of Sales Demand for Products A and B

Based on an expected value approach, the firm should select product B rather than A. The expected profits of each possible action are as follows:

Product A:
$2(300,000 \text{ units}) - \$400,000 = \$200,000$
Product B:
$2(305,000 \text{ units}) - \$400,000 = \$210,000.$

Several observations are appropriate at this point. First, the respective probabilities for each product, used in Table 1, add to 1.00. Furthermore, the possible demand levels (events) are assumed to be mutually exclusive and also exhaustive. That is, the listing is done in such a way that no two events can happen simultaneously and any events *not* listed are assumed to have a zero probability of occurring. Herein are three important (basic) concepts of probability analyses.

Secondly, the probability distributions may have been assigned by using historical demand data on similar products, or the weights may be purely subjective in the sense that there is no historical data available. Even if the probability distributions are entirely subjective, this approach still has merit. It allows the estimator to express his uncertainty about the sales estimate. An estimate of sales is necessary to make a decision. Hence, the question is *not* whether an estimate must be made, but simply a question of the best way to make and express the estimate.

Now, suppose that the expected value of sales for each product is 300,000, as shown in Table 3. In this example, it is easy to see that the firm would *not* be indifferent between products A and B, even though the expected value of sales is 300,000 units in both cases. In the case of product

A, for example, there is a .1 chance that sales will be only 100,000 units, and in that case, a loss of $200,000 would be incurred (i.e., $2 × 100,000 units − $400,000). On the other hand, there is a .3 chance that sales will be above 300,000 units and if this is the case, higher profits are possible with product A than with product B. Hence, the firm's attitude toward risk becomes important. The expected value (or the mean of the distribution) is important, but so is the "spread" in the distribution. Typically, the greater the "spread," the greater the risk involved. A quantitative measure of the spread is available in the form of the standard deviation of the distribution, and this concept and its application will be refined later in the paper.

THE NORMAL PROBABILITY DISTRIBUTION

The preceding examples were highly simplified and yet the calculations are relatively long and cumbersome. The possible sales volumes were few in number and the probability distribution was discrete, that is, a sales volume of 205,762 units was considered an impossible event. The use of a continuous probability distribution is desirable not only because the calculation will usually be simplified but because the distribution may also be a more realistic description of the uncertainty aspects of the situation. The normal probability distribution will be introduced and used in the following analysis which illustrates the methodology involved. This distribution, although widely used, is not appropriate in all situations. The appropriate distribution depends on the decision problem and should, of course, be selected accordingly.

DEMAND	P(A)	E.V.(A)	P(B)	E.V.(B)
100,000 units	.1	10,000	—	—
200,000 units	.2	40,000	—	—
300,000 units	.4	120,000	1.00	300,000
400,000 units	.2	80,000	—	—
500,000 units	.1	50,000	—	—
	1.00		1.00	
Expected Sales Demand		300,000		300,000

Table 3

The normal probability distribution is a smooth, symmetric, continuous, bell-shaped curve as shown in Figure 1. The area under the curve sums to 1. The curve reaches a maximum at the mean of the distribution and one-half the area lies on either side of the mean.

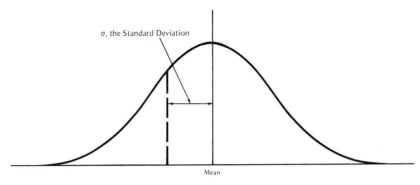

The Normal Probability Distribution

Figure 1

On the horizontal axis are plotted the values of the appropriate unknown quantity or random variable; in the examples used here, the unknown quantity is the sales for the coming periods.

A particular normal probability distribution can be completely determined if its mean and its standard deviation, σ, are known. The standard deviation is a measure of the dispersion of the distribution about its mean. The area under any normal distribution is 1, but one distribution may be "spread out" more than another distribution. For example, in Figure 2, both normal distributions have the same area and the same mean. However, in one case the σ is 1 and in the other case the σ is greater than 1. The larger the σ, the more spread out is the distribution. It should be noted that the standard deviation is not an area but is a measure of the dispersion of the individual observations about the mean of all the observations—it is a distance.

Since the normal probability distribution is continuous rather than discrete, the probability of an event cannot be read directly from the graph. The unknown quantity must be thought of as being in an interval. Assume, for example, that the mean sales for the coming period is estimated to be 10,000 units and the normal distribution appears as in Figure 3. Given Figure 3, certain probability statements can be made. For Example:

> 1. The probability of the actual sales being between 10,000 and 11,000 units is .20. This is shown by area C. Because of the symmetry of the curve, the probability of the sales being between 9,000 and 10,000 is also .20. This is shown by shaded area B. These probabilities can be given a frequency interpretation. That is, area C indicates that the actual sales will be between 10,000 and 11,000 units in about 20% of the cases.

> 2. The probability of the actual sales being greater than 11,000 units is .30 as shown by area D.

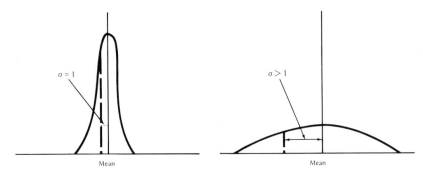

Normal Probability Distributions with Different Standard Deviations

Figure 2

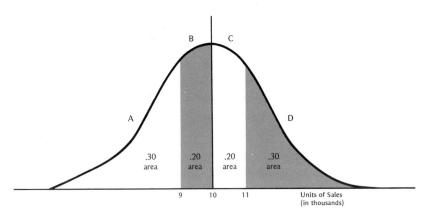

Figure 3

3. The probability of the sales being greater than 9,000 units is .70, the sum of areas B, C, and D.

Given a specific normal distribution, it is possible to read probabilities of the type described above directly from a normal probability table.

Another important characteristic of any normal distribution is that approximately .50 of the area lies within $\pm .67$ standard deviations of the mean; about .68 of the area lies within ± 1.0 standard deviations of the mean; .95 of the area lies within ± 1.96 standard deviations of the mean.

As was mentioned above, normal probabilities can be read from a normal probability table. A partial table of normal probabilities is given in Table 4. This table is the "right tail" of the distribution; that is, probabilities of the unknown quantity being greater than X standard deviations from the mean are given in the table. For example, the probability of the unknown quantity being greater than the mean plus $.35\sigma$ is .3632. The distribution tabulated is a normal distribution with mean zero and standard deviation of 1. Such a distribution is known as a standard normal distribution. However, any normal distribution can be standardized and hence, with proper adjustment, Table 4 will serve for any normal distribution.

X	0.00	0.05
.1	.4602	.4404
.3	.3821	.3632
.5	.3085	.2912
.6	.2743	.2578
.7	.2420	.2266
.8	.2119	.1977
.9	.1841	.1711
1.0	.1587	.1469
1.1	.1357	.1251
1.5	.0668	.0606
2.0	.0228	.0202

Table 4. Area Under the Normal Probability Function

For example, consider the earlier case where the mean of the distribution is 10,000 units. The distribution was constructed so that the standard deviation is about 2,000 units.[1] To standardize the distribution, use the following formula, where X is the number of standard deviations from the mean:

$$X = \frac{\text{Actual sales} - \text{Mean sales}}{\text{Standard deviation of the distribution}}$$

To calculate the probability of the sales being greater than 11,000 units, first standardize the distribution and then use the table.

$$X = \frac{11,000 - 10,000}{2,000}$$

$$= .50 \text{ standard deviations.}$$

The probability of being greater than .50 standard deviations from the mean, according to Table 4, is .3085. This same approximate result is shown by Figure 3, that is, area D is .30.

[1]To see why this normal distribution has a standard deviation of 2,000 units, remember that the probability of sales being greater than 11,000 units is .30. Now examine Table 4, and it can be seen that the probability of a random variable being greater than .5 standard deviations from the mean is .3085. Hence, 1,000 units is about the same as ½ standard deviations. So, 2,000 units is about 1 standard deviation.

THE NORMAL DISTRIBUTION USED IN C-V-P ANALYSIS

The normal distribution will now be used in a C-V-P analysis problem, assuming that sales quantity is a random variable. Assume that the per-unit selling price is $3,000, the fixed cost is $5,800,000, and the variable cost per unit is $1,750. Breakeven sales (in units) is calculated as follows:

$$S_B = \frac{\$5,800,000}{\$3,000 - \$1,750} = 4,640 \text{ units.}$$

Furthermore, suppose that the sales manager estimates that the mean expected sales volume is 5,000 units and that it is equally likely that actual sales will be greater or less than the mean of 5,000 units. Furthermore, assume that the sales manager feels that there is roughly a ⅔ (i.e., .667) chance that the actual sales will be within 400 units of the mean. These subjective estimates can be expressed by using a normal distribution with mean $E(Q) = 5,000$ units and standard deviation $\sigma_q = 400$ units. The reason that σ_q is about 400 units is that, as mentioned earlier, about ⅔ of the area under the normal curve (actually .68) lies within 1 standard deviation of the mean. The probability distribution is shown in Figure 4.

The horizontal axis of Figure 4 denotes sales quantity. The probability of an actual sales event taking place is given by the area under the probability distribution. For example, the probability that the sales quantity will exceed 4,640 units (the breakeven point) is the shaded area under the probability distribution (the probability of actual sales exceeding 4,640 units).

The probability distribution of Figure 4 can be superimposed on the profit portion of the traditional C-V-P; this is done in Figure 5. The values for price, fixed costs, and variable costs are presumed to be known with certainty. Expected profit is given by:

$$E(Z) = E(Q) (P-V) - F = \$450,000,$$

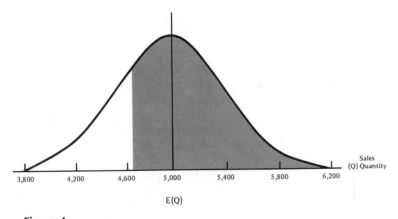

E(Q)

Figure 4

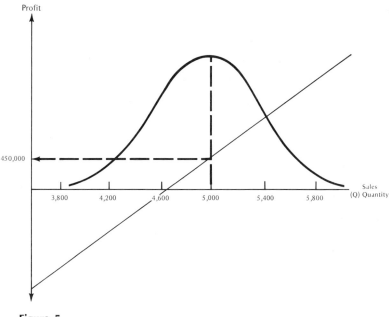

Figure 5

where

$$
\begin{aligned}
E(Z) &= \text{Expected Profit} \\
E(Q) &= \text{Expected Sales} \\
P &= \text{Price} \\
V &= \text{Variable Cost} \\
F &= \text{Fixed Cost.}
\end{aligned}
$$

The standard deviation of the profit (σ_z) is:

$$
\begin{aligned}
\sigma_z &= \sigma_Q \times \$1{,}250 \text{ contribution per unit} \\
&= 400 \text{ units} \times \$1{,}250 = \$500{,}000.
\end{aligned}
$$

Since profits are directly related to the volume of sales, and since it is the level of profits which is often the concern of management, it may be desirable to separate the information in Figure 5 which relates to profit. Figure 6 is a graphical illustration of the relationship between profit level and the probability distribution of the profit level. A number of important relationships can now be obtained in probabilistic terms. Since the probability distribution of sales quantity is normal with a mean of 5,000 units and a standard deviation of 400 units, the probability distribution of profits will also be normal with a mean, as shown earlier, of $450,000 and a standard deviation of $500,000.

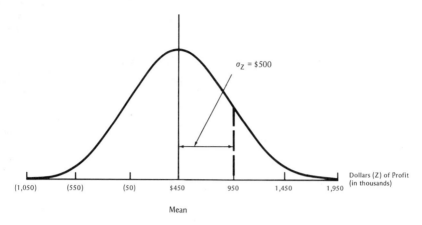

Figure 6

Using the probability distribution shown in Figure 6, the following probabilities can be calculated (using Table 4).

1. The probability of at least breaking even: This is the probability of profits being greater than zero and can be calculated by summing the area under the distribution to the right of zero profits. This probability can be calculated as 1 – (the probability of profits being less than zero). Since the distribution is symmetric, Table IV can be used to read left tail as well as right tail probabilities. Zero profits fall .9 standard deviations to the left of the mean

$$\left(\text{i.e.,} \quad \frac{\$450 - 0}{\$500} \ = \ .9\right).$$

Hence, the probability of profits being less than zero is:

$$P \ (\text{Profits} < .9\sigma \text{ from the mean}) \ = \ .184.$$

Therefore

$$P \ (\text{Profits} > 0) \ = \ 1 - .184 \ = \ .816.$$

2. The probability of profits being greater than $200,000.

$P \ (\text{Profits} > \$200,000)$

$$= \ 1 - P \left(\text{Profits} < \frac{450 - 200}{500} \ \sigma \text{ from the mean}\right)$$

$$= \ 1 - P \ (\text{Profits} < .5\sigma \text{ from the mean})$$

$$= \ 1 - .3085 \ = \ .692.$$

3. The probability of the loss being greater than $300,000.

P (Loss > $300,000)

$$= P \left(\text{Loss} > \frac{450 - (-300)}{500}, \text{ or } 1.5\sigma \text{ from the mean} \right)$$

$P = .067.$

The question of how the above information can be used now arises. The manager, in choosing between this product and other products or other lines of activity, can probably improve his decision by considering the risk involved. He knows that the breakeven sales is at a level of 4,640 units. He knows that the expected sales are 5,000 units which would yield a profit of $450,000. Surely, he would benefit from knowing that:

    1. The probability of at least reaching breakeven sales is .816,

    2. The probability of making at least $200,000 profit is .692,

    3. The probability of making at least $450,000 profit is .50,

    4. The probability of incurring loses, i.e., not achieving the breakeven sales volume, is (1.816, or .184),

    5. The probability of incurring a $300,000 or greater loss is .067, etc.

If the manager is comparing this product with other products, probability analysis combined with C-V-P allows a comparison of the risk involved in each product, as well as a comparison of relative breakeven points and expected profits. Given the firm's attitude toward and willingness to assume risk (of losses as well as high profits), the decision of choosing among alternatives should be facilitated by the above analysis.

SEVERAL RELEVANT FACTORS PROBABILISTIC

It is evident from the above discussion that profit, Z, is a function of the quantity of sales in units (Q); the unit selling price (P); the fixed cost (F); and the variable cost (V). Up to this point P, F, and V were considered only as given constants, so that profit was variable only as a function of changes in sales quantity. In the following discussion, P, F, and V will be treated in a manner similar to Q, i.e., as random variables whose probability distribution is known. Continuing the example from the preceding section, let:

Variable	Expectation (Mean)	Standard Deviation
Sales Quantity (Q)	$E(Q') = 5,000$ units	$\sigma_{Q'} = 400$ units
Selling Price (P)	$E(P') = \$3,000^2$	$\sigma_{P'} = \$50^2$
Fixed Costs (F)	$E(F') = \$5,800,000^2$	$\sigma_{F'} = \$100,000^2$
Variable Costs (V)	$E(V') = \$1,750^2$	$\sigma_{V'} = \$75^2$

For purposes of illustration, the random variables will be assumed to be independent, so that no correlation exists between events of the different random variables.[3] In this case, the expected profit $E(Z')$ and the related standard deviation σ_z', can be calculated as follows:

$$
\begin{aligned}
E(Z') &= E(Q')\,[E(P') - E(V')] - E(F') \\
&= \$450,000. \\
\sigma_z'^{4} &= \$681,500.
\end{aligned}
$$

Note that when factors other than sales are treated as random variables, the expected profit is still $450,000 as in the previous cases. However, the profit's risk as measured by the standard deviation is increased from $500,000 to $681,500. The reason for this is that the variability in all of the components (i.e., sales price, cost, etc.) will add to the variability in the profit. Is this change in the standard deviation significant? The significance of the change is a value judgment based on a comparison of various probabilistic measures and on the firm's attitude toward risk. Using a normal distribution, Table 5 compares expected profits, standard deviations of profits, and select probabilistic measures for three hypothetical products.

In all three situations, the proposed products have the same breakeven quantity—4,640 units. The first case is the first example discussed where sales quantity is the only random variable. The second case is the one just discussed, that is, all factors are probabilistic. In the third case, the assumed product has the same expected values for selling price, variable cost, fixed cost, and sales volume, but the standard deviations on each of these random variables have been increased to

$$
\begin{aligned}
\sigma_{Q''} &= 600 \text{ (instead of 400 units)}; \\
\sigma_{P''} &= \$125 \text{ (instead of \$50)}; \\
\sigma_{F''} &= \$200,000 \text{ (instead of \$100,000)}; \\
\text{and } \sigma_{V''} &= \$150 \text{ (instead of \$75).}
\end{aligned}
$$

---

[2]The mean and standard deviation for P, F, and V can be established by using the same method described earlier. That is, the sales manager may estimate a mean selling price of $3,000 per unit and, given the above information, he should feel that there is roughly a $\frac{2}{3}$ probability that the actual sales price per unit will be within $50 of this mean estimate.

[3]This assumption is made to facilitate computation in the example. Where correlation among variables is present the computational procedure must take into account the values of the respective covariances.

[4]For the case of independent variables given here, σ_z', is the solution value in the equation:

$$\sigma_z = \sqrt{[\sigma_Q^2\,(\sigma_p^2 + \sigma_v^2) + E(Q')^2\,(\sigma_p^2 + \sigma_v^2) + [E(P') - E(V')]^2\,\sigma_Q^2 + \sigma_F^2]}$$

| | PRODUCTS | | |
	(1)	(2)	(3)
Expected profit	$450,000	$450,000	$ 450,000
Standard deviation of profit	$500,000	$681,500	$1,253,000
The probability of:			
(a) at least breaking even	.816	.745	.641
(b) profit at least +$250,000	.655	.615	.564
(c) profit at least +$600,000	.382	.413	.456
(d) loss greater than $300,000	.067	.136	.274

*Note: The above probabilities, in some cases, cannot be read from Table 4. However, all probabilities come from a more complete version of Table 4.

Table 5. Comparison of Expected Profits, Standard Deviations of Profits, and Select Probabilistic Measures*

Table 5 shows the relative "risk" involved in the three new products which have been proposed. The chances of at least breaking even are greatest with product 1. However, even though the standard deviation of the profit on product 3 is over twice that of product 1, the probability of breaking even on product 3 is only .17 lower than product 1. Likewise, the probability of earning at least $250,000 profit is higher for product 1 (which has the lowest σ) than for the other two products.

However, note that the probability of earning profits above the expected value of $450,000 (for each product) is *greater* for products 2 and 3 than for 1. If the firm is willing to assume some risk, the chances of high profits are improved with product 3, rather than with 2 and 1. To offset this, however, the chance of loss is also greatest with product 3. This is to be expected, since product 3 has the highest standard deviation (variability) as far as profit is concerned.

The best alternative cannot be chosen without some statement of the firm's attitude toward risk. However, given a certain attitude, the proper choice should be facilitated by using probability information of the type given in Table 5. As an example, suppose that the firm's position is such that any loss at all may have an adverse affect on its ability to stay in business. Some probability criteria can, perhaps, be established in order to screen proposals for new products. If, for example, the top management feels that any project which is acceptable must have no greater than a .30 probability of incurring a loss, then projects 1 or 2 would be acceptable but project 3 would not.

On the other hand, the firm's attitude toward risk may be such that the possibility of high profit is attractive, provided the probability of losses can be reasonably controlled. In this case, it may be possible to set a range within which acceptable projects must fall. For example, suppose that the firm is willing to accept projects where the probability of profits being greater than $600,000 is at least .40, provided that the probability of a loss being greater than $300,000 does not exceed .15. In this case, project 2 would be acceptable, but project 3 would not. Given statements of attitude toward risk of this nature, it seems that a probability dimension added to C-V-P analysis would be useful.

SUMMARY AND CONCLUSION

In many cases, the choice among alternatives is facilitated greatly by C-V-P analysis. However, traditional C-V-P analysis does not take account of the relative risk of various alternatives. The interaction of costs, selling prices and volume are important in summarizing the effect of various alternatives on the profits of the firm. The techniques discussed in this paper preserve the traditional analysis but also add another dimension—that is, risk is brought in as another important decision factor. The statement of probabilities with respect to various levels of profits and losses for each alternative should aid the decision maker once his attitude toward risk has been defined.

13.
TOWARD PROBABILISTIC PROFIT BUDGETS*

William L. Ferrara
and
Jack C. Hayya

Practical techniques have recently been developed for business applications of probability concepts so that they can be easily integrated with profit planning. This paper shows how some of these techniques can be used in the construction of probabilistic profit budgets, i.e., budgets that display expected values and a probability interval for every item.

RELATED STUDIES AND LITERATURE

The accounting literature does not specify how probabilistic profit budgets are constructed. A 1960 study on profit planning by executives, for example, makes no mention of probabilistic approaches to profit budgets.[1]

The 1966 *Statement of Basic Accounting Theory*, encourages accountants to adopt probabilistic financial statements, but does not offer any guidelines.[2] Byrne, *et al*, offer similar encouragement when they state that decision-tree and network concepts ". . . may be a better way of utilizing the double-entry principle—at least when probability distributions are to be compounded for such purposes as . . . projection of profit-and-loss state-

---

*From *Management Accounting*, October 1970, pp. 23–28. Copyrighted 1970 by National Association of Accountants. Reprinted by permission. The authors are indebted to Joseph Mackovjak (now with General Electric) who provided simulation expertise and other valuable assistance.

[1]Leon E. Hay, "Planning for Profits—How Some Executives are Doing It," *The Accounting Review*, April 1960, pp. 233–237.
[2]A Statement of *Basic Accounting Theory*, American Accounting Association, 1966, pp. 38, 59, and 65.

ment categories along with related balance-sheet and flow-of-funds analysis."[3]

Magee,[4] Hertz,[5] and Jaedicke and Robichek[6] focus on issues related to probabilistic profit budgets. Magee develops a detailed decision-tree in calculating the expected net present value of alternative capital investments. Hertz also deals with capital investments, but uses computer simulation to derive expected discounted return on investment and a probability distribution which expresses the variability of expected return on investment. Jaedicke and Robichek handle uncertainty in cost-volume-profit analysis by assuming that uncertainty is in the form of a normal probability distribution.

Coughlan,[7] Hespos and Strassman,[8] Springer, Herlihy, Mall and Beggs[9] offer, in ascending order, some of the more detailed approaches to preparing probabilistic financial statements.

Coughlan uses discrete probability distributions to calculate expected net receipts. His treatment of probability intervals, however, is incomplete.

Hespos and Strassman, like some afore-mentioned authors, deal with investment decisions. They expand the treatment of risk analysis in decision-trees by substituting continuous probability distributions for the discrete probabilities at the chance event nodes.

Springer, Herlihy, Mall and Beggs use an analytic technique and Monte Carlo to estimate probability intervals for net profit. In this respect, their work is similar to ours.

The intent of this paper is to integrate three probabilistic techniques suggested in the literature with profit budgets. The PERT-like and probability-tree approaches used here emphasize most likely and mean values as well as measures of variability for each item in the income statement. Monte Carlo is used to simulate probability intervals for complex distributions that are too difficult to treat analytically.

[3]R. Byrne, A. Charnes, W. W. Cooper, and K. Kortanek, "Some New Approaches to Risk," The Accounting Review, January 1968, p. 33.

[4]John F. Magee, "How to Use Decision Trees in Capital Investment," Harvard Business Review, September–October 1964, pp. 79–96.

[5]David B. Hertz, "Risk Analysis in Capital Investment," Harvard Business Review, January–February, 1964, pp. 95–106, and "Investment Policies that Pay Off," Harvard Business Review, January–February 1968, pp. 96–108.

[6]R. K. Jaedicke and A. A. Robichek, "Cost-Volume-Profit Analysis Under Conditions of Uncertainty," The Accounting Review, October 1964, pp. 914–926.

[7]John W. Coughlan, "Profit and Probability," Advanced Management Journal, April 1968, pp. 53–69.

[8]Richard F. Hespos and Paul A. Strassman, "Stochastic Decision Trees for the Analysis of Investment Decisions," Management Science, August 1956, pp. 244–259.

[9]Clifford H. Springer, Robert E. Herlihy, Robert T. Mall, and Robert I. Beggs, Probabilistic Models, Richard D. Irwin, Inc., Homewood, Ill., 1968: Of particular relevance are chapters 4 and 5.

THE TYPICAL PROFIT BUDGET

Let us assume that the profit budget in a single-product company is as shown in Exhibit 1. The direct-costing format of Exhibit 1 facilitates the use of break-even and cost-volume-profit analysis. Fixed costs are classified into managed and committed costs. Managed fixed costs are those costs which can be modified in the short run. Committed fixed costs are those which cannot be modified in the short run. The distinction between variable, managed and committed costs in this model is not only useful, it is particularly appropriate (as will become clear) in the preparation of probabilistic budgets.

Sales (100,000 units @ $10)		$1,000,000
Variable costs		
Manufacturing ($5 per unit)	$500,000	
Marketing ($.50 per unit)	50,000	550,000
Marginal contribution		$ 450,000
Managed fixed costs		
Manufacturing	$ 20,000	
Marketing	10,000	
Administrative	40,000	70,000
Short-run margin		$ 380,000
Committed fixed costs		
Manufacturing	$180,000	
Marketing	40,000	
Administrative	60,000	280,000
Net income before tax		$ 100,000
Tax — 50%		50,000
Net income after tax		$ 50,000

Exhibit 1. Profit Budget for Year Ending June 197X

The segregation of fixed costs into managed and committed fixed costs gives rise to the "short-run margin." This margin is the contribution to earnings for which managers can be held accountable in a given budget period. The short-run margin further shows that committed costs are an obstacle which must be hurdled before a net profit is realized.

The weakness of Exhibit 1, and other models like it, is that they give no indication of the potential variability of the various estimates used. It is clear that the items in the budget are subjective estimates of most likely values, i.e., estimates of what is most probable in terms of revenues, costs and profits. The function of probabilistic profit budgets is to extend such models to indicate the variability of each budget item.

OPTIMISTIC, PESSIMISTIC AND MOST LIKELY VALUES

Consider first the "three-level" estimates referred to as optimistic, pessimistic and most likely values. Such a "three-level" profit budget can be easily prepared, as shown in Exhibit 2.

	PESSIMISTIC	MOST LIKELY	OPTIMISTIC
Sales ($10 per unit)	$800,000	$1,000,000	$1,100,000
Variable costs			
Manufacturing	408,000	500,000	528,000
Marketing ($.50 per unit)	40,000	50,000	55,000
Marginal contribution	$352,000	$ 450,000	$ 517,000
Managed fixed costs			
Manufacturing	10,000	20,000	30,000
Marketing	10,000	10,000	10,000
Administrative	25,000	40,000	40,000
Short-run margin	$307,000	$ 380,000	$ 437,000
Committed fixed costs			
Manufacturing	180,000	180,000	180,000
Marketing	40,000	40,000	40,000
Administrative	60,000	60,000	60,000
Net income before tax	$ 27,000	$ 100,000	$ 157,000
Tax — 50%	13,500	50,000	78,500
Net income after tax	$ 13,500	$ 50,000	$ 78,500

*The data are based on Exhibit 1 with optimistic, most likely, and pessimistic values for sales volume and variable costs being 110,000, 100,000, 80,000 and $4.80, $5.00, $5.10, respectively. Unit variable costs are assumed to vary inversely with volume. Committed costs and unit variable marketing cost are assumed to be certain; some managed costs are modified to reflect changing volume levels.

Exhibit 2. Profit Budget for Year Ending June 197X*

It is evident that the three-level estimates of Exhibit 2 are more informative than the most likely one of Exhibit 1. For example, Exhibit 2 shows that net income after tax may be as low as $13,500 or as high as $78,500. The lone use of the most likely estimate of $50,000, as in Exhibit 1, can therefore be misleading.

From the data of Exhibit 2, one can calculate means and standard deviations for sales, variable costs, and marginal contribution by using the PERT formulas[10] or through probability-tree analysis. If we are to use the PERT

---

[10]The PERT formulas for the standard deviation (σ) and the mean (μ) are:

$$\sigma = \frac{b - a}{6}$$

$$\mu = \frac{1}{3} \left[2m + \frac{1}{2} (a + b) \right]$$

Where "b" is the optimistic estimate, "a" is the pessimistic estimate and "m" is the most likely estimate.

formulas, the person who is providing the estimates must be made aware that a most likely estimate is a mode rather than a mean, and that the pessimistic and optimistic estimates are assumed to be six standard deviations apart.

PROBABILITY-TREE ANALYSIS: GENERAL

A more useful method for the preparation of probabilistic profit budgets is probability-tree analysis.[11] Probability-tree analysis is a generalization of the PERT method.

In using probability-tree analysis, probability estimates must be made for every level of volume and variable manufacturing cost considered. Thus, in our case, probabilities are assigned to each of the three sales and variable manufacturing cost levels as indicated in Exhibit 3. The probabilities (the p's and q's) assigned to each level are usually applicable to ranges whose midpoints are used in the calculations.

The budget variables under consideration in Exhibit 3 are sales, variable manufacturing cost, variable marketing cost, managed costs, committed costs, and net income after tax. The nine combinations in the exhibit result

Volume (price = $10)	Variable Manufacturing Cost	Variable Marketing Cost	Managed Costs	Committed Costs	Net Income After Tax-50% (NIAT)	Joint* Probability (JP)	Combination	JP X NIAT
	$5.10	$0.50	$45,000	$280,000	$13,500	0.06	1	$ 810
	q = .2							
80,000	$5.00	$0.50	$45,000	$280,000	$17,500	0.18	2	3,150
p = .3	q = .6							
	$4.80	$0.50	$45,000	$280,000	$25,500	0.06	3	1,530
	q = .2							
	$5.10	$0.50	$70,000	$280,000	$45,000	0.10	4	4,500
	q = .2							
100,000	$5.00	$0.50	$70,000	$280,000	$50,000	0.30	5	15,000
p = .5	q = .6							
	$4.80	$0.50	$70,000	$280,000	$60,000	0.10	6	6,000
	q = .2							
	$5.10	$0.50	$80,000	$280,000	$62,000	0.04	7	2,480
	q = .2							
110,000	$5.00	$0.50	$80,000	$280,000	$67,500	0.12	8	8,100
p = .2	q = .6							
	$4.80	$0.50	$80,000	$280,000	$78,500	0.04	9	3,140
	q = .2		Expected Value of Net Income after Tax					$44,710

*Joint probabilities are calculated by multiplying the probabilities on the path (the succession of branches) moving toward each outcome.

Exhibit 3. Tree Diagram of Basic Problem Including Expected Values

---

[11] The probability-tree analysis used in this study differs from formal decision-tree analysis in that all nodes in the probability-tree are chance event nodes.

by considering the three sales estimates to be independent of the three variable manufacturing cost estimates.[12]

In Exhibit 3, variable marketing costs, managed costs and committed costs are assumed to be non-probabilistic. The exhibit shows net income after tax (NIAT) for each of the nine combinations and the expected value (the average or mean value) of NIAT.

The expected value of NIAT in Exhibit 3 [$\Sigma(\text{NIAT})JP$] is $44,710. On the other hand, the corresponding result for Exhibit 2, as calculated by use of the PERT formula for the mean, turns out to be $48,666. The two results differ because they are based on two different models.

PROBABILITY-TREE ANALYSIS AND PROFIT BUDGETS

In Exhibit 4 the expected value (μ) and the standard deviation (σ) of every item in the income statement is presented. The normal distribution and probability intervals[13] of $\pm 2\sigma$ or $\pm 3\sigma$ from the mean cannot be used here since the probability distributions under consideration are not normal. They are discrete probability functions, i.e., functions where the random variable must assume distinct values.

It may be preferable to use the coefficient of variation rather than a probability interval in describing variability for discrete probability distributions of the type shown in Exhibits 3 and 4. The coefficient of variation is the percentage relationship between the standard deviation and the mean. The calculated values of this coefficient are presented in Exhibit 4 for each item in the income statement.

The coefficient of variation is a useful tool for planning and control purposes. From the point of view of planning, the coefficient of variation predicts the potential variability of budgeted items. A high coefficient of variation, for example, indicates that an outcome (e.g., actual sales) has relatively large variations about the budgeted value. From the point of view of control, differences between budgeted and actual outcomes are understood more meaningfully when they are related to the coefficient of variation.

Exhibit 5 summarizes Exhibit 4 in the format of an income statement. The three columns provide the mean, the standard deviation and the coefficient of variation.

An alternative format is presented in Exhibit 6, which displays the 100 percent and the 90 percent probability intervals (or ranges) for the budget

---

[12]Exhibits 2 and 3 represent different models. The model of Exhibit 2 assumes that volume and variable manufacturing costs are inversely related. The model of Exhibit 3 assumes them to be independent.

[13]Referred to as confidence intervals when the parameter to be estimated is not known.

items. As the terms imply, the 100 percent probability interval includes all the elements in the distribution, whereas a 90 percent probability interval excludes five percent in each of the two tails of the distribution. Probability intervals are obtained from Exhibit 4 by inspection as explained below.

Clearly the highest and lowest possible values for an item would contain a 100 percent probability interval. This can be obtained readily from Exhibit 4. The 90 percent range, on the other hand, is arbitrarily chosen in this instance because it fits the distribution of the nine possible values for each item shown in Exhibit 4. The highest value for each item has a probability of 0.04, while the lowest value for each item has a probability of 0.06. Thus the 90 percent range is determined by excluding the highest and lowest values for each item (with the exception of sales). By definition, the 90 percent probability interval as it has been presented here is slightly off center.

The probabilistic income statements of Exhibits 5 and 6 provide more information than the three-level format of Exhibit 2. The improvement results from attaching probabilities to sales and unit variable manufacturing cost. The choice of any of these formats, however, depends on managerial needs and preferences.

A MODEL WITH CONTINUOUS DISTRIBUTION

Thus far we have considered two general approaches to preparing probabilistic income statements, i.e., the three-level and the probability-tree approaches. We now consider the construction of a probabilistic income statement for a model with continuous probability distributions.

Description of the Model

The assumptions of the model are listed in Exhibit 7. Note that basic data (e.g., price, mean volume, or mean-unit variable manufacturing cost) similar to the previous illustrations are adopted. Again the model is for a single-product firm. The main variables (volume and unit variable manufacturing cost) are normally distributed and statistically independent with known means and standard deviations. A relevant range for volume (80,000 $\leq Q \leq$ 120,000), but not for unit variable manufacturing cost, is assumed. In addition, two costs are functions of volume. These are managed manufacturing cost and managed administrative cost. The former has a linear and the latter a quadratic relationship with volume. The other costs, and also unit price are constant.

The model presented may not be representative of the typical firm. Nevertheless, it is useful for gaining insight into the construction of probabilistic profit budgets.

Combination	1	2	3	4	5	6	7	8	9
					DOLLARS IN THOUSANDS				
Joint Probability	.06	.18	.06	.10	.30	.10	.04	.12	.04
Sales	$800	$800	$800	$1,000	$1,000	$1,000	$1,100	$1,100	$1,100
Variable costs									
Manufacturing	408	400	384	510	500	480	561	550	528
Marketing	40	40	40	50	50	50	55	55	55
Marginal contribution	352	360	376	440	450	470	484	495	517
Managed costs									
Manufacturing	10	10	10	20	20	20	30	30	30
Marketing	10	10	10	10	10	10	10	10	10
Administrative	25	25	25	40	40	40	40	40	40
Short-run margin	307	315	331	370	380	400	404	415	437
Committed costs	280	280	280	280	280	280	280	280	280
Net income before tax	$ 27	$ 35	$ 51	$ 90	$ 100	$ 120	$ 124	$ 135	$ 157
Tax @ 50%	13.5	17.5	25.5	45	50	60	62	67.5	78.5
Net income after tax	$ 13.5	$ 17.5	$ 25.5	$ 45	$ 50	$ 60	$ 62	$ 67.5	$ 78.5

IN DOLLARS

	Expected value*	σ²***	σ	Coefficient of Variation***
Sales	$960,000	$12,400,000,000	$111,400	11.6%
Variable costs				
Manufacturing	478,080	3,164,913,600	56,300	11.8%
Marketing	48,000	31,000,000	5,560	11.6%
Marginal contribution	433,920	2,623,033,600	51,200	11.8%
Managed costs				
Manufacturing	19,000	49,000,000	7,000	36.8%
Marketing	10,000	0	0	—
Administrative	35,500	47,250,000	6,870	19.4%
Short-run margin	369,420	1,462,363,600	38,250	10.4%
Committed costs	280,000	0	0	—
Net income before tax	89,420	1,462,363,600	38,240	42.8%
Tax @ 50%	44,710	365,590,900	19,120	42.8%
Net income after tax	44,710	365,590,900	19,120	42.8%

* Σ x_1 $p(x_1)$ where the x_1 are the values of each combination and the $p(x_1)$ are the joint probabilities assigned to each x_1.

*** Σ $[x_1{}^2$ $p(x_1)] - \mu^2$ where μ is the expected value (mean).

*** $\frac{\sigma}{\mu}$, the % that σ is the mean.

Exhibit 4. Calculation of Expected Values, Standard Deviations, and Coefficient of Variation for all Income Statement Items

	EXPECTED VALUE	STANDARD DEVIATION	COEFFICIENT OF VARIATION
Sales	$960,000	$111,400	11.6%
Variable costs			
Manufacturing	478,080	56,000	11.8
Marketing	48,000	5,560	11.6
Marginal contribution	$433,920	51,220	11.8
Managed fixed costs			
Manufacturing	19,000	7,000	36.8
Marketing	10,000	0	0
Administrative	35,500	6,870	19.4
Short-run margin	$369,420	38,240	10.4
Committed fixed costs			
Manufacturing	180,000	0	0
Marketing	40,000	0	0
Administrative	60,000	0	0
Net income before tax	$ 89,420	38,240	42.8
Tax—50%	44,710	19,120	42.8
Net income after tax	$ 44,710	19,120	42.8

Exhibit 5. Profit Budget for Year Ending June 197X

Difficulties Associated with the Construction of Probability Intervals When the Probability Distributions are Not Readily Identifiable

To estimate a 95 percent probability interval for the various budget items, we must know how these items are distributed.[14] If these items are normally distributed, or if they belong to distributions that are tabulated, it would be a simple matter to obtain the desired distribution limits. However, in spite of the simplifying assumptions of our model, difficulties associated with identifying the proper distributions occur.

These difficulties increase as one progresses from the top to the bottom of the income statement. This is especially true with regard to the "short-run margin" and the "net income before and after tax" since these items are functions of a product of two normal variables, a linear function of a normal variable and a quadratic function of a normal variable.[15] Without knowing the specific or approximate distribution of these functions one cannot hope to obtain a probability interval for the items under consideration.

---

[14] The probability interval could be set at whatever level desired if 95 percent is considered inappropriate.

[15] The Short-Run Margin, $SRM = 60,000 + Q(8.75 - v) - .64(10^{-5})Q^2$, where Q is the volume, v is the unit variable manufacturing cost, and Q and v are independently and normally distributed. Net income before and after tax is of the same form.

	EXPECTED VALUE	100% RANGE	90% RANGE
Sales	$960,000	$800,000 – $1,100,000	not applicable
Variable costs			
Manufacturing	478,080	384,000 – 561,000	400,000 – 550,000
Marketing	48,000	40,000 – 55,000	40,000 – 55,000
Marginal contribution	$433,920	352,000 – 517,000	360,000 – 495,000
Managed fixed costs			
Manufacturing	19,000	10,000 – 30,000	10,000 – 30,000
Marketing	10,000	–	–
Administrative	35,500	25,000 – 40,000	25,000 – 40,000
Short-run margin	$369,420	307,000 – 307,000	315,000 – 415,000
Committed fixed costs			
Manufacturing	180,000	–	–
Marketing	40,000	–	–
Administrative	60,000	–	–
Net income before tax	$ 89,420	27,000 – 157,000	35,000 – 135,000
Tax — 50%	44,710	13,500 – 78,500	17,500 – 67,500
Net income after tax	$ 44,710	13,500 – 78,500	17,500 – 67,500

Exhibit 6. Profit Budget for Year Ending June 197X

1. Volume (Q) is normally distributed with estimated mean, μ_Q = 100,000 units, standard deviation, σ_Q = 10,000 units, and relevant range 80,000 $\leq$ Q $\leq$ 120,000.

2. Sales price is constant at $10 per unit.

3. Unit variable manufacturing cost (v) is normally distributed with estimated mean, μ_v = $5.00 and standard deviation, σ_v = $0.20.

4. Volume (Q) and unit variable manufacturing cost (v) are statistically independent.

5. Managed manufacturing cost (Cm mfg) has the following linear relationship with volume (Q):

   Cm mfg = $20,000 + $\dfrac{1}{2}$ (Q - 100,000),

   within a relevant range: 80,000 $\leq$ Q $\leq$ 120,000.

6. Managed administrative cost (Cm ad) has the following quadratic relationship with volume (Q):

   Cm ad = -$40,000 + 0.25 Q + 0.64 ($10^{-5}$ Q^2)

   within a relevant range: 80,000 $\leq$ Q $\leq$ 120,000.

7. All other costs are constant: managed marketing ($10,000), committed manufacturing ($180,000), committed marketing ($40,000), committed administrative ($60,000), and variable marketing ($0.50 per unit).

Exhibit 7. Assumed One-Product Company Model

The distribution of these functions can be derived with involved numerical and mathematical techniques. By using simulation, however, we can more easily derive such probability intervals.

PROBABILISTIC INTERVALS THROUGH SIMULATION

The model described in Exhibit 7 was simulated by computer and the mean and a 95 percent probability interval for each budget item was determined. The result is the profit budget of Exhibit 8.

The simulation program involved 1000 iterations; for in this type of problem, experience indicated that 1000 iterations yield a reasonable approximation to the theoretical distribution.[16] We have partially verified this in our case as test runs of 3000 iterations did not produce significantly different results.

---

[16] Additional information concerning how many iterations are appropriate in this type of problem is available in: R. W. Conway, "Some Tactical Problems in Digital Simulation," *Management Science*, October 1963, p. 49; and Daniel Teichroew, "A History of Distribution Sampling Prior to the Era of the Computer and its Relevance to Simulation," *Journal of the American Statistical Association*, March 1965, pp. 27–49.

	EXPECTED VALUE	95% PROBABILITY INTERVAL*	
Sales	$1,002,146	$807,746 –	$1,195,900
Variable costs			
Manufacturing	500,452	406,370 –	600,546
Marketing	50,123	40,387 –	59,795
Marginal contribution	$ 451,571	366,022 –	548,412
Managed fixed costs			
Manufacturing	20,111	10,387 –	29,795
Marketing	10,000**	–	
Administrative	49,937	20,825 –	70,049
Short-run margin	$ 371,523	314,057 –	433,914
Committed fixed costs			
Manufacturing	180,000**	–	
Marketing	40,000**	–	
Administrative	60,000**	–	
Net income before tax	$ 91,523	34,057 –	153,914
Tax – 50%	45,762	15,682 –	75,870
Net income after tax	$ 45,761	15,682 –	75,870

*Determined by dropping the upper and lower 2½ percent of the 1000 iterations.
**Costs which are constant do not have a probability interval since they are considered "certain."

Exhibit 8. Profit Budget for Year Ending June 197X

SUMMARY AND CONCLUSIONS

This paper presents three methods for the construction of probabilistic profit and loss statements: the three-level, the probability-tree and the continuous distribution approaches.

The paper begins with a typical profit and loss statement which displays most likely values. Valuable information, however, is added to budgeted profit and loss statements if every item in those statements displays a mean and a probability interval. The mean is an expected value—what the value of the item would be on the average if we are afforded a large number of trials. The probability interval, on the other hand, tells us that a stated percentage of the distribution of a budget item falls within a given range. Thus the probability interval serves as a measure of variability for the budget item. Other indices of variability suggested are, of course, the standard deviation and the coefficient of variation.

In models with continuous distributions, it is recommended that Monte Carlo simulation be used where the probability distributions in question are difficult to handle analytically. One thousand iterations usually yield an accurate approximation of the desired distributions.

THREE
Capital Budgeting

For long-range decisions about proposed capital outlays and methods of financing equipment, discounted cash-flow methods can be used to incorporate cash flows into the analysis of investment opportunities, and to recognize the fact that the use of money involves a cost for interest so that dollars to be received or costs to be incurred in future periods have a different present value from those that are received or incurred today. The cost model used in the replacement of equipment example in Article 1 does not incorporate the time value of money.

For evaluating capital budgeting decision projects, management may apply such methods as: (1) the financial-statement method; (2) the payback method; and (3) the discounted cash-flow methods (internal rate of return, net present value, and the present value index). Article 14, "Methods of Capital Project Selection," serves as an introduction for this section about investments in long-lived assets and demonstrates the application of the methods listed above.

The financial statement method is identified by different titles (accountant's rate-of-return, book-value method, return on assets) that cover variations in application. In applying the method, net income from the investment proposal can be estimated according to accepted methods of accrual accounting and related to the total cost of capital assets to be acquired. The article discusses the problem of determining the total cost of an investment project to be used in the analysis, and the disagreement over the proper treatment of depreciation.

The payback method measures the time it will take to recover the cost of the investment. Annual returns are measured before deducting depreciation. The method does not consider cash flows received after the payback period and it ignores the time value of money. A variation of the method, the discounted payback method, discounts cash flows to their present value before the payback period is determined. The payback method does not measure the profitability of an investment and this is a major weakness. In spite of limitations the method is still widely used.[1]

The time-adjusted or internal rate-of-return method of discounted cash flow requires that a rate of interest be determined that equates the discounted value of the projected cash flows for each year of the life of the proposed project to the cost of the initial investment. Thus, the cash flows are discounted at some rate of interest such that the net present value of the

---

[1] In "Limit DCF in Capital Budgeting," *Harvard Business Review*, September–October 1968, pp. 133–139, Eugene N. Lerner and Alfred Rappaport indicate that the relatively slow acceptance of discounted cash flow may be due to difficulty in projecting cash flows for more than a few years into the future, or the preference for the guide of a payback benchmark on the part of decision makers concerned with risk taking and who have strong liquidity preferences. They also propose that the failure of the discounted cash-flow methods to gain wider acceptance may result from management not incorporating a consideration of earnings to be reported to stockholders into the model, and they discuss the imposition of an "earnings-growth constraint" into capital budgeting models.

project will be zero; this rate of interest (to be compared to a minimum acceptable rate of return) is called the internal rate of return (IRR).[2]

In contrast to the internal rate of return, the net present-value method does not solve for an interest rate but assumes a minimum desired rate of return (hurdle rate), discounts the projected cash flows for each year of the life of the project at this rate, and compares the present or discounted value of the cash flows with the initial investment. If the discounted value of the cash flow is greater than ($>$) the initial investment, the project can be accepted; if less than ($<$) the initial investment, the project is rejected.

Capital budgeting can involve a variety of problems which include: income tax considerations that affect the amount and timing of cash flows, unequal lives for alternative investments, cost of capital considerations, sensitivity analysis (where the impact of changes in predetermined estimates and problem parameters are examined before management makes a decision), and uncertainty concerning an investment proposal and assigning probabilities to cash inflows and outflows. Article 14 notes important problems for capital budgeting, and gives references for discussions about the various problems.

The problem of unequal lives for alternative investments complicates the capital investment decision. For a decision alternative, new equipment may be expected to have a five-year life, but present equipment may be estimated to have only three years of life remaining. The analyst has to consider some common termination date for comparison purposes and to adjust the alternative projects to that date. The comparison may be made for the remaining life of the old equipment, and it is then necessary to determine the residual value of the new equipment at the end of the three-year life of the old equipment. The comparison may also be made over the longer time period of five years. This requires that the cost of replacing the old equipment at the end of three years be estimated. It is necessary to estimate the residual value of the replacement equipment two years after that, i.e., at the end of the five-year time period.[3]

At the theoretical level, the minimum acceptable rate of return on a capital project is the cost of capital. The cost of capital concept is discussed

---

[2]An article by Victor H. Brown, "Rate of Return: Some Comments on Its Applicability in Capital Budgeting," *The Accounting Review*, January 1961, pp. 50–62, considers the merits of the internal rate of return as well as its complexities and limitations. The article includes a discussion of the important reinvestment assumption implicit in this method. Near the end of the article, a section is included about alternative evaluation techniques, and under this heading the payoff or payback period and the differential present worth or net present-value method are considered.

In addition to quantitative techniques for capital investment analysis, qualitative analysis is important; management judgment is needed about such factors as rate of return, cash flow, timing, and asset lives. See Stanley B. Henrici, "Eyeing the ROI," *Harvard Business Review*, May–June 1968, pp. 88–97. The article discusses rate of return, net present value, and stresses qualitative considerations for the investment decision.

[3]For a discussion of the unequal life problem where discounted cash flow is used, see Ezra Solomon, "The Arithmetic of Capital Budgeting Decisions," *Journal of Business*, April 1956, pp. 124–129.

in Part V, Article 24, "A New Way to Measure and Control Divisional Performance."[4] The application of sensitivity analysis for the long-lived asset investment decision is discussed in Article 15, "Use of Sensitivity Analysis in Capital Budgeting." Sensitivity analysis is applied for cash budgeting purposes in Part II of this book and for linear programming in Part VI. The problem of uncertainty and capital budgeting decisions is covered in Articles 16 through 18.

Article 16, "Investment Policies That Pay Off," discusses conventional ways of dealing with risk and uncertainty in making capital investment decisions. The sophisticated tool of computer simulation, as it relates to risk analysis and the investment decision, is an important part of the article. With this tool, management can examine risk consequences and compare the probable payoffs of various investment alternatives. Inherent in the article is the Monte Carlo method of simulation. Article 17, "Monte Carlo Simulation," was written to explain the method, and the article applies the operations research tool to aid management with capital budgeting decisions involving uncertainty. Article 18, "Stochastic Decision Trees for the Analysis of Investment Decisions," builds on risk analysis; sensitivity analysis can be used with the model and the method is suitable for computer simulation.

[4]Problem III-Q8, a problem for study included in Appendix B of this book, shows a cost of capital computation. Also see Dean S. Eiteman, "A Closer Look at Cost of Capital," *Management Accounting*, July 1967, pp. 57–63.

14.
METHODS OF CAPITAL PROJECT SELECTION*

C. Stevenson Rowley

The decision to undertake a capital investment project is one of the most significant decisions that a corporation can make; it involves a substantial commitment of funds over an extended period of time. Such a decision is particularly perilous today when all types of costs are rising and uncertainties concerning economic conditions abound. Interest in the problem of capital project selection is evident from the frequency with which articles on this topic have appeared in this journal; two recent articles have presented the theory of discounted cash flow and some of the problems encountered in the use of discounted cash flow analysis.[1] This article examines the alternative methods of capital project selection, several of which involve the use of discounted cash flows.

One of the most recent examinations of practice concerning capital budgeting decisions was conducted by the National Association of Accountants in 1967. Their findings revealed that of the twenty-eight major companies examined, fourteen used the financial statement method of analysis, fourteen used the discounted cash flow method, and nearly all used the payback method of analysis as a supplementary test.[2] These results may be compared with an earlier (1960) study of 116 companies: where only one

*From *Managerial Planning*, March/April, 1973, pp. 33–40. Reprinted by permission of the publisher. This article is based on an article published in the *Arizona Business Bulletin*, January 1971. Permission was obtained from the editor of *Arizona Business*.

[1]F. M. Kirby and J. J. Paulos, "The Theory of Discounted Cash Flow," *Managerial Planning*, XVIII, No. 4 (January/February 1970), 1–8, and Surendra S. Singhvi, "Discounted Cash Flow Analysis and the Reinvestment Assumption," *Managerial Planning*, XX, No. 1 (July/August 1971), 27–30.

[2]National Association of Accountants, Research Report No. 43: *Financial Analysis to Guide Capital Expenditure Decisions* (New York: N.A.A., 1967), p. 3.

196

method of analysis was used, 49 percent used the financial statement method, 23 percent used the discounted cash flow method, and 28 percent used the payback method; where more than one method of analysis was used, the respective percentages were 34, 23, and 37.[3] These findings are summarized in Table 1.

Method Used	FREQUENCY OF USE			
	1967 (n = 28)[a]		1960 (n = 116)[b]	
	As A Primary Method	As A Secondary Method	Used Alone	Used With Other Methods
Financial Statement Method	50%		49%	34%
Discounted Cash Flow Method	50%		23%	23%
Payback Method		100%	28%	37%
Other				6%
	100%	100%	100%	100%

[a] National Association of Accountants, Research Report No. 43: *Financial Analysis to Guide Capital Expenditure Decisions* (New York: N.A.A., 1967), p. 3.
[b] James H. Miller, "A Glimpse at Practice in Calculating and Using Return on Investment," *N.A.A. Bulletin*, XLI, No. 10 (June 1960), 72–74.

Table 1. Methods of Capital Investment Analysis in Use

The apparent conclusions from an examination and comparison of these two studies are:

1. The discounted cash flow method of analyzing capital investment opportunities has increased in popularity in recent years.

2. The financial statement method, although much maligned in recent years, still enjoys wide use.

3. The payback method is used extensively as a supplementary test of capital investment decisions.

The applications and implications of these three methods will now be examined in detail.

---

[3] James H. Miller, "A Glimpse at Practice in Calculating and Using Return on Investment," *N.A.A. Bulletin*, XLI, No. 10 (June 1960), 72–74.

ALTERNATIVE METHODS OF ANALYSIS

The Financial Statement Method

This method is identified by different titles that cover a number of variations in application. Among these designations are: accountant's rate-of-return, book-value method, and return on assets. The general approach is derived from the return-on-investment ratio, net income/total assets, used frequently by financial analysts to measure company performance. In its simplest form, the method is applied in the analysis of individual capital investment projects in a manner identical to its application to overall company performance; that is, income from the investment proposal is estimated according to accepted methods of accrual accounting and related to the total cost of the capital assets to be acquired. In this application, however, two problems are encountered: (1) failure to include all of the assets involved in the project, and (2) disagreement over the proper treatment of depreciation.

Undertaking a capital investment project usually involves more than the acquisition of fixed assets; for example, there may be significant outlays for research and development which, under accepted accounting practice, may be charged as expense in the period of incurrance rather than recognized as additional costs of the capital project. There may also be substantial increases in working capital, such as receivables and inventories, that represent a part of the total investment but may be ignored under an accounting definition of capital assets.

The problem of depreciation concerns the question of whether the asset base used to measure the return on investment should be gross assets or assets net-of-depreciation; some authorities argue that because the investment is being recovered in the annual depreciation charge, the amount of capital committed to the project over its life is less than the initial investment. The effect of capital recovery through depreciation may be recognized by measuring the return on average investment (usually calculated as one-half the initial investment where depreciation is determined on a straight-line basis and salvage value is negligible) or by adding the annual depreciation charge back to net income calculated on an accrual basis (in effect measuring the return as cash flow).[4] The two most frequently used methods of computing the accounting return on investment are: (1) net income/total investment, and (2) net income/average investment. Obviously, the second method will yield a rate of return twice that of the first and must be interpreted in that context. An example of these alternative approaches to applying the financial statement method is presented in Exhibit 1.

---

[4]For a more detailed examination of these alternatives, see Edwin A. Bowen, "Problem Areas in Use of Discounted Cash Flow for Investment Valuations," *N.A.A. Bulletin*, XLIV, No. 12 (August 1963), 12.

Investment Proposal

Estimated cost: $1,300,000
Estimated useful life: 5 years
Estimated salvage value: zero
Method of depreciation: straight-line

Estimated Revenues and Expenses
(Thousands of dollars)

	YEAR					
	1	2	3	4	5	Total
Revenue	$ 500	$1,000	$2,000	$2,500	$2,000	$8,000
Expenses: Depreciation	260	260	260.	260	260	1,300
Other	400	750	1,400	1,750	1,400	5,700
	660	1,010	1,660	2,010	1,660	7,000
Income before taxes	$ (160)	$ (10)	$ 340	$ 490	$ 340	$1,000
Income taxes (40%)	0	0	136	196	136	468
Loss carry forward[a]	0	0	(68)	0	0	(68)
Net taxes	0	0	68	196	136	400
Income after taxes	$ (160)	$ (10)	$ 272	$ 294	$ 204	$ 600

Computation of Accounting Rate of Return

On Total Investment

Average return = $600 ÷ 5 = $120
Total investment = $1,300
Return on investment = $120 ÷ $1,300
= 9.2%

On Average Investment

Average return = $120
Average investment = $1,300 ÷ 2
= $650
Return on investment = $120 ÷ $650
= 18.4%

[a]($160 + $10) × .40

Exhibit 1. Financial Statement Method of Analyzing A Capital Investment Opportunity

The proposed project in Exhibit 1 requires an investment of $1,300,000, and it is estimated that net income after taxes over the life of the project will total $600,000. Average annual income, therefore, is $120,000; return on total investment is 9.2 percent and return on average investment is 18.4 percent. The second rate is twice that of the first because the denominator used in its calculation is one-half that of the first. The decision to accept or reject the project based on this information would depend on the company's criteria for an acceptable accounting rate of return.

The Discounted Cash Flow Method

Under the financial statement method of analyzing investment opportunities, return on investment is defined as net income determined by accrual accounting and annual net income is usually calculated as an average of the total net income expected to be received during the life of the project. The use of accrual accounting ignores differences between cash flows and net income and the use of project-life averages ignores deferrals over periods and inequalities between periods. For example, if in Exhibit 1 no revenue was received in years 1–4 and $8,000 was received in year 5, average income as calculated by the financial statement method would still be $120,000. The discounted cash flow (DCF) methods incorporate cash flows and the time value of money into the analysis. There are three general approaches to analyzing capital investment opportunities by discounted cash flow: (1) the net present value method, (2) the present value index, and (3) the internal rate of return.

The Net Present Value Method
Under this method of analysis, all cash inflows and outflows associated with a capital investment project are discounted to their present value; if the net present value (NPV) of the project is positive, the project is accepted; if negative, the project is rejected. The nature of the cash inflows and outflows should be similar to the revenues and expenses determined by accrual accounting; however, the timing of the inflows and outflows will differ from the timing of revenues and expenses.

The investment proposal considered in Exhibit 1 may be analyzed by the NPV method. It will be assumed that the only difference between cash flows and accrual accounting is in the recognition of depreciation. Under this assumption all revenues are received as cash and all expenses except depreciation are paid in cash in the year of recognition. The $1,300,000 cost of the investment, however, although charged in equal amounts to the five periods to determine net income was a cash outflow only at the beginning of the first period. For simplicity, it is assumed that all other cash flows occurred at the end of each respective year and that the relevant interest rate was based on annual compounding. The distortion caused by these latter assumptions is insignificant at normal rates of interest. In Exhibit 2 the net present value of this investment proposal is calculated (to the nearest thousand dollars) to be $152,000 when the cash flows are discounted at 8 percent to the date of initiation of the project (year zero). Under the NPV method of analyzing capital investment proposals, the criterion for acceptance is a positive (i.e., greater than zero) net present value; therefore according to the analysis in Exhibit 2 the investment proposal should be accepted.

Several points in the analysis deserve clarification. (1) The analysis is one of opportunity cost; the alternative to investing in this proposal is the opportunity to invest $1,300,000 elsewhere to earn an 8 percent return compounded annually for five years. (2) Discounting to the date of initiation of the project is a matter of convenience and convention—the purpose of the procedure is to equate all the cash inflows and outflows over time to a single point in time. (3) Acceptance or rejection of a proposal depends

Estimated Cash Inflows and Outflows[a]
(Thousands of dollars)

	0[b]	1	2	3	4	5	Total
				YEAR			
Operating receipts	$ 0	$ 500	$1,000	$2,000	$2,500	$2,000	$8,000
Operating disbursments	0	400	750	1,400	1,750	1,400	5,700
Tax payments	0	0	0	68	196	136	400
Capital outlay	1,300	0	0	0	0	0	1,300
Total outflows	1,300	400	750	1,468	1,946	1,536	7,400
Net cash flows	($1,300)	$ 100	$ 250	$ 532	$ 554	$ 464	$ 600

Discounted Cash Flow
(Thousands of dollars)

YEAR	NET CASH FLOW (A)	PRESENT VALUE FACTOR (8%)[c] (B)	PRESENT VALUE AMOUNT (AxB)
0	-$1,300	1.000	-$1,300
1	100	0.926	93
2	250	0.857	214
3	532	0.794	422
4	554	0.735	407
5	464	0.681	316
	$ 600		$ 152

[a] See Exhibit 1 for presentation of items in income statement form.
[b] Represents beginning of year 1; all other items are assumed to occur at the end of their respective years.
[c] Present value of a dollar due in n periods at 8% interest; may be found in any published compound interest table.

Exhibit 2. Net Present Value Method of Analyzing A Capital Investment Opportunity

on the discount rate (e.g., 8 percent) used. Let us consider these points in order.

The sum of the present value of the net cash flows of each of the five years is $1,452,000 ($93 + $214 + $422 + $407 + $316); this may be interpreted as indicating that $1,452,000 would have to be invested at 8 percent to yield the cash flows that will be produced by investing $1,300,000 in this capital project.

This point may be alternatively confirmed by examining Point 2. If the net cash flows for each year, as listed in Exhibit 2, are compounded to the termination date of the project (the end of year five) the net future value of the investment is $223,000. In other words, if the expected net cash flows from the capital project were invested each year at 8 percent, the company would earn $223,000 *more* over the five-year period than if the funds for the capital project were directly invested in an alternative opportunity yielding 8 percent. Whether the flows are discounted to the present or compounded to the future, the conclusion is the same—if the net value is positive, the project should be undertaken. The important factor is that events occurring at different points in time are equated at the same point in time.

The third point noted for clarification was the dependence of the decision on the interest rate used to discount the cash flows. The proposal examined in Exhibit 2 was accepted when the cash flows were discounted at 8 percent. If these same cash flows were discounted at 15 percent, however, the net present value of the investment proposal would be −$126,000, and the proposal would be rejected. It was noted that the interpretation of the information obtained by the financial statement method of analysis (Exhibit 1) depended on the criteria concerning an acceptable rate of return. Here also the selection of the appropriate interest rate to be used in discounting the cash flows depends on the criteria for an acceptable rate of return.

The Present Value Index Method

In the examples previously presented, the question before management was the acceptance or rejection of a single investment proposal. The decision with which management is more likely to be faced, however, is the selection of the most acceptable project from a set of mutually exclusive proposals. Let us assume that the project presented in Exhibit 2, called Project A, must be compared with a second proposal, Project B. It is estimated that Project B will require an investment of $248,000 now and will return cash flows of $100,000 at the end of each of the next five years. The net present value of Project B, discounted at 8 percent, is $152,000, identical to Project A. The two projects yield the same net present value over the same period of time; on what basis should management select one or the other? Intuitively it may seem that the project that requires the smaller investment, Project B, is the more attractive; the present value index (PVI) provides substantive support for this intuition.

The index is computed by dividing the present value of the cash-flow return by the present value of the cost of the investment. An example of this calculation is presented in Exhibit 3. It can be seen that judged by its PVI Project B is more attractive than Project A. In fact if we introduce a third project, C, identical to B in all respects except cost which is $100,000 higher, its PVI too is higher than Project A; however, its NPV is $100,000 lower. The present value index recognizes a variable in capital investment analysis, the relative cost of projects, that is concealed in the net present value analysis; the index indicates the number of dollars of return (present value of annual net cash flows) that will be earned for each dollar invested.

	PROJECT A[a]	PROJECT B	PROJECT C
Present value of cash-flow return (A)	$1,452,000	$400,000	$400,000
Present value of investment outlays (B)	$1,300,000	$248,000	$348,000
Net present value (A − B)	$ 152,000	$152,000	$ 52,000
Present value index (A ÷ B)	1.12	1.61	1.15

[a] See Exhibit 2.

Exhibit 3. Present Value Index Method of Analyzing Capital Investment Opportunities

The Internal Rate of Return Method

The cash flows from Project A have been discounted at interest rates of 8 and 15 percent, resulting in a NPV of + $152,000 and − $126,000 respectively. The cash flows can be discounted at some rate of interest such that the NPV of the project will be zero; this rate of interest is called the internal rate of return (IRR). The IRR may also be interpreted as the rate of interest that the investment must earn such that its terminal value is zero. For Project A the IRR must be between 8 and 15 percent; somewhere within that range the NPV changes from positive to negative. The only way to discover precisely where the change occurs, that is, where the NPV is zero, is by trial and error. An analysis to determine the IRR for Project A is presented in Exhibit 4. The change in the sign of the NPV occurs some-

		Project A			
		ELEVEN PER CENT		TWELVE PER CENT	
Year	Net Cash[a] Flows (A)	Present Value[b] Factor (B)	Present Value Amount (A × B)	Present Value[b] Factor (C)	Present Value Amount (A × C)
0	−$1,300	1.000	−$1,300	1.000	−$1,300
1	100	0.901	91	0.893	89
2	250	0.812	203	0.797	199
3	532	0.732	389	0.712	379
4	554	0.659	365	0.636	352
5	464	0.594	276	0.567	263
	$ 600		$ 24		−$ 18

Interpolation: $24 − (−$18) = $42; $24 ÷ $42 = 0.57; IRR = 11.0% + 0.57% = 11.6%

[a] See Exhibit 2.
[b] Present value factors may be found in any published compound interest table.

Exhibit 4. Internal Rate of Return Method of Analyzing Capital Investment Opportunities (in thousands of dollars)

where between 11 and 12 percent and by interpolation can be fixed more precisely at 11.6 percent; therefore the IRR for Project A is 11.6 percent. The IRR of Projects B and C are, respectively, 29.2 and 13.3 percent.

Like the present value index the IRR recognizes the relative cost of investment proposals in measuring their relative attractiveness. The IRR method does not require the selection of a specific rate of interest (e.g., 8 percent) to be used to discount the cash flows; however, it does require the determination of a minimum acceptable rate of return against which to compare the IRR of a particular project.

Payback Method

In the 1960 study by Miller, the payback method of analyzing capital investment opportunities was the second most popular method when used alone and the most popular when several methods were used; in the 1967 study by the N.A.A., the payback method was used by almost all companies as a secondary method of analysis.[5] The popularity of the payback method may be attributed in large part to its ease of calculation and comprehension. Simply explained, the payback method analyzes a proposal in terms of the time it will take to recover the cost of the investment. Because the focus of attention is the recovery of the cost, annual returns are measured before deducting depreciation; therefore payback is measured in terms of approximate cash flow. The payback periods for Projects A, B, and C are, respectively, 3.8, 2.5, and 3.5 years; the computations for Project A are presented in Exhibit 5.

	PROJECT A	
Year	Net Cash[a] Flow	Cumulative Cash Flow
0	−$1,300	−$1,300
1	100	− 1,200
2	250	− 950
3	532	− 418
4	554	+ 136
5	464	+ 600

Payback Period $= 3 + \dfrac{418}{554} = 3.8$ years

[a] See Exhibit 2.

Exhibit 5. Payback Method of Analyzing Capital Investment Opportunities (in thousands of dollars)

[5] See Table 1.

The most serious criticism of the payback method is that it ignores the cash flows received after the payback period; a secondary criticism is that it ignores the time value of money. For example, if the cash flows of Project C, $100,000 a year, were expected to be received for ten rather than five years, the NPV of the project, discounted at 8 percent, would more than double to $323,000 and the IRR would almost double to 26.0 percent. On the other hand, if the cash flows were expected to be received for only four years, the NPV at 8 percent would become negative, − $17,000, while the IRR would be more than halved to 5.8 percent. In both cases, however, the payback period for Project C would remain unchanged at 3.5 years because the payback method ignores all cash flows beyond the payback period.

In response to the criticism that the payback method ignores the time value of money, a variation of the method, known as the payback method with interest or discounted payback method, has been developed.[6] In its application the method is identical to the traditional payback method with the exception that the cash flows are discounted to their present value before the payback period is determined. The discounted payback periods for Projects A, B, and C are, respectively, 4.5, 2.9, and 4.2 years; the computations for Project A are presented in Exhibit 6. The relative position of the three projects does not change; Project B still has the shortest payback period and Project A the longest. The discounted payback method does indicate, however, that because of the time value of money, recovery of the investment in the project may take longer than is indicated by the traditional payback method. The discounted payback method still ignores any cash flows beyond the payback period, and its use introduces a prob-

	PROJECT A	
Year	Discounted Cash Flow[a]	Cumulative Cash Flow
0	−$1,300	−$1,300
1	93	− 1,207
2	214	− 993
3	422	− 571
4	407	− 164
5	316	+ 152

$$\text{Payback Period} = 4 + \frac{164}{316} = 4.5 \text{ years}$$

[a]See Exhibit 2.

Exhibit 6. Discounted Payback Method of Analyzing Capital Investment Opportunities (in thousands of dollars)

[6]See Alfred Rappaport, "The Discounted Payback Period," *Management Science*, II, No. 4 (July–August 1965), 30–36.

lem common to the NPV and PVI methods, the selection of an appropriate discount rate.

The payback method is defended at the practical level with arguments about the uncertainty of estimates concerning future events. If the estimated cash flows of Project C were expected to continue for ten years, the businessman would be inclined to ignore this information because of the uncertainty associated with estimates of events expected to occur more than three or four years in the future. At the theoretical level, the payback method has been defended because it can be demonstrated mathematically that when the life of the project is relatively long the reciprocal of the payback period is a good approximation of the IRR.[7]

Summary of Alternative Methods
The following methods of analyzing capital projects have been discussed:

> Financial statement method
> Discounted cash flow methods
> > Net present value method (NPV)
> > Present value index method (PVI)
> > Internal rate of return method (IRR)
> Payback methods
> > Traditional payback method
> > Discounted payback method

Three hypothetical projects were examined. Information obtained by the various methods of analysis concerning these three projects is presented in Table 2 (a); in Table 2 (b) the three projects are ranked according to the information obtained. The PVI, IRR, and payback methods produce the same rankings; these differ from those produced by the financial statement and NPV methods. The rankings of the PVI and IRR methods reflect recognition of project costs relative to returns; Project B produces the same return as C with a smaller investment and both produce a larger return relative to project costs than does Project A. The fact that the payback rankings are identical to the PVI and IRR rankings is partly coincidental and partly explained by the equal lives of the projects. As demonstrated, if the life of Project C was shortened by one year, it would be ranked as the least attractive by all of the discounted cash flow methods but its payback ranking would be unchanged. The ranking produced by the NPV method is a consequence of ignoring the relative cost of the projects, and that produced by the financial statement method is a consequence of using accrual accounting information and project-life averages.

[7]A complete statement of this argument may be found in Myron J. Gordon, "The Payback Period and the Rate of Profit," *Journal of Business*, XXVIII, No. 4 (October 1955), 253–60.

Table 2 (a)

Comparison of Projects By Alternative Methods of Capital Investment Analysis

Method of Analysis

Project	FINANCIAL STATEMENT[a] On Total Investment	DISCOUNTED CASH FLOW			PAYBACK (YEARS)	
		Net Present Value	Present Value Index	Internal Rate of Return	Standard Method	Discounted Method
A	9.2%	$152,000	1.12	11.6%	3.8	4.5
B	20.2%	$152,000	1.61	29.2%	2.5	2.9
C	8.6%	$ 52,000	1.15	13.3%	3.5	4.2

Table 2 (b)

Ranking of Projects by Alternative Methods of Capital Investment Analysis

RANK						
1st	B	A[b]	B	B	B	B
2nd	A	B[b]	C	C	C	C
3rd	C	C	A	A	A	A

[a] Return calculated on total investment; return on average investment would be twice the return on total investment.

[b] By this method Projects A and B are equally attractive and therefore tied for first rank.

Table 2

The popularity of the financial statement and payback methods may be explained by their familiarity and ready availability of the necessary information; the data can be collected within the accrual accounting framework, and an understanding of the principles of present value and the use of compound interest tables is not required. Even the users of the financial statement method concede that it may produce misleading information. Arguments in favor of the payback method may be valid *if* one accepts limitation of the time horizon to three or four years as the best procedure for dealing with uncertainty. Writers have long argued that the discounted cash flow method is the most theoretically sound procedure for analyzing capital investment opportunities. Acceptance of the discounted cash flow method, however, merely changes the nature of the problem from the direct selection of acceptable proposals to the selection of an acceptable rate of return to be used either directly to discount cash flows or as a standard against which to compare the IRR of an investment proposal.

OTHER CONSIDERATIONS

The purpose of this article was to examine some of the more popular procedures for analyzing capital investment opportunities. By so limiting the scope many important considerations concerning capital investment decisions have been ignored. These considerations will not be explained in detail but will be noted briefly.

Several references were made to an acceptable rate of return on a capital project; at the theoretical level the minimum acceptable rate to a company is its cost of capital. Much has been written on the problem of determining a company's cost of capital;[8] at this writing the problem is still unresolved.

Reference was also made to the problem of uncertainty concerning estimates about an investment proposal. This problem may be explicitly recognized in the analysis by assigning probabilities to estimates of cash inflows and outflows, or it may be recognized implicitly in the selection of an acceptable rate of return. A technique that is useful in determining the consequences of uncertainty is sensitivity analysis whereby the impact of possible departures from predetermined estimates may be examined before a decision concerning the proposal is reached.[9]

A number of sophisticated articles have been written exploring the relative merits of the NPV and IRR methods. Among the more interesting questions raised are the reinvestment assumptions implicit in both procedures and the unusual situation where an investment proposal has more than one internal rate of return.[10] An understanding of the first question requires some understanding of the problems involved in the determination of the cost of capital; the second problem is relatively unimportant because of the infrequency with which the problem occurs.

Another problem ignored in this article was the analysis of the total capital budget and the related problem of capital rationing. Based on the PVI and IRR methods of analysis, Project B, requiring an investment of $248,000, appears to be the most attractive alternative. This conclusion might be different if a decision was being made within the framework of a total annual capital budget of two million dollars.[11] On the other hand, the most attractive long-run alternative for the company might be to invest its funds in short-term marketable securities in anticipation of more attractive capital investment opportunities in future years; however, multi-period analysis usually requires the use of mathematical programming.[12]

Finally, the most significant factors in an analysis are the estimates of the cash flows on which the analysis is based. These may be developed within

---

[8]Many of the articles on this and the following topics may be found in two excellent collections of readings: Stephen H. Archer and Charles A. D'Ambrosio, ed., *The Theory of Business Finance* (New York: The Macmillan Co., 1967), and Ezra Soloman, ed., *The Management of Corporate Capital* (Chicago: The Free Press of Glencoe, 1959).

[9]William C. House, Jr., N.A.A. Research Monograph No. 3, *Sensitivity Analysis in Making Capital Investment Decisions* (New York: National Association of Accountants, 1968).

[10]For an excellent discussion of these questions, see James H. Lorie and Leonard J. Savage, "Three Problems in Rationing Capital," *Journal of Business*, XXVIII, No. 4 (October 1955), 229–39.

[11]See Charles T. Horngren, *Cost Accounting: A Managerial Emphasis* 2nd ed. (Englewood Cliffs, N.J.: Prentice-Hall, Inc., 1967), p. 455.

[12]See H. Martin Weingarten, *Mathematical Programming and the Analysis of Capital Budgeting Problems* (Englewood Cliffs, N.J.: Prentice-Hall, Inc., 1963).

the accrual accounting system or outside it by industrial engineers or cost accountants; the estimates may be point estimates or probability distributions; they may be constrained within a limited time horizon and subjected to sensitivity analysis. However the estimates are determined and revised, the output of any method of analyzing capital investment opportunities can be no better than the estimates that are the input of the analysis.

15.

USE OF SENSITIVITY ANALYSIS IN CAPITAL
BUDGETING*

William C. House

> *Any investment always involves an estimate of the ex-*
> *pected rate of return. But no one can guarantee that the*
> *estimate will be correct. What a company can do, however,*
> *is calculate the possible degree of error in its estimate and*
> *weigh this against the alternative uses of its capital.*

The anticipated rate of return on investment is one of the principal criteria
used by corporate managements in deciding whether to accept or reject a
proposed capital expenditure. Like any forecast, however, the rate of return
estimate may prove to be inaccurate.

Estimates of rates of return are based on forecasts of such elements as
sales volumes, selling prices, product purchase or production prices, operating expenses, capital investment outlays, and project economic lives. Any
or all of these forecasts may be erroneous, and the result may be an actual rate of return that falls far below what has been anticipated.

Thus, management needs some method for determining the likelihood
and amount of such errors before making a final decision to accept or reject
a given proposal. It is sometimes possible to develop probability distribution curves that indicate the likelihood of occurrence of specific rates of
return for individual projects. If enough information is available about the
outcomes of similar past proposals, then management can make its choice
on the basis of expected values (i.e., the values with the highest probability
of occurrence) derived from a probability distribution of rates of return. In
many cases, however, capital investment proposals represent unique events
for which there is little or no relevant past experience. Then expected
values cannot be determined objectively, and the likelihood of errors cannot be predicted.

---

* From *Management Services (Management Adviser)*, September–October 1967, pp.
37–40. Copyright © 1967 by the American Institute of Certified Public
Accountants, Inc. Reprinted by permission.

It is always possible, however, to calculate in advance what effect errors in estimation would have on the estimated rates of return and thus to determine the significance of such errors. The appropriate technique to use is that of sensitivity analysis. Its application, illustrated by means of a case example, is explained in this article.

Analysis of the sensitivity to error of rates of return is the process of determining whether small changes in various estimates cause significant changes in estimated rates of return. If management finds that a 5 or 10 percent error in forecasting a certain estimate (e.g., production costs) will cause the estimated rate of return for a given project to decline below the estimated rate of return for a competing project or below a prescribed minimum figure, it will probably decide to investigate more thoroughly the likelihood of changes in production costs before making a final decision to accept or reject the project under consideration. On the other hand, if management discovers that a relatively large error (e.g., 25 or 30 percent) must occur in forecasting production costs before the estimated rate of return is affected significantly, then further efforts to reduce errors in forecasting production costs may not be deemed economically justifiable.

Even when estimated rates of return are sensitive to errors in certain estimates (i.e., a small change in an estimate causes a significant change in the estimated rates of return), management may not always be able to reduce significantly either the likelihood or the impact of estimating errors. However, knowing the conditions of sensitivity puts management in a better position to decide if the risks are large enough to cause the rejection of investment proposals under consideration.

MEASUREMENT

The sensitivity of estimated rates of return to errors in estimates cannot be measured precisely for several reasons. First, management must base its analysis of the relationships among the variables which affect the rates of return on past experience; these relationships, however, may not hold completely true in the future. Second, in its examination of the sensitivity of rates of return to errors in estimating individual variables, management may have to ignore the fact that a change in one estimate (e.g., sales volume) may cause changes in another estimate (e.g., operating expenses) because such cause and effect relationships are difficult to measure. Third, autocorrelation[1] may exist between two or more estimates for a given variable, distorting what appears to be the sensitivity or insensitivity of estimated rates of return to errors in estimation.

---

[1] Autocorrelation is, to a certain extent, the dependence of the estimated value of a variable in one year on the value of that variable in a previous year. Thus, a 5 percent change in selling prices in one year may actually cause a change of more or less than 5 percent in selling prices the next year. See Michael J. Brennan, *Preface to Econometrics*, Southwestern Publishing Co., Cincinnati, Ohio, 1960, p. 348.

Thus, lack of actual data on how one estimate will vary if another is altered may make it difficult for management to determine the precise effects of errors of estimation on estimated rates of return. However, management does not need to know precisely the sensitivity of estimated rates of return to errors in estimation. If the relative differences in the effects of errors in estimating various elements can be determined, management will be able to identify the estimates that deserve further attention. Selection of estimates to investigate more thoroughly can be made on the basis of whether or not the sensitivity of estimated rates of return to errors in any given estimate is significant.

SIGNIFICANCE

How can management determine whether a significant degree of sensitivity of rates of return to errors in estimation exists if sensitivity cannot be measured precisely? Two major guidelines are helpful. First, a stated degree (e.g., 10 percent) of error in an estimate must cause the estimated rate of return for a proposal to decline below that for a competing proposal or some prescribed minimum figure. Second, the stated degree of change in the estimate being considered must be within a range of error (e.g., 10 percent) considered to be feasible, based on management's past experience or its subjective evaluations. When both these conditions are met, the sensitivity of rates of return to errors in estimation can be said to be significant.

If the sensitivity of a measure of return to errors in a given estimate is significant (i.e., a stated degree of error in the estimate would cause management to reverse its decision to accept a given proposal), what can management do? It should examine such estimates more thoroughly or collect more information in an effort to reduce errors in forecasting and the likelihood of making the wrong choice.[2] It may need to recalculate the estimates of rates of return on the basis of new underlying data, perhaps using discounted measures of return.

The changes that occur in estimated rates of return when the basic estimates are changed are difficult to compare for two reasons. If the estimated rates of return for the different projects vary widely, the same amount of change in estimated rates of return for any two given proposals may not have the same significance for both proposals. If both simple and discounted rates of return with different original values are calculated for each proposal, the changes in these values caused by any particular error in

---

[2]An incorrect decision is one that management could have avoided if more complete information about the future had been available. It may be possible for management to reduce its uncertainty about expected values of estimates by applying managerial resources to the task of improving its accuracy in forecasting. This, in turn, would decrease the likelihood of management's selecting projects which would have been rejected if more complete information had been available.

estimation may not be comparable. To solve these problems, the sensitivity of estimated rates of return to errors in estimation can be measured in terms of the percentage increase or decrease from base-case values for rates of return resulting from errors of a given size.

More valid comparisons of the sensitivity of different estimated rates of return to errors in the estimates for the same project or of the same rates of return for different projects can be made by stating the change in the estimated rates of return as a function of a percentage deviation from the original estimated values. This approach surmounts many of the difficulties ordinarily encountered in comparing rates of return for projects of different sizes and/or different measures of return when base-case values are different.

CASE EXAMPLE

The following case example illustrates some of the significant aspects of the application of sensitivity analysis applied to a capital investment decision. The table below shows the discounted cash flow rate of return for an oil company manufacturing project based on original estimates or base-case assumptions. The effects of 10 percent changes in various estimates used to compute the discounted cash flow rate of return are also shown. It can be seen that 10 percent errors in certain estimates (sales prices and raw materials costs, for example) are much more significant than errors in other estimates in terms of their effect on the discounted cash flow rate of return.

| | DISCOUNTED CASH FLOW RATES OF RETURN[1] | | | |
Likely Maximum Error in Given Estimate	Base-Case	Base-Case Revised	Increase (Decrease)	Percentage[2] Change
10% decrease in estimated sales prices	12.0%	4.7%	(7.3)%	60.8%
10% decrease in estimated sales volume	12.0%	10.1%	(1.9)%	15.8%
10% increase in estimated raw material cost	12.0%	7.4%	(4.6)%	38.3%
10% increase in estimated processing cost	12.0%	11.6%	(0.4)%	3.3%
10% increase in estimated overhead/ maintenance cost	12.0%	11.4%	(0.6)%	5.0%
10% increase in capital investment	12.0%	11.2%	(0.8)%	6.7%

[1]Based on an estimated economic life of 20 years.
[2]Calculated by dividing the increase or decrease in the discounted cash flow from the base-case figure by the base-case discounted cash flow rate of return.

Table 1. Sensitivity Analysis of a Manufacturing Project

Let us assume further that the management of the oil company in question has established a cutoff rate of return of 8 percent for all manufacturing projects. The base-case discounted cash flow rate of return for this proposal is 12 percent, well above the cutoff rate. If the base case estimates are used to compute the discounted cash flow rate of return, the project will probably be accepted.

However, a 10 percent decrease in sales prices or a 10 percent increase in raw material cost will cause the discounted cash flow rate of return to decline below the cutoff rate of 8 percent. Therefore, an investment decision based on the discounted cash flow rate of return in this case is sufficiently sensitive to errors in estimates of sales prices and raw materials costs to justify further investigation of the accuracy of such estimates before accepting the proposal in question. Errors of 10 percent in the remaining four estimates do not cause the discounted cash flow rate of return to decline to or below the cutoff point. Therefore, further investigation of the accuracy of these estimates is not required.

If there are no formal cutoff points in effect, the percentage changes that occur in the discounted cash flow rate of return when various estimates are altered by a fixed percentage can be used as a gauge of the significance of such errors. In the case cited, a 10 percent decrease in estimated sales prices causes a 60.8 percent decrease in the discounted cash flow rate of return (from the base-case figure) and a 10 percent increase in raw materials cost causes the discounted cash flow rate of return to decline 38.3 percent. A ten percent decrease in sales volume causes the discounted cash flow rate of return to decline by 15.8 percent. Errors of 10 percent in processing cost, overhead/maintenance cost, and capital investment cause the discounted cash flow rate to decline by 7 percent or less.

These results indicate that a decision to invest in this project (on the basis of the discounted cash flow rate of return) is very sensitive to errors in estimates of sales prices and of raw materials costs and moderately sensitive to errors in estimates of processing cost, overhead/maintenance costs, and capital investment. Assuming that management cannot investigate the accuracy of all estimates more thoroughly, it would seem advisable to concentrate on the most significant estimates (i.e., sales prices, raw material costs, and possibly sales volume).

Some would argue that much the same information as that shown here can be obtained using conventional breakeven analysis. However, the use of a discounted measure of return within the sensitivity analysis framework offers several important advantages. First, it permits cash flows to be related to invested capital; this cannot be done easily with breakeven analysis, and the productivity of capital may be impossible to portray in a meaningful manner. Second, it gives consideration to the time value of money while breakeven analysis does not. Finally, breakeven analysis is based on the assumption that the variables being considered are linearly related. In actual practice this may not be true. The sensitivity analysis approach does not require a strictly linear relationship among the variables being considered.

IMPLICATIONS FOR MANAGEMENT

Determining, among a selected group of estimates, those in which errors have the most significant impact on measures of return and identifying cases in which calculation of discounted rates of return gives significantly different results from calculation of simple measures of return could be extremely helpful to management. It would indicate which estimates must be forecast more precisely than others if a correct investment decision is to be made and when the use of a discounted rate of return is economically justifiable. Such information will aid management in allocating scarce managerial resources such as time, money, and effort to the process of measuring and reducing or eliminating the risks involved in capital budgeting.

The amount of information sensitivity analysis can convey to management is limited. The approach outlined here would not permit management to draw precise conclusions about possible combinations of errors in estimating significant variables and the resultant effects on estimated rates of return. Nor would it indicate what effect a change in one estimate might have on another estimate. Despite these drawbacks, information about the effects of errors in estimation on the choice of capital investments may be significant for management since it will often indicate where the greatest risks in making investments lie.

Fortunately, determinations of the sensitivity of rates of return to errors in estimates need not be precise to be useful to management. If the relative difference between the effects of error in various estimates on rates of return is known, management will often be able to determine which estimates deserve more attention than others and in what cases the use of discounted as opposed to simple rates of return is economically justified.

16.
INVESTMENT POLICIES THAT PAY OFF*

David B. Hertz

Recent research findings point to a practical way for most companies to improve their capital investment decision making and maximize the chances of attaining their long-term dollars-and-cents investment objectives. Explaining the methods and results of this research, the author discusses conventional approaches to risk and describes a more sophisticated approach, involving the use of computer-based risk analysis techniques to compare probable payoffs.

In the next 12 months, U.S. businessmen, acting for the most part on the basis of painstaking staff analyses, will commit an estimated $65 billion to promising new capital investment projects. Two or three years later, when the long-term financial results of those investments are beginning to take shape, a good many of these same businessmen will be suffering the pangs of the big loser at Las Vegas. For, despite all the high-priced staff time and the board-level soul-searching that go into them, most capital investment decisions remain an incongruous blend of the slide rule and the roulette wheel. Consider some recent evidence.

The president of a big international corporation told me recently, "I can't understand why our investment policy hasn't worked the way we expected." Some years ago, he explained, the executive committee had decided that every capital investment, to be acceptable, would have to show an estimated before-tax average annual return on capital of 20%. The rule had been scrupulously followed; yet actual results had averaged 14%. "And we've got some of the best analysts in the business," added the frustrated president.

In another large and sophisticated company engaged in diversified manufacturing operations, barely half of the new investments during the past ten years are now expected to reach the break-even point—and less than half of those will reach or exceed their predicted return on investment. (On the other hand, some of the winners will be much larger than anticipated.)

The executive committee of a major chemical company is facing a real dilemma. It currently requires each proposed capital project to show an

---

*From *Harvard Business Review*, January–February 1968, pp. 96–108. Reprinted by permission of *Harvard Business Review*. Copyright © 1971 by the President and Fellows of Harvard College; all rights reserved.

expected return of at least 12% after taxes (16% for high-risk investments). Applying this policy, the executive committee has not turned down a single capital investment proposal for the past two years. Results from recent investments, however, have been alarmingly uneven. To provide a better screen for future proposals, and hopefully to improve investment results, a new policy requiring a three-year payback period plus a discounted cash flow return of 8% has been recommended to the committee. The members of the committee do not know what to do.

Capital investment decisions, it would seem, are still more art than science—and often more gamble than art. The reasons, moreover, are fairly obvious.

Any investment decision is (or should be) concerned with a choice among the available alternatives, and it is always subject to an unknown future environment. Actual future costs, markets, and prices will inevitably differ from any single set of assumptions used as a framework for weighing proposals. Moreover, a variety of criteria—payback, average annual return, net present value, internal ROI—may be used as yardsticks for proposals. And, despite much theoretical discussion, it has been hard for management to guess what difference, if any, the choice of a particular yardstick would make in actual long-term dollars-and-cents results. In short, lacking any way to test out the ultimate financial impact of a given investment policy, management literally has had no way of knowing whether it might have done better.

Research results recently obtained by McKinsey & Company through analysis and computer simulation of the investment process indicate that there is a practical way for most companies to make sure that the policies they do choose have the greatest chance of meeting their objectives. Specifically, management can answer these questions with confidence:

> Historically, has our investment policy given us the highest possible return, consistent with the risks we have accepted?
> How much risk have we been accepting in our investment decisions? Is this consistent with the risks that top management really wants to accept?
> Have we been using the best criteria for investment selection, considering long-term corporate objectives? Have we been taking adequate account of uncertainty?
> Given the investment alternatives that are available to us and the risks we are willing to accept, what *investment policy* will maximize the earnings-per-share performance of our investments over the long run?

To understand how these questions can be answered and to clarify the methods and results of our research, it will be useful to compare some current approaches to risk, and then to explore the concept of an effective investment policy.

RISK AND THE FUTURE

The exact course of future events is unknown when investment choices are made, and uncertainty creates risk. There are two conventional ways of dealing with risk and uncertainty, and one less conventional method that is gaining acceptance.

"Best-Guess" Estimates

A simple, widely used conventional approach is to express one's assumptions about the key variables affecting future costs, revenues, and investment requirements in terms of single-point estimates based on the best information available to management at the time the forecast is made. The calculated outcome of the investment, based on these "best guesses," is judged acceptable if it exceeds a specified criterion of return or payback. If the project is considered particularly risky, the hurdle may be raised—in effect, requiring a "risk premium," an idea carried over from the early days of insurance.

Exhibit 1 shows how difficult it is to determine an acceptable risk premium, even in a simple case. Using very reasonable ranges for each of the variables involved (e.g., a best guess of 200,000 units for sales volume, with a range from 175,000 to 225,000 units), it demonstrates that the outcome, in terms of average return on investment, may vary anywhere from 0% to 56.5%. Thus, as Exhibit 1 demonstrates, this approach has a fatal weakness: if the actual outcome for any variable is significantly different from the estimate, the actual results of the investment may be *very* much different from those projected; simply raising the hurdle may not help much.

$$\text{ROI} = \frac{(\text{Price} \times \text{Unit sales}) - (\text{Costs})}{(\text{Investment})}$$

Best-guess estimates:	Likely ranges:
Price = $5.00	Price = $5.00 to $5.50
Costs = $800,000	Costs = $700,000 to $875,000
ROI = 20%	Sales = 175,000 to 225,000 units
Sales = 200,000 units	Investment = $950,000 to $1,100,000
Investment = $1,000,000

Worst case: $\dfrac{5.0 \times 175,000 - 875,000}{1,100,000} = \dfrac{0}{1,000,000} = 0\% \text{ ROI}$

Best case: $\dfrac{5.5 \times 225,000 - 700,000}{950,000} = 56.5\% \text{ ROI}$

Exhibit 1. Drawbacks of Single-Point Estimates

In an attempt to overcome this weakness, many managements follow the practice of supplementing their best-guess estimates with other values for each variable, e.g., a "high" (optimistic) and a "low" (pessimistic) value. By permuting the values for each variable in repeated calculations, it is then possible to see what variations might occur if the best guesses are not all on target—as in fact they are highly unlikely to be.

With no information as to the *likelihood* of a given outcome, however, the decision maker has not added much to his assessment of the uncertainty. He has a better idea of what he may be letting the company in for, but he has little real information about what he ought to *expect*. To be sure, managements can and do try out various investment criteria—e.g., payback period, ROI, and net present value—to see whether each seems to yield good results under varying conditions. But they have not really been able to predict the ultimate financial results of using particular criteria.

"Forced-Fit" Forecasts

The second conventional way around the difficulties of an unknown future—a way that seems to have special appeal to marketing-oriented companies—is to acknowledge freely all the uncertainties surrounding the estimated outcome of a new investment and then to wave them away on the grounds that the actual outcome can be forced to fit the estimate. For example, if sales fall short of target, various measures—ranging from heavier advertising to a shake-up of the sales force—can be applied to get the desired results. And since the precise circumstances in which these tactics might be applied cannot be known in advance, there is no point in worrying until the time comes; "something will always turn up."

Of course, this micawberish view completely misses the point. If one can be certain of achieving a particular set of results, the uncertainty disappears, and so, in large measure, does the problem of investment policy. If one cannot, the uncertainty and the problem remain. The striking proportion of marketing failures among new products (estimates range from 30% to 80%, depending on definitions) belies the optimism of the micawbers.

Risk-Based Profiles

A third method of dealing with uncertainty, which is less conventional but more sophisticated, has recently been gaining adherents. Some years ago I suggested that the risks inherent in an investment could be directly assessed through computer simulation.[1] In this method, called risk analysis, the first step is to identify the leverage factors that will influence the key variables determining future costs and revenues for example, capacity will influence sales volume; timing of market entry will influence price; and so

---

[1] See my article "Risk Analysis in Capital Investment," *Harvard Business Review*, January–February 1964, p. 95. [Editors' Note: Also see page 245 (Article 17) in this book, and the discussion of Monte Carlo simulation, pp. 235–246.]

forth. The next step is to weigh all of the available information—e.g., historical trends, growth of markets, likely price changes—about each of these leverage factors and then, from this information, to develop the "uncertainty profile" for each key variable.

Estimates of revenues from a proposed new plant, for example, might indicate that there is a two-thirds chance of their falling within ± $40,000 of an "expected"—or average over the long run—$250,000 a year, that there is only one chance in ten of their falling below $180,000, but that there is also one chance in ten that they will exceed $350,000. These estimates are used to define a probability distribution curve for future revenues which is called the "uncertainty profile." These profiles for the elements that enter into an investment project are sometimes determined from historical or other objective data, but they are more likely to be subjective estimates by those most familiar with the various parts of the overall proposal.

Gathering and analyzing the data needed to construct such uncertainty profiles may pose difficult communications problems, it should be noted. For example, does a marketing executive know what it means to say, "Product A has at least a 90% chance of achieving a 15% return on investment five years out?" Can he learn to think in these terms? Solving such communications problems is part of the process of developing a rational and effective investment policy. It is not, however, the issue addressed in this article.

Once an "uncertainty profile" has been established for each key investment project variable, we can repeatedly sample from the distributions of these variables shown in their uncertainty profiles. Using a computer, we calculate the financial outcome of the combined variables each time we sample, and thus simulate the range of probable outcomes from the proposed investment in terms of the particular investment criterion to be used or tested. From the results of these simulations, a probability distribution or "risk profile" of the criterion can be built up.

Exhibit 2 shows the steps employed in simulating the possible outcomes of a given investment and in determining the risk profile. Such profiles can be developed for any criterion that management may wish to use. Exhibit 3 shows the payback, average ROI, and discounted ROI profiles of a hypothetical investment.

Of two investments, one is clearly better than the other if it offers a greater probability of achieving any given level of return. In this situation risk analysis permits management to distinguish without question among more and less desirable investments. For example, in Part I of Exhibit 4 we see that Investment A is a better bet than Investment B at all values of return—that is, it *dominates* Investment B.

But one investment alternative is *not* always dominant. Consider the case of Investments X and Y in Part 2 of Exhibit 4. Here, Investment X is more likely than Investment Y to attain at least a 10% return on investment but less likely to bring in a 40% return. In cases of this kind—and they are

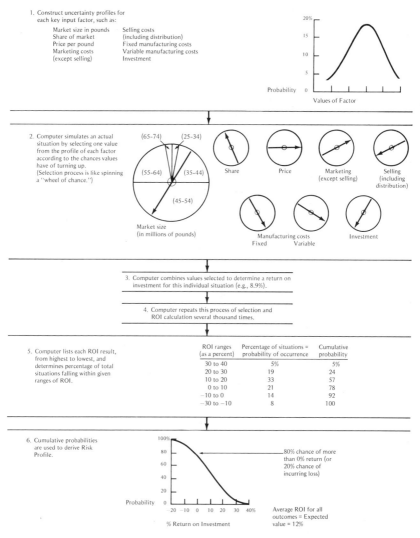

Exhibit 2. Example of Risk-Analysis Simulation

numerous—the questions of which investment to select and how to go about establishing a policy to guide the choice have hitherto gone unanswered.

To be sure, in using risk profiles management is availing itself of all, not just part, of the quantitative information that can be put together on the investment possibilities. And more information in the hands of management should mean better decisions. But the question of how to use this information remains. Before it can be answered, we need a clear conception of the nature and function of an investment policy.

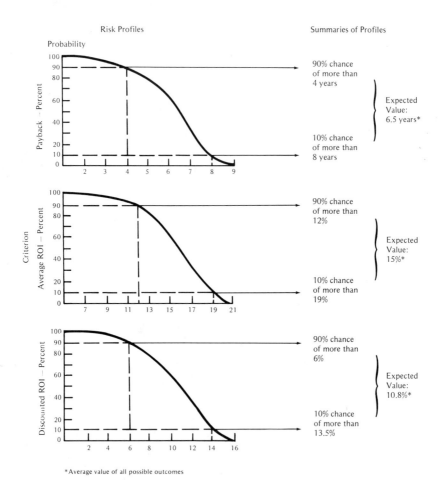

*Average value of all possible outcomes

Exhibit 3. Risk-Analysis Results Using Different Criteria

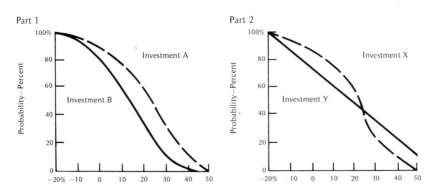

Return on Investment—Percent

Exhibit 4. Examples of "Best-Choice" Investment Alternatives

NATURE OF POLICY

Any investment policy, if it is to guide management's choices among available investment alternatives, must embody two components: (1) *one or more criteria* by which to measure the relative economic attributes of investment alternatives, and (2) *decision rules*—which may or may not make use of risk analysis or otherwise seek to take uncertainty into account—for selecting "acceptable" investments.

The criteria have been the subject of much analysis and discussion. They include payback period, which is simply the number of years required for the investment to return its costs; average annual percent return on average funds employed; net present value measures; and internal rates of return, calculated on a discounted cash flow basis.[2] On the other hand, the rules for making choices, particularly under uncertainty, have been largely left up in the air.[3] Of course, no preestablished policy can take into account all the considerations—human, organizational, strategic, and financial—that typically enter into a major capital investment decision. In this article, however, I am concerned strictly with the question of financial policy, which does lend itself to rigorous formulation.

Dual Role

A consistent and adequate investment policy has a double function. In the short run, it should indicate which investments should be chosen to achieve the financial objectives of the corporation. In the long run, it should serve as a basis for identifying or developing investment alternatives that are likely to match the policies selected. In other words, it serves as a basis for both (a) *acting on* and (b) *communicating about* investment alternatives.

Screening Proposals
In the first instance, an investment policy may be regarded as a screen which will "pass" certain investment proposals and reject others. The screen may be coarse or fine, tight or loose, high-risk or low-risk—depending on management's knowing or unknowing choice. Through the screen will pass the acceptable investment proposals that will form management's "investment set."

Once it is understood that a risk profile attaches, willy-nilly, to all investments and that this profile varies with the criteria chosen even

---

[2] For a comprehensive discussion of these measures and their relative merits, see Harold Bierman, Jr. and Seymour Smidt, *The Capital Budgeting Decision* (New York: The Macmillan Company, 1966).

[3] An interesting and provocative discussion of such rules will be found in R. M. Adelson, "Criteria for Capital Investment: An Approach Through Decision Theory," *Operational Research Quarterly*, Vol. 16, No. 1; Adelson approaches the problems suggested in this article and provides, along with a useful list of references, an excellent analytical discussion of the difficulties in presently used methods.

though based on the same estimates of underlying real-world phenomena, it becomes clear that a policy with a "determinate," or single-point-based, decision-rule component is a very coarse screen indeed—if it can be called a screen at all. In any case, as we shall see, such a "determinate" policy is ineffective; it will not guide management to making the best use of its investment funds, no matter what the company's financial objectives may be.

Risk-based policies, on the other hand, may specify how management would prefer to trade off the chances of low return against the chances of high return. For example, would it prefer a virtual certainty of no loss coupled with a virtual ceiling on gains over 20% after taxes—or would it accept a one-in-ten chance of significant loss for the sake of a one-in-ten chance of very high gain?

Exhibit 5 shows how one specific policy may be defined by the criterion to be used and the rules to be followed in screening investments in terms of their risk profiles. These rules, which make explicit management's entrepreneurial or risk-taking attitudes, do allow consistent investment choices.[4] The methods described in this article assume that uncertainty—that is, the spread of distribution of potential returns around the "expected value," or average of all outcomes—is a useful measure of risk. It is generally accepted that the further the return might exceed the expected value, the further it could also fall short—and lucky indeed is the company to which this principle does not apply.

---

1. Criterion to be used as a measure of investment worth: Before-tax return on investment, on a discounted cash flow basis

2. Rules to be used to screen investments based on risk profiles of proposed projects:
   Accept proposals that have—
   a. Expected value (average of all outcomes) of 5% or greater
   b. One chance in ten that the ROI will exceed 25%
   c. Nine chances in ten that the ROI will exceed 0%

Exhibit 5. Example of Risk-Based Investment Policy

Communicating alternatives
In the second instance, an investment policy can be a powerful communications tool. It enables top management to make known in advance to those responsible for developing investment proposals what sort of projects the company seeks. The object is to control the selection and development of alternatives so that they reflect the gains the company wants to make and the risks it is willing to undergo to achieve them.

---

[4] See Ralph O. Swalm, "Utility Theory—Insights Into Risk Taking," *Harvard Business Review*, November–December 1966, p. 123.

In theory, of course, this function could be served by policy statements such as: "All investments must have an estimated average return on capital employed of 12% or more after taxes." But, on the practical level, the complexity of most present-day investment projects and the multitude of future variables to which they are subject rob such statements of most of their usefulness. This is why top management today, confronted with requests for capital, so often finds that the only significant response it can make is to approve the results of all the analyses that have previously taken place at divisional and staff levels.

With a risk-based policy, using one or more criteria and such rules as shown in Exhibit 5, management still has no guarantee that all or any of the available investments will pass through the screen. But it does have a better, more specific means for discriminating among proposed investments. And it also has a tool for testing out its own procedures for developing investment proposals and for checking out alternative policies. To analyze its own past investments and requests for capital, a company can estimate the risk profiles of these past investments and determine (a) whether it has been consistent in its past selections and (b) what changes in the mix selected would be indicated by different policy choices.

This analysis, however, still will not indicate what is the best investment policy overall—that is, what impact the choice of a particular criterion, such as net present value, payback, or return on investment, has on the likely outcome of specific real-world variables, such as costs and revenues, or what differences there are (again, in terms of real-world financial results) between high-risk and low-risk screens. In this connection I think it is important to note that the criteria are mathematically derived in fairly complicated ways from real-world events, such as sales, price changes, equipment installations, and so on. Since the uncertainty profiles of the events must be used to determine the final risk profile of the criterion, simulation methods are required.

"EFFICIENCY" CONCEPT

Most managements would like to have investment policies that both maximize financial results over the long run and minimize uncertainty or risk. Seeking additional returns, however, normally entails accepting additional uncertainty—that is, risk. If two policies produce the same average result (e.g., the same average earnings per share over a five-year period), the one that involves less "variability" (or uncertainty as to the outcome) for the same yield is a more desirable or "efficient" policy. Conversely, of two policies entailing the same variability, the one producing the higher expected return ("expected" meaning the average of all outcomes) is obviously the better policy. Variability is best measured in terms of the probability distribution of the values within which the actual results are likely to fall.

Standard Deviation

The spread or variability of a risk profile can be measured by the size of the standard deviation, which represents the spread around the expected value of the criterion encompassing two-thirds of all the actual outcomes. Thus, if one can simulate the financial results of investments selected on the basis of a particular policy, the expected return—along with the standard deviation of the financial results obtained with that policy—will indicate the "efficiency" of the investment project set selected under that policy. (With this simulation, the distributions of the uncertainty profiles of revenues, costs, and investments in a specific year are combined. These combinations are linear, and we can expect the results to be normally distributed.)

The expected return and the standard deviation can be plotted on a graph to show the effectiveness of any policy, and a line can then be drawn through the points of greatest yield for a given standard deviation. This line is called the *efficiency frontier* because it represents the best return management can get for a given variance—unless, of course, management either (a) finds a policy that will yield a greater return on investment for no more variance, or (b) develops investment proposals with different uncertainty profiles that provide project choices with less variance for equivalent returns.

Exhibit 6 illustrates how the average returns—in this case, earnings per share—are plotted against the standard deviation of those earnings to give an efficiency frontier.[5] Each point on the graph represents the financial results to be expected from a combination of investments selected by passing the same group of proposals through the screen of a particular investment policy. (The results shown in this exhibit were obtained by simulating the operation of a company using this policy for 15 years.)

Policies A, B, and C lie on the efficiency frontier because each produces the maximum earnings per share for a given degree of risk. Policies D, E, and F do not lie on the frontier because none of them produces, for a given standard deviation, as much earnings as management could obtain by using a different policy. Policy F, for example, is better than E because it earns $4.00 against $2.95 for the same risk (15% standard deviation); but it is worse than A, which produces earnings of $6.50 at a standard deviation of 16%. An efficient policy at 15% standard deviation should produce average earnings of approximately $6.25 per share.

Specific policies can, of course, be developed to fill in the entire efficiency frontier curve. For example, the simulation can take into account the capital structure of a real or hypothetical firm, both currently and in the (uncertain) future, thereby dealing effectively with the problem of the marginal cost of capital.

[5] In *Portfolio Selection: Effective Diversification of Investments* (New York: John Wiley & Sons, Inc., 1959), Harry M. Markowitz develops a similar concept; the method he describes does not, however, select investments with reference to their risk characteristics; see Michael L. Ruby, "The Current State of Chance-Constrained Programming," *Systems Research Memorandum, No. 181,* The Technological Institute, Northwestern University, August 1967.

Policy	Simulation results	
	Average earnings per share*	Percentage standard deviation
A	$6.50	16%
B	7.10	20
C	3.00	5
D	5.75	20
E	2.95	15
F	4.00	15

*Under reasonable assumptions of depreciation, life of investments, initial conditions, and so forth.

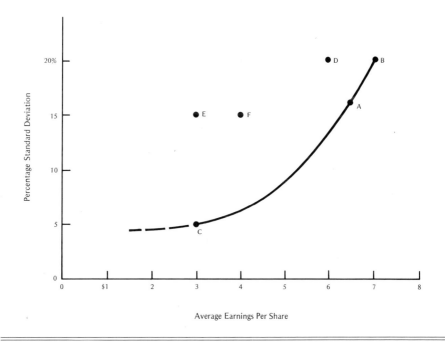

Exhibit 6. Comparing Investment Policies

If the objective of an investment policy is to maximize average long-term earnings or yield for a given variation of those earnings or that yield, there is literally no reason why a management that has calculated its own efficiency frontier should use a policy that is not on that frontier. By definition, such a policy entails more variability in investment results and/or a lower expected return than the company is in fact obliged to accept. A management that wants to invest rationally—that is, wants to optimize results—has every reason, therefore, to locate its efficiency frontier and continually strive to improve it.

RESEARCH RESULTS

How practicable is the concept of efficient investment sets (on the efficiency frontier) and effective investment policies that will lead to a choice
of such sets? In terms of actual investment results, what light does it throw
on the choice of particular investment criteria, such as payback period,
average annual return, and the like? To help answer these questions, a
computer model was developed that made it possible to simulate the effects
of various policies, operating over a period of years, on the financial results
of a hypothetical company which selects annually from a wide range of
investment proposals. Generally acceptable accounting procedures were
used to determine financial results. Straight-line depreciation was used,
and a fixed percentage dividend, along with a constant allowable debt
ratio, was required to be paid where profits were available. At initial
start-up each simulation run had standard conditions of assets, earnings,
and so forth.[6]

Seven-Step Simulation

As input to the computer simulation model, we developed three sets of 37
hypothetical investments. Each of the hypothetical investments, in turn,
was characterized by uncertainty profiles for each of the three key variables
for each year of the particular investment: sales, costs, and investment
requirements. The computer simulation involved seven steps:

> 1. Choose an investment policy by (a) selecting a financial criterion
> (or criteria) and (b) establishing decision rules. Except in the case of
> single-point estimates, these rules specified criterion values, along
> with a minimum expected value, at the 10% and 90% probability
> points on the criterion-risk profile (see Exhibit 5).
>
> 2. From the uncertainty profiles of key variables for each
> investment given in the available investment set, develop risk
> profiles for each.
>
> 3. Screen investments against policy, and accept all those that pass
> the screen, subject to realistic constraints on size and number of
> investments to be made in a given year.
>
> 4. Simulate the financial performance of the chosen investments
> over a 15-year period, selecting at random the operating results for
> each year from the individual uncertainty profiles for the
> investment project in order to obtain one set of operating results for
> that investment for each year.

---

[6]This simulation was programmed for an IBM 7094 computer by my colleague at
McKinsey & Company, Joan Morthland Bush.

5. Combine the various revenues, costs, and investment requirements for each of the years, and then compute the yearly financial results for this investment set.

6. Repeat the entire process until a stable distribution of the financial results for the policy chosen and the investments available has been built up. Determine the average or expected value and the standard deviation of the key financial results.

7. Repeat for other policies and other sets of investment alternatives.

Policies Tested

For each of the three investment sets, investment policies covering conservative, medium-risk, and high-risk screens were tested. The conservative ones required a very high probability of no loss along with moderate expectations, while the high-risk ones accepted significant chances of loss but required good chances of high gains.

Exhibit 7 shows the nature of the policies used for the test, illustrating the low-risk and high-risk policies. (Note that single-point determinate policies—not shown on the exhibit—were also included in the tests.) The investments available were varied, ranging from short-term to longer-term payouts, with cash investment requirements sometimes extending into later years.[7] The simulation was repeated 500 times for each policy and each set of investments, and the financial results were calculated for each year of a 15-year period. The average of each financial result and its standard deviation was determined for each year and for the combination of the last five years of the runs.

General Findings

Exhibit 8 shows the results of all the runs, plotted on a standard index basis, for the new investments selected. As can be seen, these results permit us to draw at least four general conclusions.

First, there is a wide gap in financial performance between some commonly used investment policies and those policies that lie on the efficiency frontier.

Second, risk-based policies consistently give better results than those using single-point, determinate decision rules. Using determinate decision rules, one cannot compensate for high risk by raising the level-of-return hurdle; single-point estimates produce, at best, half the return for a given degree of risk, no matter how the required return level is raised or lowered.

---

[7]On a single-point basis, the investments ranged from 1.9 years to 6.8 years for payback, from 16.9% to 47.2% average annual return, and from 7.5% to 77% ROI-dcf.

CRITERION	CONSERVATIVE POLICY			HIGH-RISK POLICY		
	90% PROBABILITY OF DOING BETTER THAN	EXPECTED VALUE BETTER THAN	10% PROBABILITY OF DOING BETTER THAN	90% PROBABILITY OF DOING BETTER THAN	EXPECTED VALUE BETTER THAN	10% PROBABILITY OF DOING BETTER THAN
1. Payback (years to recover investment)	7	5	—	10	4	2
2. Average annual proceeds/ investment (percent)	15%	20%	—	– 5%	15%	45%
3. ROI-dcf (percent)	10%	15%	—	–10%	10%	35%
4. NPV-dcf* Discount rate:						
10	1.0					
15		1.0		1.0		
45						1.0

*The indicated values are ratios of NPV of cash flow at the specified discount rates, divided by the present value of the investment.

Exhibit 7. Examples of Investment Policies (after tax)

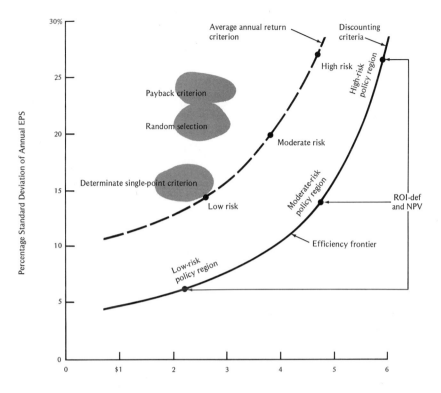

Exhibit 8. Investment Policy Simulation

Third, long-term financial results are highly dependent on the risk accepted for a given return or on the return achieved for a given degree of risk. Thus, on the efficiency frontier, to get a long-term average of $6 per share, management would have to accept fluctuations on the order of 45% in two years out of three, whereas it could get only $3 if it decided to accept a probable fluctuation no greater than 10%.

Fourth, some investment criteria are empirically better than others. Whenever growth is a goal—that is, whenever results are measured on an earnings-per-share (EPS) basis—net present value (NPV) and internal discounted cash flow return (ROI-dcf), both of which are based on discounting future returns, are superior to criteria, such as average annual return, which do not take the time value of money into account. At 25% annual standard deviation, for example—that is, accepting one chance in three of the results falling outside ± 25% of the expected values in any given year—the discounting criterion gives expected EPS of $5.50 while the non-discounted criterion gives $4.10, or 25% less.

(Policies that produce equivalent financial results for NPV and ROI-dcf can also be developed. That is, by specifying appropriate values for (a) the discount rate and (b) the probability of achieving a particular ratio of the NPV of the cash flow stream to the NPV of the investment, one can obtain exactly the same screen for investments as is provided by specific risk-based values of the ROI-dcf criterion.)

Although payback period is still an extremely popular criterion, it turns out to be an extremely crude, inconsistent, and inefficient yardstick from the standpoint of actual financial results. Thus all the investments selected with payback criteria showed higher variances and lower returns than the others.

A more general conclusion to be drawn from this simulation project is that the same approach can profitably be used by management to evaluate its past investments, to determine its efficiency frontier, and to select efficient investment policies that more accurately reflect its risk preferences.

Note that the results shown in Exhibit 8 are charted in terms of standard deviation—that is, the vertical coordinate of any point on the chart represents the range of variation that may be expected *two-thirds of the time* in the results of a particular policy. If management is unwilling to accept one chance in six of results falling below this range, it will have to accept a lower average return.

How much lower depends, of course, on what odds are acceptable. If, for example, assurance is wanted that results will fall above a given boundary five-sixths of the time, *one standard deviation* must be subtracted from average earnings per share for each policy on the efficiency frontier, thereby creating a new curve inside the efficiency frontier as shown in Exhibit 9. Or, if management has a still more conservative attitude toward risk and wants a 19-to-1 probability of a given range of results—that is, an assurance that results will fall below the range indicated for a given return only 1 time in 20—*two standard deviations* may be subtracted, giving still another curve along which the returns offered by particular policies can be located.

Of significance here is the fact that different risk preferences, as exemplified by different risk boundaries, dictate different investment policy choices. Thus, in the situation illustrated by Exhibit 9, Policy C provides an expected return of $5.50 with a ± 25% standard deviation. Since these are typical Gaussian or normal distributions, we know that one standard deviation (25% × $5.50) subtracted from the mean will give a value—approximately $4.10 in this case—below which no more than one-sixth of the possible future values may be expected to fall. Two standard deviations subtracted would mean no more than a 1-in-20 chance of getting less than $2.70.

In the example a *very* conservative management might wish to accept no more than a 1-in-200 risk. In this case Policy A would offer the best return possible; all others would give less after subtracting three standard deviations. For a management inclined to moderate risk, however, Policy B is the best choice; it offers a 19-in-20 chance of getting $3.15 or better.[8]

[8]William J. Baumol has suggested a somewhat similar approach to stock portfolio selection in "An Expected Gain-Confidence Limit Criterion for Portfolio Selection," *Management Science*, October 1963, p. 174.

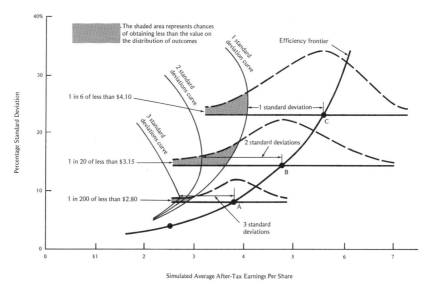

Exhibit 9. Determining Risk Boundaries on the Efficiency Frontier

Which risk boundary is used determines which investment policy is best; which boundary to select depends on management's willingness to assume risk. Moreover, the risk aversion inherent in any policy can be assessed by determining the risk boundary on which that policy gives better results than all others. The fewer standard deviations one must subtract to define a frontier on which a given policy is best, the greater is the indicated willingness to accept risk.

CONCLUSION

Computer simulation offers corporate management, for the first time, a tool that will enable it to examine the risk consequences of various investment policies. As the research reported in this article shows, the development of a good investment policy involves four requirements:

1. The determination of risk profiles for all investments.

2. The use of a discounting measure (either discounted internal rate of return or an equivalent net present value) for assessing the merit of an investment proposal.

3. The establishment of alternative screening rules for investment proposals.

4. The determination of risk boundaries for the alternative policies.

It should be clear that the same policy will not necessarily show the same risk characteristics (or risk boundaries) when used to screen different classes of investments. In one application, for example, a diversified chemical company found that the projects proposed by various divisions—overseas, heavy chemical, and so on—varied widely in their efficiency frontiers, and therefore entailed different risks for the same policies. Having decided what level of risk it wished to assume for each of the businesses, management was able to choose its policies accordingly.

Moreover, the company was able to determine the level of investment in each class of projects that would combine with investment levels and risks in other classes to maximize its chances of achieving its long-range growth goals. With the aid of simulation, it was able to establish ceilings and targets in the various investment classes and to describe in detail the screens or policies to be used to make choices in each of them. This enabled division managers and staff personnel to understand management's objectives and to develop more appropriate and promising investment alternatives.

Using the same approach, other companies can now examine in detail the kind of investment opportunities generated by various segments of their businesses and select investment policies that will give them firmer control over their long-term growth. Top executives can analyze their own prejudices and test out the historical effects of inconsistent and irrational choices on their companies' long-term financial results. In short, top management can get back in the driver's seat, in charge of the most important element of the corporate future—effective investment for growth.

17.
MONTE CARLO SIMULATION*

Henry R. Anderson

> *An operations research tool to cope with capital budgeting decisions involving uncertainty.*

Decision making under conditions of uncertainty is high on the list of problem areas in today's rapidly changing business world. Decisions have to be made about events that may take place five or ten years into the future. If a wrong decision is made, the time factor compounds the costliness of the error to the business organization. Such decisions involve a large degree of risk and it is the decision maker's task to minimize that risk while still trying to optimize the results of the decision.

Operations research and the computer can be used by decision makers to reduce the risk caused by uncertainties. This paper will outline briefly the area of operations research, including in the discussion its definition, solution categories and models or tools. The major portion of the paper, however, will describe and illustrate the Monte Carlo method, an operations research tool used exclusively for analyzing problems involving uncertainty. Although the applicability of the computer will not be illustrated, the reader should keep in mind that the entire Monte Carlo model is readily adaptable to the language of the computer.

OPERATIONS RESEARCH

There have been many attempts to define operations research but, in most of the definitions, the scope of O.R. has been limited to one or two small areas. In the past, operations research has been associated with such vaguely defined terms as "quantitative methods," "systems analysis," and

*From *Managerial Planning*, January/February 1970, pp. 26–32. Reprinted by permission of the publisher.

"management science." Ronald V. Hartley, in his article "Operations Research and Its Implications for the Accounting Profession," collected a number of ideas and formulated the following definition of operations research:

> Operations research is a collective effort of many types of talent concentrating on the application of the scientific method to the development of predictive models which describe the stable patterns of order underlying certain business operations and thereby enabling the provision of quantitative information which is helpful in solving executive-type problems.[1]

In reviewing Hartley's definition, the terms "collective effort," "scientific method," "predictive models" and "provision of quantitative information" help to illustrate the complexity of the area. The scope of operations research, then, is difficult to delineate. It includes the construction of models and the design of new systems for solving management problems. The solution of day-to-day problems, however, are not included within the scope of operations research.

Methodology

The methodology of operations research is distinguished by two major characteristics. As was pointed out in its definition, O.R. is interdisciplinary in nature. It calls for a team approach utilizing one or more of the following basic sciences: mathematics, physics, chemistry, biology, physiology, sociology, economics and business, and engineering. O.R.'s second characteristic is that it is scientific. This means that the various analyses are structured in some orderly and logical manner. Utilizing the mathematical and statistical tools that an operations research man has at his command, the following steps are used in solving problems: (a) recognition of the existence of a problem; (b) determination of the goal; (c) selection of the decision variables; (d) construction of a mathematical model to describe the activity; (e) solution of the model; and (f) translation of the solution into procedures for the firm.[2]

Solution Categories of Operations Research

There are many problem solving techniques which have been classified as operations research tools or methods. Techniques usually associated with the field of operations research include linear programming, Monte Carlo

---

[1]Ronald V. Hartley, "Operations Research and Its Implications for the Accounting Profession," *Accounting Review*, April 1968, p. 321.

[2]William H. Jean, "Operations Research for the Accountant," *Management Accounting*, February 1968, p. 27.

process, inventory theory, replacement theory, queueing theory, statistical decision theory, game theory, PERT/CPM, capital budgeting and dynamic programming. Nearly all of these generally accepted O.R. techniques, however, can be placed into one of three categories; (1) analytic solutions, (2) numerical solutions, and (3) simulation solutions.[3]

Analytic Solutions
Formal mathematical deduction processes are used to obtain the analytic solutions. The mathematical expression

$$SP = f(A) \qquad \text{where } SP = \text{selling price}$$
$$A = \text{advertising outlay}$$

is a model which represents a sub-system of an industrial decision model. In the equation, SP is a variable the value of which depends upon the value of the independent variable A. By controlling the value of A, SP may be given some desired value. Utilizing the capabilities of differential calculus, it is possible to find values of A for which SP assumes a minimum or maximum value. A formal deductive process of the type used above represents an analytic solution method.

Numerical Solutions
In a numerical solution, the relationships of variables are still formalized but the solution is obtained through a less formal trial and error procedure. Instead of using established mathematical techniques to find the value of the independent variable, a sequence of arbitrary values is substituted into the equation. The substitution process is continued until a particular value of A is found for which SP has a satisfactory value. Numerical solutions are used in cases where either no analytic method is applicable or when analytic methods are inconvenient to apply. The basic linear programming problem is an example of a numerical type of solution.

Simulation Solutions
Finding solutions to problems through simulation processes is the third problem solving category of operations research. In a simulation experiment, a set of "synthetic" variables, which represents a set of real-world variables, is manipulated with the objective of making determinations about the real-world system being studied.[4] A simulation study begins with an abstract simplified model. The model is then operated in a real-world fashion, generating output data which should be similar to that of the real world. Through experimentation with simulation (adding variables to make it more complete and accurate), the model is perfected.

---

[3] W. W. Thompson Jr., *Operations Research Techniques*, Columbus, Ohio: Charles E. Merrill Books, Inc., 1967, p. 4.

[4] Ibid., p. 5.

Simulation is employed usually in situations where a series of relatively simple subsolutions is the best approach to the solution of a problem. In addition, it is useful in instances where a statement of the mathematical relationships is very complex. Simulation also provides the only convenient means of solution to problems in which several of the relevant variables are probabilistic. (This particular area will be elaborated upon later in the paper.)

SIMULATION AND THE MONTE CARLO METHOD

Many problems in business involve very complex stochastic processes which cannot be analyzed directly. A stochastic process is a sequence of trials or experiments whose outcomes are random rather than deterministic in nature.[5] In the business field, simulation and the Monte Carlo technique have been applied to the study of a business system or a portion of a system.

The essential elements in simulation are (1) the construction of the mathematical model of the process being investigated and (2) a sample of inputs, based on either actual inputs or synthetic data. Once the model has been constructed and the input data formalized, the model is operated to simulate a real-world situation. The yield is a sample of outputs based on a sample of inputs. The ultimate purpose is to infer from the data generated how the corresponding real-world system would function under similar circumstances. Very often the analysis is aimed at discovering the behavior characteristics of a system as it operates over time. In addition, the decision maker may want to analyze the nature of variations which take place in the characteristics as the system operates.

Random Variables

Many of the models employed in simulation processes are constructed using random variables. A random variable is a variable which may have any one of a range of values, the exact value of which is determined by a chance process which can be described in the form of a probability distribution.[6] Care must be taken to clearly define the behavior of the random variable in the model. Describing, in numerical form, the value of the variable and its related probability distribution will satisfy the definition requirement.

---

[5]Roger L. Burford, *Introduction to Finite Probability*, Columbus, Ohio: Charles E. Merrill Books, Inc., 1967, p. 44.

[6]C. William Emory and Powell Niland, *Making Management Decisions*, Boston: Houghton Mifflin Company, 1968, p. 213.

The Monte Carlo Method

Monte Carlo simulation is a type of analysis which is concerned with simulating systems which are influenced by stochastic elements. In any simulation process which produces output units having measurable characteristics, variations will be expected to occur. If the generating system is stochastic, the variations are attributable to some system of chance causes. A probability distribution is a function which describes this kind of variation in terms of the relative likelihood of particular values. In other words, a probability distribution specifies the behavior pattern of a corresponding stochastic process.

The Monte Carlo method is described as the generation of artifacts from an idealized model by means of random numbers.[7] Monte Carlo models can be applied when the problem under analysis involves variables whose values are determined by stochastic experiment. The problem must contain one or more random variables and sufficient data must be available so that the probability distributions for the variables can be constructed. Monte Carlo is a process of simulation which operates in a replica of the problem area and manipulates the strategic factors in a way that enables the decision maker to arrive at the best decision. It is a process involving sensitivity analysis. The values of one variable can be changed so as to reflect the resulting changes to the other variables and to the model itself.

Monte Carlo simulation, then, is a technique for generating synthetic output data which are representative of the real world. This is accomplished by sampling the probability distribution which represents the actual process. If the probability distribution is a good representation of the actual system, and if the sampling procedure is applied correctly, the data produced by the simulation will be very similar to the data observed by operating the real world process.

The Steps of the Monte Carlo Process
The Monte Carlo procedure is as follows:[8]

> 1. Determine the probability distribution for the variable of interest. The distribution can be formulated by sampling the actual data or through subjective estimates of the process.

> 2. Convert the distribution to a cumulative distribution function. This involves restating the distribution in terms of "X or greater" where X is the variable of interest.

> 3. Select, at random, a sequence of numbers having values with a uniform 0 to 100 distribution. These can be chosen from structured

---

[7] Arthur Brodshatzer and Oliver Galbraith III, "Making Decisions More Rationally—The Application of Monte Carlo," *NAA Bulletin*, August 1963, p. 34.
[8] W. W. Thompson Jr., op. cit., p. 136.

random number charts or from good random number generators which are available as subroutines for computer programs.

4. From the list of random numbers, determine a corresponding list of values for the variable of interest. The object is to produce for the random variable a cumulative distribution identical to the one derived in steps (1) and (2).

The example in the following section will illustrate the procedure outlined above.

CASH FLOW ANALYSIS IN THE CAPITAL BUDGETING DECISION

Monte Carlo simulation is associated usually with queuing problems, but its application is not limited only to waiting line situations. The Monte Carlo process can be employed in any situation involving decisions based upon uncertain or probabilistic data of future events. To illustrate the Monte Carlo process, an example could have been formulated around an inventory problem involving a queue. However, the capital budgeting decision area was selected because it utilizes more than one type of operations research solution and is, itself, a recognized O.R. model.

Exhibit 1 is a model of the capital budgeting decision process. The final decision is the end result of weeks of gathering and interpreting the information relevant to the decision. As viewed in this paper, the capital budgeting decision process begins with the formulation of the problem and ends with the appraisal of the results of the final decision. Before the final data can be subjected to the discounted cash flow analysis, (one of many techniques used in arriving at the final decision), the elements of the cash flow model must be projected for the period relevant to the decision. Therefore, the decision maker must have at his disposal expected values for each of the variables and their degree of interdependence before he can compute the expected cash flow for the proposed project.

The Problem

The decision maker is concerned about the amount of uncertainty that will be carried into the final decision if he simply makes a subjective single-valued estimate for each of the ten variables. These amounts will be based almost entirely on intuition while the influence of the various interdependencies will be unknown. In an attempt to reduce the degree of uncertainty in a projected cash flow situation, the decision maker should elect to use two classes of operations research solutions, analytic and simulation solutions.

The following examples will be limited to the computation of the expected value of the selling price, E (SP). Similar processes can be used to

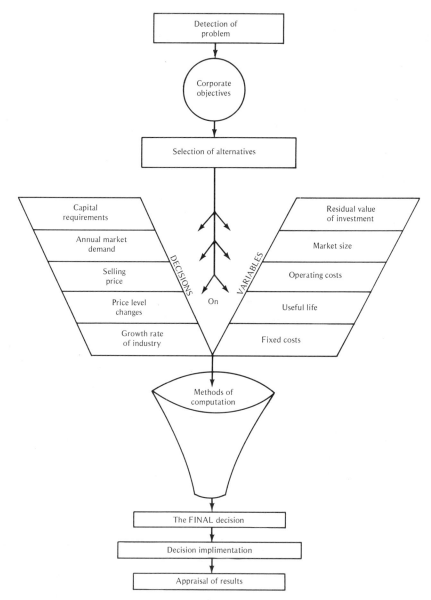

Exhibit 1. The Capital Budgeting Decision Process

determine the expected values of the other variables. From past data, it is assumed that the selling price was found to be dependent upon advertising (A), market share (MS), quality of product (QP), variable costs (VC) and fixed costs (FC). Stated in an analytic solution form, the model of the selling price would be:

$$SP = f \, (A, \, MS, \, QP, \, VC, \, FC).$$

The solution to the problem of determining the expected selling price consists of two parts, (a) determining the values of the independent variables by use of the Monte Carlo process and (b) solving the model for the dependent variable, SP, using the analytic solution.

Monte Carlo and the
Independent Variables

On a per unit basis, this example will assume that one of the independent variables, variable cost, is constant. Expected selling price will be solved on a per unit basis and can then be extended by total demand when the dependent variable, expected market demand, is computed. Another independent variable, fixed cost, is deterministic in nature and will vary only from the influence of market share. Because two of the five variables are deterministic, it will only be necessary to apply Monte Carlo simulation to the remaining three, advertising, market share and quality of product.

Step One
The first step in the Monte Carlo process is to determine a probability distribution for each probabilistic variable. Exhibit 2 shows the probability distributions, formulated from subjective estimates and intuition based on data of prior years, for the variables in question. Advertising was found to be normally distributed with a mean of $300,000 and a standard deviation of $100,000. For all practical purposes, then, the range of advertising expenditures will be between $0 and $600,000. Market share was found also to be normally distributed with a mean of 2,000,000 units and a standard deviation of 500,000 units. In the past, quality of product had been measured according to decimal ratings which could range from .5 to .8. In this particular type of product line, quality was found to be very necessary and the resulting distribution was skewed to the right.

Step Two
The next step is to convert the distributions into cumulative distribution functions. The result of this procedure is illustrated also in Exhibit 2. As was stated earlier, this involves the restatement of the probability distribution in terms of the cumulative frequency of the variable as the range is plotted from left to right.

Step Three
The third step is to select, at random, a sequence of numbers having values with a uniform 0 to 100 distribution. This may be accomplished by using a table of random numbers or a computer subroutine for generating random numbers.

Step Four
The last step is to determine a corresponding sequence of values for the variable of interest from the sequence of random numbers. The figures in

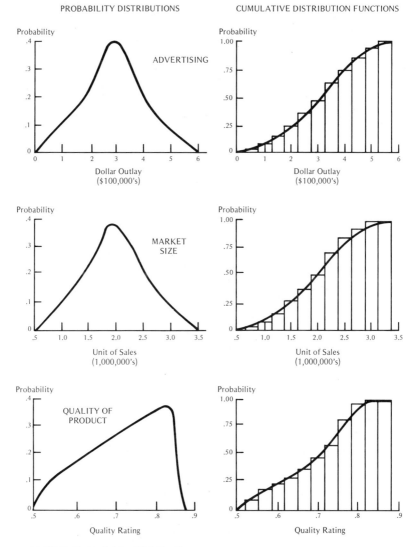

PROBABILITY DISTRIBUTIONS   CUMULATIVE DISTRIBUTION FUNCTIONS

Exhibit 2. Variable Distributions

Exhibit 3 represent a partial simulation for the variable, Advertising. At this point, the Monte Carlo process has generated a series of simulated experiences which should represent possible real-world results.

The Analytic Solution for The Dependent Variable

The general model for the determination of the selling price was:

$$SP = f (A, MS, QP, VC, FC).$$

From the probability distribution for advertising the following probabilities and random number ranges were determined:

P(A)	ADVERTISING EXPENDITURE	RANGE FOR RANDOM NUMBERS
.1	$100,000	00–09
.2	200,000	10–29
.4	300,000	30–69
.2	400,000	70–89
.1	500,000	90–99

Using 10 random numbers for illustrative purposes, the various simulated expenditures would appear as follows:

RANDOM NUMBER**	ADVERTISING EXPENDITURE SIMULATED BY RANDOM NUMBER
15	$200,000
46	300,000
48	300,000
93	500,000
39	300,000
06	100,000
72	400,000
91	500,000
14	200,000
36	300,000

**Taken from a standard random number table. The values for advertising, determined from the random numbers, are each substituted into the equation for SP. A large number of experiments are required before a realistic Expected Value for SP can be generated.

Exhibit 3. Simulation of Advertising Expenditures

Through analysis of past experiences it is possible to refine this function and restate it for one specific company. Assuming that price per unit is a function of the independent variables, the formula may be restated hypothetically as follows:

$$SP = 3.92 \ (A/MS) + 0.375 \ (QP) + VC + (FC/MS).$$

If the independent variables were simulated 2000 times through a sequence of 2000 random numbers, the values generated in each of the 2000 experiments could be substituted into the equation. The result would yield a probability distribution for the dependent variable, selling price. Extending the various probabilities times the computed values for the selling price would yield its expected value.

The value of one of the original ten variables has now been determined. The decision maker has simulated the situation and, in doing so, has reduced significantly the degree of risk and uncertainty inherent in the variable, selling price. The same process should be used for the remaining nine variables. The resulting cash flow figure in the capital budgeting model should resemble closely the actual real-world figure.

CONCLUSION

In David B. Hertz's article, "Risk Analysis in Capital Investment,"[9] he states that the kind of uncertainty that is involved in the estimate of each variable can be evaluated ahead of time through simulation. His case studies have tested this point successfully. Inherent in his process is the Monte Carlo method of simulation.

From the description of the Monte Carlo method, the literature devoted to this area and the illustration of the use of simulation on the capital budgeting model, the following conclusions can be drawn:

1. Simulating a decision model enables the decision maker to gain insight into the interrelationships of the variables and their influence on the final outcome. The areas of uncertainty in the capital budgeting model arise because this type of decision involves new, untested costing, pricing and marketing policies. The decision maker is unsure of the outcome of a model based on variables whose values are structured around intuition and estimation.

2. Monte Carlo simulation has been proven as a reliable testing device for probabilistic decision variables.

3. Simulation through the use of random numbers yields experiences similar to those of the real world. The decision maker no longer has to wait for actual results before appraising his decision. Through simulation and the computer, the appraisal process can be started before the decision is made.

BIBLIOGRAPHY

Books

Burford, Roger L., *Introduction to Finite Probability,* Columbus, Ohio: Charles E. Merrill Books, Inc., 1967.

Emory, C. William and Niland, Powell, *Making Management Decisions,* Boston: Houghton Mifflin Company, 1968.

---

[9]David B. Hertz, "Risk Analysis in Capital Investment," *Harvard Business Review,* January–February 1964, p. 105. [Editors' Note: See the discussion of risk analysis by David B. Hertz, pp. 219–221 (Article 16) in this book.]

Hein, Leonard W., *The Quantitative Approach to Managerial Decisions*, Englewood Cliffs, New Jersey: Prentice-Hall, Inc., 1967.

Hillier, Frederick S. and Lieberman, Gerald J. *Introduction to Operations Research*, San Francisco: Holden-Day, Inc., 1967.

Miller, David W. and Starr, Martin K., *Executive Decisions and Operations Research*, Englewood Cliffs, New Jersey: Prentice-Hall, Inc., 1960.

Simone, Albert J., *Probability: An Introduction With Applications*, Boston: Allyn and Bacon, Inc., 1967.

Thompson, W. W. Jr., *Operations Research Techniques*, Columbus, Ohio: Charles E. Merrill Books, Inc., 1967.

Van Der Veen, B., *Introduction to the Theory of Operational Research*, New York: Springer-Verlag, Inc., 1966.

Williams, Thomas H. and Griffin, Charles H., *The Mathematical Dimension of Accountancy*, Cincinnati, Ohio: South-Western Publishing Company, 1964.

Articles

Belda, Bertrand J., "Operations Research at Work," *NAA Bulletin* (August 1965), 51–55.

Bierman, Harold Jr., "Probability, Statistical Decision Theory, and Accounting," *The Accounting Review* (July 1962), 400–405.

Brodshatzer, Arthur, and Galbraith, Oliver III, "Making Decisions More Rationally—The Application of Monte Carlo," *NAA Bulletin* (August 1963), 33–42.

Hartley, Ronald V., "Operations Research and Its Implications for the Accounting Profession," *The Accounting Review* (April 1968), 321–332.

Hertz, David B., "Risk Analysis in Capital Investment," *Harvard Business Review* (January–February 1964), 95–106.

Hiller, Frederick S., "The Derivation of Probabilistic Information For The Evaluation of Risky Investments," *Management Science* (April 1963), 443–457.

House, William C. Jr., "The Usefulness of Sensitivity Analysis in Capital Investment Decisions," *Management Accounting* (February 1966), 22–29.

Irish, Robert R., "Managerial Use of Operations Research," *NAA Bulletin* (April 1965), 19–24.

Jean, William H., "Operations Research for the Accountant," *Management Accounting* (February 1968), 27–31.

Lorie, James H. and Savage, Leonard J., "Three Problems in Rationing Capital," *The Journal of Business* (October 1955), 229–239.

Magee, John F., "How to Use Decision Trees in Capital Investment," *Harvard Business Review* (September–October 1964), 79–96.

Mood, Alex M., "Diversification of Operations Research," *Operations Research* (March–April 1965), 169–178.

Secrest, Fred G., "From Bookkeeping to Decision Theory," *Management Accounting* (December 1966), 3–9.

Vatter, William J., "The Use of Operations Research in American Companies," *The Accounting Review* (October 1967), 721–730.

18.

STOCHASTIC DECISION TREES FOR THE
ANALYSIS OF INVESTMENT DECISIONS*

Richard F. Hespos
and
Paul A. Strassman

This paper describes an improved method for investment decision making. The method, which is called the stochastic decision tree method, is particularly applicable to investments characterized by high uncertainty and requiring a sequence of related decisions to be made over a period of time. The stochastic decision tree method builds on concepts used in the risk analysis method and the decision tree method of analyzing investments. It permits the use of subjective probability estimates or empirical frequency distributions for some or all factors affecting the decision. This application makes it practicable to evaluate all or nearly all feasible combinations of decisions in the decision tree, taking account of both expected value of return and aversion to risk, thus arriving at an optimal or near optimal set of decisions. Sensitivity analysis of the model can highlight factors that are critical because of high leverage on the measure of performance, or high uncertainty, or both. The method can be applied relatively easily to a wide variety of investment situations, and is ideally suited for computer simulation.

Investment decisions are probably the most important and most difficult decisions that confront top management—for several reasons. First, they involve enormous amounts of money. Investments of U.S. companies in plant and equipment alone are approaching $50 billion a year. Another $50 billion or so goes into acquisition, development of new products, and other investment expenditures.

Second, investment decisions usually have long-lasting effects. They often represent a "bricks and mortar" permanence. Unlike mistakes in inventory decisions, mistakes in investment decisions cannot be worked off in a short period of time. A major investment decision often commits management to a plan of action extending over several years, and the dollar

---

*From *Management Science*, August 1965, pp. B244–B259. Reprinted by permission of the authors and *Management Science*.

penalty for reversing the decision can be high. Third, investments are implements of strategy. They are the tools by which top management controls the direction of a corporation.

Finally, and perhaps most important, investment decisions are characterized by a high degree of uncertainty. They are always based on predictions about the future—often the distant future. And they often require judgmental estimates about future events, such as the consumer acceptance of a new product. For all of these reasons, investment decisions absorb large portions of the time and attention of top management.

Investment decision making has probably benefited more from the development of analytical decision-making methods than any other management area. In the past 10 or 15 years, increasingly sophisticated methods have become available for analyzing investment decisions. Perhaps the most widely known of these new developments are the analytical methods that take into account the time value of money. These include the net present value method, the discounted cash flow method, and variations on these techniques [4, 13]. Complementary to these time-oriented methods, a number of sophisticated accounting techniques have been developed for considering the tax implications of various investment proposals and the effects of investments on cash and capital position [2, 12, 16]. Considerable thought has been given to the proper methods for determining the value of money to a firm, or the cost of capital [12, 13]. The concepts of replacement theory have been applied to investment decisions on machine tools, automobile fleets, and other collections of items that must be replaced from time to time [16].

In a somewhat different direction, techniques have been developed for the selection of securities for portfolios. These techniques endeavor to select the best set of investments from a number of alternatives, each having a known expected return and a known variability [11]. In this context, the "best" selection of investments is that selection that either minimizes risk or variability for a desired level of return, or maximizes return for a specified acceptable level of risk. (In general, of course, it is not possible to minimize risk and maximize return simultaneously.) The application of these techniques to corporate capital budgeting problems is conceivable but not imminent.

In the evolution of these techniques, each advance has served to overcome certain drawbacks or weaknesses inherent in previous techniques. However, until recently, two troublesome aspects of investment decision making were not adequately treated, in a practical sense, by existing techniques. One of these problems was handling the uncertainty that exists in virtually all investment decisions. The other was analyzing separate but related investment decisions that must be made at different points in time.

Two recent and promising innovations in the methodology for analyzing investment decisions now being widely discussed are directed at these two problems. The first of these techniques is commonly known as risk analysis [6, 8]; the second involves a concept known as decision trees [9, 10, 15].

Each of these techniques has strong merits and advantages. Both are beginning to be used by several major corporations.

It is the purpose of this article to suggest and describe a new technique that combines the advantages of both the risk analysis approach and the decision tree approach. The new technique has all of the power of both antecedent techniques, but is actually simpler to use. The technique is called the stochastic decision tree approach.

To understand the stochastic decision tree approach, it is necessary to understand the two techniques from which it was developed. A review of these two techniques follows.

A REVIEW OF RISK ANALYSIS

Risk analysis consists of estimating the probability distribution of each factor affecting an investment decision, and then simulating the possible combinations of the values for each factor to determine the range of possible outcomes and the probability associated with each possible outcome. If the evaluation of an investment decision is based only on a single estimate—the "best guess"—of the value of each factor affecting the outcome, the resulting evaluation will be at best incomplete and possibly wrong. This is true especially when the investment is large and neither clearly attractive nor clearly unattractive. Risk analysis is thus an important advance over the conventional techniques. The additional information it provides can be a great aid in investment decision making.

To illustrate the benefit of the risk analysis technique, Figure 1 shows the results of two analyses of an investment proposal. First, the proposal was analyzed by assigning a single, "best guess" value to each factor. The second analysis used an estimate of the probability distribution associated with each factor and a simulation to determine the probability distribution of the possible outcomes.

The best-guess analysis indicates a net present value of $1,130,000, whereas the risk analysis shows that the most likely combination of events gives the project an expected net present value of only $252,000. The conventional technique fails to take into account the skewed distributions of the various factors, the interactions between the factors, and is influenced by the subjective aspects of best guesses. Furthermore, the conventional analysis gives no indication that this investment has a 48 percent chance of losing money. Knowledge of this fact could greatly affect the decision made on this proposal, particularly if the investor is conservative and has less risky alternatives available.

The risk analysis technique can also be used for a sensitivity analysis. The purpose of a sensitivity analysis is to determine the influence of each factor on the outcome, and thus to identify the factors most critical in the investment decision because of their high leverage, high uncertainty, or both. In a sensitivity analysis, equally likely variations in the values of each

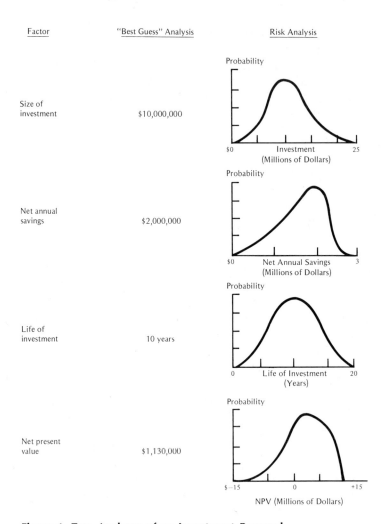

Figure 1. Two Analyses of an Investment Proposal

factor are made systematically to determine their effect on the outcome, or net present value. Figure 2 shows the effect of individually varying each input factor (several of which are components of the net cash inflow).

This analysis indicates that manufacturing cost is a highly critical factor, both in leverage and uncertainty. Knowing this, management may concentrate its efforts on reducing manufacturing costs or at least reducing the uncertainty in these costs.

Risk analysis is rapidly becoming an established technique in American industry. Several large corporations are now using various forms of the technique as a regular part of their investment analysis procedure [1, 3, 7, 17, 18]. A backlog of experience is being built up on the use cf the technique, and advances in the state of the art are continually being made

AN UNFAVORABLE CHANGE OF 10 PERCENTILES FROM THE MEAN VALUE IN THIS FACTOR	WHICH CORRESPONDS TO A PERCENTAGE CHANGE OF	WOULD REDUCE NPV BY
Annual net cash flow		
Sales level	12	17
Selling price	10	21
Manufacturing cost	18	58
Fixed cost	4	6
Amount of investment	5	12
Life of investment	12	30

Figure 2. Use of Sensitivity Analysis to Highlight Critical Factors

by users. For example, methods have been devised for representing complex interrelationships among factors. Improvements are also being made in the methods of gathering subjective probability estimates, and better methods are being devised for performing sensitivity analysis.

One aspect of investment decisions still eludes the capabilities of this technique. This is the problem of sequential decision making—that is, the analysis of a number of highly interrelated investment decisions occurring at different points in time. Until now no extension of risk analysis has been developed that can handle this problem well.

A REVIEW OF DECISION TREES

The decision tree approach, a technique very similar to dynamic programming, is a convenient method for representing and analyzing a series of investment decisions to be made over time (see Figure 3). Each decision point is represented by a numbered square at a fork or node in the decision tree. Each branch extending from a fork represents one of the alternatives that can be chosen at this decision point. At the first decision point the two alternatives in the example shown in Figure 3 are "introduce product nationally" and "introduce product regionally." (It is assumed at this point that the decision has already been made to introduce the product in *some* way.)

In addition to representing management decision points, decision trees represent chance events. The forks in the tree where chance events influence the outcome are indicated by circles. The chance event forks or nodes in the example represent the various levels of demand that may appear for the product.

A node representing a chance event generally has a probability associated with each of the branches emanating from that node. This probability is the likelihood that the chance event will assume the value assigned to

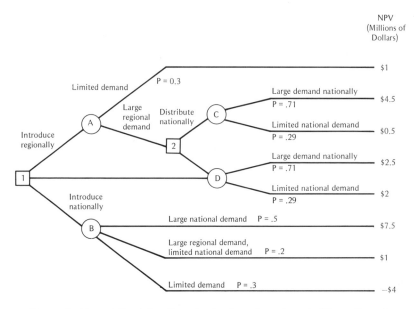

Figure 3. Use of Decision Tree to Analyze Investment Alternatives for Introduction of a New Product

the particular branch. The total of such probabilities leading from a node must equal 1. In our example, the probability of achieving a large demand in the regional introduction of the product is 0.7, shown at the branch leading from node A. Each combination of decisions and chance events has some outcome (in this case, net present value, or NPV) associated with it.

The optimal sequence of decisions in a decision tree is found by starting at the right-hand side and "rolling backward." At each node, an expected NPV must be calculated. If the node is a chance event node, the expected NPV is calculated for *all* of the branches emanating from that node. If the node is a decision point, the expected NPV is calculated for *each* branch emanating from that node, and the highest is selected. In either case, the expected NPV of that node is carried back to the next chance event or decision point by multiplying it by the probabilities associated with branches that it travels over.

Thus, in Figure 3 the *expected* NPV of all branches emanating from chance event node C is $3.05 million ($4.5 × .71 + $–0.5 × .29). Similarly, the expected NPV at node D is $2.355 million. Now "rolling back" to the next node—decision point 2—it can be seen that the alternative with the highest NPV is "distribute nationally," with an NPV of $3.05 million. This means that, if the decision maker is ever confronted with the decision at node 2, he will choose to distribute nationally, and will expect an NPV of $3.05 million. In all further analysis he can ignore the other decision branch emanating from node 2 and all nodes and branches that it may lead to.

To perform further analysis, it is now necessary to carry this NPV backward in the tree. The branches emanating from chance event node A have an overall expected NPV of $2.435 million ($1 × 0.3 + $3.05 × 0.7). Similarly, the expected NPV at node B is 2.75 million. These computations, summarized in Figure 4, show that the alternative that maximizes expected NPV of the entire decision tree is "introduce nationally" at decision point 1. (Note that in this particular case there are no subsequent decisions to be made.)

One drawback of the decision tree approach is that computations can quickly become unwieldy. The number of end points on the decision tree increases very rapidly as the number of decision points or chance events increases. To make this approach practical, it is necessary to limit the number of branches emanating from chance event nodes to a very small number. This means that the probability distribution of chance events at each node must be represented by a very few point estimates.

As a result, the answers obtained from a decision tree analysis are often inadequate. The single answer obtained (say, net present value) is usually close to the expectation of the probability distribution of all possible NPVs. However, it may vary somewhat from the expected NPV, depending on how the point estimates were selected from the underlying distributions and on the sensitivity of the NPV to this selection process. Furthermore, the decision tree approach gives no information on the range of possible outcomes from the investment or the probabilities associated with those outcomes. This can be a serious drawback.

In the example in Figures 3 and 4, the decision tree approach indicated that introducing the product nationally at once would be the optimal strategy for maximizing expected NPV. However, the NPV of $2.75 million is simply the mean of three possible values of NPV, which are themselves representative of an entire range of possible values, as shown in Figure 5a. Comparing the range of NPVs possible under each possible set of decisions shows a vastly different view of the outcome (see Figure 5, b and c).

Alternative	Chance Event	Probability of Chance Event	Net Present Value	Expected NPV
Introduce product nationally	Large national demand	.5	$ 7.5	
	Large regional, limited national demand	.2	1.0	$2.75
	Limited demand	.3	−4.0	
Introduce product regionally *(and distribute nationally if regional demand is large)*	Large national demand	.5	4.5	
	Large regional, limited national demand	.2	−0.5	2.44
	Limited demand	.3	1.0	
Introduce product regionally *(and do not distribute nationally)*	Large national demand	.5	2.5	
	Large regional, limited national demand	.2	2.0	1.95
	Limited demand	.3	1.0	

Figure 4. Net Present Value of Investment Alternatives for Introduction of a New Product

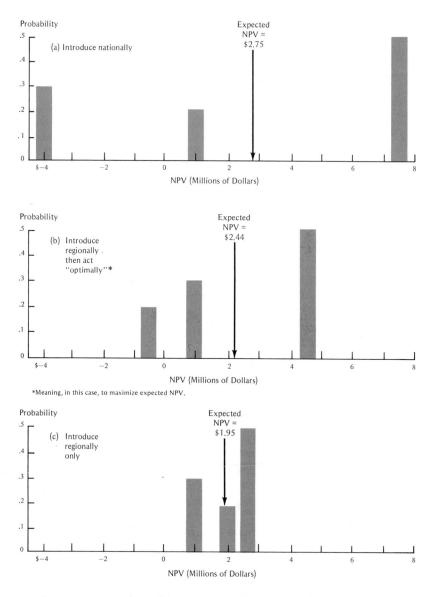

Figure 5. Range of Possible Outcomes for Each of Three Alternatives

Although the first alternative has the highest expected NPV, a rational manager could easily prefer one of the other two. The choice would depend on the utility function or the aversion to risk of the manager or his organization. A manager with a linear utility function would choose the first alternative, as shown in Figure 6a. However, it is probably true that *most* managers would *not* choose the first alternative because of the high chance of loss, and the higher utility value that they would assign to a loss, as

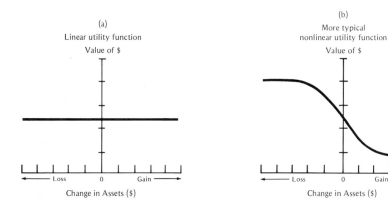

Figure 6. Examples of Utility Functions

shown in Figure 6b. This conservatism in management is, to a large extent, the result of the system of rewards and punishments that exists in many large corporations today. Whether it is good or bad is a complex question, not discussed here.

In spite of these shortcomings, the decision tree approach is a very useful analytical tool. It is particularly useful for conceptualizing investment planning and for controlling and monitoring an investment that stretches out over time. For these reasons, the decision tree approach has been, and will continue to be an important tool for the analysis of investment decisions.

COMBINING THESE APPROACHES: STOCHASTIC DECISION TREES

The complementary advantages and disadvantages of risk analysis and decision trees suggest that a new technique might be developed that would combine the good points of each and eliminate the disadvantages. The concept of stochastic decision trees, introduced in the remainder of this article, is intended to be such a combination.

The stochastic decision tree approach is similar to the conventional decision tree approach, except that it also has the following features:

>   All quantities and factors, including chance events, can be represented by continuous, empirical probability distributions.
>   The information about the results from any or all possible combinations of decisions made at sequential points in time can be obtained in a probabilistic form.

The probability distribution of possible results from any particular combination of decisions can be analyzed using the concepts of utility and risk.

A discussion of each of these features follows.

Replacement of Chance Event Nodes by Probability Distributions

The inclusion of probability distributions for the values associated with chance events is analogous to adding an arbitrarily large number of branches at each chance event node. In a conventional decision tree, the addition of a large number of branches can serve to represent any empirical probability distribution. Thus in the previous example, chance event node B can be made to approximate more closely the desired continuous probability distribution by increasing the number of branches, as shown in Figure 7, a and b. However, this approach makes the tree very complex, and computation very quickly becomes burdensome or impractical. Therefore, two or three branches are usually used as a coarse approximation of the actual continuous probability distribution.

Since the stochastic decision tree is to be based on simulation, it is not necessary to add a great many branches at the chance event nodes. In fact, it is possible to reduce the number of branches at the chance event nodes to one (see Figure 7, c). Thus, in effect, the chance event node can be *elimi-nated*. Instead, at the point where the chance event node occurred, a random selection is made on each iteration from the appropriate probabilistic economic model such as the break-even chart shown in Figure 8 and the value selected is used to calculate the NPV for that particular iteration. The

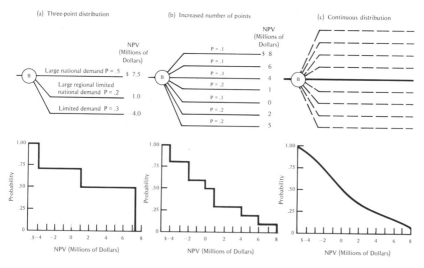

Figure 7. Probability Distributions at Chance Event Nodes

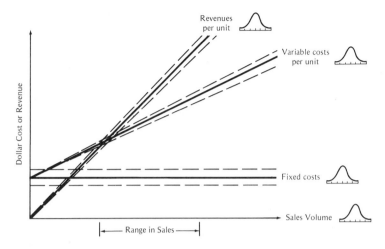

Figure 8. Typical Probabilistic Economic Model Used to Select Values of Factors at Chance Event Nodes

single branch emanating from this simplified node then extends onward to the next management decision point, or to the end of the tree. This results in a drastic streamlining of the decision tree as illustrated in Figure 9.

Replacement of all Specific Values by Probability Distributions

In a conventional decision tree, factors such as the size of the investment in a new plant facility are often assigned specific values. Usually these values are expressed as single numbers, even though these numbers are often not known with certainty.

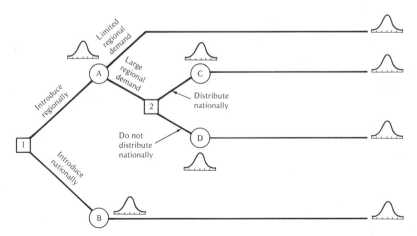

Figure 9. Simplified Decision Tree

If the values of these factors could be represented instead by probability distributions, the degree of uncertainty characterizing each value could be expressed. The stochastic decision tree approach makes it possible to do this. Since the approach is basically a simulation, any or all specific values in the investment analysis can be represented by probability distributions. On each iteration in the simulation, a value for each factor is randomly selected from the appropriate frequency distribution and used in the computation. Thus, in the example, NPV can be calculated from not only empirical distributions of demand, but also probabilistic estimates of investment, cost, price, and other factors.

Evaluating all Possible
Combinations of Decisions

Since this stochastic decision tree approach greatly simplifies the structure of the decision tree, it is often possible to evaluate by complete enumeration all of the possible paths through the tree. For example, if there are five sequential decisions in an analysis and each decision offers two alternatives, there are at most 32 possible paths through the decision tree. This number of paths is quite manageable computationally. And since most decision points are two-sided ("build" or "don't build," for example), or at worst have a very small number of alternatives, it is often feasible and convenient to evaluate all possible paths through a decision tree when the stochastic decision tree approach is used.

Why is it sometimes desirable to evaluate all possible paths through a decision tree? As the inquiry into the risk analysis approach showed, decisions cannot always be made correctly solely on the basis of a single expected value for each factor. The roll-back technique of the conventional decision tree necessarily deals only with expected values. It evaluates decisions (more exactly, sets of decisions) by comparing their expectations and selects the largest as the best, in all cases.

However, the stochastic decision tree approach produces *probabilistic* results for each possible set of decisions. These probability distributions, associated with each possible path through the decision tree, can be compared on the basis of their expectations alone, if this is considered to be sufficient. But alternative sets of decisions can *also* be evaluated by comparing the probability distributions associated with each set of decisions, in a manner exactly analogous to risk analysis. (The details of this technique are discussed in the next section.) Thus, the stochastic decision tree approach makes it possible to evaluate a series of interrelated decisions spread over time by the same kinds of risk and uncertainty criteria that one would use in a conventional risk analysis.

In a large decision tree problem, even with the simplifications afforded by the stochastic decision tree approach, complete enumeration of all possible paths through the tree could become computationally impractical, or the comparison of the probability distributions associated with all possible paths might be too laborious and costly.

In such a case, two simplifications are possible. First, a *modified* version of the roll-back technique might be used. This modified roll-back would take account of the probabilistic nature of the information being handled. Branches of the tree would be eliminated on the basis of dominance rather than simply expected value [7]. For example, a branch could be eliminated if it had both a lower expected return and a higher variance than an alternative branch. A number of possible sets of decisions could be eliminated this way without being completely evaluated, leaving an efficient set of decision sequences to evaluate in more detail.

Computation could also be reduced by making decision rules before the simulation, such that if, on any iteration, the value of a chance event exceeds some criterion, the resulting decision would not be considered at all. This has been done in the example shown in Figure 3. If a limited demand appears at node A, national introduction of the product will not be evaluated. In the simulation, if demand were below some specified value, the simulation would not proceed to the decision point 2. This technique only saves computation effort—it does not simplify the structure of the tree, and if the criterion is chosen properly, it will not affect the final outcome.

Recording Results in the Form of Probability Distributions

It has already been shown that probability distributions are more useful than single numbers as measures of the value of a particular set of decisions. The simulation approach to the analysis permits one to get these probability distributions relatively easily. It is true that the method smacks of brute force. However, the brute force required is entirely on the part of the computer and not at all on the part of the analyst.

The technique is simply this: On each iteration or path through the decision tree, when the computer encounters a binary decision point node, it is instructed to "split itself in two" and perform the appropriate calculations along *both* branches of the tree emanating from the decision node. (The same logic applies to a node with three or more branches emanating from it.) Thus, when the computer completes a single iteration, an NPV will have been calculated for each possible path through the decision tree. These NPVs are accumulated in separate probability distributions. This simulation concept is illustrated in Figure 10.

At the completion of a suitable number of iterations, there will be a probability distribution of the NPV associated with each set of decisions that it is possible to make in passing through the tree. These different sets of decisions can then be compared, one against the other, in the usual risk analysis matter, as if they were alternative investment decisions (which in

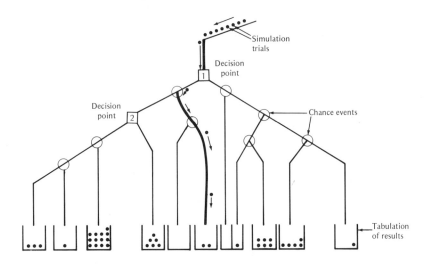

Figure 10. The GPSS Concept of Decision Trees with Risk Simulation

fact they are). That is, they can be compared by taking into account not only the expected return, but also the shape of each probability distribution and the effects of utility and risk. On the basis of this, one can select the single best set of decisions, or a small number of possibly acceptable sets. These sets of sequential decisions can then be evaluated and a decision whether or not to undertake the investment can be made by comparing it to alternative investments elsewhere in the corporation or against alternative uses for the money.

An Example

To illustrate the kinds of results that can be expected from a stochastic decision tree analysis, the new product introduction problem described earlier has been solved using this method. The results are shown in Figure 11.

The differences in the expected values of the outcomes can now be seen in proper perspective, since the results show the relationship of the expected values to the entire distribution of possible outcomes. Moreover, the expected values of these distributions will not necessarily be identical with expectations resulting from the conventional decision tree approach, because:

1. The interdependencies among the variables were not accounted for by the conventional approach.

2. The small number of point estimates used to approximate an entire distribution under the conventional approach did not utilize all the available information.

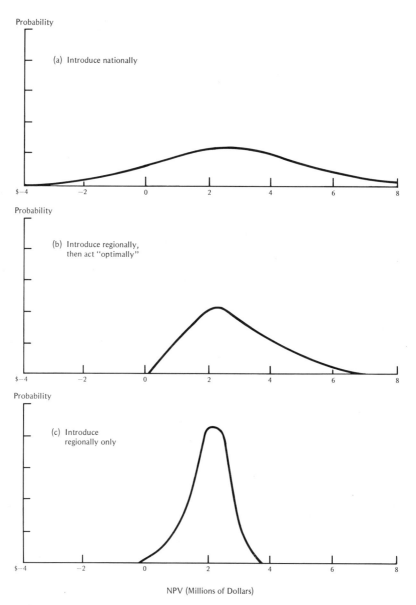

Figure 11. Results of Stochastic Decision Tree Analysis

With the three alternatives presented in this form, it is easier to understand why a rational manager might choose an alternative other than the one with the highest expected value. Presented with the full range of possible outcomes related to each alternative, he can select that alternative most consistent with his personal utility and willingness to take risk.

USING THE STOCHASTIC DECISION TREE APPROACH

Stochastic decision trees described here combine the best features of both risk analysis and conventional decision trees and are actually simpler to construct and use than either of these. The steps for collecting data and conceptualizing the problem are the same for the stochastic decision tree approach as they are for the risk analysis approach. These steps are:

1. Gather subjective probability estimates of the appropriate factors affecting the investment.

2. Define and describe any significant interdependencies among factors.

3. Specify the probable timing of future sequential investment decisions to be made.

4. Specify the model to be used to evaluate the investment.

The stochastic decision tree approach is ideally suited to the computer language known as General Purpose Systems Simulator (GPSS) [5, 14]. Although the language is not now capable of handling very complex interdependencies without certain modifications, it permits the solution of a very wide range of investment problems.

The structuring and solving of several sample problems have indicated that the stochastic decision tree approach is both easy to use and useful. The example in Figures 4, 5 and 6 shows emphatically how the stochastic decision tree approach can detect and display the probable outcomes of an investment strategy that would be deemed optimal by the conventional decision tree approach, but that many managements would definitely regard as undesirable. Other work is being done on both sample problems and real world problems, and on the development and standardization (to a limited extent) of the computer programs for performing this analysis.

SUMMARY

The stochastic decision tree approach to analyzing investment decisions is an evolutionary improvement over previous methods of analyzing investments. It combines the advantages of several earlier approaches, eliminates several disadvantages, and is easier to apply.

REFERENCES

1. Anderson, S. L. and Haight, H. G., "A Two-by-Two Decision Problem," *Chemical Engineering Progress*, Vol. 57, No. 5, May 1961.

2. Anthony, Robert N. (Editor), *Papers on Return on Investment,* Harvard Business School, Boston, 1959.

3. "Chance Factors Meaning and Use," Atlantic Refining Company, Producing Department, July 1962.

4. Dean, Joel, *Capital Budgeting,* New York: Columbia University Press, 1951.

5. Gordon, G., "A General Purpose Systems Simulator," *IBM Systems Journal,* Vol. I, September 1962.

6. Hertz, David B., "Risk Analysis in Capital Investment," *Harvard Business Review,* January–February 1964.

7. Hess, Sidney W. and Quigley, Harry A., "Analysis of Risk in Investments Using Monte Carlo Technique," Chemical Engineering Progress Symposium Series No. 42, Vol. 59.

8. Hillier, Frederick S., Stanford University, "The Derivation of Probabilistic Information for the Evaluation of Risky Investments," *Management Science,* April 1963.

9. Magee, John F., "Decision Trees for Decision Making," *Harvard Business Review,* July–August 1964.

10. Magee, John F., "How to Use Decision Trees in Capital Investment," *Harvard Business Review,* September–October 1964.

11. Markowitz, Harry, *Portfolio Selection, Efficient Diversification of Investments,* New York: John Wiley and Sons, 1959.

12. Masse, Pierre, *Optimal Investment Decisions,* Prentice-Hall, 1962.

13. McLean, John G., "How to Evaluate New Capital Investments," *Harvard Business Review,* November–December 1958.

14. Reference Manual General Purpose Systems Simulator II, IBM, 1963.

15. Schlaifer, Robert, *Probability and Statistics for Business Decisions,* McGraw-Hill, 1959.

16. Terborgh, George, *Business Investment Policy,* Machinery and Allied Products Institute, Washington, D.C., 1958.

17. Thorne, H. C. and Wise, D. C., American Oil Company, "Computers in Economic Evaluation," *Chemical Engineering,* April 29, 1963.

18. "Venture Analysis," Chemical Engineering Progress Technical Manual, American Institute of Chemical Engineers.

FOUR
Forecasting

DETERMINING COST BEHAVIOR PATTERNS FOR
PLANNING AND DECISION MAKING

SALES VOLUME FORECASTING

COST ESTIMATION

The articles in Part IV are concerned with techniques that can be used to determine fixed and variable elements of cost (necessary for such purposes as alternative decision problems where variable cost elements can be relevant, flexible budgeting, breakeven analysis, linear programming problems where contribution margins of sales minus variable cost can be relevant information) and/or to develop forecasted costs and sales so that this information can be used in budgeting and decision making.

Forecasting techniques may be classified along the following lines:[1]

1. *Extrapolation techniques.* These procedures utilize past changes in only the *variable of interest* as a basis for future projection of that variable; as such the only "independent" variable is time. Illustrations of extrapolation techniques are various types of naive models, time-series decomposition and exponential smoothing.

2. *Correlation techniques.* These procedures utilize past relationships between the variable to be forecasted and *other* variables (e.g., disposable income, customer inventory levels) which are thought to be related to the variable being forecasted. The forecast problem thus involves two major tasks: (a) quantifying the past relationship between the dependent variable and the so-called "independent" variables, and (b) forecasting values of the independent variables as a necessary step before making a forecast of the dependent variable. In so-called "lead-lag" models, the forecaster may be able to identify a fairly long and stable leading series early enough to forecast the lagged variable (without first forecasting the leading variable). If so, uncertainty still surrounds the stability of the functional relationship which links the two variables together.

3. *Econometric techniques.* These procedures are usually expressed as being "less empirical" than correlative models in the sense that they are based upon some *underlying theory* about the relationships that exist among a set of economic variables. A set of equations may be stated which reflect how the phenomena should be interrelated (if the theory holds), and parameters of the models are estimated by statistical analysis of past data.

4. *Polling techniques.* Although all forecasting involves judgment, polling techniques are probably the least "formal" of the procedures enumerated above. As the name suggests, various executives are polled with regard to the sales outlook, and these opinions may be "averaged" or combined in some manner as to reflect the opinions of company personnel closest to the market situation. Although this

[1]Paul E. Green and Donald S. Tull, *Research for Marketing Decisions*, 2nd ed. © 1970, pp. 550–551. Reprinted by permission of Prentice-Hall, Inc., Englewood Cliffs, New Jersey. A background discussion about these techniques is included in an article by Richard J. Tersine, "Forecasting: Prelude to Managerial Planning," *Managerial Planning*, July/August 1975, pp. 11–17, 23.

procedure is looked upon as less "scientific" than other techniques, it might more fairly be called *less explicit* in the sense that the process by which executives make judgments from a variety of source data and experience is not understood. These procedures, however, may lead to fairly accurate forecasts and can serve as an independent check on the "reasonableness" of forecasts derived from more explicit models.

As listed above, extrapolation techniques include time-series decomposition (trend, cyclical, and seasonal analysis where a dependent variable, sales, is a function of the independent variable, time, such as a year), naive models where the value for the most recent period is used as a forecast for the next period, and exponential smoothing. Article 19, "Forecasting in the Short Term," includes a discussion of the extrapolation techniques of moving averages and exponential smoothing. An editors' note following problem IV-Q7 shows how least-squares regression analysis (a correlation technique) can be adapted for use in a time-series problem about sales forecasting.[2]

Article 20 discusses correlation techniques. Provided there is a linear relationship between cost and volume, correlation techniques, such as the scatter diagram and the least-squares method, can be used to fit a straight line to observed values of cost and volume in order to separate cost into fixed and variable elements and to develop an equation that may be used to predict or forecast a value for cost—the dependent variable. Sales can be forecast using the least-squares method when the sales are determined as a function of only one independent variable.

Using the least-squares method, an equation is developed for the relationship between two related variables (a dependent and an independent variable), and the equation can be used to predict the value for the dependent variable provided the analyst knows the value for the independent variable.

The equation for a straight line is $Y = a + bX$. If a mixed cost (a cost with fixed and variable elements) is being predicted by using an equation developed from past data, then Y represents total cost, a can represent fixed cost, b, the increase in cost per unit increase in volume, and X might represent units or dollars of volume. Once the values of a and b are determined, then it is possible to determine the calculated value of Y from $Yc = a + bX$. The Yc is used for the predicting equation in order to distinguish between a calculated Y and observed values of Y from the past data we are using to find the values of a and b. The least-squares method allows us to calculate a and b mathematically.

[2] An article by Tim Coldicott, "Forecasting in the Long Term," *Accountancy*, October 1973, pp. 23–32 includes a discussion of the extrapolation technique of time series. The article discusses curve fitting and provides important complementary information for the application of the statistical methods of simple and multiple regression discussed in this section of the book.

The values of a and b in the equation $Y = a + bX$ can be calculated by solving the two simultaneous equations below. Note that Σ = sum and n = number of observations.

$$(1) \quad \Sigma Y = na + b\,(\Sigma X)$$
$$(2) \quad \Sigma XY = a\,(\Sigma X) + b\,(\Sigma X^2)$$

Also, the following can be used to calculate the values of a and b:

$$b = \frac{n\,(\Sigma XY) - (\Sigma X)\,(\Sigma Y)}{n\,(\Sigma X^2) - (\Sigma X)^2}$$

$$a = \frac{(\Sigma Y)\,(\Sigma X^2) - (\Sigma X)\,(\Sigma XY)}{n\,(\Sigma X^2) - (\Sigma X)^2}$$

A simpler formula for the value of a can be used if the value of b has been determined. It is

$$a = \frac{\Sigma Y}{n} - \frac{b\,(\Sigma X)}{n}$$

The discussion of simple regression analysis in Article 20 shows the use of the formula for b and the simplified formula for a.

Article 20 states that the coefficient of correlation (a measure of the closeness with which two or more variables are associated), may be determined as the square root of the coefficient of determination. The sign (i.e., + or –) used for the coefficient of correlation would be the sign from b in the regression equation. The article shows how to calculate and interpret the coefficient of determination (r^2 or d), but does not show how to calculate or interpret the coefficient of correlation. If the coefficient of correlation (r) is ± 1, the correlation of the dependent and independent variables is perfect, and if it is zero, there is no correlation. A positive correlation means that as the independent variable increases, the dependent variable increases, and the function results in a line that slopes upward to the right. Conversely, a negative correlation means the dependent variable decreases as the independent variable increases. The coefficient of correlation can be calculated as:

$$r = \frac{n\,\Sigma XY - (\Sigma X)\,(\Sigma Y)}{\sqrt{[n\,\Sigma X^2 - (\Sigma X)^2]\,[n\,\Sigma Y^2 - (\Sigma Y)^2]}}$$

The coefficient of determination (r^2) explains the proportion of the variance in the dependent variable (direct manufacturing cost of the case problem in Article 20) which is associated with the independent variable (sales volume in the problem). In addition to the formula given in Article 20 for calculating r^2 or d, it can be determined as:

$$1 - \frac{\text{Unexplained Variance}}{\text{Total Variance}} \quad \text{or} \quad 1 - \frac{\Sigma(Y - Y_c)^2}{\Sigma(Y - \overline{Y})^2}$$

In addition to the formula given in Article 20 for calculating the standard error of estimate, a simpler formula to use for calculating the measure is

$$s_{Y.X} = \sqrt{\frac{\Sigma Y^2 - a \Sigma Y - b \Sigma XY}{n - m}}$$

The formula can be used where the regression analysis is based on sample data and the regression line is fitted by the method of least squares. In the denominator, m = the number of constants (2). This simplified formula does not require the calculation of Yc values for the paired observations (see page 293); the calculations using the Article 20 formula become more tedious as the number of paired observations increases.

However, a computer program can be used to calculate the a and b values, r, r^2, and standard error of the estimate, etc.; the user of the program does not have to make the tedious calculations involved for a problem such as presented in Article 20. The program user needs to obtain the problem observations, enter them into a computer in the manner prescribed by the program instructions, understand the use of the a and b values and the measures r, r^2, standard error of estimate, and needs to be able to interpret the computer printout for the particular program used to calculate the various values.

In discussing correlation and regression analysis, Spurr and Bonini state:

> The statistical tools of correlation and regression analysis were developed to estimate the closeness with which two or more variables were associated and the average amount of change in one variable that was associated with a unit increase in the value of another variable. The term "regression" refers specifically to the measurement of this relationship. The more general term "correlation" includes regression analysis as well as certain other measures, such as the correlation coefficient.[3]

Multiple regression analysis may be used where management is aware of the presence of more than one independent variable that affects the dependent variable, or where tests of the simple regression equation (coefficient of correlation, coefficient of determination) indicate that only a portion of the dependent variable is determined by one independent variable; the remaining portion must be associated with other relevant factors or represent random variations. The availability of a computer makes it practicable to use multiple regression analysis where many independent variables are involved.

Article 20, "The Limitations of Profit Graphs, Breakeven Analysis and Budgets," begins with a discussion of the profit graph and the underlying

---

[3] William A. Spurr and Charles P. Bonini, *Statistical Analysis for Business Decisions* (Homewood, Ill.: Richard D. Irwin, Inc., 1967), p. 551. Also see, Lee Smith, Ralph W. Estes, and Thomas C. Committee "A Warning on Misuse of Linear Regression," *Managerial Planning*, January/February 1974, pp. 29–34.

assumptions for the graph; then the scatter diagram is discussed. The major emphasis of the article is on correlation analysis. The article applies the least-squares method of simple regression analysis to a firm's data, includes a computer printout for the problem, and emphasizes the importance of multiple regression analysis. The article includes tests to determine if there is a definite relationship between the dependent and independent variables (t test and F test) and contains additional important information about an equation such as the coefficient of determination and the standard error of estimate. The title of the article originally was chosen because the discussion emphasizes as a possible weakness or limitation of breakeven analysis and profit graphs the showing of a dependent variable (cost) as simply a function of one independent variable (some measure of volume). The essential weakness of simple regression analysis and a possible limitation of breakeven analysis and profit graphs is that the dependent variable is often materially affected by more than one independent variable, and therefore multiple regression analysis is important.

An editors' note following problem IV-Q5 expands the discussion in Article 20 on the determination and use of t-values (t-values help analysts determine confidence in the value of the regression coefficient (b) as a predictor), and shows the development of confidence intervals for the regression coefficient. A confidence interval can be used to express the amount of sampling error in the sample statistics chosen from a population, and the editors' note shows the use of the standard error of the b regression coefficient and an appropriate t-value to determine a 95 percent confidence interval. For a 95 percent confidence interval, we can state that the true B of the entire population is within the interval or range with a probability of 0.95 that this is correct.

Article 21, "How to Get a Better Forecast," applies multiple regression analysis for the purpose of forecasting sales. The article presents important requirements that should be met before the analysis is performed. For example, some of the factors chosen by management as independent variables may be correlated. This is the problem of multicollinearity, and means that certain variables are not independent but move together in the same direction and at the same approximate rate. This and other problems for applying the method are emphasized in the article.

A manager can use the computer to develop multiple regression equations for the purpose of forecasting. A computer program can be used that allows variables to be selected in a series of steps and in the order of their importance for the equation to explain the dependent variable. A stepwise multiple regression program is used in determining whether or not additional independent variables are needed and which variables are especially relevant for inclusion in an equation. Article 22, "Stepwise Multiple Regression in Planning Simulations and Forecasting," shows the application of this important tool that can be used in sales forecasting and cost estimation. The discussion includes an explanation of the development and use of the sales function for a computer simulation problem.[4]

Article 23, "Effects of Learning on Cost Projections," is a comprehensive article about the mathematical aspects of learning-curve application to cost projections. Some industries fall into a category between those that produce a single item to meet a customer's order and those that mass-produce a product. For the industries that fall between single-item production to special order and mass production—the aircraft industry, for example—the result has been that there is a *learning effect* and improvement in productivity of labor when the job or activity is repeated.

The learning curve can be applicable during initial stages of production such as the start-up phase of the production process for a product. If a product is produced over and over again for a long enough time, as is the case for mass-produced goods, eventually, no more increases in productivity will result and standard costs for the product can be established. But for products where "relatively small numbers of very complicated items" are produced, the learning-curve model is useful for labor cost projection purposes and for the control of direct labor.[5]

Learning curves may be applied for determining initial estimates of labor hours for a proposed order, for scheduling men and machines, for determining labor efficiency, etc. An overall or composite learning curve may need to be broken down into detailed curves, such as curves for the specific type of production work performed. Management could use learning curves for many specific activities involved in a project. Separate curves may be used for control once a contract has been received, while a combined or overall curve may be used for an original estimate.[6]

The learning curve provides a reducing standard or benchmark for labor hours as production increases, and is in line with the realities of production for certain types of manufacturing activity. The basis for the application of the learning curve can be stated as: "Every time you double the quantity, the unit hours will be reduced by a fixed percentage." For example, with an 80 percent learning curve as cumulative production is doubled, the average per unit time for all the units produced is reduced by 20 percent.

---

[4]Managers may use a computer simulation in planning for a coming period. A detailed set of equations or model (see the discussion under econometric techniques at the beginning of this introduction for Part IV) is developed for a specific business environment. Using a simulation model with a computer enables managers to try alternative decisions and to predict results prior to actually making a decision. See James C. T. Mao, "Essentials of Computer Simulation," *Financial Executive*, October 1967, pp. 55–62; and R. C. Raymond, "Use of the Time-Sharing Computer in Business Planning and Budgeting," *Management Science*, April 1966, pp. B-363–B-381. The latter article includes mathematical equations for a planning problem and shows the preparation of a computer program in BASIC for use in obtaining problem solutions.

[5]See Marvin L. Taylor, "The Learning Curve—A Basic Cost Projection Tool," *NAA Bulletin*, February 1961, pp. 21–26.

[6]See Rolfe Wyer, "Learning Curve Techniques for Direct Labor Management," *NAA Bulletin*, July 1958, Section 2.

For cost estimation purposes, the learning curve may be applicable, not only to direct labor, but to labor-associated costs; for example, where variable overhead can be determined as a function of direct labor hours. It should be noted that for manufacturing activities where the learning curve can be applied, the average time per unit decreases as production quantities are doubled, and that in this context the average time refers to the cumulative average time per unit (i.e., the average time for each unit of the total quantity of units produced); it does not refer to the quantities produced in particular lots.

19.
FORECASTING IN THE SHORT TERM*

Peter Dohrn

We often have to make decisions with uncertain knowledge of the future. Investing in plant for new products or expansion, ordering raw materials for production in three month's time, providing for cash to fund next year's sales are some of these decisions. Whenever there is a long interval between making a decision and seeing its effects, the decision maker will forecast.

In practice, we classify the methods of forecasting according to the time over which the forecast has to be made. For convenience, "short term" and "long term" are usually taken to be the categories.

Short-term forecasts are made for tactical reasons and usually cover less than a year. They do not normally involve a change in fixed assets. Historical information is the main ingredient. Sales forecasts which are used as a basis for ordering materials and for production and inventory control are the most important examples. From the accountant's point of view, short-term forecasting is associated with revenue forecasts and provision of working capital and cash.

Nearly all forecasts made beyond the period of one year would be termed long-term forecasts, with most being made with a time limit of five years, but some extending up to 50 or more. They are made for strategic reasons, including investment in plant or other changes in fixed assets and resources. Because the time span is longer, purely historical information is less relevant, and often it is not available at all.

In this article, some techniques and problems of applying short-term sales forecasts in practice will be described.

---

*From *Accountancy*, July 1973, pp. 15–17. Reprinted by permission of the author and the editor.

Short-term sales forecasts rely heavily on past history and in many cases are based on it entirely. The methods used depend on averages and curve fitting to smooth the past demand, and projecting the results over the desired period into the future. Trends and seasonal effects can be included if desired.

The method to be adopted will depend on the purpose of the forecast, the sales pattern so far exhibited by the product, and the amount which management is willing to spend to reduce uncertainty. If the purpose of the forecast is to decide quantities of raw materials to be bought for use in food manufacture, the method might include an allowance for seasonal demand.

If forecasts used to decide stock levels are inaccurate, high levels of safety stock are required. If a forecast is being used to decide finished stock levels of expensive consumer goods, it will be worth going to some trouble and expense to improve the precision of the results to keep stocks as low as possible.

Some of the main methods are described below. All of the illustrations deal in calendar months, but the period can cover any constant length of time. If periods are of uneven length, such as four weeks—four weeks—five weeks, they can be brought to the same base by multiplying the demand for five-week periods by $4/5$ and the forecast for five-week periods by $5/4$. Seasonal methods can also be used as an alternative to this procedure.

1. MOVING ANNUAL TREND

Most accountants will be familiar with the moving annual trend or MAT —not to be confused with the moving annual total. The MAT is a moving average on the most recent 12-months' history, and is also called the 12-month moving average. The method is described in Inset 1, at the end of this article, using 21 months of demand data for a spare part. The results are illustrated in Figure 1.

Reference to Figure 1 shows two important features of the MAT. The first of these is that it smooths the data and gives a good indication of trend. The second is that it lags somewhat behind the data; in effect, it is recording the position six months ago.

One feature of the MAT is that it eliminates seasonal effects. This may be an advantage or a disadvantage, depending on whether or not one wants to account for them.

2. MOVING AVERAGE

We can reduce the lag by lowering the time over which the moving average is taken. The smaller the period of the moving average, the smaller the lag. A forecast based on a four-month moving average lags two months behind the data—that is, by half the period over which the moving average is

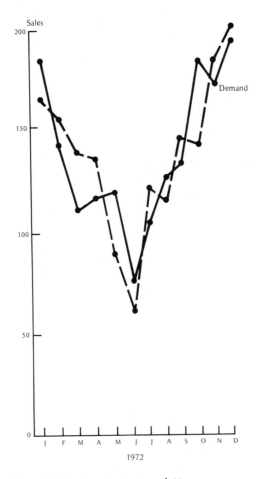

Figure 1. MAT and EMA (see Insets 1 and 2)

taken. However, reducing the period of the moving average makes the forecast less smooth.

Four-month moving averages were calculated for the same data as in Inset 1. The moving average for November 1971 was:

$$\frac{5 + 15 + 5 + 21}{4} = 11.5$$

which should be compared with 8.8 obtained with the MAT. The others were calculated similarly. By August 1972 the forecast had reached 20.5 and the errors ranged from −9.5 to 11.5. Fluctuations were greater, but the response to trend was much more rapid.

One way of reducing the effective lag in the forecast is to apply a greater weight to the more recent data. For example, we could multiply last month's demand by 4, the month before by 3, the month before that by 2 and the one before that by 1. The total would be divided by 4 + 3 + 2 + 1 = 10 to give a "weighted" moving average over 4 periods. However, this would be tedious.

3. EXPONENTIAL MOVING AVERAGES

A method which has the advantage of giving the greatest weight to the most recent value, but simplifies the arithmetic very much is the exponential moving average. It is best represented by a formula:

this month's forecast = $(1 - \alpha)$ (last month's forecast) + α (last month's demand)

α is a number less than 1, often around .2. With α equal to .2, if the forecast for last month were 251 and demand at 172, then:

$$\text{forecast} = 0.8 \times 251 + 0.2 \times 172 = 235.$$

This is a very simple sum to do every month. It can be made even simpler by rearranging the formula in such a way that only one multiplication is needed:

this month's forecast = last month's forecast + α (last month's error).

Note that the error is (actual demand − forecast) and it must have the correct sign as shown in the insets. Just to prove that this gives the same answer, with the data used previously:

$$\text{forecast} = \frac{251 + 0.2\,(172 - 251)}{251 - 0.2 \times 79} = 235.$$

The procedure as applied in practice is illustrated in Inset 2. The results are plotted on Figure 1 with the moving annual trend. Note that this forecast also lags somewhat behind the data, and that it fluctuates more than the MAT.

For most practical short-term forecasts, the simple exponential moving average technique described in Inset 2 is sufficient. However there are some practical points to be noted when using this technique.

The choice of the smoothing constant α is a problem which frequently confronts forecasters. Usually we try to find the value of α which gives the lowest errors, and procedures for doing this have been devised. If α is small, say .05, it will give a very smooth forecast. On the other hand, if it is as large as .5 the forecast will follow actual values much more closely but will fluctuate widely month by month.

Experienced forecasters will vary the constant to suit conditions at any time. For example, if a product is subject to a rise in demand over a few months they might increase α from .2 to .5 so that the forecast will rapidly follow the rise, and reduce it again when demand settles down at the new level.

4. SEASONAL EFFECTS

The sales of many products are influenced by the time of the year. A simple extension of the method of exponential moving averages allows for seasonal effects to be taken into account. The main feature is the use of "month constants" which are calculated from past data. At least one full year, and preferably more, is required for the month constants to be calculated. They are found by the formula:

$$\text{month constant} = \frac{12 \times \text{sum of demands for that month}}{\text{total demand for whole period}}.$$

Month constants are also called seasonal weights. Note that only complete years are used. So, if two years' data were available and January sales were respectively 26 and 19 items, with total sales over the period 649 items, the January month constant would be given by:

$$\text{month constant for January} = \frac{12 \times (26 + 19)}{649} = 0.83.$$

As a check, the 12-month constants should add up to 12. The procedures are shown in Inset 3. Figure 2 shows how the forecasts actually fitted.

PRACTICAL POINTS

No matter how good the techniques are, some situations are still not provided for and some questions are left unanswered. Two of them are:

> What do we do when there is little or no information on previous demand?
> How do we decide whether a forecast is good or bad or whether it should be improved?

The broad answer to the first question is that the less information there is to go on, the more judgment must be built into the forecast. It is possible to perform the mechanical work of calculating an exponential moving averages forecast after only three or four months' information has been obtained. However, it is difficult to measure reliability of forecasts made in this way, and they must be used with care.

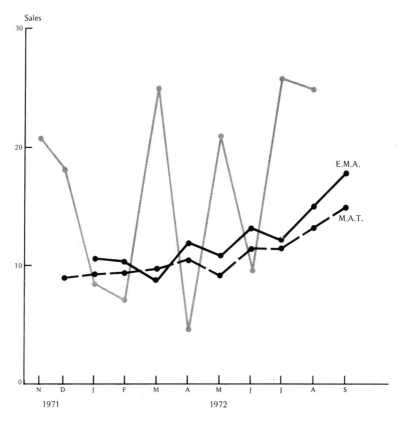

Figure 2. Seasonal Forecast (see Inset 3)

There are three main reasons why a forecast may be bad. It may be bad because it does not track a trend quickly enough, or because it does not show seasonal effects clearly, or because it does not keep up with the normal variability of demand. If the forecast is lagging behind a trend, the errors will tend to have consistently the same sign, or to be larger in one direction than the other.

Forecasts lagging behind an upward trend will have large positive errors and vice versa—see Inset 1. One of the best-known ways of detecting this effect is called Trigg's tracking signal, after its discoverer. A simple rule, much less complex than the tracking signal, is to note only the signs of the errors. If five consecutive errors are of the same sign, the forecast may be out of control and should be reset.

The way in which the forecast is reset depends very much on particular conditions. One quick way of resetting a forecast is to make a new forecast equal to the average of the last four months' demands, and raise the smoothing constant α to 0.3 for a few months.

INSET CALCULATIONS

Procedure: Inset 1

Column 3 is the series of demands under consideration.

Column 4 is the moving sum of the 12 demands in column 3. Thus for November 1971 the moving annual total is given by $10 + 12 + 2 + \ldots + 21 = 106$. The next total, for December 1971, is found by adding demand for December 1971 to 106 and subtracting demand for December 1970, that is:

$$106 + 17 - 10 = 113$$

and so on.

Column 5 is the 12-month moving average, found by dividing column 4 by 12. This is the forecast for the following month and, with decreasing reliability, for subsequent months.

Column 6—the error is the difference between demand for a month and the forecast for that month. Thus for December the demand is 17 and the forecast 8.8, calculated in November. The difference is $17 - 8.8$ which is 8.2. Similarly for January 1972 the error is:

$$9 - 9.4 = 0.4.$$

(1) YEAR	(2) MONTH	(3) DEMAND	(4) MOVING ANNUAL TOTAL	(5) FORECAST (12-MONTH MOVING AVERAGE)	(6) ERROR
1970	Dec	10			
1971	Jan	12			
	Feb	2			
	Mar	11			
	Apr	19			
	May	4			
	June	0			
	July	2			
	Aug	5			
	Sept	15			
	Oct	5			
	Nov	21	106	8.8	
	Dec	17	113	9.4	8.2
1972	Jan	9	110	9.2	− 0.4
	Feb	7	115	9.6	− 2.2
	Mar	25	129	10.8	15.4
	Apr	5	115	9.6	− 5.8
	May	21	132	11.0	11.4
	June	10	142	11.8	− 1.0
	July	26	166	13.8	14.2
	Aug	25	186	15.5	11.2

Inset 1. Twelve-Month Moving Average

Procedure: Inset 2

Column 3 is the same demand series as shown in Inset 1, but in this case we do not need to carry all of the demand for the previous 12 months.

Column 4 is 0.2 × the error, column 6.

Column 5—the forecast is found from the previous forecast plus column 4. This is the forecast for the next and subsequent months. For December 1971 therefore the forecast is given by 8.8 + 1.6 = 10.4, and for January 1972, 10.4−0.3 = 10.1. The first figure in the column is the same as the initial forecast from the 12-month moving average.

Column 6, the error, is demand minus forecast. For December 1971 the error is:

$$17 - 8.8 = 8.2.$$

(1) YEAR	(2) MONTH	(3) DEMAND	(4) 0.2 × ERROR	(5) FORECAST	(6) ERROR
1971	Nov			8.8	
	Dec	17	1.6	10.4	8.2
1972	Jan	9	−0.3	10.1	− 1.4
	Feb	7	−0.6	9.5	− 3.1
	Mar	25	3.1	12.6	15.5
	Apr	5	−1.5	11.1	− 7.6
	May	21	2.0	13.1	9.9
	June	10	−0.6	12.5	− 3.1
	July	26	2.7	15.2	13.5
	Aug	25	2.0	17.2	9.8

Inset 2. Exponential Moving Average

Procedure: Inset 3

Column 3 is the demand series.

Column 4, the error, is equal to demand this period minus forecast made last period for this period. For example in March, error = 108 − 140 = −32.

Column 5 is 0.2 times the error, corresponding to Column 4 in Inset 2.

Column 6, the average, is given by the last period's average plus column 5. In March this was:

$$139 + (-6) = 133.$$

The starting value of 137 is the average of the previous years' sales.

Column 7 contains the month constants which were calculated as described in the text. As a check, these should add up to 12.

Column 8, the forecast, is given by the average for this month times next month's weight. The forecast made in April for May is:

$$129 \times 0.70 = 90.$$

In May for June it is:

$$135 \times 0.45 = 61.$$

If the forecasts are being made two months ahead, for example in May for July, the forecast is found from this month's average × the weight two months ahead. Therefore the forecast made in May for July will be:

$$135 \times 0.87 = 117.$$

Column 9 is the adjustment to be made to the month constants in column 7 for next year. These are found from the formula:

$$\text{month constant adjustment} = \frac{0.2 \times \text{error}}{\text{average}}$$

$$= 0.2 \times \frac{\text{Column 4}}{\text{Column 6}}$$

0.2 is the smoothing constant for the adjustment, which does not need to be the same as the smoothing constant used in column 5. In January 1973 the month constant will be 1.22 + .02 = 1.24.

(1)	(2)	(3)	(4)	(5) 0.2 ×	(6)	(7) MONTH	(8)	(9) MONTH CONSTANT
YEAR	MONTH	DEMAND	ERROR	ERROR	AVERAGE	CONSTANTS	FORECAST	ADJUSTMENT
					137		167	
1972	Jan	184	17	3	140	1.22	153	0.02
	Feb	149	− 4	−1	139	1.09	140	−0.01
	Mar	108	−32	−6	133	1.01	134	−0.05
	Apr	114	−20	−4	129	1.01	90	−0.03
	May	119	29	6	135	0.70	61	0.04
	June	75	14	3	138	0.45	120	0.02
	July	104	−16	−3	135	0.87	113	−0.02
	Aug	126	13	3	138	0.84	145	0.02
	Sept	131	−14	−3	135	1.05	144	−0.02
	Oct	184	40	8	143	1.07	183	0.06
	Nov	174	− 9	−2	141	1.28	199	−0.01
	Dec	194	− 5	−1	140	1.41	174	−0.01

Inset 3. Seasonal Forecast

20.

THE LIMITATIONS OF PROFIT GRAPHS, BREAKEVEN ANALYSIS, AND BUDGETS* [SIMPLE AND MULTIPLE REGRESSION, CORRELATION]

Donald L. Raun

INTRODUCTION

A sound knowledge of cost-volume-profit behavior and cost interrelationships is essential to many business decisions. Information which is easily understood but may not represent reality can lead to costly errors in judgment in business decisions.

The management accountant certainly has a responsibility to provide management with something more than simply data. He has a responsibility to provide analyzed data, or useful information, for specific purposes. Yet he has a grave responsibility to avoid employing oversimplified techniques, or partial analysis, which may be misused or misunderstood by management. Therefore, the management accountant must be thoroughly familiar with the weaknesses, or limitations, of the techniques he employs, as well as the basic assumptions which are implied. Furthermore, he must seriously consider alternative methods of analysis which may enable him to provide more useful information.

The following case example and discussion has four major purposes:

1. To present the application and limitations of the scatter graph and least squares methods of studying the cost-volume-profit relationships of a company.
2. To present the possible weaknesses or limitations of breakeven analysis and profit graphs.
3. To review some of the major statistical techniques of evaluating the significance of relationships.

*From *The Accounting Review*, October 1964, pp. 927–945. Reprinted by permission of the author and the American Accounting Association.

4.   And, to present the application of multiple regression analysis, with the aid of a computer, to determine the cost-volume-profit relationship.

THE PROFIT GRAPH

The president of the Standard Tire Company requested that the controller explain why he did not prepare a breakeven analysis, or profit graph, for the S. T. Company. The president had been talking to the owner of another retread tire company who explained that the profit graph is a useful tool that every manager should have. The president had been given a copy of the other company's profit graph, Exhibit 1.

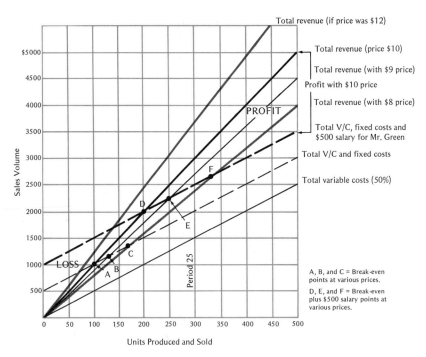

Exhibit 1. The Profit Graph of Mr. Green's Company

The president had been told that by referring to Exhibit 1 he could readily answer the following questions:

1.   What is the expected breakeven point at various prices?
2.   What are the expected costs at various volumes?
3.   What is the expected profit at various prices and volumes?

4.   What is the effect of increasing the fixed costs?
5.   What is the required volume to cover all costs plus provide a salary for Mr. Green of $500?

The controller of the S. T. Company explained that the profit graph is certainly a very neat and easily understood representation of cost-volume-profit relationship, but that in most cases it does not represent reality. It may turn out to be very misleading if used other than as an academic tool. The assumptions upon which the profit graph rests essentially succeed in assuming away the problem. With these assumptions, the problem is so simplified that there really is no problem in terms of reality.

The Usual Assumptions

As Professor Horngren points out, the following assumptions usually apply to the typical breakeven analysis, or profit graph:

1.   The behavior of costs and revenues has been reliably determined and is linear over the relevant range. (Breakeven analysis can be used even if behavior is not linear.)
2.   Costs may be resolved into fixed and variable elements.
3.   Fixed costs remain constant over the volume range on the breakeven chart.
4.   Variable costs fluctuate proportionately with volume. (The economist's breakeven chart assumes a unit variable cost that changes with the rate of production.)
5.   Selling prices are to be unchanged. (The economist assumes that price changes may be needed to spur sales volume.)
6.   Prices of the cost factors are to be unchanged.
7.   Efficiency and productivity are to be unchanged.
8.   Sales mix will be constant.
9.   Revenue and costs are being compared with a common activity base (for example, sales value of production, or units produced).
10.   All factors have been established on a going-concern basis in the light of expected economic, industry, and company situations.
11.   Changes in beginning and ending inventory levels are insignificant in amount.[1]

An Additional Assumption Required

There is another basic assumption that should be added and separately stated to emphasize its importance.

---

[1]Horngren, Charles T., *Cost Accounting: A Managerial Emphasis* (Englewood Cliffs: Prentice-Hall, Inc., 1962), p. 48.

12. It is assumed that volume is the only relevant factor affecting cost. Or, it is assumed, that if other factors do exist that they were all held constant in the past, when the experience observations were made, and that they will be held constant in the future.

Actual experience with historical cost data shows that correlations with volume are often poor as indicated by a more or less random arrangement of the plotted points on the scatter chart. This is explained by the fact that numerous factors in addition to volume cause costs to vary. In a study of cost-volume relationships it is necessary to assume that these non-volume factors affecting costs will remain constant for the period during which the conclusions are to be applied.[2]

THE SCATTER GRAPH

This last assumption seems to be neglected by many writers on methods of cost-volume analysis. Yet it is probably the most important and limiting assumption underlying the profit graph.[3]

If we refer to Information Table-A, we can prepare Graphs A-E. Graphs A, B, and D present the relationship between volume and various components of the total variable costs, direct manufacturing cost, other variable costs, and variable sales efforts. Graph C presents the relationship between volume and total variable costs. In each case the relationships are considerably different and present a wide dispersion of points. Finally, Graph E represents the profit graph for the Standard Tire Company based on the information presented in Graphs A, B, C, and D.

Let us now examine Graph A most carefully to determine its usefulness for profit planning. The same analysis can be made of the other graphs. Graph A presents a scatter graph of the relationship between direct manufacturing costs (direct labor, direct material, and direct overhead costs) and volume. The data from which this graph was developed are provided in Information Table-A, columns 1 and 3. Of the total variable cost elements, we would expect that direct manufacturing costs would have the best relationship with volume.

The accountant, assuming that the cost is directly variable and knowing that there should be no direct manufacturing cost at zero volume, would tend to draw a line from the zero point bisecting the scatter points. Thus

[2] *The Analysis of Cost-Volume-Profit Relationships*, NACA Research Report, Combined Research Series 16, 17, and 18 (December 1949), p. 12.

[3] For further discussions of the subject, see Joel Dean, "Cost Structure of Enterprises and Break-Even Charts," *American Economic Review*, May 1948, pp. 153–164; and John H. Kempter, "Break-Even Analysis—Common Ground for the Economist and the Cost Accountant," *NACA Bulletin*, February 1949.

PERIOD	(1) SALES @ $10/UNIT	(2) SALES EFFORTS[1]	(3) DIRECT COSTS	(4) COST CONTROL EFFORTS[2]	(5) TOTAL D.C. AND V/C (2) + (3) + (4)
6	$12,216	$ 926	$7,131	$ 382	$ 8,439
7	11,000	945	6,931	524	8,400
8	11,000	1,111	5,694	766	7,571
9	12,836	1,617	5,975	963	8,555
10	16,697	2,438	7,139	1,377	10,954
11	15,033	1,144	8,580	415	10,139
12	14,035	1,138	8,984	530	10,652
13	14,035	1,277	8,380	992	10.649
14	14,980	1,514	7,907	863	10,284
15	17,979	2,175	8,100	1,235	11,510
16	17,259	1,242	9,365	430	11,037
17	16,922	1,269	9,931	315	11,515
18	16,922	1,321	9,213	366	10,900
19	17,015	1,507	8,694	377	10,578
20	19,133	1,722	8,138	409	10,269
21	16,592	1,343	8,322	624	10,289
22	15,490	1,408	7,367	1,002	9,777
23	15,490	1,564	6,196	1,654	9,414
24	17,562	2,125	7,025	2,188	11,338

[1] The Sum of Sales Salaries, Advertising, Product Research and Bad Debt expense.
[2] The Sum of Supervisory control efforts, methods development and maintenance.

Information Table A. The Standard Tire Company (Periods 6–25)

one-half of the points would be on one side of the line as shown by line #1. It should be noted that the points are widely scattered about the line indicating something less than a desired relationship.

An alternative is to use the least squares method of calculating the line of best fit. The result of this approach will be line #2. Line #1 and line #2, on Graph A, are obviously quite different yet they both purport to describe the same relationship. In theory they should be identical, but in practice they may be quite different because of the assumptions mentioned in the above paragraph. The scatter graph line indicates a cost of $5.00 per unit, whereas, the least squares method indicates a cost of $2.64 per unit. Furthermore, the latter method indicates a cost of $3781 for direct manufacturing cost even though no units are produced. The company knows that this is not a statement of fact from their experience.

Finally, from the company's experience and additional analysis they know that the optimum relationship is $4.00 per unit direct labor cost, as described by line #3. This relationship was experienced in periods 23, 24, and 25.

How can we explain the difference between the company's experience and the results of our analysis? How useful for planning purposes is the scatter graph or least squares method?

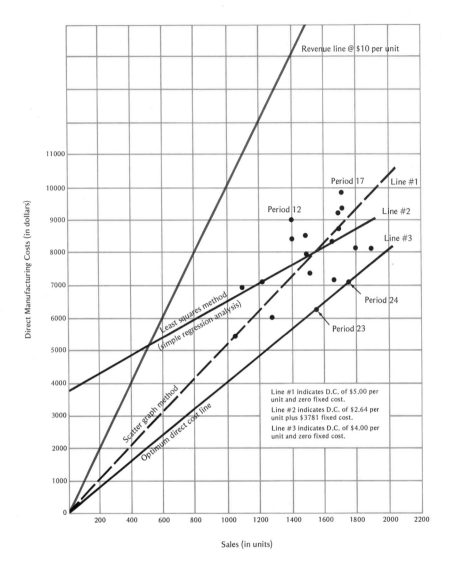

Graph A. The Relationship of Direct Cost to Sales Volume (Periods 6–24). The Standard Tire Company—Scatter Graph

PROVING THAT OTHER RELEVANT FACTORS DO, OR DO NOT, EXIST

Let us approach the problem as follows:

1.   We shall select the null hypothesis, that is, that there is no relationship between direct manufacturing cost and volume.

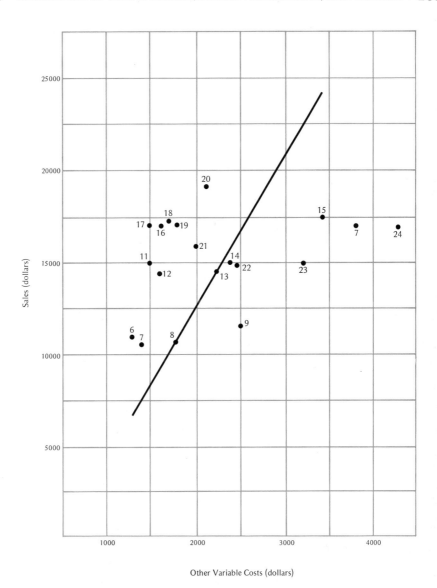

Other Variable Costs (dollars)

Graph B. The Relationship Between Other Variable Costs and Sales Volume. The Standard Tire Company

We shall attempt to prove, or disprove, this hypothesis by simple regression analysis and the t test. Is the relationship significantly different from a random relationship?

2.   If there is a significant relationship, we shall attempt to determine how much of the variation is associated with volume by calculating the coefficient of determination, the r^2

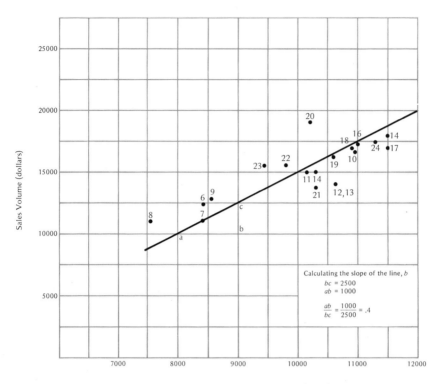

Graph C. The Relationship Between Volume and Direct Costs Plus Other Variable Costs. The Standard Tire Company

value. How much of the variation is associated with factors other than volume?

3.   If a major portion of the variation in direct manufacturing cost is associated with volume, we shall calculate the standard error of the estimate. The standard error of the estimate will approximate the range within which our estimates may fall in relationship to the actual direct manufacturing cost. How much of a difference should we expect between our estimate and the actual cost?

4.   Finally, if we discover that a major portion of the variation in direct manufacturing cost is associated with factors other than volume, we shall attempt to specifically identify these additional factors, and their relationships to direct manufacturing cost. How much of the variation is associated with these additional identified factors? How much of a variance should be expected between our estimate and actual

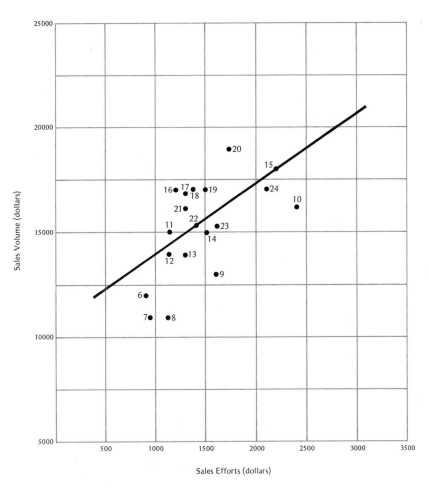

Graph D. The Relationship Between Sales Volume and Variable Sales Efforts (Periods 6–24). The Standard Tire Company

if we employ these additional factors and their coefficient in our equation?

SIMPLE REGRESSION ANALYSIS

The basic information for the calculation of the regression equation is provided in Information Table-B. The regression equation describes a relationship between the sample observations of direct costs (Y), and the respective observations of volume (X). It is limited by the sample size and range of the sample. If it is significantly greater than a random relationship,

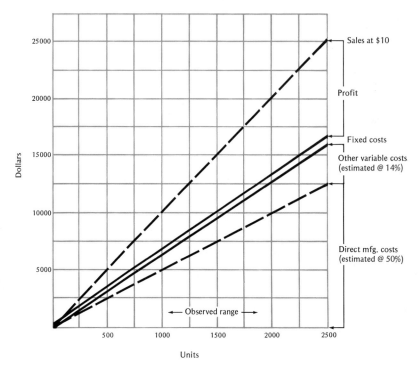

Graph E. The Profit Graph of the Standard Tire Company.

the equation will describe the relationship only within the observed range of the sample. The following steps are necessary to accomplish the task.

1.   *The calculation of the value of b:* (the regression coefficient)

$$b = \frac{N(\Sigma XY) - (\Sigma X)(\Sigma Y)}{N(\Sigma X^2) - (\Sigma X)^2}$$

N =   20 (the number of observations)
X =   (the sales volume in units)
Y =   (the total direct manufacturing cost in dollars)
ΣXY =   277,229,000 (the sum of XY)
ΣX =   32,710 (the sum of X)
ΣX^2 =   58,147,100 (the sum of X^2)
$(\Sigma X)^2$ =   1,069,944,100 (the sum of the X's squared)

then

$$b = \frac{20(277,229,000) - (32,710)(162,000)}{20(58,147,100) - (1,069,944,100)}$$

$$b = \$2.64$$

OBSERVATIONS PERIODS	X SALES IN UNITS	Y TOTAL DIRECT COSTS	X²	XY
6	1,220	$ 7,100	1,488,400	8,662,000
7	1,100	6,900	1,210,000	7,590,000
8	1,100	5,700	1,210,000	6,270,000
9	1,280	6,000	1,638,400	7,680,000
10	1,670	7,100	2,788,900	11,857,000
11	1,500	8,600	2,250,000	12,900,000
12	1,400	9,000	1,960,000	12,600,000
13	1,400	8,400	1,960,000	11,760,000
14	1,500	7,900	2,250,000	11,850,000
15	1,800	8,100	3,240,000	14,580,000
16	1,730	9,400	2,992,900	16,262,000
17	1,690	9,900	2,856,100	16,731,000
18	1,690	9,200	2,856,100	15,548,000
19	1,700	8,700	2,890,000	14,790,000
20	1,910	8,100	3,648,100	15,471,000
21	1,660	8,300	2,755,600	13,778,000
22	1,550	7,400	2,402,500	11,470,000
23	1,550	6,200	2,402,500	9,610,000
24	1,760	7,000	3,097,600	12,320,000
25	3,500	13,000	12,250,000	45,500,000
Totals	32,710	$162,000	58,147,100	277,229,000

Information Table B. The Standard Tire Company

2. The calculation of the value of a: (the constant, or intercept)

$$a = \frac{\Sigma Y}{N} - \frac{b\,(\Sigma X)}{N}$$

$$a = \frac{162,000}{20} - \frac{\$2.64\,(32,710)}{20}$$

$$a = \$3781$$

3. The calculation of the estimated direct manufacturing cost by the regression formula

$Y_c = a + bX$

$Y_c =$ estimated direct manufacturing cost
$a = \$3781$
$b = \$2.64$
$X_u = $ # of units produced and sold, $Xd/\$10$
$X_d = $ dollar sales volume, $X_u\ (\$10)$
$Y_c = \$3781 + \$2.64\ (X_u)$
$Y_c = \$3781 + .264\ (X_d)$

At this point, we have described a relationship between direct manufacturing cost (Y) and volume (X). But it should be emphasized that by this method it is possible to show a relationship between direct manufacturing cost and any factor, whether it is relevant or not. *Therefore, we need to determine if this is a meaningful relationship.*

Testing for the Significance of a Relationship

In order to discover whether or not a calculated regression coefficient is significantly greater than zero, we may use a procedure referred to as the *t* test, which is applicable to both large and small samples.

The *t* test involves two steps:

1. a. The calculation of the *t*-value of the coefficient. The information for the calculation is presented in Information Table-C.

$$t = \sqrt{\dfrac{\dfrac{\Sigma(Y_c - \overline{Y}_c)^2}{n}}{\dfrac{\Sigma(Y_c - Y)^2}{N-2}}}$$

$$= \sqrt{\dfrac{\dfrac{32{,}420{,}821}{1}}{\dfrac{18{,}246{,}221}{18}}} = 5.65$$

where:

Y_c = estimated direct manufacturing cost
$\overline{Y}_c$ = the mean of Y_c
Y = actual direct manufacturing cost
n = number of independent variables
N = number of observations in sample
Σ = summation

See the Information Table-C for the calculations of major elements of the formula.

b. An alternative method of calculating *t* is as follows:

$$t = \frac{\text{Regression Coefficient}}{\text{Standard Error of Regression Coefficient}} = \frac{.26405}{.04668} = 5.65$$

(See the computer analysis for values of above)

2. The second step requires that we refer to a *t* table to determine the significant level of our calculated *t*-value. Most statistics

Y	Y_c	$(Y_c - Y)$	$(Y_c - Y)^2$	$(Y_c - \bar{Y_c})$	$(Y_c - \bar{Y_c})^2$	$(Y - \bar{Y})$	$(Y - \bar{Y})^2$
7,100	7,002	−98	9,604	−1,098	1,205,604	−1,000	1,000,000
6,900	6,686	−214	45,796	−1,414	1,999,396	−1,200	1,440,000
5,700	6,686	+986	972,196	−1,414	1,999,396	−2,400	5,760,000
6,000	7,161	+1,161	1,347,921	−939	881,721	−2,100	4,410,000
7,100	8,191	+1,091	1,190,281	+91	8,281	−1,000	1,000,000
8,600	7,742	−858	736,164	−385	128,164	+500	250,000
9,000	7,478	−1,522	2,316,484	−622	386,884	+900	810,000
8,400	7,478	−922	850,084	−622	386,884	+300	90,000
7,900	7,742	−158	24,964	−358	128,164	−200	40,000
8,100	8,534	+434	188,356	+434	188,356	0	0
9,400	8,349	−1,051	1,104,601	+249	62,001	+1,300	1,690,000
9,900	8,243	−1,657	2,745,649	+143	20,449	+1,800	3,240,000
9,200	8,243	−957	915,849	+143	20,449	+1,100	1,210,000
8,700	8,270	−430	184,900	+170	28,900	+600	360,000
8,100	8,825	+725	525,625	+725	525,625	0	0
8,300	8,165	−135	18,225	+65	4,225	+200	40,000
7,400	7,874	+474	224,676	−226	51,076	−700	490,000
6,200	7,874	+1,674	2,802,276	−226	51,076	−1,900	3,610,000
7,000	8,429	+1,429	2,042,041	+329	108,241	−1,100	1,210,000
13,000	13,023	+23	529	+4,923	24,235,929	+4,900	24,010,000
162,000	161,995		18,246,221		32,420,821		50,660,000

$$\bar{Y} = 8100 \qquad \bar{Y_c} = 8100$$

$$\bar{Y} = \text{mean of } Y = \frac{162,000}{20} = 8100$$

Y = actual direct manufacturing cost
Y_c = estimated direct manufacturing cost
$(Y_c - Y)$ = the variance

Information Table C. The Standard Tire Company (Periods 6–25)

texts provide a table of values of t.[4] In our case, with a sample of 20 observations and 2 factors, n (degrees of freedom) is 18 (20−2). The t table indicates the following values:

$$3.92 = .001 \text{ level of significance } (P)$$
$$2.87 = .01 \quad \text{level of significance}$$
$$2.10 = .05 \quad \text{level of significance}$$
$$.69 = .5 \quad \text{level of significance}$$

Since our calculated t-value is 5.65, b (the coefficient) is significant at the .001 level. This simply means that there is

---

[4] See Croxton and Cowden, *Applied General Statistics* (New York: Prentice-Hall, Inc., 1946), p. 875.

less than 1 chance in 1000 that the regression coefficient, 2.64, could have resulted from a random relationship. *Therefore, there appears to be a definite relationship between X and Y in our example.*

The F Test

The *F* test really answers the same question as the *t* test: What chance is there that this is simply a random relationship? On the other hand, the *t*-value is calculated for each regression coefficient in the formula, whereas the *F* value is calculated for the total equation. In a simple regression (one factor *(X)*) formula, the *t* value squared equals the *F* value.

$$t^2 = F$$

The *F* value is equal to the ratio of:

$$F = \frac{\dfrac{\Sigma(Y_c - \overline{Y}_c)^2}{n}}{\dfrac{\Sigma(Y_c - Y)^2}{N - 2}} = \frac{\dfrac{32{,}420{,}821}{1}}{\dfrac{18{,}246{,}221}{18}} = 31.98$$

In the *F* test, we refer to an *F* table[5] to determine the significance of the formula in comparison to a random relationship. In our case with 20 observations and one independent factor, an *F* value of

$$4.351 = .05 \quad \text{level of significance}$$
$$8.096 = .01 \quad \text{level of significance}$$
$$14.820 = .001 \quad \text{level of significance}$$

Again we conclude that there is little or no chance that the formula describes a random relationship.

The r² Test—Coefficient of Determination

Even though we have discovered that the formula which describes the relationships is significant, we still need to answer the question: *How closely can values of the dependent variable (direct manufacturing cost) be estimated from values of the independent variable (sales volume)?*

Since the coefficient of determination (r^2, or *d*) is the most direct and unequivocal way of stating the proportion of the variance in the dependent factor (direct cost) which is explained by the independent factor (volume), it should be used in preference to the correlation coefficient, *r*. The coeffi-

---

[5]Ibid., p. 878.

cient of determination will tell us what percentages of the variation in direct cost is associated with volume. In our example, 64% of the variation in direct cost is associated with volume.

The coefficient of determination is calculated as follows (see Information Table-C):*

$$d = r^2 = \frac{\Sigma(Y_c - \overline{Y}_c)^2}{\Sigma(Y - \overline{Y})^2} = \frac{32,420,821}{50,660,000} = .64$$

The correlation coefficient (r) is the $\sqrt{d}$, or $\sqrt{r^2}$. Thus:

$$r = \sqrt{.64} = .80$$

or

$$d = r^2 = .80^2 = .64$$

If 64% of the variation in direct cost is associated with volume, *then 36%, the remainder, must be associated with some other relevant factors, or represent random variations.* With 36% of the variation in direct cost unaccounted for we can hardly expect our formula to provide a very accurate estimate of direct cost. *What will be the approximate possible error of our estimate?*

The Standard Error of Estimate

The standard error of the estimate approximates the range of possible error in our estimate of direct cost. It is calculated as follows (see Information Table-C):

$$S_{yx} = \sqrt{\frac{\Sigma z^2}{N - 2}}$$

or

$$S_{yx} = \sqrt{\frac{\Sigma(Y - Y_c)^2}{N - 2}} = \sqrt{\frac{18,246,221}{18}}$$

$$= \sqrt{1,013,678} = \$1006$$

Accordingly, in this case, we can expect two-thirds of the new estimates made by the equation to fall within approximately ±$1006 of the true value (one standard deviation), or, we can expect 95% of our estimates to be approximately within ±2(1006), or $2012 of the true value (two standard deviations). Finally, we can expect that 99% of our estimates of direct manufacturing cost, estimated by the formula $(Y = 3781 + .264 (X))$, will

---

* Editors' Note: The numerator for r^2 shows $\Sigma (Y_c - \overline{Y}_c)^2$. In this problem, $\overline{Y}$ and $\overline{Y}_c$ are 8100. The numerator appears in statistics books as $\Sigma (Y_c - \overline{Y})^2$. See the alternative formulas listed in the introductory discussion for Part IV.

be within $\pm 3(1006)$, or \$3018 of the actual direct manufacturing cost (three standard deviations).[6]

IMPROVING OUR ABILITY TO ESTIMATE

It should be obvious at this point that if we could identify additional relevant factors which have a high correlation with direct manufacturing cost, we could improve our ability to estimate. The additional relevant factors will, if they exist, account for part, or possibly all, of the 36% variation unaccounted for by volume. By identifying other relevant factors and their coefficients, we will end up with a multiple regression formula of the form

$$Y = a + b_1X_1 + b_2X_2 + b_3X_3, \text{ etc.}$$

If we can develop a formula which has a coefficient of determination approaching 1.0 and a standard error of estimate approaching 0.0, and a standard error of regression coefficients which approaches 0.0, we can estimate direct manufacturing cost with considerably less error. We can approach these goals with the aid of multiple regression analysis and the computer.

THE APPLICATION OF THE COMPUTER

As shown in Computer Printout-A, the IBM 7094 computer employing the UCLA-BIMD-06 programs accomplishes identically the same task that we have just completed. The computer accomplished the same task in 0.8 of a minute. In addition the preparation time was less than 10 minutes, preparing the input data on IBM cards, etc.

If we examine the Computer Printout-A we will discover that with the exception of a few items, all of the information presented can be directly related to our previous discussion. As shown in Computer Printout-B, this same computer program can be used for multiple regression analysis. Computer Printout-B indicates that by relating six independent variables (instead of just one—volume) we can obtain a coefficient of determination of .9655. Also our standard error of estimate is reduced to \$477 rather than

---

[6]Actually, the error in an estimate in this example could be almost double these figures because the method assumes the following:

1. That the regression coefficient is the true value of the total population.
2. That the population is represented by a normal distribution.

See Robert Ferber, *Statistical Techniques in Market Research* (New York: McGraw-Hill Book Company, Inc., 1949), pp. 390–393, for methods for correcting for these assumptions. [Also see the EDITORS' NOTE TO IV-Q5.]

Computer Printout A. Employing the IBM 7094 and the BIMD-06 Program (see Information Tables B and C for explanation)

Problem No.   1-0
No data transformation

Sample size   20
No. of variables   2   No. of variables deleted   0   (for variables deleted, see below)
Dependent variable is now no.   2

Coefficient of determination   0.6400
Multiple corr. coefficient   0.8000

Sum of squares attributable to regression   32419936.75000
Sum of squares of deviation from regression   18240063.25000

Variance of estimate   013336.84375
Std. error of estimate   1006.64633

Intercept (a value)   3781.47858
Std. error of intercept   795.98410

ANALYSIS OF VARIANCE FOR THE MULTIPLE LINEAR REGRESSION

Source of Variation	D.F.	Sum of Squares	Mean Squares	F Value
Due to regression	1	32419936.75000	32419936.75000	31.9932
Deviation about regression	18	18240063.25000	1013336.84375	
Total	19	50660000.00000		

Variable No.	Mean	Std. Deviation	Reg. Coeff.	Std. Error of Reg. Coe.	Com-puted T Value	Partial Corr. Coe.	Variance Added	Prop. Var.
1	16355.00000	4947.03229	0.26405	0.04668	5.65626	0.79997	32419936.75000	0.63995
2	8100.00000	1632.88573						

Comp. check on final coeff.   0.26405

Measure of efficiency (Std. error of est./Reg. coeff.)   3812.34662

Variables deleted   0

$1006. The computer program indicates that the equation to estimate direct costs should take the following form:

$$Y = -584 + 3.94X_1 - 1.74X_2 - 1.87X_5$$
$$- .52X_8 - .71X_{11} + 676X_{14}$$

Computer Printout A (continued). Table of Residual

OBSERVATION	Y VALUE	Y ESTIMATE	RESIDUAL	(RES.* 100)/Y EST.
1	7100.00000	7002.87640	97.12360	1.39
2	6900.00000	6686.01758	213.98242	3.20
3	5700.00000	6686.01758	−986.01758	−14.75
4	6000.00000	7161.30579	−1161.30579	−16.22
5	7100.00000	8191.09692	−1091.09692	−13.32
6	8600.00000	7742.21362	857.78638	11.08
7	9000.00000	7478.16461	1521.83539	20.35
8	8400.00000	7478.16461	921.83539	12.33
9	7900.00000	7742.21362	157.78638	2.04
10	8100.00000	8534.36060	−434.36060	−5.09
11	9400.00000	8349.52625	1050.47375	12.58
12	9900.00000	8243.90674	1656.09326	20.09
13	9200.00000	8243.90674	956.09326	11.60
14	8700.00000	8270.31165	429.68835	5.20
15	8100.00000	8824.81445	−724.81445	−8.21
16	8300.00000	8164.69202	135.30798	1.66
17	7400.00000	7874.23810	−474.23810	−6.02
18	6200.00000	7874.23810	−1674.23810	−21.26
19	7000.00000	8428.74097	−1428.74097	−16.95
20	13000.00000	13023.19360	−23.19360	−0.18

TEST OF EXTREME RESIDUALS

Ratio of ranges for the smallest residual	0.188
Ratio of ranges for the largest residual	0.215
Critical value of the ratio at alpha = .10	0.401

This is all the output for this problem.

Four of the variables selected for multiple regression analysis (see the B printout) have better than a 99% level of significance as indicated by the t-values. Variables X_{14} and X_{11} have levels of significance of approximately 90% and 85% respectively. The variables which have been deleted have levels of significance of less than 75%. The Table of Residuals compares the actual Y with Y estimated by the formula.

In this particular example, the following possible relevant factors were analyzed by the UCLA BIMD program employing the IBM 7094 Computer.

X_1 = sales volume in units—current period
X_2 = supervisory control efforts—current period (t)
X_3 = supervisory control efforts—previous period $(t-1)$
X_4 = supervisory control efforts—two periods ago $(t-2)$
X_5 = method development—current period (t)
X_6 = method development—previous period $(t-1)$
X_7 = method development—two periods ago $(t-2)$

Computer Printout B

Problem No.   1-1
No data transformation

Sample size   28
No. of variables   7   No. of variables deleted   8   (for variables deleted, see below)
Dependent variable is now no.   15

Coefficient of determination   0.9655
Multiple corr. coefficient   0.9826

Sum of squares attributable to regression   133696746.00000
Sum of squares of deviation from regression   4783302.00000

Variance of estimate   227776.28516
Std. error of estimate   477.25914

Intercept (a value)   −584.74329
Std. error of intercept   890.23930

ANALYSIS OF VARIANCE FOR THE MULTIPLE LINEAR REGRESSION

Source of Variation	D.F.	Sum of Squares	Mean Squares	F Value
Due to regression	61	33696746.00000	22282791.00000	97.8275
Deviation about regression	21	4783302.00000	227776.28516	
Total	27	69240024.00000		

Variable No.	Mean	Std. Deviation	Reg. Coeff.	Std. Error of Reg. Coe.	Computed T Value	Partial Corr. Coe.	Prop. Var.
1	1822.32143	768.03441	3.93954	0.28002	14.06858	0.95083	0.14129
2	691.75000	812.64760	−1.74274	0.32675	−5.3361	−0.75849	0.64504
5	749.85714	852.17785	−1.87064	0.32908	−5.68451	−0.77853	0.13187
8	212.96428	376.55814	−0.52367	0.34912	−1.49997	−0.31108	0.00179
11	200.85714	325.13743	−0.71386	0.40804	−1.74950	−0.35666	0.00666
14	4.22429	1.82561	676.33557	139.23582	4.85748	0.72739	0.03881
15	6588.25000	2264.70541					

Comp. check on final coeff.   676.33587

X_8 = maintenance—current period (t)
X_9 = maintenance—previous period $(t-1)$
X_{10} = maintenance—two periods ago $(t-2)$
X_{11} = equipment replacement—current period (t)
X_{12} = equipment replacement—previous period $(t-1)$
X_{13} = equipment replacement—two periods ago $(t-2)$
X_{14} = previous periods cost/unit

Computer Printout B (continued). Table of Residual

OBSERVATION	Y VALUE	Y ESTIMATE	RESIDUAL	(RES.* 100)/Y EST.
1	5445.00000	6095.37500	−650.37500	−10.67
2	5140.00000	5593.22363	−453.22363	−8.10
3	7120.00000	6331.12750	788.87250	12.46
4	6435.00000	7096.31647	−661.31647	−9.32
5	6657.00000	6964.99713	−307.99713	−4.42
6	5698.00000	5922.97577	−224.97577	−3.80
7	6045.00000	5992.77637	52.22363	0.87
8	7029.00000	6341.91913	687.08087	10.83
9	8565.00000	8608.78076	−43.78076	−0.51
10	8960.00000	8651.12549	308.87451	3.57
11	8358.00000	8319.45496	38.54504	0.46
12	8184.00000	8252.31287	−68.31287	−0.83
13	7840.00000	8252.50354	−412.50354	−5.00
14	10840.00000	10087.77600	752.22400	7.46
15	8613.00000	8462.46313	150.53687	1.78
16	9248.00000	8868.79248	379.20752	4.28
17	8575.00000	8548.98901	26.01099	0.30
18	8056.00000	8397.00525	−341.00525	−4.06
19	8517.00000	8409.86292	107.13708	1.27
20	7719.00000	7251.15778	467.84222	6.45
21	4542.00000	4550.95404	−8.95404	−0.20
22	3960.00000	4086.11752	−126.11752	−3.09
23	3720.00000	3419.73911	300.26089	8.78
24	7560.00000	8462.94604	−902.94604	−10.67
25	4025.00000	4234.39935	−209.39935	−4.95
26	2860.00000	2938.99890	−78.99890	−2.69
27	2695.00000	2648.76178	46.23822	1.75
28	2065.00000	1680.15477	384.84523	22.91

TEST OF EXTREME RESIDUALS

Ratio of ranges for the smallest residual	0.159
Ratio of ranges for the largest residual	0.071
Critical value of the ratio at alpha = .10	0.342

Similar programs are available for all major computer systems. These computer programs may be used for linear or curvilinear analysis.

CONCLUSION

Breakeven analysis and the profit graph may be satisfactory stepping stones to obtain a better understanding of operational analysis. They may be more of an academic tool rather than a tool of reality. In any case, if they are believed to be useful tools for profit planning in a particular case, simple regression analysis, the t test, or F test, the r^2 test, and standard error of estimate may be calculated to improve our understanding of the usefulness of profit graphs, or breakeven analysis.

In our case, being able to estimate direct manufacturing cost within $1000, or $2000, or $3000, when the mean cost experienced has been $8100, does not appear to be a satisfactory goal. Nor does it appear to be satisfactory to assume a direct manufacturing cost relationship of $5.00 per unit, or $2.64 per unit, when $4.00 per unit is the optimum relationship. Such a goal may be especially unsatisfactory if we can improve our estimate appreciably with the aid of a computer and multiple regression analysis providing we understand operational analysis. Further analysis may permit us to better control and improve cost relationships. Finally, we may be able to improve our ability to aid in profit planning and budgeting.

21.

HOW TO GET A BETTER FORECAST*

George G. C. Parker
and
Edilberto L. Segura

One benefit of the computer's ability to assimilate huge quantities of data is its indispensable aid to complex, statistical methods of forecasting, particularly regression analysis. With this tool the user can analyze the level of, say, sales compared to such variables as the number of new households, income, and interest rates. Its major advantage is the high degree of precision and reliability it affords. In this article the authors show, through an extended example, how the method works and how it is superior to more subjective, less scientific forecasting procedures.

More accurate forecasts of company performance have become increasingly important to management and the investment community alike in today's complex business environment. Such estimates are used, for example, to formulate financial strategy, assess liquidity, and predict stock prices over time.

In the face of a nearly universal desire for better forecasts, there remains a conspicuous gap between the conventional methods of forecasting often used and the more powerful and precise statistical methods available through creative employment of the computer. While statistically based forecasts cannot, of course, eliminate uncertainty about the future, the quality of forecasts can be dramatically improved by mathematical analysis of the trends and relationships that have prevailed in the past.

A computer-aided forecasting technique which has gained wide use in recent years is regression analysis. It attempts objectively to define the extent of movement over time in one variable (such as sales or earnings) relative to others (income, population, and new construction, for example).

---

*From *Harvard Business Review*, March–April 1971, pp. 99–109. Reprinted by permission of *Harvard Business Review*. Copyright © 1971 by the President and Fellows of Harvard College; all rights reserved.

Its main contribution is the precision with which it measures statistical relationships and indicates their reliability. Moreover, through regression, it is feasible to analyze far greater quantities of data than is possible with any intuitive or manual method.

In this article we explain the technique and show the results that can be obtained by forecasting using regression. We will go through an actual example in detail to illustrate the application of statistically based estimates and to compare them with forecasts produced under more traditional and subjective methods.

It is not our purpose here to discuss the statistical theory that underlies the regression technique; that is available elsewhere.[1] Rather, we concentrate on the types of data used in regression and on understanding the results.

RATIONALE FOR REGRESSION

Managers, of course, make forecasts every day of earnings, inventory turnover, and other critical aspects of their businesses. They range from the totally subjective to the rigidly scientific.

A subjective, "seat of the pants" approach could be that of a group of experienced sales executives who meet to offer their estimates of next year's volume. The sales vice-president gathers a consensus from their collective judgment and combines it with his own to arrive at a forecast.

Although such unscientific forecasts frequently turn out to be inaccurate, many seasoned managers continue to use them because they are unable to identify or explain the exact relationships of the external factors which they believe influence their operations, even if they can identify the factors themselves. In the absence of systematic definition and testing, they substitute conjecture for real analysis.

Another frequently used method involving less guesswork is simple extrapolation. To get a sales forecast, the vice-president may assemble data from the last four or five years and plot them on a graph to "read a trend."

In this case the manager merely attempts, through visual inspection or fitting a curve by manual means, to identify a pattern. He is not trying to understand the basis of these trends or their subtleties; instead he is presuming that future results will move along essentially the same path as past results.[2]

Such methods, no matter how unscientific, often suffice for the user. Indeed, a recent study indicates that simple extrapolation of trends in sales

---

[1]See, for example, Norman Draper and Harry Smith, *Applied Regression Analysis* (New York: John Wiley & Sons, Inc., 1966); and Lucy Joan Slater, *FORTRAN Programs for Economists* (Cambridge, England: Cambridge University Press, 1967).

[2]For a discussion of this technique, see James W. Redfield, "Elements of Forecasting," *Harvard Business Review*, November 1951, p. 81.

and earnings has been fairly adequate as a predictor.[3] Nevertheless, the demand for more precise forecasting techniques has increased, resulting in wider use of regression analysis.[4]

Regression is a mathematical procedure that takes account of the relationship of, say, sales volume to various external indicators which are thought to have significant influence on it. Regression is more powerful than subjective estimation because it enables the forecaster to measure explicitly the apparent association between variables over time, thus eliminating a large portion of the guesswork. If the user finds a statistical association between a level of growth in sales and the movement of four or five other variables, then this relationship becomes the basis of the forecast itself.

While use of regression still remains outside the normal corporate forecasting process, it has come into increasing usage by many large companies in recent years. They are generally those companies that have made the greatest strides in using the computer as a management tool, rather than merely as an accounting device. For instance:

> The American Can Company for several years has used a regression technique to estimate sales on the basis of numerous external factors. For example, to forecast beer-can demand, the company has used an equation that correlates sales to income levels, number of drinking establishments per thousand persons, and age distribution of the population.
>
> Through regression analysis, Eli Lilly and Company has correlated the sale of pharmaceuticals with disposable income.
>
> The RCA Sales Corporation uses mathematical techniques to forecast sales of television sets, radio sets, and phonographs. Analysis at this company has concentrated on identifying the most important of more than 300 economic variables that might logically be connected with sales of RCA products.
>
> Armour & Company has found that it can accurately predict the number of cattle to be slaughtered in future months by using such explanatory variables as range-grass conditions and steer-corn price ratios.

Unquestionably, the ability of the computer to digest vast quantities of data and the advent of easy accessibility to EDP devices have spread the use of regression analysis. Calculations that would take hours or even days to do by hand can be made with relative ease and great speed using computerized regression routines.

---

[3]John G. Cragg and Burton G. Malkiel, "The Consensus and Accuracy of Some Predictions of the Growth of Corporate Earnings," *Journal of Finance*, March 1968, p. 67.

[4]For a discussion of regression techniques used for another purpose, see Gordon R. Conrad and Irving H. Plotkin, "Risk/Return: U.S. Industry Pattern," *Harvard Business Review*, March–April 1968, p. 90 (especially the supplement and appendix, available with reprints of the article).

The availability of computer programs required to make the calculations has put the use of regression analysis within easy reach of small and medium-sized companies that cannot afford their own programming staffs. These programs can be employed in conjunction with the many commercial time-sharing service bureaus located throughout the country.

FORECASTING SALES

Beginning with an attempt to predict sales, clearly the first step is to pinpoint those factors that are assumed to affect sales and to be associated with sales. These factors may cover a broad range, and it is perhaps impossible to formulate a truly exhaustive list of the economic variables that might have some bearing.

Nonetheless, through regression we can analyze a large number of these variables and identify those that have been most important in an explanatory (predictive) way over the years. When more than one explanatory variable is included in the analysis, the technique is called multiple regression.

In the example used in this discussion we develop a forecast of sales and earnings for an actual (but disguised) company in the home furnishings industry, which we shall call the Cherryoak Company. First we assume that sales in this industry are sensitive to such factors as:

New marriages
New housing starts
Disposable personal income
Trend over time

Formulating the Equation

It is safe to say that most experienced observers, both within and outside the home furnishings field, have certain preconceived notions about the effects of these variables on sales of home furnishings. Through the regression technique, however, one can measure precisely how large and how significant each of them is in its historical relationship to total sales. These various relationships can be described by means of this industry sales regression equation:

$$S = B + B_m(M) + B_h(H) + B_i(I) + B_t(T), \text{ where}$$

$S =$ Gross sales for year;
$B =$ Base sales, or starting point from which other factors have influence;
$M =$ Marriages during the year;
$H =$ Housing starts during the year;
$I =$ Annual disposable personal income;
$T =$ Time trend (first year $= 1$, second year $= 2$, third year $= 3$, etc.).

B_m, B_h, B_i, and B_t represent the amount of influence on sales of the factors M, H, I, and T. We use the subscripts m, h, i, and t to identify which variable each B refers to. These B terms, called regression coefficients, indicate the extent of the relationship between the dependent variable, left-hand side of the equation, and each independent variable, right-hand side.

The B values of this equation or relationship can be estimated by regression on the basis of real data, as we will show.

The estimation of the relationships suggested by the equation generally requires the use of several years' data; obviously, a meaningful correlation can hardly be maintained when trends are measured only for a very short time. And when more than one variable is being correlated with Cherryoak's sales, as we are doing in this example, the number of years of observations should be increased to make sure the results have reasonable statistical significance.

While there is no definitive cutoff point for the minimum number of years of data that are required, a period of five years is a general rule of thumb when only one variable is being analyzed, and eight years is a minimum with two. A longer time span is necessary with three or more variables, as is the case in our example.[5]

In the analysis of the Cherryoak Company we used 24 years of data, covering the period 1947–1970. The data for each of the variables used in the regression appear for reference in Exhibit I.

Results via the computer in an initial regression of the data in Exhibit I show this pattern:

$$S = 49.85 - 0.068M + 0.036H + 1.22I - 19.54T$$

To use these results to forecast company sales for 1971, we must introduce numerical estimates for the independent variables in the equation. Thus, estimated marriages in 1971 are inserted for M, housing starts for H, and so on.[6] The combination of the estimates for the independent variables with the regression coefficients appearing in the equation will yield an initial estimate for Cherryoak's sales, S.

Before we can use the relationship with confidence, however, we must do two things. First, we must make a judgment as to the accuracy and reliability of the regression results; and second, we must determine whether we can formulate another equation that would give results as good, or even better.

---

[5]For additional discussion of this point, see Taro Yamane, *Statistics, An Introductory Analysis,* 2nd edition (New York: Harper & Row Publishers, Inc., 1967), pp. 579–583.

[6]Data are available through the *Survey of Current Business,* published monthly by the Department of Commerce, and through newsletters issued by the leading Federal Reserve city banks.

YEAR	HOUSING STARTS (H) [THOUSANDS]	DISPOSABLE PERSONAL INCOME (I) [$ BILLIONS]	NEW MARRIAGES (M) [THOUSANDS]	COMPANY SALES (S) [$ MILLIONS]	TIME (T)
1947	744	158.9	2,291	92.920	1
1948	942	169.5	1,991	122.440	2
1949	1,033	188.3	1,811	125.570	3
1950	1,138	187.2	1,580	110.460	4
1951	1,549	205.8	1,667	139.400	5
1952	1,211	224.9	1,595	154.020	6
1953	1,251	235.0	1,539	157.590	7
1954	1,225	247.9	1,546	152.230	8
1955	1,354	254.4	1,490	139.130	9
1956	1,475	274.4	1,531	156.330	10
1957	1,240	292.9	1,585	140.470	11
1958	1,157	308.5	1,518	128.240	12
1959	1,341	318.8	1,451	117.450	13
1960	1,531	337.7	1,494	132.640	14
1961	1,274	350.0	1,527	126.160	15
1962	1,327	364.4	1,547	116.990	16
1963	1,469	385.3	1,580	123.900	17
1964	1,615	404.6	1,654	141.320	18
1965	1,538	436.6	1,719	156.710	19
1966	1,488	469.1	1,789	171.930	20
1967	1,173	505.3	1,844	184.790	21
1968	1,299	546.3	1,913	202.700	22
1969	1,524	590.0	2,059	237.340	23
1970	1,479	629.6	2,132	254.930	24

Source: Statistical Abstract of the United States (Washington, Bureau of the Census).

Note: Company sales and disposable per-capita income have been adjusted for the effect of inflation and appear in constant 1959 dollars.

Exhibit 1. Data for Twenty-four Years (1947–1970) Used in Performing Regression Analysis to Forecast 1971 Sales of Cherryoak Company

Gauging Reliability

There are three supplementary statistics that are generally used to test the validity of the equation results. They are: (1) the coefficient of determination (R^2), (2) the "t-value" of the individual regression coefficients in the equation, and (3) the standard error of estimate for the equation as a whole. Each of these deserves some brief explanation.

1. *The coefficient of determination* (R^2). This index shows how good the equation is; that is, it indicates the proportion of the variation in company sales explained by the equation.

The value of .92 obtained in this case means that a very large proportion of the company sales level year-to-year is explained by the number of housing starts, disposable income, marriages, and a time trend. This is a high degree of correlation (1.00 is perfect), and it would appear that the relationships in the equation would be quite useful for forecasting.

2. *The t-values.* These figures pertain to the reliability of the relationship between each independent variable and the dependent variable. We shall not attempt to explain the mathematics involved. Suffice it to say that the computer indicates the B coefficients in the initial regression to have these t-values:

B	B_m	B_h	B_i	B_t
1.2	−3.1	2.0	8.4	−7.3

It is an often-accepted practice to consider as meaningful only those variables with a t-value of at least ±2.0. On this basis we could have confidence in the significance of all of the variables in the equation with the exception of the constant term. The significance of these variables does not mean, however, that the equation cannot be improved.

3. *Standard error of the estimate.* This figure represents the error or imprecision of the regression equation in fitting the historical data. One normally expects about one-third of the actual results (sales in this case) to be outside a range of plus or minus one standard error from the estimate of the regression equation, and one twentieth to be outside a range of plus or minus two standard errors from the regression estimate. Naturally, the smaller the standard error of estimate, the better the regression results.

The proportion of observations outside the above-noted ranges assumes that there are many years of data in the sample on which the regression is based. With relatively few observations, such as in our example, the expectation of these "outliers" is somewhat higher.

The standard error of the initial regression equation tested is 11.9. This means that if we estimate one year into the future, we can expect, with some confidence, that two thirds of the time our estimate of company sales will be in a range of ±$11.9 million around annual sales.

Since the standard error of the estimate is based on historical data only, there is no simple rule for translating this statistic into an estimate of the error that would pertain to a forecast of future years. But the forecast error will be incrementally larger than the standard error the further into the future the forecast is made.

Improving the Equation
One of the greatest advantages of regression as an analytical tool is that it permits testing of many different variables with little additional effort or computer time. Having fed all of the data in Exhibit 1 into the computer,

we can easily modify the formulated equation by changing some of the independent variables where other variables seem more rational.

For instance, we might decide to drop the variable connected with new marriages because there is no apparent reason why new marriages would be *negatively* associated with sales. Yet this is what emerged from the initial regression. This apparent association without causality (to be discussed later) does not seem to be a good foundation for a forecast, so we test a second equation that drops new marriages as a variable and substitutes last year's sales (S_{t-1}).

The idea behind this modification is that a key element in predicting sales this year is how well sales did last year. (This, in effect, incorporates a major principle of extrapolation into the estimate. Variables relating to prior years are commonly referred to as "lagged variables," since their relationship with the dependent variable is in the nature of a delayed response.)

A second modification is using housing starts in the prior year (H_{t-1}) as a predictor of sales in the current year. This allows for the lag one would expect between the time that construction of housing begins and the time that the first occupants start buying home furnishings.

The revised equation including both modifications then is:

$$S = B + B_{s-1}S_{t-1} + B_{h-1}H_{t-1} + B_iI + B_tT$$

The results, with the corresponding t-values below them, are:

$$S = -33.51 + 0.373S_{t-1} + 0.033H_{t-1} + 0.672I - 11.03T$$
$$\quad\;\; -2.1 \qquad 2.8 \qquad\quad 2.4 \qquad\quad 5.7 \qquad -5.1$$

Coefficient of determination (R^2) = .95
Standard error of the estimate = 9.7

It is apparent that we have made an improvement in the overall percentage of variation in sales that the equation explains. The R^2 has increased from .92 to .95, and the standard error of the estimate has been reduced from $11.9 million to $9.7 million. We cannot be sure whether this improvement is due to an improved equation or to the effect of adding a new variable based on the previous year's sales. At any rate, we have a substantially more accurate set of relationships.

Sensitivity Analysis
Obviously, any errors in the measurement or estimation of the independent variables will similarly result in errors in the estimation of the dependent variable. One way of dealing with this problem is through sensitivity analysis.

Although it is possible to compute the exact mathematical effect on the sales forecast if estimates of the independent variables are wrong, a simpler and more popular expedient is to recompute the estimates assuming different levels for the uncertain variables on the right-hand side of the equation.

If the forecast for disposable income, say, was thought to be subject to a forecasting error of ± 10%, the regression equation could be applied using the most likely income estimate, a high estimate, and a low estimate. This is called "sensitivity analysis" because it examines the sensitivity of the prediction to variations in any of the other variables on which the prediction is based.

Regression vs. Extrapolation

Having obtained a reliable basis for prediction, we shall compare the results achieved using the second equation with the results obtainable through a less rigorous approach. Exhibit 2 indicates the difference between actual sales and the sales predicted in the 1947–1970 period using the second, improved regression equation.

YEAR	ACTUAL SALES	PREDICTED SALES	DIFFERENCE	RATIO OF ACTUAL SALES TO PREDICTED SALES
1947	92.29	93.04	−.75	.99
1948	122.44	117.72	4.72	1.04
1949	125.57	136.91	−11.34	.92
1950	110.46	129.33	−18.87	0.85
1951	139.40	128.65	10.75	1.08
1952	154.02	154.90	−.88	.99
1953	157.59	144.88	12.71	1.09
1954	152.23	145.17	7.06	1.05
1955	139.13	135.64	3.49	1.02
1956	156.33	137.44	18.89	1.13
1957	140.47	149.27	−8.80	.94
1958	128.24	134.99	−6.75	.95
1959	117.45	123.56	−6.11	.95
1960	132.64	127.31	5.33	1.04
1961	126.16	136.52	−10.36	.92
1962	116.99	124.20	−7.21	.94
1963	123.90	125.56	−1.66	.99
1964	141.32	134.79	6.53	1.05
1965	156.71	156.61	.10	1.00
1966	171.93	170.59	1.34	1.01
1967	184.79	187.90	−3.11	.98
1968	202.70	198.75	3.95	1.02
1969	237.34	227.95	9.39	1.04
1970	254.93	263.92	−8.99	.96

Exhibit 2. Differences in Actual Sales of Cherryoak Company (1947–1970), and Sales Predicted by Multiple Regression (in millions of dollars)

In most years the estimates of the regression equation are within three or four percentage points of actual sales. The greatest deviations occur in 1956, when the regression estimate was 13% below actual, and in 1950, when it was 15% above.

Comparison of these figures with a simple linear extrapolation (straight-line trend) based on the five years prior to the forecast gives the results shown in Exhibit 3. The coefficient of determination for the linear computation in the 1952–1970 period is .86, as against .95 for the regression equation.

YEAR	ACTUAL SALES	ESTIMATES BY REGRESSION	ESTIMATES BY EXTRAPOLATION
1947	92.29	—	—
1948	122.44	—	—
1949	125.57	—	—
1950	110.46	—	—
1951	139.40	—	—
1952	154.02	154.90	142.45
1953	157.59	144.87	153.47
1954	152.23	145.17	169.69
1955	139.13	135.64	173.25
1956	156.33	137.44	147.77
1957	140.47	149.28	147.71
1958	128.24	134.99	140.11
1959	117.45	123.56	129.29
1960	132.64	127.31	114.89
1961	126.16	136.53	113.90
1962	116.99	124.21	121.72
1963	123.90	125.56	120.15
1964	141.32	134.79	122.60
1965	156.71	156.61	132.73
1966	171.93	170.60	153.84
1967	184.79	187.90	181.98
1968	202.70	198.75	200.25
1969	237.34	227.95	217.34
1970	254.93	263.92	250.70

Exhibit 3. Comparison of Actual Sales with Sales Estimated by Regression and by Linear Extrapolation of Most Recent Five-Year Trend (1952–1970) (in millions of dollars)

The conclusion is that the multiple regression technique goes farther in making rational estimates based on past relationships than does a continuously updated straight-line extrapolation. The comparison is graphically portrayed in Exhibit 4.

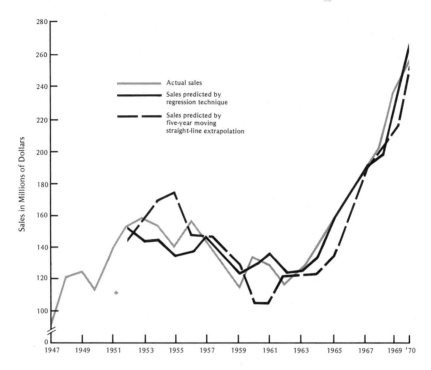

Exhibit 4. Graphic Display of Results Shown in Exhibit 3

FORECASTING EARNINGS

The next step is a prediction of the Cherryoak Company's profits. We can adopt the same approach as before, using a regression equation with cost estimates as the dependent variable and sales or some other factor as the independent variable. If costs were being correlated with sales through regression, the equation would be:

$$E = B + B_s S$$

The symbol E means expense and the symbols B and B_s represent fixed and variable expenses, respectively. This type of representation reflects the pattern of most corporate expenses, where there is a level of expenses that is constant (at least in the short run) and another level that fluctuates proportionately with sales activity. The regression equation identifies each of these components and can be used to test the movement of virtually all types of expenses, including wages and salaries, raw materials, and administrative costs.

In addition to expenses that are sensitive to sales levels, certain costs are determined by reference to other factors. For example, depreciation is more closely related to the level of net fixed assets than to changes in revenues. Interest expense is a function of the amount and terms of debt outstanding and is not specifically related to sales. Usually, it is unnecessary to apply regression techniques to estimate these kinds of expenses, since they are known by management and are predictable.

In the case of Cherryoak, however, information about expected depreciation and interest charges was not available. So we formulated several regression equations to examine how depreciation moved with changes in the level of fixed assets and interest moved with changes in the level of debt outstanding.

Added to the element of fluctuation in costs caused by changes in sales activity is the effect of a basic trend in costs over time. This can be analyzed by including time (T) as an additional variable. With certain cost categories, time is significant; with others, it clearly is not. Only by running the sample data through the regression routine is it possible to make a judgment on this.

We ran several regressions of historical relationships of costs to sales (S), net fixed assets (NFA), or debt outstanding (DO) to see what results emerged. And we made a final regression to equate income taxes (IT) with income before taxes (IBT).

Thus, using the data for 1957–1969 shown in Exhibit 5, we obtained the following summary of cost patterns:

Raw materials costs:

$$M = -3250.87 + 0.4092(S) + 516.99(T)$$
t-values -2.5 33.2 4.1
$R^2 = .99$

Wages and salaries:

$$WS = 4119.78 + 0.2895(S)$$
t-values 5.4 58.9
$R^2 = .99$

Other costs:

$$C = 0.1665(S) - 232.927(T)$$
t-values 42.8 -3.0
$R^2 = .98$

Depreciation:

$$Dp = 0.0598(NFA) + 85.70(T)$$
t-values 22.9 7.4
$R^2 = .98$

Interest:

$$I = 0.0256(DO) + 65.08(T)$$
t-values 2.8 4.2
$R^2 = .75$

Sales taxes:

$$ST = 0.0167(S) + 157.67(T)$$
t-values 9.3   4.5
$R^2 = .93$

Income taxes:

$$IT = 0.5198(IBT) - 55.05(T)$$
t-values 32.7   −2.5
$R^2 = .95$

The results of these seven regression equations yield several conclusions that might be expected. Each equation was determined only after testing several variables and selecting those that were statistically significant, that is, with a t-value greater than 2.0. Those variables that did not help explain variations in costs were not included.

YEAR	RAW MATERIALS	WAGES AND SALARIES	ADMINISTRATIVE AND OTHER EXPENSES	DEPRECIATION AND AMORTIZATION	INTEREST	SALES TAXES	INCOME TAXES
1957	56,188	44,248	22,759	1,610	354	2,553	6,437
1958	50,013	40,524	21,736	1,488	502	2,453	5,882
1959	45,218	38,758	19,227	1,619	531	2,520	4,762
1960	51,730	42,577	19,882	2,041	493	2,836	6,847
1961	50,969	41,759	20,586	1,883	493	2,963	3,597
1962	48,669	38,139	17,633	2,495	578	2,667	3,299
1963	51,914	39,895	19,359	2,510	680	3,115	3,451
1964	58,789	45,222	21,433	2,555	745	4,015	4,181
1965	64,721	49,207	25,109	2,671	742	4,127	4,492
1966	72,038	53,298	26,697	2,691	873	4,129	5,671
1967	78,536	56,730	27,610	2,994	997	5,425	5,292
1968	86,147	63,039	31,241	3,345	1,294	5,450	5,698
1969	100,395	73,575	36,333	3,584	1,143	5,364	8,402

Exhibit 5. Operational and Other Expenses of Cherryoak Company (1957–1969) (in thousands of dollars)

In some equations time was a significant variable, while in others it did not help explain the movement of these costs. Similarly, in some cases the constant term (indicating a constant bottom level on costs) was significant; in others it was not. Wages and salaries, for instance, have a highly significant fixed-cost component, and do not tend to fluctuate greatly with sales.

Perhaps it is unnecessary to mention, but we should caution that interpretation of each equation should cover the entire equation. Obviously, the negative constant term in the first equation, for example, does not mean that materials costs would be negative at zero sales. It merely means that when the data have been run through the computer, the best equation to describe the relationships of the variables in that element of expenses includes a negative constant term.

The great advantage of doing independent regressions for the different cost categories is that it enables the company to modify the forecasted costs easily by considering various expectations about future events that might indicate changes in only a single expense category.

Comparison with Extrapolation

Using the seven cost equations tested, we can obtain an estimate for each element of cost and, adding them together, obtain a total cost estimate for each year. Subtracting the total cost figure from Cherryoak's predicted sales volume gives us a forecast of net earnings.

To show the predictive accuracy of the regression technique, we made hypothetical predictions of Cherryoak's earnings for 14 previous years, using our cost equations. The correlations with actual earnings are shown in Exhibit 6. Then we compared our regression-based forecasts for the most recent nine years with earnings estimated by a five-year moving straight-line extrapolation, as we did in our discussion of sales forecasts. The comparison is shown numerically in Exhibit 7 and graphically in Exhibit 8.

The coefficient of determination of the regression estimates in Exhibit 7 is .93, as against .68 for the extrapolation. The .93 figure covering the most recent nine years is somewhat better than the R^2 of .84 which we obtained for the 14-year period represented in Exhibit 6, but in both cases regression performed measurably better than extrapolation.

PROBLEMS OF APPLICATION

As we have demonstrated, regression analysis is a useful forecasting tool. But it is not without its pitfalls, which can lead the unwary into severe biases or gross errors in results. We shall discuss four of the most important ones:

> 1. *Two-way causation.* A single equation like the one we employed to estimate Cherryoak's sales assumes a one-way direction of influence; that is, sales are presumed to be influenced by the number of housing starts, level of income, and the other independent variables, but not vice versa.
>
> If, however, we introduce other factors influencing sales, such as product price or the amount of advertising the company employs, it is likely that sales will, in turn, influence these variables. This is what is called "two-way causation" or "simultaneity." The presence

YEAR	ACTUAL EARNINGS	PREDICTED EARNINGS	DIFFERENCE	RATIO OF ACTUAL EARNINGS TO PREDICTED EARNINGS
1957	6,321	6,945	−624	0.91
1958	5,641	5,965	−323	0.95
1959	4,815	5,083	−268	0.95
1960	6,234	4,955	1,279	1.25
1961	3,910	5,396	−1,486	0.73
1962	3,510	4,206	−696	0.84
1963	2,976	4,069	−1,093	0.73
1964	4,380	4,382	−2	1.00
1965	5,641	5,407	232	1.02
1966	6,533	5,971	562	1.09
1967	7,206	6,587	619	1.10
1968	6,486	6,784	−298	0.96
1969	8,544	8,192	352	1.04
1970*	9,366	9,840	−474	0.95

*At the time of preparation of this article, Cherryoak's 1970 earnings were available, but a cost breakdown was not. We based our estimates on relationships developed from pre-1970 data.

Exhibit 6. Differences in Actual Earnings of Cherryoak Company (1957–1970) and Earnings Predicted by Multiple Regression (in thousands of dollars)

YEAR	ACTUAL EARNINGS	ESTIMATES BY REGRESSION	ESTIMATES BY EXTRAPOLATION
1957	6,321	—	—
1958	5,642	—	—
1959	4,815	—	—
1960	6,234	—	—
1961	3,910	—	—
1962	3,510	4,206	4,115
1963	2,976	4,069	3,272
1964	4,380	4,382	2,368
1965	5,641	5,407	2,809
1966	6,533	5,971	5,383
1967	7,206	6,587	7,221
1968	6,486	6,787	8,531
1969	8,544	8,192	7,782
1970	9,366	9,840	8,609

Exhibit 7. Comparison of Actual Earnings with Profits Estimated by Regression and by Linear Extrapolation of Most Recent Five-Year Trend (1962–1970) (in thousands of dollars)

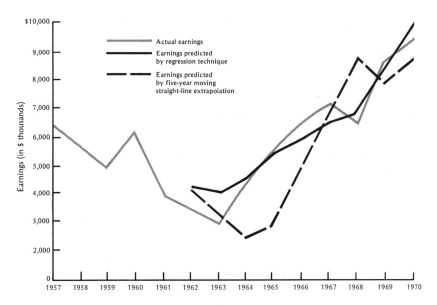

Exhibit 8. Graphic Display of Results Shown in Exhibit 7

of two-way causation makes the single equation model of standard regression analysis less than adequate.

In such cases other equations that take account of the effect of sales on the other variables must be estimated simultaneously with the original equation. For example, if sales (S) are considered to be affected by price (P) and disposable personal income (I), we have to take into account the fact that prices and, perhaps, another variable, like production (Pd), are in turn affected by the level of sales. The system of equations to be estimated then is:

$$S = A_0 + A_1(P) + A_2(I)$$
$$P = B_0 + B_1(S) + B_2(Pd)$$

Other equations that can be added include the relationships of quantities produced and sold of competitive and complementary products, their prices, and relationships of production to several inputs, such as labor, capital, and raw materials.

The great additional difficulty in application of simultaneous equations is sometimes offset by the better results obtained, mainly when the user wants forecasts for more than one year ahead.

The extension of regression analysis into simultaneous equations is considerably beyond the scope or purpose of this discussion. Nonetheless, it is worth mentioning them because they are coming into increasing use, particularly in building macroeconomic models, in corporate as well as in governmental planning offices.

2. *Multicollinearity.* This is the problem that arises when some of the independent variables are not independent of each other. Such

a situation would have arisen in our example if we had correlated population with sales as well as disposable income with sales, since both variables have shown a strong association with each other in the past. The problem here is that it is difficult to measure the extent of their *separate* effects on sales.

When multicollinearity exists, the best procedure is to drop one of the variables. If this is not done, however, the forecasting result will not be affected if the planner expects the intercorrelation between the independent variables to continue in the future.

3. *Autocorrelation.* This problem occurs when the equation systematically "overpredicts" for some periods and "underpredicts" for others. Such consistent (as opposed to random) errors could be caused by the omission of critical variables from the equation.

If no additional important variables can be found, an alternative is to use results of the prior year as an extra explanatory variable. This is precisely what we did in our example of the sales forecasts. Usually the test for autocorrelation is made by the computer routine and is labeled as such.

4. *Apparent association without causality.* It occasionally happens that regression can indicate high levels of correlation between variables in historical data where there is no reason for any cause-and-effect relationship to exist. For example, professors' salaries have been shown to be highly correlated with per-capita liquor consumption. This correlation, however, cannot be presumed to have any causal rationale, and consequently it would be very tenuous as a basis for prediction.

The user of regression analysis should always strive to isolate those independent variables thought to have some rational cause-and-effect connection with the dependent variable, since it is primarily those types of relationships that can be presumed to continue in the future.

CONCLUDING NOTE

We have tried here to put computer-assisted forecasting into a management perspective. The scientific approach to forecasting, especially the regression technique, exploits managers' *knowledge* of the various factors important to business operation better than any intuitive or nonanalytical method can.

Forecasting, however, remains an imprecise art; clearly, subjectivity and good judgment will continue to play a crucial role in it. This element must remain as long as the future refuses to replicate the past in both substance and detail.

Nonetheless, through the technique of scientific, computer-assisted forecasts, subjective and speculative conclusions about the nature of the past can be made more explicit and more accurate in terms of their implications. This, in itself, is a useful and important step forward.

22.

STEPWISE MULTIPLE REGRESSION IN PLANNING SIMULATIONS AND FORECASTING*

*Donald L. Anderson
and
Donald L. Raun*

INTRODUCTION

Multiple regression analysis relates a dependent variable Y to more than one independent variable, X_1, X_2, X_3, etc. The essential weakness of simple regression analysis is that the dependent variable is often materially affected by more than one independent variable. Assume that for a simple linear regression the coefficient of determination is .64: if additional relevant factors (independent variables) can be identified, we may improve our ability to estimate by using multiple regression analysis.

A multiple regression equation can be written in the form:

$$Y = a + b_1X_1 + b_2X_2 + b_3X_3 + \ldots$$

In the equation, Y is the dependent variable, the term a represents the value of Yc (the calculated value of Y) when each X is zero. The b_1, b_2, b_3 terms are the coefficients of the independent variables, and each coefficient represents the change in the dependent variable Y per unit change in the appropriate X (b_1 and X_1, for example) but with the other independent variables held constant.

As the number of independent variables increases, there is an increase in the number of equations that must be solved and the computations become more time consuming; the computer can help make it feasible for management to use multiple regression models.

If we want to determine the calculated value of Y, i.e., Yc, where the multiple regression solution shows 8 for the intercept a and where b_1 equals 1.5, b_2 equals 2.5 and b_3 equals 4, then the calculated value of Y can be determined from $Yc = 8 + 1.5\,(X_1) + 2.5\,(X_2) + 4.0\,(X_3)$.

---

*Printed by permission of the authors.

Some of the factors chosen by management as independent variables for a multiple regression problem may be correlated. This is the problem of multicollinearity, and means that certain variables are not independent but move together in the same direction and at the same approximate rate. The problem of multicollinearity was mentioned to point out the fact that there are important requirements for the data used for a multiple regression analysis. The multicollinearity problem and other problems that need to be considered in applying the method are discussed in the preceding article by Parker and Segura, "How to Get a Better Forecast." The article explains the use of multiple regression analysis in forecasting sales and earnings and discusses tests to determine the reliability of equation results (see Gauging Reliability, and Improving the Equation).[1]

STEPWISE MULTIPLE REGRESSION

Management can analyze independent variables affecting a dependent variable using a stepwise multiple regression program and a computer. The computer can print out a step solution so that the variables added in each step are in order of importance and unimportant variables can be discarded. We discuss the application of stepwise multiple regression below.

For the following discussion, the dependent variable is identified as variable number 1, and the independent variables are identified as variables numbered 2 through 8 (see Exhibit 1 attached at the end of this paper). The meaning of the identification letters above the columns numbered 1 through 8 in Exhibit 1 is part of the discussion (see model 9) in a subsequent section about the sales volume function for a simulation problem called the Standard Company; an understanding of the identification letters is not needed for the present discussion.

It should be noted that some of the input items in Exhibit 1 have minus signs in front of them and the column headings indicate this results from the subtraction of certain figures for determining the value for an independent variable. In the case of variable 1, which is the dependent variable, a minus sign means there has been a decrease for the percentage change in

---

[1] In discussing cautions for the use of multiple regression analysis, William A. Spurr and Charles P. Bonini, *Statistical Analysis for Business Decisions* (Homewood, Ill.: Richard D. Irwin, 1967), pp. 608–610, state: "The use of multiple regression formulas in making inferences implies the assumptions that the residuals $z = Y - Y_c$ are (1) clustered around a rectilinear (not curved) plane, (2) independent of each other (3) uniform in their scatter, and, for small samples, (4) normally distributed. If these assumptions are not valid, conclusions from multiple regression analysis may be very misleading. Yet they are often overlooked because of the ease in running a computer program and the difficulty of checking the assumptions mathematically. A simple graphic check is to first plot the original variables against each other, . . . and then, after running the program, to plot the residuals against each independent variable. . . . The residuals can then be checked visually for these conditions." (The deleted information in the above quotation refers to charts in the book where data is plotted.) See Robert E. Jensen, "A Multiple Regression Model for Cost Control—Assumptions and Limitations," *The Accounting Review*, April 1967, pp. 265–273.

volume. The symbol Δ is used in the column heading to represent change in the variable. If we attempt to determine company sales as a function of a number of independent variables, we might develop an equation by analyzing the absolute amounts from past observations for the dependent and independent variables. Again, because in our example the dependent variable represents percentage change in volume, and we use the difference between amounts for certain variables, there can be negative values for the input data.

Once the identification code for the stepwise multiple linear regression program has been entered into the computer, the program user is asked to enter how many variables and observations for the variables will be involved in the problem. For a problem with eight variables (one dependent and seven independent) and fifteen past observations for each variable, the user would enter 8 after the question about number of variables, and 15 after the question about number of observations.

The observed values (actual values) for the 8 variables can be entered into the computer by using a terminal and typing all the values for variable 1, then all the values for variable 2, etc.; they also can be entered from a data file. By entering the numbers 8 and 15 before the problem data, the computer counts fifteen observations for a variable before moving on to classify the next fifteen observations for another variable and so on in sequence. The user can ask for a listing of the data, and the computer prints eight columns numbered 1 through 8 for each of the variables with 15 rows or observations for each column.

The solution printout (Exhibit 1) starts with the listing of the data. Note that for this problem the data was not entered from a terminal, but from a data file that stores the information. VOL 73 is the code used for the data file that contains the volume function information for the Standard Company.

The user is asked to specify the number for the independent variable; 1 is typed in and appears on the solution printout after the listing of the variables and observations. On the printout, the user's responses are underlined. The solution printout then shows seven steps concerned with the seven independent variables being considered for the equation to determine the dependent variable. The Exhibit 1 solution shows the independent variables ranked in the order 6, 7, 3, 8, 2, 5, 4 after all the steps have been completed. Variable number 1 is the dependent variable and is not included in one of the steps.

A table of residuals that uses each of the seven independent variables can be printed out as part of the solution. The table shows the observed value for the dependent variable as −.303 for observation 1. The observed value is a minus figure because the dependent variable 1 represents a percentage change in volume and the volume had decreased. Thus, variable 1 does not represent total sales volume in units, although this can be determined using the step 7 equation; this is shown in a subsequent section about the Standard Company problem.

The estimated value for the dependent variable (Y estimated) is shown in the table of residuals as −.302 for observation 1; this results from using the equation from the seventh step of the printout. Step 7 contains all the independent variables (2 through 8). We used more independent variables in an earlier printout (the variables are based on data for an actual firm) but the variables contained in step 7 are the ones we include for the multiple regression equation. Step 7 shows .999 for the cumulative proportion reduced (R^2, or the multiple correlation coefficient squared) and .004 is the standard error of estimate.

In discussing how many independent variables should be used for a multiple regression equation, Hughes and Grawoig state:

> Because we use computers to relieve the tedium of mathematical calculations, we now find it increasingly easy to include more and more variables in a regression model. We reason fallaciously that the main objective of the analysis is to obtain as high a value of R^2 as is possible. The inclusion of an additional variable inevitably increases this value. So we continue, indiscriminately, to include another and still another independent variable.
>
> Yet it is not desirable to have too many variables in a regression equation. We should include only those variables that are believed likely to make an important contribution to the effectiveness of the predicting equation. Generally, three or four carefully chosen variables will provide a satisfactory relationship. With too many variables in the predicting equation, there is always the problem of obtaining observations to be applied in subsequent predictions. The interpretation of the effect of each individual variable becomes quite involved. Valuable degrees of freedom are lost, and this can have a serious consequence when the sample is small. Lastly, simplicity is itself almost always a virtue.[2]

Steps 3 and 4 below are from a computer solution for a stepwise multiple regression problem (IV-Q10). The printout shows:

```
STEP 3
VARIABLE ENTERED ...................... 4
SUM OF SQUARES REDUCED IN THIS STEP ..........    143.248
PROPORTION OF VARIANCE OF Y REDUCED .........       .003
CUMULATIVE SUM OF SQUARES REDUCED ..........  53624.758
CUMULATIVE PROPORTION REDUCED ..............       .997 OF 53776.496
FOR 3 VARIABLES ENTERED
    MULTIPLE CORRELATION COEFFICIENT .............      .999
    F-VALUE FOR ANALYSIS OF VARIANCE ............  1295.812
    STANDARD ERROR OF ESTIMATE ..................    3.714
       VARIABLE NO           REG. COEFF.
           5              4.681056E − 01
           2              1.142754E + 00
           4             −1.289336E + 00
       INTERCEPT         −1.607419E + 01
DO YOU WISH TO GO TO THE NEXT STEP? YES
```

[2] Ann Hughes and Dennis Grawoig, *Statistics, A Foundation for Analysis* (Reading, Mass.: Addison-Wesley Publishing Co., 1971), p. 375.

STEP 4
VARIABLE ENTERED 3
SUM OF SQUARES REDUCED IN THIS STEP 1.167
PROPORTION OF VARIANCE OF Y REDUCED 000
CUMULATIVE SUM OF SQUARES REDUCED 53625.924
CUMULATIVE PROPORTION REDUCED ....   .997 OF 53776.496
FOR 4 VARIABLES ENTERED
    MULTIPLE CORRELATION COEFFICIENT 999
    F-VALUE FOR ANALYSIS OF VARIANCE 890.373
    STANDARD ERROR OF ESTIMATE 3.880

VARIABLE NO.	REG. COEFF.
5	4.680053E−01
2	1.166517E+00
4	−1.278208E+00
3	−7.296275E−01
INTERCEPT	−5.781215E+00

ALL VARIABLES ARE ENTERED.
SPECIFY WHETHER YOU WISH TO PRINT THE TABLE OF RESIDUALS BY TYPING YES
OR NO. NO

After step 3 has been completed, R^2 is .997 and the standard error of estimate is 3.714, but the standard error of estimate increases to 3.880 in step 4. For the multiple regression equation, we could include the variables 5, 2, and 4, as listed in step 3. Note that 1 is the dependent variable and 2, 3, 4, and 5 are the possible independent variables. When some of the independent variables used in a multiple regression equation are not independent of each other (see multicollinearity in Article 21), this affects the reliability of *individual* variables in the regression, but may not alter the predictive power of the *total* regression equation because the standard error of estimate may not be increased.[3] In order to determine intercorrelation between the independent variables, a correlation matrix program from a statistical package of computer programs can be used (see the editors' note to VI-Q17).

For the Exhibit 1 problem, we use the independent variables listed in step 7. For calculating a Y estimated value by using the step 7 equation, it is necessary to know that in a printout, E−01 after a regression coefficient means the decimal should be moved one place to the left. E+00 means the decimal should not be moved, and E+01 means the decimal should be moved one place to the right. E−04 for the step 7 intercept means the decimal should be moved four places to the left. The −.302 Y estimated for observation 1 results from −.0005 −.147(variable 2) + .125(variable 3) + .041(variable 4) + .59(variable 5) + .308(variable 6) + .376(variable 7) + .354(variable 8). The values for the variables are those relevant for observation 1. Thus, −.0005 −.147(.7020) + .125(.1280) + .041(−.1260) + .59(−.0540) + .308(−.5780) + .376(0.000) + .354(0.000) = −.302.

---

[3] See Spurr and Bonini, op. cit., pp. 610–611; also, Lawrence A. Gordon, "Comment on the Value of R^2 in Regression Analysis," *The Accounting Review*, April 1972, pp. 356–357, and a reply pp. 358–359.

Explanation of the Problem Used for the Stepwise Multiple Regression

As previously indicated, the data for the above discussion came from the volume function of a profit planning simulation problem that we identify as the Standard Company. The volume function for the problem was developed using a stepwise multiple linear regression program. The variables used appear in the column headings of Exhibit 1; the symbols used for the variables are explained following model 9 on page 325.

Statement of the Problem
If we review the performance of three companies in some period (assume period 26), we find that the sales volume and sales effort decisions were as follows:

	Company		
Period 26	1	2	3
Sales Volume, Units	1249	1418	1447
Sales Effort Decisions (per unit sold)			
Price	$10.46	$10.64	$10.92
Advertising	.72	.72	.83
Product Research	.01	.98	.01
Credit Policy (Planned Bad Debt Losses)	.16	.34	.17
Sales Salaries	.01	.01	.65
Totals	$ .90	$ 2.05	$ 1.66

What would the sales volume of Company No. 1 have been if management had budgeted as follows?

Price	$10.00
Advertising	.90
Product Research	1.00
Credit	.60
Sales Salaries	1.40

Determining the Relevant Factors
If we simplify the problem by assuming that the sales effort factors for Companies 1, 2 and 3 have a similar effect on sales volume, then it appears that varying the budgets affects the sales volume. We can test this assumption by employing a decision simulation, proceeding to vary one factor while we hold all other factors constant, thus testing various alternative sets of decisions. Another method of testing the assumption is to employ stepwise multiple regression and the computer to identify the relevant factors and their relationship to sales volume (Exhibit 1).

Building the Decision Model
The results of either type of analysis can be represented by mathematical models as follows:

(1)	V	=	− .15(Price)
(2)	V	=	+ .125(Advertising)
(3)	V	=	+ .04(Product Research)
(4)	V	=	+ .6(Credit)
(5)	V	=	+ .3(Sales Salaries)
(6)	V	=	+ .375(Advertising of Previous Period)
(7)	V	=	+ .36(Product Research of Previous Period)

where

$$V \;=\; \text{a percentage change in sales volume.}$$

The above models may be combined into one model as follows:

$$(8) \quad V \;=\; -.15(P) + .125(A) + .04(PR) + .6(CR) + .3(SS) + .375(A{-}1) + .36(PR{-}1)$$

Actually, if we also allow the competitors' price, advertising, product research, credit, and sales salaries to vary, we discover *the strategic factors are the differences between our budget on a factor* and the average of the industry. Thus, the complete model (see step 7 of Exhibit 1) is:

$$(9) \quad V \;=\; -.15(P1{-}P) + .125(A1{-}A) + .04(PR1{-}PR) + .6(CR1{-}CR) + .3(SS1{-}SS) + .375[(A1{-}1){-}(A{-}1)] + .36\,[(PR1{-}1){-}(PR{-}1)]$$

(The intercept from step 7 of Exhibit 1 is −.0005; it can be part of model 9 but is not included here. Model 9 is the volume function as we use it for the Standard Company simulation problem. Note that variable 1 is the dependent variable (% change in volume) and is not listed as part of the step 7 printout. Variables 2 through 8 are the independent variables.)

where:

V	=	a percentage change in volume from the previous period
P1	=	price per unit, Company No. 1
P	=	price per unit, average for industry, (Price Co. No. 1 + Co. No. 2 + Co. No. 3)/3
A1	=	advertising per unit, Co. No. 1
A	=	advertising per unit, average of industry
PR1	=	product research per unit, Co. No. 1
PR	=	product research per unit, average of industry
CR1	=	credit per unit, Co. No. 1
CR	=	credit per unit, average of industry
SS1	=	sales salaries per unit, Co. No. 1
SS	=	sales salaries per unit, average of industry
A1−1	=	advertising per unit of previous period, Co. No. 1
A−1	=	advertising per unit of previous period, average of industry
PR1−1	=	product research per unit of previous period, Co. No. 1
PR−1	=	product research per unit of previous period, average of industry

A model to predict the actual sales volume (rather than the percentage change in volume) would appear as follows:

$$(10) \quad V1 \; = \; V_{-1}[-.15(P1-P) + .125(A1-A) + .04(PR1-PR) + .6(CR1-CR) \\ + .3(SS1-SS) + .375((A1-1)-(A-1)) + .36((PR1-1)-(PR-1))] \\ + V_{-1}$$

where:

$V1$	=	sales volume in units for the current period, Co. No. 1
V_{-1}	=	sales volume in units for the previous period, Co. No. 1

Testing the Model
The following data were obtained from period 25:

V_{-1}	=	1372 units
$A1-1$	=	.20
$A-1$	=	.20
$PR1-1$	=	.10
$PR-1$	=	.10

We can use Model No. 10 above to predict the sales volume of Company No. 1 for period 26 as follows:

$$V1 \; = \; 1372[-.15(10.46-10.67) + .125(.72-.7567) + .04(.01-.333) \\ + .6(.16-.223) + .3(.01-.223) + .375(.20-.20) + .36(.10-.10)] + 1372$$
$$V1 \; = \; 1251$$

The model predicts that the sales volume of Company No. 1 would be 1251 with the decision strategy employed. On the basis of this limited test, it appears to be a useful model to predict the results of decision strategies for the sales volume.

Prediction	1251
Actual	1249 (see the problem information p. 324)

Note that the mathematical model shows that a plus 30-cent differential amount budgeted for each of the factors has the following effect on sales volume:

Price	− 4.500%
Advertising	+ 3.750%
Product Research	+ 1.200%
Credit	+ 18.000%
Sales Salaries	+ 9.000%

Exhibit 1. Stepwise Multiple Linear Regression

DO YOU WANT INSTRUCTIONS (YES OR NO)? NO
NUMBER OF VARIABLES — 8
NUMBER OF OBSERVATIONS — 15
ENTER DATA FILE NAME OR TERMINAL — VOL 73

DO YOU WANT EVERYTHING LISTED (YES OR NO)? YES

VARIABLE OBS	%ΔVOL 1	(P1–P)* PRICE 2	(A1–A) ADVERTISING 3	(PR1–PR) PRODUCT RESEARCH 4	(CR1–CR) CREDIT POLICY 5
1	–.3032	.7020	.1280	–.1260	–.0540
2	–.3494	.6120	–.6460	.4720	–.1200
3	.2797	–.8460	.3020	.6580	–.0520
4	.4736	–.1060	.0880	–.3800	–.1060
5	–.1782	.0320	–.0040	–.4300	.0580
6	–.2562	–.0400	.1040	–.3300	–.0300
7	–.0683	–.7140	.4820	–.1900	–.1820
8	.0225	.2560	.3800	–.1000	–.0980
9	.1054	.0340	.4360	–.1440	–.0020
10	.1563	–.7180	.4840	.0460	–.0680
11	.1340	.0760	.4140	–.0100	–.0480
12	.0232	–.0280	.3660	.2300	–.1740
13	–.0611	.3120	.4300	.1760	–.2120
14	.0109	.3000	0.0000	–.1800	–.0260
15	–.1689	–.2080	.2400	.1460	–.0620

VARIABLE OBS	(SS1–SS) SALES SALARIES 6	(A1–1)– (A–1) 7	(PR1–1)– (PR–1) 8
1	–.5780	0.0000	0.0000
2	–.4120	.1200	–.1260
3	.6360	–.6460	.4720
4	.5920	.3020	.6580
5	–.2840	.0880	–.3800
6	–.2840	–.0040	–.4300
7	–.1400	.1040	–.3300
8	–.1460	.4820	–.1900
9	–.1340	.3800	–.1000
10	–.2600	.4360	–.1440
11	–.2400	.4800	.0460
12	–.2780	.4140	–.0100
13	–.2900	.2400	.1460
14	–.4700	.3600	.2300
15	–.4320	0.0000	–.1800

* See page 325 for the meaning of the identification symbols.

DEPENDENT VARIABLE — 1
DO YOU WISH TO DELETE ANY VARIABLES (YES OR NO)?   NO

VARIABLE	SUMS	AVERAGES	DEVIATIONS	CORRELATION
2	−.33600000	−.02240000	.45658496	−.51522921
3	3.20400000	.21360000	.29374839	.45547521
4	−.16200000	−.01080000	.30644487	.00624057
5	−1.17600000	−.07840000	.07207219	−.04917125
6	−2.72000000	−.18133333	.34639504	.79737827
7	2.75600000	.18373333	.29166308	.12441237
8	−.33800000	−.02253333	.30212057	.71373807

STEP 1

VARIABLE ENTERED 6
SUM OF SQUARES REDUCED IN THIS STEP 44724217
PROPORTION OF VARIANCE OF Y REDUCED 63581210
CUMULATIVE SUM OF SQUARES REDUCED 44724217
CUMULATIVE PROPORTION REDUCED . . . .   .63581210 OF .7034

FOR 1 VARIABLE ENTERED
    MULTIPLE CORRELATION COEFFICIENT 79737827
    F-VALUE FOR ANALYSIS OF VARIANCE 22.69585956
    STANDARD ERROR OF ESTIMATE 14037768
        VARIABLE NO.   REG. COEFF.
            6   5.159834E-01
        INTERCEPT   8.158273E-02

DO YOU WISH TO GO TO THE NEXT STEP (YES OR NO)? YES

STEP 2

VARIABLE ENTERED 7
SUM OF SQUARES REDUCED IN THIS STEP 14365640
PROPORTION OF VARIANCE OF Y REDUCED 20422600
CUMULATIVE SUM OF SQUARES REDUCED 59089857
CUMULATIVE PROPORTION REDUCED . . . .   .84003810 OF .7034

For 2 VARIABLES ENTERED
    MULTIPLE CORRELATION COEFFICIENT 91653592
    F-VALUE FOR ANALYSIS OF VARIANCE 31.50893198
    STANDARD ERROR OF ESTIMATE 09683328
        VARIABLE NO.   REG. COEFF.
            6   6.325983E-01
            7   3.739062E-01
        INTERCEPT   3.402987E-02

DO YOU WISH TO GO TO THE NEXT STEP (YES OR NO)? YES

STEP 3

VARIABLE ENTERED 3
SUM OF SQUARES REDUCED IN THIS STEP 02841828
PROPORTION OF VARIANCE OF Y REDUCED 04040023
CUMULATIVE SUM OF SQUARES REDUCED 61931685
CUMULATIVE PROPORTION REDUCED . . . .   .88043833 OF .7034

FOR 3 VARIABLES ENTERED
   MULTIPLE CORRELATION COEFFICIENT 93831676
   F-VALUE FOR ANALYSIS OF VARIANCE 27.00091068
   STANDARD ERROR OF ESTIMATE 08743929
      VARIABLE NO.   REG. COEFF.
           6   5.931228E-01
           7   3.254730E-01
           3   1.623132E-01
      INTERCEPT   1.100362E-03

DO YOU WISH TO GO TO THE NEXT STEP (YES OR NO)? YES

STEP 4

VARIABLE ENTERED 8
SUM OF SQUARES REDUCED IN THIS STEP 04150067
PROPORTION OF VARIANCE OF Y REDUCED 05899852
CUMULATIVE SUM OF SQUARES REDUCED 66081752
CUMULATIVE PROPORTION REDUCED . . . .   .93943685 OF .7034

FOR 4 VARIABLES ENTERED
   MULTIPLE CORRELATION COEFFICIENT 96924551
   F-VALUE FOR ANALYSIS OF VARIANCE 38.77922735
   STANDARD ERROR OF ESTIMATE 06526964
      VARIABLE NO.   REG. COEFF.
           6   4.358736E-01
           7   2.859743E-01
           3   2.023444E-01
           8   2.445587E-01
      INTERCEPT   −2.319690E-02

DO YOU WISH TO GO TO THE NEXT STEP (YES OR NO)? YES

STEP 5

```
VARIABLE ENTERED . . . . .  2
SUM OF SQUARES REDUCED IN THIS STEP . . . . . . . . . .     .02335119
PROPORTION OF VARIANCE OF Y REDUCED . . . . . . . . .     .03319671
CUMULATIVE SUM OF SQUARES REDUCED . . . . . . . . . .     .68416871
CUMULATIVE PROPORTION REDUCED . . . . . . . . . . . . . .     .97263357 OF .7034

FOR 5 VARIABLES ENTERED
    MULTIPLE CORRELATION COEFFICIENT . . . . . . . . . . . . .     .98622186
    F-VALUE FOR ANALYSIS OF VARIANCE . . . . . . . . . . . .   63.97400597
    STANDARD ERROR OF ESTIMATE . . . . . . . . . . . . . . . . .     .04624820
        VARIABLE NO.              REG. COEFF.
             6                  3.066790E-01
             7                  3.403298E-01
             3                  9.720625E-02
             8                  3.363848E-01
             2                 -1.505632E-01
        INTERCEPT              -3.545705E-02
```

DO YOU WISH TO GO TO THE NEXT STEP (YES OR NO)? <u>YES</u>

STEP 6

```
VARIABLE ENTERED . . . . .  5
SUM OF SQUARES REDUCED IN THIS STEP . . . . . . . . . .     .01785556
PROPORTION OF VARIANCE OF Y REDUCED . . . . . . . . .     .02538397
CUMULATIVE SUM OF SQUARES REDUCED . . . . . . . . . .     .70202428
CUMULATIVE PROPORTION REDUCED . . . . . . . . . . . . . .     .99801754 OF .7034

FOR 6 VARIABLES ENTERED
    MULTIPLE CORRELATION COEFFICIENT . . . . . . . . . . . . .     .99900828
    F-VALUE FOR ANALYSIS OF VARIANCE . . . . . . . . . . . .  671.23195870
    STANDARD ERROR OF ESTIMATE . . . . . . . . . . . . . . . . .     .01320274
        VARIABLE NO.              REG. COEFF.
             6                  2.917075E-01
             7                  3.560605E-01
             3                  1.176893E-01
             8                  3.707383E-01
             2                 -1.545870E-01
             5                  5.193827E-01
        INTERCEPT              -4.033734E-03
```

DO YOU WISH TO GO TO THE NEXT STEP (YES OR NO)? <u>YES</u>

STEP 7

VARIABLE ENTERED   4
SUM OF SQUARES REDUCED IN THIS STEP 00125886
PROPORTION OF VARIANCE OF Y REDUCED 00178964
CUMULATIVE SUM OF SQUARES REDUCED 70328314
CUMULATIVE PROPORTION REDUCED . . . .   .99980718 OF .7034

FOR 7 VARIABLES ENTERED
   MULTIPLE CORRELATION COEFFICIENT 99990358
   F-VALUE FOR ANALYSIS OF VARIANCE 5185.13954413
   STANDARD ERROR OF ESTIMATE 00440186

VARIABLE NO.	REG. COEFF.
6	3.076220E-01
7	3.757662E-01
3	1.249644E-01
8	3.539868E-01
2	−1.465147E-01
5	5.901592E-01
4	4.132175E-02
INTERCEPT	−5.239830E-04

RESIDUALS (YES OR NO)? YES

DO YOU WANT TO FIND RESIDUALS FOR ALL OF
THE OBSERVATIONS (YES OR NO)? YES

TABLE OF RESIDUALS

OBSERVATION	Y OBSERVED	Y ESTIMATED	RESIDUAL	RES. PCNT. OF EST.
1	−.303	−.302	−.001	.312
2	−.349	−.348	−.001	.255
3	.280	.278	.002	.753
4	.474	.476	−.003	−.555
5	−.178	−.178	−.000	.063
6	−.256	−.254	−.002	.840
7	−.068	−.072	.003	−4.743
8	.022	.016	.006	36.621
9	.105	.108	−.003	−2.409
10	.156	.160	−.004	−2.199
11	.134	.134	−.000	−.102
12	.023	.023	.001	2.614
13	−.061	−.058	−.003	5.923
14	.011	.005	.006	123.891
15	−.169	−.167	−.002	1.029

TEST OF EXTREME RESIDUALS
   RATIO OF RANGES FOR THE SMALLEST RESIDUAL 12586452
   RATIO OF RANGES FOR THE LARGEST RESIDUAL 30206950
   CRITICAL VALUE OF THE RATIO AT ALPHA = .10 47200000

23.
EFFECTS OF LEARNING ON COST PROJECTIONS*

Edwin A. Bump

The problem of projecting costs affects the management of most business entities. Accurate predictions of the amounts and the timing of cost incurrence are essential to provide a basis for informed decision making. The need for accurate predictions is particularly acute for new product evaluation decisions since the quality of these decisions determines the long-run profitability of the firm. Yet, by the very nature of these decisions, the amount and quality of available data are extremely limited.

With the importance attached to cost projections in product evaluation decisions, it is not surprising that a number of methods have been developed and are in regular use to provide these data.[1] Within the context of cost projection techniques, the purpose of this article is to discuss the effects of learning theory, to illustrate its potential for use in product evaluation decisions, and to review the related financial planning and cost control aspects of such decision.

COST PROJECTIONS

Most cost projections are based on some derived average cost per unit. By its very nature, an average presumes some level of production. If some form of learning is present (although possibly undefined), use of this constant

---

[1]Probably the most common techniques of cost projection are based on engineering standards and recent experience. The first is commonly used in job shops and in construction. The second appears frequently in mass production industries. Another approach to cost estimation considers data from similar products or operations and adjusts it for anticipated changes and contingencies.

332

average cost underestimates the actual unit costs in the early stages of production and overestimates the actual unit costs in the later stages. If the N units used in deriving the average cost are actually produced, the unit errors in estimation balance to zero. This effect is illustrated in Exhibit 1 in the Areas A and A'. If N = 200, the areas of over and underestimation (A' and A) are equal. If N ± Y units are actually produced, aggregate over- or underestimation occurs since these areas are not equal. In addition, a constant, standard, or average cost does not facilitate control if particular unit costs can realistically be expected at levels more or less than this amount.

One of the problems with using an average value (regardless of its ability to forecast accurately average costs) is in its inability to consider the timing dimensions of expected costs. The timing of cost incurrence is very crucial

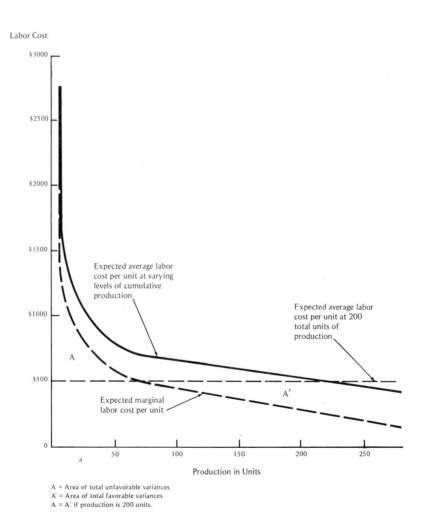

Exhibit 1. Average and Marginal Cost Curves

to capital budgeting and financial planning. In making new product evaluation decisions, the application of time (or learning-based) cost predictions can affect planning and control functions. In the area of planning, such cost predictions appear useful in deciding whether or not to produce and in coordinating financial resource requirements. These costs are also useful as a base for product cost control decisions.

THE PLANNING FUNCTION

The desirability of producing a new product is generally cast in a capital budgeting format for evaluation. It begins when an idea for a product is discussed. At that time, guesstimates of the relevant data inputs are made and are applied in a loose evaluative format to eliminate from further consideration any obviously undesirable or infeasible products. The remaining product proposals are then evaluated in terms of the desirability of continued development to obtain better data. After a series of these informal evaluations, a conscious effort is made to evaluate market potential, sales pricing, costs, and other relevant decision-making parameters. Engineering and product design groups are likely to determine production means and methods and establish design specifications. Quite probably a prototype or two is completed and market reactions are sought. With the data and subjective opinions obtained from these efforts, an evaluation occurs to determine whether or not to manufacture the product. At this point, the learning curve may be useful in projecting costs and capacity to produce.

Although the learning phenomenon has been recognized in many industries, the cost projection techniques typically employed do not consider its impact.[2] Instead, cost projections for purposes of capital budgeting and cost control are usually based on assumptions of constant unit costs.[3] To improve the estimates of these costs, consideration should be given to the effects of learning on labor usage. In addition, the use of learning curves should facilitate cost control, permit improved estimates of attainable production levels, and allow for better financial planning.

---

[2]In addition to the aircraft industry and other businesses having high labor inputs, studies indicate learning factors in parts assembly, the manufacture of subcomponents, in production from processing units of a refinery, in maintenance operations, in the electric industry, in steel production and others. See for example: Winfred B. Hirschmann, "Profit From The Learning Curve," *Harvard Business Review*, January–February 1964; R. W. Conway and A. Schultz, Jr., "The Manufacturing Process Function," *The Journal of Industrial Engineering*, January–February 1959; and N. Baloff, "Startups in Machine-Intensive Production Systems," *Journal of Industrial Engineering*, January 1966.

[3]The expected value (single dollar amount) of cost appears most frequently.

THE LEARNING CURVE

A learning curve describes the observed improvement in operations as these operations are repeated.[4] The basis supporting the theory of learning is quite simple. The focus is on the worker. As he works, he learns. The more often he repeats an operation, the more efficient he becomes. This increase in efficiency results in a reduction of the labor input per unit of product. These rather commonplace observations were transformed into a useful concept when it was discovered that the rate of improvement is regular enough to be predictable and included entire operations as well as the more common focus on direct labor hours and costs.[5]

Intensive study revealed that whenever the total quantity of units produced doubled, the cumulative average hours of labor input declined by a constant percentage—approximately 20 percent in the aircraft industry. "Because this rate of improvement seemed to prevail so consistently, it was concluded that the aircraft industry's rate of learning was approximately 80 percent. . . ."[6] The 80 percent learning rate means that if the first unit produced requires 100 hours, the "cumulative average" time for producing a total of two units should be 80 hours per unit (80% of 100) and the cumulative average time to produce a total of four units should be 64 hours per unit. A cumulative average time of 80 hours for two units implies that the second unit required a "marginal" 60 hours for its production [(100 + 60) ÷ 2 = 80]. Similarly, a cumulative average of 64 hours for four units implies the marginal time required for the last two units of 96 hours [(160 + 96) ÷ 4 = 64]. It is important to clearly maintain a distinction between "cumulative average" and "marginal" production times.

The phenomenon of learning discussed above can be expressed mathematically as:

$$Y = aX^b$$

where:

> Y = The average number of hours per unit required to produce a total of X units

---

[4]T. P. Wright is generally credited with the development of the theory of learning curves based on his attempts to measure manufacturing progress in the airplane industry, although others have refined and added to the theory. Wright focused on direct labor hours and the reductions in labor time per unit as workers gained experience. As the cumulative number of planes produced increased, unit costs were reduced and more planes could be produced with the same work force and facilities. Further, it was found that this "learning process" repeated itself whenever a new type of airplane was put into production and the pattern of learning occurred with considerable regularity. For a discussion, see Conway and Schultz, op. cit.

[5]Frank J. Andress, "The Learning Curve as a Production Tool," *Harvard Business Review*, January–February 1954.

[6]Ibid., p. 88.

$$a \quad = \quad \text{The number of hours required to produce the first unit}$$
$$X \quad = \quad \text{The cumulative number of units to be produced}$$
$$b \quad = \quad \text{The index of learning[7] (log of learning rate} \div \text{log of 2)}$$

To solve for Y, we must first convert the equation to its logarithmic form:

$$\log Y = (\log a) + b \ (\log X)$$

For example, let:

$$a \quad = \quad 100 \text{ hours for the first unit}$$
$$X \quad = \quad 4 \text{ units}$$
$$b \quad = \quad \log .80/\log 2 = -.3219$$

Then

$$\log Y \quad = \quad \log 100 + (-.3219) \log 4$$
$$Y \quad = \quad 64$$

If the total time, T, to produce X units is desired, both sides of the above formula are multiplied by X to yield:

$$T = YX = aX^{(b + 1)}$$

If the approximate time required to produce any specific unit, N, is desired, the formula is adapted as follows:

$$U = (b + 1) \ aN^{b}$$

where U is the approximate time for the Nth unit and (b + 1) is a conversion factor. Values for b and (b + 1) are listed in Exhibit 2.

A graphic portrayal is useful in visualizing learning curve relationships. Exhibits 3 and 4 depict 80 percent learning curves on arithmetic and logarithmic coordinate scales, respectively, for the hypothetical data described above. While the hyperbola in Exhibit 3 appears convex due to the arithmetic scales, its conversion to the logarithmic form results in a linear transformation (upper curve in Exhibit 4). This linearity is an important quality. It facilitates testing for learning behavior, it is useful for estimating the rate of learning, and it is an indication of the reliability of the learning parameter.

In addition to the plot in Exhibit 4 of the cumulative average labor hours required for all units produced up to any particular point, the time for the

---

[7]If the learning rate is less than 100 percent, b will be negative and if greater than 100 percent it will be positive (negative learning).

LEARNING RATE	(b)	(b + 1)	LEARNING RATE	(b)	(b + 1)
70%	−.5146	.4854	83%	−.2688	.7312
71%	−.4942	.5058	84%	−.2516	.7484
72%	−.4739	.5261	85%	−.2345	.7655
73%	−.4541	.5459	86%	−.2176	.7824
74%	−.4345	.5655	87%	−.2009	.7991
75%	−.4150	.5850	88%	−.1845	.8155
76%	−.3959	.6041	89%	−.1681	.8319
77%	−.3771	.6229	90%	−.1520	.8480
78%	−.3585	.6415	91%	−.1361	.8639
79%	−.3401	.6599	92%	−.1204	.8796
80%	−.3219	.6781	93%	−.1047	.8953
81%	−.3041	.6959	94%	−.0892	.9108
82%	−.2863	.7137	95%	−.0740	.9260

b = log of learning rate/log 2

Exhibit 2. Learning-Rate Factors

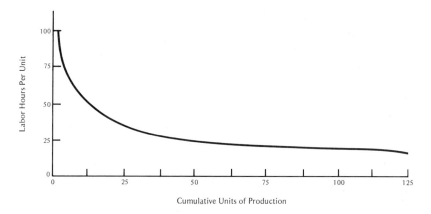

Exhibit 3. Learning Curve on Arithmetic Coordinates

Nth unit is also plotted. It is represented by the lower line and it approximates the labor hours required for any particular unit. The upper and lower lines are parallel except for the first few units produced.

THE CAUSAL FACTORS

Despite the original focus and subsequent emphasis on the increase in labor productivity in learning, the patterns of learning are not inherently limited to labor paced operations. Baloff indicates that the ". . . learning

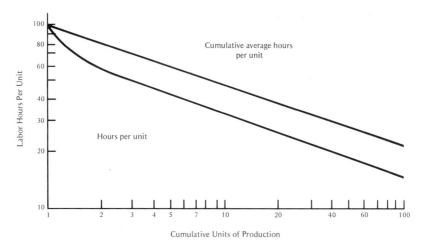

Exhibit 4. Learning Curve on Logarithmic Coordinates

phenomenon has been empirically verified in a number of product and process startups in several different forms of mechanized or automated manufacture."[8] Conway and Schultz, on the other hand, suggest the adaptation efforts of engineers and supervisory personnel (may) greatly overshadow the effect of direct labor learning of a fixed task in producing the overall gains in productivity that are experienced.[9] They argue, in effect, that the performance of various supportive activities, such as improved work methods, tooling and design, and other similar support endeavors by indirect labor accounts for the major gains in labor productivity.

In the literal sense, the distinction between the effect of learning by workers and the effect of a whole series of other factors which contribute to productivity is necessary to explain the causes of the learning phenomenon observed in machine-paced industries. It is well to recognize that the individual factors may sometimes be in opposition and sometimes in harmony, and that the separation of these factors is next to impossible.[10] This may cause the actual data to appear as blips and to be distributed around the theoretical curve. In line with this reasoning, technological progress may also be said to represent a form of learning.

CASE STUDY

The B & PA Manufacturing Company is about to make a production decision on new blidgets. The data gathered indicate that the product has a cumulative expected demand of 200 units over a five-year period at a unit

---

[8]N. Baloff, "The Learning Curve—Some Controversial Issues," *Journal of Industrial Economics*, July 1966, p. 277.

[9]Conway and Schultz, op. cit.

[10]Andress, op. cit., p. 89; see also Conway and Schultz, op. cit., p. 42.

sales price of $3,500. The annual sales distribution is expected to be 25, 40, 60, 40, and 35 units per year for the respective five years. The program would require an immediate investment of $100,000 in equipment having a five-year expected life and no salvage value. To be acceptable, the B & PA Company requires a minimum 15 percent rate of return.[11] Based on engineering studies for 200 units of production, the following average variable costs were estimated: direct material, $1,000; direct labor ($5 per hour), $500; variable factory overhead (100 percent of direct labor), $500; variable selling and administration (10 percent of sales price), $350. In addition to these costs, other fixed operating costs are estimated at $15,000 per year.

From studies of the development and production of other similar products, the Company has determined that an 80 percent learning rate is applicable to labor and variable factory overhead.[12] The 100 hour average labor time was derived by considering this learning factor and the 880.6 hours of labor required to produce the two prototypes.

Cash-Flow Analysis

Using the predicted average costs detailed above, the production decision is evaluated by using typical capital budgeting techniques. Annual cash flows from production and sale of X units equal $3,500X_j - $2,350X_j - $15,000 for the jth year (where $j = 1, 2, 3, 4,$ and 5). By comparing the present value of these cash flows at a 15 percent annual discount rate to the investment requirement of $100,000, the production decision may be made. Exhibit 5 summarizes the necessary computations. The net present value in favor of production equals $1,181.

A more meaningful cash-flow analysis would include the time-related learning-based costs. The use of learning-based costs requires a calculation of the expected labor times to produce each of the annual demands. We begin with the data on the average production time for the first two units which are used to derive the approximate time to complete the first unit (the a value). The a value is then used to derive cumulative average production times, Y, to meet cumulative demands. These cumulative average times are multiplied by the cumulative demand to yield cumulative time requirements. The difference between cumulative times is the marginal production time required to meet annual demand. The computations for the first two years' demands will illustrate this procedure.

To calculate the time implied for the first unit, we proceed as follows. We know the total time to produce the first two units is 880.6 hours and the cumulative average hour per unit $Y = 880.6/2 = 440.3$ hours. We also know

[11]To avoid unnecessary complexities, the effects of taxes are ignored.
[12]No distinction of pre vs. during production factors is made to keep the illustration fairly simple. For discussion of this distinction, see Conway and Schultz, op. cit., pp. 41–42.

YEAR	(1) PRODUCT DEMAND	(2) TOTAL CONTRIBUTION MARGIN*	(3) FIXED COSTS	(4) NET CASH FLOW (2) – (3)	(5) DISCOUNT FACTOR 15%	(6) DISCOUNTED NET CASH FLOW (4) x (5)
	——Investment——			$(100,000)	1.0000	$(100,000)
1	25	$28,750	$15,000	13,750	.8696	11,957
2	40	46,000	15,000	31,000	.7561	23,439
3	60	69,000	15,000	54,000	.6575	35,505
4	40	46,000	15,000	31,000	.5718	17,726
5	35	40,250	15,000	25,250	.4972	12,554
					Net present value	$ 1,181

*$3,500 revenue—$2,350 variable costs

Exhibit 5. Production Analysis with Constant Average Costs and 15 Percent Rate of Return

that $b = -.3219$ for the 80 percent learning rate. By using the logarithmic form of the equation: $Y = aX^b$, we can solve for a.

$$\begin{aligned} \log Y &= (\log a) + b\,(\log X)\\ \log 440.3 &= \log a + (-.3219)\log 2\\ a &= 550.4 \end{aligned}$$

To calculate the cumulative average time required for the first 25 units, we set $a = 550.4$, $X_1 = 25$, $b = -.3219$, and solving, $Y = 195.3$ average hours per unit. Multiplying by 25 units indicates that the cumulative time to produce the first 25 units is 4,882 hours.

To calculate the cumulative average time required for the first 65 units (years 1 and 2 total demand), we set $a = 550.4$, $X_2 = 65$, $b = -.3219$, and solving, $Y = 143.6$ average hours per unit. Multiplying by 65 gives cumulative time for the first 65 units of 9,334 hours; of which 4,882 were required for the first 25 units. Thus, the marginal time to produce the second year's demand of 40 units is 4,452 hours.

The analysis would continue in the above manner to derive the annual marginal production times. These values are summarized in Exhibit 6 (Column 2) as a part of the revised analysis of the production decision. While the decision format remains the same as shown in Exhibit 5, the timing of the cost inputs changes. The annual cash flow now equals $3,500X_j - $1,350X_j - $10LT_j - $15,000$ (where LT is the marginal labor time required to meet demand of X units in period $j = 1, 2, 3, 4$ and 5).[13] Exhibit 6

---

[13]The illustration assumes the learning rate applies to variable factory overhead as well as direct labor.

Year	(1) Product Demand	(2) Marginal Labor Hours Required	(3) Revenues (1) × $3,500	(4) Labor and Var. Factory Overhead Cost (2) × $10	(5) Other Costs $15,000 + ($1,350) (1)	(6) Net Cash Flow (3) − (4) + (5)	(7) Discount Factor 15%	(8) Discounted Cash Flow (7) × (6)
			——————— Investment ———————			$(100,000)	1.0000	$(100,000)
1	25	4,882	$ 87,500	$48,820	$48,750	(10,070)	.8696	(8,757)
2	40	4,452	140,000	44,520	69,000	26,480	.7561	20,022
3	60	5,204	210,000	52,040	96,000	61,960	.6575	40,739
4	40	3,018	140,000	30,180	69,000	40,820	.5718	23,341
5	35	2,444	122,500	24,440	62,250	35,810	.4971	17,805
						Net present value		$ (6,850)

Exhibit 6. Production Analysis with Learning-Based Costs and 15 Percent Rate of Return

summarizes the required computations and indicates a net present value of a negative $6,850.

The difference between the net present values in the two analyses is $8,031. This difference is strictly due to alterations in the timing of cost incurrence. As indicated by this example, improved cost projection using a learning function can have a significant effect on decisions. If the learning rate had been 90 percent, the difference between the two net present values would have been $3,410 and the analysis using learning-based cost predictions would still yield a negative net present value.

Implications for Financial Planning

Based on the data from Exhibit 6 and the assumptions preceding its preparation, the product does not appear to meet the criteria for production. If the product is accepted for production (as was indicated by the original analysis in Exhibit 5), the planning for financial resources and manpower requirements may present some problems. The differences in annual cash flows indicate a difference of $23,820 in the first year alone [$13,750 − ($10,070)]. This represents an unexpected financial drain on the firm that must be satisfied since the product will not generate positive cash flows until sometime during the second year.

If manpower planning for the first year is based on 2,500 direct labor hours (100 average hours times 25 units of demand), the firm will be understaffed. The learning-based estimate of labor requirements to produce the first 25 units is 4,882 hours. Meeting expected demands may thus require additional staffing and overtime. Such crisis production with its concomitant disruptive impacts might be avoided and a smooth flow of production facilitated with the learning-based projections.

The Control Function

Learning-based cost projections can also have an effect on the control function. In the above case study, the expected labor hours, labor cost and variable overhead costs per unit will not be attained until approximately the 60th unit is produced. This is determined for the example by using the formula $U = (b + 1) aN^b$ where $U = 100$; $(b + 1) = .6781$; $a = 550.4$ and $b = -.3219$ and then solving for N. Each unit produced prior to the 60th will require more than 100 labor hours. Each unit produced after the 60th will require less than 100 labor hours. This effect in terms of labor cost is illustrated in Exhibit 1 by the average labor cost per unit at 200 units and the marginal cost per unit lines. Unfavorable variances will be expected for labor and variable factory overhead for all units prior to the 60th unit, and favorable variances would be expected for production in excess of 60 units. Such variances, if unanticipated, could lead to investigation costs, revision of plans, and other costly managerial reactions.

Behavioral Implications

The behavioral implications of constant cost projections or standards are worthy of mention. For example, an expectation of favorable variances is indicated for units produced after the 60th unit. Emphasis is placed on "expected" since there may be a tendency for workers who have met the standard to become complacent and hence reduce or negate further improvement. While it is not the purpose of this article to discuss the behavioral implications of standards on employee performance, it is well to recognize that incentive for further improvement may well be lacking and hence the 100 hour cumulative average time per unit for 200 units may never be attained.[14]

CONCLUSION

Problems in estimating costs affect most managerial decisions. This article has considered learning curve theory as a basis for projecting costs and illustrated how its use may permit more accurate cost predictions. Its potential effects on managerial planning and control decisions are enormous.

The potential for improving cost projections and the decisions emanating from these projections has been demonstrated within the format of a capital budgeting evaluation involving a new product. The illustrative case indicated that the refinements in cost prediction (particularly in the timing of cost incurrence) from using learning-based costs could be significant. Even though the aggregate cost projections are equal under constant average

---

[14]For a basic reference to the behavioral aspects of control systems, see William J. Bruns, Jr. and Don T. DeCoster, eds., *Accounting and Its Behavioral Implications*, McGraw-Hill Book Company, New York, N.Y., 1969.

and learning-based costs, the timing of incurrence of cost components is improved.

In addition to the differences between production decisions resulting from average versus learning-based costs, learning-based costs provide potentially better data for purposes of financial planning, work scheduling and cost control.

FIVE

Performance Evaluation and Control

Part V is concerned with the measurement and control of performance relative to some plan or goal of the company. This subject involves a broad area of coverage. We have included a discussion about the measurement and control of divisional performance, involving the concepts of rate of return on investment and residual income. Also discussed are responsibility accounting reports and behavioral considerations in the design of reports to motivate performance. Standard costs can be used both for product costing and control purposes. An article is included that is concerned with analyzing the effectiveness of the traditional standard cost variance model for the purpose of control. The use of probability and statistics for determining whether or not to investigate a variance from budget and/or standard is part of this section. Also, we have included an article about transfer pricing. Transfer pricing has implications for performance reporting and for the problem of goal congruence for company segments and the company as a whole.

Article 24, "A New Way to Measure and Control Divisional Performance," reviews the problems that arise when decentralized operations are controlled by the return on investment technique. The article proposes a residual income method to align divisional and corporate goals.

In setting standards and budgets, an understanding of the psychological aspects of these systems is important because the systems involve people. Unless the company personnel have a desire to cooperate in setting and/or to accomplish a plan, for example a standard cost budgeting system, the plan may not succeed.[1] The motivation of people is an important consideration in the designing of accounting system reports. A discussion of the problem of motivation and the implication for the accounting system

---

[1] See Michael Schiff and Arnie Y Lewin, "The Impact of People on Budgets," *The Accounting Review*, April 1970, pp. 259–69; Selwyn Becker and David Green, Jr., "Budgeting and Employee Behavior," *Journal of Business*, October 1962, pp. 392–403. The April 1964 *Journal of Business* contains a reply by Andrew C. Stedry to the article by Becker and Green and a rejoinder to the reply. Also see Article 8 in Part II ("Budgeting: Functional Analysis and Behavioral Implications"); J. Ronen and J. L. Livingstone, "An Expectancy Theory Approach to the Motivational Impacts of Budgets," *The Accounting Review*, October 1975, pp. 671–685; William J. Bruns, Jr. and John H. Waterhouse, "Budgetary Control and Organization Structure," *Journal of Accounting Research*, Autumn 1975, pp. 177–203; Robert J. Swieringa, "A Behavioral Approach to Participative Budgeting," *Management Accounting*, February 1975, pp. 35–39.

Budgets necessarily incorporate the effects of project decisions. For discussions of behavioral considerations and decision making, see Article 6 in Part I ("Accounting Information and Decision-Making: Some Behavioral Implications"); Yuji Ijiri, Robert K. Jaedicke and Kenneth E. Knight, "The Effects of Accounting Alternatives on Management Decisions," *Research in Accounting Measurement*, edited by Robert K. Jaedicke, Yuji Ijiri, Oswald Nielsen (Evanston, Ill.: American Accounting Association, 1966), pp. 186–199; Ronald N. Taylor, "Psychological Determinates of Bounded Rationality: Implications for Decision-Making Strategies," *Decision Sciences*, July 1975, pp. 409–429.

For a discussion of the congruence of risk-taking attitudes and behavior, including a section about the budget as an evaluation standard, see Hiroyuki Itami, "Evaluation Measures and Goal Congruence Under Uncertainty," *Journal of Accounting Research*, Spring 1975, pp. 73–96.

is the subject of Article 25, "The Role of the Firm's Accounting System for Motivation."[2]

Article 26 is concerned with the standard cost variance model. To realize an optimum profit plan, management needs to be able to evaluate and control the detailed company operations by departments, cost centers, products, etc. To do this, management may desire to know what a reasonable relationship should be between cost and production for a specific activity. Management can develop a standard cost budgeting system and variance analysis reports for this purpose.

In using a standard cost system, a manager compares performance with a predetermined standard or goal. Standards may be based on optimum efficiency, expected efficiency, or attainable standards based on past realized efficiency.[3] By comparing actual and standard costs, management can develop variance reports which are used to indicate activities that may require management action in order to realize future cost improvement. For control purposes, the standard cost system may be designed to develop such variances as material price and efficiency variances, labor rate and efficiency variances and spending and efficiency variances for the variable manufacturing overhead.[4]

For control purposes, the actual performance can be compared with the planned performance, and variances from the budgeted and/or standard

---

[2]For a discussion of departmental contribution margin statements, rather than conventional income statements for performance evaluation purposes, see Article 2 in Part I ("Contribution Margin Analysis by Company Segments—Three Uses").

[3]Because actual performance may not approach any optimum or desired standard, management could be concerned more with raising the average level of performance than attempting to meet an optimum standard. Therefore, a variance comparison may be based on "what is likely, rather than exclusively on the basis of what ought to be" (see Raymond E. Miles and Roger C. Vergin, "Behavioral Properties of Variance Controls," *California Management Review*, Spring 1966). In this type of comparison, a change in the actual performance from the expected or likely performance will be reflected in the variance, and if the change is not favorable, action can be taken to attempt to identify and remedy the cause of the variance.

[4]In conventional standard cost accounting analysis, labor is treated as a variable cost. An article by Charles R. Purdy and Donald E. Ricketts, "Analysis of Rate, Efficiency, and Utilization Variances," *Management Accounting*, November 1974, pp. 49–52 considers the determination of standard cost variances for labor where labor is not in fact variable.

A fixed overhead variance can have quite different control implications for management than a variable overhead variance. For evaluating capacity utilization plans and for directly measuring the effects of volume on profits, an article by Charles T. Horngren, "A Contribution Margin Approach to the Analysis of Capacity Utilization," *The Accounting Review*, April 1967, pp. 254–264 proposes the use of lost contribution margins. The author indicates that for measuring the effects of volume on profits, the inclusion of fixed overhead costs in variance analysis has little economic significance because historical fixed costs "unitize total costs that are not affected by current fluctuations in volume."

Professor Horngren's article shows the usual way of computing efficiency variances for variable costs (direct material, direct labor, and variable overhead), and indicates that the same approach is commonly taken to calculate a fixed overhead efficiency variance. However, he stresses inefficiency can be revealed by reports about the control of variable costs. An efficiency variance for fixed overhead is not that useful for management because how effectively or ineffectively facilities are utilized does not change the amount of currently incurred fixed costs.

figures are developed. A total system, or company profit plan, should include the detailed goals for specific functional areas of the business. Managers need information about the variances that require their attention. Cost variances from budget that are within the area of responsibility of a manager, and for costs that are controllable by that manager, may be reported to him for possible control action. Not all controllable variances need to be reported. Under the "management by exception" principle, only significant deviations from budget are reported.

Article 26, "Analyzing the Effectiveness of the Traditional Standard Cost Variance Model," extends the traditional model, which shows planned and actual results, by incorporating a consideration of what output should have been. A section of the article uses calculus in the determination of an optimum output. For a background discussion about differential calculus, useful in understanding the application in the article, the reader is referred to Article 36, "Optimization."

The problem of when a variance from budget or standard should be investigated is an important one for management. The following quotation is from Article 27.

> ... one of the most important problems that arises is to decide when a variance is worthy of investigation. If the variance is small in amount or results from uncontrollable factors, or if future operations would not improve even if the cause of the variance was determined, management would prefer not to waste time and money investigating such variations. On the other hand, if investigation will result in substantial future savings and more efficient operations, management will probably want the variance investigated.
>
> The problem of when to investigate is an important part of the control process. The best conceived budget or control procedures will be ineffective unless the decision of when to investigate a variance is made in a reasonable manner.

Whether or not a variance should be investigated may be determined by management using business judgment or intuition. However, quantitative models using probability, statistics, and techniques developed for statistical quality control purposes can be applied. In Article 27, "A Use of Probability and Statistics in Performance Evaluation," quantitative techniques are applied for the problem of investigation of variances.[5]

Article 28, "Quantitative Models for Accounting Control," includes an explanation that, in effect, is a review of the application of a statistical control model, and then the author discusses a control system based on modern decision theory (i.e., Bayesian statistics). The system incorporates subjective probability. A model based on classical statistics results in a

---

[5]For a discussion about control charts, see Edwin W. Gaynor, "Use of Control Charts in Cost Control," *N.A.C.A. Bulletin* [*Management Accounting*], June 1954.

decision on the basis of objective evidence. The author states: "Insistence on objective evidence before making a decision is unrealistic, for objective evidence may be lacking, too expensive, or a new process may be involved, etc."

Article 29 is concerned with transfer pricing. Contribution margin statements or full divisional profit statements may be useful for different management purposes if the divisions for which they are prepared are for the most part independent. In the case where a segment of the business (i.e., profit center, division, department, etc.) acts as a supplier of a product, a part or a service to some other segment, some form of transfer price needs to be used if contribution margin statements or full profit statements are to be prepared for the different segments.

The determination of transfer prices is complicated and can be affected by economic and legal considerations (for example, income taxes and property taxes may affect the setting of transfer prices), the specific management decisions for which transfer prices may be contemplated, performance evaluation considerations,[6] and considerations with regard to the autonomy of different segments of the business.

If some form of transfer price is to be used, it is necessary to understand possible advantages and disadvantages of the base used to determine the transfer price. For example, if a market price is to be used as a transfer price, it is especially difficult to determine the transfer price where an alternative to interdivisional business is not permitted. Cost, because it may contain charges for less than efficient production, can result in problems for performance evaluation and motivation. Negotiation results in statements that are affected by the differing negotiating abilities of managers.

Transfer prices can be used for decentralized operations, for profit center reporting and decisions, etc., but it may be that for some decisions the centralization of control over them by top management will result in optimal decisions for the firm as a whole. An economic analysis may show that the use of transfer prices by a firm does not aid management in optimizing the profit for the company as a whole; if the objective of the company is to maximize profit, it may be helpful to consider the company as one profit entity for that purpose.

A number of approaches to approximating a transfer price have been developed. Some of these are indicated by the above discussion. Article 29, "A Transfer Pricing System Based on Opportunity Cost," is concerned with the problem of approximating a transfer price. Much like the problem of cost allocation—even though an attempt is made to determine a transfer price for some purpose in a "reasonable manner"—the selection of a transfer price is necessarily arbitrary. If transfer prices are needed to determine contribution margins or profits, it may be better not to prepare

---

[6]See William L. Ferrara, "Accounting for Performance Evaluation and Decision Making," *Management Accounting*, December 1976, pp. 13–19.

performance evaluation reports that show either a contribution or a profit for a segment of the business. However, even though transfer prices are not perfect, they may be used by management because they aid in the attainment of given objectives for a firm.

If transfer prices are to be used by management, it is important to realize that one form of transfer price may not be useful for all management purposes and it may be necessary to use transfer prices that differ depending on the specific purposes for which they are applied.[7]

Article 29 first discusses the economic foundation of a transfer pricing system and its limitations. This is useful information for the transfer price problems included in the problem section of this book: The article includes behavioral problems, presents a significant new idea of "motivation costs" to resolve conflict, and discusses an approach to solving the transfer price problem based on opportunity cost. Article 29 uses the concept of opportunity cost from the linear programming model. In Case 1 of Article 29, the price of a transferred product X_1 is set at the opportunity cost or the shadow price of resources utilized in its production instead of being used to produce X_2. Shadow prices are part of the discussion of linear programming in Article 30 (the sections about computer solution of linear programming problems, and sensitivity analysis).[8]

The concept of opportunity cost from the linear programming model can be used in decision making. For an article that links accounting tools for planning and control with programming (the discussion includes transfer pricing), see J. M. Samuels, "Opportunity Costing: An Application of Mathematical Programming," *Journal of Accounting Research*, Autumn 1965, pp. 182–191; also see Richard H. Bernhard, "Some Problems in

[7]For examples, see Harold Bierman, Jr., "Pricing Intracompany Transfers," *The Accounting Review*, July 1959, pp. 429–432.

[8]For every linear programming problem, there is a closely related problem called its dual. In a dual problem, the objective function is minimized instead of maximized. The optimal values of the dual variables are called shadow prices. In Article 30, "Linear Programming," shadow prices are the coefficients in the last row (except for the RHS value) of the optimal solution tableau of the primal problem (maximization of profit problem—Valvton Company). For a problem with 3 constraints, there are 3 dual variables. Assume these are labeled y_1, y_2, and y_3 for the Valvton Company problem of Article 30. The variables y_1, y_2, and y_3 represent, respectively, the marginal value associated with one additional unit (hr.) of lathe time, one additional unit (hr.) of grinder time, and one additional unit (lb.) of steel. In the dual problem, the objective is to minimize the total marginal value of all resources, subject to the constraints that the marginal value of the required resource for each product must be not less than that product's profit. Note that the marginal value (additional profit) sets an upper limit on cost for acquiring an additional resource unit.

As discussed in Article 30, when a slack variable (identified as S) is zero, it shows that the corresponding resource is completely utilized. The associated shadow price is the increase in the value of the objective function if an additional unit of that resource becomes available. Thus, in the optimal solution for the Valvton Company problem, $S_1 = 0$, so that all 750 hours of lathe time are being utilized. Since y_1, or the shadow price, equals 2 (see the 2 in the last row of Table 7, Article 30), an additional hour of lathe time would increase the total profit by $2. When a slack variable is positive, the corresponding resource is not being completely utilized, so its marginal value is zero. Since $S_2 = 50$, in the Valvton Company problem, there are 50 hours of grinder time unused, and an additional hour of grinder time has zero value.

Applying Mathematical Programming to Opportunity Costing," *Journal of Accounting Research*, Spring 1968, pp. 143–148.

The transfer price and opportunity cost discussion of Article 29 uses the dual solution for a programming problem. In Article 29, the solution values are given. They were obtained using the decomposition principle, and for references about the mathematical operational steps the author includes a bibliography at the end of the article. See the brief discussion of the decomposition principle in Appendix A (of this book) Section 4.2 Suboptimization.

24.

A NEW WAY TO MEASURE AND CONTROL DIVISIONAL PERFORMANCE*

Roger Clayden

The decentralized corporation, in which the corporate entity is divided into portions that are considered small enough for traditional general management, is now well established as an organizational format. In many cases these divisions are involved in different markets, have different performance histories, and undoubtedly have different planning strategies.

An increasingly popular but nonetheless hazardous method of measuring and controlling decentralized investment centers is the so-called return on investment technique. The purpose of this article is to review the problems of using the return on investment technique for control of decentralized investment centers and to suggest another technique, the residual income method, which better aligns divisional goals with those of the corporation.

There has been some argument over the distinction between decentralization and divisionalization. In this article the terms are treated as synonymous and as referring to delegation of responsibility for the planning, the execution, and the profitability of operations.

The reasons for decentralization can be classified into two main categories:

Operational—Sometimes technological or geographical specialties make each division essentially independent. In the case of conglomerate acquisition there may also be the desire to retain an old system—at least for the time being.

* From *Management Services (Management Adviser)*. September–October 1970, pp. 22–29. Copyright © 1970 by the American Institute of Certified Public Accountants, Inc. Reprinted by permission. Editors' Note: This article discusses ROI and residual income. Also see William L. Ferrara, "Probabilistic Approaches to Return on Investment and Residual Income," *The Accounting Review*, July 1977, pp. 597–604.

Motivational—In a very large company long chains of command result in an impersonal organization structure. Decentralization of decision making provides local motivation and encourages internal competition, taking advantage of developed traits common in the make-up of the industrial manager.

To achieve the benefits expected from decentralization it is, of course, essential that top management have the means both to measure and to control the actions of its division managers. In fact, the desire of top management for better control is always a major factor in any decision to decentralize. It has always been obvious that profits alone are an inappropriate measure of performance because some divisions are several times as large as others. A technique is necessary for comparing and contrasting the performance and prospects of the separate divisions, and the one that has gained the broadest acceptance is the "return on investment ratio" (ROI), sometimes called "return on assets employed."

In a 1966 survey of major United States industrial corporations Mauriel and Anthony[1] found that of 2,658 respondents 60 percent were using the investment center concept, 21 percent were using profit centers but not investment centers, and 74 percent of decentralized companies were using ROI or a similar technique. In some industrial groups the percentage using ROI was considerably higher—86 percent for scientific instrument manufacturers, for example. The authors concluded that divisional ROI had not only become an established performance measurement but had also displaced profit as the most widely used basis for measuring the performance of divisional managers.

The predominance of ROI is not difficult to understand. The economic prospects of a corporation are broadly defined by the price investors are willing to pay for a share in the company's future. Since the overall return on investment for the company is an essential ingredient of any decision the prospective investor makes, it is natural that the top managements of decentralized companies should want to delegate responsibility along the same lines. In this way the division manager should be motivated to make the same decisions that would have been made by top management. However, while theory and practice support the thesis that the division manager will react to the stimulus of the ROI control, an analysis of the economics of his decisions will show that in many cases they may not be in accord with the objectives of top management.

THE CONTROL PROBLEM

Unfortunately, the application of a simple ROI indicator to decentralized investment centers is fraught with hidden dangers. As early as 1956, Ralph J. Cordiner, an advocate of decentralization, stated:

---

[1] John J. Mauriel and Robert N. Anthony, "Misevaluation of Investment Center Performance," *Harvard Business Review*, March–April 1966, p. 98.

> The traditional measures of profits such as return on investment, turnover, and percentage of net earnings to sales provide useful information. But they are hopelessly inadequate as measures to guide the manager's effectiveness in planning for the future of business—the area where his decisions have the most important effects.[2]

Nevertheless, as was reported earlier in this article, ROI is now firmly established in the hierarchy of measurement techniques and furthermore is probably used as a basis for long-range business decisions more often than any other factor.

Professor John Dearden of Harvard, a leading critic of existing ROI methods, has written several articles on this and related subjects for the *Harvard Business Review*. He classifies the inherent limitations of ROI into two types: "technical" and "implementation." "The first type," he says, "are those conditions which cause incongruities between divisional objectives and company goals, and which result in motivating division managers to take uneconomic actions. The second type includes those conditions that result from the inability, under many circumstances, to evaluate accurately the profit performance of division managers."[3]

This paper is concerned solely with the first type of limitation. Its objective is to formulate criteria that will align divisional goals with those of the company.

GOAL INCONGRUITY

To explain how simple ROI can lead to divisional decisions that are not in the best interests of the company, let us look at a few examples.

Division A is mature and produces an ROI of 30 percent. Division B is young and has a target ROI rate of 5 percent. Both divisions are considering increasing inventory for seasonal demand. Division A will not add an inventory of $100,000 unless it can yield at least $30,000 that year since a lower yield will reduce divisional ROI; Division B, however, will add inventory of $100,000 even though it yields only $5,000. Let us assume that the additional capital for this inventory can be directly attributed to a short-term bank loan at 8 percent. We can see vividly that Division A may be foregoing up to $22,000 of additional profit to the company. Division B, however, could equally well reduce total profits by as much as $3,000.

Let us consider now the same two divisions contemplating the purchase of a piece of cost-saving equipment. Assume that it would be operating the same number of hours in each case, saving the same number of dollars.

[2]Ralph J. Cordiner, *New Frontiers for Professional Managers*, McGraw-Hill Book Company, New York, 1956, p. 95.
[3]John Dearden, "The Case Against ROI Control," *Harvard Business Review*, May–June 1969, p. 124.

Clearly there is a range of returns which would be attractive to one division but unattractive to the other. From the corporate viewpoint, however, the capital acquisition uses the same source of funds and produces the same profits.

As time goes on, Division A's performance drops at a rate of 5 percent per year because of a diminishing market, until it eventually falls below the company average. However, at the lower ROI, Division A is motivated to increase its inventory and purchase additional warehouse space, thus artificially enhancing its twilight years to the detriment of the corporation.

These are some examples of obvious anomalies that may result from ROI controls. In general, the limitations of simple ROI can be grouped into the following categories:

1. *Current Investment.* The use of a different target rate for each division will not maximize profits realized from the company's management of liquid assets.

2. *Fixed Asset Investment.* Certain methods employed for including fixed assets in the investment base can lead to unfortunate management. If any technique is used that does not charge to the division the capital loss from scrapping an asset, then a division manager may be tempted to dispose of any asset that is not yielding his target ROI. The problem is even greater if fixed assets are constantly valued at cost (as in the gross book value method).

3. *Allocations.* To make divisional and corporate ROI comparable, centralized assets are apportioned according to some measure. While these allocations may appear neat and tidy from a bookkeeping standpoint, they can be just as misleading as allocated expenses are in costing. Consider the division that found it could get its data processing done by a service bureau for $20,000 a year more than it was paying the company's unit. However, the asset value of the facility was apportioned according to usage, and in this case $100,000 was allocated. If the divisional ROI objective were 30 percent, then the additional cost of $20,000 would be more than offset by the reduction of $100,000 in its asset base. It is more than likely, however, that such an action would not be in the best interests of the company as a whole.

4. *Transfer Pricing.* The problem of intracompany pricing is a result of decentralization, not of the use of ROI per se. However, since ROI control is often the only common quantitative measure among divisions, it is frequently expected to supply the solution. There is no doubt that transfer pricing can be a serious administrative problem, especially in companies whose divisions perform sequential tasks (such as the oil industry). Where divisions are heavily dependent on each other, price manipulation can play havoc with ROI controls.

COST OF CAPITAL

Capital funds come from three major sources: stockholder's equity, long-term debts, and short-term debts.

The cost of new equity capital can be measured approximately by the following formula:

$$C_e = \frac{E_0}{P_0} + g \text{ (after Bierman and Smidt[4])}$$

where

C_e	=	cost of equity capital
E_0	=	current earnings per share
P_0	=	current net value per share (cost of issue deducted)
g	=	expected annual percentage rate of increase in future earnings expressed as a decimal fraction.

Another source of new equity capital is retained earnings. The cost of retained earnings has been a point of argument,[5] but for the purpose of this analysis we shall assume that some cost C_r can be established that can be related to the cost of capital from common stock issue. A popular estimator is:

$$C_r = \frac{E_0}{P_0} (.80) + g$$

The .80 factor makes a rule-of-thumb allowance for the tax benefits of retained earnings to the investor.

The cost of long-term debt capital is the current effective interest rate for long-term securities held by the company's creditors. Because the market price for bonds may change from time to time, the nominal interest rate for the bonds cannot be used, and an effective interest rate must be calculated by selecting the rate that makes the present worth of all future payments equal to the market price.

Short-term debt capital comes from several sources; bank or institutional loans, trade credits, customer prepayments, accrued expenses, and accrued taxes are the most important. There is no one interest rate that can be applied to such debt, and in certain cases an average rate could be misleading, particularly since it is sometimes possible to assign the cost to some capital asset that has been used as the collateral for the borrowed funds.

The cost of debt capital (short- or long-term) can, however, be calculated with reasonable accuracy. If we exclude any fluctuation in the national economy that will seriously affect the value of bonds, then, since the future

[4]Harold Bierman, Jr., and Seymour Smidt, *The Capital Budgeting Decision*, The Macmillan Company, New York, 1964, p. 135.

[5]Benson Hunt, Charles M. Williams, and Gordon Donaldson, *Basic Business Finance*, Richard D. Irwin, Inc., Homewood, Illinois, 1966, pp. 427–430.

interest payments are certain costs, it is possible to establish a cost for the capital. If equity capital were also able to yield such a certain benefit, the same argument would apply, but under such conditions, of course, the investor would be unable to differentiate between the two, and there would be no need for alternative sources of capital.

In reality, finding the cost of equity capital is not a simple analytical task. The name itself is misleading because it suggests a definite price paid for new capital whereas the "cost" is the return expected from the use of the capital in a future that is far from certain. Furthermore, any changes in the capitalization of a company may result in a change in the market price for its stock. Uncertainties like these make the measurement of capital cost more difficult; they must be considered in any analysis. As Ezra Solomon points out:

> If the purpose of a target or minimum rate is simply to prevent unwise investment decisions, it is easy to set a rate high enough to avoid such sins of commission. But its purpose is also to ensure that investment proposals which can be expected to increase net present worth are not rejected. This requires a more exact basis for setting screening standards, and for altering them in the light of changes in the capital markets and variations in the quality of returns expected from the investment or reinvestment of funds. The problem is a complex one. . . .[6]

Some companies allow for these uncertainties by increasing the target rate of return as a hedge against risk. If all the proposals considered for investment bore the same degree of uncertainty, then the technique might have some validity. But the chances are that risk will not be apportioned consistently and that relatively risk-free investments will be foregone because their expected yield is below the target rate, even though it is above the expected average rate of return.

It is essential, then, to set a real target rate through analysis of past performance, through a forecast of desired future performance, or through a combination of both. When capital comes from several sources, the target rate must be calculated by taking a weighted average of the component costs. In the method for performance evaluation that is proposed in this article, the measurement of capital costs from its various sources is an indispensable prerequisite.

RESIDUAL INCOME

We have considered the anomalous decisions that might result from the use of ROI. There are two basic problems. The first is the fact that a single criterion is being used for both measurement and control. This criterion is

---

[6]Ezra Solomon, *Theory of Financial Management*, Columbia University Press, New York, 1963, p. 35.

supposed to guide the manager in his decision making, which looks to the future, and to afford an evaluation of his performance, which looks to the past. Unless an extremely long evaluation period is used (at least three years), the two are likely to be out of phase. Divisions with poor perform-ance, for example, will be set achievable target rates, which will be used to make investment decisions that will extend their poor performance for years to come. The second problem arises because, in order to arrive at a single divisional ROI, a single target rate of return has to be used for all classes of investment—and this technique is unable to accommodate the short-term changes in a company's financial position.

These disadvantages are the trade-off for simplicity. ROI is easy to under-stand and is appealing to the ratio cult of business and finance. However, while it is not possible to devise a technique as compact as ROI that doesn't also have its pitfalls, it is possible to develop a technique that is equally simple to understand and avoids most of those pitfalls. This technique is a development of the concept of residual income.

To equal the company's target ROI, a division must make a certain profit using the assets it has. If it exceeds the target ROI, then its profits also exceed its share of the target profit level. The excess profit is called residual income. In principle, it is as if the division were borrowing its capital at an interest rate equal to the company's target rate. If the capital charge were made at a single rate for all assets, the control method would encounter some of the problems of ROI. However, it is possible to expand the residual income method so that different classes of assets can collect different capi-tal charges, a capability not available with ROI.

The fixed assets of the division will collect a capital charge equal to the long-term cost of capital for the corporation (or an assignable charge such as mortgage interest). Part of the company's current assets will also be using capital from equity or long-term debt, but the remainder will proba-bly be financed by short-term debt capital from bank loans, trade credits, etc. A case is sometimes put for the indistinguishability of capital em-ployed; in other words, no asset class can be said to use capital from any specific source. But, while there is some interdependency of capital, within certain limits we can see that that argument is invalid. It may be possible, for example, to borrow from a banker in order to increase receivables. It would be a frivolous banker who would loan money to finance specialized equipment for a research venture (without some other collateral).

MULTIPLE CAPITAL CHARGING

A simplified capital charge schedule for a division might appear as in Fi-gure 1. The cost of long-term capital is at a rate of 20 percent, so that assets employing this capital are so charged. The portion of the division's current assets to be charged at the long-term rate is a decision for top management. The charge may be allocated simply as a percentage of sales or by compari-son with other companies in the same business as the division. Whichever method is used, the total of all the capital in the company charged at this rate must be equal to the company's long-term liabilities. In Figure 1 several assets have been charged at rates other than 20 percent. There are $1,000,000 of accounts receivable charged at 8 percent, for example. This means that loan capital at 8 percent has been allocated against excess receivables held by the division. The division has a warehouse (Building No. 5) financed by a mortgage at an interest rate of 6 percent on the debt outstanding ($1,000,000).

ASSET CLASS	ASSET VALUE (000'S)	CAPITAL RATE	CAPITAL CHARGE (000'S)	ADDITIONAL CAPITAL APPROVED (000'S)
Current Assets:				
Cash	$ 5,000	20%	$ 1,000	$ 100
Acc. Rec.	10,000	20	2,000	200
	1,000	8	80	0
Inventories	15,000	20	3,000	0
	0	5	0	2,000
Others	3,000	20	600	0
Fixed Assets:				
Land & Buildings	20,000	20	4,000	100
Building No. 5	1,000	6	60	0
Equipment	10,000	20	2,000	200
	$65,000		$12,740	

Figure 1. A Divisional Capital Charge Schedule

The capital charge for each asset is then calculated as shown in the next column. The current capital charges for the division's $65 million of assets total $12,740,000. If the division were an average performer for the company, its ROI would be $12,740,000 ÷ $65,000,000 or 19.6 percent. If it were expected to yield this rate of return on all capital, it might mistakenly get rid of receivables costing the company only 8 percent or a building costing 6 percent. The possibility of an uneconomic decision if its ROI were higher or lower than average has been discussed. Let us see now how the capital charge method can direct the division manager to make correct decisions.

In the last column of Figure 1 are listed capital amounts that are available for the division's use during the next fiscal period. Long-term capital has been allocated according to the capital budget; the division in the example has planned an expansion, and capital has been set aside for this expansion. This does not mean that absolutely no other funds can be made available. As with any capital budget, a review period must be established at a frequency sufficient to avoid financial traffic jams caused by changes in divisional plans. An annual review may be sufficient, but in a young company without financial stability it may be necessary to review divisional budgets as often as quarterly.

In our case, when the finance budget for the year was prepared, a capital excess was forecast, and a decision was made to buy short-term securities at 5 percent with the capital unless it could be better employed within the company. It was further decided that this capital should be offered to the divisions for increasing inventory levels. Although the division in the example is paying 20 percent on its current inventory, it can add up to $2,000,000 more inventory at only 5 percent. However, because this cheap capital may be available for only a short period (two years, say) an advisory note would be included to prevent the division from increasing its inventory excessively.

If we look now at receivables, we can see that a $200,000 budgeted increase is available at 20 percent. No additional capital is available at 8 percent. It might seem peculiar that, with an expected capital excess, increasing receivables should be made unattractive. But this is a hypothetical example designed to demonstrate the method, so let us assume that top management believes that the company's receivables are getting out of hand and have been a reason for the fall in the price of its stock.

DIVISIONAL GOALS

The example has shown how, in principle, the division manager will be motivated to make decisions in the best interests of the company. So far, however, we have not set a target, except perhaps that profits should exceed the capital cost. The actual target is set in much the same way as a divisional ROI target, but, instead of dividing the target profit by the asset base, we subtract the capital charge for the assets from the target profit level. The final goal for the division is the residual income, which can be improved by either reducing assets or increasing profits in much the same way as an ROI target.

With this method it is possible that divisions with performances below average for the company will be set a negative goal. Technically this is no problem, but motivationally it may be distasteful. Fortunately, for reasons that will be explained in the next section, the problem will arise less frequently than we might at first expect.

ASSET MEASUREMENT

With the ROI technique it is common to allocate centralized assets. The reason for this, as was explained previously, is to produce a ratio that can be related to the world outside. The knowledge of this ratio is certainly useful: first, for measurement, because the comparison of a division's performance with outside competitors provides an important perspective for both top management and the division manager; second, to facilitate long-range planning where a division's growth and potential are conveniently quantified. However, from the standpoint of control, the inclusion of centralized assets is completely erroneous. In order to allocate assets, it is necessary to devise a convenient rule, e.g., so many dollars for each sales dollar or so many dollars for each fixed asset dollar used by the division. Whatever the rule, the division is able to reduce its allocated assets more directly by lowering its allocation base than it can by reducing its use of the centralized assets.

The same argument applies to the residual income method, and therefore we can make a general rule that only assets controlled by the division should be included in its capital charge schedule. The only exception to the rule occurs where an allocated asset is truly dependent upon the size of the allocation base. An example of this is cash. More often than not the company has one central banking function and divisions do not control their own cash. However, an increase in a division's activity will immediately increase the cash required for payroll, for example. Proper allocation of cash to the capital charge schedule is important to prevent a division from overrating the benefits of increased activity.

What about the increase in headquarters faciliities necessary to accommodate continually expanding divisions? Perhaps the simplest answer is another question: What happens to the excess facilities that result from divisional reductions? Apart from the problem of finding a suitable allocation base, the headquarters changes would not be proportional to divisional changes—especially in the case of marginal variations. If it is important to allocate an asset, then the basis must be carefully chosen to avoid the pitfalls mentioned.

When assets are not allocated, the algebraic sum of the residual incomes from all divisions is equal to the capital charge for the unallocated assets. The existence of this divisional excess has a beneficial by-product; it means that fewer divisions will be set negative targets for residual income—a problem discussed earlier.

At the beginning of this section, the possibility was discussed that top management may want to make comparisons among divisions and between its own divisions and outside competitors. The residual income method does not always offer as convenient a comparison as ROI. However, all the information required for the ROI calculation has been collected in order to measure residual income, and it is therefore a simple matter to calculate an ROI. If an ROI is calculated, of course, it must not be involved in the formal procedure for measuring divisional performance.

REMAINING PROBLEMS

The residual income method resolves some, but not all, of the problems associated with ROI. The most significant problem remaining is that of setting a value for depreciable assets.

A piece of equipment may be purchased that is expected to yield a rate of return equal to the long-term capital charge rate. As the asset gets older, its book value decreases, and, consequently, so does the capital charge. If the operating benefits produced by the piece of equipment are uniform, then the residual income from it increases with time (see figure 2). This not only makes the residual income measurement inconsistent, but it may also deter a division manager from making an investment because of the short-range reduction in residual income that would follow. Straight-line depreciation was used in the example. If an accelerated depreciation method were used, the variation would be even greater.

| | NET BOOK VALUE | | CASH FLOW | CAPITAL | RESIDUAL INCOME | |
YR.	AT START OF YEAR	AVERAGE FOR YEAR	AFTER TAX	CHARGE AT 15%	BEFORE DEPREC.	AFTER DEPREC.
1	100,000	90,000	30,000	13,500	16,500	−3,500
2	80,000	70,000	30,000	10,500	19,500	− 500
3	60,000	50,000	30,000	7,500	22,500	2,500
4	40,000	30,000	30,000	4,500	25,500	5,500
5	20,000	10,000	30,000	1,500	28,500	8,500

Figure 2. Effect of Decreasing Book Value on Residual Income

To overcome this problem, the annual capital charge plus the depreciation must be constant and should be equal to the capital recovery amount for the asset over its useful life. However, to prevent the improper disposition of assets, they must always appear on the asset list at their salvage value—or at as good an approximation as possible. The existence of these two constraints makes the problem theoretically insoluble.

Anthony has suggested a solution which he calls the annuity method.[7] He achieves the constant capital recovery amount by having an increasing rate of depreciation which compensates for the decreasing capital charge. The asset, therefore, decreases in book value slowly at first and then more rapidly as time goes on. While no depreciation method consistently values assets at their salvage value, the annuity method rarely comes even close. The tax laws being what they are, the annuity method would also be unattractive for cost accounting, so that in order to use the method two sets of records would have to be maintained.

There is a far simpler, albeit artificial, means of fixing the capital charge for depreciable assets. Property ledgers are usually kept in a form that shows the depreciation period for the asset and either the number of years'

[7]Robert N. Anthony, John Dearden, and Richard F. Vancil, *Management Control Systems: Cases and Readings*, Richard D. Irwin, Inc., Homewood, Illinois, 1965, p. 343.

reserves that have accrued or the number of years' depreciation remaining. It is possible—and, if the files are on EDP equipment, easy—to subtotal these assets according to their remaining life. When this has been done, the capital charge can be calculated by multiplying each subtotal by the appropriate future benefit charge rate (see Figure 3). This way the capital charge will be equal to the expected benefits from investments uniformly yielding the company's target rate of return. Therefore, at all times assets will be valued at net book value, while the capital charge will be commensurate with the annual benefit expected from a wise investment decision.

Let r = target rate of return for equipment investment.

n = number of years of depreciation (useful life) remaining.

An item of equipment should be retained if the present value of the future benefits resulting from its use is greater than current salvage value. For this to be true, the annual future benefit must be equal to the capital recovery amount at $r\%$ for n years (assuming a uniform series).

Define the future benefit capital charge for n years remaining:

$$f_n = \text{(Salvage value)} \times \text{(crf-}r\%\text{-n)}$$

where $\text{(crf-}r\%\text{-n)} = \dfrac{r(1 + r)^n}{(1 + r)^n - 1}$ is the capital charge rate.

This charge includes recovery of principal. If depreciation is recovered separately, then the capital charge

$$f_n = \text{(Salvage value)} \times \text{(crf-}r\%\text{-n)} - \text{(Depreciation)}.$$

Note: In practice it will often be necessary to assume that the salvage value is equal to the net book value of the asset.

Figure 3. Future Benefit Method of Capital Charging

As is shown in Figure 4, the method has one drawback: An investment that produces the uniform benefits originally expected of it actually shows a residual income increasing with time. The reason for this is that a uniform benefit does not recover the principal uniformly; the interest component is higher in the early years. The only way to make the residual income uniform is to have an increasing rate of depreciation as in the annuity method. The disadvantages of this method have been explained.

Let us review again the purpose and technique of the residual income method. The division manager needs to be motivated to make economic decisions. At any point in time the division manager will be faced with two alternatives: either to scrap or to retain an asset. The basis of his decision should be to compare the present value of future benefits with the salvage value for the asset. If we accept the idea of a uniform benefit (which does not apply in every case but is the best generalization available), then, in the marginal case, the forecast uniform annual benefit will be equal to the

*YRS. OF LIFE REMAINING, N	AVERAGE NET BOOK VALUE	AFTER TAX CASH FLOW	(crf-15%-n)	CAPITAL CHARGE f_n	RESIDUAL INCOME
5	$100,000	$30,000	.30	$30,000	$ 0
4	80,000	30,000	.35	28,000	2,000
3	60,000	30,000	.44	26,400	3,600
2	40,000	30,000	.62	24,800	5,200
1	20,000	30,000	1.15	23,000	7,000

*Beginning of year used to facilitate calculation

Figure 4. Use of the Future Benefit Method for Capital Charging

forthcoming capital charge, and, therefore, the manager will be properly motivated by the capital charge to make an economic decision.

What of the excess residual income from older assets? Will the manager's performance look better than it actually is? The answer is no, because the residual income target is simply set as the difference between projected profit and capital charge. There is no absolute measure of residual income. The important consideration is that the future benefit method of capital charging for depreciable assets directs the division manager to make decisions that will increase his residual income and at the same time improve the performance of the company.

Finally the problem of transfer pricing deserves comment. Many pages have been written on methods for equitable transfer pricing, and it is generally agreed that where an outside market price is available this should be charged internally. In the more complex case of no outside market there is little agreement. In this situation, the residual income method should be used with the selling division's residual target set at zero. The buying division thus indirectly pays for the use of the selling division's assets. If the buying division contemplates an increase in sales, then its cost analysis allows for the increase in assets necessary to operate the selling division. Thus, the system is self-compensating.

SUMMARY

This article has demonstrated that, while ROI is an appealing method for division measurement and control because of its simplicity and its independence of divisional size, its use will often lead to divisional decisions that are not in the best interests of the company. Supplementary controls may be used to minimize these unfortunate decisions, but the very presence of these additional restrictions will remove the motivational benefits that make decentralization attractive.

The residual income method overcomes the deficiencies of ROI if it is applied in the following manner:

> 1. Capital charges should be made at various rates, according to the cost of capital employed by each type of asset.

> 2. Assets should be valued at their worth to the company. If assessments of value are not possible annually, then the net book value of an asset should be used as an alternative.

> 3. The future benefit method should be used for charging capital costs against depreciable assets.

> 4. Intracompany prices should be fixed at the open market price if prices are known. When there is no market price, the selling division should set its prices so as to earn zero residual income. A division that falls partly into the latter category must apportion its assets so as to yield zero residual income on the assets used for intracompany business.

By using these techniques, top management will align the goals of its division managers with those of the company and prevent a manager from making decisions that will improve the performance of his division but at the same time lower the overall performance of the company.

25.

THE ROLE OF THE FIRM'S ACCOUNTING SYSTEM FOR MOTIVATION*

George J. Benston

INTRODUCTION

Motivating employees to work for the goals of the firm has long been one of management's most important and vexing problems. The search for methods that motivate effectively, that induce the employee to work harder for the firm's goals, led to experimentation with a wide diversity of devices.[1] In recent years, several writers emphasized that the firm's accounting system has a direct influence on the motivation of managers.[2] This paper (a) surveys the available findings of research done in the behavioral sciences and organization theory as they bear on motivation, and (b) critically examines the accounting system and reports in the light of such findings.

---

*From *The Accounting Review*, April 1963, pp. 347–354. Reprinted by permission of the author and the American Accounting Association.

[1]See M. S. Viteles, *Motivation and Morale in Industry*, New York: W. W. Norton and Co., 1953.

[2]C. Argyris, *The Impact of Budgets on People*, New York: The Controllership Foundation, 1952.

"Tentative Statement on Cost Accounting Concepts Underlying Reports for Management Purposes," *The Accounting Review*, 1956, Vol. 31, p. 188.

R. Anthony, "Cost Concepts for Control," *The Accounting Review*, 1957, Vol. 32, pp. 229–234.

N. Bedford, "Cost Accounting as a Motivation Technique," *N.A.C.A. Bulletin*, 1957, pp. 1250–1257.

A. Stedry, *Budget Control and Cost Behavior*, Englewood Cliffs, N.J.: Prentice-Hall, 1960.

Part I surveys the literature related to motivation and organizational structure and concludes that the decentralized[3] form of organization provides the conditions in which effective motivation can occur. In the light of Part I and other evidence, the accounting system and reports are critically evaluated in Part II. The major conclusions of Part II are that:

> 1. The empirical research reinforces and justifies the recent emphasis on the virtues of responsibility accounting. Responsibility accounting provides an effective overall aid to decentralization and, hence, while indirect and not as dramatic as some proposed direct uses (such as "proper" budgets or standards), perhaps is more important for effective motivation.

> 2. The evidence does not support the unqualified use of accounting reports as direct motivating factors. Indeed, there is evidence that the direct use of budgets can lead to a reduction in effective motivation. Nevertheless, there are positive aspects to the direct use of accounting reports.

I. MOTIVATION AND ORGANIZATIONAL STRUCTURE

The motivation of employees may be attempted by the use of a very large variety of techniques, applied in a number of ways. Among these techniques are direct wage incentives, participation schemes, goal setting, and morale boosters. These may be offered directly to the employee by the firm in a centralized fashion (by the personnel department, for example), or indirectly, by the department head in a decentralized firm.[4] Since even a cursory examination of the literature on motivation leads to the realization that the specific techniques of motivation are of almost infinite variety, this paper will concentrate on the problem of application. Indeed, the survey of the literature presented below led the writer to conclude that the organizational structure of the firm is very important for the successful application of motivation techniques, especially with respect to the ordinary

---

[3]Decentralization, as used in this paper and in organization theory generally, refers to the vesting of authority and responsibility in the department manager or supervisor for the day-to-day conduct of departmental operations. The department in question need not be physically or organizationally separate from the rest of firm. The title "department manager" and the organizational grouping "department," then, signify any supervisory position and work group for which authority and responsibility over specific tasks are delegated and for which accounting reports are prepared. With this system of organization, the department manager is given the authority to operate his department and supervise his employees as he would do if he were an individual entrepreneur.

[4]In a small firm, these two procedures of application may merge, since the central decision maker is in direct contact with the employees.

worker.[5] The influence of organizational structure on motivation, then, is examined below.

Decentralization and Centralization

The organizational structure of decentralization is one in which managers and employees are in direct and continuous contact. This face-to-face relationship facilitates the manager's perception of the needs and goals of his workers. With the authority given him by decentralization, the manager can provide those specific rewards and penalties that are effective for motivating individual workers and groups. Thus, he is in a good position to persuade them to accept the goals of the firm as their own (or as not opposed to their goals) and work to achieve these ends.

In contrast, centralization and large size make perception of the workers' needs difficult. Communication between the decision makers and those who carry out their decisions becomes complicated and subject to more interference ("noise").[6] And, as a study of ten voluntary associations revealed, ordinary members become more passive and disassociated from the central purposes of the organization and leaders become further removed from the activities they plan.[7]

In addition, research at Sears, Roebuck and Co. revealed that organizational size alone unquestionably is one of the most important factors in determining the quality of employee relationships: "the smaller the unit, the higher the morale and vice versa."[8] And, a study of two British motorcar factories demonstrated that the size factor affects productivity directly. Significant (though low) correlations were found between output and size, the smaller work groups showing consistently larger output in each factory.[9]

However, the existence of small groups, per se, is not a sufficient condition for motivation. Workers may feel a greater sense of belonging if they work in smaller, more cohesive groups, but they will not necessarily be motivated toward fulfilling the goals of the organization. Some writers, notably Argyris (who has done extensive research at Yale's Labor and Management Center), believe that it is inevitable that the ordinary worker fight

---

[5]The motivation of managers and other executives similarly is affected by organizational structure. However, since published findings that dealt with the motivation of executives specifically could not be found, the major emphasis in this paper is on the motivation of the ordinary worker.

[6]T. M. Whitin, "On the Span of Central Direction," *Naval Research Logistics Quarterly*, 1954, Vol. 1, p. 27.

[7]F. S. Chapin and J. E. Tsouderos, "Formalization Observed in Ten Voluntary Associations: Concepts, Morphology, Process," *Social Forces*, 1955, Vol. 33, pp. 306–309.

[8]J. C. Worthy, "Organization Structure and Employee Morale," *American Sociological Review*, 1950, Vol. 15, p. 173.

[9]R. Marriott, "Size of Working Group and Output," *Occupational Psychology*, 1949, Vol. 23, p. 56.

the organization. He writes that the organization characterized by ". . . task specialization, unity of direction, chain of command, and span of control . . . may create frustration, conflict and failure for the employee. He may react by regressing, decreasing his efficiency, and creating informal systems against management."[10]

This tendency for informal organizations to be created has been explored extensively.[11] Selznick, for example, writes that

> "In every organization, the goals of the organization are modified (abandoned, deflected, or elaborated) by processes within it. The process of modification is effected through the informal structure."[12] After reviewing several empirical studies, he concludes that "the day-to-day behavior of the group becomes centered around specific problems and proximate goals which have primarily an internal relevance. Then, since these activities come to consume an increasing proportion of the time and thoughts of the participants, they are—from the point of view of actual behavior—*substituted* for the professed goals."[13]

The Motivation of Small Groups

There also is ample evidence that these informal groups can work to increase or decrease productivity, depending on whether or not the workers perceive that the organization's goals are not contrary to theirs.[14] Two types of procedures have been proposed to cope with this problem. One, the direct approach, involves an immediate attempt by top management to influence the worker through direct wage incentive plans, company-wide incentive plans, and group discussions. The other, the indirect approach, gives primary responsibility and authority to the department manager to motivate his workers effectively.

The direct approach is often effective but it is also difficult to administer successfully. Direct incentive plans are not feasible generally unless a

---

[10] C. Argyris, "The Individual and Organization: Some Problems of Mutual Adjustment," *Administrative Science Quarterly*, 1957, Vol. 2, p. 1.

[11] For example see C. I. Barnard, *The Functions of the Executive*, Cambridge, Mass.: Harvard University Press, 1938; J. A. March and H. A. Simon, *Organizations*, New York: John Wiley and Sons, 1958; P. Selznick, "An Approach to a Theory of Organization," *American Sociological Review*, 1943, Vol. 8, pp. 47–54; and H. A. Simon, *Administrative Behavior*, New York: The Macmillan Co., 1947.

[12] Ibid., p. 47.

[13] Ibid., p. 48. (Emphasis appears in the original.)

[14] For example see L. Berkowitz, "Group Standards, Cohesiveness and Productivity," *Human Relations*, 1954, Vol. 7, pp. 509–519; D. Cartwright and A. Zander, "Group Pressures and Group Standards," in *Group Dynamics*, Second Edition, D. Cartwright and A. Zander, eds., Evanston, Illinois: Row, Peterson and Co., 1960, pp. 165–188; S. Schachter, N. Ellertson, D. McBride, and D. Gregory, "An Experimental Study of Cohesiveness and Productivity," *Human Relations*, 1951, Vol. 4, pp. 229–238, and W. F. Whyte and others, *Money and Motivation*, New York: Harper, 1955.

homogeneous product is produced under repetitive conditions.[15] Also, attempts to promote individual increases in productivity usually are disruptive and detrimental to efficiency where the employees' tasks are interrelated.[16] Company-wide incentive plans have had a spotty record of success.[17] They seem to work best where there is a long history of trust between labor and management or an unusual person as chief executive of the company.[18] However, efforts to impose company-wide incentive plans in other situations have been generally unsuccessful. Group discussions also do not appear to be reliable. A famous experiment conducted in an American plant on the effect of group discussions on productivity and worker acceptance of change produced negative results when replicated in Norway.[19]

The indirect approach makes the informal group's goals synonymous with the organization's goal through effective company leadership of the informal group. The firm then can take advantage of the demonstrated positive relationship between group goals and productivity (cited above).[20] Also, this approach does not rule out the use of direct techniques when and where they are deemed feasible.

The Role of the Department Manager

The indirect approach can be effected most readily in the decentralized firm. The department manager, who is likely to understand and accept the firm's goals,[21] can be assigned the task of leading the informal group. In assigning the department manager this role, the departmentalized firm can take advantage of the probability that the informal grouping of workers will

---

[15] W. B. Wolf, *Wage Incentives as a Management Tool*, New York: Columbia University Press, 1957.

[16] P. M. Blau, *The Dynamics of Bureaucracy*, Chicago: University of Chicago Press, 1955, chapter IV; M. Deutch, "The Effects of Cooperation and Competition Upon Group Process," in *Group Dynamics*, Second Edition, op. cit. footnote 14, pp. 414–448; and E. J. Thomas, "Effects of Facilitative Role Interdependence on Group Functioning," *Human Relations*, 1957, Vol. 10, pp. 347–366.

[17] J. N. Scanlon, "Profit Sharing: Three Case Studies," *Industrial and Labor Relations Review*, 1948, Vol. 2, pp. 58–75.

[18] See J. F. Lincoln, *Lincoln's Incentive System*, New York: McGraw-Hill, 1946.

[19] L. Coch and J. R. P. French, Jr., "Overcoming Resistance to Change," *Human Relations*, 1948, Vol. 1, pp. 512–532; and J. R. P. French, Jr., J. Israel, and D. As, "An Experiment on Participation in a Norwegian Factory," *Human Relations*, 1960, Vol. 30, pp. 3–19.

[20] See footnote 14.

[21] Research that examined the motivation of managers, as distinct from production workers, could not be found. However, managers are in more direct and continual contact with the firm's policy makers than are ordinary workers. Hence, they are likely to assume the goals of top-management (see evidence cited in footnotes 14 and 22). Also, top management can exercise control over the performance and possibly the motivation of department managers through budgets and accounting reports of performance (as discussed below).

follow the formal department organization. Task specialization and frequent interaction provide this cohesiveness.[22]

It is very important that the organization-oriented manager assume the leadership role, for when he abdicates or is incapable in his role as leader, an informal leader arises.[23] Without a management-oriented leader, the drives of workers for satisfaction are often channeled into nonproductive or destructive practices.[24] This behavior is to be expected, since the effort necessary for high production rarely is satisfying in itself. Indeed, many empirical investigations have shown that there seldom is positive, but occasionally negative, correlation between productivity and job satisfaction.[25]

The factors that are likely to make the department manager an effective leader also are a product of decentralization. Bass, who considers much of the literature on leadership, concludes that the effective supervisor satisfies the needs of his subordinates.[26] Since these needs are diverse, any number of leadership styles have been found to work in a variety of situations. Thus, the organizational structure must allow the manager the freedom and authority to reward his workers. Freedom is necessary so that the manager can adapt his methods to the particular needs of his group. And, the employees will respond to the demands of the manager only if he has enough influence to make the employees' behavior pay off in terms of actual benefits.[27]

Decentralization also is effective in encouraging the manager to use a style of leadership that promotes effective motivation. It was found in several empirical studies that the fewer the restraints put upon a group (within limits), the more it produced.[28] Kahn and Katz have done extensive research on this aspect of motivation. They find that "Apparently, close supervision can interfere with the gratification of some strongly felt needs."[29] They go on to observe that "There is a great deal of evidence that

[22] J. M. Jackson, "Reference Group Processes in a Formal Organization," *Sociometry*, 1959, Vol. 22, pp. 307–327. Also reprinted in *Group Dynamics*, Second Edition, op. cit., footnote 14.

[23] R. L. Kahn and D. Katz, "Leadership Practices in Relation to Productivity and Morale," in *Group Dynamics*, Second Edition, op. cit., footnote 14, pp. 554–570.

[24] W. F. Whyte and others, op. cit., footnote 14.

[25] A. H. Brayfield and W. H. Crockett, "Employee Attitudes and Employee Performance," *Psychological Bulletin*, 1955, Vol. 52, pp. 396–424; and R. L. Kahn and N. C. Morse, "The Relationship of Productivity to Morale," *Journal of Social Issues*, 1951, Vol. 7, pp. 8–17.

[26] B. M. Bass, *Leadership, Psychology, and Organizational Behavior*, New York: Harper and Bros., 1960. The bibliography of this work includes 1155 items.

[27] D. C. Petz, "Influence: A Key to Effective Leadership in the First Line Supervisor," *Personnel*, 1952, Vol. 29. A similar conclusion is reached by Fiedler for military and sports groups. He concludes that ". . . leadership traits can become operative in influencing group productivity only when the leader has considerable power in the group." (F. E. Fiedler, "The Leader's Psychological Distance and Group Effectiveness," in *Group Dynamics*, Second Edition, op. cit., footnote 14, p. 605). Kahn and Katz also reached this conclusion (op. cit., footnote 22, p. 561), as do W. S. High, R. D. Wilson, and A. Comrey, "Factors Influencing Organizational Effectiveness VIII," *Personnel Psychology*, 1955, Vol. 8, p. 368.

[28] R. M. Stogdill, *Individual Behavior and Group Achievement*, New York: Oxford University Press, 1959, p. 272.

[29] R. L. Kahn and D. Katz, op. cit., footnote 22, p. 560.

this factor of closeness of supervision, which is very important, is by no means determined at the first level of supervision. . . . The style of supervision which is characteristic of first-level supervisors reflects in considerable degree the organizational climate which exists at higher levels in the management hierarchy."[30] Thus decentralization, which is characterized by the autonomy of action given the department manager by top management, serves both to allow the managers the necessary freedom and authority needed for motivation and to encourage them to supervise their workers effectively.

II. ACCOUNTING SYSTEMS AND MOTIVATION

Decentralization, which provides the motivational advantages described above, is aided by the firm's accounting system. In fact, many students of decentralization agree with E. F. L. Brech's conclusion (in a review of British experience with decentralization):

> By whatever arrangements and procedures, decentralization necessitates provision for the periodic review of performance and progress and the expression of approval.[31]

This need is met by the firm's accounting system. Top management can afford to give authority to the department manager, since it can control the basic activities of the department with the help of accounting reports of performance. Furthermore, accounting reports and budgets may serve as reliable means of communication, wherein top management can inform the manager of the goals of the firm that it expects him to fulfill.

Responsibility Accounting

More specifically, the findings surveyed above reinforce the recent emphasis on responsibility accounting. In making the smallest areas of responsibility the fundamental building blocks of the accounting system, accountants facilitate effective motivation. With a system of responsibility accounting, top management can afford to widen its span of control and allow operating decisions to be made on a decentralized basis. Correlatively, assigning costs to the individual managers who have control over their incurrence is a factor in encouraging these managers to exercise effectively their authority to motivate their supervisees. The managers' performance in this regard is measured by the accounting reports, which are likely to be an incentive for the effective motivation of the managers.

---

[30]Ibid., p. 560.
[31]E. F. L. Brech, "The Balance Between Centralization and Decentralization in Managerial Control," *British Management Review*, 1954, Vol. 12, p. 195.

Budgets and Motivation

Indeed, several writers have proposed that accounting reports be used as a direct factor for effective motivation. The most extensive examination of the use of budgets as a tool for motivation was made by Stedry, who measured the effect of various budgets on an individual's level of aspiration as a method of determining the differences in motivation on these budgets.[32] His experiment, in which the subjects attempted to solve problems for which they received budgets and were rewarded for achievement, resulted in the following determinations:

> The experimental results indicate that an "implicit" budget (where the subject is not told what goal he must attain) produced the best performance, closely followed by a "medium" budget and a "high" budget. The "low" budget, which was the only one which satisfied the criterion of "attainable but not too loose," resulted in performance significantly lower than the other budget groups.
>
> However, there is a strong interaction effect between budgets and the aspiration level determination grouping. The group of "high" budget subjects who received their budgets prior to setting their aspiration levels performed better than any other group, whereas the "high" budget group who set their aspirations before receiving the budget were the lowest performers of any group.[33]

After presenting arguments to the effect that firms probably do not operate at optimal efficiency, Stedry concludes that ". . . it seems at least reasonable to suppose that it is a proper task of budgetary control to be concerned with strategies for constant improvement in performance."[34] He implies that the budget should be used to motivate department managers. The function of the budget would be to raise the manager's level of aspiration and thereby increase his level of performance, rather than to inform him of top management's goals and decisions.

Stedry briefly notes, but does not really consider, the effects of accounting reports on the setting of aspiration levels. His experiment was deliberately designed so that the subjects would not have knowledge of their performance.[35] The budget then became their primary point of reference.[36] But would this happen where the managers had knowledge of their previous performance to compare with the budget that is supposed to motivate them to new productive heights?

It is likely that department managers can make a fairly accurate estimate of their performance. The experience of time study engineers can be noted, since the setting of a rate for a particular job is analogous to the setting of a

---

[32] Op. cit., footnote 2.
[33] Ibid., pp. 89–90.
[34] Ibid., p. 147.
[35] Ibid., p. 71.
[36] Ibid., p. 82.

budget for a department. In both situations the attempt is made to motivate the worker to produce more by setting high standards. But, as many articles, texts, and case studies attest, the worker almost always can gauge his performance. The worker generally will fight a "tight" rate by refusing to produce efficiently, because of his fear that the "carrot" will always be pushed ahead every time he attempts to overtake it.[37] There is no reason to expect department managers to be less perceptive than factory workers.

In an actual situation, the department manager probably would compare his estimate of his performance with the budget to see how well he did. This means that the manager would have knowledge of his success or failure. Several experimenters have examined the effect of this knowledge on aspiration levels. Lewin, Dembro, Festinger, and Sears, in an often quoted review and analysis of the literature to 1944 conclude that ". . . generally the level of aspiration will be raised and lowered respectively as the performance (attainment) reaches or does not reach the level of aspiration."[38]

The effects of success and failure are difficult problems for the would-be budget manipulator. Stedry's findings indicate that a high budget (one technically impossible of attainment) produced the best performance where the subject received it before setting his level of aspiration. The attainable low budget produced the worst results. But in working conditions, assuming knowledge, the high budget probably will result in failure for the department manager and, consequently, in lowering his level of aspiration (motivation) and performance.[39] The budget manipulator, then, must either give the manager false reports about his performance or attempt to set the budget just enough above the manager's perception of his performance to encourage him.

The first alternative, false reports, is a potentially dangerous procedure and is likely to be quite expensive. Performance reports would have to be secretly prepared. This would make accounting data on the department's actual operations (needed for economic decisions) difficult to obtain, since the department manager could not be consulted. Also, this procedure must be based on the assumption that the manager will believe a cost report, even if it conflicts with his own estimates. The validity of this assumption is denied in a study by Simon, Guetzkow, Kozmetsky, and Tyndall:

---

[37] See W. F. Whyte and others, op. cit., footnote 14, Chapter 3, "Setting the Rate," for a delightful description of this practice.

[38] K. Levin, T. Dembro, L. Festinger, and P. Sears, "Level of Aspiration," in *Personality and the Behavioral Disorders*, Vol. I., J. McV. Hunt, ed., New York: Ronald Press, 1944, p. 337. A comprehensive test of the hypothesis stated by Lewin, *et al.*, which confirmed it, was made by I. L. Child and J. W. M. Whiting, "Determinants of Level of Aspiration: Evidence from Everyday Life," *Journal of Abnormal and Social Psychology*, 1949, Vol. 44, p. 314. Similar results are reported by I. M. Steisel and B. D. Cohen, "Effects of Two Degrees of Failure on Level of Aspiration in Performance," *Journal of Abnormal and Social Psychology*, 1951, Vol. 46, pp. 78–82.

[39] This may have happened even in Stedry's experiment, since he found that the poorest performance occurred where the subjects determined their aspiration levels before they were given the high budget.

Interview results show that a particular figure does not operate as a norm, in either a score-card or attention-directing sense, simply because the controller's department calls it a standard. It operates as a norm only to the extent that the executives and supervisors, whose activity it measures, accept it as a fair and attainable yardstick of their performance. Generally, operating executives were inclined to accept a standard to the extent that they were satisfied that the data were *accurately recorded*, that the standard level was *reasonably attainable*, and that the variables it measured were *controllable* by them.[40]

The second alternative open to the budget manipulator is rather difficult to effect. The manager's level of aspiration must be measured, and his perception of his performance level must be estimated. However, measurement of an individual's aspiration level is not a well-developed science. Some fairly successful, though crude, procedures for measuring level of aspiration have been developed. Unfortunately, they depend on the subject's verbal response to questions about the goal explicitly to be undertaken, such as the score expected (not hoped for) in a dart-throwing contest.[41] The usefulness of this technique, for a work situation is limited, since the employee has an incentive to state a false, low goal and thus avoid failure. A more precise measure has been developed by Siegel,[42] but the technique itself restricts it to highly artificial conditions. Thus, it is doubtful that the use of budgets for motivation can be effective except in carefully selected situations.

The direct influence of the budget on motivation may be more effective than is indicated above if the budget is a participation budget, rather than an imposed budget of the type used by Stedry. In a forthcoming article, Becker and Green present evidence and arguments to show that participation in budget making in conjunction with the comparison and reviewing process may lead to increased cohesiveness and goal acceptance by the participants.[43] If this goal acceptance is at a higher level than previous goals, the aspiration level of the participants has been raised and should lead to increased production.[44]

---

[40]H. A. Simon, H. Guetzkow, G. Kozmetsky, and G. Tyndall, *Centralization vs. Decentralization in Organizing the Controllers Department*, New York: The Controllership Foundation, in 1954, p. 29. (Emphasis appears in the original.)

[41]K. Levin, T. Dembro, L. Festinger, and P. Sears, op. cit., footnote 38.

[42]S. Siegel, "Level of Aspiration and Decision Making," *Psychological Review*, 1957, Vol. 64, pp. 253–263.

[43]S. Becker and D. Green, Jr., "Budgeting and Employee Behavior," *The Journal of Business*, 1962, Vol. 35, pp. 392–402.

[44]For a fuller treatment of ths subject see the Becker and Green paper, in which is discussed the conditions under which cohesiveness, goal acceptance, and productivity can be lowered as well as increased.

Accounting Reports of Performance and Motivation

Budgets are not the only accounting reports that may be used for motivation. Accounting reports of performance also have a direct effect on motivation by giving the department manager knowledge of his performance. Most of the published experiments on this subject consider the effects of knowledge on the learning or performance of physical tasks. However, the general findings reported ought to be relevant to the effect of accounting information on the manager's performance. Ammons surveyed most of the literature in this area (to 1956) and reached the following generalizations that seem applicable to the present problem:[45]

> Knowledge of performance affects rate of learning and level reached by learning.
>
> *Knowledge of performance affects motivation.* The most common effects of knowledge of performance is to increase motivation.
>
> The more specific the knowledge of performance, the more rapid improvement and the higher the level of performance.
>
> The longer the delay in giving knowledge of performance, the less effect the given performance has.
>
> When knowledge of performance is decreased, performance drops.

However, overemphasis of departmental costs reports may have undesirable effects, since accounting data often does not measure fulfillment of the firm's goals. Ammons notes that "It is very important to keep in mind *what* the subject is motivated to do when knowledge of performance increases his motivation. Often he is motivated to score higher, not necessarily to learn the task faster and better. He may then resort to taking advantage of weaknesses in the apparatus, learning habits which are of no value or actually lead to poorer performance when he later attempts to learn a similar task."[46] Overemphasis of accounting reports has been found to result from this behavior.[47] Where the reports became the sole criteria for evaluating performance, managers resorted to such anti-productive techniques as delayed maintenance, bickering over cost allocations, and even falsification of inventories. Thus, recognition of the positive motivational aspects of accounting reports should not lead to the conclusion that they can be used

---

[45] R. B. Ammons, "Effects of Knowledge of Performance: A Survey and Tentative Theoretical Information," *Journal of General Psychology*, 1956, Vol. 54, pp. 283–290. (Emphasis appears in the original.)

[46] Ibid., p. 280.

[47] See C. Argyris, op. cit., footnote 10; P. W. Cook, Jr., "Decentralization and the Transfer Price Problem," *Journal of Business*, 1955, Vol. 27, p. 87; and V. F. Ridgeway, "Dysfunctional Consequences of Performance Measurements," *Administrative Science Quarterly*, 1956, Vol. 1, pp. 240–247.

without limits. Indeed, the history of the search for "the key to motivation" indicates that people's needs are too diverse and changeable to be satisfied by any single device or mechanically applied procedure.

CONCLUSION

Decentralization contributes to effective motivation. The firm's accounting system facilitates decentralization and hence has an indirect but important impact on motivation. The direct use of accounting reports, such as budgets, for motivation can result in reduced performance, if the budget is imposed on the department manager. However, a participation budget may be effective in increasing motivation. Also, accounting reports of activities aid motivation by giving the manager knowledge of his performance.

In short, the accounting system facilitates decentralization, which is conducive to effective motivation. Furthermore, the careful use of accounting reports can directly contribute toward effective motivation by expressing goals and by supplying knowledge of performance.

26.

ANALYZING THE EFFECTIVENESS OF THE TRADITIONAL STANDARD COST VARIANCE MODEL*

Joel S. Demski

A fundamental, yet largely unexplored tenet in accounting is that accounting is utilitarian in nature. The implication is that both accounting theory construction and practice should be based on user requirements. Unfortunately, these requirements remain largely unknown. Two consequences follow: First, accounting—in both its external and internal versions—continues to rely on general purpose models for such activities as periodic income determination and profit variation analyses (to the extent that such models exist). Second, current empirical research is largely limited to defining utility in terms of predictive ability rather than in terms of specific decision consequences.[1]

In internal accounting, however, user requirements are now known to the extent that well-structured decision models are employed in certain managerial decision processes. It therefore becomes appropriate to examine the utility of the traditional accounting model in those situations. This paper conducts such an examination.

The analysis is divided into three sections. The first establishes a framework by viewing the management process as an adaptive control process. The second then contrasts the information provided by the traditional standard cost variance model with that required by the management pro-

---

*From *Management Accounting*, October 1967, pp. 9–19. Copyrighted 1967 by National Association of Accountants. Reprinted by permission.

[1]See for example, William H. Beaver, "Financial Ratios as Predictors of Business Failure" (unpublished Ph.D. dissertation, Graduate School of Business, University of Chicago, 1965) and Philip Brown, "The Predictive Abilities of Alternative Income Concepts: with Special References to Assets Amortized Under Certificates of Necessity" (paper presented to the Workshop in Accounting Research, Graduate School of Business, University of Chicago, Spring, 1966).

cess, as described in the first section. Finally, the third section suggests an operational extension of the traditional standard cost model, designed to provide superior control information.

THE MANAGEMENT CONTROL PROCESS

Jaedicke observes that:

> A survey of the accounting and management literature seems to indicate that the control process is generally thought of in three ways. First, control is sometimes defined as the analysis of present performance in the light of some standard or goal in order to determine to what extent accomplishment measures up to the plan or standard. . . . An intermediate sort of concept defines control as a process of securing conformity to a plan. This concept holds that after the variance or deviation from the plan is discovered, the next step is to take corrective action. . . . A third concept of control stresses the idea of information *feedback*. That is, data collected as part of the control process might be systematically reported and used in future planning decision.[2]

The essential difference between the intermediate and broad conception is that the latter envisions the deviation data as being input both to the response decision—immediate corrective action—and to what might be termed the planning process. The former, however, concentrates only on the immediate corrective action. The narrow conception, on the other hand, concentrates only on the analysis of performance *per se*.

The broad response and feedback conception of the control process will be followed here. The reason for this preference is that the control system viewed in its entirety must encompass feedback and response considerations.

The narrow conception of the control process, being inadequate in its analytical implications, can be summarily dismissed as bordering on the naive. It is simply not possible to discuss the quality of information generated without considering the use to be made of that information.

The same argument can also be used to dispose of the intermediate conception, because it ignores the important use of current information as feedback into the planning model. For any deviation of an actual result from the expected result, the avoidability (or controllability) of the deviation must be assessed. If it were avoidable, it can be suppressed. Were it not avoidable, two further aspects must be considered: (1) Its statistical significance and (2) the (immediate) response—that is, should the existing program be altered?

---

[2]R. K. Jaedicke, "Accounting Data for Purposes of Control," *Accounting Review*, April 1962, p. 181.

If we are to be concerned with the "task of communicating information on the objectives to be accomplished, providing a means for evaluation of performance, learning and instigation of remedial action,"[3] we are compelled to look at this task in its entirety, including feedback into the planning model (learning and remedial action). The implication is that the traditional planning-control dichotomy is artificial and misleading to the extent that this feedback is important.

Perhaps enlisting the aid of a schematic representation of the control process being discussed will clarify this point. Consider Exhibit 1. The lower, individual task portion of the diagram depicts the usual interpretation of the control process. That is, control is usually veiwed as being task oriented—where the term task is used in a broad sense (referring to any undertaking or piece of work). But in a strict literal sense we must also recognize the need for control of this typical (task) control system—hence the diagram's upper portion.

The purpose of the multiple task control portion of the diagram, then, is to control the organization's set of task control systems. For example, the operation of an individual oil refinery in an integrated oil firm may be viewed in terms of the diagram's task control portion; but control of this individual refinery's management is exercised by the multiple task control portion.

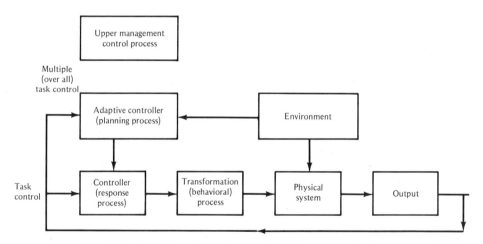

Note: Taken in part for S. Chang, *Synthesis of Optimum Control Systems*, McGraw-Hill, New York, 1961, E. B. Roberts, "Industrial Dynamics: the Design of Management Control Systems," *Management Controls: New Directions in Basic Research*, ed. C. P. Bonini, R. K. Jaedicke, and H. M. Wagner, McGraw-Hill, New York, 1964, pp. 102–26, and G. Shillinglaw, "Divisional Performance Review: An Extension of Budgetary Control," *Management Controls: New Directions in Basic Research*, ed. Bonini et. al., McGraw-Hill, New York, 1964, pp. 149–63. The horizontal line indicates that not all of the usual information flows between the multiple and task control processes have been included.

Exhibit 1. The Control Process

[3]Z. Zannetos, "Some Thoughts on Internal Control Systems of the Firm," *Accounting Review*, October 1964, pp. 867–868.

As becomes obvious, the diagram in Exhibit 1 could easily be extended to represent each individual level in any organization. However, our objectives are adequately served by limiting the diagram as shown.

Given a set of objectives, the function of the planning model or adaptive controller is to receive environmental and feedback measures and determine the ideal or optimum output. This, in turn, is transmitted to the decision transformation process (via the controller) where the decision is transformed into instructions for the controlled system. Following this, actual results are measured and transmitted to the controller or response model where actual and optimum results are used as a basis for making a response decision which is transmitted, in turn, to the decision transformation process, and so on. But the optimum in this response decision need not be the one originally transmitted to the controller. The optimum may have changed as the result of further environmental measures and/or additional feedback from the controlled system and the purpose of the upper management control process is to make certain that all of this is done correctly.[4]

The adaptive controller's function, as indicated, is to receive environmental and feedback inputs and to generate an ideal or optimum program. In many instances today this type of decision process exists in well-defined form—that is, it

> ... is well structured to the extent that it satisfies the following criteria:
>
> 1. It can be described in terms of numerical variables, scalar and vector quantities.
> 2. The goals to be attained can be specified in terms of a well-defined objective function—for example, the maximization of profit or the minimization of cost.
> 3. There exist computational routines (*algorithms*) that permit the solution to be found and stated in actual numerical terms. . . .[5]

Examples are provided by successful application of the inventory, linear programming, queuing, and linear decision rules for employment and production models (although this is not to deny that there are qualitative factors in these decision processes).

---

[4] Further note in conjunction with the diagram that the term decision process is used in a broad sense. It refers either to quantitative, well-defined decision processes, or to qualitative, judgment oriented decision processes. Also, while the planning, response, behavioral and upper management processes are depicted as separate decision processes in the diagram, this is certainly not an artifact. They are certainly not independent; in many instances, the same manager will make all four types of decisions. We separate them in the diagram in order to emphasize the fact that different information flows are associated with each of the processes and that different degrees of quantification may be associated with each.

[5] H. Simon and A. Newell, "Heuristic Problem Solving: The Next Advance in Operations Research," *Operations Research*, January–February 1958, p. 5.

The function of the controller or response process is to make a decision in response to observed divergences between optimum and actual results. These divergences are the result of prediction errors, control failures (failures to maintain or obtain specific programs), measurement errors, model errors (errors or approximations in constructing and using the planning, response or transformation models), and/or the stochastic nature of some underlying variables. Because of the necessity of separating the impact of these various causal factors and of predicting the time path of the perceived deviation, the response decision is at once critical and difficult.

Work has been done in such areas as assessing the statistical significance of a given deviation,[6] making the decision to investigate a deviation in the hope of determining the specific causal factors involved,[7] exploring the sensitivity of the planning model to estimation errors,[8] and simulating the transient characteristics of specified systems using certain decision rules.[9] The fact remains, however, that these items of research must be combined and supplemented before the response decision process can be synthesized to the extent that we are able to specify and successfully implement a well-defined response model. At present, these decisions remain in the realm of judgment or heuristic decision making.

The unfortunate implication for the present analysis is that in supplying control information, we must postulate the existence of some such heuristic response decision process and then indulge in the inextricable task of determining the inputs to this process.[10]

Once a response decision is made, it is relayed to the transformation process. In essence, the transformation process is a behavioral model; it takes an optimum plan or response and generates a set of specific instructions designed to achieve the plan or response.

Research has been done on such items as the motivational impact of budgets and standards[11] and incentive systems.[12] However, we shall not be

---

[6]See, for example, A. J. Duncan, "The Economic Design of $\overline{X}$ Charts used to Maintain Current Control of a Process," *Journal of the American Statistical Association*, June 1956, pp. 228–242 or Z. Zannetos, "Standard Costs as a First Step to Probabilistic Control: A Theoretical Justification, an Extension and Implications," *Accounting Review*, April 1964, pp. 296–304.

[7]See H. Bierman, Jr., *Topics in Cost Accounting and Decisions*, McGraw-Hill, New York, 1963.

[8]See C. Holt, J. Muth, F. Modigliani, and H. Simon, *Planning Production, Inventories, and Work Force*, Prentice-Hall, Englewood Cliffs, N.J., 1960 or C. Van de Panne and P. Bosje, "Sensitivity Analysis of Cost Coefficient Estimates: The Case of Linear Decision Rules for Employment and Production," *Management Science*, October 1962, pp. 82–107.

[9]See J. W. Forrester, *Industrial Dynamics*, McGraw-Hill, New York, 1964.

[10]As we shall see, while the response decision process has not been completely synthesized, we do know that one of the major inputs to the process is an analysis of the differences between actual and ideal results.

[11]See, for example, C. Argyris, "Human Problems with Budgets," *Harvard Business Review*, January–February 1953, pp. 97–110; and A. C. Stedry, *Budget Control and Cost Behavior*, Prentice-Hall, Englewood Cliffs, N.J., 1960.

[12]See M. Haire, "Psychological Research on Pay," *Management Controls: New Directions in Basic Research*, ed. C. P. Bonini, R. K. Jaedicke, and H. M. Wagner, McGraw-Hill, New York, 1964, pp. 277–281.

concerned with the behavioral aspects of control theory, although the various components in the diagram are by no means independent. Major emphasis is placed instead on analyzing the nature of the data required for efficient control systems apart from the manner by which the data will or will not be used in the transformation process.

Finally, superimposed on this repeating sequence of decision-action-measurement-evaluation (the lower loop in the diagram), is a planning horizon. The planning model is constructed on the basis of some finite horizon and is periodically re-solved with these, periodic, results being used as the basis for a formal change (for example, a production run) in the specified program.

This task control system, in turn, is controlled or monitored by the upper management control process. This process is conceptually similar to the task control system's response process in that action is taken on the basis of divergences between optimum and actual results. This implies that the process requires as inputs what results were obtained by the task control system and what these results could have been according to the decision model. And, as in the case of the task system's response process, this upper-level process is regarded as being judgment or heuristic oriented.

This, then, is the control process. It

> ... encompasses the technique used to identify the need for action and to review possible action alternatives as well as the ultimate control action itself. ... Management has four basic methods or approaches to the control of internal operations:
>
> 1. Control by planning and decision making.
> 2. Control by scheduling, direction and supervision.
> 3. Control by follow-up response to feedback comparison.
> 4. Control by manipulation.[13]

The essential point to grasp in describing the firm's control system is that we are assuming a coupled organizational-environmental relationship which can be viewed in terms of what, in automatic control theory, is called a self-optimizing or adaptive control system. That is, we are describing a situation where

> ... the statistics of the inputs and the plant dynamics are not completely known or are gradually changing.[14]

[13]G. Shillinglaw, "Divisional Performance Review: An Extension of Budgetary Control," *Management Controls: New Directions in Basic Research*, ed. C. P. Bonini, R. K. Jaedicke, and H. M. Wagner, McGraw-Hill, New York, 1964, p. 152.
[14]S. Chang, *Synthesis of Optimum Control Systems*, McGraw-Hill, New York, 1961, p. 255.

THE TRADITIONAL ROLE OF ACCOUNTING
IN THE CONTROL PROCESS

The traditional role of accounting in the control process centers around use of the standard costing and flexible budgeting techniques. Following the establishment of performance standards (for example, expected prices, labor time standards, and so on) and an optimum output program, the cost aspects of this program are used to establish the budget for the period. A linear relation between total standard cost and some volume index of production is usually assumed. Actual cost is them compared with budgeted (standard) cost through the well-known techniques of standard cost variance analysis in order to isolate the effect of each specific deviation.

These techniques can be succinctly summarized by resorting to some algebraic notation. Omitting units, let

$$
\begin{aligned}
TC &= \text{total standard cost for the period,}\\
F &= \text{standard fixed overhead cost for the period,}\\
P_L &= \text{standard price of direct labor,}\\
Q_L &= \text{standard quantity of direct labor,}\\
P_M &= \text{standard price of direct material,}\\
Q_M &= \text{standard quantity of direct material,}\\
V &= \text{standard volume for actual output, and}\\
c &= \text{standard variable overhead per unit of volume.}
\end{aligned}
$$

Then,

$$TC = F + P_L Q_L + P_M Q_M + cV$$

where we note that volume is the independent variable.[15] Now let primed (') values denote actual results,

$$
\begin{aligned}
F' &= F + \Delta F\\
P_L' &= P_L + \Delta P_L\\
P_M' &= P_M + \Delta P_M\\
Q_L' &= Q_L + \Delta Q_L\\
Q_M' &= Q_M + \Delta Q_M\\
V' &= V + \Delta V\\
c' &= c + \Delta c
\end{aligned}
$$

The total difference between actual and standard cost *for the actual output is:*

$$
\begin{aligned}
TC' - TC &= (F + \Delta F) + (P_L + \Delta P_L)(Q_L + \Delta Q_L) + (P_M + \Delta P_M)(Q_M + \Delta Q_M)\\
&\quad + (c + \Delta c)(V + \Delta V) - F - P_L Q_L - P_M Q_M - cV\\
&= \Delta TC\\
&= P_L \Delta Q_L + \Delta P_L Q_L + \Delta P_L \Delta Q_L + P_M \Delta Q_M + \Delta P_M Q_M + \Delta P_M \Delta Q_M + c\Delta V\\
&\quad + \Delta cV + \Delta c\Delta V + \Delta F
\end{aligned}
$$

---

[15] That is, total cost is assumed to be a function of volume. To be rigorous in our description, we should express the labor and material quantities as functions of volume. However, the exposition is facilitated by following the description presented.

$P_L \Delta Q_L$ is usually called the direct labor efficiency variance, $Q_L \Delta P_L + \Delta P_L \Delta Q_L$—the direct labor wage rate variance,[16] $P_M \Delta Q_M$—the direct material usage variance, $Q_M \Delta P_M + \Delta P_M \Delta Q_M$—the direct material price variance, $c \Delta V$—the overhead efficiency variance, and $\Delta c V + \Delta c \Delta V + \Delta F$—the overhead spending variance (using a three variance method of overhead analysis).

In an absorption costing system there would also be a volume or capacity variance arising from the difference between standard and absorbed fixed cost for the period. Such refinement, however, is not germane to the present analysis.

This is the essence of the traditional standard cost variance analysis technique. It subdivides the total difference between actual and standard cost for the standard amount produced and attempts to factor out the individual contributions to this difference of each deviation—that is, of ΔP_L, ΔQ_L, ΔP_M, ΔQ_M, Δc, ΔV and ΔF. The factoring, of course, is limited by the existence of joint product terms.

This traditional role has also been expanded to include revenues of the products produced, as in the familiar breakeven and cost-volume-mix (or profit variation) analyses. The latter is merely an extension of the above techniques to include product mix and selling price deviations, thereby focusing on the difference between actual and budgeted net income instead of between actual and budgeted cost.

As becomes obvious, the usefulness of these techniques is dependent upon, among other things, proper selection of the type of standard to be employed. Numerous types can be found in the literature. Horngren, for example, lists the three broad categories of basic, ideal, and currently attainable;[17] and for each category we could add ex post and ex ante versions. But much more important than the fact of variety is the fact that selection must be predicated on anticipated use of the resultant variance information. Here the distinction between the planning, response, behavioral and upper management decision processes being discussed becomes critical.

The planning model requires currently attainable inputs, where it is recognized that these data are ex ante in nature. They are also temporal in nature. As information in the form of feedback from current operations and additional environmental information is obtained, the ex ante data are either confirmed or altered. These confirmations and alterations then form part of the basis for the succeeding planning decisions.

---

[16]This, of course, assumes that price variances are isolated as the materials are consumed, not when they are purchased. The latter situation is preferrable from a control standpoint, but is not included in the algebraic description because of the notational burden that inclusion would impose.

[17]C. T. Horngren, Cost Accounting: A Managerial Emphasis, Prentice-Hall, Englewood Cliffs, N.J., 1962, pp. 138–39.

As noted previously, explicit discussion of the inputs to the behavioral model is beyond the scope of this inquiry. There is sufficient evidence to suggest that different types of standard may produce different results.[18] Therefore, we cannot argue in favor of some particular type without examining the behavioral process in detail.

Passing mention, though, should be made of the fact that one of the more common techniques used in the transformation process is performance evaluation where actual performance is compared with what it should have been in order to facilitate learning and motivation.[19] Exactly how and in what form this is accomplished is determined by the behavioral model; but whatever its form (for example, fictitious indicators of what should have been) *ex post* information is an input to the evaluation process.

The response and upper management decision processes require as inputs the results which were obtained (actual performance) and the results which could have been obtained. This implies that the proper standard to be used in supplying variance information for these two processes is a standard based on actual conditions—that is,

> . . . those that would have been incorporated in the [original] plan if the actual conditions had been known in advance.[20]

We shall call this an *ex post* (currently attainable) standard.

In order to fully describe what results could have been obtained, the response and upper management processes also require a determination of the optimum program implied by the *ex post* standards and decision model. We shall call this program the *ex post* (optimum) program. Its determination and synthesis, the tasks of *ex post* analysis, are discussed in the following section.

Thus, we see that the control process requires information flows related to planned results, actual results and *ex post* optimum results. The traditional accounting model does not convey all of this information. It conveys planned and actual results; and, in addition, if the budget is revised to reflect actual events (that is, if *ex post* standards are used), it will also convey what performance should have been obtained for the output actually achieved. Otherwise, it will convey what performance was anticipated for the output actually achieved. In either event, the traditional variance model, because it treats volume as the independent or exogenous variable, reports divergencies between planned and actual output and between actual and (some definition of) standard cost for the actual output. It does not, however, report what output should have been. Explicit discussion of the proposed *ex post* system will further clarify this important distinction.

---

[18] See, for example, Argyris, op. cit., Haire, op. cit., and Stedry, op. cit.
[19] See, for example, Z. Zannetos, op. cit., pp. 860–868.
[20] Shillinglaw, op. cit., p. 151.

THE PREFERRED ROLE OF EX-POST ANALYSIS

Ex post analysis is an extention of the traditional accounting analysis to include program or output revisions. It is primarily concerned with linking the planning model to the response model through generation of an ex post optimum program. The net result is a system that simultaneously monitors both performance and the original plan.

This analysis differs from the traditional accounting technique in two important respects. First, actual results are compared with ex post optimum results instead of with either ex post or ex ante standard results for the output actually obtained. That is, output is viewed as an endogenous (internal) rather than exogenous (external) variable. Second, all the inputs to the planning model are incorporated into the analysis, not just those cost (or cost and revenue) factors present in the optimum program.

These two differences are not independent because all inputs to the planning model must be incorporated into the analysis in order to determine the ex post program. On the other hand, we could conceive of a system that formally reported only ex post optimum performance for certain inputs—for example, one that reported only the opportunity cost associated with variances in a traditional standard cost system. For this reason the two differences are treated somewhat independently in the following discussion.

IMPORTANCE OF PROGRAM ALTERATIONS

The importance of comparing actual performance with ex post optimum performance, instead of with standard performance for the standard volume produced, can be indicated by a brief review of some elementary aspects of the economic theory of the firm. In doing this we shall primarily concentrate on the relevance of the information for the response decision.

In economic theory, the firm is viewed as determining its optimum output mix and quantities on the basis of its cost and demand functions. Consequently, when either of these functions changes (or differences between actual and predicted results are obtained), a new output decision is required: whether to alter the optimum output and, if so, in what manner. Quite obviously this new output decision depends on the costs and benefits associated with alteration of the existing output.

Consider the typical marginal revenue vs. marginal cost situation given in Exhibit 2, where we assume that the firm produces a single product. (To rule out the possibility of measurement error, we shall also assume that the standard is the marginal cost curve.)

The maximizing firm, facing a marginal revenue curve of MR and a marginal cost curve of MC_0 will produce at output level X_0. If the marginal cost curve subsequently shifts unavoidably to MC_1, the firm will move from output level X_0 to X_1. Since it cannot now obtain its original cost curve,

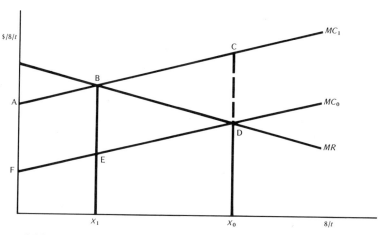

Exhibit 2

MC_0, the firm is maximizing profit by producing at level X_1. Hence, there is no foregone opportunity associated with the event. However, had the firm chosen to remain at X_0 in response to the unavoidable shift from MC_0 to MC_1, it would forego obtainable profit represented by area BCD. That is, the opportunity cost of this failure to move to the new optimum output level is represented by area BCD.

If, on the other hand, the shift to MC_1 had been avoidable, the firm would maximize profit by remaining at X_0 and suppressing the avoidable increase in marginal cost. If it does not suppress the increase and remains at X_0, it foregoes obtainable profit represented by area ACDF; if it moves to X_1, the opportunity cost is represented by area ABDF.

In contrast, regardless of whether the shift in marginal cost could have been avoided, the traditional accounting model produces a cost figure of ACDF if the firm remains at X_0 or ABEF if it moves to X_1.

Considering the various possible combinations of output level and avoidable shifts in the marginal cost curve we get the following variances provided by the traditional accounting model and opportunity cost variances provided by the proposed ex post model:

Shift in MC_0	Actual Output	Optimum Output	Accounting Variance	Opportunity Cost
Avoidable	X_0	X_0	ACDF	ACDF
Avoidable	X_1	X_0	ABEF	ABDF
Unavoidable	X_0	X_1	ACDF	BCD
Unavoidable	X_1	X_1	ABEF	0

The *ceteris paribus* approach of the traditional accounting model does not consider optimum adjustment to the changed conditions; it merely says that the cost of the deviation is the difference between actual and standard results for the output produced. In contrast, the *mutatis mutandis* approach of *ex post* analysis does consider optimum adjustment; it gauges significance by determining the opportunities foregone as a result of the deviation and failure to respond to it.

Perhaps a numerical example will clarify these issues:

Example 1

Consider a firm with total revenue (TR) and total cost (TC_0) curves given by TR = 500 X − X² and TC_0 = 100X + X² + 1000 units. Optimum output X_0 is determined as follows:

TR	=	500 X − X²	TC_0	=	100X + X² + 1000
MR	=	dTR/dX = 500 − 2X	MC_0	=	dTC_0/dX = 100 + 2X
		Optimum output:	MR	=	MC_0
			500 − 2X	=	100 + 2X
			400	=	4X
			X	=	100 units

The associated profit is $19,000
  TR(100) − TC_0(100) = 500(100) − (100)² − 100(100) − (100)² − 1000 = $19,000

If the cost curve now unavoidably shifts to TC_1 = 300X + X² + 1000, the new optimum output, X_1, would be:

TR	=	500X − X²	TC_1	=	300X + X² + 1000
MR	=	dTR/dX = 500 − 2X	MC_1	=	dTC_1/dX = 300 + 2X
		Optimum output:	MR	=	MC_1
			500 − 2X	=	300 + 2X
			200	=	4X
			X	=	50 units

and the maximum profit would be $4,000.

Suppose, now, that the firm does not respond to this shift in its cost function and remains at output level X_0. It will experience a loss of $1,000 instead of the $4,000 profit it could have obtained by moving to X_1. That is, the opportunity cost associated with not anticipating the shift and subsequent failure to respond to it is $5,000. The traditional accounting model, on the other hand, would report a variance of $20,000 under these circumstances.

The traditional and opportunity cost variances associated with the various output level and avoidability possibilities are presented in Exhibit 3. Note that because actual and standard revenues are identical in the example, the accounting profit variance is the difference between actual and standard costs.

Thus, if our objective is to analyze differences between actual and ideal results, we need to consider *ex post* optimum performance instead of standard performance for the standard volume produced. Implied changes in output mix and quantities need to be explicitly recognized. Then, and only then, can we compare actual results with what these results should have been. Quite clearly such an approach requires that we monitor all inputs to the planning model and not just those cost (or cost and revenue) factors present in the optimum program.

SHIFT IN TCo	ACTUAL OUT-PUT	OPTI-MUM OUTPUT	STAN-DARD COST	ACTUAL COST	ACCOUNT-ING VARIANCE	OPTI-MUM PROFIT	ACTUAL PROFIT	OPPOR-TUNITY COST
Avoidable	100	100	$21,000	$41,000	$20,000	$19,000	($1,000)	$20,000
Avoidable	50	100	$ 8,500	$18,500	$10,000	$19,000	$4,000	$15,000
Unavoidable	100	50	$21,000	$41,000	$20,000	$ 4,000	($1,000)	$ 5,000
Unavoidable	50	50	$ 8,500	$18,500	$10,000	$ 4,000	$4,000	0

Exhibit 3

IMPORTANCE OF MONITORING ALL PLANNING MODEL INPUTS

The effect of not monitoring all inputs to the planning model can be amply demonstrated with a simple example using the assignment model:[21]

Example 2

"A department head has four subordinates and four tasks to be per-formed. The subordinates differ in efficiency, and the tasks differ in their intrinsic difficulty. His estimate of the times each man would take to perform each task is given in the effectiveness matrix below. How should the tasks be allocated, one to a man, so as to minimize the total man-hours"?

		Man			
		I	II	III	IV
	A	8	26	17	11
Task	B	13	28	4	26
	C	38	19	18	15
	D	19	26	24	10

The optimum allocation is to make the following assignments:
    A-I, B-III, C-II, D-IV
which results in 41 total labor hours.
Assume, now that the time for man II to do task D was erroneously estimated and should have been 3 hours. This implies that the assignment should have been:
    A-I, B-III, C-IV, D-II
with a resultant labor hour total of 30 hours.

Under these circumstances a traditional standard cost system would report no variance whatever—in spite of the fact that 11 more labor hours than necessary were used to accomplish the four tasks. Expanding the scope of the traditional system to encompass all factors in the assignment decision would, on the other hand, result in a variance of 11 labor hours, appropriately costed.

---

[21]Adapted from M. Sasiene, A. Yaspen, and L. Friedman, *Operations Research,* John Wiley and Sons, New York, 1961, p. 185.

SUMMARY

We see, then, that ex post analysis is an extension of traditional standard cost variance analysis techniques in two important related directions: (1) provision is made for revision of the (ex ante) optimum program and (2) all factors in the output decision are included in the analysis. It is anticipated, ignoring issues of the cost and value of information, that this extension will provide meaningful and valuable information for the managerial function of acting on exceptions which result from either the controlled process or established goals themselves falling outside of control limits.

By introducing into the analysis optimal variation of the planned output, the proposed ex post system establishes a framework which depicts the best that might have been done, given the actual circumstances encountered during the period. The resultant opportunity cost variances are potentially useful in such areas as (1) reviewing the period's operations, (2) future planning, (3) deciding if and how to alter a current program, (4) judging the effectiveness of the task control system and (5) evaluating performance.[22]

This suggested approach to generation of control information, of course, can be pursued only in those situations where a well-defined planning model is in operation. And, to be certain, the implications of such a combined approach are only beginning to be explored.[23]

---

[22] We should perhaps note that our description of the traditional accounting model, being strictly algebraic, does not give a true measure of the information provided by the system when the data are analyzed by a competent analyst. But this does not weaken the significance of the preceding discussion because our competent analyst is much better off with the ex post system than with the traditional system. The latter will signal certain deviations but in a complex model the accounting variables are likely to represent an aggregation of a number of individual model inputs. In such a situation, the analyst must search for causal deviations. Similarly, deviations signaled by the accounting model may, in part, be manifestations of deviations in elements not included in the accounting model; or worse yet, such deviations may not be signaled at all (as in Example 2). And, finally, even if the analyst could glean all deviations from the accounting model he would still be faced with the task of assessing their effect on the program. For example, he would have to assess the effect of a given deviation on other responsibility centers. The accounting model cannot provide this information.

[23] See J. S. Demski, "Variance Analysis: An Opportunity Cost Approach with a Linear Programming Application," (unpublished Ph.D. dissertation, Graduate School of Business, University of Chicago, 1967).

27.
A USE OF PROBABILITY AND STATISTICS IN PERFORMANCE EVALUATION*

Harold Bierman, Jr.,
Lawrence E. Fouraker,
and
Robert K. Jaedicke

In the modern business enterprise, a widely used technique for perform-ance evaluation is the budget (the term budget as used here includes standard cost systems). The budgeting procedure consists of (1) setting a standard or budgeted amount for each cost classification for the coming period; (2) comparing actual performance with the budget or standard; (3) reporting and analyzing the variances of the actual performance from the budgeted performance; and (4) taking action consistent with the analysis (for example, removing the cause of unfavorable variances).

In the third step of this procedure, one of the most important problems that arises is to decide when a variance is worthy of investigation. If the variance is small in amount or results from noncontrollable factors, or if future operations would not improve even if the cause of the variance was determined, management would prefer not to waste time and money inves-tigating such variances. On the other hand, if investigation will result in substantial future savings and more efficient operations, management will probably want the variance investigated.

The problem of when to investigate is an important part of the control process. The best conceived budget or control procedures will be ineffec-tive unless the decision of when to investigate a variance is made in a reasonable manner. Yet, this problem has received little attention in the accounting literature. The traditional discussion of the problem is in terms of business judgment and intuition. The purpose of this article is to de-scribe a quantitative model for solving the decision problem of when to

*From The Accounting Review, July 1961, pp. 409–417. Reprinted by permission of the authors and the American Accounting Association.

investigate a variance. The model to be discussed draws on some concepts related to probability and statistics. These concepts will be briefly developed and explained as they are needed.

DECISION FACTORS

In deciding whether or not to investigate a variance, the following factors should be considered:

1. The probability that the variance resulted from random, noncontrollable causes.
2. The reward which will result if a variance is investigated, together with the associated probability of this reward.
3. The cost of investigation.

The model to be discussed will incorporate the above factors.

THE GENERAL PROCEDURE

In establishing the budget for the coming period, management would be required to establish a budgeted amount and the probability distribution of the actual cost about the budget amount. Suppose the cost item in question is the cost of secretarial services in a particular division of the company. The person responsible for the budget would be required to submit a budgeted amount for the coming year. This amount is, in a sense, an *expected* amount or an average (mean) expected expenditure. The amount would be set assuming normal efficiency and so that variances from this mean because of random, noncontrollable causes are equally likely to be on either side of the budgeted mean.

With this specific instruction, the amount to be budgeted is defined. This amount may be somewhat different from the amount which is usually budgeted. For example, it is sometimes argued that the budget should be set at a high level of efficiency. In such a case, the variance that results is generally unfavorable. Actually, if this latter budget philosophy is desired by management the model being presented could be modified accordingly. However, if the budget mean is established so that unfavorable and favorable *random* (noncontrollable) variances from this mean are approximately equally likely, it is possible to fit a normal probability distribution to the expected cost for the coming period. Based on this probability distribution, acceptable ranges for cost variances can be established and the probability that any variance, regardless of amount, has resulted from random causes can be determined.

THE NORMAL PROBABILITY DISTRIBUTION

At this point, a short discussion of the normal probability distribution is offered before applying it in the cost control model.

The normal distribution has a probability density function which is a smooth, symmetric, continuous, bell-shaped curve as shown in Figure 1. The area under the curve sums to 1. The curve reaches a maximum at the mean of the distribution and one-half the area lies on either side of the mean.

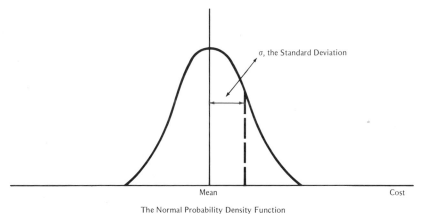

The Normal Probability Density Function

Figure 1

On the horizontal axis is plotted the values of the appropriate unknown quantity; in our model the unknown is the amount of cost for the coming period.

A particular normal probability distribution can be completely determined if its mean and its standard deviation, σ, are known. The standard deviation is a measure of the dispersion of the distribution about its mean. The area under any normal distribution is 1, but one distribution may be spread out more than another distribution. For example, in Figure 2, both normal distributions have the same area and the same mean. However, in one case the σ is 1 and in the other case the $\sigma > 1$. The larger the σ, the more spread out is the distribution. It should be noted that the standard deviation is not an area but is a measure of the dispersion of the individual observations about the mean of all the observations—it is a distance.

Since the normal probability distribution is continuous rather than discrete, the probability of an event cannot be read directly from the graph. The unknown quantity must be thought of as being in an interval. Assume, for example, that the mean cost for the coming period is $10,000 and the

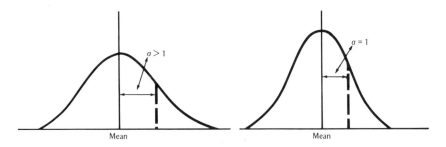

Normal Probability Distributions with Different Standard Deviations

Figure 2

normal distribution appears as in Figure 3. Given Figure 3, certain probability statements can be made. For example:

1. The probability of the actual cost being between $10,000 and $11,000 is .20. This is shown by area C. Because of the symmetry of the curve, the probability of the cost being between $9,000 and $10,000 is also .20. This is shown by shaded area B. These probabilities can be given a frequency interpretation. That is, area C indicates that the actual cost will be between $10,000 and $11,000 in about 20% of all cases.
2. The probability of the actual cost being greater than $11,000 is .30 as shown by area D.
3. The probability of the cost being greater than $9,000 is .70, the sum of areas A, B, and C.

Given a specific normal distribution, it is possible to read probabilities of the type described above directly from a normal probability table.

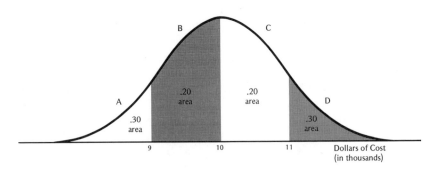

Figure 3

Another important characteristic of any normal distribution is that approximately .50 of the area lies within ±.67 standard deviations from the mean; about .68 of the area lies within ±1.0 standard deviation of the mean; .95 of the area lies within ±1.96 standard deviations of the mean.

As was mentioned above, normal probabilities can be read from a normal probability table. A partial table of normal probabilities is given in Table 1. This table is the "right tail" of the distribution; that is, probabilities of the unknown quantity being greater than X standard deviations from the mean are given in the table. For example, the probability of the unknown quantity being greater than .309 is .3483. The distribution tabulated is a normal distribution with mean zero and standard deviation of 1. Such a distribution is known as a standard normal distribution. However any normal distribution can be standardized and hence, with proper adjustment, Table 1 will serve for any normal distribution.

X	0.00	0.05	0.09
.1	.4602	.4404	.4247
.3	.3821	.3632	.3483
.5	.3085	.2912	.2776
.6	.2743	.2578	.2451
.7	.2420	.2266	.2148
.8	.2119	.1977	.1867
.9	.1841	.1711	.1611
1.0	.1587	.1469	.1379
1.5	.0668	.0606	.0559
2.0	.0228	.0202	.0183

Table 1. Area Under the Normal Density Function

For example, consider the earlier case where the mean of the distribution is $10,000. The distribution was constructed so that the standard deviation is about $2,000. To standardize the distribution, use the following formula, where X is the number of standard deviations from the mean:

$$X = \frac{\text{Actual cost} - \text{Mean cost}}{\text{Standard deviation of the distribution}}.$$

To calculate the probability of the cost being greater than $11,000, first standardize the distribution and then use the table.

$$X = \frac{\$11,000 - \$10,000}{\$2,000}$$

$$= .50 \text{ standard deviations}$$

The probability of being greater than .50 standard deviations from the mean, according to Table 1, is .3085. This same approximate result is shown by Figure 3, that is, area D is .30. Note that if the distribution is standard to begin with, the formula still holds because the mean is zero and standard deviation is 1.

THE BUDGET AMOUNT AND THE RANGE

Having described some of the properties of the normal distribution, it is now possible to use this distribution in the cost control model. As an example, suppose the secretarial department supervisor must establish a budget amount for the coming period. The supervisor would estimate the standard deviation by assigning subjective probabilities to possible variances from the budgeted amount. Alternatively, if he can answer a question such as the following, an estimate of the standard deviation can be made:

1. "If 50-50 betting odds are to be established that the cost falls within some range, it being equally likely that the cost will be above or below that range, what range of cost should be chosen?" or,
2. "There is a 50-50 chance that cost variances from random, noncontrollable causes will be larger than some amount. What is that amount?"

If either of these questions is answered, a budget range can be established *within which* the actual cost is expected to fall one-half the time if *variances from the budgeted mean are random, noncontrollable variances.*
Assume this question is posed to the supervisor of the secretarial department and the budget mean is $10,000. Also, the supervisor feels there is a 50–50 chance that the actual cost will be within $\pm$$600 of the mean. This type of estimate could easily be made an integral part of the budget procedure and estimation will become easier as experience is gained.
With the information from the above questions, a probability significance range can be established using the normal probability distribution as an approximation of the expected cost performance. Remembering that about one-half the area under a normal curve lies within $\pm$.67 standard deviation of the mean, the normal probability distribution can be uniquely determined as follows:

$$2/3\sigma = \$600$$
$$\sigma = \$900.$$

The mean of the distribution is $10,000, the budgeted amount. The budget situation is shown in Figure 4.

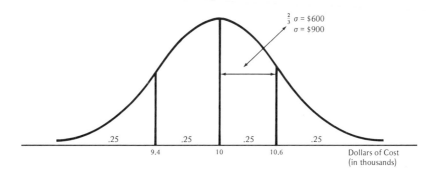

Figure 4

Having identified the particular normal distribution (mean = $10,000, σ = $900), it is possible to compute the probability that secretarial costs will vary from the mean by any amount (the variance resulting from random noncontrollable causes). For example, if actual secretarial costs were $11,800 investigation would undoubtedly be called for because a variance of $1,800 is 2 standard deviations from the mean, i.e.

$$\frac{(\$11,800 - \$10,000}{\$900} = 2).$$

The probability of an unfavorable variance this large or larger occurring from random, noncontrollable causes is only .0228 (see Table 1).

IS INVESTIGATION DESIRABLE?

Two measures have been developed for deciding whether or not to investigate a variance. They are the size of the variance and the probability of the variance resulting from random, noncontrollable causes. In conventional procedure, only the first measure is usually provided.

At this point, the two measures can be combined in a manner that will suffice for many situations. Figure 5 is a cost control decision chart that provides a guide to the investigation decision in terms of the probability of the variance and the size of the variance. Figure 5 pertains to unfavorable variances. It should be noted that both favorable and unfavorable variances can be investigated. The investigation of favorable variances is designed to discourage the practice of overestimating the budgeted cost in order to have favorable variances and thus avoid investigation. Also, investigation might serve to identify unusually capable performance as well as unusually bad performance. Although the following discussion will stress unfavorable variances, the analysis will apply equally well to favorable variances.

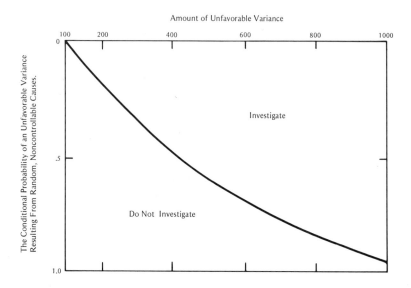

Figure 5. Cost Control Decision Chart: Unfavorable Variances

Figure 5 shows that either of two situations may give rise to an investigation of a cost variance. One is the occurrence of a variance which, based on budgeted mean cost and the standard deviation, is unlikely to occur. Secondly, a variance (which is not unreasonable in terms of the probability of occurrence) may be so large in absolute amount relative to the financial position of the company that it must be investigated. Thus, both the probability significance and the economic significance of the variances are important in deciding when to investigate. Both of these factors are incorporated in Figure 5.

The curve separating the "investigate" and "do not investigate" areas can conceivably be determined by management on the basis of judgment. Once the determination is made, the cost analyst has a good guide to action and both the probability and dollar criteria are incorporated in this guide. Note that the investigate region starts with some positive amount, in this case $100, because the variance must be equal to or greater than the cost of investigation before it is eligible for examination. Also, the probability shown in Figure 5 is conditional on an unfavorable variance having occurred.

The exact location of the curve will depend on how intensively management wishes to control costs. If the "investigate" area is made considerably larger than the "do not investigate" area, the expense of conducting cost analysis may be larger than the value of the information obtained. In setting the areas, management should equate the expense of investigation and the expected value of the information obtained. This might be done by judgment but it can also be quantified. If judgment will suffice, the quantitative method to be described will not be needed.

DERIVATION OF THE INVESTIGATE REGION: MINIMIZING EXPECTED COST

The derivation of the "investigate" and "do not investigate" regions should be done on the basis of a consistent decision rule: choose that act which will minimize the expected cost. The two possible acts from which this choice must be made are as follows:

Act 1. Investigate the variance.
Act 2. Do not investigate the variance.

Assume an unfavorable variance in amount (d). The decision—investigate or do not investigate—depends upon the probabilities of the two possible states of affairs which have caused the variance. These two states are:

State 1—the variance was caused by factors beyond the control of management, or
State 2—the variance was caused by factors within the jurisdiction and control of management.

If state 1 is the true state, investigation is wasted; if state 2 is the true state, investigation will presumably result in a reward. The reward will be in the form of a rebate or a future cost saving. Table 2, a conditional cost table, summarizes the above information.

In Table 2, C represents the cost of investigating the unfavorable variance. This cost will be incurred if an investigation is made but will not be incurred if investigation is not undertaken. If an investigation is not made (act 2) the cost will not be incurred. However, if state 2 is the true state, the company will incur a cost due to not investigating a variance that can be

	ACTS		CONDITIONAL PROBABILITIES OF STATES GIVEN AN UNFAVORABLE VARIANCE HAS OCCURRED
STATES	(1) INVESTIGATE	(2) DO NOT INVESTIGATE	
(1) The unfavorable variance resulted from noncontrollable causes.	C	0	P
(2) The unfavorable variance resulted from controllable causes.	C	L	$(1-P)$
Expected Cost of Act	C	$L(1-P)$	1.00

Table 2. Conditional Cost Table

controlled. This latter cost is called L.[1] It is assumed that L is greater than C; otherwise investigation would never be undertaken. Given an unfavorable variance, the probability of that variance resulting from noncontrollable causes is P, where $P \geqslant 0$. Hence, $(1 - P)$ is the probability of state 2.

The expected cost of each act is calculated by multiplying each conditional cost by its respective probability and summing. The results are shown at the bottom of the table. The expected cost of investigating the variance is C, i.e., $[C(P) + C(1 - P)]$; the expected cost of not investigating is $(1 - P)L$. If the expected cost of investigating is less than the expected cost of not investigating, the appropriate act would be to investigate. Thus, the following decision rules may be formulated:

$$C < (1 - P)L, \text{ Investigate.}$$
$$C > (1 - P)L, \text{ Do not investigate.}$$

If the expected cost of the two acts are equal the decision maker is indifferent between the two possible acts. The probability value, P_c, which establishes this equality is the critical probability that separates the two possible acts for the unfavorable variance being considered. Hence:

If P (the actual probability) $< P_c$, then $C < (1 - P)L$ and investigation is warranted.
If $P > P_c$, then $C > (1 - P)L$, and investigation is not warranted.

Since P_c, is needed to establish the "investigate" and "do not investigate" areas, it is necessary to solve for P_c in terms of L and C. That is:

$$C = (1 - P)L,$$
$$P_c = \frac{L - C}{L}.$$

The cost control group must estimate L and C for various possible variances for a given budget activity and derive the critical probability in the manner indicated above.[2] If C is some fixed cost and if L is a linear function of the unfavorable deviation, then the resulting cost control chart will resemble Figure 5. For an example, assume $C = 100$ and $L = d$, where d is an unfavorable variance. For different variances it is possible to determine the curve separating the investigate and do not investigate areas as follows:

---

[1]In situations where the inefficiency will be repeated, L should be defined as the present value of the costs that will be incurred in the future if an investigation is not made now.

[2]The above relationship, $P_c = L - C/L$ can be checked at the extremes to see if it agrees with common sense. For example, assume $C = 0$; then $P_c = 1$ and the rule would say to investigate if $P < 1.0$, which it always will be, given that an unfavorable deviation has occurred. If the cost of investigation is zero, all deviations should be investigated. At the other extreme, if $C = L$, the $P_c = 0$, and the rule would say do not investigate when $P > P_c$, or $P > 0$, which will always be the case.

$d = L$	C	$L - C$	$Pc = L - C/L$
100	100	0	0
200	100	100	.50
400	100	300	.75
600	100	500	.83
800	100	700	.875
900	100	800	.888
1,000	100	900	.90

Given these critical probabilities, the related cost control decision chart is shown in Figure 6.

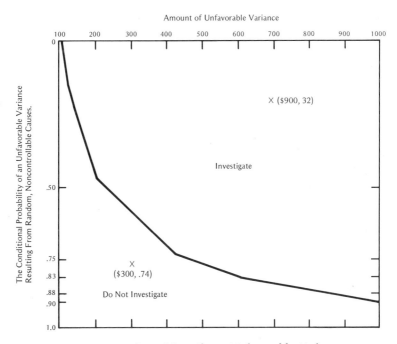

Figure 6. Cost Control Decision Chart: Unfavorable Variances

An illustration of the use of Figure 6 can now be given. Assume, as in the earlier example, that the budgeted amount for secretarial services is $10,000. The standard deviation of the normal probability distribution is calculated to be $900. Suppose the actual cost is $10,900. The probability of an unfavorable variance of $900 or more is calculated as follows:

1. $\dfrac{\$10,900 - \$10,000}{\$900}$ = One standard deviation.

2. The probability of being one or more standard deviations from the mean according to Table 1 is about .1587.
3. However, .1587 is a probability based on a scale running from zero to .5. Since a scale of zero to one is used in Figure 6, this probability can be converted by dividing by .5.* Hence, the probability to be used for Figure 6 is:

$$\frac{.1587}{.50} = .3174 \text{ or } .32.$$

According to Figure 6, the variance of $900 would be investigated since the combination of ($900, .32) falls in the "investigate" region, i.e., .32 < .888, the critical probability

$$\left(P_c = \frac{\$900 - \$100}{\$900} = .888\right).$$

On the other hand, suppose the unfavorable variance was $300.

1. $\dfrac{\$10,300 - \$10,000}{\$900} = .33$ standard deviations.
2. The probability of being greater than .33 standard deviation from the mean according to Table 1 is about .37.
3. The applicable probability for Figure 6 is .37/.50 = .74.

A non-recurring variance of $300 would not be investigated since ($300, .74) falls in the "do not investigate" region

$$\left(P_c = \frac{\$300 - \$100}{\$300} = .667\right).$$

SUMMARY AND CONCLUSIONS

There is a need in cost and budgetary control for information on the significance of cost variances. The conventional tests of absolute or relative dollar magnitudes are inadeequate. The probability of a variance resulting from random, noncontrollable causes is also important. By using the properties of a normal probability distribution, it is possible to devise a method for computing the probability significance of cost variances. By combining the costs and rewards of investigation with the associated probabilities, a model can be constructed to aid in the decision of when a variance should be investigated.

---

*The .3174 is a conditional probability; that is, the probability of an event, given that another event (in this case, an unfavorable variance) has already occurred.

In the illustrative model presented in this article, the formal distribution has been used. In some cases, the cost characteristic may make the assumption of normality unrealistic. There is no reason why the analysis could not be modified to accommodate some other probability distribution and also some other budget philosophy. However, the normal distribution is easy to work with and in most cases it is probably a reasonable approximation, particularly if the budget philosophy is not one of selecting the lowest possible budgeted amount (highest possible efficiency). Given any definite budget philosophy, a reasonable probability distribution could be chosen and the remaining analysis would be much the same as that suggested above. Such analysis should facilitate management by exception as applied to cost control.

28.
QUANTITATIVE MODELS FOR
ACCOUNTING CONTROL*

Mohamed Onsi

Accounting control is an important function of accounting. It is defined as that process which discovers and reports information enabling managers to correct or prevent unfavorable conditions. Accounting control is concerned both with the discovery of deviations and their prompt minimization.

This article examines the basic control aspects of three control models: (1) the traditional accounting model employing standard costing, (2) an accounting model based on classical statistical theory, and (3) an accounting control model based on modern decision theory. The main characteristics of and differences among the three accounting control models will be discussed, and are summarized in Exhibit 1.

TRADITIONAL ACCOUNTING CONCEPTS OF CONTROL

Two criteria are currently used to decide whether to investigate deviations from standard. They are (1) the absolute size of a deviation or (2) the relative size of a deviation, unfavorable or favorable. The magnitude of these criteria depend upon management judgment and experience.[1] A 3% departure from standard may be considered normal under certain circumstances. How does management decide that an historic 3% departure from standard is no longer acceptable? The traditional model does not provide information which indicates when the informal limit becomes

---

*From The Accounting Review, April 1967, pp. 321–330. Reprinted by permission of the author and the American Accounting Association.

[1] See A. W. Patrick, "A Proposal for Determining the Significance of Variations from Standard," The Accounting Review, October 1957, p. 587.

outmoded. Tests are needed to determine whether the observed deviation is within normal expectations or requires investigation.

There are two possible approaches to this information: a model based on classical statistical theory and model based on modern decision theory (i.e., Bayesian statistics). A model based on classical statistics uses a mathematically derived long-run frequency distribution as a basis for setting control limits. However, a model based on decision theory uses subjective or personal probabilities for making informed decisions. Other differences will be noted later.

ACCOUNTING CONTROL MODEL
BASED ON CLASSICAL STATISTICS

The accounting control model based on classical statistics assumes that (1) standard cost is equal to the mean of a normal probability distribution, (2) standards are developed as ranges, not as point estimates, (3) the allowable deviation is represented by the size of the control limits, and (4) investigation is exercised when one or more consecutive observations lie outside the control limits. This model assumes that two types of variations from standard will emerge. The first is "chance variation" due to random causes, and the second is "assignable variation" which is attributable to systematic causes.[2] The first variation should not be investigated, while the latter should be.

Standard cost is the expected or average cost from which deviations are measured. By assuming that these deviations are normally distributed, the management accountant hypothesizes that favorable and unfavorable deviations due to random causes will fall equally on either side of the standard. Probability analysis permits establishing the range of variations within which deviations are attributed to chance, and limits are then set so that random variations due entirely to non-controllable causes are identified and ignored. This analysis requires that both the mean of the unit-cost distribution and its standard deviation be known. Both are determined from past data adjusted to represent the current situation.[3]

Determination of the upper and lower control limits for non-investigated variations depends upon the relative weight assigned to two types of possible error. These are:

I. The error of investigating when it is unnecessary, investigating a deviation which is due to random influences, i.e., Type I error, α.

[2]See Owen L. Davis (ed.), *Statistical Methods in Research and Production with Special Reference to the Chemical Industry* (Oliver & Boyd, 1954), p. 212.

[3]See: Alex L. Hart, "Using Probability Theory for Economy in Cost Control," *N.A.C.A. Bulletin*, October 1956, pp. 257–263; James C. Stephenson, "Quality Control to Minimize Cost Variances," *N.A.C.A. Bulletin*, October 1956, pp. 264–275; Earle N. Martin, "We Studied and Applied Statistics for Control," *N.A.C.A. Bulletin*, October 1955, pp. 219–237.

ELEMENTS	THE TRADITIONAL ACCOUNTING CONTROL MODEL	ACCOUNTING CONTROL MODEL BASED ON CLASSICAL STATISTICS	ACCOUNTING CONTROL MODEL BASED ON DECISION THEORY
NATURE OF CONTROL	1. Based on a point estimate	1. Based on a range estimate	1. Based on the expected value of information that will be obtained based on investigation
	2. Based on management judgment	2. Based on scientific analysis	2. Based on judgment and scientific analysis
	3. Developed after all facts are known	3. Developed as a preventive control model	3. Developed as a preventive and time oriented control model based on the sample outcome
	4. Developed as deterministic feedback control model	4. Based on stochastic feedback control processes	4. Based on stochastic and adaptive feedback control processes
CRITERIA OF CONTROL (INVESTIGATE OR DO NOT INVESTIGATE)	1. If the absolute size of a deviation is large	1. If the deviation (one or more) falls outside the control limits	1. If the probability to revise a standard is high
	2. If the relative size of a deviation is large	2. If the deviations have a certain trend, even if they fall in the range of allowable magnitude	2. If the cost of uncertainty is large in a decision to investigate based on a priori probability
		3. If the absolute amount of a deviation is financially significant	
BASIC REQUIREMENTS NECESSARY TO EXERCISE CONTROL	1. The establishment of standards based on engineering judgment	1. The knowledge of the $\bar{x}$ and σ of unit-cost	1. The knowledge of all basic values of red deviations and the expected cost of each value, not the $\bar{x}$ or σ
		2. The ability to determine the range of allowable deviations, i.e., 1 or 2 or 3σ	2. The ability to determine the a priori probability. It can be revised later by obtaining more information
		3. The assumption that past conditions of production will remain the same in the future	3. The assumption concerning the repetition of the manufacturing process or that past conditions remain the same in the future is not required
		4. The distribution of cost is a normal frequency distribution	4. Normal distribution is not necessary to the development of the model

II. The error of failing to investigate when there is in fact a non-random deviation from standard, i.e., Type II error, β.

In setting control limits, one tries to minimize the penalties from an erroneous decision. Operationally, it is desirable to balance Type I error and Type II error with the degree of risk prevailing in a certain situation. The degree of risk which should be accepted depends on: (1) the absolute amount of deviation, i.e., a deviation of a large amount may be investigated even if it is not significant in terms of its probability of occurrence; (2) the nature of the problem and the consequences of a decision based on this information. The consequences depend not only on dollar value, but also on such intangible factors as the effect of the report on human motivation and level of aspiration. The accountant, in addition, should consider: (1) the cost of unnecessary investigation and (2) the cost of not preventing inefficiency in terms of spoilage, rework, or warranty costs due to the failure to effect the level of control that is needed. This cost is measured as equal to the present value of future costs due to inefficiency. If the cost of investigation is high relative to possible losses, the control limits should be relatively large (say more than 1σ). If the potential loss is high relative to the cost of investigation, control limits should be tight (say 1σ or less).[4]

The accountant, accordingly, faces two possibilities: (1) if the sample size is predetermined, the risk of one type of error can be reduced only by increasing the risk of the other type; and (2) if the risk of making both types of errors is to be controlled, the sample size must not be fixed in advance and should be determined from the specifications of the probabilities of error. Decision rules are developed based on balancing the cost of sampling against the order and magnitude of the consequences of the two types of errors.

The accountant should be on the alert to discover promptly the occurrence or the possibility of a shift in standards. This is done by observing the trend of consecutive observations even though they are still within the control limits.[5] The greater the shift of standard cost from that originally planned, the sooner the shift is likely to be detected. The operating characteristics curve is used to indicate the probability of committing Type II error for various shifts in standard cost above or below the initial standard in the control model.[6] It shows the risk of stating that costs are under

---

[4]The size of the sample and its subgroups and the frequency of taking such samples are problems to be solved in relation to each particular situation. See Acheson T. Duncan, *Quality Control and Industrial Statistics* (McGraw-Hill Book Co., Inc., 1952), pp. 294–296.

[5]It is assumed that successive observations are independent. If such an assumption is rejected based on the assumption that cost observations are dependent random variables and the standard is subject to a stochastic process, the "significant test" approach is no longer applicable. When the probability of deciding that the process is out of control depends on the values of previous observations, the control models must be based on cumulative series. See G. A. Barnard, "Control Charts and Stochastic Processes," *Journal of the Royal Statistical Society*, Series B, No. 2, 1959, pp. 239–271.

[6]See: John D. Heide, *Industrial Process Control by Statistical Methods* (McGraw-Hill Book Co., Inc., 1952), pp. 102–123; Duncan, pp. 305–314.

control at the designated standard, if a cost value falls within the control limits when the standard is actually at a different value. The accountant can also use the power curve to determine the probability of rejecting a cost observation as coming from the population of the original standard cost, when in fact the standard cost has shifted to another value.

Investigation may be required when two or more consecutive deviations fall outside (or within) the same control limit. Two or more points in succession falling outside the control limit give stronger evidence of a shift in standard cost than does a single point outside the control limit. This technique is based on the theory of runs. The probability that a specific number of deviations would fall on the same side of the standard cost can be calculated if the probability of a deviation falling above the standard is known.[7]

The model uses both the average $(\overline{X})$ and the range (R) control charts. There are situations in which the cost observations plotted on the average chart are shown out of the control limits, while, if plotted on the range chart, they are shown within the range limit, and vice-versa. The causes of the variations should be determined, and corrective action may be required. If the accountant waits, say, to the end of a week or month to make a decision to investigate, the variations may offset each other, and any shift in the average for a short period of time will not be detected. Conventional cost analysis fails to spot the deviations in this instance.

The prior model, however, does have some operational difficulties as follows:

1. It is based on a procedure for coming to a decision to investigate purely on the basis of objective evidence, given a certain accepted prespecified risk or error. Insistence on objective evidence before making a decision is unrealistic, for objective evidence may be lacking, too expensive, or a new process may be involved, etc.

2. It does not make an explicit structural use of prior information and the a priori probability of the unknown parameter. A decision should be made using both prior information and current objective evidence.[8]

---

[7] Wilfrid J. Dixon and Frank J. Massey, Jr., *Introduction to Statistical Analysis* (McGraw-Hill Book Co., Inc., 1957), pp. 287–289.

[8] While the classical approach ignores the a priori probability, the user of the approach takes account of such information in his decisions. For example, a rasonable manager will insist on a higher level of significance (smaller α) before rejecting a null hypothesis representing a strongly held belief, on the basis of given sample evidence, as compared with a null hypothesis representing only a weak conjecture. See Jack Hirshleifer, "The Bayesian Approach to Statistical Decision—An Exposition," *The Journal of Business*, October 1961, p. 478; William Fellner, *Probability and Profit* (Richard D. Irwin, Inc., 1965), p. 62 and pp. 192–198; and Morris Hamburg, "Bayesian Decision Theory and Statistical Quality Control," *Industrial Quality Control*, December 1962, p. 11.

3. It does not make formal use of the risks of error of each decision rule as a function of the possible values of the parameter or standard.

A model based on Bayesian statistics will provide a solution to some of these problems.

ACCOUNTING CONTROL MODEL
BASED ON MODERN DECISION THEORY

A control model based on the Bayesian approach will:

1. De-emphasize the confidence-interval estimate. The decision is based on both sample evidence and the consideration of both economic loss and prior belief, especially if losses due to one type of error are larger or more serious than those due to the other type of error.

2. Incorporate into the analysis subjective a priori probability as a useful and logically consistent formalization of the prior state of information about the parameter.

3. Not require the determination of α and β as in the classical model. However, the economic importance of each type of error and prior information as to the likelihood of the different parameter values are put in the analysis.

4. Provide a systematic analysis to determine sample size. An optimum sample size can be obtained by balancing the sampling cost against the gains in terms of reduction in risk of error.

5. Provide a procedure to select the best action minimizing expected loss to take in a many-action situation, given the entire subjective probability distribution of the parameter. The model makes explicit and systematic use of the opportunity cost concept to evaluate the worth of each action relative to the best possible action for the given state of nature.

Operationally, to the extent that the budget committee (composed of the managerial accountant and others) can set the probability of a given event under conditions of uncertainty, modern decision theory is a practical tool. The budget committee, through cooperation and experience, can develop a subjective probability distribution approximating reality. Modern decision theory then provides a good method for choosing the best act in the face of uncertainty.[9] Subjective probability here refers to personal judgment. It is

---

[9]The theory of probability allows us "to make more effective use of our judgment and experience by assigning probabilities to those events on which our experience and judgment bear most directly rather than to events which will actually determine costs, but with which we have had relatively little direct experience." Robert Schlaifer, *Probability and Statistics for Business Decisions* (McGraw-Hill Book Co., Inc., 1959), p. 333.

subjective in the sense that two reasonable men may assign different probabilities to the same event. This does not mean, however, that a reasonable man assigns probabilities arbitrarily; he does so based on his experience and in cooperation with the appropriate individuals in his organization. We can assume that if two reasonable men had roughly the same experience, each would assign roughly the same probability. In this sense, probability is subjective, but it is revised by acquiring more information.

There are two basic assumptions underlying the development of this model. First, the managerial accountant decides whether to investigate based on incomplete information. He takes periodic samples of units of output every hour or every day or whatever period is decided upon as economical and advantageous, depending on what is being checked. His decision is based on this random sample, which is a good representation of the population. Such an immediate decision incurs a degree of risk in the sense that it should be the same decision that would be made had the accountant waited until the end of the period when historic results are known. This kind of uncertainty is a new dimension in accounting, and it requires the use of a tool of analysis to decrease risk. Second, the accountant is not only interested in analyzing total variances into price and efficiency variances after the actual results are known, but is also interested in expanding his control function to reporting on whether the process is stable. In doing so, he is interested in two things: (1) that the defective units are controlled within normal expectation and (2) that the standard quantities of raw material, labor hours, and variable overhead per unit are controlled within the prescribed range. If the process is accepted as in control, cost is expected to be within the predetermined range, and deviations, if any, are minimum.[10] This is the essence of the expansion of the accounting control function if accounting data are to be of help in making immediate decisions on whether investigation is necessary.

The accountant can base his decision to investigate on the available prior information, or he may decrease the risk of such a decision by delaying it until he acquires additional information. To obtain additional information, he takes a sample from the deviations occurring during this period.[11] The a priori probability assigned to each value of the basic random variables, i.e., the proportion of deviations, will be revised according to information obtained from this evidence, and the best act under uncertainty can be made. The value of such additional information obtained from the sample is equal to the difference between the expected loss of a decision based on the a priori probability and the expected loss of the same decision based on the a posteriori probability plus the cost of sampling. If, under a given a priori probability distribution, the cost of uncertainty[12] is very small, sam-

---

[10]In a relatively short period of time, deviations may not be minimum.

[11]Assuming Bernoulli process, the conditional probabilities will be calculated from the binomial tables for the given sample size.

[12]The cost of uncertainty, which is a measure of the expected value of information, is equal to the expected opportunity loss of the best decision under a given probability distribution, i.e., minimum opportunity loss of cost of sampling and defective and spoiled units.

pling is likely to cost more than it is worth, and a decision can be made without a large degree of risk. Conversely, if the cost of uncertainty is large, the expected value of information is likely to be equal to or greater than the cost of sampling.

Accounting control under decision theory, accordingly, is based on the expected value of information which may be obtained from investigation. The value of information is measured by comparing the reduction of expected cost of the proposed initial decision with the cost of sampling and not by the reduction of the magnitude of the standard deviation, as in classical statistics.

To develop this model operationally, assume that we have a highly automated process in which the cost of material is an important element. The standard cost of material is set, and the expected normal deviation of defective units is determined.[13] If actual deviations are within an expected norm, investigation is not required. If they exceed an expected norm, it is assumed that the process is out of control and that corrective action is needed.

Production through this process, which is considered a cost center, is divided into equal intervals of time. Assume that production in each period of time is 200 units, and the proportion (p) of normal defective units is .01, or 2 defectives. The defective unit will cost $0.50 to rework. The cost of investigation is $3.00. The accountant could wait until the end of each interval to find out whether the process is under control; but, if it is not, it is too late to inform management. The company would suffer the cost of inefficiency and waste. On the other hand, investigating the process at each interval may be too expensive. Accordingly, at the beginning of each interval, the accountant takes a sample from which he decides whether the process is under control or out of control. There are two acts available:

1. "Accept" Process A as being under control; the proportion of deviation of defective units is within normal expectations (say .01).

2. "Reject" Process A as being out of control; the proportion of deviation of defective units is more than normally expected (more than .01).

If Process A is accepted, the conditional expected number of deviations in this interval is equal to 2, i.e., 200p, and p is equal to .01. The expected cost of reworking these deviations is $0.50 × 2 = $1.00. However, if the

---

[13]The term deviation is used here not to denote the amount of variation from the mean or standard. It indicates the departure from the expected value (standard) and not the value of the departure itself, in order to isolate the effect of any changes in prices. However, given a standard price, this physical measure can be translated into a dollar value. Whenever the word deviation is used in this section, it means the deviation of defective units. In cost accounting literature, it is assumed that if defective units are within normal expectation (say p = .01) it is treated as a production cost. The cost of those defective units exceeding normal expectation (say (p) more than .01) is treated as a loss. Cost accounting literature does not indicate how the accountant can provide timely information to management to control these events. This analysis provides one solution.

proportion of deviations is .05 (10 deviations), the expected cost of reworking these deviations will be $5.00. The conditional expected cost analogy
for each possible event (p) of this act is shown in Table 1.[14]

(p) OF THE BASIC RANDOM VARIABLE, I.E., DEVIATIONS[15]		COST	
		ACCEPT	REJECT
.01 (normally	2 defectives	$ 1.00*	$4.00
.05 expected)	10 defectives	$ 5.00	4.00*
.10	20 defectives	10.00	4.00*
.15	30 defectives	15.00	4.00*
*The best act according to each value of (p).			

Table 1. The Conditional Cost Payoff

If the process is rejected, the expected cost of reworking the deviations is
$1.00 [$100.00 p = $100 (.01)], and the cost of investigation is $3.00, so
that the total is $4.00. This cost is the same for each value of (p), since we
assume that by investigation the deviations will only be within normal
expectations, i.e., 2 deviations.

DEVELOPMENT OF THE A PRIORI PROBABILITY

From past records and experience, assume that the budget committee finds
the frequency distribution of deviations to be as shown in Table 2.

PROPORTION OF DEVIATION	RELATIVE FREQUENCY
.01	.5
.05	.2
.10	.2
.15	.1
	1.0

Table 2. The A Priori Distribution of Deviations

---

[14]The relevant costs in this analysis are "opportunity losses," that is, the additional
losses incurred by not making the correct decisions with respect to investigating the process.
[15]These deviations are assumed to be both collectively exhaustive events and
mutually exclusive events.

As long as there is no new information indicating a change in any variable affecting the process, one can assume that the a priori probability distribution of Process A deviations in any new interval of time remains the same.

Using this information, the unconditional expected costs of the two acts (accept or reject) are calculated and shown in Table 3.

(p) OF DEVIATIONS	A PRIORI PROBABILITY	COST OF ACCEPTANCE		COST OF REJECTION	
		CONDITIONAL	EXPECTED	CONDITIONAL	EXPECTED
.01	.5	$ 1.00	$ .50	$4.00	$2.00
.05	.2	5.00	1.00	4.00	.80
.10	.2	10.00	2.00	4.00	.80
.15	.1	15.00	1.50	4.00	.40
	1.0		$5.00		$4.00

Table 3. Unconditional Expected Costs

From Table 3, the unconditional expected cost of rejecting that the process is under control is $1.00 less than the unconditional expected cost of acceptance. Therefore, the best decision is to investigate Process A as out of control.

DEVELOPMENT OF A POSTERIORI PROBABILITY

Before basing a decision to accept or reject entirely on past experience, we may need additional information concerning current performance. A sample of 20 is taken from Process A. It is found that the cost per unit is within normal expectations, and, accordingly, the "red deviation" is zero. The question is whether this is an indication that the process is under control and therefore that no action is required. The results of this sample will be used to revise the a priori probabilities as shown in Table 4.

Using this information, the posterior unconditional expected costs are calculated and tabulated in Table 5.

On the basis of both past data and information obtained from the sample, the expected cost of acceptance that the process is under control is $1.91 less than the expected cost of rejection. Therefore, the best decision is to accept Process A as being under control.

(p) OF DEVIATIONS	A PRIORI PROBABILITY	LIKELIHOOD Pb (r = 0, n = 20p)	JOINT PROBABILITY[16]	A POSTERIORI PROBABILITY[17]
		P(A/R)	P(A, R)	P(R/A)
.01	.5	.818	.4090	.804
.05	.2	.358	.0716	.141
.10	.2	.122	.0244	.048
.15	.1	.039	.0039	.007
	1.0		.5089	1.000

Table 4. A Posteriori Probabilities

(p) OF DEVIATIONS	A POSTERIORI PROBABILITY	COST OF ACCEPTANCE CONDITIONAL	EXPECTED	COST OF REJECTION CONDITIONAL	EXPECTED
.01	.804	$ 1.00	$ .804	$4.00	$3.216
.05	.141	5.00	.705	4.00	.564
.10	.048	10.00	.480	4.00	.192
.15	.007	15.00	.105	4.00	.028
	1.000		$2.094		$4.000

Table 5. A Posteriori Unconditional Expected Costs

THE EXPECTED OPPORTUNITY LOSS CONCEPT

The previous two decisions can also be based on another important concept, i.e., opportunity loss. The conditional opportunity loss of any act (to accept or reject), given a particular value of the deviation (.01, .05, .10, .15), is equal to the difference between the cost of that act and the cost of the act that would be the best possible for that value of deviation. These values are obtained (shown in Table 6) by taking each entry in each row and subtract-

---

[16]The "multiplication rule" is used to compute the joint probabilities as follows:

$$P(A, R) = P(R)P(A/R) = .5 \times .818 = .4090$$

[17]Bayes' Theorem is used to calculate the a posteriori probability as follows:

$$P(R/A)$$
$$= \frac{P(R,A)}{P(A)} = \frac{P(R)\,P(A/R)}{P(R)\,P(A/R) + P(B)\,P(A/B)}$$
$$= \frac{\text{Joint probability of "red" and "accept"}}{\text{Marginal probability of "accept"}}$$
$$= \frac{.4090}{.5089} = .804$$

ing from it the starred entry (representing the best act in this case) in the same row.

(p) OF DEVIATIONS	ACT	
	ACCEPT	REJECT
.01	$ 0.00	$3.00
.05	1.00	0
.10	6.00	0
.15	11.00	0

Table 6. Conditional Opportunity Loss

The expected opportunity loss, based on the a priori probability, can be calculated as detailed in Table 7. This means that if Process A is rejected and, accordingly, is investigated, the expected loss will be $1.00 less than if it is accepted as being under control and not investigated. This difference is equal to that shown in Table 3. The best decision is the same as that based on Table 3, namely, to investigate Process A.

However, on the basis of the sample information given before, the expected opportunity loss based on the a posteriori probability distribution can be calculated as detailed in Table 8.

(p) OF DEVIATIONS	A PRIORI PROBABILITY	LOSS OF ACCEPTANCE		LOSS OF REJECTION	
		CONDITIONAL	EXPECTED	CONDITIONAL	EXPECTED
.01	.5	$ 0.00	$0	$3.00	$1.50
.05	.2	1.00	.2	0.00	0
.10	.2	6.00	1.2	0.00	0
.15	.1	11.00	1.1	0.00	0
	1.0		$2.5		$1.50

Table 7. Prior Expected Losses

(p) OF DEVIATIONS	A POSTERIORI PROBABILITY	LOSS OF ACCEPTANCE		LOSS OF REJECTION	
		CONDITIONAL	EXPECTED	CONDITIONAL	EXPECTED
.01	.804	$ 0.00	$0	$3.00	$2.412
.05	.141	1.00	.141	0	0
.10	.048	6.00	.288	0	0
.15	.007	11.00	.077	0	0
	1.0		$ .506		$2.412

Table 8. A Posteriori Expected Losses

On the basis of this sample information, the posterior expected loss if Process A is not investigated is $1.91 less than if the process is investigated. This difference is equal to the difference between the corresponding costs in Table 5. The best decision is the same as that based on Table 5, i.e., to accept Process A and not investigate.

The value of information obtained from this sample is equal to the reduction of the cost of uncertainty, which is the expected loss of the best decision for the given probability distribution, that is, the irreducible loss due to action under uncertainty. The cost of uncertainty is $1.50 under the prior distribution and $.51 under the posterior distribution. Thus, not more than $1.00 should be paid for the information of this sample. If the cost of a sample is more, the value of information obtained does not justify its cost.

The model, however, will not be free from operational problems such as: (1) the difficulty in setting the a priori probability distribution; (2) the difficulty of measuring utility in decisions where the expected monetary value does not apply because managers' attitudes toward risk vary. For example, the latter may exist when large gains or losses are involved. However, these problems will not keep the method from having wide use. Operational techniques are under study which can be used to overcome some of these problems and provide additional solutions to these temporary difficulties.

SUMMARY NOTE

The preceding control models have introduced refinements in the use of accounting information as means of control. Standards in an accounting budget should be expressed within a range. The cost of material or labor for a given level of output in a certain process or for a departmental budget should not be estimated as one value, the deviation from which has to be investigated. If the observed costs occur within a specified range, there is no need to report such deviation in the accounting report to the responsible individual as a deviation to be examined. Only those deviations outside this range, favorable or unfavorable, should be reported as red deviations requiring investigation. Accounting control should be time oriented in the sense that the system immediately reports a deviation when it is discovered and points out a corrective action based on trend, incomplete information, and probabilities.

The budget committee, of which the managerial accountant is a member, should assign the a priori probability of the different values of deviation. This probability can subsequently be revised upon the receipt of any additional information. The managerial accountant will then be using probability theory to select the best act which determines whether to investigate. In this way he will spend less time on mechanics and more time on creative analysis and evaluation. His function in the company is thus advanced to a more constructive position as an effective participant in policymaking.

29.
A TRANSFER PRICING SYSTEM
BASED ON OPPORTUNITY COST*

Mohamed Onsi

With decentralization of decision making and creation of profit centers in multi-product organizations, the transfer pricing system becomes an acute problem. To arrive at an optimal solution, or at an approximation to it, both accounting and economic thought have recommended certain solutions.[1] However, some of the suggested solutions have shortcomings that cannot be ignored or assumed to be insignificant. The problem is material when the performance of a divisional manager is measured based on profit, and incentive compensation is so determined.

In this paper the economic foundation of a transfer pricing system and its limitations will be briefly presented. A new transfer pricing system is suggested, based on an opportunity cost concept. The advantages of this approach, compared to others, will be discussed.

THE ECONOMIC TRANSFER
PRICING SYSTEM

When there is a market price for intermediate goods, they are transferred according to such a price, assuming that the goods transferred are produced in a competitive market where the supplying center cannot influence the sales price in the open market by its own output decision. Pricing

---

*From The Accounting Review, July 1970, pp. 535–543. Reprinted by permission of the author and the American Accounting Association.

[1]See: David Solomons, Divisional Performance (Financial Executives Research Foundation, 1965), pp. 212–228, and Jack Hirshleifer, "Internal Pricing and Decentralized Decisions," in Management Controls, ed. by C. P. Bonini, R. K. Jaedicke and H. M. Wagner, (McGraw-Hill, 1964), pp. 27–37.

intermediate goods according to market price has the advantage of motivating the supplying center to reduce its cost as much as possible and emphasize innovation and research and development, since it will be to its advantage.

However, if there is no market price for the intermediate goods, then the volume which Profit Center A should produce and that which Profit Center B should demand, ideally, is at that level where the MC_A is equal to the NMR_B. Operationally, however, the profit center manager, in this case, may behave according to one of two possibilities: (1) as *a simple maximizer* of his own profit, or (2) as a *cooperator* who is concerned with maximizing total joint profits.

The Simple Maximizer Case

If the selling profit center (A) is in a monopolistic position, he will keep the price of the intermediate goods at P_2 (Exhibit 1) and will produce at a level equal to that demanded, OBd_2; that is, the volume where the buying center equates its own $NMR_B = P_2$. The profit area of Center A lies between the P_2 line and his MC_A line. This area is larger than his profit if he accepts lowering the price to P^*, where $MC_A = NMR_B$ and corresponds to the ideal volume X. On the other hand, if the buying profit center (B) is in a monopsonistic position, it will force the selling center (A) to set the price at P_1 and produce a volume OAS_1, where it equates its own $MC_A = P_1$. This results in a maximization of profit for center B, as shown in the area between the NMR_B line and P_1. This profit area is larger than that of a

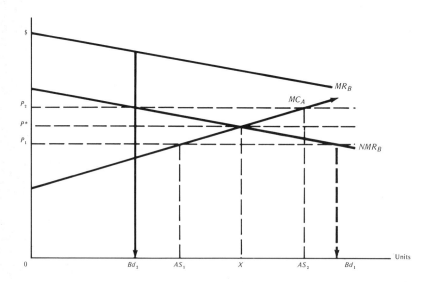

Transfer Price is Equal to $MC_A = NMR_B$

Exhibit 1

transfer price set at P^*. The total profit of both centers, however, is smaller than the joint profit that can be achieved if both centers set the transfer price at P^*.

The Cooperative Case

In this second case, in which the profit center manager is a *cooperator* concerned with maximizing total joint profits; the volume produced will be optimal from the corporate point of view. Total profit will be a maximum and larger than that under the first case, but the distribution of such profits is not clear-cut (see Exhibit 2).

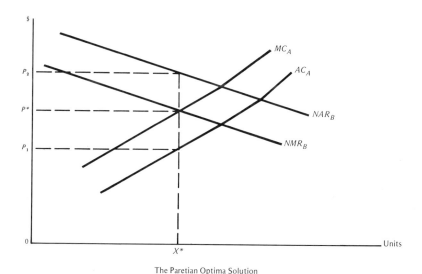

The Paretian Optima Solution

Exhibit 2

If Profit Centers A and B are conceived to maximize their combined profits, the volume of transferred goods is the quantity OX^*, for which MC_A = NMR_B, and the ideal price is P^*. However, in such a situation where the buyer is obliged to buy from within, there is no guarantee that the price is going to be P^*, even if they are cooperative. The transfer price, in other words, is indeterminate, i.e., between P_1 and P_2. That is to say, the transfer price can be negotiated somewhere between ANR_B and AC_A (e.g., the average net revenue for Center B and the average cost of Center A for the volume OX^*).

If the transfer price is negotiated at P_1 for the optimal volume OX^*, Center A receives zero profits and Center B receives the total joint profit. If the transfer price is negotiated at P_2, Center A will receive the total joint profit and Center B receives zero. So, operationally, the negotiated transfer price is in a range with P_2 as an upper limit and P_1 as a lower limit, and the actual transfer price somewhere in between. This negotiated transfer price is set after reaching the optimal product volume and not before.

To overcome such a limitation, it is believed that the budget committee should be in a position to receive the necessary information from each profit center, establish the volume which maximizes corporate profit (OX^*), and set the price at P^*. The accounting practice of pricing the transfer goods as equal to variable costs, approximating marginal costs, is felt to yield such an optimal volume. However, imposing a transfer price does not guarantee an optimal solution. The reason is that the selling profit center knows the rules of the game and, as a result, it adjusts its level of accuracy in estimating variable costs according to its belief in the accuracy of other centers' estimations. This managerial response is feasible especially when the selling profit center is not given the option to produce another product that is more profitable.

Another weakness in the economic transfer system is its failure to provide incentive for a center manager to reduce his MC below the determined level ($MC_A = NMR_B$). Suppose that the transfer price of intermediate goods is $8.00/unit.[2] If the supplying profit center discovers a new method for producing such goods at $7.00/unit, should this be the new price for transferred goods according to the $MC_A = NMR_B$? If the answer is yes, there is no motivation or reward for the innovating supplying profit center, since the receiving profit center will reap all the profit increment, while the supplying center breaks even. Should the transfer price remain at $8.00/unit, the receiving profit center will find no incentive to remix its production or increase its output to take advantage of the relatively cheaper input prices. As a solution to this problem, it is suggested, violating the main principle of $MC_A = NMR_B$, that the supplying profit center should charge $8.00/unit for additional units over that budgeted volume. Another solution is that the supplying center will negotiate a lump sum grant or subsidy from the receiving center as a condition for continuous cost reduction and innovation.[3] While this is a deviation from the theoretical principle (e.g., P is determined having $MC = MR$), its purposes are motivationally oriented.

Another operational difficulty stems from the assumption that there are no constraints (physical or monetary) on the resources available for each profit center in producing the volume OX^* that is optimal based on $MC = MR$. This assumption is not realistic, because each profit center has certain constraints, either manpower, capacity, etc. If these constraints are not explicitly dealt with in the system, the theoretical solution is no longer a pragmatic one.

---

[2]Remember that we are assuming, in the entire discussion, no cost interdependence, i.e., MC_A is independent from the MC_B. If the marginal cost of (A) (which is P^*) depends also on the volume of output of the final product (B), through common cost savings, the level of over-all marginal costs of the final product B for the organization is not equal to the sum of MC_A & MC_B. The analysis in such a case will be different.

[3]Jack Hirshleifer, "On the Economics of Transfer Pricing," *Journal of Business* (July 1956), pp. 172–184.

To solve these problems, a new approach to solving the transfer price problem based on an opportunity cost concept is needed. Opportunity cost is used here with cost accounting derived surrogates. This approach takes into consideration in arriving at the optimal solution the physical and financial constraints that exist at divisional levels and at the top corporate level. While the transfer price under this system is determined based on the decomposition principle, the final suggested price is not necessarily equal to it as we will show later. Since we will not discuss the mathematical operational steps of solving a case using the decomposition principle, a bibliography at the end of this article is a representative reference for this purpose.* In addition, we will show how this approach, with some motivational factors, can induce a profit center manager to act in the right direction and lessens his reason to manipulate cost estimates. This approach works as follows.

TRANSFER PRICE AND OPPORTUNITY COST

If Profit Center (A) transfers a part of its goods to Profit Center (B), and there is an outside market price, the transferred goods are priced equal to the market price, which represents the opportunity cost of not selling to outsiders.

If there is no market price, the transferred goods still should be priced equal to the opportunity cost of diverting divisional (A) resources into producing such goods, instead of producing another kind of goods that has an outside market. In developing the framework of this system, two cases will be differentiated.

I. Profit Center (A) transfers product X_1, that has no outside market price, to Profit Center (B). However, Profit Center (A) also produces X_2, which has a known market price.[4]

In this case, the price of the transferred product X_1 is equal to the opportunity cost or the shadow price of resources utilized in its production instead of being used to produce X_2. The following example is written in a linear programming model:

$$\text{Max } \pi = C_1X_1 + C_2X_2 = ?X_1 + 8X_2$$
$$\text{subject to:}$$
$$\text{Process I } 3X_1 + 6X_2 \leqslant 60$$
$$\text{Process II } 2X_1 + 4X_2 \leqslant 40$$
$$X_1, X_2 \geqslant 0$$

---

*Editors' Note: See the brief discussion of the decomposition principle in Appendix A (of this book) Section 4.2 Suboptimization.

[4]This is assuming that X_2 has a free competitive market, and that the organization will be able to sell all it produces of X_2. If this assumption is released, the analysis still can be applied, although it gets complicated.

Since the market price of product X_1 is unknown, we will first *a priori* assume that Profit Center A will maximize its profit by producing only X_2. The optimal solution is to produce 10 units of X_2, yielding a contribution margin of $80.00 and shadow price of $W_1 = 8/10$ and $W_2 = 8/10$. No idle capacity is available.

If Profit Center A is to produce X_1, it will divert a portion of its resources devoted to producing X_2 to produce X_1. For example, to reduce X_2 by 1 unit, it will increase X_1 by 2 units. Such a substitution rate will maintain the total contribution margin ($80.00) at the same level. This means that if Profit Center A is to produce (X_1), it should charge Profit Center B, $7.00/ unit in order to maintain its profitability intact. The $4.00/unit represents the opportunity cost of profit foregone by not producing X_2, calculated as follows:

$$C_1 = a_{11}W_1 + a_{12}W_2$$
$$= \left(3 \times \frac{8}{10}\right) + \left(2 \times \frac{8}{10}\right)$$
$$= \frac{24}{10} + \frac{16}{10} = \frac{40}{10} = \$4.00$$

Sales price = Variable costs + Contribution margin = 3.00 + 4.00 = $7.00

If the preceding example had resulted in idle capacity with the optimal solution, it would create motivational problems that the operating manager of Profit Center A may find difficult to ignore. For example, assume that the preceding example is the same, except for a change of the coefficient a_{22}.

$$\text{Max} = CX_1 + C_2X_2$$
$$?X_1 + 8X_2$$
$$\text{subject to:}\quad 3X_1 + 6X_2 \leqslant 60$$
$$2X_1 + 3X_2 \leqslant 40$$
$$X_1,\quad X_2 \geqslant 0$$

The solution is to produce 10 units of X_2, with a contribution margin of $80.00. However, process II has an idle capacity of 10 hours and, accordingly, $W_2 = 0$. Process I has dual evaluator of $W_1 = 1\frac{1}{3}$. The substitution rate is still 2 units of X_1 for 1 unit of X_2, requiring X_1 to be priced at $7.00/unit. However, if Profit Center A is being asked to completely divert its resources into producing X_1, it will produce 20 units of X_1, yielding the same contribution margin of $80.00. There is no idle capacity in process II, however. The center manager will hardly accept the utilization of all of his center's resources and still receive the same contribution margin. Theoretically, this is explainable on the grounds that the idle capacity of a slack variable is considered cost-free, assuming that such idle capacity cannot be leased, rented, or have its utilization deferred to next year without a reduction in its value. If these conditions are not met, the opportunity cost concept will require that the transfer price of X_1 be more than $7.00/unit to account for such additional profit foregone. If this is not accounted for, the manager of Profit Center A may believe that top corporate policy favors Profit Center B, because it does not reward his profit foregone.

The previous example also raises a crucial problem operationally. The shadow price value of W_1 and W_2 depends on the contribution margin of X_2 per unit and its required [A] coefficients. If the CM is high, the values of the dual evaluators will be high, and vice versa, assuming that the [A]'s are the same. If it happens that X_2 is the most profitable product for Center A, the transfer price for X_1 will be so high that Profit Center B may not be able to pay. The opposite may also be possible, leaving Profit Center A at a disadvantage. While such operational problems have long-run implications for policy planning, in the short run it is a situation to reckon with! A suggested solution is that the corporate level may use dual pricing for motivating reasons, since its total profit is still optimal because the volume of both centers is determined by the system.

It is not advisable to obtain the optimal solution for Profit Center A first, and then that of Profit Center B.[5] This procedure usually leads to dis-economies or suboptimal solution for the company as a whole. To over-come such a difficulty, a solution for the combined efforts of both centers has to be obtained. If such an optimal solution, company-wise, put Profit Center A at a disadvantage, the system should provide a motivational solution to induce and maintain the divisional manager's motivation in the right direction, or at least minimize the chance of moving in the wrong motivational direction. Motivation costs (the difference between the cent-er's maximization figure and that resulting from the corporate optimal solution) should be credited to Center A's profitability plan. If this is not done, conflict between the division's goal and that of the corporation moves into full gear, especially when the reward system is based on each center's profit. These points are illustrated in the following example:

	Profit Center A	*Profit Center B*
	Max $C_1X_1 + C_2X_2$	$C_3Y_1 + C_4Y_2$
	$?X_1 + 8X_2$	$(10 - C_1X_1)Y_1 + 5Y_2$
subject to:		
	$3X_1 + 6X_2 \leqslant 60$	$4Y_1 + 5Y_2 \leqslant 28$
	$2X_1 + 4X_2 \leqslant 40$	$3Y_1 + 2Y_2 \leqslant 14$
	$X_1, X_2 \geqslant 0$	$Y_1, Y_2 \geqslant 0$

To solve this problem, maximizing profit from a corporate point of view, assume that the variable cost of X_1 is \$3.00/unit, and that one unit of X_1 is needed to produce one unit of Y_1. This makes the net contribution margin of $Y_1 =$ \$7.00/unit.

A linear programming model based on decomposition is as follows:[6]

---

[5]This is due to the fact that Profit Center A acts as a simple maximizer, and, as such, forces Center B to behave in the same way, leading to suboptimization. See the example illustrated above.

[6]See: George Dantzig and Philip Wolf, "Decomposition Principles for Linear Programming, *Operations Research* (February 1960); and George Dantzig, *Linear Programming and Extensions* (Princeton University Press, 1963); Chapters 22–24.

	PLAN I			PLAN II			PLAN III	
Production	Center (A)	Center (B)	Production	Center (A)	Center (B)	Production	Center (A)	Center (B)
Y_2 = 5 units		$25.00	Y_2 = 1 units		$ 5.00	Y_2 = 4 units		$20.00
Y_1 = 0 units		0	Y_1 = 4 units		28.00	Y_1 = 2 units		14.00
X_1 = 0 units	0		X_1 = 4 units	0		X_1 = 2 units		
X_2 = 10 units	$80.00		X_2 = 8 units	$64.00		X_2 = 9 units	$72.00	
S_1 = 0 hours			S_1 = 0 hours			S_1 = 0 hours		
S_2 = 0 hours			S_2 = 0 hours			S_2 = 0 hours		
S_3 = 3 hours			S_3 = 7 hours			S_3 = 0 hours		
S_4 = 4 hours			S_4 = 0 hours			S_4 = 0 hours		
Divisional Profit	$80.00	$25.00		$64.00	$33.00		$72.00	$34.00
Corporate Profit	$105.00			$97.00			$106.00	

Exhibit 3. Different Operating Profitability Plans

$$
\begin{aligned}
\text{Max } \pi(X, Y) = \quad & 0X_1 + 8X_2 + 7Y_1 + 5Y_2 \\
& -X_1 \qquad\quad + Y_1 && \leq\ 0 \\
& 3X_1 + 6X_2 && \leq 60 \\
& 2X_1 + 4X_2 && \leq 40 \\
& \qquad\qquad\quad 4Y_1 + 5Y_2 \leq 28 \\
& \qquad\qquad\quad 3Y_1 + 2Y_2 \leq 14 \\
& \quad X_1, \quad X_2, \quad Y_1, \quad Y_2 \geq 0.
\end{aligned}
$$

Master Budget

The mathematical solution of such a case is illustrated in Exhibit 3, where the feasible plans and optimal one are shown.[7] The slack variables (S_1, S_2, S_3, S_4) corresponding to each plan are also shown, indicating any idle capacity in the corresponding process of each profit center.

For the corporation as a whole, plan III is optimal. However, if we look at the solution from the point of view of each profit center, do we reach the same conclusion?

From the Profit Center B's point of view, plan III is optimal. From Profit Center A's point of view, it is not, since plan I is its optimal program. Would the manager of Profit Center A accept plan III, knowing what this means for his incentive compensation at the end of the year? Will the rate of return on his divisional investment reflect a fair measure of his performance if he accepts plan III?

What is the source of the problem and how should it be solved? The problem arises from the fact that the intermediate good X_1 is priced equal to its marginal (variable) costs. No contribution margin is given to Profit Center A, meaning that Profit Center B has captured all the gains yielded from this process itself, without sharing it with Profit Center A. This reflects unfair treatment. Accounting literature argues for the distribution of the joint profit of $7.00/unit of (X_1, Y_1) between both centers, either through bargaining or by means of an equalization rate based on the ratio of production cost in both centers related to (X_1, Y_1). This accounting solution, as seen in this example, leads to suboptimization.[8] If a fair and equitable distribution is to be followed, Profit Center A should be given the profit foregone as a result of producing X_1. This means that the operating budget of Center A, if plan III is adopted, should be increased by $8.00 as motivation costs. Profit Center B's additional contribution, as a result of

---

[7] No top corporate constraints are assumed. If any exist, the problem can still be solved, using the decomposition principle. The operating costs of each center are assumed to be independent of the level of activity of the other center and linear. Also, any additional sales of Y's will not reduce the external demand for X_2. These two conditions are called technological independence and demand independence consecutively. However, there is a demand interdependence for Y_1 and X_1; the demand of X_1 is derived from that of Y_1. If the demand for X_2 and Y_2 is interrelated, the problem still can be solved, although it gets complicated.

[8] If Center A charges B a sales price of $8.00/unit of X_1, using the accounting equalization method, Center B finds it in its best interest not to buy X_1 and not to produce Y_1. Center B will produce 5 units of Y_2 and yield CM of $25.00, and Center A will then produce 10 units of X_2 yielding CM of $80.00. The total of $105.00 (equal to plan I) is a suboptimization case.

further processing X_1 to Y_1, is \$1.00. This is the additional gain the company obtained by encouraging the production of (X_1, Y_1). If the corporate level does not adhere to such an opportunity cost approach, budgetary conflict arises between the profit center managers and the corporate level.

The previous solution in general, however, raises two important implications:

> 1. If product X_2 is highly profitable, the opportunity cost of producing X_1 is high. If product Y_1, which uses X_1 as input, is not so profitable as to afford paying such opportunity costs, the company as a whole will be better off by not producing Y_1. However, if product Y_1 should be produced in order to meet a contract commitment, or as a result of a policy decision, this decision is a top corporate decision and not a center one. The profit (or loss) consequence of such a decision should be isolated. Center A should not be penalized by a decision not of its own.

> 2. If product X_2 is not highly profitable, the opportunity cost of producing X_1 will be less, and Profit Center B may be in an advantageous position. Profit Center A should not blame Profit Center B for this condition. Profit Center A would be well advised, if the demand for X_2 is decreasing and profitability is declining, to shift its resources to a new product. In the short run, however, Profit Center A should not ask Profit Center B to subsidize its operation and increase its profits.

These two implications do not necessarily require that the top corporate level use motivation costs in profitability planning, as in the case above.

II. *Profit Center (A) produces both product X_1 and product X_2 for Profit Center (B), and there are no market prices for either product.*

In this case, Profit Center A, in reality, is not a profit center. It will function the same if it is treated as a cost center,[9] or is joined with Profit Center B to compose one large profit center. The latter may require a change in the organization's structure, which may be justifiable to minimize the undesirable motivational consequence of a system based on "games" if the price of suboptimization is too high for the company to bear!

SUMMARY

Under the assumption $MC_A = NMR_B$, the supplying profit center is not motivated to change the relative use of various factors of production in response to changes in factor prices, since these favorable effects will pass

---

[9]If it is treated as a cost center, it will have a zero marginal contribution which a budgetary system should accept. Its performance can be evaluated in terms of cost control and volume attainment.

over to the buying profit center. In addition, the profit center selling the final product will be motivated either to manipulate its sales by delaying them to next year, if this year is especially profitable, or to increase its production inventory level so that a part of its overhead will be capitalized, leading to an increase of its profit if it is originally unfavorable. This will affect the production of intermediate goods. To prevent this, the corporate level watches the inventory level and asks for an explanation if it exceeds a certain level. Another solution is that the buying division commits itself to acquire a certain volume. These methods are partial solutions to the problem.

We have shown that using variable costs, approximating marginal costs, to price transfer goods has several limitations since this approach ignores several strategic factors. Also, we have shown that using the accounting equalization method leads to suboptimization and that any solution to a transfer pricing system cannot ignore the motivational conflict that is pertinent. We have used "motivation costs" to reduce the level of conflict due to the transfer pricing system. As a result, arriving at an optimal solution based on opportunity costs from the company's point of view, accepted by profit centers, is feasible.

REFERENCES ON THE DECOMPOSITION PRINCIPLE

1. A. Charnes and W. W. Cooper, *Management Models and Industrial Application of Linear Programming*, Vols. I, II (John Wiley & Sons, 1961).

2. G. B. Dantzig, *Linear Programming and Extensions* (1963).

3. —— and P. Wolfe, "The Decomposition Principle for Linear Programs," *Operations Research*, Vol. 8 (1960), pp. 101–111.

4. Warren E. Walker, "A Method for Obtaining the Optimal Dual Solution to a Linear Program Using the Dantzig-Wolfe Decomposition," *Operations Research* (March–April 1969), pp. 368–370.

5. Adi Ben-Israel and Philip D. Roberts, "A Decomposition Method for Interval Linear Programing," *Management Science* (January 1970), pp. 374–387.

6. David P. Rutenberg, "Generalized Networks, Generalized Upper Bounding and Decomposition for the Convex Simplex Method," *Management Science* (January 1970), pp. 396–401.

7. William J. Baumol and Tibor Fabin, "Decomposition Pricing for Decentralization and External Economics," *Management Science* (September 1964), pp. 1–32.

8. Jerome E. Hass, "Transfer Pricing in a Decentralized Firm," *Management Science* (February 1968), pp. 310–331.

9. C. S. Colantoni, R. P. Manes and A. Whinston, "Programming, Profit Rates and Pricing Decisions," *The Accounting Review* (July 1969), pp. 467–481.

10. Andrew Whinston, "Pricing Guides in Decentralized Organization," *New Perspective in Organizational Research*, edited by W. W. Cooper, et al. (John Wiley and Sons, 1964), pp. 405–448.

11. Edwin V. W. Zschau, *A Primal Decomposition Algorithm for Linear Programming*, Ph.D. Thesis (Graduate School of Business, Stanford University, December 1966).

SIX
Additional Applications of Quantitative Techniques

LINEAR PROGRAMMING

INVENTORY CONTROL

PERT/COST RESOURCE ALLOCATION

MATRIX APPLICATIONS

OPTIMIZATION AND DIFFERENTIAL CALCULUS

Business decision problems can involve a consideration of both quantitative and nonquantitative factors. For the quantitative models, mathematical and statistical techniques can be applied to help solve the business problem. Quantitative techniques, such as probability, the least-squares method, and multiple regression analysis have been discussed in other sections of this book. This section contains articles about linear programming, inventory control, PERT, the application of matrix methods in management accounting, and the use of differential calculus for optimization purposes.

Although some decisions may be made with a disregard for "scientific thinking" and the use of quantitative techniques to aid in evaluating alternatives, successful decision making primarily involves:

1. A clear and timely perception of the problem, its limits and components.
2. The selection, collection, and interpretation of the relevant factors.
3. A method of integrating the strategic factors to facilitate evaluation of the alternatives and to formalize the decision process for future reference, analysis, and improvement.

Quantitative techniques and the use of a computer aid the accountant, analyst, and manager in evaluating alternatives, and are useful tools for a rigorous and systematic decision-making process.

LINEAR PROGRAMMING

Linear programming is a mathematical method for considering a number of interacting variables simultaneously, and calculating the best possible solution for a given problem for the stated limits or constraints of the problem. The method helps management minimize costs or maximize profits. For example, linear programming can be applied to product-mix problems concerned with maximizing profits resulting from two or more products the firm sells, with sales prices and costs given, and subject to limits or constraints imposed by production facilities, financial limitations, and demand, so that the total contribution resulting from the product mix will be maximized. Some other possible uses for linear programming include: determining combinations of machines and manpower, material mixes, and utilizing storage facilities; this latter use involves a special case of the simplex method of linear programming called the transportation method.

The use of a computer for the solution of the simplex method of linear programming has made linear programming practicable for business problems. In practice, where a number of variables may be involved, obtaining solutions by any other means than a computer is really not feasible. Also, the man-hours required for the solution of a problem where a computer is not used may not allow the solution to be obtained quickly enough to be of use to a decision maker.

The technique of linear programming is useful for planning and decision-making purposes and, when used in this manner, is part of a forward-looking analysis. In contrast, using the conventional accounting model for a product-mix problem tends to be a post-mortem analysis in that the statements that result from operations are compared with statements of prior periods or with standards; as part of this analysis, volume and mix variances, to select two examples, may be determined to help management obtain clues for possible improvements in profits. It should be noted that even relatively simple product-mix problems, involving few relevant factors and restrictions, can be virtually impossible to solve by trial-and-error methods.

In Article 30, "Linear Programming," the graphic method of linear programming is explained first. This is useful to introduce the subject. For a product-mix problem, we can attempt to maximize an objective function made up of the separate margins over variable costs (contribution margins) for each of the products included in the analysis, while remaining within the range set by the limiting factors. Once the objective function and the restrictions (i.e., constraints) have been determined, different techniques may be used to compute the optimum solution. The graphic approach can aid a decision maker in visualizing a linear programming problem, but is only useful for very simple problems with two or perhaps three variables.

The use of a computer to perform the calculations for the simplex method of linear programming, which is an iterative, step-by-step process, facilitates the application of linear programming to problems involving many and complex variables. With the aid of a computer for obtaining solutions, we are able to expand the restrictions of a problem so that our analysis can be made completely flexible and realistic for business decisions. The major problem, of course, is the determination of such parameters as the demand schedule for specific products and the cost coefficients for the products.

In a linear programming problem, a solution which satisfies all of the constraints is called a feasible solution. A solution which satisfies all of the constraints and occurs at an extreme point or vertex (see the Article 30 discussion of extreme points for the graphic method) is called a basic feasible solution. In the simplex method, we start with an initial basic feasible solution and move to successive basic feasible solutions until the optimal solution is reached. For actual business problems, in addition to determining the optimal solution we may want to perform sensitivity analysis to determine the effect on the solution of changes in constraints or objective function coefficients.

Linear programming computer routines can provide tableau and basis printout data and these are often used to determine the effect on the optimal solution of changes in constraints or objective function coefficients. Article 30 explains the optimal tableau (computer solution of linear programming problems), and the use of tableaus in sensitivity analysis. The latter involves right-hand side (RHS) and profit ranging. Working with the optimal solution tableau, it is usually possible to determine the effect of changes without working the problem over again. For example, assume that after the optimal tableau is determined the available amount of a resource is changed (either up or down), the profit will increase or decrease by the value of the shadow price associated with the slack variable for the resource. If the optimal basis remains feasible, it is not necessary to calculate a new optimal solution to determine the change in profit. However, we need to find the permissible range for the amount of a resource such that the shadow price is applicable. To aid in understanding the ranging computations, the article includes a discussion of the computational procedure of the simplex algorithm.

For questions concerned with the interpretation of a tableau and involving sensitivity analysis, see VI-Q3 parts 9 through 12. For 9, 10, and 11, see the computer solution of linear programming problems section of Article 30. Part 12 involves sensitivity analysis and ranging. See the note following part 12 which discusses the solution for that question and which refers to the sensitivity analysis discussion of Article 30. For an example prepared to tie together the material on optimal solutions and sensitivity analysis, see the problem and solution at the end of Article 30. Problem VI-Q16 demonstrates the use of linear programming, the computer and sensitivity analysis. Computer printouts are included with the problem.

QUANTITATIVE TECHNIQUES AND INVENTORY MANAGEMENT

Decision problems concerned with determining optimum levels of inventory can benefit by the application of quantitative techniques; these can include economic order quantity, reorder point calculations, and the application of the Monte Carlo method to inventory problems involving uncertainty of demand and/or lead time.[1]

---

[1]Monte Carlo analysis is a method that can be used to simulate and generate a schedule of events which would be expected to occur in random fashion. The method can be useful as a technique for computer simulation of business problems for planning purposes. For a discussion of the specialized technique of Monte Carlo analysis, the reader is referred to Donald L. Raun, "The Application of Monte Carlo Analysis to an Inventory Problem," The Accounting Review, October 1963, pp. 754–758. This article extends the application of Monte Carlo analysis to an inventory problem, makes reference to the use of a computer for generating random numbers, is concerned with determining the optimum order point, and presents a numerical example of the application of Monte Carlo analysis for the uncertainty of demand and/or lead time problem.

In order to minimize the total long-run cost of materials used in production, a manufacturer must determine the quantity of materials to buy and the time for the purchase. To answer these questions, economic order quantity (EOQ) and order point or reorder point tabulations or formulas may be prepared.

All inventory situations have certain general characteristics, each involving some aspects of cost, service, and usage. One characteristic is that as inventory increases, the cost of storing the goods will increase, but the cost resulting from an inability to fill orders will decrease. Quantitative methods may be used in making inventory decisions with the objectives of minimizing total cost but providing an acceptable level of goods to satisfy the anticipated or expected demand rate.

Article 31, "Inventory Control," presents a broad outline of the objectives and problems involved in the control of inventory, including such considerations as the possible methods to use in determining safety-stock levels and how to determine estimates for the cost parameters to be included in inventory models. The article also presents the classic economic order quantity (EOQ) formula that can be used in deciding "how much of an item is replenished at a time," as well as the formula for the reorder point that can be used in determining "when the item is replenished."[2]

The editors recommend that the article, "Inventory Control," and Problem VI-Q6, for which an answer has been included in this book, be studied as a unit. Problem VI-Q6 requires the application of the economic order quantity formula, the determination of the reorder point, and the determination of the cost of a stockout. Stockout costs may be determined from certain costs that are incurred with respect to back orders, and also might include such estimates as an amount for lost goodwill resulting from not being able to supply customers.

The economic order quantity formula can be modified for determining an economic manufacturing lot size. The formula can be modified to take into consideration setup costs (such as labor cost for preparing machines for production), and the holding cost of the work-in-process inventory.[3]

---

[2] The classic EOQ theory approach does not consider the effect that the payment terms imposed by suppliers of inventory purchased can have on the "real" investment in inventory. By using more exact measurements for formula parameters, for example, considering payment terms, there can be an impact on the determination of reorder quantities. This modification for the EOQ formula is discussed in an article by Robert G. Bunch, "The Effect of Payment Terms on Economic Order Quantity Determination," *Management Accounting,* January 1967, pp. 53–63.

[3] For a discussion concerned with applying the EOQ formula for determining units per production run for company manufactured items, and including a consideration of work-in-process inventories, see Subodh Bhattacharjee, "Economic Manufacturing Lot Size," *Journal of Industrial Engineering,* March–April 1957, pp. 119–126.

PERT—PROGRAM EVALUATION AND
REVIEW TECHNIQUE

PERT or PERT/Time can be a useful control tool for management in that it helps coordinate various parts of a project by determining critical activities that can cause problems for the time completion of a project. It uses a network technique to show the relationship between the steps of a complex project. PERT/Cost involves a network where time and cost estimates for activity are included, and management can see the effect of decisions involving trade-offs of time and cost. This can aid management in obtaining the optimum allocation of resources such as labor and equipment that could be used in project completion. The readings about PERT are included in Articles 32 and 33, "PERT/Cost Resource Allocation Procedure" and "A Note on PERT/Cost Resource Allocation."

MATRIX METHODS

Matrix algebra can be used to solve systems of linear equations (see matrix inversion in Article 34). Examples of techniques for which matrix applications may be useful include linear programming (for example, the classic product-mix problem),[4] game theory, and Markov chains used in solving business problems.

Article 34, "An Introduction to Matrix Operations in Accounting," is concerned with the matrix operations of addition, subtraction, multiplication, and inversion. Article 35, "A Proposal for Condensing Diverse Accounting Procedures," discusses the application of matrix methods in management accounting; included are reciprocal relationship problems such as allocating costs of service departments to producing departments, equivalent unit determination, profit sharing bonus plans, and matrix bookkeeping.

AN OPTIMUM SOLUTION AND DIFFERENTIATION

Differentiation (differential calculus) is used for determining the slope of a line tangent to a curve at a point (see Article 36). This concept can be used for marginal analysis and for problems that involve determining relative maximum and minimum points of a function. For example, differentiation could be used by management in an attempt to seek an optimum solution (minimum cost) for a combination of factors of production.[5] Also, differ-

---

[4]See Edwin Heard, Constantine Konstans, and James Don Edwards, "Demonstrating the Conceptual Significance of the Matrix Inverse," *Accounting Review,* April 1974, pp. 377–381.

[5]An example of a cost minimization problem would be an attempt by managers to obtain the optimum solution for a combination of expenditures for repairs plus maintenance and where a unit of maintenance can be substituted for a unit of repairs. Given a total cost for maintenance plus repairs, an attempt is made to find the number of units to be interchanged to minimize total cost. This can be accomplished by using a basic principle of differential

entiation could be used for problems concerned with the optimum pricing policy for profit maximization.

Article 36, "Optimization," discusses an optimum price problem and shows how to determine and use the first and second derivatives for a function (see the discussion about first and second derivatives in footnote 5 of this introductory discussion). The article includes differentiation formulas or rules for obtaining the derivatives of various types of functions. The second derivative for a problem is the derivative of the first derivative. The second derivative is used in Article 36 to indicate whether a maximum point has been reached on the profit and price curve. The point is a maximum if the second derivative is negative. A positive second derivative shows that a point is a minimum, and when a second derivative is zero, the point is neither a maximum nor a minimum.

Article 37, "An Application of Curvilinear Break-Even Analysis," applies differential calculus; the article can aid the reader in understanding the concept of the derivative. Also, see an article by Thomas A. Morrison and Eugene Kaczka, "A New Application of Calculus and Risk Analysis to Cost-Volume-Profit Changes," *The Accounting Review*, April 1969, pp. 330–343. The authors use differential calculus to develop a formula and solution for the problem of changes in selling price which result in changes in quantities demanded. The article extends breakeven analysis in that C-V-P, under the application, would not be handicapped by a consideration of only a selected few possible alternatives. When plotted, the quadratic equation for volume changes related to price changes results in a parabola, and the maximum profit can be calculated by using differential calculus.

---

calculus. See Carl L. Moore and Robert K. Jaedicke, *Managerial Accounting*, 3rd ed. (Cincinnati, Ohio: South-Western Publishing Co., 1972), pp. 299–304 for a sample problem and explanation of how to use derivatives (differential calculus) to obtain the solution.

The following briefly describes the problem. The problem assumes maintenance cost is $300, and that for each unit of maintenance (X) added, the cost increases by X^2; if two units of maintenance are added the cost would be $X^2 + \$300$ or $2(2) + \$300 = \$304$. Repair cost is $800, and for each decrease of a unit of repairs, the cost can be reduced by $8; the equation is $800 - 8X$. The maintenance and repair units are defined so that an increase in a unit of maintenance is balanced by a decrease in a unit of repairs; therefore, X is used to represent maintenance or repair units. The combined cost equation is $C = X^2 - 8X + 1100$. Following the rules of differentiation, $2X - 8$ is the first derivative. The exponent of the factor is multiplied by the coefficient of the factor to obtain a new coefficient, and the exponent is reduced by one. Thus, $2 \cdot X^{2-1} - 1 \cdot 8X^{1-1} = 2X - 8$. The fixed constant (1100) is eliminated in differentiation. Setting the first derivative equal to zero, and then solving for the critical value of X results in X = 4. The combined cost for maintenance and repairs is $1,100. If 4 units are interchanged, the combined cost will be $16 - 32 + 1100 = \$1,084$. The second derivative is 2, i.e., $1 \cdot 2X^{1-1}$; the constant (-8) drops out. Note that the second derivative (2) is determined as the derivative of the first derivative ($2X - 8$). Because the second derivative is positive, the point f(4) is the minimum point of a function and the combined minimum cost will be $1,084 for the problem.

For a brief review of the concepts of calculus (differential calculus concerned with determining the rate of change of a function, and integral calculus concerned with finding a function where its rate of change is given), and for examples of the rules (listed in Article 36) for obtaining the derivatives of various types of functions, and the use of the second derivative in locating relative maxima and minima, see Ann Hughes and Dennis Grawoig, *Statistics: A Foundation for Analysis* (Reading, Mass.: Addison-Wesley Publishing Company, 1971), pp. 474–479.

30.
LINEAR PROGRAMMING*

Richard E. Trueman

Of all the well-known operations research models, linear programming and related techniques have been by far the most productive, as measured by their effective application to the solution of a great variety of large-scale problems in business and industry. The advent of the high-speed digital computer has made it practical to solve with incredible speed problems involving hundreds or even thousands of decision variables.

Since virtually all real-world linear programming problems are solved by computer, the emphasis will be placed on learning the basic concepts of linear programming, rather than on the attainment of any particular expertise in the manual solution of small linear programming problems. The interpretation of a computer solution will be discussed and the results of such a solution will be extended through the technique of sensitivity analysis. The preparation of linear programming problems for computer solution will also be covered.

Basically, linear programming is a deterministic mathematical technique which involves the allocation of scarce resources in an optimal manner on the basis of a given criterion of optimality. Frequently, the criterion of optimality is either maximum profit or minimum cost, depending on the type of problem. The following are but a few examples of some types of problems that have been tackled and solved utilizing linear programming techniques:

---

*From *An Introduction to Quantitative Methods for Decision Making*, 2nd. ed. by Richard E. Trueman. Copyright © 1977, 1974 by Holt, Rinehart and Winston. Reprinted by permission of the author and Holt, Rinehart and Winston. Selected material from pp. 212–267 was jointly edited by Richard E. Trueman and Donald L. Anderson. More comprehensive coverage of linear programming topics can be found in the Trueman text or in the many texts devoted solely to linear programming and related mathematical programming models.

Product-Mix Selection. A company can manufacture several different products, each of which requires the use of limited production resources, such as machine time, process time, and labor time. What quantity of each product should be produced in order to maximize profit?

Minimum-Cost Diet. A hospital wishes to provide its patients with meals which are balanced, varied, and meet certain minimum nutritional requirements. What is the minimum-cost selection of food items which will meet these constraints?

Blending Problems. A chemical product can be made from a variety of available raw materials, each of which has a particular composition and price. Subject to availability of the raw materials and to minimum and maximum constraints on certain product constituents, what is the minimum-cost blend?

Production Planning. A company faces a certain expected demand each month for a manufactured product. Considering the initial number of units in inventory, the available production capacity, constraints on production, employment, and inventory levels, and all relevant cost factors, what is the minimum-cost production plan over the planning horizon of n months?*

* Editors' Note: For a capital budgeting application (the determination of expected cash flow for a machine used in the production process), see Walter J. Thurn, Sr., "A Systems Approach to Cash Flow Determination," *Management Accounting*, February 1973, pp. 29–31. Also see the applications in Articles 3 and 29.

GRAPHICAL APPROACH

The basic concepts of linear programming can best be illustrated and explored by a simple example. For the case of two decision variables (often called activity variables), a graphical solution can be readily developed, and this pictorial representation can yield very valuable insights. (For three decision variables, a graphical solution is possible but rather unwieldy; beyond three decision variables, a graphical solution is no longer possible.)

It should be clearly pointed out that the graphical approach to solving linear programming problems is a completely impractical method of solution for realistic problems. Nevertheless, it is extremely useful in explaining the basic concepts and techniques of linear programming, and that alone justifies its use.

Example 1

Consider the production planning decision of the Valvton Company, which makes valves and pistons. Both valves and pistons must be machined on a lathe and processed on a grinder. The pistons must also be polished. Each valve and each piston requires a certain amount of steel. Table 1 summarizes the amount of each resource (machine time and steel, in this case) used in the manufacture of one valve and one piston. The table also presents the unit profit for both valves and pistons and the amount of each resource available weekly. Valvton wishes to determine the values of the decision variables, the number of valves and pistons to be produced, which maximize profit, subject to the constraints on available machine time and steel.

	GRINDER TIME (HR)	LATHE TIME (HR)	POLISHING TIME (HR)	STEEL (LB)		UNIT PROFIT ($)
Each valve requires	0.3	1.0	0	1.0	and yields	3
Each piston requires	0.5	1.5	0.5	1.0	and yields	4
Available resources	300	750	200	600		

Table 1. Resource Requirements

Restrictions Imposed by Limited Resources

In the problem formulation phase of a linear programming problem, we investigate the effect of only one resource at a time, so let us take them in order, as presented in Table 1.

1. Grinder Time

With 300 hours of grinder time available, suppose only valves were to be produced:

$$\text{Maximum valve production} = \frac{300 \text{ hr}}{0.3 \text{ hr/valve}} = 1000 \text{ valves.}$$

On the other hand, if only pistons were to be produced:

$$\text{Maximum piston production} = \frac{300 \text{ hr}}{0.5 \text{ hr/piston}} = 600 \text{ pistons.}$$

Or, we could produce any combination of valves and pistons which did not require more than 300 hours of grinder time.

The two data points developed (1000 valves, 0 pistons; and 0 valves, 600 pistons) define the endpoints of the line representing the grinder time restriction, as plotted in Figure 1.

Within the triangle formed by the two axes and the linear function representing the grinder time restriction, any combination of valves and pistons is feasible, *considering only grinder resources* and, of course, the obvious restriction that the quantity of valves and pistons must be non-negative. The region above and to the right of this triangle represents

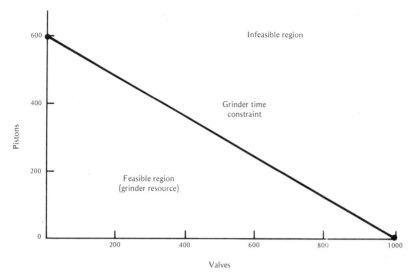

Figure 1

combinations which are infeasible because of grinder time limitations. For any combination of valves and pistons lying on the line representing the grinder time restriction, the grinder resource will be fully utilized. For any such combination lying within the shaded area, which we call the *feasible region*, there will be excess grinder time.

At this point, we might look at the data of Table 1 and observe that it will clearly be impossible to produce 1000 valves, since the limited amount of steel available will permit a maximum of 600 valves to be manufactured. This is absolutely true, but each constraint must be considered separately during the problem formulation phase. During the solution phase, the interaction of the different constraints will be taken care of "automatically" by the computational algorithm, which is what we call the computing procedure.

2. Lathe Time

Examining next the availability of lathe time, we could apply all 750 hours to the production of 750 valves, to the production of 500 pistons, or to any combination of valves and pistons not using more than 750 hours of lathe time. These data are graphed in Figure 2, along with the restrictions due to grinder time.

From the graph, it is apparent that the constraint on lathe time availability is more restrictive than that of grinder time availability. As a consequence, the feasible region, for both grinder and lathe resources, is the region defined by the latter resource alone. We say that the lathe time constraint dominates the grinder time constraint, and the grinder time constraint is, therefore, *redundant*.

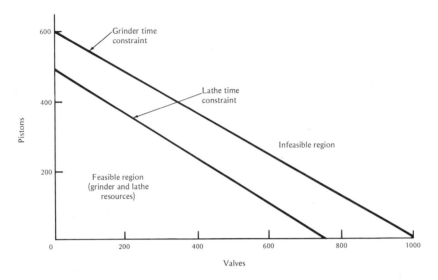

Figure 2

3. Polishing Time

Since valves require no polishing, their production is not limited by the amount of polishing time available. Maximum piston production would be 400, with 200 hours available and 0.5 hour polishing time per piston. The resultant constraint line will be parallel to the horizontal axis, at a value of 400 pistons.

4. Steel

With valves and pistons both taking 1.0 pound of steel per unit, maximum valve or piston production would be 600 units. This constraint is represented by a line connecting the points (600 valves, 0 pistons; and 0 valves, 600 pistons).

In Figure 3, the steel and polisher constraints have been added, but the redundant grinder time constraint is not shown. The feasible region is now a polygon, instead of a triangle. The arrows on each given constraint line indicate the direction of the feasible region, which is determined by the sign of the constraint inequality. If that sign were reversed, the feasible region would be on the opposite side of the line.

Graphical Determination of Optimality

Having determined the feasible region, considering all resources, we can now work toward an optimal solution. To do this, we will set up a system of linear inequalities.

The first thing to do is to introduce a suitable notation for this problem.

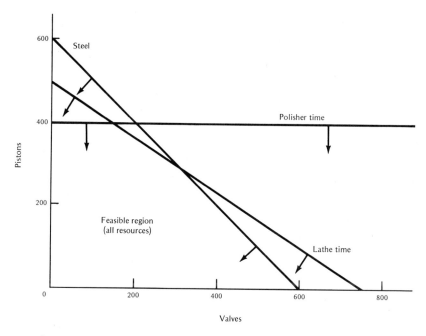

Figure 3

$$
\begin{aligned}
\text{Let } v &= \text{number of valves produced,}\\
p &= \text{number of pistons produced,}\\
z &= \text{total profit in dollars.}
\end{aligned}
$$

The constraints, which define the limitations placed on the decision variables, may now be written as follows:

Grinder time constraint	$0.3v + 0.5p \le 300$
Lathe time constraint	$1.0v + 1.5p \le 750$
Polishing time constraint	$0.5p \le 200$
Steel constraint	$1.0v + 1.0p \le 600$
Nonnegativity constraints	$v \ge 0, p \ge 0$

The first four constraints, which involve the limitation of scarce resources, are called *restrictions,* and they are written as $\le$ inequalities. The final nonnegativity constraints are necessary because we cannot produce a negative quantity of valves or pistons.

As we observed earlier, the constraint on grinder time is not a factor in the analysis, since at least one constraint is more restrictive; thus, we do not have to consider the first constraint. (Actually, in this particular example, both the lathe time and the steel constraints are more restrictive than the grinder time constraint.)

The function to be optimized (maximized or minimized) is called the *objective function.* In this profit maximization problem, the objective function represents the total profit obtained from any specified combination of valves and pistons. Since each valve earns $3 profit and each piston $4 profit, the objective function is:

$$\text{maximize } z = 3v + 4p.$$

For any value of z, the objective function represents a line with constant slope. The value of the slope will always be equal to the negative of the ratio of the coefficient of the variable plotted on the horizontal axis to the coefficient of the variable plotted on the vertical axis. In this example, v is on the horizontal axis and p on the vertical axis, so the slope is $-3/4$, or -0.75. As the value of z increases, we can visualize a line moving parallel to itself and away from the origin. We can easily plot several such lines by specifying a value for z, setting v to zero, and solving for p to get one point on the line, and then setting p to zero and solving for v to get a second point. We used this same general procedure to plot the constraint lines. The table below gives values which establish three lines (with arbitrary z values).

	Point 1		Point 2	
z	v	p	v	p
600	0	150	200	0
1200	0	300	400	0
1800	0	450	600	0

These three lines are shown in Figure 4 superimposed on the feasible region. It should be apparent that we can achieve a higher profit than $1800 by moving as far as possible in the direction of increasing profit, which in this case is away from the origin. The line representing maximum profit is that line which just touches the edge of the feasible region. In the figure this line is shown as line AB, which touches the edge of the feasible region at the point where the lathe time and steel constraint lines intersect. The optimal product mix can be determined by simultaneously solving these two constraint equations:

$$
\begin{aligned}
1.0v + 1.5p &= 750 \\
-(1.0v + 1.0p &= 600) \\
\hline
0.5p &= 150, \\
p &= 300.
\end{aligned}
$$

Substituting this value of p in either of the two constraint equations, we get

$$v = 300.$$

Therefore, the maximum achievable profit is

$$z = (3)(300) + (4)(300) = \$2100.$$

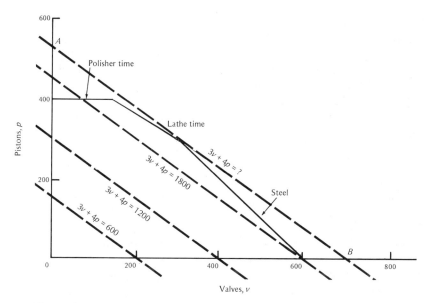

Figure 4

The equation of the objective function line yielding the maximum profit is thus $3v + 4p = 2100$.

Observe carefully that the optimal solution point can never be an interior point of the feasible region. This is always true, since any solution at an interior point can always be bettered by moving in the direction of increasing profit, perpendicular to the objective function line. If there is a single (unique) optimal solution, the optimal solution point must be at a vertex of the feasible region.

ASSUMPTIONS IN LINEAR PROGRAMMING MODELS

Although it has not been stated explicitly up to this point, in all linear programming models there are three basic assumptions which must be met in order for such models to be applicable.

Proportionality

The amount of each resource used (or requirement supplied) and the associated contribution to profit (or cost) must be exactly proportional to the value of each decision variable, often called its activity level. For example, if the number of valves produced were halved, the total amount of each resource required in the manufacture of valves would also be halved, as would the total profit contribution from valves.

Divisibility
The decision variables must be allowed to assume a continuous range of values. (In such problems as that of the Valvton Company, where we wished to determine the optimal production quantity of individual items, it is clear that we cannot produce a fractional piston or valve. However, we assume that with the given optimal resource allocation, any fractional items to be produced will be partially completed during a given time period and then finished during the next time period.) If any of the variables can assume only integer values or are limited to a discrete number of values, we no longer have a linear programming model but a discrete programming model. Such models tend to be much more complex than linear programming models and will not be covered in this text.

Additivity
The total amount of each resource utilized (or requirement supplied) and the total profit (or cost) are equal to the sum of the respective individual amounts. Thus, in a feed blending example, the total amount of nutrient A is exactly equal to the sum of the amount of nutrient A contributed by the first commercial feed and that contributed by the second commercial feed. The total cost of the feed mixture equals the cost for the given amount of the first commercial feed plus the cost for the given amount of the second commercial feed.

These three postulates mean that all constraints and the objective function must be characterized by linear relationships. In addition, we have assumed that the linear programming model is completely deterministic, having no stochastic elements.

SIMPLEX METHOD

As we have indicated, the graphical approach to linear programming is useful only to illustrate basic concepts and not to solve practical problems, which typically have many decision variables, not two or three. We will now discuss in some detail the simplex method, an algebraic approach to the solution of any linear programming problem. Although more efficient computational techniques have been developed for the solution of large problems (some having thousands of variables and equations), the version of the simplex algorithm presented here illustrates the principles involved in solving linear programming problems. We will study it, not as an end in itself, but primarily to provide a foundation for the later study of post-optimality analysis of computer solutions. As a matter of interest, many of the specialized computational techniques for large linear programming problems are actually variants of the simplex method.

Let us work with Example 1, the product-mix problem previously solved graphically. Before actually getting into the simplex algorithm, we will need to set up the problem algebraically and define some fundamental concepts. The set of governing constraints, which are inequalities, can be converted to equations by the addition of what are called *slack variables*.

$$
\begin{array}{llll}
v + 1.5p & + S_1 & & = 750 \text{ (lathe time constraint)} & (1) \\
0.5p & + S_2 & & = 200 \text{ (polishing time constraint)} & (2) \\
v + p & & + S_3 & = 600 \text{ (steel constraint)} & (3) \\
-3v - 1p & & + z & = 0 \text{ (objective function)} & (4)
\end{array}
$$

where

$S_1 =$ lathe time slack (unused resource), in hours,
$S_2 =$ polisher time slack (unused resource), in hours,
$S_3 =$ steel slack (unused resource), in pounds,
$z =$ value of the objective function—to be maximized,

and

$v, p, S_1, S_2, S_3 \geqslant 0.$

The slack variables, as noted in their definitions, represent unused resources. For example, since it takes 1.0 hour of lathe time per valve and 1.5 hours of lathe time per piston, a product mix consisting of 100 valves and 120 pistons would require a lathe time totaling $(1.0)(100) + (1.5)(120) = 280$ hours. With 750 hours of lathe time available, the unused amount of this resource would be $750 - 280 = 470$ hours. This would be the value of the lathe time slack, S_1. This value could have been determined directly from Equation (1) by substituting the values $v = 100$ and $p = 120$ and solving for S_1.

Excluding the value z of the objective function, there are five variables in the problem. Only two of them are decision variables, or what are frequently called activity variables. The other three variables are slack variables, representing unused resources. The variable z is not a decision variable, since its value depends on the value of those variables appearing in the objective function. Incidentally, although the objective function looks different than before, it has not changed. All we have done is to place all the variables on the left-hand side of the equation.

At this point, we introduce some terminology which has become commonly accepted in the analysis of linear programming models. Any solution of the problem satisfying all the constraints is called a *feasible solution*. As we observed earlier, we will be interested only in a feasible solution which occurs at an extreme point, or vertex. Such a solution is called a *basic feasible solution*. In general, with n decision variables and m inequality constraints (restrictions) requiring m slack variables, any basic feasible solution will have at most m variables with nonzero values. These "nonzero" variables are called *basic variables*, and the set of basic variables is often called the *basis*. The "zero" variables are termed *nonbasic variables*. The term "basic" comes from the condition that, using the simplex algorithm, we always solve a system of m equations in $m + n$ unknowns by setting n variables to zero and then solving the resulting system of m equations in m unknowns, giving a unique *basic solution*. A basic solution will be infeasible if it contains any variables with negative values, but we will always work with a basic feasible solution. We will find that the simplex algorithm starts with an initial basic feasible solution, moving to successive basic feasible solutions and terminating when the optimal basic feasible solution has been reached.

In Figure 5, we show again the feasible region, this time with each vertex numbered. At each vertex, two of the five variables must be zero, since there are three constraint equations and there must be one and only one basic (nonzero) variable for every constraint equation. The graph shows only the values of the two decision variables, but by noting which two of the five variables are zero at each vertex, we can readily solve for the values of the other three variables. Table 2 shows the value of all variables and the associated profit z.

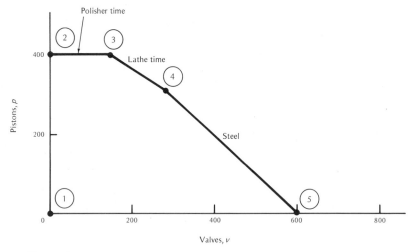

Figure 5

A brief discussion of Table 2 may be helpful. To show how the numbers are derived, consider vertex 3, for example. Since vertex 3 is on both the polisher time and the lathe time constraint lines, all available polisher time and lathe time is being used. The slack variables S_1 and S_2 associated with these resources must therefore be zero. From Equation (2), p must then be 400. Substituting this value of p in Equation (1), v must equal 150, since S_1 is zero. Going to Equation (3), we now find that S_3 must be 50, since $v + p = 550$. From the objective function, Equation (4), z equals \$2050. Note that at vertex 4, where S_1 and S_3 are zero, we have to solve Equations (1) and (3) simultaneously to get the values of v and p.

Although it is theoretically possible to enumerate all basic feasible solution points, it is computationally quite impractical to do so, since the number of such solutions could be as large as $(m + n)!/(m!n!)$. The simplex algorithm provides us with an efficient algebraic technique for

Vertex Number	"Zero" Variables	VARIABLES		SLACK VARIABLES			Profit ($)
		Valves v	Pistons p	Lathe Time (hr) S_1	Polisher Time (hr) S_2	Steel (lb) S_3	z
1	v, p	0	0	750	200	600	0
2	v, S_2	0	400	150	0	200	1600
3	S_1, S_2	150	400	0	0	50	2050
4	S_1, S_3	300	300	0	50	0	2100
5	p, S_3	600	0	150	200	0	1800

Table 2. Basic Feasible Solutions

moving from one basic feasible solution to another basic feasible solution until the optimal solution is reached. The steps of the procedure are listed below for problems where the constraints are all in the form of restrictions.

1. Choose an initial basic feasible solution.

2. Examine the objective function and determine whether there is at least one nonbasic variable which would improve the solution if its value were increased from its current value of zero. If so, choose the nonbasic variable which, for each unit increase in its value, yields the greatest increase in the value of the objective function. (We call this nonbasic variable the "entering variable.") If no such improvement is possible, stop—the optimal solution has been reached.

3. For the entering variable, increase its value until a current basic variable is forced down to a value of zero. We call this current basic variable the "departing variable."

4. With the exception of the constraint equation where the departing variable has been forced to zero, eliminate the entering variable from all other equations, including the objective function. Go back to step 2.

In Table 2, as the solution moved from one vertex to an adjacent vertex, the second column shows that it was always true that one of the two nonbasic ("zero") variables went into the solution as a basic variable (the entering variable) and was replaced by a previously basic variable (the departing variable).

The development of each new basic feasible solution, always moving toward an optimal solution, is called an *iteration*. (A flow chart of the simplex algorithm is shown later, in Figure 6, after the computational procedure has been explained in some detail.)

The initial basic feasible solution is obtained in a very straightforward manner. We start at the origin by setting all activity variables (v and p) to zero. From equations (1) to (3), we can immediately see that $S_1 = 750$, $S_2 = 200$, and $S_3 = 600$. The profit z is zero, from equation (4). Obviously, we can do better, since we produce nothing and utilize none of the available resources. Clearly, the solution can be improved by increasing either v or p. As a general rule, the entering variable will be that variable with the highest per-unit profit contribution. In this example, each unit of v contributes \$3, while each unit of p contributes \$4. Therefore, we want to bring in as many units of p as possible. (We could select as the entering variable that variable which yields the greatest *total* profit, but this involves considerably more computational effort. Such effort has not, in general, paid off by reducing the overall computational time to arrive at an optimal solution.) Note that we make only one interchange of variables at a time, in order to make certain that we move from one basic feasible solution to another.

The required calculations will turn out to be quite straightforward because of the particular form of the equations involved. An examination of Equations (1) to (4) will show that they meet two primary conditions: (1) each constraint equation contains exactly one basic variable, and that variable has a coefficient of one; (2) each basic variable appears in one and only one constraint equation and does not appear in the objective function. A set of equations meeting these conditions is said to be in *canonical form*. In the simplex algorithm, the equations will always be in canonical form. We will first state the simplex procedure and then illustrate it using the Valvton problem, Example 1.

Always working from a canonical set of equations, the procedure is basically as follows.

1. The variable with the most negative coefficient in the z (objective function) equation is selected as the entering variable. In case of a tie, an arbitrary selection may be made. If none of the z equation coefficients are negative, stop—the optimal solution has been reached.

2. In each constraint equation, if the coefficient of the entering variable is positive, divide that coefficient into the RHS (right-hand side) value, to get what we can call a *test ratio*. (If the coefficient of the entering variable is zero or negative, ignore this equation, since this constraint cannot limit the value of the entering variable.) Choose, as the so-called *pivot equation*, that equation which has the smallest test ratio. The departing variable will be the current basic variable in the pivot equation. The coefficient of the entering variable in the pivot equation is called the *pivot element*.

3. All coefficients in the pivot equation are divided by the pivot element, and the entering variable now becomes the basic variable in that equation. We call this equation the new pivot equation, and it becomes the initial constraint equation in the next canonical set, although its row position need not change.

4. In the new pivot equation, solve for the value of the entering variable. Use the resultant expression to replace (and thus eliminate) the entering variable in all equations other than the pivot equation, including the z equation.

5. Multiply out and combine terms to form the new set of canonical equations, including the pivot equation. Specify the solution. Go to step 1.

Although we will stress the importance of computer solution of linear programming problems, we will now show, for completeness, how the computational procedures of the simplex algorithm can be mechanized.

Computational Procedure of the Simplex Algorithm

The linear system of equations in the linear programming model can be conveniently represented in tabular form. By "detaching" the variable symbols from their coefficients, leaving an array of numbers representing the coefficients and constant terms, we now have what is called a *tableau*, in linear programming jargon. For the example problem, the initial tableau is shown in Table 3. (The data on grinder time have been eliminated, because the grinder time constraint is redundant, being dominated by at least one other constraint. This redundant constraint would be handled properly, but its inclusion would only complicate the calculations.)

BASIS	v	p	S_1	S_2	S_3	RHS
S_1	1	1.5	1	0	0	750
S_2	0	0.5	0	1	0	200
S_3	1	1	0	0	1	600
z	−3	−4	0	0	0	0

Table 3. Initial Tableau

The symbol for each variable appears at the head of the column of its detached coefficients, and RHS stands for right-hand side value, as mentioned earlier. Note that the variable z does not appear as a column entry. This is customary, since the detached coefficients for the variable representing the value of the objective function will always be the same—a one in the final (objective function) row and zeroes in all other rows. Adding this column would therefore contribute no useful information. From the data of Table 3, the variables constituting the basis are readily identified. As we have noted, the basic variable in a given constraint equation will have a coefficient of one in that equation and a coefficient of zero in all the other equations, including the objective function. The computational procedures here take advantage of the column alignment of coefficients and also generally use the term "row" in place of "equation."

1. Select the column containing the nonbasic variable with the most negative coefficient in the z (objective function) row. The variable in that column, frequently called the *pivot column*, will be the entering variable. If none of the z row coefficients are negative, stop—the optimal solution has been reached.

From the tableau in Table 4, which is a "working copy" of Table 3, the pivot column is marked by an arrow below -4, the most negative value for a nonbasic variable in the z row. The entering variable is p.

2. In each constraint row, if the coefficient of the entering variable is positive, divide that coefficient into the RHS value, to get the test ratio. (If the coefficient of the entering variable is zero or negative, ignore this row, since this constraint cannot limit the value of the entering variable.) Choose, as the *pivot row*, that row which has the smallest test ratio. The departing variable will be the current basic variable in the pivot row. The coefficient of the entering variable in the pivot row is called the pivot element.

In the tableau of Table 4, all coefficients of the entering variable are positive in the constraint equations, and the resulting test ratios are shown in the last column of that table. Since the smallest test ratio appears in row 2, that becomes the pivot row, and it is marked by an arrow. The departing variable is the current basic variable in that row, S_2. The pivot element, the coefficient in both the pivot row and the pivot column, is 0.5, which is asterisked in the table.

BASIS	v	p	S_1	S_2	S_3	RHS	TEST RATIO
S_1	1	1.5	1	0	0	750	750/1.5 = 500
→S_2	0	*0.5	0	1	0	200	200/0.5 = 400
S_3	1	1	0	0	1	600	600/1 = 600
z	-3	-4	0	0	0	0	
		↑					

Table 4. Tableau I (initial tableau)

3. *All* coefficients in the pivot row are divided by the pivot element, and the entering variable now becomes the basic variable

in that row. We call this equation the new pivot equation, and it becomes the initial constraint equation in the next tableau, although its row position does not change. (Preserving the order of the constraint equations will be useful in later analyses, but it is not a requirement of the solution process.)

Dividing the pivot row, row 2, by the pivot element, 0.5, we get the initial constraint equation of the next tableau, as shown in row 2 of Table 5 (see page 452). The basic variable in this new pivot equation is now p, the entering variable.

> 4. In all rows other than the pivot row, including the z row, eliminate the coefficient of the entering variable by substituting for the entering variable its algebraic equivalent, using the new pivot equation. (As will be shown, this can be done by multiplying the pivot equation coefficients by the coefficient of the entering variable and subtracting.) These equations become the new constraint equations and the new objective function.

For the first constraint equation in Table 4, the coefficient in the pivot column is 1.5, so we subtract 1.5 times the new pivot equation (the second constraint equation in Table 5), thereby eliminating the coefficient of p in the new equation. The result, in coefficient form, is shown below.

v	p	s_1	s_2	s_3	RHS
1	1.5	1	0	0	750
$-(0$	1.5	0	3	0	600)
1	0	1	-3	0	150

The resulting coefficients are the coefficients of the first constraint equation in Table 5.

Since the second constraint equation in Table 4 became the new pivot equation, we move on to the third constraint equation in Table 4. Its coefficient in the pivot column is 1.0, so we subtract 1.0 times the new pivot equation. This becomes the third constraint equation in Table 5.

v	p	s_1	s_2	s_3	RHS
1	1	0	0	1	600
$-(0$	1	0	2	0	400)
1	0	0	-2	1	200

Finally, to calculate the new objective function, the required multiplier of the new pivot equation is -4.

v	p	S_1	S_2	S_3	RHS
-3	-4	0	0	0	0
-(0	-4	0	-8	0	-1600)
-3	0	0	8	0	1600

This is the z row in Table 5. Now we would return to step 1.

BASIS	v	p	S_1	S_2	S_3	RHS	TEST RATIO
→ S_1	*1	0	1	-3	0	150	150/1 = 150
p	.0	1	0	2	0	400	—
S_3	1	0	0	-2	1	200	200/1 = 200
z	-3 ↑	0	0	8	0	1600	

Table 5. Tableau II

Starting with Tableau II in Table 5 and following the four-step procedure just detailed, the computations of the simplex algorithm were carried out for the next two iterations, producing Table 6 and Table 7, where the optimal solution is indicated by the absence of any negative coefficients of the nonbasic variables in the z row. The computations for these two tables are not difficult, and you can readily perform them to verify that you understand the simplex algorithm.

BASIS	v	p	S_1	S_2	S_3	RHS	TEST RATIO
v	1	0	1	-3	0	150	—
p	0	1	0	2	0	400	400/2 = 200
→ S_3	0	0	-1	*1	1	50	50/1 = 50
z	0	0	3	-1 ↑	0	2050	

Table 6. Tableau III

BASIS	v	p	S_1	S_2	S_3	RHS
v	1	0	-2	0	3	300
p	0	1	2	0	-2	300
S_2	0	0	-1	1	1	50
z	0	0	2	0	1	2100

Table 7. Tableau IV Optimal Solution

A flow chart of the simplex algorithm is shown as Figure 6.

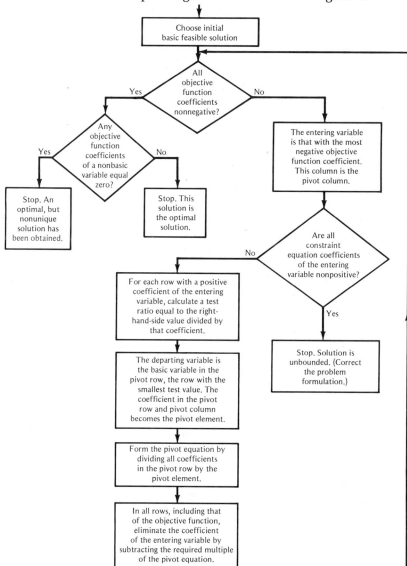

Figure 6. Flow Chart of the Simplex Algorithm

COMPUTER SOLUTION OF
LINEAR PROGRAMMING PROBLEMS

In the real world, practical linear programming problems are always solved by computer. Hand computations are completely impractical for problems other than very small ones, and even the manual solution of small problems is generally avoided because of the high probability of making arithmetic errors. Thus, after learning the fundamental concepts associated with the simplex method, it appears desirable to become acquainted with the general preparation of input data for a linear programming computer program and the analysis of the output data printed out when the optimal solution is reached.

For computer solution, the linear system of equations can be conveniently represented in tableau form, as we have demonstrated. The initial tableau for the Valvton problem is shown in Table 3.

Let us now go through the steps necessary to set up this problem for computer solution. Although a large number of linear programming computer programs are available, we will not discuss any one particular program but will illustrate the general principles involved. We will discuss the preparation of the required input data and the analysis of the most unsophisticated type of output, consisting solely of the coefficients in the final optimal tableau. This output is readily available and, although minimal, is sufficient to give us a good deal of information if we know how to analyze it.

The following numerical data must be input (in one form or another) to the program in an order dependent on the design of the particular program.

1. Number of constraint equations of each type
   a) Restrictions ("less-than" inequalities)
   b) Equalities
   c) Requirements ("greater than" inequalities)
2. Number of activity variables
3. Table of constraint equations coefficients, with the rows arranged in a given order, such as restrictions first, equalities, and then requirements
4. Column of RHS initial values
5. Objective function coefficients
6. Information as to whether this is a minimization or maximization problem

After the input data has been read in, the computer program usually supplies all required surplus, slack, and artificial variables "automatically." The program then performs the required iterations until the optimal solution is reached. At that point, as shown in Table 8, the optimal tableau is printed out. (This tableau contains the same information as that of Table 7.) Although it is admittedly not in a very handy form, the tableau contains a good deal of useful information, as we will see.

To make the interpretation a little more straightforward, the dotted lines have been drawn to set off the column of right-hand side values and the objective function row. We can now derive the following information, some of which has been discussed previously.

v	p	S_1	S_2	S_3	RHS
1	0	−2	0	3	300
0	1	2	0	−2	300
0	0	−1	1	1	50
0	0	2	0	1	2100

Table 8. Optimal Tableau

1. The RHS column gives solution values for the basic variables, which are identified as those with a coefficient of 1 in just one constraint equation and a coefficient of 0 in all other equations. Thus, v, p, and S_2 are basic variables. For each of these variables, the value of that basic variable is then equal to the RHS value in the row in which its coefficient of 1 appears. Thus, in the first row, we see that $v = 300$; in the second row, that $p = 300$; and in the third row, that $S_2 = 50$.

2. The profit z is found in the lower right-hand corner, in the objective function row and the RHS column, and is equal to $2100.

3. In the *optimal tableau*, the values in the objective function row (excluding, obviously, the RHS value) are called "shadow prices." These represent the rate of decrease (increase) in the value of the objective function for each unit increase (decrease) in the value of the associated nonbasic variable. Thus the total profit would decrease by $2 for every unit of S_1 in the solution. Since S_1 represents lathe time slack and the available lathe time is completely utilized, a unit increase in S_1 has the identical effect as a unit decrease in the amount of lathe time available. Similarly, a unit increase in S_3, steel slack, is the same as a unit decrease in steel availability, and would decrease total profit by $1.* *The shadow prices are applicable so long as the optimal basis remains feasible.*

4. The coefficients above and to the left of the dotted lines represent substitution rates for basic variables. If there is a change in the level of any nonbasic variable, its effect may be calculated, in turn, on each constraint equation by subtracting algebraically, from the RHS value, the amount of the change times the substitution rate for that variable. This is a very important feature and will be discussed in detail in the following section.

SENSITIVITY ANALYSIS

In actual practice, it is often not enough simply to obtain the optimal solution and consider the problem solved. Frequently, we would like to know the effect on the optimal solution if constraints or objective function coeffi-

---

*Editors' Note: See footnote 8 in the Part V introductory discussion.

cients change. Working from the previous optimal solution tableau, it is usually possible to evaluate numerically the effect of such changes without solving the problem again from scratch. In the analyses that follow, we will consider only changes in one variable at a time.

In the final tableau (and any other tableau, for that matter), the substitution rates represented by the various coefficients are applicable only as long as the basis does not change. Therefore, one of the first things we would like to do is to determine the range over which some of the more important factors can change without changing the basis.

Changes in Right-Hand Side Values in Original Tableau

After having obtained an optimal solution, suppose we were informed that the available amount of resource k had changed, either up or down. If the change in this resource is such that the optimal basis remains *feasible*, it will be unnecessary to calculate a new solution to determine the change in total profit. For each unit increase (decrease) in this resource, the total profit will increase (decrease) by the value of the shadow price associated with the slack variable S_k for this resource. We wish to find the permissible range for the amount of this resource such that the shadow price is applicable.

We will let Δ^+ be the maximum allowable increase and Δ^- be the maximum allowable decrease in the available amount of a given resource. There are two cases to be considered.

> *Case 1.* Resource k is not fully utilized, so that its associated slack variable S_k has a positive value. In this situation, the shadow price will always be zero, since additional units of the resource have no value. This shadow price applies for an unlimited increase in the amount of this resource, so that $\Delta^+ = \infty$. On the other hand, we could decrease this resource only until the slack vanishes, so that $\Delta^- = S_k$.

> *Case 2.* Resource k is fully utilized, so that its associated slack variable $S_k = 0$. The procedure for determining the value of Δ^- is the same as that for determining, in the simplex algorithm, how many units of the entering variable should come into the solution. In the column in which slack variable S_k appears, calculate the test ratio for each row. The smallest positive test ratio is the value of Δ^-. If there is no positive test ratio, Δ^- is unlimited. For Δ^+, the process is entirely similar, except that we consider only negative test ratios. The smallest absolute value of all negative test ratios is Δ^+. An absence of negative test ratios means that Δ^+ is unlimited.

In Table 9 are shown the calculations involved in determining the allowable range over which each of the three resource amounts can vary without

RESOURCE	ORIGINAL VALUE	SLACK VARIABLE AND ITS OPTIMAL VALUE	TEST RATIOS	MAXIMUM ALLOWABLE CHANGE Δ^-	Δ^+	ALLOWABLE RANGE
Lathe time	750 hr	$S_1 = 0$	$\dfrac{300}{-2} = -150$			(750 − 150 to 750 + 50)
			$\dfrac{300}{2} = 150$	150		600 to 800 hr
			$\dfrac{50}{-1} = -50$		50	
Polisher time	200 hr	$S_2 = 50$	—	50	∞	(200 − 50 to 200 + ∞) ≥ 150 hr
Steel	600 lb	$S_3 = 0$	$\dfrac{300}{3} = 100$			(600 − 50 to 600 + 150)
			$\dfrac{300}{-2} = -150$		150	550 to 750 lb
			$\dfrac{50}{1} = 50$	50		

Table 9. Sensitivity Analysis of RHS Values

changing the basis. The original values of the resource amounts are taken from Table 1, while the values of the slack variables and their associated test ratios are derived from the data of Table 8.

To explain the rationale behind this sensitivity analysis, consider the first Δ^- value of 150 in Table 9. If the lathe time resource were reduced from 750 to 600 hours, this would be equivalent to having the original 750 hours, but with 150 hours of lathe time slack, S_1. In the second row of Table 8, the basic variable $p = 300$. With an S_1 value of 150, p would be driven to zero. (Remember that S_3 is nonbasic, so its value is already zero.) If the lathe time resource were reduced by more than 150 hours, p would be forced out of the basis and it would be necessary to perform another iteration to determine the new optimal solution. The Δ^+ value of 50 is derived from the third row equation. If the lathe time resource were increased from 750 to 800 hours, this would be equivalent to having the original 750 hours, but with −50 hours of lathe time slack S_1. With an S_1 value of −50, the basic variable, S_2, in the third row, would be driven to zero. If S_1 were more negative, S_2 would be driven out of the basis, and the shadow price would no longer be applicable.

The polisher time resource is not fully utilized in the optimal solution, since its slack variable $S_2 = 50$. Thus, $\Delta^- = 50$, and Δ^+ is unlimited, so that the shadow price of zero applies over a range of (200 − 50) to (200 + ∞), or for polisher time ≥ 150 hours.

For the steel resource, the associated slack variable, S_3, is zero, so that the available steel is completely utilized. We then follow the same procedure as for the lathe time resource. The maximum allowable positive value is 50, so $\Delta^- = 50$, and the maximum allowable negative value is -150, so $\Delta^+ = 150$. Since the original constraint value was 600 pounds, the amount of steel could range between $600 - 50$ and $600 + 150$, or from 550 to 750 pounds, without changing the basis.

A comment on negative slack variables (used in the calculation of Δ^+ values) is in order. Earlier, we said that none of the variables in a basic feasible solution could be negative. This is still true. The concept of a negative slack variable is an artificiality, introduced after the solution process has been completed, to represent the effect of an increase in a resource. Note that our analysis of RHS value changes arrived at a range of values for the amount of each resource, and this range can never include negative values.

Having gone through all these computations, we now know the range of applicability for the shadow prices shown in the final tableau. For example, the basis would still be optimal if the lathe time were reduced by 150 hours, and, since the lathe time shadow price is $2 per hour, the resultant profit would be $2100 - (150)(2.00) = \$1800$. Lathe time could be increased by 50 hours, with an additional profit of $(5)(2.00)$, for a total profit of $2200. The first 50 hours of polisher time removed will have no effect on the solution, since we have an excess supply of this resource. Additional polisher time, in any amount, is, of course, worthless. In either case, any such change will not affect the total profit, since the shadow price of polisher time is zero. If we attempted to remove more than 50 hours of polisher time, the basis would change and we would have to perform a new iteration. As for steel, a 50 pound decrease in the available amount will drop the profit to $2100 - (50)(1)$ or $2050, whereas an additional 150 pounds would raise the profit to $2250.

Calculating the Effect on Basic Variables

Now that we know how to calculate the new profit value for permissible one-at-a-time changes in our resources, we would also like to determine the associated changes in the values of the basic variables. This is easily done. In each row, the new value of the basic variable will be equal to the RHS value in the optimal tableau minus the amount of the resource change multiplied by the coefficient of its slack variable (the substitution rate) in that equation, carefully observing its algebraic sign. For example, suppose that lathe time availability is decreased by 100 hours. This represents a positive slack of 100 hours. Remembering that S_3 is zero, the first constraint equation could be written as

$$v - (2)(100) = 300,$$

so,

$$v = 300 + 200 = 500.$$

In the second equation,

$$p = 300 - (2)(100) = 100.$$

In the third equation,

$$S_2 = 50 - (-1)(100) = 150.$$

If lathe time were to be increased by 100 hours, equivalent to a negative slack of 100, this would be outside the range of applicability and the basis would have to change, invalidating the existing shadow prices and substitution rates.

The analysis here has considered only changes in the RHS values of constraints involving restrictions, or $\leq$ inequalities. Similar analyses can be performed for changes in the RHS values for requirements constraints, which have $\geq$ inequalities.

Changes in Original Objective Function Coefficients

If the original objective function coefficients, the unit profits, of the basic decision variables change, the optimal profit will change. For each of these coefficients, we can determine the range over which they can change *without changing the basis*. Over that range, the change in profit will be equal to the change in the particular coefficient multiplied by the number of units of that variable in the optimal solution. Unlike the case where RHS values change, changes in the original objective function coefficients do not affect the values of the basic variables, so long as the basis is not changed.

Suppose we let Δ^+ be the maximum allowable increase, and Δ^- the maximum allowable decrease, in the value of the objective function coefficient for a given decision variable. The analysis depends on whether the decision variable is nonbasic or basic in the optimal solution.

Nonbasic Variable
The shadow price of a nonbasic variable is the amount by which it is unprofitable, so Δ^+ is equal to the shadow price. A greater increase would require the nonbasic variable to come into the solution. Since a decrease in the objective function coefficient would just make units of that decision variable even more unprofitable, Δ^- is unlimited. (For a minimization problem, Δ^- would equal the magnitude of the shadow price, while the value of Δ^+ would be unlimited.)

Basic Variable
Before going through the somewhat complicated explanation of the effect of a change in the objective function coefficient of a basic variable, we will show that it is not difficult to mechanize the required computations in a manner quite similar to that shown for the evaluation of resource changes.

For each nonzero coefficient in the objective function row, we calculate a test ratio equal to that coefficient divided by the coefficient which is the same column and in the row in which the variable of interest is basic. The smallest positive test ratio becomes Δ^-. If there is no positive test ratio, Δ^- is unlimited. The smallest absolute value of all negative test ratios is Δ^+. Δ^+ is unlimited if there is no negative test ratio.

Table 10 shows, for the Valvton problem data of Table 8, the analysis of the changes in the objective function coefficients of the two activity variables such that the optimal solution basis will not change.

DECISION VARIABLE	BASIC IN ROW	ORIGINAL OBJECTIVE FUNCTION VALUE*	TEST RATIOS	MAXIMUM ALLOWABLE CHANGE Δ^-	Δ^+	ALLOWABLE RANGE
v	1	\$3.00	$\frac{2}{-2} = -1$		1	(3.00 − 0.33 to 3.00 + 1.00)
			$\frac{1}{3} = 0.33$	0.33		\$2.67 to \$4.00
p	2	\$4.00	$\frac{2}{2} = 1$	1		(4.00 − 1.00 to 4.00 − 0.50)
			$\frac{1}{-2} = -0.5$		0.5	\$3.00 to \$4.50

*From Table 1

Table 10. Sensitivity Analysis of Objective Function Coefficients

When a decision variable is basic in the optimal solution, we go through a procedure generally similar in nature to that involved in analyzing the effect of a change in the amount of a resource already fully utilized in the optimal solution. Now, however, the test ratio involves the objective function coefficients rather than the RHS values. As an example of the rationale behind the calculations in Table 10, consider decision variable v, which is basic in the optimal solution. Suppose its objective function coefficient is *decreased* by an amount d. Thus, an amount dv is added to the objective function equation, which now becomes

$$dv + 2S_1 + S_3 + z = 2100.$$

Since v is a basic variable, it must be eliminated from the objective function equation, just as though v were an entering variable in a simplex iteration. (Remember that a basic variable cannot have a nonzero coefficient in the objective function.) As a basic variable, v appears only in the first constraint equation, where

$$v - 2S_1 + 3S_3 = 300,$$

so

$$v = 300 + 2S_1 - 3S_3.$$

Substituting this expression in the objective function equation, we get

$$d(300 + 2S_1 - 3S_3) + 2S_1 + S_3 + z = 2100,$$

so that

$$(2 + 2d)S_1 + (1 - 3d)S_3 + z = 2100 - 300d.$$

We set, in turn, each of the coefficients of the nonbasic variables (S_1 and S_3, in this case) to zero. We can then determine the maximum allowable change in d before a nonbasic variable would come into the solution, thus changing the basis.

For S_1: $2 + 2d = 0$,   so $d = 2/(-2) = -1$.
For S_3: $1 - 3d = 0$,   so $d = 1/3$.

With only one positive and one negative test ratio, $\Delta^- = \frac{1}{3}$ and $\Delta^+ = 1$. Thus, the original objective function coefficient of v can be increased by 1 or decreased by 0.33. With a given value of \$3, the unit profit of valves can therefore range from \$2.67 to \$4 without changing the basis. Within this range, a decrease (increase) of \$$d$ would decrease (increase) z by \$300d, since $v = 300$ in the optimal solution.

The analysis for activity variable p, which is basic in row 2 of the optimal solution, is performed in the same fashion. The unit profit for pistons could drop by as much as \$1 or increase by \$0.50 without changing the basis. Since there are 300 pistons in the optimal solution, a change of \$$d$ in the unit profit would result in a \$300d change in z.

In this small-scale example, there were no nonbasic activity variables. Suppose, however, that the optimal solution had included no values, so $v = 0$, and that the associated shadow price for v was \$1.25. Then, since the original unit profit of valves was \$3, the shadow price for v would indicate that valves were unprofitable by \$1.25. Their profit would have to be increased to more than \$4.25 before they would come into the solution. On the other hand, their original unit profit could be decreased by any amount without affecting the solution, since they would just become more unprofitable.

With only two activity variables in this problem, the change in the objective function coefficients of these variables can be interpreted graphically. If the unit profit of p is held at \$4, varying the unit profit of v from \$2.67 to \$4 causes the slope of the objective function to range between $-2.67/4 = -2/3$ and $-4/4 = -1$. Referring back to Figure 4, these are precisely the slopes of the lathe time and steel constraints, respectively, as can be verified by checking Equations (1) and (3). For any objective function whose slope falls between those limiting values, the currently optimal solution point at the intersection of the lathe time and steel constraints will remain optimal. In a similar fashion, holding the unit profit of v at \$3 and varying the unit profit of p from \$3 to \$4.50 results in a change in the objective function slope over a range of $-3/3 = -1$ to $-3/4.50 = -2/3$. This is again the range in slopes for which the current optimal solution remains optimal.

It is also worth noting that, since it is the *ratio* of the coefficients of v and p which determines the slope, any value of that ratio falling between 2/3 and 1 will not change the existing optimal solution basis. Thus, if the unit profit of v dropped to \$2 and the unit profit of p fell anywhere within the range of \$2 to \$3, the current solution would remain optimal.

Sensitivity analyses can also be performed on the constraint equation coefficients, but this becomes considerably more complicated. Since this type of analysis almost mandates the use of matrix arithmetic, which has not been discussed, it will not be covered. There is also another technique, called *parametric programming*, which extends the techniques of sensitivity analysis.

The following example is presented to tie together the material on optimal solutions and sensitivity analysis.

Example 2

A company manufactures three products, A, B, and C. Each product must be machine-processed in three departments, as shown in the following table.

| | MACHINE TIME REQUIRED (HR) | | | |
PRODUCT	Dept. 1	Dept. 2	Dept. 3	PER UNIT PROFIT CONTRIBUTION
A	1	1	2	\$30
B	2	1	1	25
C	1	2	1	35
Hours available per month	800	1000	2000	

Table 11. Problem Data

A computer LP program, after two iterations, gives the optimal tableau as in the accompanying table.

a) What is the optimal product mix?

Let x_1 = units of product A
x_2 = units of product B
x_3 = units of product C
S_1 = Dept. 1 slack, in hours
S_2 = Dept. 2 slack, in hours
S_3 = Dept. 3 slack, in hours

PRODUCT			SLACK			
A	B	C	Dept. 1	Dept. 2	Dept. 3	RHS
1	3	0	2	1	0	600
0	1	1	−1	1	0	200
0	−4	0	−3	1	1	600
0	30	0	25	5	0	25,000

Table 12. Optimal Solution

Basic variables — row 1: $x_1 = 600$
                — row 2: $x_3 = 200$
                — row 3: $S_3 = 600$
Optimal product mix: 600 units of product A, 200 units of product C.

b) What is the total profit? Check this value by totaling the profit from the individual products.

From the z row, $z = 25,000$. Total profit $= \$25,000$.

Individual profit contributions — product A: (600)(30) $=$ \$18,000
                                   — product B: (0)(25) $=$ 0
                                   — product C: (200)(35) $=$ 7,000
                                                           \$25,000

c) How many processing hours are being used in each department?

The easy way to answer this question is to utilize the values of the slacks.
Dept. 1: 800 hours available. $S_1 = $ 0.   800 hours used.
Dept. 2: 1000 hours available. $S_2 = $ 0.   1000 hours used.
Dept. 3: 2000 hours available. $S_3 = 600$.   1400 hours used.

Check by totaling machine time requirements for each product. Working from the per unit values in Table 11:

Dept. 1: (1)(600) + (2)(0) + (1)(200) $= $ 800 hours
Dept. 2: (1)(600) + (1)(0) + (2)(200) $=$ 1000 hours
Dept. 3: (2)(600) + (1)(0) + (1)(200) $=$ 1400 hours

d) For each department, determine the range over which the basis would remain unchanged.

Dept.	Original Value (hr)	Slack	Test Ratios	Allowable Δ^-	Δ^+	Range
1	800	$S_1 = 0$	600/2 $= $ 300	300		(800 − 300
			200/−1 $=$ −200		200	to 800 + 200)
			600/−3 $=$ −200		200	500 to 1000 hr
2	1000	$S_2 = 0$	600/−1 $=$ −600		600	(1000 − 200
			200/1 $= $ 200	200		to 1000 + 600)
			600/1 $= $ 600			800 to 1600 hr
3	2000	$S_3 = 600$	—	600	∞	≥ 1400 hr

e) An additional 10 hours in each department would be worth how much? Consider one department at a time.

Observe that, for all three departments, the value of 10 hours is well within the allowable range for the optimal basis to remain unchanged, so that all that has to be done is to multiply the 10 hours by the appropriate shadow price.

$$\text{Dept. 1: } (10)(25) = \$250.$$
$$\text{Dept. 2: } (10)(5) \ = \$ \ 50.$$
$$\text{Dept. 3: } (10)(0) \ = \$ \ \ 0.$$

(Since machine time in Department 3 is already in oversupply, additional time in that department is clearly worthless.)

    f) If the availability of processing time in Department 1 were increased to 900 hours, how would the solution change? (Work this out directly from the optimal tableau.) Evaluate the new profit directly and then check it by summing the individual product profits.

The value of 900 hours, which is within the allowable range for Department 1 machine time, must be expressed in terms of the slack which it represents. Since 900 hours is 100 hours more than is currently available in Department 1, this is equivalent to a negative slack, so $S_1 = -100$. The product of the value of S_1 and, in turn, each of the coefficients (substitution rates) in the column for Department 1 slack, will determine the change in the basis variables. (Remember that nonbasic variables x_2 and S_2 have a value of zero.)

$$\text{Row 1: } x_1 + \ \ (2)(-100) = \ \ \ \ 600, \ x_1 = 800 \text{ units.}$$
$$\text{Row 2: } x_3 + (-1)(-100) = \ \ \ \ 200, \ x_3 = 100 \text{ units.}$$
$$\text{Row 3: } S_3 + (-3)(-100) = \ \ \ \ 600, \ S_3 = 300 \text{ hours.}$$
$$\text{z row: } \ \ z + (25)(-100) = 25{,}000, \ \ z = \$27{,}500.$$

New solution: 800 units of product A, 100 units of product C.

$$\text{Total profit} = \$27{,}500.$$

Check: Total profit $= (800)(30) + (0)(25) + (100)(35) = \$27{,}500.$

    g) Over what range could the unit profits of the three products change, one at a time, without changing the product mix?

Product	Basic in Row	Original Profit ($)	Column Test Ratios	Δ^-	Δ^+	Allowable Range
A	1	30	30/3 = 10	10		(30 − 10
			25/2 = 12.5			to 30 + 5)
			5/−1 = −5		5	$20 to $35
B	Nonbasic	25	—	∞	30	(25 − ∞
(Product B is currently unprofitable						to 25 + 30)
by the shadow price of $30.)						≤$55
C	2	35	30/−1 = −30			(35 − 5
			25/−1 = −25		25	to 35 + 25)
			5/1 = 5	5		$30 to $60

    h) If the profit on each product, considered individually, were to drop by $2, what would be the effect on total profit?

Verify first that the $2 change is within the allowable range for all three products.

Product	Units in Optimal Solution	Profit Change ($) Per Unit	Profit Change ($) Total	New Total Profit
A	600	−2	−1200	25,000 − 1200 = $23,800
B	0	−2	0	25,000
C	200	−2	−400	25,000 − 400 = 24,600

31.
INVENTORY CONTROL*

Robert D. Niemeyer

Inventory control is concerned with establishing and maintaining desired inventory levels. In keeping with this concept, the inventory control techniques that will be discussed are directed toward unit control of inventory rather than the closely related function of accounting for inventory dollars.

Broadly stated, the basic objective of inventory control is to establish and maintain an adequate inventory level at a minimum inventory cost. Achievement of this objective requires solution to two basic problems:

Determination of desired inventory levels, weighing inventory costs against such inventory benefits as:

> Improved customer service that may result in increased sales
> Smoother production operations yielding lower production costs

Minimization of total inventory costs for a given inventory level, giving consideration to the interaction between:

> Acquisition costs
> Holding costs

An approach to the solution of these basic inventory control problems will be discussed in the following sequence:

> Methods of control
> Inventory costs
> Determination of expected inventory usage
> Other refinements

---

*From *Management Services (Management Adviser)*, July–August 1964, pp. 25–31.

There are two primary factors that must be considered in the control of inventories:

> *How much* of an item is replenished at a time
> *When* the item is replenished

These two factors control inventory levels, and through these factors, total inventory costs can be minimized for any given inventory level.

HOW MUCH

In discussing this factor, we should first look at the basic saw-tooth inventory pattern to visualize the effect of replenishment quantities on inventory levels. This basic pattern is depicted in Charts 1 and 2.

In these charts we have assumed that the "when" factor is controlled so that a replenishment is received when on-hand balance has reached zero. From Chart 1 we can also easily see that the average inventory is 100 and that this amount is also equal to one-half of the replenishment quantity. If we increase the order quantity to 300 units, we increase the average inventory to 150 units as shown on Chart 2.

WHEN

Charts 1 and 2 demonstrate that "how much" is a definite factor in determining inventory levels. Now consider the "when" factor. On these charts, the "when" factor was controlled so that a replenishment was received when the on-hand balance reached zero. However, some replenishment lead time is normally involved and this factor must be known in solving the "when" problem. Assuming a lead time of one month, we find that on our first chart the items must be ordered at the end of the first month so that replenishment will arrive when on-hand balance reaches zero. This order point could also be expressed in terms of on-hand balance as 100 units, this quantity representing expected usage during the lead-time period. So we see that lead time and expected usage are both required for determining a reorder point expressed in terms of on-hand balance. However, we have not yet considered just how the "when" factor influences inventory levels. When we do this, we find that the basic saw-tooth pattern with usage and other variations would appear as shown on Charts 3 and 4.

In Chart 3 the basic inventory pattern is disrupted by two factors found in practical inventory situations:

> Usage variations
> Lead-time variations

Basic Saw-Tooth Inventory Pattern

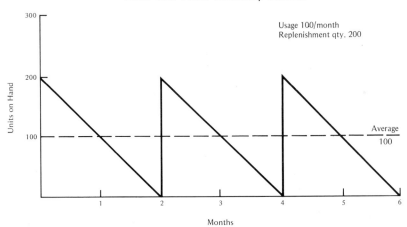

Chart 1

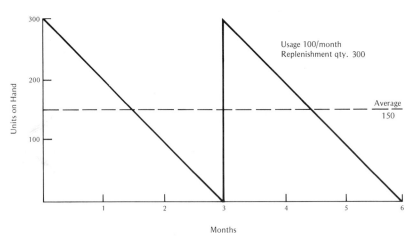

Chart 2

These charts illustrate the effect of replenishment quantities on inventory levels. Stock is replenished in quantities of 200 (Chart 1) and 300 (Chart 2).

As this chart indicates, these factors cause stock-outs when inventories are controlled under the premise that a replenishment will be received when on-hand balance reaches zero.

To provide for these inherent variations, an additional amount of stock must be carried. This additional quantity or safety stock thus makes our practical inventory chart appear as it does in Chart 4.

This protection is built into our inventory balance by the "when" factor. Under an order-point system the protection is primarily needed during the

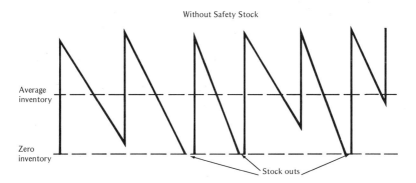

Chart 3. Practical Inventory Pattern without Safety Stock

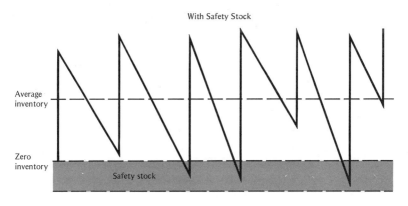

Chart 4. Practical Inventory Pattern with Safety Stock

Variations in usage and lead time may cause stock-outs (Chart 3) unless a higher inventory level is maintained (Chart 4) to provide safety stock.

replenishment (lead time) period and is obtained by adding the protection required to the reorder point expressed in terms of on-hand balance. The formula for the reorder point then becomes:

R.O.P. = (Expected usage during the lead time period) + (safety stock)

This action can probably best be shown with these new factors superimposed on our first basic chart (see Chart 5). In this illustration, we have assumed a desirable safety stock of 100 units and have accordingly increased the reorder point from 100 to 200 units. Under these conditions the average inventory becomes 200 units. It can also be seen that this average inventory is composed of two elements:

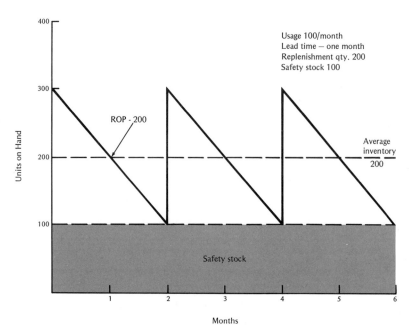

Chart 5. Basic Saw-Tooth Inventory Pattern with Safety Stock. This chart shows what happens to average inventory if the reorder point is calculated with allowance for both expected usage during the lead-time period and safety stock.

One-half of replenishment quantity
Safety stock

We have now determined a formula for development of average inventory under an order-point system:

Average inventory = (1/2 order quantity) + (safety stock)

This same formula holds approximately true under our practical inventory problem previously charted. Safety stock tends to be on the average a constant amount, while working stocks are composed of replenishment quantities, the average of which is approximately one-half of the established replenishment quantity.

Before discussing these principles of basic inventory control further, let us summarize the points that have been covered:

Replenishment quantity directly affects average inventory levels.
When to replenish stock can be expressed in terms of on-hand units as reorder point.

Reorder point = expected usage during the lead-time period plus safety stock.

Average inventory = (½ replenishment quantity) + (safety stock).

These basic rules lead normally then to the question of determining replenishment and safety-stock quantities since these two factors determine average inventory levels.

REPLENISHMENT QUANTITIES

Since replenishment (order) quantities affect average inventory levels, they affect the costs associated with having inventory (holding or carrying costs). The size of replenishment quantity also affects the frequency with which an item must be reordered. Therefore, the replenishment quantity also affects order or acquisition costs, and economic order quantity formulas consider both holding and acquisition cost factors in arriving at the best balanced or least-cost order quantity.

This relationship between the two individual cost lines and the total cost line is shown graphically on Chart 6. It can be seen that the minimum total cost occurs at the same order quantity at which the two individual lines meet. A basic economic order quantity formula can be developed from the relationships as charted.

Let—
Q = Economic order quantity in dollars
A = Annual usage in dollars
C = Cost of an order in dollars
I = Inventory carrying cost, as a decimal
Then—

$$\text{The order cost line} = \frac{CA}{Q}, \text{ and}$$

$$\text{The carrying cost line} = \frac{IQ}{2}$$

When these two are equated we have

$$\frac{CA}{Q} = \frac{IQ}{2}$$

AND

$$Q = \sqrt{\frac{2CA}{I}}$$

By additional mathematics we can also express order quantity in units as follows:

$$Q \text{ (units)} = \sqrt{\frac{2 \times C \times \text{(annual usage units)}}{I \times \text{(unit cost)}}}$$

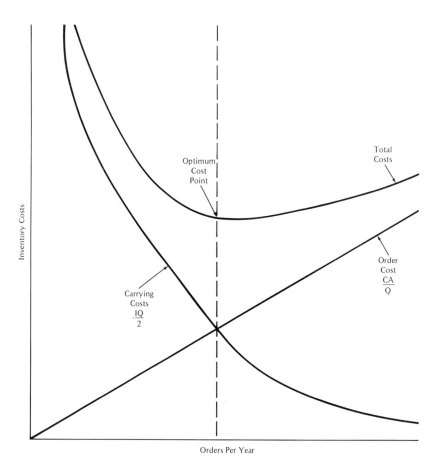

Chart 6. Graphic Presentation of Inventory Costs. The economic order quantity formula is based on the relationship between holding and acquisition costs. Total cost is lowest where the lines cross.

For example, if we assume that we annually use 100 units of an item that costs $4.00 a unit and that we have an order cost of $10.00 and an inventory carrying cost of 20 percent, our formula becomes:

$$\text{Units to Order} = \sqrt{\frac{2 \times 10 \times 100}{.20 \times 4}} = 50$$

Determination of the inventory carrying and order or acquisition costs required for application of this basic formula will be covered in a later portion of this discussion.

This basic formula, developed in the early part of this century, is in fairly widespread use in solving today's problems of inventory control. There are, however, several points that should be made regarding use of this formula.

As we shall discuss a little later, some of the costs required for application of the formula are somewhat difficult to determine precisely. It should be remembered, however, that all factors influencing the answer are under a square-root sign, which allows some latitude in the determination of these costs and acts as a sort of "forgiveness factor." In addition, while carrying or acquisition costs may be approximated and the resulting equating of the two not completely precise, the answer should be considerably better than an out and out guess or an intuitive approach.

Another limiting factor possibly to be found in the use of the formula is that when constant carrying and acquisition costs are used across a wide range of inventory items, the answers become somewhat impractical at the extreme ends of the range. That is, use of the formula may indicate that an unworkably large amount should be ordered for a low-cost item, or that too frequent orders should be placed for a high-cost item. These difficulties can be overcome by actually recognizing the variations in costs for various types of items or, in a more practical way, by limiting the answers at each end of the range.

It can also be pointed out that this basic EOQ formula does not consider all variables in the problem, an obvious example being that quantity discounts are not directly recognized. If quantity discounts are a significant factor, the difficulty may be overcome by a simple one-time computation that can be used in determining alternate order quantities from those developed by the formula.

This is done by calculating the additional cost incurred for various increased order quantities and charting these with order quantities down the side, unit cost across the top, and additional cost in the appropriate boxes. Thus the saving by quantity discount can be compared directly with the additional cost incurred because of the larger size of the order, and an intelligent decision can be made accordingly.

Another factor that must be considered in using the formula is that the computation for each order is somewhat complicated. Probably one of the reasons for the considerably extended use of this formula in recent years is the availability of electronic data processing equipment. Such equipment has made it relatively easy to compute EOQ amounts at the time of each reorder. There are, however, other methods of applying this basic formula. One practical way is to develop a table of EOQ amounts based on various ranges of annual dollar usage. While not completely precise at the extremes of each range, this method is preferable to more arbitrary determination of order quantities. Another method of applying the formula is through the use of a nomograph. An EOQ nomograph is a sort of poor man's slide rule and utilizes three equidistant parallel lines with logarithmic scales. The simplest form uses one column for monthly usage in units, the middle scale for order quantity, and the other scale for unit cost. By connecting the appropriate monthly usage with the proper unit cost, the line crosses the middle scale at the economic order quantity. Once a nomograph has been prepared, it can be published in various formats and can even be printed on the back of the requisition form for ready reference.

SAFETY-STOCK QUANTITIES

It has been demonstrated that safety-stock quantities directly affect average inventory holdings. It would then follow that safety-stock levels directly affect inventory holding or carrying costs. Since safety stock is carried to provide protection against stock-outs, the determination of safety-stock quantities requires the balancing of holding costs against outage costs (as differentiated from EOQ considerations where we were balancing holding costs against acquisition costs). As we shall discuss further under the cost portion of this presentation, the cost of an outage is somewhat difficult, if not impossible, to determine precisely. Most approaches to the development of safety-stock quantities take this fact into consideration.

There is probably no widely accepted formula for safety-stock computations as there is for determining economic order quantities. Most approaches do, however, attempt to provide safety stock that will cover *reasonable maximum usage* during the *lead-time period*. Let's take a look at some of the ways this somewhat arbitrary amount may be determined.

One method is tied in with several other inventory refinements, which will be discussed later. The key point in this method is a definition of the *maximum* amount of usage fluctuations (expressed as a percentage) for which protection would be provided. Items for which usage fluctuations are greater than or equal to the maximum considered are given maximum protection. Those for which usage fluctuations are not equal to the maximum are protected for historical actual amounts. Under this method, more consistent use items are given proportionately less safety stock than those with more erratic use patterns.

Another approach—one which requires substantial data and computing facilities—to handle safety-stock computations takes into consideration that most inventory usage patterns follow some standard statistical distribution. On this basis, percentage of outage based on standard statistical factors can be determined. Then, by computing holding costs for various levels of inventory, a chart can be prepared showing cost for various percentages of inventory coverage. Such a chart can be helpful to management in determining just how far it is willing to go in providing inventory protection.

Other safety-stock formulas take into consideration such refinements as the average size of requisition quantities. The formula used by one of the major airlines combines this feature with the statistical approach mentioned above.

In summary, it should be emphasized that considerable judgment enters into safety-stock computations, and that the answer should be designed and tempered to fit the situation. The definition that safety stock should provide protection for *reasonable* maximum usage during the lead-time period is a good guide. It remains then to apply some judgment to determine what is reasonable in any given situation.

We have now covered some basic methods of inventory control based on the fixed order quantity approach. Included in these techniques were consideration of certain costs and a requirement for an estimate of future usage. These two items:

> Costs
> Estimate of future usage
>> will be discussed next

INVENTORY COSTS

Major categories of inventory costs are:

> Acquisition costs
> Holding costs
> Outage costs

In discussing these costs it is probably best first to define each item of cost and then to consider some practical means of quantifying these various items.

Acquisition Costs

Costs related to acquisition of purchased items would include the following categories of expense:

> Requisitioning
> Purchase order (including expediting)
> Trucking
> Receiving
> Placing in storage
> Accounting and auditing:
>> Inventory
>> Disbursements

Acquisition costs pertaining to company-manufactured pieces include several of the above mentioned items, but also comprehend some different categories, notably set-up costs rather than purchase-order costs. A complete list of manufactured-item acquisition costs could include:

> Requisitioning
> Set-up
> Receiving
> Placing in storage

Accounting and Auditing:
    Inventory
    Product costs

In considering just how much of any of these costs should be applied to inventory-control decision, we again must use some rule of thumb or arbitrary methods. To begin with, records frequently are not kept in such a way that the above mentioned categories of cost are readily accessible. Very often determination of these costs must be made by special study. Then we have the problem of deciding what degree of variability should be used when these costs are applied in the EOQ formula. (This is the only computation reviewed in this presentation where acquisition costs are used.) Welch, in his book *Scientific Inventory Control*, suggests that the effect of a 25 percent change in order rate should be used as a basis for determining acquisition costs. This is a reasonably good approach because some of these costs do not increase in a straight line, but rather in a stair-step pattern. This 25 percent rule tends to give some weight to the latter condition. In any event, *all* acquisition costs should *not* be used in the standard EOQ formula, but the *variable* portion determined on some reasonable basis should be applied.

Holding or Carrying Costs

Holding or carrying costs to be considered in the solution of inventory control problems would include the following items:

    Interest
    Insurance
    Taxes
    Storage
    Obsolescence

In arriving at these costs for inventory control solutions it is probably best to consider only those items meeting the following two tests:

    Out-of-pocket expenditures
    Foregone opportunities for profit

An example of the application of these tests would be the consideration of warehouse space costs only to the extent that additional facilities would need to be acquired or that unused space could be rented for profit. These rules would also indicate that interest would be considered from the standpoint of foregone profit opportunity when sufficient capital existed in the business that money need not be borrowed to finance inventories.

Again, as with acquisition costs, holding costs are somewhat difficult to determine precisely because the usual records do not easily identify them.

In addition, problems exist with the application of the above-mentioned rules or tests. As a guide to reasonableness of holding costs that may be computed, the following table of representative cost ranges is offered:

Item	Approximate Range
Interest	4–10%
Insurance	1– 3
Taxes	1– 3
Storage	0– 3
Obsolescence	4–16
Total	10–35%

This table is a composite taken from various references and tempered with personal experience. Obviously, any extreme situation may fall outside the ranges shown, but the table should be representative of the majority of situations.

Outage Costs

This category of costs is mentioned primarily because it exists, and not because definitive rules can be set forth for computing outage costs. It was noted earlier that outages result in:

> Decreased customer service level, which *may* result in decreased sales
> Less efficient production operations
> High costs resulting from "crash" procurements

It is probably obvious that outages affect the items named above; the unanswered question in most cases is "how much?" Unless some very direct relationships exist, the cost of an outage is difficult to quantify.

The fact that answers to the determination of outage costs are approximate and arbitrary in nature does not necessarily mean, however, that their significance should be ignored. As was seen in the computation of safety stocks (where these costs apply), knowledge of the cost of alternatives enables the application of enlightened judgment to produce satisfactory answers to the problem of just how great an outage rate is acceptable.

DETERMINATION OF EXPECTED USAGE

All replenishment of inventory requires some sort of forecast for determining expected usage. This forecast can take various forms, including:

> Hunches
> Visual review of past history

Computation of average demand over a past period
Exponential smoothing of past demand
Tying past demand to a more reliable forecast
Relationship with other forecast items

This is obviously only a partial list, but it can serve as a basis for discussing forecasting methods as they relate to inventory control situations.

The first two of these categories have been included not because of their advantages but because of their widespread use. Whenever human judgment is the primary ingredient in inventory usage forecasts, the resulting answers tend to show the influence of overcompensation for the current situation. For example, when usage temporarily increases, much greater quantities are ordered. When usage then seeks its normal trend and declines, a large overstock results. Human reaction to temporary decreases in usage, on the other hand, often results in stock-outs.

The point of this discussion is that an answer arrived at in a methodical, consistent fashion is usually much more reliable over a period of time than an answer obtained by hunch. In fact, in a particular application of some of these inventory control principles, a good portion of the benefit was obtained by replacing a usage forecast based mainly on human judgment by one based on principles *consistently* applied to past usage.

In direct computation of usage forecasts, either the averaging of past demand for a selected period of time or the exponential smoothing of past demand provides an acceptable method. The characteristics of the inventory in question and the facilities available for making the computation should influence the decision as to which method to use. Exponential smoothing gives greater weight to more recent periods and has the advantage of not requiring detailed usage history for each inventory item.

In certain production situations the last two forecasting methods outlined above can be used to advantage. The use of other forecasts can probably best be illustrated by a method that utilizes the explosion of a finished item into its component and piece parts. The demand for the finished item is forecast directly and the component and piece parts then become a logical extension of that forecast.

OTHER REFINEMENTS

Two inventory control concepts that have been used successfully and have fairly broad application should also be covered in a general discussion of inventory control principles. These two are:

A-B-C approach
Use of control limits

A-B-C Approach

This concept is based on the premise that in most inventories approximately 10 percent of the items account for about 85 percent of the annual dollar usage. At the other extreme, about 75 percent of the items account for only about 5 percent of the annual dollar usage. Recognition of this situation and division of the inventory into three groups (A, B, and C) based on annual dollar usage, has commonly been called the A-B-C method.

These relationships appear to exist in virtually all inventories, and because of this, and the advantages of being able to place emphasis on the important items, this approach has begun to be used somewhat more extensively in recent years. In addition to being able to concentrate attention on the items that make the big difference in inventory results, this method also enables several different methods of control to be applied to the same inventory. An alternative to this approach is the use of the same method, but varying decision rules for each group.

In order to utilize this concept it is first necessary to analyze the inventory to determine the approximate distribution of items so that ranges for each of the A-B-C categories can be set. Chart 7 shows the distribution of inventory usage values based on an actual inventory study. In this particular case, A items were determined to be those with annual usage exceeding $1,000, B items to include those with annual usage of from $100 to $1,000, and C items to have annual usage of less than $100.

Use of Control Limits

This approach, based on statistical quality control concepts, emphasizes the management by exception technique. The key assumption in this approach is that there is a "normal," expected usage for an item and that some deviations from this expected usage will occur. Significant usage deviations are determined by control limits, and only upon such occurrences need the item be reviewed. Otherwise, with the item operating within limits, decision rules can be applied mechanically to produce desired results.

This technique can also be combined with the A-B-C approach by varying the degree of control for each of the A-B-C categories. The tighter control is obviously applied to the A items and because of the more frequent and earlier inspection of usage variances, less safety stock is required for these items. This then meets the requirement of minimizing inventory balances on the 10 percent of the items that account for 85 percent of the annual dollar usage. Also because only 10 percent of the items are being more tightly controlled, effort required for inventory administration is minimized.

We have now reviewed some of the basic principles of inventory control. This has not been a complete coverage; instead, emphasis has been placed

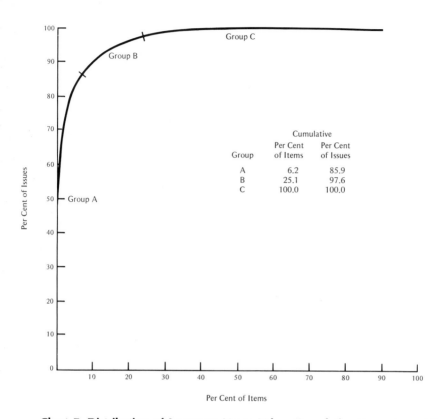

Group	Cumulative Per Cent of Items	Cumulative Per Cent of Issues
A	6.2	85.9
B	25.1	97.6
C	100.0	100.0

Chart 7. Distribution of Inventory Usage Values Cumulative Percentages. The fact that in all inventories a few items account for most of the dollar usage makes it possible to concentrate the control effort where it is most needed. This is the A-B-C approach.

on the order-point approach because it probably has the widest application in problems of inventory control and is well accepted today. The basic principles reviewed are just that—basic principles. As always, a specific solution must be worked out for the problem at hand. It is hoped that the points discussed will be helpful and can be applied in a practical way to the solution of some of these specific problems.

32.

PERT/COST RESOURCE ALLOCATION PROCEDURE*

W. R. Ross

The PERT/Cost approach to managing large and complex programs of work—e.g., weapons systems, space ventures, etc.—is receiving considerable attention by industry, government, and in the literature. Structurally, the PERT/Cost system is based upon three interrelated components—a work breakdown structure, work packages, and the network—and is designed to provide management with the tools necessary to achieve schedule and cost planning, determination, and control in those instances for which conventional management systems are inadequate.

The "resource allocation procedure," a supplement to the basic PERT/Cost system, is concerned with the problem of efficient allocation of limited resources in accomplishing work programs, and is based on the premise that activities (work efforts; usually represented by arrows) on a network are subject to time/cost trade offs.

This supplement is not considered an essential part of the PERT/Cost system. However, it serves to extend the usefulness and effectiveness of the PERT/Cost system as a management tool. While the concepts involved appear relatively simple, the implementation of the supplement usually requires considerable management education and understanding in order to insure its proper use. Maximum care is essential in the use of the resource-allocation supplement so as to obtain realistic results from its application.

The resource-allocation supplement is designed to assist the manager in the systematic development of an optimum assignment of men and equipment. This supplement is "a plan in which men and equipment are as-

* From The Accounting Review, July 1966, pp. 464–473. Reprinted by permission of the author and the American Accounting Association.

signed to the project in such a way that the technical objectives are achieved at either the lowest cost for a specified time duration, or the shortest time within a specified cost limit."[1] To do this, the procedure calls for alternate time/resource estimates for performing each activity in the segment of the program under consideration. Provided an activity can be carried out in more than one way, it is assumed that these alternative approaches will produce different cost and time estimates.

Briefly, implementation of the resource-allocation supplement requires the following:

> Management first defines the project by a network of activities with technical specifications for the work. Alternative times and costs are then estimated for each of the activities. (Any number of meaningful time-cost combinations may be estimated.)
>
> The duration of an activity is initially set at the time associated with its lowest cost alternative. Then, by selecting shorter time/higher cost points on certain critical-path activities, time is "bought" on the critical path until the project duration is equal to or slightly less than the target duration.[2]

It should be pointed out that while the overall PERT/Cost system is intended as a planning and control aid for entire work programs, the resource-allocation supplement can be used in planning small groups of associated activities from a larger network.

PRELIMINARY PROCEDURAL STEPS

The steps to be followed in the application of the time/cost trade-off portion of the resource-allocation supplement are summarized below and illustrated in Figure 1.

> Step 1. Construct the network or portion thereof under consideration. For simplicity in illustration, a network of only three activities has been assumed with event C representing the desired end objective.
>
> Step 2. Obtain alternate time/cost estimates for each activity. These are "discrete" time/cost intersect points for performing each activity. The manager may determine as many discrete intersect points as desired and practical. The graphs in Figure 1a show the alternative times and costs estimated for each of the three activities. Where it is

---

[1] *DOD and NASA Guide: PERT/Cost—"Systems Design"* (Washington, D.C.: Department of Defense and National Aeronautics and Space Administration, June 1962), p. 108.

[2] Ibid., p. 109.

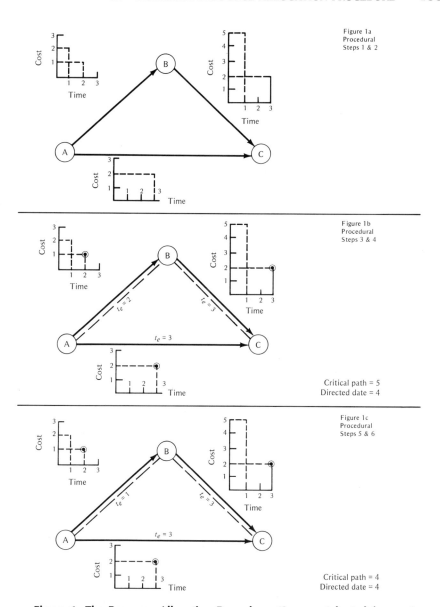

Figure 1. The Resource Allocation Procedure. (Source: Adapted from—An Introduction to the PERT/Cost System for Integrated Project Management—, Special Projects Office, Department of the Navy, Washington, D.C., Figure 14.)

possible to extend the duration of a project it may be possible to reduce costs for a variety of reasons, including: (1) better preliminary planning, (2) reduction of overtime wages, (3) less premium purchasing, (4) less rework cost, or (5) a different approach in accomplishing the task. The alternative time/cost estimates submitted by the managers for the three activities in Figure 1 are as follows:

Activity A–B: 2 weeks/$1,000
1 week/$2,000

Activity B–C: 3 weeks/$2,000
1 week/$5,000

Activity A–C: 3 weeks/$2,000 (assumed work can be accomplished in only one way).

Step 3. Select the lowest cost alternate for each activity. For the illustrative example, this is the following:

Activity A–B $1,000
Activity B–C 2,000
Activity A–C 2,000
Total Cost $5,000

Step 4. Calculate the critical path, using the time values associated with the costs selected in Step 3, and compare to directed date. The critical path as indicated in Figure 1b is along activities A–B and B–C and has a duration of five weeks. The directed date calls for a maximum duration of four weeks; therefore, the critical path duration exceeds the necessary target date duration.

Step 5. If the critical path is too long, it must be compressed by shortening some or all of its component activities. Select the higher cost, shorter time alternates where the ratio of increased cost to decreased time is least. This is determined by dividing the increase in cost by the decrease in time as a result of moving to the next shorter time period. For the example these ratios are:

$$\text{Activity } A\text{–}B \quad \frac{1}{1} = 1$$

$$\text{Activity } B\text{–}C \quad \frac{3}{2} = 1.5$$

Activity A–B has the least increase in time associated with a decrease in cost; therefore, this activity should be shortened to its next shorter time alternate point or the one week/$2,000 cost intersect.

Step 6. Repeat Step 5 until the length of the critical path conforms to the directed date. In the example presented, iteration of Step 5 is unnecessary since the estimated duration has been reduced to four weeks and conforms to the directed date for the project (Figure 1c).[3]

---

[3] These steps were adapted from Special Projects Office, Department of the Navy, *An Introduction to the PERT/Cost System for Integrated Project Management*, Sec. IV-B; and *DOD and NASA Guide: PERT Cost*—"Systems Design," pp. 108–112.

In effect, if the critical path time exceeds the desired duration, time is "bought" until the required estimated duration is achieved. In buying this time, several additional important considerations must be kept in mind.

COMBINATION REDUCTION OF ACTIVITIES

First, where several alternate time/cost points exist for the critical path activities being operated on, a combination of reductions may be the best. This can be illustrated as follows. Suppose that the critical path consists of the three activities and their related time/cost estimates as presented in Figure 2. The lowest cost is $9,000 with a time duration of twenty-three weeks:

Activity	Lowest Cost	Related Time (Weeks)
A–B	$4,000	8
B–C...............................	2,000	7
C–D...............................	3,000	8
Totals	$9,000	23

Suppose that the directed date specifies a maximum duration of some number less than twenty-three weeks—in brief, that the critical path needs to be reduced. Application of the resource-allocation procedure calls for computing the ratio of increased cost to decreased time for each of the alternative points other than those associated with the lowest cost (Figure 3). Now, the critical path can be systematically transformed from the minimum-cost, maximum-time plan to the minimum-time, maximum-cost plan, always making the optimum choice as illustrated in Figure 4.

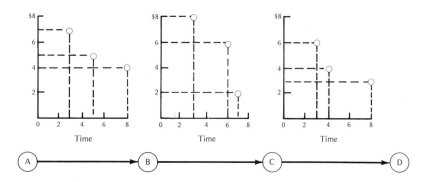

Figure 2. Three Activity Critical Path and Related Time/Cost Estimates

With the information developed in the worksheet of optimal cost/time plans (Figure 4), management can select the plan that conforms to the di-

Activity	Lowest Cost Cost/Time	Second Lowest Cost Actual Cost/Time	Change Cost/Time	Ratio	Third Lowest Cost Actual Cost/Time	Change Cost/Time	Ratio
A-B	$4 / $8	$5 / $5	$1 / $3	0.33	$7 / 3	2 / 2	1.00
B-C	$2 / 7	$6 / 6	$4 / 1	4.00	$8 / 3	$2 / 3	.67
C-D	$3 / 8	$4 / 4	$1 / 4	0.25	$6 / 3	$2 / 1	2.00

(Cost in thousands of dollars; time in weeks)

Figure 3. Computation of Activity Increased Cost/Decreased Time Ratios

ACTIVITIES

Description	A-B Time	A-B Cost	B-C Time	B-C Cost	C-D Time	C-D Cost	TOTAL Time	TOTAL Cost
Minimum cost, maximum time plan	8	$4	7	$2	8	$3	23	$ 9
Select cheapest time reduction (C-D = .25)					−4	+1	−4	+1
Revised Plan A	8	$4	7	$2	4	$4	19	$10
Select next cheapest time reduction (A-B = .33)	−3	+1					−3	+1
Revised Plan B	5	$5	7	$2	4	$4	16	$11
Select next cheapest time reduction (A-B = 1)*	−2	+2					−2	+2
Revised Plan C	3	$7	7	$2	4	$4	14	$13
Select next cheapest time reduction (C-D = 2)					−1	+2	−1	+2
Revised Plan D	3	$7	7	$2	3	$6	13	$15
Select next cheapest time reduction (B-C = 4)			−1	+4			−1	+4
Revised Plan E	3	$7	6	$6	3	$6	12	$19
Select next cheapest time reduction (B-C = .67)			−3	+2			−3	+2
Minimum time, maximum cost plan	3	$7	3	$8	3	$6	9	$21

*Note that although activity B-C has a ratio of .67 associated with its "Third Lowest Cost," the ratio attributable to its "Second Lowest Cost" is 4 and has not been selected to this point. This illustrates that it is necessary to consider the shortest time periods for each activity in sequence. (Cost in thousands of dollars; time in weeks.)

Figure 4. Worksheet of Optimal Cost/Time Plans

rected date with assurance of minimum cost for such a plan. If there is no specific plan that meets exactly the directed duration, then the next plan shorter than the directed duration can be selected (e.g., if the directed duration is fifteen weeks, then it would be necessary to select Revised Plan C). With the desired duration determined in advance, it is unnecessary to complete the worksheet past the point of the revised plan that meets the duration criteria.

Care must be exercised to avoid buying excessive time when selecting the "cheapest time reduction" which finally reduces the duration to the desired plan. For instance, suppose that it becomes necessary to "buy" two weeks time, and further assume that movement to the next shorter times of two activities results in the following ratios:

$$\text{Activity X-Y:} \quad \frac{\text{Increase in Cost \$4,000}}{\text{Decrease in Time 5 weeks}} = .80$$

$$\text{Activity Y-Z:} \quad \frac{\text{Increase in Cost \$3,000}}{\text{Decrease in Time 2 weeks}} = 1.50$$

If the lower ratio (.80) is selected, then excessive cost of $1,000 is incurred because two weeks of time could have been bought on activity Y–Z for $3,000 as opposed to buying the excessive five weeks time at a cost of $4,000 on activity X Y.

CRITICAL PATH SHIFT

A second consideration in "buying" time along the critical path is the possibility that another path may become critical as a result of shortening the original critical path. It may become necessary simultaneously to reduce the duration of two or more paths in such a situation. Also, since PERT/Cost is a dynamic management tool, certain critical path activities on which time is bought to reduce total duration in the original planning network may end up on a slack path as the network times are continuously subject to change. In this or any other case, the slack paths require review and, if possible, replanning at lower cost and longer duration so long as they do not become critical.

TIME AND FIXED-COST CONSIDERATIONS

While it may be possible to include fixed overhead in the estimates to determine the alternative time/cost points, this would likely prove to be a cumbersome and unnecessary task. Nevertheless, it is essential that fixed costs be scrutinized closely to determine their relationship to the overall planning of a complex work program.

Figure 5 illustrates the effect that fixed overhead can have on total project cost. In this example, it is assumed that fixed overhead is one million dollars per year and that there are four feasible plans for completing the project. The five-year plan has a variable cost of $5.4 million and would be rejected since the four-year plan has a variable cost of only $5.2 million. The purpose for including the five-year plan is to demonstrate that there is

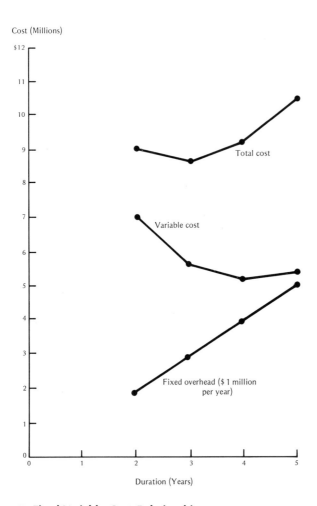

Figure 5. Fixed/Variable Cost Relationships

a saturation point to variable cost reduction at which it becomes costlier to extend the duration.

The four-year plan has the lowest variable cost ($5.2 million), but a higher total cost than the three-year plan which has a variable cost of $5.6 million. The $0.6 million lesser total cost of the three-year plan over the four-year plan is attributable to the fact that the reduction in fixed cost of $1 million more than offsets the $0.4 million increase in variable costs.

Finally the two-year plan has $1 million less fixed cost than the three-year plan, but $1.4 million more variable cost for a net increase in total cost of $0.4 million. From strictly a total-cost point of view, the three-year plan is the best of those available.

It should be noted that the alternative feasible plans are at discrete time/cost intersects and that the lines in Figure 5 are merely for readability and do not indicate continuous time/cost relationships. The value of calculating continuous time/cost curves for significant projects is doubtful. Whereas this is a reasonable approach to determining optimum quantities for continuous production, continuous time/cost curves are usually not applicable in the case of one-time programs of work.

Finally, the effect of optimizing one segment (activity or continuous group of activities) of the work program on other segments must be analyzed. Figures 6 and 7 can be used to illustrate this relationship. In both illustrations it is assumed that there are two work segments (A and B) to be completed and that the following time/cost alternatives have been determined:

Duration	Costs (Millions)					
	Segment A			Segment B		
(years)	Variable	Fixed	Total	Variable	Fixed	Total
1	$16	$ 2	$18	$31	$1	$32
2	11	4	15	31	2	33
3	8	6	14	24	3	27
4	7	8	15	18	4	22
5	11	10	21	12	5	17

These time/cost relationships are plotted in Figure 6. If A and B are completely independent of each other (one does not have to be completed before the other can start) and it is desirous to complete these at the lowest possible cost, then A would be performed in three years at a cost of $14 million and B would be performed in five years at a cost of $17 million—a total combined cost of $31 million. The maximum duration could be cut to four years, but at a cost increase of $5 million (A in three years for $14 million + B in four years for $22 million = $36 million). Further time reductions at increased cost could similarly be made. If for technical reasons it is imperative that A and B be completed simultaneously, then a program of four years duration at a total combined cost of $37 million is optimal. Again, the duration could be reduced with increases in cost.

The effect of reducing time on the critical path must be measured not only on the critical path but on other paths as well. For example, to reduce a critical path by twenty weeks to the next discrete alternative may require an increase in cost along that path of only $50,000, and this may be desirable in management's judgment. However, if a reduction of twenty weeks in this path causes a second path to become critical, then a different decision may be forthcoming. If the second path becomes critical by sixteen weeks, then the real over-all time gained is only four weeks. Management may not be willing to spend $50,000 to gain four weeks. A further reduction in the second path may be extremely costly and thus undesirable, or it may be impossible.

Using the time/cost data for A and B presented above and assuming that A must be completed before B can commence, what is the optimal plan for

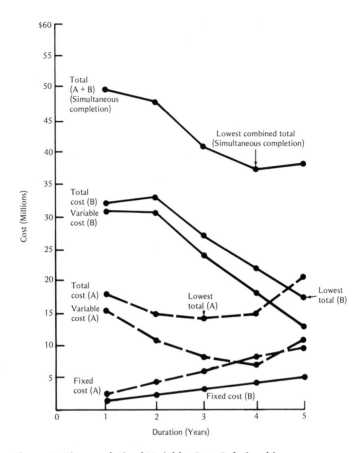

Figure 6. Time and Fixed/Variable Cost Relationships

various total durations? Figure 7 is a matrix of the various combinations of time/cost plans available.

A plan of eight years duration (A = 3; B = 5) provides the lowest possible cost of $31 million. Shorter durations and their associated lowest cost combinations are next listed:

Duration (Years)			Combined Costs
A	+ B	= Total	(Millions)
2	5	7	$32
1	5	6	35
1	4	5	40
1	3	4	45
2	1	3	47
1	1	2	50

The nine- and ten-year plans have total combined costs exceeding the costs for the eight-year plan and certain other combinations having a lesser dura-

Segment A		Segment B									
Year/Cost (millions)		1	$32	2	$33	3	$27	4	$22	5	$17
		Total Time/Cost Plans Where A Must Be Complete Prior to Starting B									
		Years	Cost	Years	Cost	Years	Cost	Years	Cost	Years	Cost
1	$18	2	$50	3	$51	4	$45	5	$40	6	$35
2	$15	3	$47	4	$48	5	$42	6	$37	7	$32
3	$14	4	$46	5	$47	6	$41	7	$36	8	$31
4	$15	5	$47	6	$48	7	$42	8	$37	9	$32
5	$21	6	$53	7	$54	8	$48	9	$43	10	$38

Figure 7. Matrix of Total Time/Cost Combinations

tion. The matrix in Figure 7 provides data necessary to management in making the optimum combination choice for a given duration. As an example, if a six-year maximum duration is desired, then there are five combinations of A and B with the cost ranging from $35 million to $53 million. Using the matrix, the lowest cost combination of $35 million (A = 1; B = 5) can be determined; and it can also be ascertained that no shorter total duration plan provides a lower cost.

LEVELING RESOURCES UTILIZATION

After arriving at the desired plan, using the resource-allocation techniques described to this point, loading charts by resource categories and time periods should be developed. The purpose of these loading charts is to display the possible over- and under-utilization of resources. This will assist management in leveling out peaks and valleys in resource utilization. While graphs can be developed for various categories of resources, probably the most useful application of this leveling process is in manpower loading. This is illustrated in Figures 9 and 10, using the network in Figure 8. Suppose that two hundred hours of manpower skill "A" are required weekly for each activity in progress during that week. If each activity in the network is started as early as possible, the schedule of activities would appear as in Figure 9a and the manpower loading requirements for manpower skill "A" would appear as in Figure 9b. As can be seen in Figure 9b, the manpower requirements are quite erratic, ranging from a peak of 800 man-hours to a minimum of 200 man-hours per week. Needless to say, such a schedule of manpower requirements would create a number of problems relative to hiring, layoff, overtime, and idle time.

Figure 10 shows the effects of rescheduling certain activities to smooth out the manpower requirements for Skill "A". The schedule of activities in Figure 10a still permits completion in nineteen weeks, but starting times of certain activities on slack paths have been shifted in order to attain the

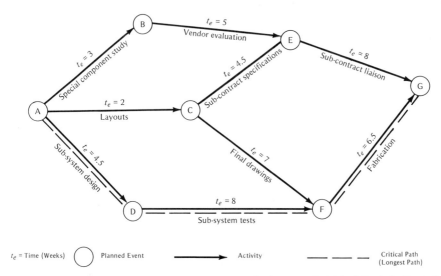

Figure 8. PERT Network with Expected Times and Critical Path Indicated. (Source: Adapted from—An Introduction to the PERT/Cost System for Integrated Project Management—, Special Projects Office, Department of the Navy, Washington, D.C.)

leveling of manpower requirements as indicated in Figure 10b. Manpower skill "A" demands for this second schedule are much more compatible with the job of maintaining and scheduling a work force.

It is highly unlikely that the assumption of 200 skill "A" man hours per week for each activity in progress is a realistic one; certain activities might require varying quantities of this skill and some may require no skill "A" manpower at all. The assumption, however, is a feasible one for explaining and illustrating simply the process of resource utilization leveling. In a real situation it may even become necessary to shorten or lengthen certain activities to attain the smoothing effects desired. Also there will undoubtedly be some compromise between the various resources involved in the leveling process.

RECAPITULATION

Commencing with the steps outlined under the caption "Preliminary Procedural Steps" above, which determine the lowest time/cost alternatives consistent with the directed date, application of the resource-allocation procedure is completed by evaluating the effects of (1) combination reductions of activities, (2) critical path shifts, (3) variable/fixed cost relationships, and (4) leveling over- and underutilization of resources. The full utilization of this supplement requires both quantitative analysis and in-

SCHEDULE OF ACTIVITIES

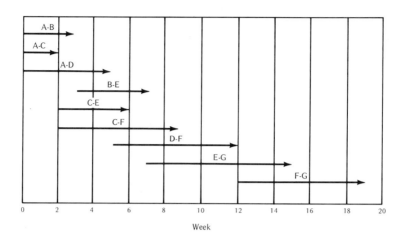

MANPOWER REQUIREMENTS
(SKILL A)

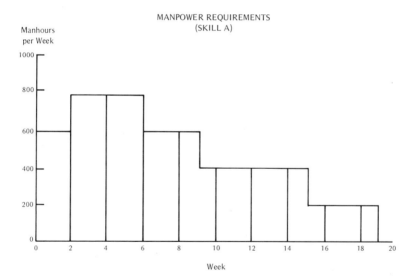

Figure 9. Schedules of Activities and Manpower Loading Requirements for Manpower Skill A (based on Network in Figure 8, each activity started as early as possible)

formed management judgment. Although the resource-allocation procedure is not considered absolutely essential in using the PERT/Cost system, the factors considered in its application must necessarily be an integral part of any well developed PERT/Cost plan. Therefore, where the procedure per se is not used, the factors involved must be considered by management even though this consideration may be an informal approach.

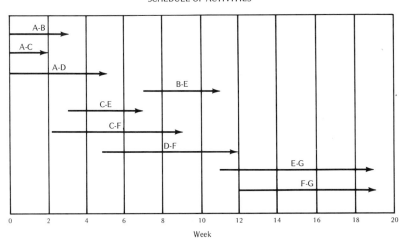

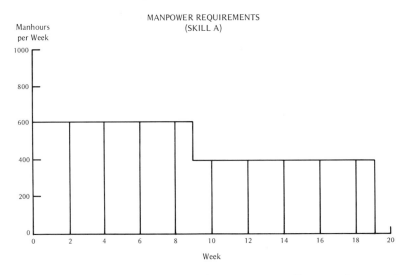

Figure 10. Schedule of Activities and Manpower Loading Requirements for Manpower Skill A (based on Network in Figure 8, activities started so as to level manpower requirements)

The application of the resource-allocation procedure to an entire network of several hundred or even thousands of activities would be a formidable task. As mentioned earlier, however, this supplement finds its primary usefulness in planning small groups of associated activities which represent only a minor portion of the overall program of work. Formal application of the procedure may be restricted to work segments involving high costs and critical paths, and to work segments involving the use of substantial amounts of a certain resource where original network plans make some leveling of the planned requirements for this resource desirable. The effects of replanning one segment of work on other parts of the overall project must be determined and evaluated when the resource-allocation procedure is applied on only selected portions of the entire network.

Editor's Note: PERT/Time (Question VI-Q9). For a concise explanation of PERT (PERT/Time), see Peter P. Schoderbek, "PERT-Its Promises and Performance," *Michigan Business Review*, Vol. 17, No. 1 (1965), pp. 25–32. PERT formulates a network of the activities required to implement project objectives. Activities (arrows) represent time-consuming tasks. Events (circles) do not consume time and represent the beginning or end of activities. PERT highlights critical activities. If less time is used in one part of the network, then labor and equipment can be used in other activities to meet completion dates or reduce the time required for completion.

Because time completion is uncertain, PERT utilizes a weighted time average of three estimates (a = optimistic time, m = most likely, b = pessimistic time) to arrive at an expected elapsed time. The most likely time is weighted four times as heavily as the others. Question VI-Q9 refers to the 1-4-1 method. The formula is

$$t_e = \frac{a + 4m + b}{6}$$

The earliest expected date at which an event can take place T_E is determined by "summing all activity times (t_e) through the most time-consuming chain of events from the beginning event to the given event." The longest path in the network is the path that would affect the completion date of the entire project. This is the critical path, and activities on the path are the critical activities; they consume the most time in the network. Other paths are slack paths because they have some leeway, but there is no slack for the critical activities. For example, the slack time on path 1-7-8-6 (see VI-Q9) equals 3.4, determined as 20.8 (the T_E for the project or 4.2 + 4.2 + 3.0 + 2.1 + 7.3) minus 17.4 (the sum of all activity times (t_e) for the path or 4.2 + 3.6 + 5.0 + 4.6).

Slack for an event is calculated by using (1) the latest allowable date (T_L) an event can take place without affecting the completion date of the project, and (2) the earliest expected date the activity can be completed (T_E). The T_L for an event (say 9) is determined by subtracting the t_e following the event (i.e., 5.2) from the T_L for the next event (event 6) where $T_L = 20.8$. (The T_L for event 6 results from path 1-2-3-4-6 and is the sum of the t_e values of 4.2 + 4.2 + 3.0 + 2.1 + 7.3 = 20.8.) The T_E for event 9 is determined as 4.2 + 7.1 = 11.3. The slack for an event equals T_L minus T_E. Therefore, the event 9 slack is 15.6 − 11.3 = 4.3.

PERT (PERT/Time) aids management in interchanging resources when slack exists in a network. Under the system, alternative courses of action or even alternative networks can be simulated to determine the effects of changes before making a decision.

The PERT/Cost system integrates both time and cost information as part of the network. As discussed in Article 32, the resource-allocation supplement to the basic PERT/Cost system assists the manager in an optimum assignment of men and equipment.

33.

A NOTE ON PERT/COST RESOURCE ALLOCATION[1] *

F. A. Bailey

With reference to the excellent article by W. R. Ross in the July 1966 issue of *The Review* [Article 32], the computation of costs for a combination reduction of activities will not always indicate the minimum cost for a specified duration even if the computation provides a plan for the exact time duration required.

Dynamic programming provides a method of dealing with this type of problem. The objective is to find the minimum cost for a given time taken to reach D from A. The principle of optimality requires that if there are two ways of covering any part of the route in the same time, only the least cost method should be considered. The calculation proceeds as follows:

	A–B			*B–C*			Combined *A–C*	
	Time	Cost		Time	Cost	Plan	Time	Cost
1	8	$4	1	7	$2	1-1	15	$ 6
						2-1	12	$ 7
2	5	$5	2	6	$6	3-1	10	$ 9
3	3	$7	3	3	$8	2-3	8	$13
						3-3	6	$15

The schedule for A–C includes only those routes which are acceptable. For example, compare the following combinations:

---

*From *The Accounting Review*, April 1967, p. 361. Reprinted by permission of the author and the American Accounting Association.

[1]"PERT/Cost Resource Allocation Procedure," *The Accounting Review*, July 1966, pp. 464–473; at page 468. [Editors' Note: See page 486 (Article 32) in this book.]

A–B	1	8 hours $ 4		2	5 hours $5
B–C	2	6 hours $ 6		1	7 hours $2
Combined	1-2	14 hours $10		2-1	12 hours $7

The combination of 2-1 taking 12 hours at a cost of $7 is a better method in that both time and cost are less. Therefore, 1-2 is not considered.

If A–C is combined with C–D on the same basis the following schedule results:

Combined A–D		
Plan	Time	Cost
1-1-1	23	$ 9
1-1-2	19	$10
2-1-2	16	$11
3-1-2	14	$13
3-1-3	13	$15
2-3-2	12	$17
3-3-2	10	$19
3-3-3	9	$21

This is similar to the schedule produced by Professor Ross; but there are two important differences:

> 1. Revised plan E [see Figure 4, p. 486] is shown to be inferior to plan 2-3-2 in that it costs $2 more for the same time.

> 2. An additional plan (3-3-2) is revealed which reduces the time to 10 hours for a cost of $19 against 12 hours in plan E.

This schedule is a complete list of least-cost plans. If the desired time does not coincide with a plan on the list the next plan with a shorter time may be chosen in the knowledge that excess time is not being bought.

All alternatives have been considered in the computation, and those which have been rejected are inferior to those appearing on the final schedule.

34.
AN INTRODUCTION TO MATRIX
OPERATIONS IN ACCOUNTING*

Yow-Min R. Lee
and
Donald L. Anderson

Applications of matrix operations in accounting have been growing rapidly with the increasing use of computers for data processing. The purpose of this paper is to familiarize students in business with basic matrix operations useful in solving accounting problems. Matrix operations consist of addition, subtraction, multiplication, and inversion and these are explained in the paper. Division is not defined in matrix algebra. Instead the concept of arithmetical division is replaced by reciprocal multiplication. The reciprocal of a matrix is called the inverse of the matrix. In addition to explaining the determination of the inverse of a matrix, its use in obtaining solutions for systems of linear equations is shown in an example.

DEFINITION AND SUBSCRIPT NOTATION
FOR A MATRIX

A matrix is a rectangular array of elements (i.e., numbers, symbols) which can be used to describe problems involving relations between the elements. A matrix may be represented by a letter. For example:

$$A = \begin{bmatrix} 2 & 3 & 4 & 1 \\ 1 & 0 & 2 & 1 \end{bmatrix}$$

Column ↓ ← Row

The size or order of a matrix is determined by the number of rows and columns contained in the matrix, and can be referred to as the dimensions of a matrix. Matrix A with 2 rows and 4 columns has the order 2 by 4. To indicate its dimensions, the matrix can be written as $A_{2 \times 4}$.

---

*Printed by permission of the authors.

In subscript notation, the A matrix can be written as:

$$A = \begin{bmatrix} a_{11} & a_{12} & a_{13} & a_{14} \\ a_{21} & a_{22} & a_{23} & a_{24} \end{bmatrix}.$$

Note that a_{11} refers to the element in row 1 and column 1 of matrix A, a_{12} refers to the element in row 1 and column 2, and so on. The subscript notation can be shortened by using a_{ij} to represent the typical element of a matrix A called the ijth element of A. The first subscript (i) refers to the row that the ijth element is in, and the second subscript (j) refers to the column. The compact notation of the above matrix A is:

$$A = \{a_{ij}\} \text{ where } i = 1, 2 \text{ and } j = 1, 2, 3, 4.$$

AN EXAMPLE USED IN EXPLAINING MATRIX ADDITION, SUBTRACTION, AND MULTIPLICATION

Assume that we are interested in the total sales volumes by quarters, the differences in quarterly sales volumes, the total sales revenue, and the total cost of sales of a firm. The firm has both domestic and foreign sales. We can use matrix addition, subtraction, and multiplication to obtain the answers. We can express sales (measured in millions of units) in matrix notation by quarters of the year as follows:

$$\text{Quarter I \quad II \quad III \quad IV}$$
$$A = \begin{bmatrix} 2 & 3 & 4 & 1 \\ 1 & 0 & 2 & 1 \end{bmatrix} \begin{matrix} \text{Domestic sales volume for 19X1} \\ \text{Foreign sales volume for 19X1} \end{matrix}$$
$$B = \begin{bmatrix} 3 & 4 & 5 & 2 \\ 0 & 2 & 1 & 2 \end{bmatrix} \begin{matrix} \text{Domestic sales volume for 19X2} \\ \text{Foreign sales volume for 19X2} \end{matrix}$$

MATRIX ADDITION AND SUBTRACTION

The rule for matrix addition is that matrices must be added element by element. In order to perform this operation, matrices to be added must have the same order, i.e., the same number of rows and columns. This is called the conformable rule for addition. This operation is demonstrated by adding sales of 19X1 and 19X2 together.

$$A + B = \begin{bmatrix} 2 & 3 & 4 & 1 \\ 1 & 0 & 2 & 1 \end{bmatrix} + \begin{bmatrix} 3 & 4 & 5 & 2 \\ 0 & 2 & 1 & 2 \end{bmatrix} = \begin{bmatrix} 2+3 & 3+4 & 4+5 & 1+2 \\ 1+0 & 0+2 & 2+1 & 1+2 \end{bmatrix} = \begin{bmatrix} 5 & 7 & 9 & 3 \\ 1 & 2 & 3 & 3 \end{bmatrix}$$

Note that the result of adding two matrices is a matrix with the same dimensions as the original matrices. The addition operation does not change the fact that we are dealing with arrays of numbers and that we are not evaluating the numerical value of A and B. This fact also holds true in other matrix operations.

Matrix subtraction can be thought of as adding a negative matrix to another matrix, i.e., subtracting element by element. Thus, the comformable rule for addition must be observed. For example, the difference in sales between 19X2 and 19X1 can be calculated as follows:

$$B-A = \begin{bmatrix} 3 & 4 & 5 & 2 \\ 0 & 2 & 1 & 2 \end{bmatrix} - \begin{bmatrix} 2 & 3 & 4 & 1 \\ 1 & 0 & 2 & 1 \end{bmatrix} = \begin{bmatrix} 3-2 & 4-3 & 5-4 & 2-1 \\ 0-1 & 2-0 & 1-2 & 2-1 \end{bmatrix} = \begin{bmatrix} 1 & 1 & 1 & 1 \\ -1 & 2 & -1 & 1 \end{bmatrix}.$$

The subscript notations for the addition and subtraction of the matrices A and B of the examples are:

$$A + B = \{a_{ij}\} + \{b_{ij}\} = \{a_{ij} + b_{ij}\} \quad \text{for } i = 1, 2 \text{ and } j = 1, 2, 3, 4$$
$$B - A = \{b_{ij}\} - \{a_{ij}\} = \{b_{ij} - a_{ij}\} \quad \text{for } i = 1, 2 \text{ and } j = 1, 2, 3, 4$$

We can add or subtract more than two matrices simply by performing the addition or subtraction operations by pairs provided they have the same number of rows and columns (i.e., they are conformable). We can group the operations in any fashion we wish; this is called the associative law of addition. For example:

$$A + B - C = (A + B) - C = A + (B - C).$$

SCALAR MULTIPLICATION

Suppose the sales volume of the firm is the same as matrix A for each of the years 19X1, 19X2, and 19X3. The total sales volume can be calculated by performing pairwise addition twice in the following form:

$$A + A + A = \begin{bmatrix} 2 & 3 & 4 & 1 \\ 1 & 0 & 2 & 1 \end{bmatrix} + \begin{bmatrix} 2 & 3 & 4 & 1 \\ 1 & 0 & 2 & 1 \end{bmatrix} + \begin{bmatrix} 2 & 3 & 4 & 1 \\ 1 & 0 & 2 & 1 \end{bmatrix}$$

$$= \begin{bmatrix} 4 & 6 & 8 & 2 \\ 2 & 0 & 4 & 2 \end{bmatrix} + \begin{bmatrix} 2 & 3 & 4 & 1 \\ 1 & 0 & 2 & 1 \end{bmatrix}$$

$$= \begin{bmatrix} 6 & 9 & 12 & 3 \\ 3 & 0 & 6 & 3 \end{bmatrix}.$$

However, the above calculation of the total sales volume can be simplified by scalar multiplication. A scalar is a single number (a constant) usually denoted by λ, and the number may be positive or negative. If λ is a positive number, then the multiplication of matrix A by λ can be interpreted as adding matrix A the λ number of times. This is equivalent to multiplying every element of A by the scalar λ. For the problem where the sales volume is identical for each of the three years, we can multiply all elements of the sales volume matrix A by 3, the scalar. This can be shown as:

$$3\begin{bmatrix} 2 & 3 & 4 & 1 \\ 1 & 0 & 2 & 1 \end{bmatrix} = \begin{bmatrix} 3(2) & 3(3) & 3(4) & 3(1) \\ 3(1) & 3(0) & 3(2) & 3(1) \end{bmatrix} = \begin{bmatrix} 6 & 9 & 12 & 3 \\ 3 & 0 & 6 & 3 \end{bmatrix}.$$

The subscript notation for the above scalar multiplication is:

$$\lambda A = \{\lambda a_{ij}\} \quad \text{for } \lambda = 3, i = 1, 2 \text{ and } j = 1, 2, 3, 4.$$

In scalar multiplication, the products of scalar λ multiplied by matrix A and matrix A multiplied by scalar λ are identical, i.e., scalar multiplication is commutative, which means $\lambda A = A\lambda$.

MATRIX MULTIPLICATION

In order to obtain sales revenue, we must know the per unit sales prices. Assume sales prices in 19X1 and 19X2 are $1.00, $1.10, $1.20, and $1.00 respectively for the four quarters. We can set up the following table for arithmetical multiplication:

19X1 Sales Price	$1.00	$1.10	$1.20	$1.00
Domestic sales volume	2	3	4	1
Foreign sales volume	1	0	2	1

Domestic sales revenue = 2(1.00) + 3(1.10) + 4(1.20) + 1(1.00) = 11.1
Foreign sales revenue = 1(1.00) + 0(1.10) + 2(1.20) + 1(1.00) = 4.4

Matrix multiplication is similar to the above calculation but is in a different format. In matrix multiplication, we can write the prices as a column vector p. A column vector is a matrix consisting of only one column. We then multiply the elements of the first row of the sales volume matrix A from left to right respectively by the corresponding elements of the price column vector p from top to bottom (i.e., the row 1, column 1 element in A and the first element in vector p, the row 1, column 2 element in A and the second element in vector p, etc.) and then add the products. The sum of the products forms the first row element of the resulting product matrix Ap. Next, we multiply the elements of the second row of matrix A by the elements of the vector p and add the products to form the second row element of matrix Ap. If we have more rows in matrix A, a similar procedure is used to form the other row elements in the resulting product matrix. These operations are shown by the following example:

$$Ap = \begin{bmatrix} 2 & 3 & 4 & 1 \\ 1 & 0 & 2 & 1 \end{bmatrix} \begin{bmatrix} 1.0 \\ 1.1 \\ 1.2 \\ 1.0 \end{bmatrix} = \begin{bmatrix} 2(1.0) + 3(1.1) + 4(1.2) + 1(1.0) \\ 1(1.0) + 0(1.1) + 2(1.2) + 1(1.0) \end{bmatrix} = \begin{bmatrix} 11.1 \\ 4.4 \end{bmatrix}.$$

Assume the costs per unit are $0.60, $0.70, $0.80, and $0.60 for the four quarters in 19X1 and 19X2. We can express the costs per unit as a column vector c and apply the same procedure as stated above to obtain the total cost of goods for both domestic and foreign sales as follows:

$$Ac = \begin{bmatrix} 2 & 3 & 4 & 1 \\ 1 & 0 & 2 & 1 \end{bmatrix} \begin{bmatrix} .6 \\ .7 \\ .8 \\ .6 \end{bmatrix} = \begin{bmatrix} 2(.6) +3(.7) +4(.8) +1(.6) \\ 1(.6) +0(.7) +2(.8) +1(.6) \end{bmatrix} = \begin{bmatrix} 7.1 \\ 2.8 \end{bmatrix}.$$

Now we combine the price column vector p and cost column vector c into a matrix X. The multiplication of A by X can be thought of as the aggregation of Ap and Ac. In effect, the resulting product matrix AX is formed by setting the resulting product vectors of Ap and Ac side by side. The numerical example of multiplying A by X is as follows:

$$AX = \begin{bmatrix} 2 & 3 & 4 & 1 \\ 1 & 0 & 2 & 1 \end{bmatrix} \begin{bmatrix} 1.0 & .6 \\ 1.1 & .7 \\ 1.2 & .8 \\ 1.0 & .6 \end{bmatrix}$$

$$= \begin{bmatrix} 2(1.0) +3(1.1) +4(1.2) +1(1.0) & 2(.6) +3(.7) +4(.8) +1(.6) \\ 1(1.0) +0(1.1) +2(1.2) +1(1.0) & 1(.6) +0(.7) +2(.8) +1(.6) \end{bmatrix}$$

$$= \begin{bmatrix} 11.1 & 7.1 \\ 4.4 & 2.8 \end{bmatrix}.$$

Matrix multiplication follows the rule (the conformable rule of matrix multiplication) that the number of columns of the first matrix must be equal to the number of rows of the second matrix. Therefore, because the number of columns in matrix A (four) equals the number of rows in matrix X (four), the resulting matrix product AX can be determined.[1] In forming AX, matrix A elements can be multiplied by matrix X elements in the manner previously described for Ap and as shown directly above for AX. The matrix product AX is of the order 2 by 2. It contains the same number of rows as the first matrix or matrix A (A is of the order 2×4) and the same number of columns as the second matrix or matrix X (X is of the order 4×2).

It should be noted that matrix multiplication is not in general commutative, which means that if matrices are of such orders that the products AX and XA both exist, they usually are not equal to each other. In the problem discussed above, the matrix product AX has an order 2×2 and XA has an order 4×4; therefore, AX cannot be equal to XA (i.e., $AX \neq XA$).[2] Where A

---

[1] If A is of the order 2 by 2, and X is 2 by 3, the product AX can be determined, but the product XA does not exist, following the conformable rule of multiplication, because X has 3 columns, while A has only 2 rows. Also, note that an associative law is true for matrix multiplication provided the matrices are conformable for multiplication. Thus, $ABC = A(BC) = (AB)C$.

[2] There are two special cases to the general non-commutative property of matrix multiplication. First, multiplication involving a square null matrix is commutative. A square matrix has the same number of columns as rows. A null (zero) matrix is a matrix whose elements are all zeros (0's). A zero matrix can be any order. If A is a square matrix of order m,

is of the order 2×4, and X is 4×2, we can determine the matrix products AX and XA because both meet the rules for matrix multiplication (for the AX case, 4 columns for A and 4 rows for X and for the XA case, 2 columns for X and 2 rows for A), but realize that the resultant matrix XA does not even have the same dimensions as AX.

The subscript notation for the above example of AX is as follows:

$$A = \begin{bmatrix} a_{11} & a_{12} & a_{13} & a_{14} \\ a_{21} & a_{22} & a_{23} & a_{24} \end{bmatrix} \quad X = \begin{bmatrix} x_{11} & x_{12} \\ x_{21} & x_{22} \\ x_{31} & x_{32} \\ x_{41} & x_{42} \end{bmatrix}$$

and

$$AX = \begin{bmatrix} a_{11}x_{11} + a_{12}x_{21} + a_{13}x_{31} + a_{14}x_{41} & a_{11}x_{12} + a_{12}x_{22} + a_{13}x_{32} + a_{14}x_{42} \\ a_{21}x_{11} + a_{22}x_{21} + a_{23}x_{31} + a_{24}x_{41} & a_{21}x_{12} + a_{22}x_{22} + a_{23}x_{32} + a_{24}x_{42} \end{bmatrix}$$

$$= \begin{bmatrix} \sum\limits_{k=1}^{4} a_{1k}x_{k1} & \sum\limits_{k=1}^{4} a_{1k}x_{k2} \\ \sum\limits_{k=1}^{4} a_{2k}x_{k1} & \sum\limits_{k=1}^{4} a_{2k}x_{k2} \end{bmatrix}$$

$$= \left\{ \sum\limits_{k=1}^{4} a_{ik}x_{kj} \right\} \qquad \text{for } i = 1, 2 \text{ and } j = 1, 2.$$

MATRIX INVERSION

As stated earlier in this paper, division is not defined in matrix algebra. The concept of dividing by a matrix A is replaced by the concept of multiplying by a matrix called the inverse of A. The inverse is usually denoted by A^{-1}. One of the important uses of matrix inversion is to obtain solutions for linear equations. We will illustrate the inversion technique first by solving a single equation and then a set of simultaneous equations.

---

and 0 is also a square matrix of order m, then $A_m 0_m = 0_m A_m = 0_m$. Second, multiplication involving an identity matrix is commutative. An identity matrix is a square matrix with ones (1's) in the main diagonal elements and zeros elsewhere. It is usually denoted by I. In general, if A is a square matrix of the order n, then $A_n I_n = I_n A_n = A_n$. In order to clarify the definition of a null matrix and an identity matrix, we give the following examples:

$$0_{2 \times 3} = \begin{bmatrix} 0 & 0 & 0 \\ 0 & 0 & 0 \end{bmatrix}, \quad 0_3 = \begin{bmatrix} 0 & 0 & 0 \\ 0 & 0 & 0 \\ 0 & 0 & 0 \end{bmatrix}, \quad I_3 = \begin{bmatrix} 1 & 0 & 0 \\ 0 & 1 & 0 \\ 0 & 0 & 1 \end{bmatrix}$$

Note that 0_3 and I_3 in the above refer to a 3 by 3 matrix and that the 0_3 and I_3 notations may be used rather than $0_{3 \times 3}$ and $I_{3 \times 3}$.

Assume we want to calculate the per unit cost of a product. The total manufacturing costs are $1,800 and the total units produced are 600 units. We can set up a single equation as:

$$600x = 1,800$$

where x is the per unit cost. One way of solving for x is to multiply both sides of the equation by the reciprocal or inverse of the coefficient of x, i.e., $\frac{1}{600}$. The equation would then be shown as follows:

$$\left(\frac{1}{600}\right)600x = \left(\frac{1}{600}\right)1800$$

From this equation we determine x = 3, which is the per unit cost of the product.

This reciprocal concept can be extended to solve a set of simultaneous equations. Assume we are planning to have a $4,000 operating profit for the coming year and want to know the sales and cost of sales figures based on the past experience of the firm. From the past cost-volume-profit relationships, we estimate cost of sales as $2,000 fixed costs plus variable costs which are approximately equal to 40% of sales. Selling and administrative expenses have been 25% of cost of sales. Operating profit, by definition, is equal to sales minus cost of sales and selling and administrative expenses.

The above statements can be translated into the following equations:

$$4,000 = x_1 - x_2 - .25x_2$$
$$x_2 = 2,000 + .4x_1$$

where x_1 denotes sales and x_2 cost of sales. These equations can be restated and put into matrices as follows:

$$x_1 - 1.25x_2 = 4,000$$
$$-.4x_1 + x_2 = 2,000$$

or $Ax = b$ where

$$A = \begin{bmatrix} 1 & -1.25 \\ -.4 & 1 \end{bmatrix}, \quad x = \begin{bmatrix} x_1 \\ x_2 \end{bmatrix}, \quad \text{and } b = \begin{bmatrix} 4,000 \\ 2,000 \end{bmatrix}$$

Analogous to the solution of the single equation, we multiply both sides of the matrix equation $Ax = b$ by the inverse matrix A^{-1} and solve for the vector x (i.e., the solution values for x_1 and x_2) as follows:

	$A^{-1}Ax = A^{-1}b$	(1)
or	$Ix = A^{-1}b$	(2)
and	$x = A^{-1}b$	(3).

In the left-hand side of equation (1) above, when the inverse matrix A^{-1} and the original matrix A are multiplied, an identity matrix, I, is formed.

Therefore, in equation 2, I replaces $A^{-1}A$. *The inverse matrix* A^{-1} is defined as a matrix such that $A^{-1}A = AA^{-1} = I$. An identity matrix, I, is a square matrix (which means it has the same number of columns as rows) with ones (1's) in the main diagonal elements and zeros elsewhere. For example, the following matrix with 3 columns and 3 rows is an identity matrix.

$$I = \begin{bmatrix} 1 & 0 & 0 \\ 0 & 1 & 0 \\ 0 & 0 & 1 \end{bmatrix}$$

In this matrix, all the elements in the main diagonal, i.e., where $i = j$, are ones, which means $a_{11} = 1$, $a_{22} = 1$, and $a_{33} = 1$.

When an identity matrix is multiplied by some other matrix, the result of the multiplication gives the same matrix by which the identity matrix was multiplied. Thus, multiplying an identity matrix of the appropriate order for equation 2 by the matrix x results in just the matrix x (i.e., the vector x) that appears in equation 3. Equation 3 above $(x = A^{-1}b)$, shows that for the set of simultaneous equations given below

$$x_1 - 1.25x_2 = 4,000$$
$$- .4x_1 + x_2 = 2,000$$

if we multiple the inverse matrix A^{-1} of these equations by the b values of the equations, or 4,000 and 2,000, the vector x or the solution values for x_1 and x_2 will be obtained.

The determination of an inverse matrix and then the use of that matrix in obtaining solution values for the original equations is demonstrated below.

There are several methods for finding the inverse matrix A^{-1}. We will demonstrate only the elementary row transformation technique here. For this technique we place an identity matrix next to the A matrix. This technique converts A into A^{-1} using elementary row transformations by converting the augmented matrix $[A \mid I]$ to another augmented matrix $[I \mid A^{-1}]$. This is done in a step-by-step fashion by repeatedly applying row transformations on the entire augmented matrix $[A \mid I]$ until the part representing the matrix A is reduced to an identity matrix. The part originally composed of an identity matrix, I, will now contain the desired inverse of A or A^{-1}.

The elementary row transformation technique allows the following operations:

1. Multiply or divide every element in a row by any number except zero.

2. Add any row to or subtract any row from any other row and replace either of the two rows by the new row of algebraic sums. (A row that is added to or subtracted from any other row can be a row resulting from multiplying or dividing a row by any number except zero.)

3. Interchange any two rows.

We will illustrate the technique by calculating the inverse of A for the set of simultaneous equations given above. We form the augmented matrix first and then perform row transformations systematically. The augmented matrix is shown as:

$$\begin{array}{c} \\ R_1 \\ R_2 \end{array} \begin{array}{cc} A & \quad\quad I \\ \left[\begin{array}{cc} 1 & -1.25 \\ -.4 & 1 \end{array}\right. & \left.\begin{array}{cc} 1 & 0 \\ 0 & 1 \end{array}\right] \end{array}$$

where A is the original matrix, I an identity matrix, and R_1 and R_2 represent rows 1 and 2 respectively. Remember we want to manipulate the augmented matrix so that matrix A of the augmented matrix is converted to an identity matrix, I.

1. We start the transformation process with the upper left-hand corner of the augmented matrix. We know the first element of row 1 and column 1 must be a 1 in order to agree with the first element of an identity matrix. Since a_{11} is 1 in this example, we do not have to perform any row transformations and can move to the next step. Therefore, after step 1, for this particular example the matrix still remains:

$$\begin{array}{c} R_1 \\ R_2 \end{array} \left[\begin{array}{cc} 1 & -1.25 \\ -.4 & 1 \end{array} \;\middle|\; \begin{array}{cc} 1 & 0 \\ 0 & 1 \end{array}\right].$$

If a_{11} were some number other than 1 or zero, we could divide all elements in the first row by a_{11} in order to make a_{11} equal to 1. If a_{11} were zero, we should interchange the first row with some other row whose first element is not zero.

2. Convert the remaining elements in the first column of matrix A (i.e., $-.4$) to zero. We complete one column at a time before moving to the next column. In this example, we can multiply the first row of the augmented matrix by .4 and add the resultant products to the second row to obtain a zero for the a_{21} element. Note that by multiplying each element in row 1 by .4, we obtain $.4(1)$, $.4(-1.25)$, $.4(1)$, $.4(0) = .4, -.5, .4, 0$. Then adding the resultant products to row 2, we obtain $(-.4+.4)$, $(1-.5)$, $(0+.4)$, $(1+0) = 0$, .5, .4, 1 for the new second row elements. When this operation is completed, we have:

$$\begin{array}{c} R_1 \\ R_2 + .4R_1 \end{array} \left[\begin{array}{cc} 1 & -1.25 \\ 0 & .5 \end{array} \;\middle|\; \begin{array}{cc} 1 & 0 \\ .4 & 1 \end{array}\right].$$

3. Convert the element in row 2 and column 2 (i.e., .5) to 1. We can divide the second row of the augmented matrix above by .5, and we have:

$$\begin{array}{c} R_1 \\ R_2 \div .5 \end{array} \left[\begin{array}{cc} 1 & -1.25 \\ 0 & 1 \end{array} \;\middle|\; \begin{array}{cc} 1 & 0 \\ .8 & 2 \end{array}\right].$$

After this step is completed, the a_{22} element is 1, and the only element remaining to be converted is the a_{12} or -1.25 in the matrix resulting from step 3. In step 4, the -1.25 will be converted to zero.

4. The remaining element of column 2 in the matrix A can be converted to a zero (thereby completing the transformation of the matrix A to an identity matrix) by multiplying the second row of the above augmented matrix by 1.25 and adding the resultant products to the first row. The resultant matrix shows:

$$
\begin{matrix} R_1 + 1.25\,R_2 \\ R_2 \end{matrix}
\quad
\left[\begin{array}{cc|cc} 1 & 0 & 2 & 2.5 \\ 0 & 1 & .8 & 2 \end{array}\right].
$$

$I \qquad A^{-1}$

In this example, we have accomplished the desired inversion, because the part of the augmented matrix that originally was matrix A has been converted to an identity matrix, I. The part of the augmented matrix that originally was the identity matrix now contains the inverse of A, or:

$$
A^{-1} = \begin{bmatrix} 2 & 2.5 \\ .8 & 2 \end{bmatrix}.
$$

If we have a problem with more rows and columns than the example used here, there will be more rows and columns in the augmented matrix and a procedure similar to that used in converting the first and second columns of matrix A into the first and second columns of matrix I should be followed.

Now we are ready to obtain the solution values for x_1 and x_2 in the original equations by multiplying the inverse matrix A^{-1} from step 4 and vector b of 4,000 and 2,000 from the original equations. Thus, $x = A^{-1}b$ and can be shown numerically as:

$$
\begin{bmatrix} x_1 \\ x_2 \end{bmatrix} = \begin{bmatrix} 2 & 2.5 \\ .8 & 2 \end{bmatrix} \begin{bmatrix} 4{,}000 \\ 2{,}000 \end{bmatrix}
$$

or

$$
\begin{bmatrix} x_1 \\ x_2 \end{bmatrix} = \begin{bmatrix} 2(4000) + 2.5(2000) \\ .8(4000) + 2(2000) \end{bmatrix}
$$

and

$$
\begin{bmatrix} x_1 \\ x_2 \end{bmatrix} = \begin{bmatrix} 13{,}000 \\ 7{,}200 \end{bmatrix}.
$$

Therefore, the required sales or x_1 and cost of sales or x_2 are \$13,000 and \$7,200 respectively in order to satisfy the relationships set forth in the problem. To check the solution values, we substitute them into the original equations of:

$$
\begin{aligned} x_1 - 1.25x_2 &= 4{,}000 \\ -.4x_1 + x_2 &= 2{,}000. \end{aligned}
$$

When the x_1 and x_2 values are substituted, the equations check as shown below:

$$13,000 - 1.25(7,200) = 4,000$$
$$-.4(13,000) + 7,200 = 2,000$$

or

$$13,000 - 9,000 = 4,000$$
$$-5,200 + 7,200 = 2,000.$$

For this problem, we can determine the inverse matrix and the solution values for x_1 and x_2 by using steps 1 through 4 shown above by including the vector b along with the matrices A and I; this is shown below:

$$
\begin{array}{c} \\ R_1 \\ R_2 \end{array}
\begin{array}{cc} \overset{A}{} & \overset{I}{} \end{array}
\left[\begin{array}{cc|cc|c}
1 & -1.25 & 1 & 0 & 4,000 \\
-.4 & 1 & 0 & 1 & 2,000
\end{array} \right].
$$

We use the row transformation technique with the new augmented matrix and the result of the operations is such that the matrix A above is replaced by matrix I, the identity matrix, I above, is replaced by A^{-1} and the vector b is replaced by the vector x which contains the solution values. Thus:

$$
\begin{array}{c} R_1 \\ R_2 \end{array}
\left[\begin{array}{cc|cc|c}
1 & -1.25 & 1 & 0 & 4,000 \\
-.4 & 1 & 0 & 1 & 2,000
\end{array} \right]
$$

$$
\begin{array}{c} R_1 \\ R_2 + .4R_1 \end{array}
\left[\begin{array}{cc|cc|c}
1 & -1.25 & 1 & 0 & 4,000 \\
0 & .5 & .4 & 1 & 3,600
\end{array} \right]
$$

$$
\begin{array}{c} R_1 \\ R_2 \div .5 \end{array}
\left[\begin{array}{cc|cc|c}
1 & -1.25 & 1 & 0 & 4,000 \\
0 & 1 & .8 & 2 & 7,200
\end{array} \right]
$$

$$
\begin{array}{c} R_1 + 1.25R_2 \\ R_2 \end{array}
\left[\begin{array}{cc|cc|c}
1 & 0 & 2 & 2.5 & 13,000 \\
0 & 1 & .8 & 2 & 7,200
\end{array} \right].
$$

Again, the required sales and cost of sales to satisfy the relationships set forth in the problem are $13,000 and $7,200 respectively.

TESTING TO SEE IF AN INVERSE MATRIX EXISTS; TRANSPOSING A MATRIX

Before attempting to calculate the inverse of a matrix, a test can be made to see if an inverse exists. In a 2×2 matrix, the product of the main diagonal elements minus the product of the cross diagonal elements of matrix A is called the determinant of A denoted by $|A|$ or det A. The existence of A^{-1} requires the determinant $|A|$ to be non-zero; an explanation of why this is the case involves a discussion of another matrix inversion method than the one presented above, and is beyond the scope of this paper. However, to show how to use the test, assume the coefficients in matrix A used in the problem for matrix inversion had been listed as:

$$A = \begin{bmatrix} 1 & -1.25 \\ -.4 & .5 \end{bmatrix}, \quad \text{then } |A| = 0.$$

For the matrix above, the determinant of A equals zero because the product of the main diagonal elements $(1)(.5) = .5$ and the product of the cross diagonal elements $(-.4)(-1.25) = .5$; thus, the product of the main diagonal elements minus the cross diagonal elements or $(.5) - (.5) = 0$. This means the nonexistence of A^{-1} and that there are no unique solutions to the two simultaneous equations because they are inconsistent.

The concept of the transpose of a matrix is frequently used in matrix manipulations. The transpose of a matrix A is denoted by A^T or A'; in forming it, we interchange the rows and columns of the original matrix. The first row in A is the first column in A^T, the second row in A is the second column in A^T, and so on. For example, referring back to the matrix A of the domestic- and foreign-sales volume:

$$\text{if } A = \begin{bmatrix} 2 & 3 & 4 & 1 \\ 1 & 0 & 2 & 1 \end{bmatrix}, \quad \text{then } A^T = \begin{bmatrix} 2 & 1 \\ 3 & 0 \\ 4 & 2 \\ 1 & 1 \end{bmatrix}.$$

It follows that the transpose of a transposed matrix is the matrix itself, i.e., $(A')' = A$, and that the transpose of a row vector is a column vector and vice versa. Furthermore, the transpose of a product matrix is the product of the transposed matrices taken in reverse order, i.e., $(AB)' = B'A'$.

CONCLUDING REMARKS

We have explained the matrix operations by simple accounting examples. Additional applications of matrix algebra such as cost allocations, equivalent unit determinations, profit sharing bonus plans, statement of affairs, and matrix bookkeeping can be found in the accounting literature. See Article 35, "A Proposal for Condensing Diverse Accounting Procedures," which follows.

Most of the applications of matrix algebra involve one or more of the four matrix operations in a more involved situation, but the mathematical concepts and rules of manipulation are the same as interpreted in this paper. Even in a very complicated application of matrix operations, it is important to remember that the conformable rules must be checked before the operations of matrix addition, subtraction, and multiplication are carried out, and that the existence of an inverse can be tested before the calculation of the inverse of a matrix is attempted.

SELECTED REFERENCES

Corcoran, A. Wayne, *Mathematical Applications in Accounting* (New York: Harcourt, Brace and World, Inc., 1968).

Hadley, George, *Linear Algebra* (Reading, Mass.: Addison-Wesley Publishing Company, 1961).

Hohn, Franz E., *Elementary Matrix Algebra*, 2nd ed. (New York: The Maxmillan Company, 1964).

Livingstone, John Leslie, *Management Planning and Control: Mathematical Models* (New York: McGraw-Hill Book Company, 1970).

Shank, John K., *Matrix Methods in Accounting* (Reading, Mass.: Addision-Wesley Publishing Company, 1972).

35.

A PROPOSAL FOR CONDENSING DIVERSE
ACCOUNTING PROCEDURES*

A. Wayne Corcoran

Whenever a person proceeds from one accounting area to another, he encounters what seems to be an entirely new set of inputs, rules, definitions,
and procedures. As traditionally presented, such diverse accounting areas
as partnerships, process cost accounting, liquidation statements, consolidated financial statements, variance analysis, determining overhead absorption rates, and preparing depreciation lapse schedules—to mention but a
few—seem to be virtually unrelated. In 1953 A. C. Littleton recognized this
problem when he wrote:

> In actual historical evolution, accounting principles have been
> slowly distilled out of accounting actions. That is to say, accounting
> rules, having first been the fruits of tentative actions, grew in
> significance until they became guides to predetermined actions. As
> these accounting particulars grew increasingly diverse and com-
> plex, so did accounting actions and the accompanying rules, cus-
> toms, practices. And as this diversity of particulars falls under
> more and more critical consideration, it becomes increasingly
> advisable to decide whether there are elements of order, se-
> quence, interrelation within the mass.[1]

Not only is this lack of interrelationship annoying, bewildering, and time
consuming, but it is also unnecessary. This article advocates the use of the
mathematical tool of matrices to interrelate diverse accounting areas from a

---

[1]A. C. Littleton, *Structure of Accounting Theory*, Monograph Number 5, American
Accounting Association, 1953, p. 123.

procedural viewpoint. It shows how just a few, simple matrix manipulations may be used as substitutes for the myriad procedures now employed to accomplish allocation.

ACCOUNTING PROCEDURE STRUCTURE

Much of traditional accounting procedure involves the acquisition, valuation, and allocation of input data. Concentrating on these processes makes it possible to interrelate diverse accounting areas. Let us illustrate this idea by referring to two accounting areas that perhaps, at first glance, seem related only in that money and accounting are concerned. These areas are the preparation of process cost reports and the preparation of liquidation statements. These areas may be viewed in terms of their acquisition, valuation, and allocation phases as shown in Exhibit 1.

| **BASIC STEPS IN ACCOUNTING PROCEDURE** | | |
Process Cost Reports		Liquidation Statement
The listing of material, labor, and overhead components	Acquisition	The listing of all available assets
The determining of historical cost outlays of components	Valuation	The determining of realizable values of assets
The distribution of valued cost components to output designations	Allocation	The distributing of valued assets to various types of creditors and owners

Exhibit 1. Basic Steps in Accounting Procedure

The similarities between these areas are now more apparent. Both involve listing a set of inputs (acquisition phase), determining appropriate values for these inputs (valuation phase), and distributing the valued inputs to output destinations (allocation phase). Likewise, the differences between the two areas are evident: The inputs in process costing are data on materials, labor, and overhead while those involved in liquidation are data on all available assets. The values assigned to inputs in process costing are historical cost outlays while those in liquidation are realizable values. The output destinations in process costing are product costs while those in liquidation are claimants' equities.

Because these two accounting areas are most similar to each other in the allocation phase, it would seem that their interrelationship could best be accomplished by concentrating on allocation processes. The inputs and outputs in the various accounting areas differ, and so do the methods of input valuation. Thus, the acquisition and valuation processes are not likely to lead to extensive interrelation. This leaves us with allocation processes as the most promising avenue. We seek, therefore, the answer to the question, "Can the allocation of inputs to outputs be standardized so that diverse accounting areas may be interrelated?"

In mathematics, the framework for allocation problems is found in vector spaces, and the allocation process itself is carried out by transformation matrices. A matrix may be defined as something that consists of rows and columns of numbers. These rows and columns of numbers are referred to as vectors, and a matrix consists of one or more vectors. This is a row vector: (1, 3, −1, 4); this is a column vector:

$$\begin{bmatrix} 8 \\ 2 \\ 0 \end{bmatrix}.$$

An example of a matrix containing more than a single vector is

$$\begin{bmatrix} 2 & 1 & 0 \\ 1 & -2 & 5 \end{bmatrix}.$$

Vectors and matrices may be added and subtracted element by element, provided they have the same dimensions. For instance:

$$\begin{bmatrix} 2 & 1 & 0 \\ 1 & -2 & 5 \end{bmatrix} + \begin{bmatrix} 3 & 5 & 2 \\ 6 & -1 & 0 \end{bmatrix} = \begin{bmatrix} 5 & 6 & 2 \\ 7 & -3 & 5 \end{bmatrix}.$$

Vectors and matrices may be multiplied, provided the number of columns in the left-hand matrix equals the number of rows in the right-hand matrix. The exact procedure for multiplication is expressed in the formula:

$$c_{ik} = \sum_{j=1}^{n} a_{ij} b_{jk} = a_{i1} b_{1k} + \ldots a_{in} b_{nk}$$

$$\text{where: } \begin{aligned} i &= 1, 2, \ldots, m. \\ j &= 1, 2, \ldots, n. \\ k &= 1, 2, \ldots, r. \end{aligned}$$

Consider this problem:

$$\underset{(2 \times 3)}{\overset{A}{\begin{bmatrix} a_{11} & a_{12} & a_{13} \\ a_{21} & a_{22} & a_{23} \end{bmatrix}}} \underset{(3 \times 4)}{\overset{B}{\begin{bmatrix} b_{11} & b_{12} & b_{13} & b_{14} \\ b_{21} & b_{22} & b_{23} & b_{24} \\ b_{31} & b_{32} & b_{33} & b_{34} \end{bmatrix}}} = \underset{(2 \times 4)}{\begin{bmatrix} C \end{bmatrix}}$$

a_{ij} represents any element from Matrix A; the subscript i indicates the row number and the subscript j indicates the column number.

b_{jk} represents any element from Matrix B; the subscript j indicates the row number while the subscript k indicates the column number.

Let us substitute artibrary numerical values and see what Matrix C looks like.

$$
\overset{A}{\begin{bmatrix} 2 & 1 & 0 \\ 1 & -2 & 5 \end{bmatrix}} \overset{B}{\begin{bmatrix} -2 & 3 & -1 & 4 \\ 1 & 8 & 1 & 0 \\ 4 & 0 & 2 & 4 \end{bmatrix}} = \overset{C}{\begin{bmatrix} -3 & 14 & -1 & 8 \\ 16 & -13 & 7 & 24 \end{bmatrix}}
$$

To see how an element of Matrix C is determined, let us apply the formula to determine c_{23}.

$$
c_{23} = \sum_{j=1}^{3} a_{2j}\, b_{j3} = 1(-1) - 2(1) + 5(2) = 7.
$$

DEPRECIATION APPLICATION

Perhaps the simplest accounting application of matrix multiplication is to be found in preparing depreciation lapse schedules. Here the accountant is concerned with allocating portions of the depreciable bases of assets—the inputs of the problem—to appropriate time periods—the output designations of the problem. This problem is illustrated in Exhibit 2.[2]

Note that Matrix L arrays inputs (assets) according to outputs (time periods). This form of schedule clearly depicts allocation and is easily understood. It can be made to result from other types of matrix multiplication, but the important thing is that the more widely used the matrix schedule is the more interrelation among accounting areas will exist.

PROCESS COST APPLICATION

Let us return now to the preparation of process cost reports and statements of affairs and see how matrices may be used to further interrelate these accounting areas.

Exhibit 3 contains a generalized presentation of a matrix approach to preparing a process cost report. The dashed lines in Matrix A and Vector b

---

[2]Note that the multiplication of the vectors would yield only the body of Matrix L; the rim totals have merely been obtained by addition. Such addition could be accomplished in matrix algebra by use of sum vectors, that is, vectors all elements of which are ones. However, this use of sum vectors would only be a mathematical nicety and would needlessly complicate our example.

DEPRECIATION MATRIX

b (depreciable bases)	r (rates per time period)	L				Totals
$\begin{bmatrix} 60,000 \\ 80,000 \\ 20,000 \end{bmatrix}$	$\begin{bmatrix} .4, .3, .2, .1 \end{bmatrix}$	24,000	18,000	12,000	6,000	60,000
		32,000	24,000	16,000	8,000	80,000
		8,000	6,000	4,000	2,000	20,000
	Totals	64,000	48,000	32,000	16,000	160,000

(lapse schedule)

Exhibit 2. Depreciation Matrix

indicate partitioning. Wherever the partitions are drawn, the usual procedure of multiplication of column and row elements and the summing of individual products must be halted, and the results to that point must be entered in separate vectors.

For instance, without partitioning we would determine the elements in a product matrix, C, as was described previously, that is

$$c_{ik} = \sum_{j=1}^{n} a_{ij} b_{jk}.$$

Suppose now that Matrix A is partitioned after Columns 3 and 7 and hence Matrix B is correspondingly partitioned after Rows 3 and 7. There would be three matrices resulting from the multiplication of the separate partitioned matrices,

$$\sum_{j=1}^{3} a_{ij} b_{jk}, \qquad \sum_{j=4}^{7} a_{ij} b_{jk}, \qquad \text{and} \qquad \sum_{j=8}^{n} a_{ij} b_{jk}.$$

The separate vectors may then be added to obtain the total equivalent production vector e—which, parenthetically, could have been obtained by ignoring the partitioning and performing the multiplication Ab. The elements E_i in Vector e are used in the computation of the unit costs, U_i. The unit costs are then entered in Matrix U, and the cost report results from the multiplication UD. Exhibit 3 essentially reduces to a system of equations for solving process cost problems under the average method.

The form of Matrix U in Exhibit 3 deserves further comment. In this form—that is, with non-zero numbers on the main diagonal of the matrix and zeros everywhere else—the matrix is called a diagonalized matrix. A diagonalized matrix has a number of properties, the most interesting of which for present purposes is that the elements of Matrix R, the cost report, can be obtained by multiplying the elements of U and D in a distributive manner (that is, so to say, straight-across multiplication) rather than by

---

PROCESS COST MATRICES: AVERAGE METHOD, SINGLE PRODUCT

Equivalent Production Computation:

$$
\begin{array}{cccc}
 & & A & & b & & & & e \\
\end{array}
$$

Inputs \ Outputs	T	E	L
"Preceding"	1	1	1
"Materials"	1	f_M	g_M
"Conversion"	1	f_c	g_c

$$
\begin{bmatrix} T \\ E \\ L \end{bmatrix} = \begin{bmatrix} T \\ T \\ T \end{bmatrix} + \begin{bmatrix} E \\ f_M E \\ f_c E \end{bmatrix} + \begin{bmatrix} L \\ g_M L \\ g_c L \end{bmatrix} = \begin{bmatrix} E_p \\ E_M \\ E_c \end{bmatrix}
$$

Unit cost formula:

$$
U_i = \sum_{j=1}^{2} I_j \div E_i
$$

Cost Allocation:

$$
\begin{array}{ccc}
U & & \\
\end{array}
$$

$$
\begin{bmatrix} U_p & O & O \\ O & U_M & O \\ O & O & U_c \end{bmatrix} \begin{bmatrix} T & E & L \\ T & f_M E & g_M L \\ T & f_c E & g_c L \end{bmatrix} = \begin{bmatrix} U_p T & U_p E & U_p L \\ U_M T & U_M f_M E & U_M g_M L \\ U_c T & U_c f_c E & U_c g_c L \end{bmatrix}
$$

$$
\begin{array}{ccc}
 & D & R\ (cost\ \ report)
\end{array}
$$

KEY:

A = Matrix containing proportions of each output quantity appearing in each input category. Note that the rows (labelled) show the input categories while the columns show the output designations.

b = A vector showing the total quantities in each of the three output designations (T, E, L).

e = A vector that shows the equivalent production (E_i) for each type of input.

T = Units transferred.

E = Units in ending inventory.

L = Units lost.

f_i = Fraction of ending inventory completed in terms of input i.

g_i = Fraction of lost units completed in terms of input i.

U_i = Unit cost of input i; i = P (Preceding department's transferred production costs), M (Direct materials), C (Conversion costs).

I_j = Total cost of input I (I = P, M, C, as defined above under index i) appearing in opening inventory (j = 1) or in the costs incurred during the present period (j = 2).

E_i = Equivalent production of i.

D = Matrix composed of the equivalent production vectors.

Exhibit 3

observing the ordinary rules of matrix multiplication (which would generate the same results—but in a more complicated way). In a nutshell—a diagonalized matrix simplifies matrix multiplication.

Another advantage of the use of a diagonalized matrix in multiplication is that it results in an input-output-type matrix such as shown in Matrix R. Such a matrix arrays inputs according to outputs, and, after all, this is what allocation is all about. No other form for reporting allocations is as appealing as the input-output form. No other report format shows correspondence of inputs to outputs as well. No other report format is as easy to understand. No other report format is as simple. We shall use a numerical example to make this argument more concrete.

Exhibit 4 presents the data for an illustrative problem. The problem deals with several of the usual complicating features of process costing, including opening inventories, incomplete products received from a previous department, units "gained" through adding departmental materials, lost units, and the reallocation of lost-unit costs.

PROCESS COST PROBLEM

Key: (P, M, C) = portion of production done during present month for P (goods received from preceding department), M (departmental materials), C (departmental conversion costs).

QUANTITY DATA

Opening inventory (0, 1/4, 1/2)	40,000
Received from preceding department during period	360,000
Units added by present department	100,000
	500,000
Transferred out	320,000
Ending Inventory (1, 2/3, 1/2)	150,000
Lost units (normal loss occurring gradually during processing;	
no provision in overhead rate: 1, 2/5, 1/3)	30,000
	500,000

COST DATA

Opening inventory:		
Preceding department's costs		$ 120,000
Departmental material costs		60,000
Departmental conversion costs		60,160
Costs during month:		
Preceding department's costs		1,380,000
Departmental material costs		804,000
Departmental conversion costs		1,187,240
	TOTAL	$3,611,400

Exhibit 4

The matrix solution to the problem appears in Exhibit 5, shown below. Exhibit 5 traces the generalized presentation of Exhibit 3. Three inputs—costs from preceding department, departmental materials, and departmental conversion costs—have been allocated to three designations—units transferred, units in ending inventory, and units lost.[3] The reallocation of lost-unit costs to the transferred- and ending-inventory designations has been done in the proportion these output designations have in the equivalent production of conversion.

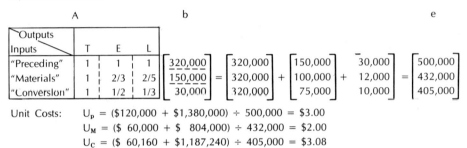

MATRIX SOLUTION TO PROCESS COST PROBLEM

Equivalent Production

	A			b		e
Outputs / Inputs	T	E	L			
"Preceding"	1	1	1			
"Materials"	1	2/3	2/5			
"Conversion"	1	1/2	1/3			

$$\begin{bmatrix} 320,000 \\ 150,000 \\ 30,000 \end{bmatrix} = \begin{bmatrix} 320,000 \\ 320,000 \\ 320,000 \end{bmatrix} + \begin{bmatrix} 150,000 \\ 100,000 \\ 75,000 \end{bmatrix} + \begin{bmatrix} 30,000 \\ 12,000 \\ 10,000 \end{bmatrix} = \begin{bmatrix} 500,000 \\ 432,000 \\ 405,000 \end{bmatrix}$$

Unit Costs: $U_p = (\$120,000 + \$1,380,000) \div 500,000 = \$3.00$
$U_M = (\$ 60,000 + \$ 804,000) \div 432,000 = \$2.00$
$U_C = (\$ 60,160 + \$1,187,240) \div 405,000 = \$3.08$

Cost Allocation:

$$\begin{array}{cc} U & D \\ \begin{bmatrix} 3.00 \\ 2.00 \\ 3.08 \end{bmatrix} & \begin{bmatrix} 320,000 & 150,000 & 30,000 \\ 320,000 & 100,000 & 12,000 \\ 320,000 & 75,000 & 10,000 \end{bmatrix} = R \end{array}$$

R
COST REPORT

	Transferred	Ending Inventory	Lost	Costs to be Accounted for
Preceding department's costs	$ 960,000	$450,000	$ 90,000	$1,500,000
Departmental material costs	640,000	200,000	24,000	864,000
Departmental conversion costs	985,600	231,000	30,800	1,247,400
Totals	$2,585,600	$881,000	$144,800	$3,611,400
Reallocation of lost costs	117,306	27,494	(144,800)	—0—
Costs accounted for	$2,702,906	$908,494	$ —0—	$3,611,400

Reallocation: $\$144,800 \left(\dfrac{320,000}{395,000}, \dfrac{75,000}{395,000} \right) = (\$117,306; \$27,494)$

Note: The totals surrounding the basic matrix, R, have been obtained merely by adding and cross adding. The multiplication UD did not produce these totals. Similarly, UD had nothing to do with reallocation.

Exhibit 5

---

[3] These outputs exhaust the set of possibilities; units can still be in process, or they can be completed, or they can be lost in some way—nothing else can take place. The matrix approach accords lost units full status as an output designation. This logical view of lost units is not found in most cost accounting texts, but it is ably put forth in Charles T. Horngren, *Cost Accounting—A Managerial Emphasis*, Prentice-Hall, Inc., Englewood Cliffs, New Jersey, 1962.

Exhibit 6 presents a conventional cost report treatment of this same process cost report. The purpose of presenting this exhibit is merely to provide something to compare with the input-output format of the cost report. It seems probable that only the initiated could follow the traditional cost report. The allocation of inputs to outputs is much more clearly presented in matrix format.

CONVENTIONAL COST REPORT

	Total Cost	Unit Cost
Costs to be accounted for:		
Cost from preceding department:		
Opening inventory	$ 120,000	—
Costs during period	1,380,000	$3.00000
Departmental costs:		
Opening inventory		
Departmental material costs	60,000	—
Departmental conversion costs	60,160	—
Costs during period:		
Departmental material costs	804,000	2.00000
Departmental conversion costs	1,187,240	3.08000
	$3,611,400	$8.08000
Adjustment for lost units	—0—	.36658
TOTAL COST TO BE ACCOUNTED FOR	$3,611,400	$8.44658
Costs accounted for:		$2,702,906
Transferred (320,000 × $8.44658)		
Ending inventory:		
Preceding department costs (150,000 × .$3.00)	$ 450,000	
Departmental material costs (100,000 × $2.00)	200,000	
Departmental conversion costs (75,000 × $3.08)	231,000	
Adjustment for lost units (75,000 × $.36658)	27,494	908,494
TOTAL COST ACCOUNTED FOR		$3,611,400

Additional computations:
Unit costs:
Preceding department costs: ($120,000 + $1,380,000) ÷ 500,000 = $3.00
Departmental material costs: ($ 60,000 + $ 804,000) ÷ 432,000 = $2.00
Departmental conversion costs: ($ 60,160 + $1,187,240) ÷ 405,000 = $3.08
Adjustment for lost units:
  (30,000($3.00) + 12,000($2.00) + 10,000($3.08)) ÷ 395,000 = $.36658

Exhibit 6

To expedite the discussions ahead, we introduce a form of matrix shorthand, shown in Exhibit 7 below.

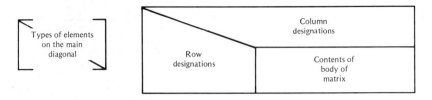

Exhibit 7. Matrix Shorthand

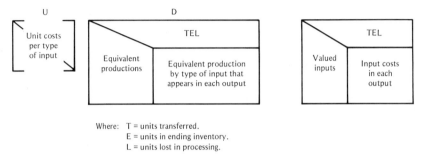

Where: T = units transferred.
        E = units in ending inventory.
        L = units lost in processing.

Exhibit 8. Process Cost Matrices

We could use this shorthand to summarize the matrices U, D, and R in Exhibit 3 as shown in Exhibit 8.

Now let us turn our attention to Exhibit 9 which contains an illustrative statement of affairs. Exhibit 9 presents the traditional format of this report, which again is probably understood only by the initiated. Exhibit 10 shows how this report would look in input-output format. The matrix format emphasizes the distribution of inputs (types of assets) to output designations (types of claimants). With the exception of the row and column totals which were obtained by addition, the matrix report results from the multiplication shown in Exhibit 11.

How well have matrices succeeded in further interrelating the process costing and statement of affairs areas? The matrix approach in both cases employed diagonalized matrices. The transformation matrices were composed of either quantities or proportions depending on whether the non-zero elements in the diagonalized matrices were dollars per unit or total dollars. Hence, the procedures of allocation in these areas are very similar under the matrix approach. The reports that resulted from matrix allocation are identical in format, and this is significant. When process costing and statements of affairs are first encountered, perhaps the single most time-consuming chore is to understand the separate report formats. Under the matrix approach only one, easy-to-understand report format is necessary.

Many accounting areas can be approached in exactly this same manner, that is, by the formulation of a diagonalized matrix and a transformation

ILLUSTRATIVE STATEMENT OF AFFAIRS

Book Value			Expected to Realize
	Assets pledged with fully secured creditors:		
$25,000	Land and buildings:		
	Estimated value	$25,500	
	Less mortgage payments—contra	15,000	$11,500
	Assets pledged with partially secured creditors:		
3,000	Bonds of X Company—deducted contra		
	Estimated value	$ 3,200	
	Free assets:		
300	Cash		300
9,000	Accounts receivable:		
	$8,000 Good		8,000
	$1,000 Doubtful		600
	$9,000		
18,700	Merchandise		19,200
	Total free assets		$39,600
	Deduct liabilities having priority—per contra		600
$56,000			$39,000

Book Value			Expected to Rank
	Liabilities having priority:		
$ 600	Accrued wages—deducted contra		
	Fully secured liabilities:		
15,000	Mortgage payable—deducted contra		
	Partially secured liabilities:		
5,000	Notes payable	$ 5,000	
	Less bonds of X Company	3,200	$ 1,800
	Unsecured liabilities:		
23,000	Accounts payable		23,000
	Net worth per books:		
12,000	Capital stock		
400	Retained earnings		
	Total unsecured liabilities		$24,800
	Excess of net free assets over unsecured liabilities		14,200
$56,000			$39,000

Exhibit 9

matrix to obtain an input-output matrix report.[4] The trick is to recognize data inputs and outputs as such and to determine the accounting criteria

---

[4] Some of the other accounting areas that can be treated this way include job-order costing, standard costing, period budgeting, primary overhead allocation, and responsibility accounting.

STATEMENT OF AFFAIRS—MATRIX FORMAT

Assets:	Liabilities Having Priority	Fully Secured Liabilities	Partially Secured Liabilities	Unsecured Liabilities	Owners	Totals
Pledged in full security (Land)	$—0—	$15,000	$—0—	$—0—	$—0—	$15,000
Pledged in partial security (Bonds owned)	—0—	—0—	3,200	—0—	—0—	3,200
Free (See note)	600	—0—	1,800	23,000	14,200	39,600
	$600	$15,000	$5,000	$23,000	$14,200	$57,800

Note: Free assets include:	Cash	$ 300
	Accounts receivable	8,600
	Merchandise	19,200
	Land & buildings ($26,500–$15,000)	11,500
		$39,600

DEFICIENCY ACCOUNT

Owners' equity per books	$12,400
Gains on realization:	
Land and buildings	1,500
Bonds of X Company	200
Merchandise	500
	$14,600
Loss on realization:	
Accounts receivable	400
Amount payable to owners in liquidation	$14,200

Exhibit 10

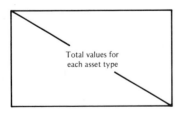 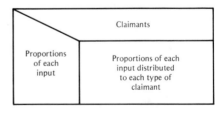

Total values for each asset type

Claimants

Proportions of each input

Proportions of each input distributed to each type of claimant

Exhibit 11. Multiplication for Statement of Affairs: Matrix Format

that govern the allocation. Usually, the accounting criteria can be reduced to simply measuring ownership or to reflecting usage. If any difficulty is encountered, it is likely to be not so much in recognizing inputs as in recognizing output designations.

BONUS-TAX COMPUTATIONS

There are other types of matrices that are important in accounting allocations. One of these is the inverse matrix. Although it would take too long to
develop matrix inversion in full here, the broad concepts can be presented
briefly if we restrict ourselves to systems in which there are two unknowns
and two equations.

Consider the situation where it is necessary to calculate simultaneously
an executive bonus based on profits after tax and a tax of some sort:

$$
\begin{aligned}
\text{Key: } B &= \text{Bonus} \\
T &= \text{Tax} \\
\$90,000 &= \text{Profits before } B \text{ and } T \\
B &= .20(\$90,000 - T) \\
T &= .50(\$90,000 - B)
\end{aligned}
$$

This system of equations can be restated and put into matrices as follows:

$$
\begin{aligned}
B + \quad .2T &= \$18,000 \\
.5B + \quad T &= \$45,000
\end{aligned}
$$

$$
\underset{A}{\begin{bmatrix} 1 & .2 \\ .5 & 1 \end{bmatrix}} \quad \underset{x}{\begin{bmatrix} B \\ T \end{bmatrix}} = \underset{b}{\begin{bmatrix} 18,000 \\ 45,000 \end{bmatrix}}
$$

It is always wise to check the matrix set-up by mentally performing the
matrix multiplication $Ax = b$ to see that the original equations are obtained.

Now, as matrix algebra is ordinarily put forth, division by a matrix is
undefined, that is, one could not solve for x by performing $x = b$ divided by
A as one would solve $5x = 20$ by performing $x = 20$ divided by 5. Instead
one must use an inverse matrix; this corresponds to solving $5x = 20$ by
performing $x = 20(.2)$. Recognize that the multiplication of a number by its
inverse yields the number 1 (for example, since the inverse of 5 is 1 divided
by $5 = .2$, we have $5(.2) = 1$). So it is with matrices; the multiplication of a
matrix A by its inverse A^{-1} yields the identity matrix, I. I has the property
that when it multiplies another matrix the product of the multiplication is
the other matrix. Note that this is the same result produced when we
multiply the number 1 by some other number, for example, $1 \times 5 = 5$.

The procedure for solving our bonus-tax problem is as follows:

$$
\begin{aligned}
Ax &= b \\
(A^{-1}A)x &= A^{-1}b \\
(Ix) &= A^{-1}b \\
x &= A^{-1}b
\end{aligned}
$$

We may form A^{-1} by interchanging the main diagonal elements of A,
putting minus signs next to the cross diagonal elements, and dividing the
resulting elements by the product of the main diagonal elements minus the

product of the cross diagonal elements (in our example: $1(1) - .5(.2) = .9$). The solution to this example is shown in Exhibit 12.

SOLUTION TO BONUS—TAX PROBLEM

$$x \quad = \quad A^{-1} \qquad\qquad b$$

$$\begin{bmatrix} B \\ T \end{bmatrix} = \begin{bmatrix} 1/9 & -.2/.9 \\ -.5/.9 & 1/.9 \end{bmatrix} \begin{bmatrix} 18,000 \\ 45,000 \end{bmatrix} = \begin{bmatrix} 10,000 \\ 40,000 \end{bmatrix}$$

This says that B = $10,000 and T = $40,000.

Exhibit 12

SECONDARY OVERHEAD ALLOCATION

Another example of a case in which this kind of matrix manipulation is useful[5] is secondary overhead allocation. Here primary overhead costs (such as indirect labor, repairs, depreciation, insurance, heat, light, power, and so forth) have been distributed to both service and production departments, and it remains necessary to reallocate service department costs to service-consuming departments (secondary allocation) so that overhead absorption rates may be determined. Deciding the percentages of services consumed involves the accountant in estimating potential and actual usage of departmental services.

Let us consider a simple illustration. Assume that the percentages reflecting usage have already been determined and are as shown in Exhibit 13.

There are two approaches to be considered: (1) the traditional approach, whereby the primary costs of the service-rendering departments are first augmented by the costs these departments are responsible for as service consumers and then the new totals are allocated to the production departments, and (2) the "linked" approach, whereby the intermediate stage is omitted since it serves no purpose.

Under the traditional approach, augmenting the service department primary costs is accomplished by solving the following system of equations:

$$S_1 = 90 + .25S_2$$
$$S_2 = 180 + .40S_1$$

---

[5] A third example involving an inverse matrix occurs in consolidated financial statements. Here the inputs are intercompany profits in inventory, fixed assets, and bonds that are made by each constituent company. The outputs are the majority and minority interests. When the intercompany relationships are entered in a matrix and adjusted to reflect effective interests, the resulting transformation matrix may be used to determine the adjusting entries to correct the various retained earnings accounts.

SECONDARY OVERHEAD ALLOCATION PROBLEM

$$P_i = \text{Service department } i.$$
$$\text{Key: } S_j = \text{Production department } j.$$

Consumers Renderers	S_1	S_2	P_1	P_2	P_3
S_1	0	40%	10%	30%	20%
S_2	25%	0	45%	20%	10%

	S_1	S_2	P_1	P_2	P_3
Primary overhead allocation totals (000 omitted)	$90	$180	$377	$307	$246
Standard Machine hours (estimated, 000 omitted)			200	50	150

Exhibit 13

The system may be stated in matrices as follows:

$$
\begin{matrix} A \end{matrix} \qquad \begin{matrix} x \end{matrix} \qquad \begin{matrix} b \end{matrix}
$$
$$
\begin{bmatrix} 1 & -.25 \\ -.40 & 1 \end{bmatrix} \begin{bmatrix} S_1 \\ S_2 \end{bmatrix} = \begin{bmatrix} 90 \\ 180 \end{bmatrix}
$$
$$\text{Total} = \qquad 270$$

The solution is:

$$
\begin{matrix} x \end{matrix} = \begin{matrix} A^{-1} \end{matrix} \qquad \begin{matrix} b \end{matrix} \qquad \begin{matrix} x \end{matrix}
$$
$$
\begin{bmatrix} S_1 \\ S_2 \end{bmatrix} = \begin{bmatrix} 1/.9 & .25/.9 \\ .40/.9 & 1/.9 \end{bmatrix} \begin{bmatrix} 90 \\ 180 \end{bmatrix} = \begin{bmatrix} 150 \\ 240 \end{bmatrix}
$$

Vector x contains the augmented service department costs.

Now the amounts in Vector x must be allocated to the production departments. Accordingly, we form Matrix P by transposing the percentages shown under the P_i and use this matrix to obtain our ultimate amounts for redistribution (shown in Vector r).

$$
\begin{matrix} P \end{matrix} \qquad\quad \begin{matrix} x \end{matrix} \qquad \begin{matrix} r \end{matrix}
$$
$$
\begin{bmatrix} .10 & .45 \\ .30 & .20 \\ .20 & .10 \end{bmatrix} \begin{bmatrix} 150 \\ 240 \end{bmatrix} = \begin{bmatrix} 123 \\ 93 \\ 54 \end{bmatrix}
$$
$$\text{Total} = \qquad 270$$

The amounts in Vector r must then be added to the primary allocation amounts for the production departments (say, Vector d) to obtain the total overhead costs (Vector t) for each production department.

$$
\begin{array}{ccc}
r & d & t \\
\begin{bmatrix} 123 \\ 93 \\ 54 \end{bmatrix} & + \begin{bmatrix} 377 \\ 307 \\ 246 \end{bmatrix} & = \begin{bmatrix} 500 \\ 400 \\ 300 \end{bmatrix}
\end{array}
$$

The amounts in Vector t would next be divided by the respective esti-mated standard machine hours to obtain the desired overhead absorption rates of $500 divided by 200 = \$2.50$, $400 divided by 50 = \$8.00$, and $300 divided by 150 = \$2.00$.

The alternate or "linked" approach recognizes the uselessness of the augmented service department totals of \$150,000 and \$240,000 (shown in Vector x). Control over the reallocated portions of these totals (that is, over \$150,000 − \$90,000 and \$240,000 − \$180,000) is typically achieved by the "departmental cross charges" of responsibility accounting. Hence, for product costing purposes the intermediate augmented service department totals may be bypassed, provided the effects of these totals are provided for.

Since matrices may be multiplied and added, it is possible to "link up" several stages of allocation. In our secondary overhead allocation example, for instance, we could proceed as follows:

$$ t = d + PA^{-1}b $$

Let us first form PA^{-1}. It would always make sense to do this where the departmental interrelationships can be expected to remain stable—as they might for planning purposes.

$$
\begin{array}{ccc}
P & A^{-1} & PA^{-1} \\
\begin{bmatrix} .10 & .45 \\ .30 & .20 \\ .20 & .10 \end{bmatrix} & \begin{bmatrix} 1/.9 & .25/.9 \\ .40/.9 & 1/.9 \end{bmatrix} & = \begin{bmatrix} .3111 & .5278 \\ .4222 & .3055 \\ .2667 & .1667 \end{bmatrix}
\end{array}
$$

We see that the equation for t holds.[6]

$$
\begin{array}{ccccc}
t & d & PA^{-1} & b & \\
\begin{bmatrix} 500 \\ 400 \\ 300 \end{bmatrix} = & \begin{bmatrix} 377 \\ 307 \\ 246 \end{bmatrix} + & \begin{bmatrix} .3111 & .5278 \\ .4222 & .3055 \\ .2667 & .1667 \end{bmatrix} & \begin{bmatrix} 90 \\ 180 \end{bmatrix} = & \begin{bmatrix} 377 \\ 307 \\ 246 \end{bmatrix} + \begin{bmatrix} 123 \\ 93 \\ 54 \end{bmatrix}
\end{array}
$$

OTHER APPLICATIONS

Matrices may be helpful in price-level work and traditional variance analysis. Let us consider the analysis of labor variances. Here the inputs

---

[6]Further discussion of this type of transformation may be found in Neil Churchill, "Linear Algebra and Cost Allocation: Some Examples," The Accounting Review, October, 1964.

involve wage rates for different categories of labor; transformation involves labor hours, and the outputs are the standard costs and variances. An example is shown in Exhibit 14.

LABOR VARIANCE ANALYSIS

Given data: Labor type A:
                                       Standard = 600 hours at $3 per hour
                                       Actual   = 640 hours at $2.75 per hour

                                Labor type B:
                                       Standard = 1000 hours at $4 per hour
                                       Actual   = 900 hours at $5 per hour

                                Labor type C:
                                       Standard = 800 hours at $2 per hour
                                       Actual   = 1000 hours at $2.50 per hour

Matrix solution:

        Key: P = standard wage rate
                                             ΔP = change in wage rate
                                      $P + \Delta P$ = actual wage rate
                                             Q = standard hours
                                            ΔQ = change in standard hours
                                      $Q + \Delta Q$ = actual hours

		A	B	C			Q	ΔQ		Standard	Net Efficiency Variance
P		3	4	2	A		600	40		$7,400	$120
ΔP		−.25	1	.50	B		1000	−100	=	$1,250	−$ 10
					C		800	200			

	Net Wage Variance	Net Mixed Variance

Note: The signs attached to the net variances may be interpreted as follows: − indicates a favorable
        variance; + indicates an unfavorable variance.

Exhibit 14

INDIVIDUAL INPUT CALCULATION

Besides organizing the calculation of variances and aggregating inputs to aid in determining the overall significance of the respective variances, the matrix approach permits ready calculation of the significance of individual input variances. For instance, since the vector of standard wage rates is arrayed on top of the rate changes vector, it would be an easy matter to determine percentages of change (for example, $-.25$ divided by $3.00 = -8\frac{1}{3}$ per cent, 1 divided by $4 = 25$ per cent, etc.). Then those percentages that exceed a stipulated amount can be further investigated. Similarly, calculations could easily be made for changes in hours. In this way, the matrix approach could be used to implement statistical "quality" control techniques.

CONCLUSIONS

This review of some of the rudiments of matrix algebra and its applications to the field of financial accounting offers a basis for putting forth the following claims:

1. With matrix algebra, inputs and outputs in the various accounting areas can be more easily recognized as such.

2. Matrix algebra can be accepted as a basic way of accomplishing the allocation of inputs to outputs.

3. Matrix algebra may be considered as offering one or two procedures to accomplish allocation instead of the myriad of procedures presently in use.

4. The input-output form of report may be recognized as being superior to most other forms. This is true not only because it is readily understood but also because it is of significant help in the interrelation of a number of diverse accounting areas.

36.

OPTIMIZATION*

*Robert J. Thierauf
and
Richard A. Grosse*

DIFFERENTIATION

Differentiation (differential calculus), sometimes called the mathematics of change, is used for determining the slope of a line tangent to a curve at a point on the curve. This concept can be directed toward the solution of important business problems.

Let us consider any curve $y = f(x)$ where y is a function of x. Suppose that curve M in Figure 1a is a graph of the function $y = f(x)$. The slope of the curve at a particular point on the curve is defined as the slope of the tangent to the curve at the given point. A tangent is defined as a straight line intersecting a curved line at only one point.

To determine the slope of curve M at point A, draw a straight line l which passes through point A and intersects M at some point B. The coordinates of point A are $[x, f(x)]$. Starting at point A on the curve and going to point B, the x and y coordinates change to their values at B from their values at A. The change in x is shown as Δx and the change in the function is shown as Δy. *The coordinates of point B become* $[x + \Delta x, f(x + \Delta x)]$. In terms of

---

the coordinates of A and B, $\Delta y = f(x + \Delta x) - f(x)$ and $\Delta x = (x + \Delta x) - x$. The slope of line AB is

$$\frac{\Delta y}{\Delta x} = \frac{f(x + \Delta x) - f(x)}{(x + \Delta x) - x}$$

$$\text{Slope } AB = \frac{f(x + \Delta x) - f(x)}{\Delta x}$$

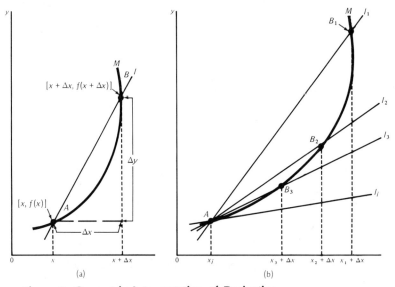

Figure 1. Geometric Interpretation of Derivative

Now imagine that several straight lines (l_1, l_2, l_3, l_i) can pivot at a fixed point A, as in Figure 1b. As the straight lines pivot in a clockwise direction about point A, point B becomes closer to point A on curve M. It should be noted that the closer B is to A, Δx becomes increasingly smaller. As B approaches A, B approaches a position where B and A coincide. At this point (just prior to A and B coinciding), the line between A and B is tangent to the curve. For all practical purposes, A and B are now the same point. We can now state that the ratio $\Delta y/\Delta x$, the slope of the straight line through A and B, approaches the slope of the line tangent to the curve at A as Δx approaches zero. This is called the *first derivative* and is the instantaneous rate of change in the dependent variable $y(dy)$ divided by the instantaneous change in the independent variable $x(dx)$. Note that at the limit, the delta (Δ) form of the operator is expressed as a lower-case d. The equational form of this process is called differentiation and is defined by

$$\frac{dy}{dx} = \lim_{\Delta x \to 0} \frac{\Delta y}{\Delta x} = \lim_{\Delta x \to 0} \frac{f(x + \Delta x) - f(x)}{\Delta x}$$

where y is a function of x. The geometric counterpart of the derivative, then, is the slope of a line tangent to a curve at a point.

FIRST DERIVATIVE AND SECOND DERIVATIVE

The slope of a curve at a point is found by evaluating the derivative at the point. We are interested in finding points where the slope is zero or points where a tangent to the curve is horizontal. Not only is zero slope analysis helpful in plotting curves, but also it is most helpful in the determination of maximum and minimum values of a function, that is, maximum profit, minimum cost, and the like.

The procedure for finding points of zero slope is to set the first derivative equal to zero, then solve the resultant equation. The point of zero slope can be determined by the first derivative test. If the maximum point has been reached, the slope to the left is positive, while the slope to the right is negative. In effect, the slope changes from positive to negative as we traverse a maximum. On the other hand, the slope changes from negative to positive as we traverse a minimum. However, the slope does not change sign as we pass through an inflection point (a point where the curvative changes from concave downward to concave upward or vice versa). In applying the first derivative test, we evaluate the first derivative a little to the right and left of the point of zero slope. The convention is that slope is positive if the curve rises as we go to the right and negative if it descends to the right.

In the second derivative test, a point of zero slope is a maximum if the second derivative at that point is negative, a minimum if the second derivative at the point is positive. If the second derivative is zero for a point of zero slope, the test fails. It is necessary to apply the first derivative test. If the first derivative is zero, we apply the first derivative test by finding the value of the first derivative a little to the left and to the right of the point. The second and subsequent derivatives are found by repeating the process used in determining the previous derivative. The function notation for the higher derivative is

$$\frac{d}{dx}\left(\frac{d}{dx}\right) = \frac{d^2}{dx^2}, \quad \frac{d}{dx}\left(\frac{d^2}{dx^2}\right) = \frac{d^3}{dx^3}, \quad \dots, \quad \frac{d}{dx}\left(\frac{d^{n-1}}{dx^{n-1}}\right) = \frac{d^n}{dx^n}$$

Differentiation Formulas

Mathematicians have developed differentiation formulas or rules with which we are able to find the derivative of a given differentiable function. The more commonly used formulas where C is constant and u and v are functions of x are listed below. It should be pointed out that the derivative of an expression may be taken term by term when these terms are added or subtracted as shown in formulas 4 and 5 below.

Formulas for Differentiation

1. $\dfrac{d}{dx}(C) = 0$

The derivative of a constant (C) is zero.

2. $\dfrac{d}{dx}(Cx) = C\dfrac{d}{dx}(x)$

The derivative of a constant (C) times the variable (x) equals the constant times the derivative of the variable.

3. $\dfrac{d}{dx}(x) = 1$

The derivative of the variable (x) is 1.

4. $\dfrac{d}{dx}(u + v) = \dfrac{du}{dx} + \dfrac{dv}{dx}$

If u and v are functions of x, the derivative of the first function is added to the derivative of the second function.

5. $\dfrac{d}{dx}(u - v) = \dfrac{du}{dx} - \dfrac{dv}{dx}$

If u and v are functions of x, the derivative of the second function is subtracted from the derivative of the first function.

6. $\dfrac{d}{dx}(uv) = \dfrac{u\,dv}{dx} + \dfrac{v\,du}{dx}$

If u and v are functions of x, the derivative of the product uv with respect to x is the "first" (u) times the derivative of the "second" (v) plus the "second" (v) times the derivative of the "first" (u).

7. $\dfrac{d}{dx}\left(\dfrac{u}{v}\right) = \dfrac{v\dfrac{du}{dx} - u\dfrac{dv}{dx}}{v^2}$

If u and v are functions of x, the derivative of the quotient u/v is the denominator times the derivative of the numerator minus the numerator times the derivative of the denominator, all over the denominator squared.

8. $\dfrac{d}{dx}(u^n) = nu^{n-1}\dfrac{du}{dx}$

The derivative of the function (u) to a power is the original power (n) times the function (u) to the original power minus one times the derivative of the function (u) with respect to x.

9. $\dfrac{d}{dx}(\ln u) = \dfrac{1}{u}\dfrac{du}{dx}$

The derivative of the natural logarithm (u) is one over u times the derivative of the function (u) with respect to x.

10. $\dfrac{d}{dx}(e^u) = e^u\dfrac{du}{dx}$

The derivative of e to the function (u) is e^u times the derivative of the function (u) with respect to x.

These rules can be illustrated by applying them to the following problem. Consider the total sales function where $S = -1000p^2 + 10,000p$ and the total cost function where $C = -2000p + 25,000$ (where p is the price of the new product). The problem is to find the optimal price for the new product. It can be determined by using the basic equation, P (profits) equals S (total sales) minus C (total costs). The equations for S and C can be substituted into the profit equation to determine the optimum price. This is shown as follows:

$$
\begin{aligned}
P &= S - C \\
P &= -1000p^2 + 10,000p - (-2000p + 25,000) \\
P &= -1000p^2 + 10,000p + 2000p - 25,000 \\
P &= -1000p^2 + 12,000p - 25,000 \\
\frac{dP}{dp} &= -2000p + 12,000 = 0 \text{ (first derivative)} \\
2000p &= 12,000 \\
p &= \$6
\end{aligned}
$$

Inspection of the above equation $P = -1000p^2 + 12,000p - 25,000$ reveals that the variable p in the first term is squared.[1] The use of differentiation allows us to eliminate the second power in this first term.

Returning to the formulas for differentiation, the approach to this problem is to utilize the rules for the sum and difference of two functions. Whether formula 4 or 5 is used, the essence of each formula is that the derivative of such an expansion $(-1000p^2 + 12,000p - 25,000)$ must be taken term by term. The first term, $-1000p^2$, can be differentiated by using the power formula 8. The rule states that the derivative of a power is the original power (2) times a constant (-1000) with the new power being the value of the original power (2) minus one ($p^{2-1} = p$). The first term after differentiating is $-2000p$. The second term, $12,000p$, can be differentiated by using formula 2 (and formula 3). Since C is a constant of 12,000 and p is analogous to x in the formula, the resulting value, after differentiation, is $+12,000$ (12,000 × 1). The last term $(-25,000)$ requires the use of formula 1 where the constant C is zero after differentiation. Finally, the whole equation is set equal to zero in order to solve for a maximum selling price or maximum point when graphed in terms of profits.

Applying the second derivative test to determine whether we have actually solved for a maximum point, the value of the second derivative should be negative. The second derivative for this problem is as follows:

$$
\frac{d^2P}{dp^2} = -2000(1) + 0
$$

---

[1]This problem can be solved using algebra (applies only to a quadratic function):

$$
x = \frac{-b}{2a} \quad \text{or} \quad p = \frac{-(+12,000)}{2(-1000)} = \frac{-12,000}{-2000} = \$6
$$

534   ADDITIONAL APPLICATIONS OF QUANTITATIVE TECHNIQUES

Using formula 2 (and formula 3), the value of the first term is −2000 while the constant +12,000 drops out after differentiation through the use of formula 1. The sign is negative. This indicates a maximum point on the profit (y axis) and price (x axis) curve has been reached and a selling price determined that will maximize profits for the firm.

This example raises several questions. For example, how was the total sales function determined, how was the total cost function determined, what would a graphical approach indicate, what is the optimum profit to be expected, and what is the quantity that can be expected to be sold at a price of $6? This problem was presented only to show how differential calculus can be used to solve a problem that ordinary albegra cannot.*

---

*Editor's Note: An example in the next section of the Thierauf and Grosse book (not included here with the differential calculus discussion) answers these questions. For a brief discussion of a cost minimization problem see footnote 6 in the Part VI introductory discussion.

37.

AN APPLICATION OF CURVILINEAR BREAK-EVEN ANALYSIS * [PROVIDES INSIGHT INTO THE CONCEPT OF THE DERIVATIVE AND ITS APPLICATIONS]

Horace R. Givens

Curvilinear break-even analysis is made more meaningful to the student if the analytical and mathematical procedures used can be related to a simulated real world situation. To do this it is necessary to ascertain the cost and revenue data of a non-linear character, and then to derive cost and revenue equations that will form the basis of the mathematical analysis. Such an analysis was presented by Professor Travis P. Goggans in his article "Break-even Analysis with Curvilinear Functions" in the October 1965 *Accounting Review.*

The purpose of this paper is to illustrate the derivation of such equations and their subsequent use. To do this we will assume the following cost and revenue observations:

Unit Volume	Total Revenue	Total Cost
5	$ 6	$ 5
10	12	7
15	17	10
20	21	14
5	8	7
10	14	9
15	19	12
20	23	16

A useful first step in determining the cost and revenue equations is to plot the data on a scattergraph. This has been done in Illustration 1 for the cost data. Through examination of this scattergraph, we may estimate the

---

*From *The Accounting Review,* January 1966, pp. 141–143. Reprinted by permission of the author and the American Accounting Association.

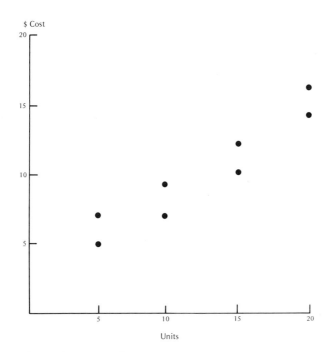

Illustration 1. Scattergraph

shape of the best line to fit this data. In order to obtain an equation for such a line we are required to use a statistical technique such as the least squares method. In Illustration 1 the data closely approximate a parabolic curve. Obviously, the data in this example have been highly stylized in order that the procedure not be obscured by unnecessary complexity in the computations. (More irregular data would be more difficult to fit, but similar procedures could be used.)

Assuming a parabolic case we would use the parabolic normal equations:

$$a(N) + b(Sx) + c(Sx^2) = S(y)$$
$$a(Sx) + b(Sx^2) + c(Sx^3) = S(xy)$$
$$a(Sx^2) + b(Sx^3) + c(Sx^4) = S(x^2y)$$

in which, for our example:

$$
\begin{aligned}
x &= \text{Any volume observation} \\
y &= \text{Any dollar observation (cost or revenue)} \\
Sx &= \text{Sum of the volume observations} \\
Sy &= \text{Sum of the dollar observations} \\
N &= \text{Number of joint cost or revenue and volume observations}
\end{aligned}
$$

Solving these three equations will result in the determination of one equation in three unknowns of the general form

$$y = a + bx + cx^2$$

that is the best-fitting equation for the data used. Inserting our cost and volume observations in these normal equations and solving for the single equation, we obtain the following cost equation:

$$y = 5 + .1x + .02x^2$$

A similar procedure may be used to determine the revenue equation. In this example, plotting the revenue data on a scattergraph reveals that it too is of parabolic character. Using the parabolic normal equations once again, we can ascertain the best-fitting equation:

$$y = 1.5x - .02x^2$$

(As may be expected, the coefficient of the constant (a) is zero in the revenue equation due to the fact that the revenue line must intersect the ordinate at the origin, the equation having no value for $x = 0$.)

Using this revenue equation in conjunction with the cost equation determined earlier, it is possible for us to compute the break-even points by setting the two equations equal and solving for the required level of volume. Thus:

$$1.5x - .02x^2 = 5 + .1x + .02x^2$$

Then,

$$0 = 5 - 1.4x + .04x^2$$

Solving this quadratic yields:

$$x = 4.037 \quad \text{and} \quad 30.963$$

The break-even levels of operation would be at these points.

The third stage involves the determination of the point of maximum profit. Economic theory tells us that this point will be reached when the marginal revenue is equal to the marginal cost. Since our cost and revenue functions are curved, the marginal cost and marginal revenue change constantly as volume changes. Therefore, within the profit area there will be a period of increasing profit as volume increases. In this area, the marginal revenue exceeds the marginal cost, and the slope of the cost line will be less than the slope of the revenue line (see Illustration 2). At higher volume levels profits will decrease as volume increases. In this area the marginal cost exceeds the marginal revenue, and the slope of the revenue line is less than the slope of the cost line. Clearly, there must be some point at which the slopes of the revenue and cost lines are equal, and this must be the point of maximum profit. To determine this point it is necessary that we take the first derivative of each of the functions, set them equal, and solve for the required volume. The derivative of the revenue equation is:

$$1.5 - .04x$$

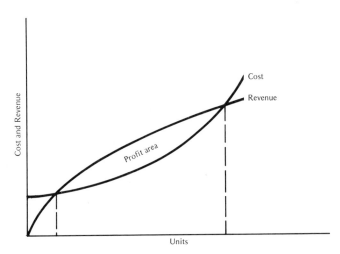

Illustration 2. Curved Cost and Revenue Functions

The derivative of the cost equation is:

$$.1 + .04x$$

Then,

$$1.5 - .04x = .1 + .04x$$

Solving for x we find the required volume level to be 17.5 units. We may test this result by evaluating the basic cost and revenue equations for this volume, a higher volume and a lower volume. By our reasoning, both higher and lower volumes must yield lower profits if our answer is correct. The following will be found by performing this evaluation:

Volume	Profit
17.0	$7.24
17.5	7.25
18.0	7.24

We may assume our answer to be correct.

CONCLUDING NOTE

A benefit often obtained by the writer in presenting such an example to students is that those whose mathematical background is weak often gain a greater insight into the concept of the derivative and its applications to real world situations through the connection drawn between the derivative and the marginal revenue and marginal cost concepts.

Caution should be exercised, however, in discussing the results of any mathematical analysis involving cost and revenue data. The complexity of the mathematical process often tends to imply a greater precision than actually exists. No accounting (or mathematical) results can be better than the raw data used. If that data has been determined wholly or in part by subjective judgments as may be the case with cost and revenue information, and further, if some form of averaging has been done, as in the use of normal equations, the results are by no means invalidated. Nevertheless, the possible qualifications must be kept in mind.

Appendix A[*]

DECISION THEORY

INFORMATION ECONOMICS

MATHEMATICAL DECISION MODELS

*American Accounting Association—Committee on
Information Systems*

[*] From "Accounting and Information Systems," *The Accounting Review*, Supplement to Vol. XLVI, pp. 300–309. Reprinted by permission of the American Accounting Association. Section 2.2 of the report—Decision Theory (General Decision Theory, Information Economics, Mathematical Decision Models) is reprinted. The report contains selected references for the subject areas.

DECISION THEORY

1. General Decision Theory

Decision Theory (or Decision Analysis) is a formal approach to decision making. As accountants, we are concerned with two types of decisions: the decisions which will be based, in part, on the information supplied by the accounting system; and the decisions accountants must make—the selection of the information system. Of course, the two decisions should be made simultaneously if the final results are to be optimal from the point of view of the total system. However, decision makers often ignore the possibility of alternative information systems in their decision making and accountants often select information systems based on experience or ad hoc analysis rather than giving formal consideration to the decisions which are based on the information supplied. Clearly, more work needs to be done on the interrelationships between these two areas if we are to implement a systems approach.

Decision Theory provides a basis for interrelating these two areas. In fact, it specifies a means of calculating the value of additional information and this approach has been extended to the valuation of alternative information systems.

A decision maker must select a course of action (i.e., make resource allocations) in an environment that is perceived as uncertain, complex, and dynamic. Recognition of uncertainty is particularly important in the evaluation of information because the prime purpose of information in decision making is the reduction of uncertainty. If uncertainty is not explicitly included in the decision analysis, any consideration of the impact of information must be made on a relatively ad hoc basis.

Formal recognition of uncertainty is desirable, but it does create certain problems with respect to the payoff measure used to evaluate alternative actions. Under uncertainty, there are a number of possible outcomes associated with each action and for each action the decision maker must specify his probability distribution over these outcomes. The payoff associated with each outcome should be such that the expected payoff[1] will be largest for the action with the set of outcomes and associated probability distribution (often called a lottery) most desired by the decision maker. A payoff measure which satisfies this requirement is referred to as a utility measure.

Accounting information has traditionally concentrated on dollar measures of outcomes and the utility of these outcomes has been largely ignored. The implicit assumption is that utility is linear with respect to dollar profit or cash flow. This assumption is due, in part, to the fact that most decision models have been deterministic and it seems reasonable to assume

---

[1]The expected payoff for a particular action is the weighted average of the payoffs of all the possible outcomes associated with that action, where the weights are the probabilities with which the outcomes will occur.

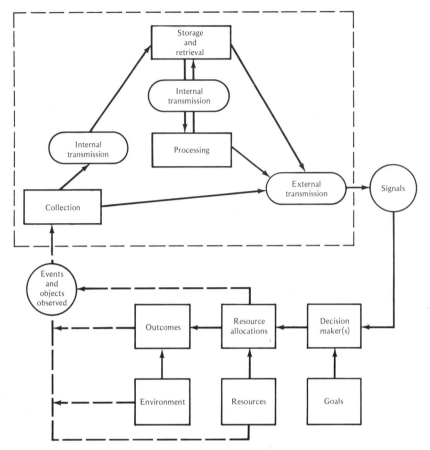

Figure 1. A Functional Model of the Information Subsystem and Its Role in the Total System. (Figure 1 is from a preceding section of the report by the Committee on Information Systems. It is included here because there are references to the figure in the discussion. For the purposes of this report, it is useful to view an organization as being composed of an operating subsystem and an information subsystem.)

Functionally, the information subsystem is the set of operations and operators which accomplish the collection, processing, storage and retrieval, and transmission of data. A simple model of the relationship between these operations and the relationship between the information system and the remainder of the total system is depicted in Figure 1.

The remainder of the system may be described as follows. The decision makers in the organization receive signals from the information system. Based on the information derived from these signals, his previous experience, and his goals, each decision maker selects resource allocations which are to be implemented. The resource allocations actually implemented and the environment at the time of these allocations determine the firm's outcomes. They also effect the resources available and the environment for future periods. The information system makes observations on some of the events and objects which make up the organization's resources, resource allocations, outcomes, and environment; it also records data that represent descriptions of what was observed. The process is then repeated and, hence, there is a time dimension to the process which is not depicted by Figure 1.

that the decision maker will prefer the action with the highest dollar profit or cash flow. Developments in capital budgeting have forced more explicit recognition of the utility issue as these developments have included explicit recognition of the uncertainty associated with the cash flows resulting from alternative projects. However, despite these developments, there has been little accounting research into the information required for payoff measures other than dollar measures.

Complexity is a second aspect of the decision maker's environment and it has several implications. First, it would probably be too costly to recognize the full range of environmental complexities in the decision analysis. Therefore, we must abstract from reality in order to make the analysis economically feasible. For example, many analyses assume a linear (or simple nonlinear) relationship between certain activities and the costs incurred. Second, all interrelated decisions are not considered simultaneously, the decision situation is typically decomposed into a number of separate decisions. This tends to lead to sub-optimization. For example, most inventory models take the demand as given and do not consider the marketing decisions which may affect that demand. Third, the simplifications outlined above create the need for predicting parameters which represent average relationships rather than actual events. Furthermore, these average relationships may not be an accurate reflection of the "true" situation. For example, the linearity assumption mentioned above leads to a prediction of the variable cost per unit of production, but there is no constant variable cost per unit if the true relationship is not linear. Consideration should be given to the impact of averaging and other simplifications on the information that should be provided.

A third aspect of the decision environment is that it is dynamic. The dynamic nature of the environment implies that decisions should recognize the impact of current actions on future results as well as the results in the current period. This fact has led to greater consideration of multiperiod decision models, i.e., models which explicitly recognize the impact of current actions on the payoff in future periods. It also means we must recognize that the magnitude of certain parameters in single period models, such as the value of ending inventory, should be derived from the future impact of current events (outcomes).

The elements of a basic decision theory model are outlined in Table A and in Figure 2. In the model, the decision maker must specify: all the alternative actions available to him; the possible outcomes of each action; the payoff associated with each outcome; and, if there is more than one outcome associated with any action, the probability with which each outcome may occur. As a comparison of Figures 1 and 2 indicates, information is not explicitly recognized in the basic decision theory model, but specification of the above elements is implicitly based on his experience and the information received prior to the decision.

To illustrate this model, consider a situation in which the decision maker must determine the production quantity of a perishable product at the start of each period. The set of possible actions may be the different quantities

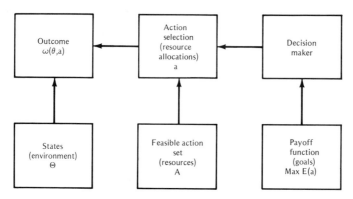

Figure 2. Basic Decision Theory Elements

Table A	A Basic Decision Theory Model
$A = \{a\}$	Set of alternative actions available to the decision maker.
$\Theta = \{\theta\}$	Set of possible states that may occur during the payoff period.
$\omega(\theta,a)$	Payoff (utility) associated with the outcome from section a and state θ.
$P(\theta)$	Prior probability that θ will occur.*
$E(a) = \sum_{\theta \epsilon \Theta} \omega(\theta,a)\,P(\theta)$	Expected payoff if action a is selected.
$E(a^*) = \max_{a \epsilon A}\,[E(a)]$	Expected payoff if the optimal action, a^*, is selected.

*Many models assume that the state is independent of the actions selected but in some situations it is desirable to assume that the probability with which a state will occur is conditional on the action selected. In this latter case we would use $P(\theta/a)$ instead of $P(\theta)$.

he could produce. An outcome is the amount produced and the amount sold, and the payoff is the revenue from the sales less the expenditures incurred by the production. The outcome from a particular action will depend on the demand for the product. Each level of possible demand is a separate state and the decision maker must specify his probability distribution over the possible levels of demand.

2. Basic Decision Theory Information Issues

While the basic decision theory model does not explicitly consider information, it does provide the foundation for a number of analyses which directly consider information issues. Perhaps the most basic information issue in decision theory is the value of perfect information. The purpose of information, in a decision making context, is to reduce the uncertainty as to the outcome that will result from each action. In decision theory this means reducing the uncertainty about which state will exist in the payoff period.

Obviously, the best any information could do would be to completely eliminate the uncertainty and thus permit the decision maker to predict, with certainty, the state that would occur.

The expected value of perfect information is the difference between (i) the expected payoff assuming that the decision maker could obtain this perfect information and would then select the best action given that information; and (ii) the expected payoff from selecting the best action given his prior information. This calculation is specified in Table B.

Table B. The Expected Value of Perfect Information

$$\text{EVIP} = \sum_{\theta \in \Theta} \left[\max_{a \in A} \; \omega(\theta, a) \; P(\theta) \right] - E(a^*)$$

(See Table A for a description of the notation).

The expected value of perfect information places an upper bound on the value of any information. If the value of perfect information is not sufficient to justify an expenditure for the additional information being considered, there is no point in obtaining it. However, if the cost of the information is less than the value of perfect information, it may pay to acquire that information. Decision theory provides a means of formally evaluating that acquisition before it is made.

In effect, the probability distribution over the set of possible states is based on the information the decision maker received prior to the analysis. If additional information is received before the action is selected, that distribution is likely to change. The procedure for formally changing that probability distribution so that it is consistent with the rules of probability is based on Bayes' Theorem.

The decision maker must specify the information processes he is considering and the signals that might be generated by each of these processes. Then he must specify the probabilistic relationship between the signals and states, plus a prior distribution over either the signals or the states. There are a number of different ways of specifying the required distributions and the approach used will depend on the decision maker's understanding of the processes involved.

The appropriate calculations are outlined in Table C. Observe that the introduction of additional information into the decision theory model brings it closer to a model of the system depicted in Figure 1. This fact is illustrated by Figure 3. The model presented in Table C and Figure 1 may be referred to as the information economics model.

3. Information Economics

The term "information economics" has been used to denote any analysis which is concerned with the trade-off between the cost of additional information (or new information systems) and the value derived from that in-

Table C. The Expected Value of Imperfect Information

Model I	
$H = \{\eta\}$	Set of alternative information processes (experiments) available to the decision maker.
$Y = \{y\}$	Set of possible signals generated by the information processes.
$P\eta(y/\theta)$	Conditional probability that signal y will be generated if the environment is in state θ and information process η is used.
$P\eta(\theta/y)$	Conditional probability that state θ will occur if the decision maker receives signal y from information process η.
$P\eta(\theta,y)$	Prior probability that state θ will occur and signal y will be generated by information process η.
$P\eta(y)$	Prior probability that signal y will be generated by information process η.

The decision maker must specify one of the three following sets of probability distributions:

    (i) $P\eta(y/\theta)$ and $P(\theta)$
   (ii) $P\eta(\theta,y)$
  (iii) $P\eta(\theta/y)$ and $P\eta(y)$

If set (i) is specified,

$$P\eta(y) \;=\; \sum_{\theta\epsilon\Theta} P\eta(y/\theta)\, P(\theta)$$

and

$$P\eta(\theta/y) = P\eta(y/\theta)\, P(\theta)/P\eta(y)\dagger$$

$\dagger$ This is an application of Bayes' Theorem:
The Probability of an Outcome given both New and Prior Information = {[The Probability of the New Information given the Outcome] × [The Probability of the Outcome given the Prior Information]} ÷ [The Probability of the New Information given the Prior Information].

The maximum expected payoff given an information process and the signal produced by that process:

$$E^*(y,\eta) \;=\; \max_{a\epsilon A} \left\{ \sum_{\theta\epsilon\Theta} \omega(\theta,a)\, P\eta(\theta/y) \right\}$$

The maximum expected payoff given the information process to be used:

$$E^*(\eta) \;=\; \sum_{\gamma\epsilon Y} E^*(y,\eta)\, P\eta(y)$$

The expected value of imperfect information (for a given information process):

$$EVII\eta = E^*(\eta) - E(a^*)$$

The expected value of a particular information process should be compared to the expected cost of that process. The information process with the largest expected *net* value is the most desirable.

formation. Recently, however, this term has been used to specifically denote those analyses which apply decision theory to the evaluation of information, and an area of study is gradually developing from these analyses. This area of study includes the traditional information analyses in decision theory (e.g., the analysis in section 2), but, in addition, it has extended the analysis to a broader range of information issues and it has given more explicit consideration to the various elements of the information system.

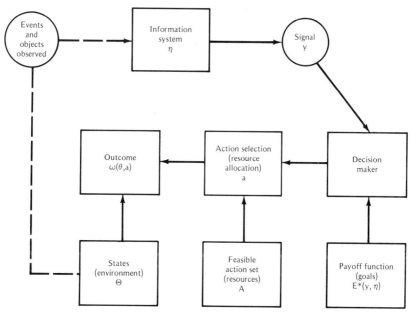

Figure 3. Information Economics Elements

Information economics provides a formal procedure for evaluating information alternatives; therefore, it provides a formal procedure for evaluating accounting alternatives (assuming of course, that the role of accounting is to provide information for decisions). Accounting has lacked such analysis in the past, at least at the formal level, but it should be a basic element in future accounting research.

Research in information economics has provided a number of useful concepts and some useful insights into issues and problems of interest to accountants. Some of these concepts and insights are briefly examined below.

3.1. Payoff Relevant Distinctions Between States

Information economics formally recognizes that the decision maker need not consider all the different possible states of the environment. Differences may be ignored if they will not affect his analysis; that is, a subset of the possible states may be combined into a single state if, for each action, the payoff is the same for all states that are combined. For example, if differences in states due to differences in the temperature in the Sahara Desert do not affect the payoff derived from the decision maker's actions, all states which are the same except for differences in this temperature may be combined together.

The set of states derived from eliminating all distinctions which do not produce payoff differences is defined to be the payoff relevant set of states (or the payoff relevant partition of the states of the environment). Perfect information about the payoff relevant states is as valuable to the decision maker as perfect information about the complete set of states of the environment.

3.2. Information System Classification and Ranking

The decision maker is primarily interested in ranking information systems in terms of their value, but some insights may be gained from classifying and ranking information systems independently from their value to a particular decision. There are at least three basic categories of information systems.[2]

First, an information system is *complete* if a different signal is produced for each state (or, at least, each payoff relevant state).

Second, an information system is *noiseless* if some signals may be produced by more than one state, but there is no doubt about which signal a given state will produce.

Third, an information system is *noisy* if at least one state may produce any one of a number of signals and at least one of these signals may be produced by more than one state.

If information systems are costless, a complete information system is the most desirable; it provides perfect information. The relative value of alternative noiseless and noisy information systems usually depends on the specifics of the decision situation; certainly a noiseless information system is not always more valuable than a noisy information system, even if the systems are costless. However, if the signals of one system can be obtained by combining or garbling[3] the signals of another system, then the latter system is at least as valuable as the first system for all decision situations.

3.3. Accuracy, Timeliness, and Relevance

An information system may be noisy because of errors in observing, processing, or communicating the information. It will also be noisy if the system does not have access to information that would permit a "noiseless"

[2] Similar categories are found in the statistical communication theory literature (e.g., Lee and Bedford (1969)), but they are mentioned in the information economics section of this report in order to tie them more closely to decision making uses of the information produced by these systems. [L. C. Lee and N. M. Bedford, "An Information Theory Analysis of the Accounting Process," *Accounting Review*, April 1969.]

[3] The signals of one system are said to be a garbling of another system's signals, if the probability distribution over the first system's signals can be considered to be conditional only on the second system's signals (i.e., the state that produced the second system's signal is irrelevant).

forecast of the state that will occur during the payoff period (such information may be impossible to obtain by any system). A distinction can be made between these two cases by recognizing that information must be based on events that precede the decision. If these events are recognized, the decision maker must specify the relationship (probably probabilistic) between the events prior to the decision and the states which occur during the payoff period; he must also specify the relationship between the prior events and the signals received.

Recognition of these prior events facilitates investigation of such issues as accuracy, timeliness, and relevance. Observation, processing, and communication errors are recognized by expressing the relationship between prior events and the signals received as a probabilistic relationship. Time delays in reporting are recognized by noting that the information system does not report on the most recent prior events; in most processes, information about these recent events would improve the forecast of the future states. If by relevance we mean the value of additional information, this may be handled by determining the value of reporting on additional prior events. This is similar to timeliness as again some events are unreported, but in this case the unreported events may be scattered throughout the prior period and it is a question of whether to report them at all, rather than determining when to report them.

3.4. Decision Rules

Information economics assumes that the action selected will be a function of the information received by the decision maker. Usually, decision theory implicitly assumes that the action selected by the decision maker will be that action which maximizes the expected payoff given the information received. This latter assumption defines what might be considered the ideal decision rule, but this is not necessarily the decision rule used and information evaluation should be based on the actual decision rule. Nonoptimal decision rules may be used because the cost of using the optimal decision rule is too costly. Furthermore, the decision rule might be determined by a decision maker who is someone other than the individual who is selecting the information system. Both of these reasons have been explored in information economics and these explorations may provide the basis for further research.

3.5. Multiple Decision Makers

Some work has been done in extending information economics to the case where there are several decision makers and their actions interact to determine the payoff. The Theory of Teams provides the most extensive investigation into this area. In the Theory of Teams all decision makers are assumed to have the same expectations about the future states and the same payoff function over possible future outcomes. Hence, it is assumed that each decision maker will select the action (i.e., use the decision rule) which maximizes the expected payoff given his information plus his knowledge about the information system and the information he is transmitting to other decision makers in the team. In such a situation, each decision maker can optimally determine (in an expected value sense) what observations he should make in the environment accessible to him and what information he should transmit to the other members of the team (recognizing the costs of observation and transmission).

A less explored area of research in the multiple decision maker case is that in which a "meta-decider" determines the information system and instructs organization members on what to observe and what to transmit. This approach can either assume that the meta-decider determines the decision rules for all decision makers or accepts the decision rules used by the decision makers, even if their goals and expectations do not agree with the meta-decider.

3.6. Multiperiod Models

Current actions typically affect the results of several future periods; current information may be used in subsequent decisions; and current information system selections often affect the systems available in future periods. These factors may require that information evaluation be based on a multiperiod model instead of the single period models often used in decision theory. Most multiperiod models use dynamic programming formulations. This permits compact expressions of the model and designates a procedure for its solution. Multiperiod models are probably too costly to solve for many regular information decisions, but they do provide a basis for research and have the virtue of pinpointing the shortcomings and assumptions implicit in single period models.

4. Mathematical Decision Models

In this section we explore some developments in mathematical decision models which have information implications. Any mathematical decision model may be formulated in terms of the basic decision theory model, but a somewhat different format is often used when the set of possible actions takes the form of activity levels which may take on a large number of possible values. In this case, an action is expressed as a vector of decision variables and the set of feasible actions is specified by constraints which limit the magnitudes which may be assigned to these variables. The different states are represented by different magnitudes of a vector of uncontrollable variables. Of course, the decision maker may assume that the magnitude of the uncontrollable variables can be predicted with certainty; this is equivalent to assuming there is only one possible state. The payoff is expressed as a function of the decision variables and the uncontrollable variables. The form of the payoff function and the constraints is often fairly simple in order to facilitate solution of the model. Models of this type are often associated with mathematical programming, which concentrates on the solution of models.

Both the payoff function and the constraints contain parameters and the decision maker must predict the magnitude of these parameters, as well as the magnitude of uncontrollable variables. Typically, the parameter predictions are assumed to be deterministic, while predictions of uncontrollable variables may be deterministic or may be represented by a probability distribution over the possible magnitudes. Accountants should be interested in these predictions as many are costs or technical coefficients whose predictions are likely to be based on information the accountant is or should be producing. Clearly, accountants should understand the information needs associated with these models. This topic has been discussed, to some extent, by the American Accounting Association's Committee on Managerial Decision Models and will not be explored here.

Instead, we wish to briefly consider some developments in mathematical modeling which specifically address themselves to information issues. The results of these developments should be of interest to accountants and accounting researchers should be interested in these techniques as a basis for further research into information evaluation.

4.1. Sensitivity Analysis

Perhaps the most widely known approach to information evaluation is sensitivity analysis. Sensitivity analysis is an examination of the impact of changes in the magnitude of parameters (or uncontrollable variables) or changes in the form of the payoff function or the constraints on the optimal payoff and the optimal magnitude of the decision variables. This analysis is usually applied after an initial prediction has been made and an initial solution to the problem has been obtained. However, the analysis may also be applied at a general level to a particular type of decision model rather than its specific application.

From an information point of view, the purpose of this analysis is to determine which parameter predictions, if any, are critical. A parameter prediction is considered to be critical if small errors in the predicted magnitude will have a significant impact on the optimal payoff. If it is possible to obtain additional information which will improve a parameter prediction, that information should be obtained if the prediction is critical and the cost of that information is within reason.

Observe that sensitivity analysis is asking essentially the same types of questions about information that were considered in information economics. However, sensitivity analysis is a more ad hoc way of asking these questions. The basic reason for the more ad hoc approach is that mathematical models usually assume that the parameter predictions are deterministic when, in fact, they are uncertain. Recognition of this uncertainty increases the complexity of the models and the resulting increase in the cost of solution may not be warranted. More research is needed to determine when it is desirable, in a cost-benefit sense, to explicitly recognize uncertainty in decision models and, also, the desired level of accuracy of predictions for various parameters in various models.

4.2. Suboptimization

It is generally recognized that we work with models which concentrate on a subset of the decisions of a firm. In so doing, these models tend to produce suboptimal decisions. That is, while the decisions may be optimal for the model constructed they are not optimal for the firm in total. However, while a model concentrates on a subset of the firm's decisions, part of the modeling process is to attempt to recognize the most important interactions with other parts of the firm. This recognition typically takes the form of constraints on the magnitudes of the decision variables or penalties (bonuses) on certain undesirable (desirable) results. These penalties are of particular interest to accountants as they are usually referred to as opportunity costs. Research into how these opportunity costs should be determined has been limited and is certainly an area for future research of interest to accountants.

One aspect of this problem that has received attention in the mathematical programming literature is the decomposition of linear and nonlinear programming problems. This problem is often equated to a firm with several decisions: the divisions have a number of decision variables under their control and are aware of certain constraints on the magnitudes of these variables; and, on the other hand, the head office is aware of certain restrictions which apply across a number of divisions, although they may not know the details of the divisions' problems.

Analysis of this type of problem usually considers the information that must be sent by the divisions to head office and from head office to divisions in order to achieve an optimal solution. A question of particular interest is whether the head office can supply prices for the use of the corporate resources which will cause the divisions to arrive at an optimal solution if they maximize divisional profit. If this is possible, the next issue is to determine what information the head office must have in order to determine the desired prices.

For example, prices are almost always insufficient for an optimal solution if the objective function is linear.[4] In fact, the objective must be strictly

---

[4]However, it is possible to generate "price schedules" which will accomplish the desired results.

concave (i.e., the marginal net revenue is strictly decreasing) if we wish to be certain that prices will be sufficient. In this latter case, the prices can be determined by an iterative procedure whereby the head office sends prices to the divisions and the divisions respond with the maximum profit they can earn and corporate resources they desire if those prices are charged. The head office uses this information to generate a new set of prices and the process is repeated until the optimal prices are determined.

This area of research should be of interest to accountants because it relates to such issues as the following: Do transfer prices exist that will motivate a division to select a set of actions which are optimal for the firm? How can such transfer prices be determined? What is the form of and how can we determine the opportunity cost of resources considered in suboptimal decision models?

In addition, extension of this research might consider questions such as the following: What is the cost of using techniques which provide opportunity costs or transfer prices which will not yield the optimal solution? What is the cost of using simple opportunity costs or transfer prices when, in fact, no simple form exists which would support an optimal solution?

Similar questions arise because most models decompose the decision situation with respect to time. That is, single period models are often used even when current actions have an impact on the payoff in future periods. Ideally, multiperiod models should be used, but they are often too costly. The question that arises is how to determine the value of the state at the end of the single period if a multiperiod model is not used, e.g., what is the value of ending inventory. Very little research has been done in this area.

4.3. Adaptive Programming

Adaptive programming is an area of modeling which recognizes the information content of observed outcomes. In this type of model, the outcome is a function of the action selected and a random event; the probability distribution describing the likelihood with which each possible event may occur is assumed to be a function of the state of the environment. The state of the environment is unknown, but it is often assumed to be constant from period to period; observations of the events (or outcomes) provide information which result in changes in the decision maker's probability distribution over the set of possible states. Examples of this type of modeling are found in the inventory literature; the alternative states might be alternative average (mean) demand rates, an event is the demand that actually occurs during a period, and an outcome is the sales made or the revenue associated with those sales. The alternative states can also be alternative types of probability distributions over demand.

The adaptive formulation may also be applied to situations in which the decision maker may take actions which will influence the state of the process. Often in this case, the state may change from period to period. An example of this type of formulation is found in research on the investigation of variances; the states refer to the condition of the process which generates the costs considered by the variances. If the process is in an undesirable condition, investigation of the cause of the variance may reflect this fact and corrective action may return the process to a desirable state. If the process is in a desirable state, there is some chance that it will go into some undesirable state in some subsequent period.

Appendix B

SELECTED MANAGEMENT ACCOUNTING QUESTIONS

Material from the Uniform CPA Examinations, Copyright © (1955–1977) by the American Institute of Certified Public Accountants, Inc., is reprinted (or adapted) with permission.

Material from the Certificate in Management Accounting (CMA) Examinations, Copyright © by the National Association of Accountants, is reprinted (or adapted) with permission.

PART ONE QUESTIONS

PROJECT PROFIT PLANNING: ALTERNATIVE DECISION
   PROBLEMS, QUANTITATIVE AND
   COMPUTER APPLICATIONS FOR
   ALTERNATIVE DECISION ANALYSIS,
   DECISION MAKING AND BEHAVIORAL
   CONSIDERATIONS

I—Q1. Accepting an Order at Less Than Full Cost (CMA)

E. Berg and Sons build custom-made pleasure boats which range in price
from $10,000 to $250,000. For the past 30 years, Mr. Berg, Sr. has determined the selling price of each boat by estimating the cost of material,
labor, a prorated portion of overhead, and adding 20% to these estimated
costs.

For example, a recent price quotation was determined as follows:

Direct Materials	$5,000
Direct Labor	8,000
Overhead	2,000
	$15,000
Plus 20%	3,000
Selling price	$18,000

The overhead figure was determined by estimating total overhead costs
for the year and allocating them at 25% of direct labor.

If a customer rejected the price and business was slack, Mr. Berg, Sr.
would often be willing to reduce his markup to as little as 5% over estimated costs. Thus, average markup for the year is estimated at 15%.

Mr. Ed Berg, Jr. has just completed a course on pricing and believes the
firm could use some of the techniques discussed in the course. The course
emphasized the contribution margin approach to pricing and Mr. Berg, Jr.
feels such an approach would be helpful in determining the selling prices
of their custom-made pleasure boats.

Total overhead which includes selling and administrative expenses for
the year has been estimated at $150,000, of which $90,000 is fixed and the
remainder is variable in direct proportion to direct labor.

Required

A. Assume the customer in the example rejected the $18,000 quotation and also rejected a $15,750 quotation (5% markup) during a slack period. The customer countered with a $15,000 offer.

    1. What is the difference in net income for the year between accepting or rejecting the customer's offer?
    2. What is the minimum selling price Mr. Berg, Jr. could have quoted without reducing or increasing net income?

B. What advantages does the contribution margin approach to pricing have over the approach used by Mr. Berg, Sr.?

C. What pitfalls are there, if any, to contribution margin pricing?

I—Q2. Accepting an Order at Less Than Full Cost When Excess Capacity Exists (CPA)

Nubo Manufacturing, Inc., is presently operating at 50% of practical capacity producing about 50,000 units annually of a patented electronic component. Nubo recently received an offer from a company in Yokohama, Japan, to purchase 30,000 components at $6 per unit, FOB Nubo's plant. Nubo has not previously sold components in Japan. Budgeted production costs for 50,000 and 80,000 units of output follow:

Units	50,000	80,000
Costs:		
Direct material	$ 75,000	$120,000
Direct labor	75,000	120,000
Factory overhead	200,000	260,000
Total costs	$350,000	$500,000
Cost per unit	$7.00	$6.25

The sales manager thinks the order should be accepted, even if it results in a loss of $1 per unit, because he feels the sales may build up future markets. The production manager does not wish to have the order accepted primarily because the order would show a loss of $.25 per unit when computed on the new average unit cost. The treasurer has made a quick computation indicating that accepting the order will actually increase gross margin.

Required

A.   Explain what apparently caused the drop in cost from $7 per unit to $6.25 per unit when budgeted production increased from 50,000 to 80,000 units. Show supporting computations.

B.   1.   Explain whether (either or both) the production manager or the treasurer is correct in his reasoning.
     2.   Explain why the conclusions of the production manager and the treasurer differ.

C.   Explain why each of the following may affect the decision to accept or reject the special order.
     1.   The likelihood of repeat special sales and/or all sales to be made at $6 per unit.
     2.   Whether the sales are made to customers operating in two separate, isolated markets or whether the sales are made to customers competing in the same market.

I—Q3. Calculation of Different Costs Related to a Decision About Taking a Special Order—Firm is at Full Capacity (CMA)

George Jackson operates a small machine shop. He manufactures one standard product available from many other similar businesses and he also manufactures products to customer order. His accountant prepared the annual income statement shown below:

	Custom Sales	Standard Sales	Total
Sales	$50,000	$25,000	$75,000
Material	$10,000	$8,000	$18,000
Labor	20,000	9,000	29,000
Depreciation	6,300	3,600	9,900
Power	700	400	1,100
Rent	6,000	1,000	7,000
Heat and light	600	100	700
Other	400	900	1,300
	$44,000	$23,000	$67,000
	$ 6,000	$ 2,000	$ 8,000

The depreciation charges are for machines used in the respective product lines. The power charge is apportioned on the estimate of power consumed. The rent is for the building space which has been leased for 10 years at $7,000 per year. The rent, and heat and light are apportioned to the product lines based on amount of floor space occupied. All other costs are current expenses identified with the product line causing them.

A valued custom parts customer has asked Mr. Jackson if he would manufacture 5,000 special units for him. Mr. Jackson is working at capacity and would have to give up some other business in order to take this business. He can't renege on custom orders already agreed to but he could reduce the output of his standard product by about one-half for one year while producing the specially requested custom part. The customer is willing to pay $7 for each part. The material cost will be about $2 per unit and the labor will be $3.60 per unit. Mr. Jackson will have to spend $2,000 for a special device which will be discarded when the job is done.

Required

    A.   Calculate and present the following costs related to the 5000 units custom order:
        1.   The incremental cost of the order.
        2.   The full cost of the order.
        3.   The opportunity cost of taking the order.
        4.   The sunk costs related to the order.

    B.   Should Mr. Jackson take the order? Explain your answer.

I—Q4. Contribution Margin (Marginal Income) Statement for a Product Showing an Operating Loss; Breakeven Point Calculation for the Problem (CPA)

The president of Eastern Company wants guidance on the advisability of eliminating product C, one of the company's three similar products, or investing in new machinery to reduce the cost of product C in the hope of reversing product C's operating loss sustained in 19_6. The three similar products are manufactured in a single plant in about the same amount of floor space and the markets in which they are sold are very competitive.

Below is the condensed statement of operating income for the company and for product C for the year ended October 31, 19_6.

Eastern Company
STATEMENT OF OPERATING INCOME
For the year ended October 31, 19_6

	All three Products	Product C
Sales	$2,800,150	$350,000
Cost of sales:		
Raw materials	565,000	80,000
Labor		
Direct	1,250,000	150,000
Indirect	55,000	18,000
Fringe benefits (15% of labor)	195,750	25,200
Royalties (1% of product C sales)	3,500	3,500
Maintenance and repairs	6,000	2,000
Factory supplies	15,000	2,100
Depreciation (straight-line)	25,200	7,100
Electrical power	25,000	3,000
Scrap and spoilage	4,300	600
Total cost of sales	2,144,750	291,500
Gross profit	655,400	58,500
Selling, general and administrative expenses:		
Sales commissions	120,000	15,000
Officers' salaries	32,000	10,500
Other wages and salaries	14,000	5,300
Fringe benefits (15% of wages, salaries		
and commissions)	24,900	4,620
Delivery expense	79,500	10,000
Advertising expense	195,100	26,000
Miscellaneous fixed expenses	31,900	10,630
Total selling, general and administrative		
expenses	497,400	82,050
Operating income (loss)	$ 158,000	$(23,550)

Required (Disregard income taxes)

A. Prepare a schedule showing the contribution of product C to
the recovery of fixed costs and expenses (marginal income) for
the year ended October 31, 19_6. Assume that each element of
cost and expense is entirely fixed or variable within the
relevant range and that the change in inventory levels has
been negligible.

B. Assume that in fiscal 19_6 the variable costs and expenses of
product C totaled $297,500 and that its fixed costs and
expenses amounted to $75,100. Prepare a schedule computing
the breakeven point of product C in terms of annual dollar
sales volume. Sales for 19_6 amounted to $350,000.

C.   The direct labor costs of product C could have been reduced by $75,000 and the indirect labor costs by $4,000 by investing an additional $340,000 (financed with 5% bonds) in machinery with a ten-year life and an estimated salvage value of $30,000 at the end of the period. However, the company would have been liable for total severance pay costs of $18,000 (to be amortized over a five-year period), and electrical power costs would have increased $500 annually.

Assuming the information given above in part "B," prepare a schedule computing the breakeven point of product C in terms of annual dollar sales volume if the additional machinery had been purchased and installed at the beginning of the year.

I—Q5. Sell or Process Further (CPA)

Items 1 and 2 are based on the following information:
    From a particular joint process, Watkins Company produces three products, X, Y, and Z. Each product may be sold at the point of split-off or processed further. Additional processing requires no special facilities, and production costs of further processing are entirely variable and traceable to the products involved. In 19_3, all three products were processed beyond split-off. Joint production costs for the year were $60,000. Sales values and costs needed to evaluate Watkins' 19_3 production policy follow:

Product	Units Produced	Sales Values at Split-Off	Additional Costs and Sales Values if Processed Further	
			Sales Values	Added Costs
X	6,000	$25,000	$42,000	$9,000
Y	4,000	41,000	45,000	7,000
Z	2,000	24,000	32,000	8,000

Joint costs are allocated to the products in proportion to the relative physical volume of output.

1.   For units of Z, the unit production cost most relevant to a sell-or-process-further decision is
    a. $5
    b. $12
    c. $4
    d. $9

2. To maximize profits, Watkins should subject the following products to additional processing
   a. X only
   b. X, Y, and Z
   c. Y and Z only
   d. Z only

I—Q6. Make-or-Buy Decision (CMA)

The Vernom Corporation, which produces and sells to wholesalers a highly successful line of summer lotions and insect repellents, has decided to diversify in order to stabilize sales throughout the year. A natural area for the company to consider is the production of winter lotions and creams to prevent dry and chapped skin.

After considerable research, a winter products line has been developed. However, because of the conservative nature of the company management, Vernom's president has decided to introduce only one of the new products for this coming winter. If the product is a success, further expansion in future years will be initiated.

The product selected (called Chap-off) is a lip balm that will be sold in a lipstick type tube. The product will be sold to wholesalers in boxes of 24 tubes for $8 per box. Because of available capacity, no additional fixed charges will be incurred to produce the product. However, a $100,000 fixed charge will be absorbed by the product to allocate a fair share of the company's present fixed costs to the new product.

Using the estimated sales and production of 100,000 boxes of Chap-off as the standard volume, the accounting department has developed the following costs:

Direct Labor	$2.00/box
Direct Materials	$3.00/box
Total Overhead	$1.50/box
Total	$6.50/box

Vernom has approached a cosmetics manufacturer to discuss the possibility of purchasing the tubes for Chap-off. The purchase price of the empty tubes from the cosmetics manufacturer would be $.90 per 24 tubes. If the Vernom Corporation accepts the purchase proposal, it is estimated that direct labor and variable overhead costs would be reduced by 10 percent and direct material costs would be reduced by 20 percent.

Required

A. Should the Vernom Corporation make or buy the tubes? Show calculations to support your answer.

B. What would be the maximum purchase price acceptable to the Vernom Corporation for the tubes? Support your answer with an appropriate explanation.

C. Instead of sales of 100,000 boxes, revised estimates show sales volume at 125,000 boxes. At this new volume additional equipment, at an annual rental of $10,000, must be acquired to manufacture the tubes. However, this incremental cost would be the only additional fixed cost required even if sales increased to 300,000 boxes. (The 300,000 level is the goal for the third year of production.) Under these circumstances should the Vernom Corporation make or buy the tubes? Show calculations to support your answer.

D. The company has the option of making and buying at the same time. What would be your answer to part C if this alternative was considered? Show calculations to support your answer.

E. What nonquantifiable factors should the Vernom Corporation consider in determining whether they should make or buy the lipstick tubes?

I—Q7. Equipment Replacement Decision—Cost Comparisons on an Annual Basis (CPA)

The controller of the Jones Manufacturing Company asks for your advice and assistance regarding the problem of whether or not they should replace their "A" machines with new and advanced "B" machines. "B" machines are capable of doubling the present annual capacity of the "A" machines. At the present time the annual finished production of the "A" machines is 2,500,000 good units. You are to assume that the increased production can be sold at the same profitable price.

The "A" machines are being depreciated by the Jones Manufacturing Co. under the straight-line method using a salvage value of 10% and a useful life of 8 years. The "A" machines cost the Jones Manufacturing Co. $175,000 plus freight and insurance of $25,000. The raw materials as they are fed into the machines are subject to heavy pressure; because of this there is a 20% waste factor on an annual basis. The waste materials have no value and are scrapped for nominal value. Direct labor costs are equal to 60% of prime costs at the present time (labor and materials are considered prime costs). The company has been purchasing its raw materials in small lots at a cost of $50.00 per 1,000 units. Factory overhead, exclusive of depreciation is applied to the manufacturing process at the rate of 20% of direct labor costs.

If the company purchases the "B" machines, certain economies will be gained. Material costs will decrease 20% because the company will be able to buy in larger quantities. In addition, the new machines have been perfected to such an extent that the waste factor will be reduced by 50%. However, because the "B" machine is much larger than the "A" machine, direct labor cost will be expected to increase by 20% of itself. Direct labor will continue to be 60% of prime cost before the increase of 20% in direct labor cost is applied. In addition to this, it is expected that the factory overhead rate will increase by 10% of itself. The life of the new machines is expected to exceed the life of the "A" machines by ¼ and the salvage value of the "B" machines will be in the same ratio as the salvage value of the "A" machines. The cost of the "B" machines, including freight and insurance of $35,000, will amount to $500,000. The company is aware of the fact that dismantling costs and installation costs will be involved, however, they do not wish to consider this factor at the present time.

Required

A. A statement of estimated cost comparisons on an annual basis. (Round to the nearest dollar.)

B. List additional factors that should be considered in deciding upon the replacement.

C. Comment briefly on the usefulness and validity of the comparisons made in part A. (See Article 14.)

I—Q8. Direct Costing—Inventory Valuation;* Variable Cost Pricing (CPA)

Items 1 and 2 are based on the following information:

Gyro Gear Company produces a special gear used in automatic transmissions. Each gear sells for $28, and the Company sells approximately 500,000 gears each year. Unit cost data for 19_6 are presented below:

---

* Direct costing is part of the Article 1 discussion. Article 9 (Part II of the book) contains a direct costing section and questions II—Q9, 10 use direct costing in preparing income statements.

	Direct material	$6.00	
	Direct labor	5.00	

		Variable	Fixed
Other costs:			
	Manufacturing	$2.00	$7.00
	Distribution	4.00	3.00

1. The unit cost of gears for direct-cost-inventory purposes is
   - a. $13
   - b. $20
   - c. $17
   - d. $27

2. Gyro has received an offer from a foreign manufacturer to purchase 25,000 gears. Domestic sales would be unaffected by this transaction. If the offer is accepted, variable distribution costs will increase $1.50 per gear for insurance, shipping, and import duties. The relevant unit cost to a pricing decision on this offer is
   - a. $17.00
   - b. $14.50
   - c. $28.50
   - d. $18.50

I—Q9. Adding Concession Business—Incremental Revenue and Incremental Cost (CPA Adapted)

The M Co., manager of an office building, is considering putting in certain concessions in the main lobby. An accounting study produces the following estimates, on an average annual basis:

Salaries		$ 7,000
Licenses and payroll taxes		200
Cost of merchandise sold:		
Beginning inventory	$ 2,000	
Purchases	40,000	
Available	42,000	
Ending inventory	2,000	40,000
Share of heat, light, etc.		500
Pro rata building depreciation		1,000
Concession advertising		100
Share of company administrative expense		400
Sales of merchandise		49,000

The investment in equipment, which would last 10 years, would be $2,000.

As an alternative, a catering company has offered to lease the space for $750 per year, for ten years, and to put in and operate the same concessions at no cost to the M Co. Heat and light are to be furnished by the office building at no additional charge.

1. What is your advice to the M Co.? Explain fully.

2. The sales amount is given as $49,000. Discuss how this amount might have been determined.

3. Discuss how probabilities can be used in estimating sales. (See I—Q10.)

I—Q10. Expected Value, Payoff Table, Decision Strategy (CMA)— Problem for Study (Partial Answer Included to Show the Construction of a Payoff Table for Part A. The Table Is to Be Completed).*

Vendo, Inc. has been operating the concession stands at the University football stadium. The University has had successful football teams for many years; as a result the stadium is always full. The University is located in an area which suffers no rain during the football season. From time to time, Vendo has found itself very short of hot dogs and at other times it has had many left. A review of the records of sales of the past five seasons revealed the following frequency of hot dogs sold.

	Total Games
10,000 hot dogs	5 times
20,000 hot dogs	10 times
30,000 hot dogs	20 times
40,000 hot dogs	15 times
	50 total games

Hot dogs sell for 50 cents each and cost Vendo 30 cents each. Unsold hot dogs are given to a local orphanage without charge.

Required

A. Assuming that only the four quantities listed were ever sold and that the occurrences were random events, prepare a payoff

---

*For additional expected value application questions see II—Q17, 18, 19.

table (ignore income taxes) to represent the four possible strategies of ordering 10,000; 20,000; 30,000; or 40,000 hot dogs.

B. Using the expected value decision rule determine the best strategy.

C. What is the dollar value of perfect information in this problem?

Answer

A. (The payoff table for A is only partially completed. Complete the table. See the explanation for 30,000 ordered and 20,000 sold that appears below the table for aid in preparing the remainder of the table.)

Probability		.1	.2	.4	.3	Expected
Order Sell		10,000	20,000	30,000	40,000	Value
10,000						
20,000						
30,000		−$4,000	$1,000	$6,000	$6,000	$4,000
40,000						

Calculation for ordering 30,000 and selling only 20,000 hot dogs

Sales 20,000 @ $0.50	$10,000
Cost of hot dogs 30,000 @ $0.30	9,000
Payoff	$ 1,000

Calculation of expected value for ordering 30,000 hot dogs

$.1(-4,000) + .2(1,000) + .4(6,000) + .3(6,000)$ = *$4,000 expected value*

B. The best strategy, using the expected value decision rule, is to order 30,000 hot dogs because on the average Vendo will earn $4,000. Note that $4,000 will be the highest of the four amounts in the expected value column after the table is completed.

C. The value of perfect information is the difference between the average profit using the best strategy against the probabilities and the average profit if Vendo knew in advance what the sales level would be each Saturday.

Average profit if Vendo knew sales level

.1(2,000)* + .2(4,000) + .4(6,000) + .3(8,000) =	$5,800
Average profit from expected value strategy	4,000
Dollar value of perfect information	$1,800

I—Q11. Contribution Margin Statements by Markets and a Decision With Regard to Dropping a Market; Adding a Product That Increases Fixed Costs and the Contribution Margin Necessary to Make the Addition Financially Feasible (CMA)

The Justa Corporation produces and sells three products. The three products, A, B, and C, are sold in a local market and in a regional market. At the end of the first quarter of the current year, the following income statement has been prepared:

	Total	Local	Regional
Sales	$1,300,000	$1,000,000	$300,000
Cost of Goods Sold	1,010,000	775,000	235,000
Gross Margin	$ 290,000	$ 225,000	$ 65,000
Selling Expenses	$ 105,000	$ 60,000	$ 45,000
Administrative Expenses	52,000	40,000	12,000
	$ 157,000	$ 100,000	$ 57,000
Net Income	$ 133,000	$ 125,000	$ 8,000

Management has expressed special concern with the regional market because of the extremely poor return on sales. This market was entered a year ago because of excess capacity. It was originally believed that the return on sales would improve with time, but after a year no noticeable improvement can be seen from the results as reported in the above quarterly statement.

In attempting to decide whether to eliminate the regional market, the following information has been gathered:

---

* .1 results from $\frac{5}{50}$; 2,000 results from 10,000 (.50−.30).

		Products	
	A	B	C
Sales........................	$500,000	$400,000	$400,000
Variable Manufacturing Expenses as a Percentage of Sales	60%	70%	60%
Variable Selling Expenses as a Percentage of Sales	3%	2%	2%

	Sales by Markets	
Product	Local	Regional
A	$400,000	$100,000
B	300,000	100,000
C	300,000	100,000

All administrative expenses and fixed manufacturing expenses are common to the three products and the two markets and are fixed for the period. Remaining selling expenses are fixed for the period and separable by market. All fixed expenses are based upon a prorated yearly amount.

Required

A. Prepare the quarterly income statement showing contribution margins by markets.

B. Assuming there are no alternative uses for the Justa Corporation's present capacity, would you recommend dropping the regional market? Why or why not?

C. Prepare the quarterly income statement showing contribution margins by products.

D. It is believed that a new product can be ready for sale next year if the Justa Corporation decides to go ahead with continued research. The new product can be produced by simply converting equipment presently used in producing Product C. This conversion will increase fixed costs by $10,000 per quarter. What must be the minimum contribution margin per quarter for the new product to make the changeover financially feasible?

I—Q12. Adding a Department—Incremental Revenue and Incremental Cost (CMA Adapted)

The management of Bay Company is considering a proposal to install a third production department within its existing factory building. With the company's present production setup, raw material is passed through Department I to produce materials A and B in equal proportions. Material A is then passed through Department II to yield product C. Material B is presently being sold "as is" at a price of $20.25 per pound. Product C has a selling price of $100 per pound.

The per pound standard costs currently being used by the Bay Company are as follows:

	Department I (Materials A&B)	Department II (Product C)	(Material B)
Prior department costs	—	$53.03	$13.47
Direct material	$20.00	—	—
Direct labor	7.00	12.00	—
Variable overhead	3.00	5.00	—
Fixed overhead:			
Attributable	2.25	2.25	—
Allocated ($\frac{2}{3}$, $\frac{1}{3}$)	1.00	1.00	—
	$33.25	$73.28	$13.47

These standard costs were developed by using an estimated production volume of 200,000 pounds of raw material as the standard volume. The company assigns Department I costs to materials A and B in proportion to their net sales values at the point of separation, computed by deducting subsequent standard production costs from sales prices. The $300,000 of common fixed overhead costs are allocated to the two producing departments on the basis of the space used by the departments.

The proposed Department III would be used to process material B into product D. It is expected that any quantity of product D can be sold for $30 per pound. Standard costs per pound under this proposal were developed by using 200,000 pounds of raw material as the standard volume and are as follows:

	Department I (Materials A&B)	Department II (Product C)	Department III (Product D)
Prior department costs	—	$52.80	$13.20
Direct material	$20.00	—	—
Direct labor	7.00	12.00	5.50
Variable overhead	3.00	5.00	2.00
Fixed overhead:			
Attributable	2.25	2.25	1.75
Allocated($\frac{1}{2}$,$\frac{1}{4}$,$\frac{1}{4}$)	.75	.75	.75
	$33.00	$72.80	$23.20

Required

A. If (1) sales and production levels are expected to remain constant in the foreseeable future, and (2) there are no foreseeable alternative uses for the available factory space, should the Bay Company install Department III and thereby produce product D? Show calculations to support your answer.

B. Instead of constant sales and production levels, suppose that under the present production setup $1,000,000 additions to the factory building must be made every 10 years to accommodate growth. Suppose also that proper maintenance gives these factory additions an infinite life and that all such maintenance costs are included in the standard costs which are set forth in the text of the problem. Describe how the analysis that you performed in part A would be changed if the installation of Department III shortened the interval at which the $1,000,000 factory additions are made from 10 years to 6 years? Be as specific as possible in your answer.

I—Q13. Lease Evaluation

Work III—Q7. The question requires the application of a present value interest table. (See Article 14 and/or the explanation for part 6 of III—Q7.)

I—Q14. Decision Making and Behavioral Implications

Define relevant information for decisions. Also, write what you consider to be the main themes and possible implications for decision making of the discussion in the article, "Accounting Information and Decision-Making: Some Behavioral Hypotheses."

PART TWO QUESTIONS

PERIOD PROFIT PLANNING: FINANCIAL
        MODELING AND BUDGETING, PROFIT
        PLANNING AND COST-VOLUME-PROFIT
        ANALYSIS, PROBABILISTIC PROFIT BUDGETS

II—Q1. Strategic Decisions and Procedures for Developing the Annual Profit Plan (CMA)—Problem for Study (Answer Included for Part A)

Arment Co. has sales in the range of $25–30 million, has one manufacturing plant, employs 700 people, including 15 national account salesmen and 80 traveling sales representatives. The home office and plant is in Philadelphia, and the product is distributed east of the Mississippi River. The product is a line of pumps and related fittings used at construction sites, in homes, and in processing plants. The company has total assets equal to 80% of sales. Its capitalization is: accruals and current liabilities 30%, long-term debt 15%, and shareholders' equity 55%. In the last two years sales have increased 7% each year, and income after tax has amounted to 5% of sales.

Required

    A.   Strategic decisions by top management on a number of important topics serve as a basis for the annual profit plan. What are these topics, and why are they important?

    B.   What specific procedures will be followed each year in developing the annual profit plan?

Answer for Part A

A.   The following topics are among those considered by top management to be strategic planning issues.

1. What are overall objectives of the firm?
2. What markets will be served?
3. What channels of distribution will be utilized?
4. What form of organization structure will be suited to the firm's objectives and activities?
5. What basic financial structure will be employed?
6. What intensity of research and development will be planned?

Decisions with regard to the above and similar topics are important because they give the firm the objectives to be reached and provide the basic methods to be used to reach the objectives. The annual profit plan includes the specific activities required to carry out the strategic plans and to reach the firm's objectives.

II—Q2. Budgeting and Behavioral Considerations (CMA)

The operating budget is a very common instrument used by many businesses. While it usually is thought to be an important and necessary tool for management, it has been subject to some criticism from managers and researchers studying organizations and human behavior.

Required

A. Describe and discuss the benefits of budgeting from the behavioral point of view.

B. Describe and discuss the criticisms leveled at the budgeting processes from the behavioral point of view.

C. What solutions are recommended to overcome the criticism described in part B?

II—Q3. For a problem about the effectiveness of a budget procedure for planning and controlling operations, the use of return on assets to evaluate performance, and the effect of the performance measurement system on the behavior of managers, see V—Q4.

II—Q4. Financial Modeling and "What If" Budgeting

A. In the article, "Financial Modeling and 'What If' Budgeting," how is the sales forecast determined?

B. Evaluate the usefulness of the sales forecast assumption used in the article.

C. How might such factors as product mix, action of competitors, economic conditions, consumer demand, etc., be given consideration in projecting or forecasting sales? (Forecasting is the subject of Part IV of this book.) Should these factors be considered in developing "what if" questions? Explain.

D. How can your answer to part C modify or change the model used in the article?

II—Q5. Comprehensive Budgeting Question—Determining Finished Goods Production and Raw Material Purchases from Budgeted Sales Figures; Projected Income Statement; Cash Forecast (CPA)—(Partial Answer Included, for A.1 and A.2; Answer for Part B—the Projected Income Statement)

Modern Products Corporation, a manufacturer of molded plastic containers, determined in October 19_8 that it needed cash to continue operations. The Corporation began negotiating for a one-month bank loan of $100,000 which would be discounted at 6 per cent per annum on November 1. In considering the loan, the bank requested a projected income statement and a cash budget for the month of November.
The following information is available:

1. Sales were budgeted at 120,000 units per month in October 19_8, December 19_8 and January 19_9, and at 90,000 units in November 19_8.
    The selling price is $2 per unit. Sales are billed on the 15th and last day of each month on terms of 2/10 net 30. Past experience indicates sales are even throughout the month and 50 percent of the customers pay the billed amount within the discount period. The remainder pay at the end of 30 days, except for bad debts which average ½ percent of gross sales. On its income statement, the corporation deducts from sales

the estimated amounts for cash discounts on sales and losses on bad debts.

2.   The inventory of finished goods on October 1 was 24,000 units. The finished goods inventory at the end of each month is to be maintained at 20 percent of sales anticipated for the following month. There is no work in process.

3.   The inventory of raw materials on October 1 was 22,800 pounds. At the end of each month the raw materials inventory is to be maintained at not less than 40 percent of production requirements for the following month. Materials are purchased as needed in minimum quantities of 25,000 pounds per shipment. Raw material purchases of each month are paid in the next succeeding month on terms of net 30 days.

4.   All salaries and wages are paid on the 15th and last day of each month for the period ending on the date of payment.

5.   All manufacturing overhead and selling and administrative expenses are paid on the 10th of the month following the month in which incurred. Selling expenses are 10 percent of gross sales. Administrative expenses, which include depreciation of $500 per month on office furniture and fixtures, total $33,000 per month.

6.   The standard cost of a molded plastic container, based on "normal" production of 100,000 units per month, is as follows:

Materials—½ pound	$ .50
Labor	.40
Variable overhead	.20
Fixed overhead	.10
Total	$1.20

Fixed overhead includes depreciation on factory equipment of $4,000 per month. Over- or under-absorbed overhead is included in cost of sales.

7.   The cash balance on November 1 is expected to be $10,000.

Required

Prepare the following for Modern Products Corporation assuming the bank loan is granted. (Do not consider income taxes.)

A. Schedules computing inventory budgets by months for
1. Finished goods production in units for October, November and December.
2. Raw material purchases in pounds for October and November.

B. A projected income statement for the month of November.

C. A cash forecast for the month of November showing the opening balance, receipts (itemized by dates of collection), disbursements and balance at end of month.

Partial Answer for A.1 and A.2

A.1

Modern Products Corporation
Schedule Computing Finished Goods Production Budget (Units)
For October, November, and December 19_8

	October	November	December
Budgeted sales—units	120,000		
Inventory required at end of month	18,000		
Total to be accounted for	138,000		
Less inventory on hand at beginning of month	24,000		
Budgeted production—units	114,000		

A.2

Schedule Computing Raw Materials Inventory Purchase Budget (Pounds)
for October and November 19_8

	October	November
Budgeted production—pounds (½ lb. per unit)	57,000	
Inventory required at end of month	19,200	
Total to be accounted for	76,200	
Less inventory on hand at beginning of month	22,800	
Balance required by purchase	53,400	
Budgeted purchases—pounds (based on minimum shipments of $25,000 lbs. each)	75,000	

Answer for B

Modern Products Corporation
Projected Income Statement
for the Month of November

Sales (90,000 units at $2)		$180,000
Less: Cash discounts on sales	$ 1,800	
Estimated bad debts (½% of gross sales)	900	2,700
Net sales		177,300
Cost of sales:		
Standard (90,000 units at $1.20)	108,000	
Add under-absorbed overhead (standard production		
of 100,000 units less budgeted production of		
96,000 units equal 4,000 units times $.10)	400	108,400
Gross profit on sales		68,900
Expenses:		
Selling (10% of gross sales)	18,000	
Administrative ($33,000 per month)	33,000	
Interest expense	500	51,500
Net income		$ 17,400

II—Q6. High-Low Method; Use of a Flexible Budget Formula; Flexible Budgets and Direct Costing (CPA)

A. Items 1 and 2 are based on the following information:
    Maintenance expenses of a company are to be analyzed for purposes of constructing a flexible budget. Examination of past records disclosed the following costs and volume measures:

	Highest	Lowest
Cost per month	$39,200	$32,000
Machine hours	24,000	15,000

1. Using the high-low-point method of analysis, the estimated variable cost per machine hour is
    a. $1.25
    b. $12.50
    c. $0.80
    d. $0.08

2. Using the high-low technique, the estimated annual fixed cost for maintenance expenditures is
    a. $447,360
    b. $240,000
    c. $230,400
    d. $384,000

3.   Adams Corporation has developed the following flexible-budget formula for annual indirect-labor cost:

Total cost = $4,800 + $0.50 per machine hour

Operating budgets for the current month are based upon 20,000 hours of planned machine time. Indirect-labor costs included in this planning budget are
a. $14,800
b. $10,000
c. $14,400
d. $10,400

B.   The following annual flexible budget has been prepared for use in making decisions relating to product X.

	100,000 Units	150,000 Units	200,000 Units
Sales volume	$800,000	$1,200,000	$1,600,000
Manufacturing costs:			
Variable	300,000	450,000	600,000
Fixed	200,000	200,000	200,000
	500,000	650,000	800,000
Selling and other expenses:			
Variable	200,000	300,000	400,000
Fixed	160,000	160,000	160,000
	360,000	460,000	560,000
Income (or loss)	$(60,000)	$ 90,000	$ 240,000

The 200,000 unit budget has been adopted and will be used for allocating fixed manufacturing costs to units of product X; at the end of the first six months the following information is available:

	Units
Production completed	120,000
Sales	60,000

All fixed costs are budgeted and incurred uniformly throughout the year and all costs incurred coincide with the budget.

Over- and under-applied fixed manufacturing costs are deferred until year-end. Annual sales have the following seasonal pattern:

	Portion of Annual Sales
First quarter	10%
Second quarter	20
Third quarter	30
Fourth quarter	40
	100%

4. The amount of fixed factory costs applied to product during the first six months under absorption costing would be
   a. Overapplied by $20,000
   b. Equal to the fixed costs incurred
   c. Underapplied by $40,000
   d. Underapplied by $80,000
   e. None of the above

5. Reported net income (or loss) for the first six months under absorption costing would be
   a. $160,000
   b. $80,000
   c. $40,000
   d. ($40,000)
   e. None of the above.

6. Reported net income (or loss) for the first six months under direct costing would be
   a. $144,000
   b. $72,000
   c. $0
   d. ($36,000)
   e. None of the above

7. Assuming that 90,000 units of product X were sold during the first six months and that this is to be used as a basis, the revised budget estimate for the total number of units to be sold during this year would be
   a. 360,000
   b. 240,000
   c. 200,000
   d. 120,000
   e. None of the above

II—Q7. Budget Preparation and Comparing Actual and Budget Amounts (CMA Adapted)

The Melcher Co. produces farm equipment at several plants. The business is seasonal and cyclical in nature. The company has attempted to use budgeting for planning and controlling activities, but the variable nature of the business has caused some company officials to be skeptical about the usefulness of budgeting to the company. The accountant for the Adrian plant has been using a system he calls "flexible budgeting" to help his plant management control operations.

The company president asks him to explain what the term means, how he applies the system at the Adrian plant and how it can be applied to the company as a whole. The accountant presents the following data as part of his explanation.

Budget data for 19_3

Normal monthly capacity of the plant in direct labor hours			10,000 hours
Material costs	6 lbs. @	$1.50	$9.00 unit
Labor costs	2 hours @	$3.00	$6.00 unit

Overhead estimate at normal monthly capacity [5000 units]

Variable (controllable):	
Indirect labor	$6,500
Indirect materials	$ 600
Repairs	$ 750
Total variable	$7,850
Fixed (non-controllable):	
Depreciation	$3,250
Supervision	$3,000
Total Fixed	$6,250
Total Fixed and Variable	$14,100

Planned units for January 19_3	4,000
Planned units for February 19_3	6,000

Actual data for January 19_3

Hours worked	8,400
Units produced	3,800
Costs incurred:	
Material (24,000 lbs.)	$36,000
Direct Labor	25,200
Indirect Labor	6,000
Indirect Materials	600
Repairs	1,800
Depreciation	3,250
Supervision	3,000
Total	$75,850

Required

   A.   Prepare a budget for January.

   B.   Prepare a report for January comparing actual and budgeted
        costs for the actual activity for the month.

   C.   Can flexible budgeting be applied to the nonmanufacturing
        activities of the company? Explain your answer.

II—Q8. Potential Uses of a Variable Budget (CPA)

Department A is one of 15 departments in the plant and is involved in the
production of all of the six products manufactured. The department is
highly mechanized and as a result its output is measured in direct machine
hours. Variable (flexible) budgets are utilized throughout the factory in
planning and controlling costs, but here the focus is upon the application
of variable budgets only in Department A. The following data covering a
time span of approximately six months were taken from the various
budgets, accounting records, and performance reports (only representative
items and amounts are utilized here):

On March 15, 19_1 the following variable budget was approved for
the department; it will be used throughout the 19_2 fiscal year
which begins July 1, 19_1. This variable budget was developed
through the cooperative efforts of the department manager, his
supervisor and certain staff members from the budget department.

19_2 Variable Budget — Department A

Controllable Costs	Fixed Amount Per Month	Variable Rate Per Direct Machine Hour
Employee salaries	$ 9,000	
Indirect wages	18,000	$.07
Indirect materials		.09
Other costs	6,000	.03
	$33,000	$.19

On May 5, 19_1 the annual sales plan and the production budget
were completed. In order to continue preparation of the annual
profit plan (which was detailed by month) the production budget

was translated to planned activity for each of the factory departments. The planned activity for Department A was:

	For the 12 months ending June 30, 19_2				
	Year	July	Aug.	Sept.	Etc.
Planned output in direct machine hours	325,000	22,000	25,000	29,000	249,000

On August 31, 19_1 the manager of Department A was informed that his planned output for September had been revised to 34,000 direct machine hours. He expressed some doubt as to whether this volume could be attained.

At the end of September 19_1 the accounting records provided the following actual data for the month for the department:

Actual output in direct machine hours	33,000
Actual controllable costs incurred:	
Employee salaries	$ 9,300
Indirect wages	20,500
Indirect materials	2,850
Other costs	7,510
	$40,160

Required

The requirements relate primarily to the potential uses of the variable budget for the period March through September 19_1.

A.   What activity base is utilized as a measure of volume in the budget for this department? How should one determine the range of the activity base to which the variable rates per direct machine hour are relevant? Explain.

B.   The high-low point method was utilized in developing this variable budget. Using indirect wage costs as an example, illustrate and explain how this method would be applied in determining the fixed and variable components of indirect wage costs for this department. Assume that the high-low budget values for indirect wages are $19,400 at 20,000 direct machine hours and $20,100 at 30,000 direct machine hours.

C.   Explain and illustrate how the variable budget should be utilized:

1. In budgeting costs when the annual sales plan and production budget are completed (about May 5, 19_1 or shortly thereafter).
2. In budgeting a cost revision based upon a revised production budget (about August 31, 19_1 or shortly thereafter).
3. In preparing a cost performance report for September 19_1.

II—Q9. Absorption and Direct (Variable) Costing in Projected Income Statements (CPA)

Management of Bicent Company uses the following unit costs for the one product it manufactures:

	Projected Cost per Unit
Direct material (all variable)	$30.00
Direct labor (all variable)	19.00
Manufacturing overhead:	
Variable cost	6.00
Fixed cost (based on 10,000 units per month)	5.00
Selling, general and administrative:	
Variable cost	4.00
Fixed cost (based on 10,000 units per month)	2.80

The projected selling price is $80 per unit. The fixed costs remain fixed within the relevant range of 4,000 to 16,000 units of production.

Management has also projected the following data for the month of June 19_6:

	Units
Beginning inventory	2,000
Production	9,000
Available	11,000
Sales	7,500
Ending inventory	3,500

Required

Prepare projected income statements for June 19_6 for management purposes under each of the following product-costing methods:

1. Absorption costing with all variances charged to cost of goods sold each month.

2. Direct (variable) costing.

Supporting schedules calculating inventoriable production costs per unit should be presented in good form. Ignore income taxes.

II—Q10. Effect of Sales Volume and Production Volume on Net Income Under Absorption Costing and Direct Costing (CMA)

Sun Company, a wholly owned subsidiary of Guardian, Inc., produces and sells three main product lines. The company employs a standard cost accounting system for record-keeping purposes.

At the beginning of 19_4, the president of Sun Company presented the budget to the parent company and accepted a commitment to contribute $15,800 to Guardian's consolidated profit in 19_4. The president has been confident that the year's profit would exceed budget target, since the monthly sales reports that he has been receiving have shown that sales for the year will exceed budget by 10 percent. The president is both disturbed and confused when the controller presents an adjusted forecast as of November 30, 19_4 indicating that profit will be 11 percent under budget. The two forecasts are presented below:

SUN COMPANY
Forecasts of Operating Results

	Forecasts as of	
	1/1/_4	11/30/_4
Sales	$268,000	$294,800
Cost of Sales at Standard	212,000*	233,200
Gross Margin at Standard	$ 56,000	$ 61,600
Over- (Under-) Absorbed Fixed Manufacturing Overhead	—	<6,000>
Actual Gross Margin	$ 56,000	$ 55,600
Selling Expenses	$ 13,400	$ 14,740
Administrative Expenses	26,800	26,800
Total Operating Expenses	$ 40,200	$ 41,540
Earnings before Tax	$ 15,800	$ 14,060

*Includes fixed manufacturing overhead of $30,000.

There have been no sales price changes or product mix shifts since the 1/1/_4 forecast. The only cost variance on the income statement is the under-absorbed manufacturing overhead. This arose because the company produced only 16,000 standard machine hours (budgeted machine hours were 20,000) during 19_4 as a result of a shortage of raw materials while its principal supplier was closed by a strike. Fortunately Sun Company's finished goods inventory was large enough to fill all sales orders received.

Required

A.   Analyze and explain why the profit has declined in spite of increased sales and good control over costs.

B.   What plan, if any, could Sun Company adopt during December to improve their reported profit at year end? Explain your answer.

C.   Illustrate and explain how Sun Company could adopt an alternative internal cost reporting procedure which would avoid the confusing effect of the present procedure.

D.   Would the alternative procedure described in Part C be acceptable to Guardian, Inc. for financial reporting purposes? Explain.

II—Q11. Cash Forecast—Multiple Choice (CPA)

A.   Tomlinson Retail seeks your assistance to develop cash and other budget information for May, June, and July 19_3. At April 30, 19_3, the company had cash of $5,500, accounts receivable of $437,000, inventories of $309,400, and accounts payable of $133,055.
     The budget is to be based on the following assumptions:

   Sales
   a.   Each month's sales are billed on the last day of the month.
   b.   Customers are allowed a 3% discount if payment is made within ten days after the billing date. Receivables are booked gross.
   c.   Sixty percent of the billings are collected within the discount period, 25% are collected by the end of the month, 9% are collected by the end of the second month, and 6% prove uncollectible.

Purchases

a. Fifty-four percent of all purchases of material and selling, general, and administrative expenses are paid in the month purchased and the remainder in the following month.

b. Each month's units of ending inventory is equal to 130% of the next month's units of sales.

c. The cost of each unit of inventory is $20.

d. Selling, general, and administrative expenses of which $2,000 is depreciation, are equal to 15% of the current month's sales.

Actual and projected sales are as follows:

19_3	Dollars	Units
March	$354,000	11,800
April	363,000	12,100
May	357,000	11,900
June	342,000	11,400
July	360,000	12,000
August	366,000	12,200

1. Budgeted cash disbursements during the month of June 19_3 are
    a. $292,900
    b. $287,379
    c. $294,900
    d. $285,379

2. Budgeted cash collections during the month of May 19_3 are
    a. $333,876
    b. $355,116
    c. $340,410
    d. $355,656

3. The budgeted number of units of inventory to be purchased during July 19_3 is
    a. 15,860
    b. 12,260
    c. 12,000
    d. 15,600

B. The Dilly Company marks up all merchandise at 25% of gross purchase price. All purchases are made on account with terms of 1/10, net/60. Purchase discounts, which are recorded as miscellaneous income, are always taken. Normally, 60% of each month's purchases are paid for in the month of purchase while the other 40% are paid during the first 10 days of the first month after purchase. Inventories of merchandise at the end of each month are kept at 30% of the next month's projected cost of goods sold.

Terms for sales on account are 2/10, net/30. Cash sales are not subject to discount. Fifty percent of each month's sales on account are collected during the month of sale, 45% are collected in the succeeding month, and the remainder are usually uncollectible. Seventy percent of the collections in the month of sale are subject to discount while 10% of the collections in the succeeding month are subject to discount.

Projected sales data for selected months follows:

	Sales on Account—Gross	Cash Sales
December	$1,900,000	$400,000
January	1,500,000	250,000
February	1,700,000	350,000
March	1,600,000	300,000

4. Projected gross purchases for January are
   a. $1,400,000
   b. $1,470,000
   c. $1,472,000
   d. $1,248,000
   e. None of the above

5. Projected inventory at the end of December is
   a. $420,000
   b. $441,600
   c. $552,000
   d. $393,750
   e. None of the above

6. Projected payments to suppliers during February are
   a. $1,551,200
   b. $1,535,688
   c. $1,528,560
   d. $1,509,552
   e. None of the above

7. Projected sales discounts to be taken by customers making remittances during February are
   a. $5,250
   b. $15,925
   c. $30,500
   d. $11,900
   e. None of the above

8. Projected total collections from customers during February are
   a. $1,875,000
   b. $1,861,750
   c. $1,511,750
   d. $1,188,100
   e. None of the above

C. Preparation of a Cash Forecast Model (CMA)—Problem for Study (Answer Included)

Over the past several years, the Programme Corporation has encountered difficulties estimating its cash flows. The result has been a rather strained relationship with its banker.

Programme's controller would like to develop a means by which he can forecast the firm's monthly operating cash flows. The following data was gathered to facilitate the development of such a forecast.

1. Sales have been and are expected to increase at .5% each month.
2. 30% of each month's sales are for cash; the other 70% are on open account.
3. Of the credit sales, 80% are collected in the first month following the sale and the remaining 20% are collected in the second month. There are no bad debts.
4. Gross margin on sales averages 25%.
5. Programme purchases enough inventory each month to cover the following month's sales.
6. All inventory purchases are paid for in the month of purchase at a 2% cash discount.
7. Monthly expenses are: Payroll—$1,500; Rent—$400; Depreciation—$120; Other cash expenses—1% of that month's sales. There are no accruals.
8. Ignore the effects of corporate income taxes, dividends and equipment acquisitions.

Required

Using the data above, develop a mathematical model the controller can use for his calculations. Your model should be capable of calculating the monthly operating cash inflows and outflows for any specified month.

Answer

S = current month's sales
t = number of months in the future the forecast is desired

Sales t months from now
$$= S(1.005)^t$$

Collections t months from now
$$= .3S(1.005)^t + (.8)(.7)S(1.005)^{t-1}$$
$$+ (.2)(.7)S(1.005)^{t-2}$$
$$= .3S(1.005)^t + .56S(1.005)^{t-1} + .14S(1.005)^{t-2}$$

Purchases t months from now
$$= .75S(1.005)^{t+1}$$

Cash payments t months from now*
$$= (.98)(.75)S(1.005) \quad + .01S(1.005)^t + 1{,}900$$
$$= .735S(1.005)^{t+1} + .01S(1.005)^t + 1{,}900$$

II—Q12. Cash Budgets, Projected Income Statements, Sensitivity Analysis (CPA Adapted) [Prepared by Yow-Min R. Lee]

The Standard Tire Company is preparing its cash budget for the fiscal year 19_5. You have been requested to assist in the preparation of a monthly cash budget and a projected monthly income statement. The following information is available regarding the company's operations:

1. Sales for November and December of last year were $500,000 and $600,000 respectively. The predicted sales for January through December of 19_5 are as follows:

    $360,000, $420,000, $600,000, $540,000, $480,000, $400,000
    $350,000, $550,000, $500,000, $400,000, $600,000, $800,000

2. All sales are made on account. Sales terms call for a 2% discount if paid within the month of sale. 70% of the billing will be collected within the discount period, 20% by the end of the month after sale, 8% in the following month and 2% will be uncollectible.

3. There is a basic inventory of $120,000 always kept in stock. In addition, the company replenishes the basic inventory whenever a sale is made, i.e., purchases equal sales for each month. Assume that 60% of the purchase is paid in the month of purchase and within the discount period, terms 3/10, n/30, and that the remainder is paid in full in the month after purchase.

---

*If it is assumed that the discounts were included to arrive at the 25% gross margin, then the (.98) in the first expression would not appear.

4. Fixed selling and administrative expenses are $80,000 and $70,000 respectively per month. Variable selling expense amounts to 10% of gross sales while variable general and administrative expense averages 5% of gross sales.

5. Cost of goods sold averages 50% of gross sales. The income tax rate is assumed to be 50%, which is payable quarterly according to income tax regulations.

6. The desired cash balance each month is $50,000. Payment on a loan is $10,000 a month for the first six months without interest.

Required

A. Prepare a cash budget and a projected income statement for January and February manually.

B. Use the computer and the CASHB program to prepare a cash budget and a projected income statement for January through December. (See Article 10.)

C. Change several of the parameters, rerun the program and explain the results.

II—Q13. Cost-Volume-Profit Analysis Terms, Breakeven Calculation Questions (CPA)

A. Cost-volume-earnings analysis (breakeven analysis) is used to determine and express the interrelationships of different volumes of activity (sales), costs, sales prices, and sales mix to earnings. More specifically, the analysis is concerned with what will be the effect on earnings of changes in sales volume, sales prices, sales mix, and costs.

Required

a. Certain terms are fundamental to cost-volume-earnings analysis. Explain the meaning of each of the following terms:
    1. Fixed costs
    2. Variable costs

3. Relevant range
4. Breakeven point
5. Margin of safety
6. Sales mix

b. Several assumptions are implicit in cost-volume-earnings analysis. What are these assumptions? (See Article 20.)

c. In a recent period, Zero Company had the following experience:

Sales (10,000 units © $200) $2,000,000

	Fixed	Variable	
Costs:			
Direct material	$ —	$ 200,000	
Direct labor	—	400,000	
Factory overhead	160,000	600,000	
Administrative			
expenses	180,000	80,000	
Other expenses	200,000	120,000	
Total costs	$540,000	$1,400,000	1,940,000
Net income			$ 60,000

Each item below is independent.

1. Calculate the breakeven point for Zero in terms of units and sales dollars. Show your calculations.

2. What sales volume would be required to generate a net income of $96,000? Show your calculations.

3. What is the breakeven point if management makes a decision which increases fixed costs by $18,000? Show your calculations.

B. Freedom, Inc., management has performed cost studies and projected the following annual costs based on 40,000 units of production and sales:

	Total Annual Costs	Percent of Variable Portion of Total Annual Costs
Direct material	$400,000	100%
Direct labor	360,000	75
Manufacturing overhead	300,000	40
Selling, general and administrative	200,000	25

Required

1. Compute Freedom's unit selling price that will yield a projected 10% profit if sales are 40,000 units.

2. Assume that management selects a selling price of $30 per unit (40,000 units). Compute Freedom's dollar sales that will yield a projected 10% profit on sales assuming the above variable-fixed costs relationships are valid.

II—Q14. Breakeven Point Calculation for a Single Product and for Composite Units (CPA)

The Dooley Co. manufactures two products, baubles and trinkets. The following are projections for the coming year.

| | Baubles | | Trinkets | | |
	Units	Amount	Units	Amount	Totals
Sales	10,000	$10,000	7,500	$10,000	$20,000
Costs:					
Fixed		2,000		5,600	7,600
Variable		6,000		3,000	9,000
		8,000		8,600	16,600
Income before taxes		$ 2,000		$ 1,400	$ 3,400

1. Assuming that the facilities are not jointly used, the breakeven output (in units) for baubles would be
   a.   8,000
   b.   7,000
   c.   6,000
   d.   5,000

2. The breakeven volume (dollars) for trinkets would be
   a. $8,000
   b. $7,000
   c. $6,000
   d. $5,000

3. Assuming that consumers purchase composite units of four baubles and three trinkets, the composite unit contribution margin would be
    a. $4.40
    b. $4.00
    c. $1.33
    d. $1.10

4. If consumers purchase composite units of four baubles and three trinkets, the breakeven output for the two products would be*
    a.   6,909 baubles; 6,909 trinkets
    b.   6,909 baubles; 5,182 trinkets
    c.   5,000 baubles; 8,000 trinkets
    d.   5,000 baubles; 6,000 trinkets

5. If baubles and trinkets become one-to-one complements and there is no change in The Dooley Co.'s cost function, the breakeven volume would be
    a. $22,500
    b. $15,750
    c. $13,300
    d. $10,858

6. If a composite unit is defined as one bauble and one trinket, the composite contribution margin ratio would be
    a.   7/10
    b.   4/7
    c.   2/5
    d.   19/50

* Editor's Note: Company Breakeven and Product Mix.

Assume a company has two products X and Y, and that 2X are sold for every Y. X has a selling price of $12 and Y a selling price of $8, variable costs are $6 for X and $4 for Y, and fixed costs are $25,000 and $23,000 respectively. The company breakeven point needs to consider the product mix. Using the formula

$$\frac{\text{Fixed Cost}}{\dfrac{\text{SP/unit} - \text{VC/unit}}{\text{SP/unit}}}$$

where SP = selling price and VC = variable cost, the overall company breakeven would be calculated as:

$$\frac{\$25,000 + \$23,000}{\dfrac{(2x\$12 + 1x\$8) - (2x\$6 + 1x\$4)}{(2x\$12 + 1x\$8)}} = \frac{\$48,000}{\dfrac{\$32-16}{\$32}} = \frac{\$48,000}{\dfrac{\$16}{\$32}} = \$96,000$$

Also, $48,000 divided by (SP/unit – VC/unit) or
$48,000 divided by $16 = 3,000 packages of 2X and 1Y
3000 x 2 x $12 = $72,000 sales of X at breakeven
3000 x 1 x $ 8 = 24,000 sales of Y at breakeven
                96,000 company breakeven

If we use the average contribution margin per unit
of $16 , then $48,000 ÷ 16/3 = 9000 units, i.e., 2/3 of 9000 = 6000 units
     3 units
of X and 1/3 of 9000 = 3000 units of Y.

II—Q15. Cost-Volume-Profit Analysis and Planning (CPA)

The president of Beth Corporation, which manufactures tape decks and
sells them to producers of sound reproduction systems, anticipates a 10%
wage increase on January 1 of next year to the manufacturing employees
(variable labor). He expects no other changes in costs. Overhead will not
change as a result of the wage increase. The president has asked you to
assist him in developing the information he needs to formulate a reasonable product strategy for next year.

You are satisfied by regression analysis that volume is the primary factor
affecting costs and have separated the semivariable costs into their fixed
and variable segments by means of the least squares criterion. You also
observe that the beginning and ending inventories are never materially different. (Regression analysis is discussed in Part IV, Article 20.)

Below are the current year data assembled for your analysis:

Current selling price per unit .... $ 80.00

Variable cost per unit:
 Material .... $ 30.00
 Labor 12.00
 Overhead 6.00
  Total .... $ 48.00
Annual volume of sales .... 5,000 units
Fixed costs $51,000

Required

Provide the following information for the president using cost-volume-
profit analysis:

A. What increase in the selling price is necessary to cover the 10% wage increase and still maintain the current profit-volume-cost ratio?

B. How many tape decks must be sold to maintain the current net income if the sales price remains at $80.00 and the 10% wage increase goes into effect?

C. The president believes that an additional $190,000 of machinery (to be depreciated at 10% annually) will increase present capacity (5,300 units) by 30%. If all tape decks produced can be sold at the present price and the wage increase goes into effect, how would the estimated net income before capacity is increased compare with the estimated net income after capacity is increased? Prepare computations of estimated net income *before* and *after* the expansion.

II—Q16. Breakeven Formulas for Different Company Alternatives; Probability (CPA)—(Answer Included for A.1 as an Aid in Determining Solutions for this Problem)

Notil Industries, Inc. recently established the Mocon Division (not a separate corporation) to manufacture and market a new type computer. Notil's executive committee is considering various financing methods and requests that you make a profit-volume analysis and advise the committee of the probable results of several alternatives available.

Required

A. Engineering estimates indicate that the variable cost of manufacturing a unit will be $20,000. It is estimated that the variable cost of selling a unit will be $10,000 if the sales price should be set at $50,000 per unit. State and federal income taxes are estimated at 55 percent of net income before taxes (disregard the investment credit).

It is also estimated that Mocon will incur fixed costs totaling $4,000,000 per year including depreciation. Notil must secure an additional $10,000,000 to finance the Mocon Division. Notil plans to issue at par either stocks or bonds and Mocon must bear the financing cost in addition to other costs.

Compute the number of units which must be sold annually at $50,000 per unit to pay all costs, meet any dividend requirement and comply with the stated objective under each of the following alternatives (show your computations):

1. 6% nonparticipating, cumulative, preferred stock is issued.
2. 5% bonds are issued.
3. 5% bonds are issued, and Notil requires that Mocon contribute 6 percent of its sales to be credited to Notil Industries' retained earnings for internal financing and future expansion.
4. 5% bonds are issued, and Notil requires that Mocon contribute annually both $100,000 to be paid out as dividends to Notil's common stockholders and 6 percent of Mocon's sales to be credited to Notil's retained earnings for internal financing and future expansion.

B. Mocon will have 72 salesmen. Market surveys indicate that each salesman should sell an average of one unit every three months if the sales price of the computer is set at $50,000 per unit and that no salesman is likely to sell more than one unit in any month.

Compute the following (show your computations):

1. The probability that any individual salesman will sell a computer in any one month.
2. The average number of units that Mocon can expect to sell per month at $50,000.

C. The market surveys also indicated that each salesman should be expected to sell one unit every four months if the sales price should be set at $60,000 per unit. Reduced sales would cause the variable cost of selling a unit to increase to $12,000. Notil's executive committee requests that you

1. Recompute requirement "A.4" under this alternative.
2. Advise them whether to set the sales price at $50,000 or $60,000. Explain why the sales price should be set at the amount you recommend.

Answer for A.1

Unit Sales Necessary if Stock is Issued

$$US = \frac{FC + \frac{D}{1-TR}}{MC} = \frac{\$4,000,000 + \frac{.06 \times \$10,000,000}{1 - .55}}{\$50,000 - \$30,000} = 266.7 \text{ units}$$

Round up to 267 units (impossible to sell part of a unit).

Where: US   =   unit sales
        FC   =   fixed cost
        D   =   dividends on stock
        TR   =   tax rate
        MC   =   marginal contribution per unit sold

An alternative computation would use the marginal contribution rate

$$\left(\frac{\$20,000}{\$50,000} = 40\%\right)$$

rather than the marginal contribution in the denominator. This would produce an answer expressed in dollars of sales, which would be divided by
the selling price per unit ($50,000) to determine unit sales.

II—Q17. Probability—Expected Unit Sales Level (CPA Adapted)

A sales office of Helms, Inc., has developed the following probability distribution for daily sales of a perishable product.

X (Units Sold)	P(Sales = X)
100	.2
150	.5
200	.2
250	.1

1. The product is restocked at the start of each day. If the
    company desires a 90% service level in satisfying sales
    demand, the initial stock balance for each day should be
    a.   250
    b.   160
    c.   200
    d.   150
    e.   None of the above

2. What is the expected daily sales?
    a.   250
    b.   160
    c.   200
    d.   150
    e.   None of the above

3. Work part B of II—Q16.

II—Q18. Expected Value Determination, Payoff Table Discussion Question (CPA Adapted)

The Stat Company wants more information on the demand for its products. The following data are relevant:

Units Demanded	Probability of Unit Demand	Total Cost of Units Demanded
0	.10	$ 0
1	.15	1.00
2	.20	2.00
3	.40	3.00
4	.10	4.00
5	.05	5.00

1. What is the total expected value or payoff with perfect information? (See the answer to part C of I—Q10.)
   a. $2.40
   b. $7.40
   c. $9.00
   d. $9.15
   e. None of the above

2. How does a payoff table for strategies differ from the above? (See I—Q10.)

II—Q19. Schedule of Probable Sales; Present Value of Net Cash Flows (CPA)

Vernon Enterprises designs and manufactures toys. Past experience indicates that the product life cycle of a toy is three years. Promotional advertising produces large sales in the early years, but there is a substantial sales decline in the final year of a toy's life.

Consumer demand for new toys placed on the market tends to fall into three classes. About 30 percent of the new toys sell well above expectations, 60 percent sell as anticipated, and 10 percent have poor consumer acceptance.

A new toy has been developed. The following sales projections were made by carefully evaluating consumer demand for the new toy:

Consumer Demand for New Toy	Chance of Occurring	Estimated Sales in Year 1	Year 2	Year 3
Above average	30%	$1,200,000	$2,500,000	$600,000
Average	60%	700,000	1,700,000	400,000
Below average	10%	200,000	900,000	150,000

Variable costs are estimated at 30 percent of the selling price. Special machinery must be purchased at a cost of $860,000 and will be installed in an unused portion of the factory which Vernon has unsuccessfully been trying to rent to someone for several years at $50,000 per year and has no prospects for future utilization. Fixed expenses (excluding depreciation) of a cash-flow nature are estimated at $50,000 per year on the new toy. The new machinery will be depreciated by the sum-of-the-years' digits method with an estimated salvage value of $110,000 and will be sold at the beginning of the fourth year. Advertising and promotional expenses will be incurred uniformly and will total $100,000 the first year, $150,000 the second year, and $50,000 the third year. These expenses will be deducted as incurred for income tax reporting.

Vernon believes that state and federal income taxes will total 60 percent of income in the foreseeable future, and may be assumed to be paid uniformly over the year income is earned.

Required

A. Prepare a schedule computing the probable sales of this new toy in each of the three years, taking into account the probability of above average, average and below average sales occurring.

B. Assume that the probable sales computed in "A" are $900,000 in the first year, $1,800,000 in the second year, and $410,000 in the third year. Prepare a schedule computing the probable net income for the new toy in each of the three years of its life.

C. Prepare a schedule of net cash flows from sales of the new toy for each of the years involved and from disposition of the machinery purchased. Use the sales data given in part "B."

D. Assuming a minimum desired rate of return of 10 percent, prepare a schedule of the present value of the net cash flows calculated in "C." The following data are relevant:

Year	Present Value of $1.00 Due at the End of Each Year Discounted at 10 percent	Present Value of $1.00 Earned Uniformly Throughout the Year Discounted at 10 percent
1	.91	.95
2	.83	.86
3	.75	.78

II—Q20. Probabilistic Budgeting*

A profit budget is prepared for next year as follows:

	Pessimistic	Most Likely	Optimistic
Sales ($8 per unit)	$800	$1000	$1200
Variable Costs	400	375	300
Marginal Contribution	$400	$ 625	$ 900
Fixed Costs	200	200	200
Net Income Before Taxes	$200	$ 425	$ 700
Tax (40%)	80	170	280
Net Income	$120	$ 255	$ 420

Management ascribes the following probabilities to these estimates:

	Pessimistic	Most Likely	Optimistic
Sales	.2	.5	.3
Variable Costs	.3	.5	.2

Using this information, answer the following questions:

A. What is the joint probability of getting net income after taxes of $120?

B. What is the joint probability of getting net income after taxes of $420?

C. What is the probability of getting sales of $1200?

D. What is the total probability of having net income after taxes equal $180?

E. What is the expected value of net income after taxes?

II—Q21. Statement Forecasting a Manufacturer's Cash Balance (CMA)

The Jafa Corporation uses direct costing for managerial purposes and prepared their December 31, 19_3 balance sheet on a direct costing basis as follows:

---

*From Ronald M. Copeland and Paul E. Dascher, *Managerial Accounting* (Santa Barbara, Calif.: Wiley/Hamilton Publishing Company, 1974), p. 128. Reprinted with permission.

Jafa Corporation
Balance Sheet As of December 31, 19_3

Current Assets

Cash		$10,000	
Marketable Securities		50,000	
Accounts Receivable		80,000	
Inventories			
Finished Goods	$67,500		
Work in Process	45,000		
Raw Materials	9,000	$121,500	
Total Current Assets			$261,500

Long Term Assets

Equipment (factory)	$300,000		
Less: Accumulated Depreciation	72,000	$228,000	
Plant	$1,000,000		
Less: Accumulated Depreciation	180,000	$820,000	
Property		200,000	
Total Long Term Assets			$1,248,000

Other Assets

Intangibles (net)		$10,000	
Loan to Officer of Company		10,000	20,000
Total Assets			$1,529,500

Current Liabilities

Accounts Payable		$25,680	
Other Payables		10,000	
Notes Payable (one month note due January 15, 19_4)		50,000	
Current Portion of Long-term Debt (due March 31, 19_4)		50,000	
Total Current Liabilities			$135,680
Long-term Debt (8%, 10 years, interest payable December 31, repayment of principal at rate of $50,000 per year beginning in 19_4)			450,000
Total Liabilities			$585,680

Owners' Equity

Common Stock (issued and outstanding, 70,000 shares, $10 per share)		$700,000	
Retained Earnings		243,820	
Total Owners' Equity			$ 943,820
Total Equities			$1,529,500

Some recent and forecast data are:

	Actual		Forecast			
	Nov.	Dec.	Jan.	Feb.	Mar.	Apr.
Cash Sales (units)	1,200	1,200	1,000	1,000	1,000	2,000
Credit Sales (units)	10,000	10,000	8,000	8,000	8,000	20,000
Selling and Administrative Expenses	$20,000	$20,000	$20,000	$20,000	$20,000	$20,000
Fixed Manufacturing Expenses[1]	15,000	15,000	15,000	15,000	15,000	15,000

[1] excluding depreciation and amortization.

The company manufactures an automobile safety seat for children which it sells directly to a number of automobile dealers in its four state region and to retail customers through its own outlet. The selling price through their own outlet is $30; to the dealers, the price is $20.

Since all sales through its own outlet are on a cash basis and sales to dealers, all on account, have been long established, bad debts are negligible. Terms of credit sales are net 30. 60% of the credit sales are paid in the month of the sale and the remaining 40% of the credit sales are paid in the month after the sale.

Raw materials cost $5 per unit. All purchases of raw materials are on account. Accounts payable are on terms of net 30 days. 40% are paid in the month of purchase and 60% are paid in the following month. Direct labor and variable manufacturing overhead costs are $10 per unit. Direct labor and variable manufacturing overhead costs are incurred in direct proportion to the percentage of completion and paid in cash when incurred.

At the end of each month, desired inventory levels are as follows:
Raw materials—20% of next month's requirements
Work in Process—50% of next month's requirements
Finished Goods—50% of next month's requirements
Work in process is assumed to be 50% completed at the end of the month. Raw materials are added at the beginning of production.

Depreciation on the equipment is $4,000 per month and depreciation on the plant is $5,000 per month. Amortization of intangibles is $500 per month.

Selling and administrative expenses are all fixed and half are paid in the month incurred with the balance paid in the following month.

Fixed manufacturing expenses that require cash payments are paid in the month incurred.

Long-term debt-principal is to be paid each March 31, starting in 19_4 at a rate of $50,000 per year.

The loan to the officer was made on December 31, 19_3 and is due March 31, 19_4. The loan is to be repaid on March 31, 19_4 plus interest at 6% per annum.

The firm requires a minimum cash balance of $10,000 at the end of each month. If the balance is less, marketable securities are sold in multiples of $5,000 at the end of the month. If necessary, cash is borrowed in multiples of $1,000 at the end of the month. Marketable securities earn 6% per annum and the interest is collected at the end of each month. The short-term interest rate on notes payable is 12% per annum and is paid at the time the note is repaid.

Taxes are to be ignored.

Required

Prepare a statement forecasting the cash balance including any necessary cash transactions to achieve company cash management objectives for January, 19_4.

PART THREE QUESTIONS

CAPITAL BUDGETING

III—Q1. Capital Budgeting Techniques (CPA)—Problem for Study (Answer Included for Part A.)

The management of McAngus, Inc., has never used formal planning techniques in the operation of its business. The president of McAngus has expressed interest in the recommendation of its accountants that the company investigate various techniques it may use to manage the business more effectively.

McAngus, a medium-sized manufacturer, has grown steadily. It recently acquired another company located approximately 1,000 miles away. The new company manufactures a line of products which complements the present product line. Both manufacturing plants have significant investments in land, buildings, machinery, and equipment. Each plant is to be operated as a separate division headed by a division manager. Each division manager is to have virtually complete authority for the management of his division; i.e., each will be responsible primarily for the profit contribution of his division. A complete set of financial statements is to be prepared for each division as well as for the company.

The president and his immediate management team intend to concentrate their efforts on coordinating the activities of the two divisions and investigating and evaluating such things as new markets, new product lines, and new business acquisition possibilities. Because of the cash required for the recent acquisition and the cash needs for desired future expansion, the president is particularly concerned about cash flow and the effective management of cash.

Required

Construct your answer to each of the following requirements to consider known facts about McAngus, Inc., as presented in the question. Confine your answer to the accounting techniques and processes involved.

A. Explain the objectives and describe the process which McAngus can use to plan for and evaluate the long-term commitment of its resources including cash.

B. Describe three techniques including one which considers the time value of money that McAngus can use to help evaluate various alternatives in its long-range plan. Explain the advantages and disadvantages of each.

Answer for Part A

A. The process of planning for and evaluating long-term commitments of resources is normally referred to as capital budgeting. The capital budget is distinct in that it focuses on the long-term effect of resources committed. Its primary objectives are to provide management with (1) a formal process to chart its future course; (2) a means of ranking and selecting among alternative resource commitments to maximize return on investment; and (3) a program for ongoing evaluation of extant resource commitments.

   Any significant resource commitment is viewed as a project. Hence, the capital budget is composed of projects, some of which are in progress, and some of which are proposed. Each project affects significant periods of time in the ongoing life of a company. A project often involves the evaluation of alternatives and the purchase of such assets as property, plant, and equipment. It should also consider, however, any proposal or program that requires a significant resource commitment over an extended period, such as the development of new products, opening new markets, and the design and development of major computer programs.

   Once resources have been committed to a particular project, the project requires ongoing evaluation; i.e., are the project's objectives being met? If not, it needs to be evaluated in terms of whether the project should be retained as is, modified if possible, or abandoned.

   McAngus can make significant use of capital budgeting. At the division level, projects will need to be defined in terms of those elements of the plant or operation of the division over which the manager has control. On the facts given, the division manager has authority to operate his plant essentially as if it were an independent company. Hence, anything affecting his operation which has required or will require significant resource commitment over a significant period of time should form an integral part of that division's capital budget. At the top management level, the president may view each division as a project, particularly for evaluation purposes. The other described activities of top management (investigating and evaluating such things as new markets, etc.) are projects in the capital budgeting sense. These and other new proposals may be defined, analyzed, and evaluated using a variety of capital budgeting techniques available.

III—Q2. Capital Budgeting (CPA Adapted)

A. A company bought Machine 1 on March 5, 19_4, for $5,000 cash. The estimated salvage was $200 and the estimated life was eleven years. On March 5, 19_5, the company learned that it could purchase a different machine for $8,000 cash. The new machine would save the company an estimated $250 per year compared to Machine 1. The new machine would have no estimated salvage and an estimated life of ten years. The company could get $3,000 for Machine 1 on March 5, 19_5. Ignoring income taxes, which of the following calculations would best assist the company in deciding whether to purchase the new machine?
1.   (Present value of an annuity of $250) + $3,000 − $8,000
2.   (Present value of an annuity of $250) − $8,000.
3.   (Present value of an annuity of $250) + $3,000 − $8,000 − $5,000
4.   (Present value of an annuity of $250) + $3,000 − $8,000 − $4,800

B. Cost of capital is an important concept in capital budgeting. Define the term "cost of capital" and explain how it is used in capital budgeting. (For aid in defining the term, see the cost of capital discussion in the Part V article, "A New Way to Measure and Control Divisional Performance.")

C. The statistical term "expected value" is used to describe estimates of future receipts of a capital budgeting project.

Explain the meaning of the term and indicate how the method to which it applies is used in estimating future receipts. (For a discussion of the meaning and use of expected value in decision models, see Articles 5, 12, 13 and 16.)

III—Q3. Calculations for Different Quantitative Techniques Used in Making Capital Budgeting Decisions (CMA Adapted)—Problem for Study (Answer Included)

The Baxter Company manufactures toys and other short-lived fad type items.

The research and development department came up with an item that would make a good promotional gift for office equipment dealers. Aggressive and effective effort by Baxter's sales personnel has resulted in almost firm commitments for this product for the next three years. It is expected that the product's value will be exhausted by that time.

In order to produce the quantity demanded, Baxter will need to buy additional machinery and rent some additional space. It appears that about 25,000 square feet will be needed; 12,500 square feet of presently unused, but leased, space is available now. (Baxter's present lease with 10 years to run costs $3.00 a foot.) There is another 12,500 square feet adjoining the Baxter facility which Baxter will rent for 3 years at $4.00 per square foot per year if it decides to make this product.

The equipment will be purchased for about $900,000. It will require $30,000 in modifications, $60,000 for installation and $90,000 for testing; all of these activities will be done by a firm of engineers hired by Baxter. All of the expenditures will be paid for on January 1, 19_3.

The equipment should have a salvage value of about $180,000 at the end of the third year. No additional general overhead costs are expected to be incurred.

The following estimates of revenues and expenses for this product for the three years have been developed.

	19_3	19_4	19_5
Sales	$1,000,000	$1,600,000	$800,000
Material, labor and incurred overhead	400,000	750,000	350,000
Assigned general overhead	40,000	75,000	35,000
Rent	87,500	87,500	87,500
Depreciation	450,000	300,000	150,000
	$ 977,500	$1,212,500	$622,500
Income before tax	$ 22,500	$ 387,500	$177,500
Income tax (40%)	9,000	155,000	71,000
	$ 13,500	$ 232,500	$106,500

Required

A.   Prepare a schedule which shows the incremental, after tax, cash flows for this project.

B.   If the company requires a two-year payback period for its investment, would it undertake this project? Show your supporting calculations clearly.

C.   Calculate the after tax accounting rate of return for the project. (Editors' Note: How do the accounting rate of return and the time-adjusted rate of return differ?)

D.   A newly hired Business School graduate recommends that the company consider the use of the net present value analysis to study this project. If the company sets a required rate of return of 20% after taxes will this project be accepted? Show your supporting calculations clearly. (Assume all operating revenues and expenses occur at the end of the year.)

Discount Factors for 20% (Rounded off)

Period	Present Value of $1.00	Present Value of $1.00 per period received at end of period	Accumulated Value of $1.00	Accumulated Value of $1.00 per period received at end of period
1	.83	.83	1.20	1.00
2	.69	1.52	1.44	2.20
3	.58	2.10	1.73	3.64
4	.48	2.58	2.07	5.37

Answer

A. Incremental after tax cash flow (000 omitted)

	19_3	19_4	19_5
Sales	$1,000	$1,600	$800
Material, labor, overhead	400	750	350
Added rent	50	50	50
Depreciation	450	300	150
Incremental costs	900	1,100	550
Incremental income	100	500	250
Incremental taxes	40	200	100
Incremental income after taxes	60	300	150
Add back depreciation	450	300	150
Incremental operation cash flow	510	600	300
Salvage value			180
Net incremental after tax cash flow	$ 510	$ 600	$480

Cash outlay for project:

Purchase price	$ 900
Modification	30
Installation	60
Testing	90
Total	$1,080

B. The project should be undertaken if the criterion is a two-year payback.

19_3	$ 510,000
19_4	600,000
	$1,110,000

Payback is in two years, which is greater than cost of $1,080,000.

The payback period is:

$$\frac{510}{510} + \frac{570}{600} = 1.95 \text{ years}$$

C.

19_3 Income	$ 13,500
19_4 Income	232,500
19_5 Income	106,500
	$352,500

Average Income	$117,500
Average Investment*	
$1,080,000 ÷ 2 =	$540,000
Rate of return	21.9%

* The initial investment ($1,080,000) is sometimes used in this calculation.

D.   The project should be adopted if a 20% after tax rate of return is required.

<u>Present value of cash flows at 20%</u>

19_3	.83 × 510,000	=	423,300
19_4	.69 × 600,000	=	414,000
19_5	.58 × 480,000	=	278,400
	Present Value		$1,115,700

The present value of $1,115,700 is greater than the initial outlay of $1,080,000; therefore, the project more than satisfies the 20% requirement.

III—Q4. Calculations for Different Quantitative Techniques Used in Making Capital Budgeting Decisions (CMA)—(See the answer included for III—Q3)

The Beta Corporation manufactures office equipment and distributes its products through wholesale distributors.

Beta Corporation recently learned of a patent on the production of a semi-automatic paper collator that can be obtained at a cost of $60,000 cash. The semi-automatic model is vastly superior to the manual model that the corporation now produces. At a cost of $40,000, present equipment could be modified to accommodate the production of the new semi-automatic model. Such modifications would not affect the remaining useful life of 4 years or the salvage value of $10,000 that the equipment now has. Variable costs, however, would increase by one dollar per unit. Fixed costs, other than relevant amortization charges, would not be affected. If the equipment is modified, the manual model cannot be produced.

The current income statement relative to the manual collator appears as follows:

Sales (100,000 units @ $4)		$400,000
Variable costs	$180,000	
Fixed costs**	120,000	
Total costs		$300,000
Net Income before income taxes		$100,000
Income taxes (40%)		40,000
Net income after income taxes		$ 60,000

** All fixed costs are directly allocable to the production of the manual collator and include depreciation on equipment of $20,000, calculated on the straight-line basis with a useful life of 10 years.

Market research has disclosed three important findings relative to the new semi-automatic model. First, a particular competitor will certainly purchase the patent if Beta Corporation does not. If this were to happen, Beta Corporation's sales of the manual collator would fall to 70,000 units per year. Second, if no increase in the selling price is made, Beta Corporation could sell approximately 190,000 units per year of the semi-automatic model. Third, because of the advances being made in this area, the patent will be completely worthless at the end of 4 years.

Because of the uncertainty of the current situation, the raw materials inventory has been almost completely exhausted. Regardless of the decision reached, substantial and immediate inventory replenishment will be required. The engineering department estimates that if the new model is to be produced, the average monthly raw materials inventory will be $20,000. If the old model is continued, the inventory balance will average $12,000 per month.

Required

A. Prepare a schedule which shows the incremental after tax cash flows for the comparison of the two alternatives. Assume that the corporation will use the sum-of-the-year's-digits method for depreciating the cost of modifying the equipment.

B. Assuming that the incremental after tax cash flows calculated in Requirement A and the annual incomes for the two alternatives are as given in the following schedule, will Beta Corporation, if it has a cost of capital of 18%, decide to manufacture the semi-automatic collator? Use the net present value decision rule and assume all operating revenues and expenses occur at the end of the year.

Year	Incremental Cash Flow (000 Omitted)	Annual Income (000 Omitted) Manual	Annual Income (000 Omitted) Semi-Automatic
1 Beginning	− $110	—	—
1 End	+ 40	$ 24	$ 39
2 End	+ 40	24	39
3 End	+ 40	24	39
4 End	+ 50	24	39

(Interest factors appear on p. 612)

Interest Factors for 18%

Period	Present Value of $1.00	Present Value of $1.00 per period received at end of period	Accumulated Value of $1.00	Accumulated Value of $1.00 per period received at end of period
1	.85	.85	1.18	1.00
2	.72	1.57	1.39	2.18
3	.61	2.18	1.64	3.57
4	.52	2.70	1.94	5.21

C.   Calculate the accounting rate of return for each project. Using this method, would you recommend Beta manufacture the Semi-Automatic Collator? Explain.

D.   What additional analytical techniques, if any, would you consider before presenting a recommendation to management? Why?

E.   What concerns would you have about using the information, as given in the problem, to reach a decision in this case?

III—Q5. Capital Budgeting—Involves After-Tax Accounting Rate of Return, Payback Reciprocal, Net Present Value (CPA)

Items 1 through 4 are based on the following information:
The Apex Company is evaluating a capital-budgeting proposal for the current year. The relevant data follow:

Year	Present Value of an Annuity in Arrears (See III—Q7 Part 6) of $1 at 15%
1	$ .870
2	1.626
3	2.284
4	2.856
5	3.353
6	3.785

The initial investment would be $30,000. It would be depreciated on a straight-line basis over six years with no salvage. The before-tax annual cash inflow due to this investment is $10,000, and the income tax rate is 40% paid the same year as incurred. The desired rate of return is 15%. All cash flows occur at year end.

1. What is the after-tax accounting rate of return on Apex's capital-budgeting proposal?
    a. 10%
    b. 16⅔%
    c. 26⅔%
    d. 33⅓%

2. What is the after-tax payback reciprocal* for Apex's capital-budgeting proposal?
    a. 20%
    b. 26⅔%
    c. 33⅓%
    d. 50%

3. What is the net present value of Apex's capital-budgeting proposal?
    a. $(7,290)
    b. $280
    c. $7,850
    d. $11,760

4. How much would Apex have had to invest five years ago at 15% compounded annually to have $30,000 now?**
    a. $12,960
    b. $14,910
    c. $17,160
    d. Cannot be determined from the information given

---

*Editors' Note: The payback period is determined as the investment divided by the annual cash savings or cash inflow. A payback reciprocal can be determined as the annual cash savings or cash inflow divided by the investment or as 1 divided by the payback period.

A payback reciprocal quickly approximates a project's time-adjusted rate of return where the project's life is at least twice the payback period and the savings or earnings are fairly stable over the project's life. See Myron J. Gordon, "The Payoff Period and the Rate of Profit," *Journal of Business,* October 1955, pp. 253–260.

**Note that the general formula for the present value of an annuity is

$$\frac{\text{Compound Discount}}{\text{Rate (which is .15 for the problem)}} = 3.353 \text{ for this problem — Year 5 of the table}$$

3.353 × .15 = .50295 Compound Discount
$30,000 × .503 = $15,090 and
$30,000 − $15,090 = $14,910

III—Q6. Sensitivity Analysis, Monte Carlo Simulation, Probability Trees

A.   Discuss the meaning and explain the application of sensitivity analysis for capital budgeting decisions.

B.   Why might Monte Carlo simulation and probability trees be applied for the analysis of investment decisions? Briefly explain these applications.

III—Q7. Present Value and the Purchase or Leasing of New Equipment (CPA Adapted)

Madisons, Inc. has decided to acquire a new piece of equipment. It may do so by an outright cash purchase at $25,000 or by a leasing alternative of $6,000 per year for the life of the machine. Other relevant information follows:

Purchase price due at time of purchase	$25,000
Estimated useful life	5 years
Estimated salvage value if purchased	$ 3,000
Annual cost of maintenance contract to be acquired with either lease or purchase	$ 500

The full purchase price of $25,000 could be borrowed from the bank at 10% annual interest and could be repaid in one payment at the end of the fifth year. Additional information:

Assume a 40% income tax rate and use of the straight-line method of depreciation.
The yearly lease rental and maintenance contract fees would be paid at the beginning of each year.
The minimum desired rate of return on investment is 10%.
All cash flows, unless otherwise stated, are assumed to occur at the end of the year.

Selected present value factors for a 10% return are given below:

Year		Present Value of $1 Received at End of Year
0	....	1.000
1	....	.909
2	....	.826
3	....	.751
4	....	.683
5	....	.621

1. The present value of the purchase price of the machine is
   a. $25,000
   b. $22,725
   c. $22,500
   d. $2,500
   e. None of the above.

2. Under the purchase alternative the present value of the estimated salvage value is
   a. $3,000
   b. $2,049
   c. $1,863
   d. $0
   e. None of the above

3. Under the purchase alternative the annual cash inflow (tax reduction) related to depreciation is
   a. $5,000
   b. $4,400
   c. $2,640
   d. $1,760
   e. None of the above

4. Under the purchase alternative the annual after-tax cash outflow for interest and maintenance would be
   a. $3,000
   b. $2,500
   c. $1,800
   d. $1,200
   e. None of the above

5. If salvage value is not ignored, the before-tax interest rate implicit in the lease contract is
   a. 20% or more
   b. More than 10% but less than 20%
   c. Precisely 10%
   d. Less than 10%
   e. Not determinable from the above facts

6.   Determine the present value of the cash outflow from the purchase plan and the present value of the cash outflow from the lease alternative; ignore tax considerations.*

III—Q8. Evaluation of a Capital Budgeting Project to Expand Operations (CPA)—Problem for Study (Answer Included)

Niebuhr Corporation is beginning its first capital budgeting program and has retained you to assist the budget committee in the evaluation of a project to expand operations designated as Proposed Expansion Project #12 (PEP #12).

1.   The following capital expenditures are under consideration:

$ 300,000	Fire sprinkler system
100,000	Landscaping
600,000	Replacement of old machines
800,000	Projects to expand operations (including PEP #12)
$1,800,000	Total

2.   The Corporation requires no minimum return on the sprinkler system or the landscaping. However, it expects a minimum return of 6 percent on all investments to replace old

---

*Editors' Note: If lease payments are made at the end of the year, then the present value of the lease payments would be determined as $6,000(.909) + $6,000(.826) + $6,000(.751) + $6,000(.683) + $6,000(.621). However, the lease payments are made at the beginning of the year, so we multiply $6,000(1.000 + .909 + .826 + .751 + .683). For 5 periods with payments made at the beginning of the year, we pay $6,000 immediately or $6,000 × 1.000; the present value of $6,000 at the end of year 1 (i.e., the beginning of year 2) is $6,000 times .909 and so on for the beginning of years 3, 4, and 5.

To obtain the same result, we can use the present value of an ordinary annuity of 1 table (an annuity in arrears) where payments or deposits are made at the end of each period. The annuity table can be used because the lease alternative requires an equal payment each year. Where payments are made at the beginning of each period, the annuity can be referred to as an annuity in advance or an annuity due. In order to use the ordinary annuity or annuity in arrears table (where payment is made at the end of the period) for calculating the present value of an annuity due, take one less period and add 1.000 to the figure listed for that period. We use the 10% rate and select the figure for period 4 (one period less than the actual number of periods) listed in a present value of an annuity of 1 table. To the figure of 3.169 for period 4, we must add 1.000. Thus, (3.169 + 1.000) times $6,000 equals the present value of the yearly payments for rent.

In capital budgeting decisions, it is usually assumed that cash flows occur at the beginning or end of each period. In a specific setting, a case might be made for a more or less continuous flow of cash and a continuous discount factor could be considered. See Chris Luneski, "Continuous Versus Discrete Compounding For Capital Budgeting Decisions," *The Accounting Review*, October 1967, pp. 767–776.

machinery. It also expects investments in expansion projects to yield a return that will exceed the average cost of the capital required to finance the sprinkler system and the landscaping in addition to the expansion projects.

3.   Under Proposed Expansion Project #12 (PEP #12) a cash investment of $75,000 will be made one year before operations begin. The investment will be depreciated by the sum-of-the-year's-digits method over a three year period and is expected to have a salvage value of $15,000. Additional financial data for PEP #12 follow:

Time Period	Revenue	Variable Costs	Maintenance, Property Taxes, and Insurance
0–1	$80,000	$35,000	$ 8,000
1–2	95,000	41,000	11,000
2–3	60,000	25,000	12,000

The amount of the investment recovered during each of the three years can be reinvested immediately at a rate of return approximating 15 percent. Each year's recovery of investment, then, will have been reinvested at 15 percent for an average of six months at the end of the year.

4.   The capital structure of Niebuhr Corporation follows:

	Amount	Percentage
Short-term notes at 5% interest	$ 3,500,000	10%
4% cumulative preferred stock, $100 par	1,750,000	5
Common stock	12,250,000	35
Retained earnings	17,500,000	50
	$35,000,000	100%

5.   Additional data available to you are summarized below:

	Current Market Price	Expected Earnings Per Share	Expected Dividends Per Share
Preferred stock, noncallable.....	$120	—	$4.00
Common stock.................	50	$3.20	1.60

The average marginal tax rate for Niebuhr stockholders is estimated to be 25 percent.

6.   Assume that the corporate income tax rate is 50 percent.

7. The present value of $1.00 due at the end of each year and discounted at 15 percent is:

End of Year		Present Value
2 years before	0	$1.32
1 year before	0	1.15
	0	1.00
1 year after	0	.87
2 years after	0	.76
3 years after	0	.66

8. The present values of $1.00 earned uniformly throughout the year and discounted at 15 percent follow:

Year	Present Value
0–1	$ .93
1–2	.80
2–3	.69

Required

A. Assume that the cutoff rate for considering expansion projects is 15 percent. Prepare a schedule calculating the
    1. Annual cash flows from operations for PEP #12.
    2. Present value of the net cash flows for PEP #12.

B. The budget committee has asked you to check the reasonableness of the cutoff rate. You realize that one of the factors to be considered is an estimate of the average cost of capital to this firm.
    Prepare a schedule, supported by computations in good form, to compute the average cost of capital weighted by the percentage of the capital structure which each element represents.

C. 1. Assume that the average cost of capital computed in part B is: 9 percent. Prepare a schedule to compute the minimum return (in dollars) required on expansion projects to cover the average cost of capital for financing the sprinkler system and the landscaping in addition to expansion projects. Assume that it is necessary to replace the old machines.
    2. Assume that the minimum return computed in C.1 is $150,000. Calculate the cutoff rate on expansion projects.

Answer

A.1.

Niebuhr Corporation
Cash Flows from Operations for Proposed Expansion Project #12

	Year 0–1	Year 1–2	Year 2–3
Revenue	$80,000	$95,000	$60,000
Less:			
Variable costs	35,000	41,000	25,000
Maintenance, etc.	8,000	11,000	12,000
Depreciation	30,000	20,000	10,000
Total	73,000	72,000	47,000
Net income before taxes	7,000	23,000	13,000
Less income taxes @ 50%*	3,500	11,500	6,500
Net income after taxes	3,500	11,500	6,500
Add noncash expenses	30,000	20,000	10,000
Annual cash flows from operations	$33,500	$31,500	$16,500

A.2.

Present Value of Net Cash Flows for
Proposed Expansion Project #12

	Year 0–1	Year 1–2	Year 2–3	Total Present Value of Cash Flows
Annual cash flows from operations	$33,500	$31,500	$16,500	
Present value factors	.93	.80	.69	
Present value of cash flows	$31,155	$25,200	$11,385	$67,740
Less net of lump-sum outlays and recoveries:				
Cash investment, one year before 0, ($75,000 × 1.15)			$86,250	
Salvage recovery, three years after 0, ($15,000 × .66)			− 9,900	(76,350)
Present value of net cash flows for PEP #12				$(8,610)

_____

*An alternative treatment would present income taxes one year later, i.e., $3,500 in year 1–2 and $11,500 in year 2–3.

B.

Computation of Average Cost of Capital*

Capital Structure	Amount	Percentage	Effective Cost %	Average Cost
Short-term notes, 5%	$ 3,500,000	10% ×	2.50% (1) =	.25%
Preferred stock, 4%	1,750,000	5% ×	3.33% (2)	.17%
Common stock	12,250,000	35% ×	6.40% (3)	2.24%
Retained earnings	17,500,000	50% ×	4.80% (4)	2.40%
	$35,000,000	100%		5.06%

(1) 5% interest rate − (5% interest rate × 50% tax rate**) = 2.50% cost

(2) $\dfrac{\$4 \text{ annual dividend}}{\$120 \text{ market price of preferred stock}}$ = 3.33% cost

(3) $\dfrac{\$3.20 \text{ earnings per share expected}}{\$50.00 \text{ market price of common stock}}$ = 6.40% cost

(4) $\dfrac{\$3.20 \text{ earnings per share expected } (1-.25 \text{ marginal tax rate})}{\$50.00 \text{ market price of common stock}}$ = 4.80% cost

C.1.

Estimate of Minimum Return Expected

Amounts budgeted:	
Fire sprinkler system	$ 300,000
Landscaping	100,000
Replacement projects	600,000
Expansion projects	800,000
Total	1,800,000
Percentage average cost of capital	9%
Cost of capital for all budgeted investments	162,000
Less minimum return required on replacement projects ($600,000 × 6%)	36,000
Minimum return required on expansion projects to cover the cost of capital for financing the fire sprinkler system and landscaping in addition to the expansion projects	$ 126,000

C.2.

Computation of the Cutoff Rate on Expansion Projects

$$\dfrac{\text{Minimum return required on expansion projects}}{\text{Amount to be invested in expansion projects}} = \dfrac{\$150,000}{\$800,000} = 18.75\%$$

---

*Editors' Note: This is just one possible method for calculating the cost of capital.

**(1−the tax rate)

PART FOUR QUESTIONS

FORECASTING: DETERMINING COST BEHAVIOR
    PATTERNS FOR PLANNING AND
    DECISION MAKING, SALES VOLUME
    FORECASTING, COST ESTIMATION

IV—Q1. Least-Squares Method—Simple Regression Analysis

A. Problem for Study

This problem determines the values of a and b using the formula given for b in the introductory discussion for Part IV, and the alternative formula given for a; the latter formula can be used when the value of b has been determined.

Given the following observations and values for the dependent variable Y and the independent variable X, the computation of the a and b values is shown below:

Observation	Y	X	X²	XY
1	7	3	9	21
2	8	5	25	40
3	9	7	49	63
4	10	9	81	90
Sum	34	24	164	214

$$b = \frac{4(214) - 24(34)}{4(164) - 24(24)} = \frac{856 - 816}{656 - 576} = .5$$

Note the 576 in the denominator is the $(\Sigma X)^2$ or 24x24. This should not be confused with the $n(\Sigma X^2)$ amount in the denominator where each X is squared and then added together to equal 164; this amount is then multiplied by n (i.e., the number of observations—there are 4 in this problem).

The b value of .5 is the slope of the line. If we were plotting dollars of overhead cost as the dependent variable and machine hours as the independent variable, this can refer to a cost increase of 50¢ for each unit increase in machine hours.

The a value (or intercept) can be calculated as follows:

$$\frac{34}{4} - \frac{.5(24)}{4} = 8.5 - 3 = 5.5$$

The 5.5 figure can represent the fixed costs.

B. Analyzing the Relationship Between Total Factory Overhead and Changes in Direct Labor Hours (CMA)

The following statement applies to items 1 to 5.

In analyzing the relationship of total factory overhead with changes in direct labor hours, the following relationship was found to exist: $Y = \$1000 + \$2X$

1. The above equation was probably found through the use of which of the following mathematical techniques?
   a. Linear programming
   b. Multiple regression analysis
   c. Simple regression analysis
   d. Dynamic programming
   e. None of the above

2. The relationship as shown above is
   a. Parabolic
   b. Curvilinear
   c. Linear
   d. Probabilistic
   e. None of the above

3. Y in the above equation is an estimate of
   a. Total variable costs
   b. Total factory overhead
   c. Total fixed costs
   d. Total direct labor hours
   e. None of the above

4. The $2 in the equation is an estimate of
   a. Total fixed costs
   b. Variable costs per direct labor hour
   c. Total variable costs
   d. Fixed costs per direct labor hour
   e. None of the above

5. The use of such a relationship of total factory overhead to changes in direct labor hours is said to be valid only within the relevant range. The phrase "relevant range" means
    a. Within a reasonable dollar amount for labor costs
    b. Within the range of observations of the analysis
    c. Within the range of reasonableness as judged by the department supervisor
    d. Within the budget allowance for overhead
    e. None of the above

C. Regression and Correlation Analysis (CPA Adapted)

6. A quantitative technique used to discover and evaluate possible cause-and-effect relationships is
    a. Linear programming
    b. PERT
    c. Poisson distribution models
    d. Correlation analysis

7. Given actual amounts of a semivariable cost for various levels of output, which of the following will give the most precise measure of the fixed and variable components?
    a. Bayesian statistics
    b. Linear programming
    c. Scattergram approach
    d. Least-squares method

8. A quantitative technique used to make predictions or estimates of the value of a dependent variable from given values of an independent variable(s) is
    a. Linear programming
    b. Regression analysis
    c. Trend analysis
    d. Queuing theory

9. Your client, a retail store, is interested in the relationship between sales (independent variable) and theft losses (dependent variable). Using the proper formula, you compute the coefficient of correlation as .95. What can you definitely conclude about these factors (sales and theft losses)?
    a. An increase in sales causes an increase in theft losses.
    b. Movement of these factors is in opposite directions.
    c. Movement of these factors is entirely unrelated.
    d. Movement of these factors is in the same direction.

10. Given a coefficient of correlation of .95, how can the coefficient of determination be calculated? Explain what the coefficient of determination indicates for question 9.

IV—Q2. Least Squares for Determining Fixed and Variable Production Costs (CPA Adapted)

During your examination of the 19_1 financial statements of MacKenzie Park Co., which manufactures and sells trivets, you wish to analyze selected aspects of the company's operations.

Labor hours and production costs for the last four months of 19_1, which you believe are representative for the year, were as follows:

Month	Labor Hours	Total Production Costs
September	2,500	$ 20,000
October	3,500	25,000
November	4,500	30,000
December	3,500	25,000
Total	14,000	$100,000

Based upon the above information and using the least-squares method of computation with the letters listed below, select the best answer for each of questions 1 through 5.

Let a = Fixed production costs per month
b = Variable production costs per labor hour
n = Number of months
x = Labor hours per month
y = Total monthly production costs
Σ = Summation

1. The equation(s) required for applying the least-squares method of computation of fixed and variable production costs could be expressed
   a. $\Sigma xy = a\Sigma x + b\Sigma x^2$
   b. $\Sigma y = na + b\Sigma x$
   c. $y = a + bx^2$
      $\Sigma = na + b\Sigma x$
   d. $\Sigma xy = a\Sigma x + b\Sigma x^2$
      $\Sigma y = na + b\Sigma x$

2.   The cost function derived by the least-squares method
     a.   Would be linear
     b.   Must be tested for minima and maxima
     c.   Would be parabolic
     d.   Would indicate maximum costs at the point of the
          function's point of inflection

3.   Monthly production costs could be expressed
     a. $y = ax + b$
     b. $y = a + bx$
     c. $y = b + ax$
     d. $y = \Sigma a + bx$

4.   Using the least-squares method of computation, the fixed
     monthly production cost of trivets is approximately
     a. $10,000
     b. $9,500
     c. $7,500
     d. $5,000

5.   Using the least-squares method of computation, the variable
     production cost per labor hour is
     a. $2.00
     b. $3.00
     c. $5.00
     d. $6.00

6.   Note that for this particular problem the high-low point
     method (see Article 9) could have been used because for each
     increase of 1,000 labor hours the costs increased by a constant
     amount of $5,000. What advantage(s), if any, can the
     least-squares method have for problems compared to the
     high-low point method?

IV—Q3. Use the information in IV—Q2 and answer the following:

A.   Calculate the standard error of estimate. How is it used?

B.   Determine Y estimated for 4,000 labor hours, and explain
     what a 95% confidence interval means for this problem. See
     the editors' note to IV—Q5. (Note: Y' or Yc or $\hat{Y}$ can be used
     to mean the estimated value of Y.)

    C.   Calculate the coefficient of determination. Explain what it indicates for this problem.

    D.   For this problem would you recommend that the company use multiple regression analysis for estimating total costs of production? Why or why not?

IV—Q4. Use of the High-Low Method to Determine the Cost Behavior Pattern for Overhead Cost; Use of Linear Regression to Estimate Overhead Cost; Determination of Which Method (High-Low, Scattergraph, Linear Regression) to Use in Determining a Cost Behavior Pattern (CMA)

The Ramon Co. manufactures a wide range of products at several different plant locations. The Franklin Plant, which manufactures electrical components, has been experiencing some difficulties with fluctuating monthly overhead costs. The fluctuations have made it difficult to estimate the level of overhead that will be incurred for any one month.

Management wants to be able to estimate overhead costs accurately in order to plan its operation and financial needs better. A trade association publication to which Ramon Co. subscribes indicates that for companies manufacturing electrical components, overhead tends to vary with direct labor hours.

One member of the accounting staff has proposed that the cost behavior pattern of the overhead costs be determined. Then overhead costs could be predicted from the budgeted direct labor hours.

Another member of the accounting staff suggested that a good starting place for determining the cost behavior pattern of overhead costs would be an analysis of historical data. The historical cost behavior pattern would provide a basis for estimating future overhead costs. The methods proposed for determining the cost behavior pattern included the high-low method, the scattergraph method, simple linear regression, multiple regression, and exponential smoothing. Of these methods, Ramon Co. decided to employ the high-low method, the scattergraph method, and simple linear regression. Data on direct labor hours and the respective overhead costs incurred were collected for the past two years. The raw data and the scattergraph prepared from the data are as follows:

19_3	Direct Labor Hours	Overhead Costs
January	20,000	$84,000
February	25,000	99,000
March	22,000	89,500
April	23,000	90,000
May	20,000	81,500
June	19,000	75,500
July	14,000	70,500
August	10,000	64,500
September	12,000	69,000
October	17,000	75,000
November	16,000	71,500
December	19,000	78,000
19_4		
January	21,000	86,000
February	24,000	93,000
March	23,000	93,000
April	22,000	87,000
May	20,000	80,000
June	18,000	76,500
July	12,000	67,500
August	13,000	71,000
September	15,000	73,500
October	17,000	72,500
November	15,000	71,000
December	18,000	75,000

Using linear regression, the following data were obtained:

Coefficient of determination	.9109
Coefficient of correlation	.9544
Coefficients of regression equation	
Constant	39,859
Independent variable	2.1549
Standard error of the estimate*	2,840
Standard error of the regression coefficient for the independent variable**	.1437
True t-statistic for a 95% confidence interval (22 degrees of freedom)**	2.074

Required

A.   Using the high-low method (see Article 9), determine the cost behavior pattern of the overhead costs for the Franklin Plant.

---

*Consider whether the standard error of estimate is reasonable for the level of costs involved. Also consider the size of the standard error of the regression coefficient relative to the coefficient.

**See the editors' note to IV—Q5.

B.   Using the results of the regression analysis, calculate the estimate of overhead costs for 22,500 direct labor hours.

C.   Of the three proposed methods (high-low, scattergraph, linear regression), which one should Ramon Co. employ to determine the historical cost behavior pattern of Franklin Plant's overhead costs? Explain your answer completely, indicating the reasons why the other methods should not be used. (The scattergraph is shown below.)

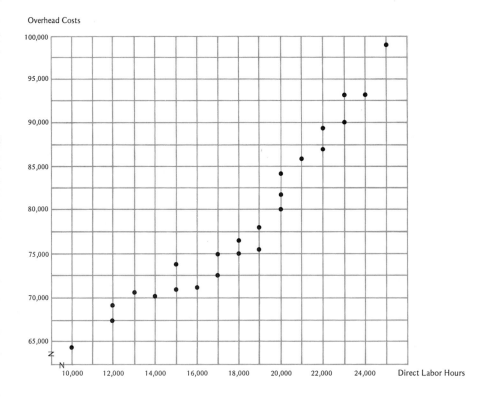

IV—Q5. Regression Analysis and Prediction (CMA)

The Johnstar Co. makes a very expensive chemical product. The costs average about $1,000 per pound and the material sells for $2,500 per pound. The material is very dangerous, therefore, it is made each day to fill the customer orders for the day. Failure to deliver the quantity required results in a shutdown for the customers and high cost penalty for Johnstar (plus customer ill will).

Predicting the final weight of a batch of the chemical being processed has been a serious problem. This is critical because of the serious cost of failure to meet customer needs.

A consultant recommended that the batches be weighed one-half way through the six-hour processing period. He proposed that linear regression be used to predict the final weight from the mid-point weight. If the prediction indicated that too little of the chemical would be available, then a new batch could be started and still delivered in time to satisfy customers' needs for the day.

Included in the report of a study made by the consultant during a one-week period were the following items:

Observation No.	Weight 3 hrs.	Final Weight	Observation No.	Weight 3 hrs.	Final Weight
1	55	90	11	60	80
2	45	75	12	35	60
3	40	80	13	35	80
4	60	80	14	55	60
5	40	45	15	35	75
6	60	80	16	50	90
7	50	80	17	30	60
8	55	95	18	60	105
9	50	100	19	50	60
10	35	75	20	20	30

Data from the regression analysis:

Coefficient of determination	0.4126
Coefficient of correlation	0.6424
Coefficients of the regression equation	
Constant	+ 28.6
Independent variable	+ 1.008
Standard error of the estimate	14.2
Standard error of the regression coefficient for the independent variable*	0.2796
The t-statistic for a 95% confidence interval (18 degrees of freedom)*	2.101

Required

A.   Using the results of the regression analysis by the consultant, calculate the estimate of today's first batch which weighs 42 lbs. at the end of 3 hours processing time.

---

* See the sampling and regression analysis note following the problem.

B.   Customer orders for today total 68 pounds. The nature of the process is such that the smallest batch that can be started will weigh at least 20 pounds at the end of six hours. Using only the data from the regression analysis, would you start another batch? (Remember that today's first batch weighed 42 pounds at the end of 3 hours.)

C.   Is the relationship between the variables such that this regression analysis provides an adequate prediction model for the Johnstar Co.? Explain your answer.

*Editors' Note: Sampling and Regression Analysis

In simple regression analysis, the usefulness of a regression equation for purposes of estimation depends on whether or not actual Y values are concentrated about the regression line or vary widely from the line. The standard error of estimate is a measure of the scatter of actual or observed values about the regression line. If we use the regression equation to make predictions for a population, and if no sampling error exists (see footnote 6 of Article 20), we can expect actual observations to fall within a range $Yc \pm 1$ times the standard error of estimate, with two chances out of three of being correct. Ninety-five percent of the observations should fall within the wider range $Yc \pm 2$ times the standard error of estimate.

In developing forecasts for a population, we use a sample of historical events and determine a regression line to represent the entire population. The equation for the true regression line is $Y = A + BX$; A and B represent the true coefficients. The values of a and b in the equation $Y = a + bX$ are based on samples, and different samples drawn from the population can result in different values. We really want the true A and B for the entire population. The values of a and b are estimates and are subject to sampling error. This editors' note is concerned with making a statistical inference about a regression coefficient. The note discusses a test to determine the significance of an explanatory relationship between X and Y (the t test in Article 20), and also discusses confidence intervals. The standard error of the regression coefficient is part of the note because it is used in the t test, and in the determination of confidence intervals.

Testing the Significance of a Relationship

The regression coefficient indicates the average change in Y for each unit of change in X. Testing for the significance of a relationship requires the calculation of a t-value and the use of a table for values of t. A t-value above 2 or 3 indicates there is a significant relationship between the variables. A zero slope for a true regression line (where $B = 0$) would be the case if there is no relationship between X and Y. Even when there is no relationship, a sample may indicate a relationship by chance. In discussing a problem where the t-value of the regression coefficient is 16 (b is 16 standard errors from $B = 0$), Spurr and Bonini state "a deviation of more than three standard errors is highly significant (except for very small samples). The chance is negligible, therefore, that a deviation as large as 16 standard errors could occur by chance. Hence, we reject the null hypothesis and accept the alternative hypothesis that there is a significant relationship between the variables."[1]

One of the formulas given in Article 20 for the t-value is

$$\frac{\text{Regression Coefficient}}{\text{Standard Error of Regression Coefficient}}$$

The article does not show the determination of the denominator (standard error of the regression coefficient—identified as Sb). *It can be determined as the standard error of estimate divided by either*

$$\sqrt{\Sigma\,(X - \overline{X})^2} \qquad or \qquad \sqrt{\Sigma X^2 - \overline{X}\Sigma X}$$

$\overline{X}$ = the mean of X.

Article 20 lists a level of significance of .01 (found in a table for values of t) for a calculated t-value of 2.87 and for 18 degrees of freedom (i.e., n -2 or 20-2 = 18 for the problem). The level of significance gives the probability of obtaining the size calculated for t by pure chance. The t-value calculated for the Article 20 problem is 5.65 and thus the probability is less than .01 that the regression coefficient could have resulted from a random relationship.

The probability or level of significance given in the article is from a table of values of t (t-distribution) that refers to the sum of the two-tailed areas under a curve. For a table listing the probabilities for one-tail, the probability or level of significance for a t-value of 2.87 is .005 and the given probability would be multiplied by 2 to obtain the .01 listed in Article 20. A table for values of t for one-tail is included at the end of this discussion. That table goes only to the .005 level of significance. In the article, the t-value is 5.65 and b (the regression coefficient) is stated to be significant at the .001 level. Note that Article 20 refers to a more extensive listing for values of t than we included in the attached table.

---

[1] William A. Spurr and Charles P. Bonini, *Statistical Analysis for Business Decisions* (Homewood, Ill.: Richard D. Irwin, Inc., 1967), p. 567.

Confidence Intervals

The standard error of the regression coefficient along with a table for values
of t can be used in determining a confidence interval. A confidence interval
can be used to express the amount of sampling error in sample statistics
chosen from a population. With a 95% confidence interval, we can state
that the true B is within the interval or range with the probability of 0.95
that this is correct.

To determine the 95% confidence interval for the regression coefficient,
we use the value of t (i.e., the t-statistic) listed in the .025 column (of a
one-tail table) for 18 degrees of freedom; again, 18 degrees of freedom assumes a problem with 20 observations, as in Article 20. The 95% confidence interval is determined as the value of b from the predicting equation
± the t-statistic times the standard error of the regression coefficient. For
the purpose of developing a 95% confidence interval with a two-tail table,
we use the t-value in the .05 column for the appropriate degrees of freedom. For a one-tail table, the same t-value columns are headed by probabilities that are ½ those in the two-tail table; thus, in developing a 95%
confidence interval, we enter the one-tail table at the .025 column rather
than the .05 column and use the t-value listed for the appropriate degrees
of freedom. Assume, for a problem with 20 observations, that the regression
coefficient is + 1.008 and the standard error of the regression coefficient for
the independent variable is 0.2796. The t-statistic for a 95% confidence
interval (18 degrees of freedom) is 2.101. Therefore, the probability is .95
that the "true" regression coefficient is between 1.008 ± 2.101(0.2796).

A regression line from a sample will also vary from a true regression line
in elevation (note that slope was discussed above). After determining an
estimate of the population regression equation, we can use it to predict Yc
for any value of X. To construct a 95% confidence interval around a point
on the regression line, we use Yc± the t-statistic times the standard error of
Yc. The 95% confidence interval for the regression line means the chances
are 95 out of 100 that the true regression line for the population is within
the interval limits. The t-statistic is for a 95% confidence interval and for n
− m degrees of freedom. The t-distribution at the end of this discussion is
used for a small sample with $n \leq 30$; for a large sample, a table of areas
under the normal curve is used. Note that for a large sample, 1.96 is used
for the 95% confidence interval. The standard error of a point (Yc) on the
regression line can be determined as follows:

$$S_{Yc} = S_{Y.X} \sqrt{\frac{1}{n} + \frac{(X - \overline{X})^2}{\Sigma (X - \overline{X})^2}}.$$

Values of t
The probabilities in the heading (.100, .050, etc.,) are for one-tail.

Degrees of freedom	$t_{.100}$	$t_{.050}$	$t_{.025}$	$t_{.010}$	$t_{.005}$
1	3.078	6.314	12.706	31.821	63.657
2	1.886	2.920	4.303	6.965	9.925
3	1.638	2.353	3.182	4.541	5.841
4	1.533	2.132	2.776	3.747	4.604
5	1.476	2.015	2.571	3.365	4.032
6	1.440	1.943	2.447	3.143	3.707
7	1.415	1.895	2.365	2.998	3.499
8	1.397	1.860	2.306	2.896	3.355
9	1.383	1.833	2.262	2.821	3.250
10	1.372	1.812	2.228	2.764	3.169
11	1.363	1.796	2.201	2.718	3.106
12	1.356	1.782	2.179	2.681	3.055
13	1.350	1.771	2.160	2.650	3.012
14	1.345	1.761	2.145	2.624	2.977
15	1.341	1.753	2.131	2.602	2.947
16	1.337	1.746	2.120	2.583	2.921
17	1.333	1.740	2.110	2.567	2.898
18	1.330	1.734	2.101	2.552	2.878
19	1.328	1.729	2.093	2.539	2.861
20	1.325	1.725	2.086	2.528	2.845
21	1.323	1.721	2.080	2.518	2.831
22	1.321	1.717	2.074	2.508	2.819
23	1.319	1.714	2.069	2.500	2.807
24	1.318	1.711	2.064	2.492	2.797
25	1.316	1.708	2.060	2.485	2.787
26	1.315	1.706	2.056	2.479	2.779
27	1.314	1.703	2.052	2.473	2.771
28	1.313	1.701	2.048	2.467	2.763
29	1.311	1.699	2.045	2.462	2.756
∞	1.282	1.645	1.960	2.326	2.576

Part of Table III (Distribution of t), Fisher and Yates, *Statistical Tables for Biological, Agricultural and Medical Research*, 6th Edition (Essex: Longman Group Limited, 1974), p. 46. Reprinted by permission.

IV—Q6. Correlation Analysis in Cash Forecasting (CMA)

Jackson Company is experiencing cash management problems. In particular, they have been unable to determine their temporary cash needs on a
timely basis. This has increased the cost of borrowing, because they have
often been unable to obtain desirable terms. Borrowing in advance would
give them better terms at a lower cost. A review of the cash flows indicates
that all factors can be adequately predicted except the expenditures for
hourly payroll and certain other expenditures. The cash receipts can be
accurately determined because Jackson's customers are all reliable and pay
on an identifiable schedule within the two calendar months following the
sale. The payments for raw materials are similarly predictable because they
are all paid in the calendar month subsequent to the purchase. Disbursements for monthly fixed obligations, such as lease payments, salaried personnel, etc., are known well in advance of the payment dates.

In an attempt to better forecast cash changes for the next month, the
company conducted a statistical analysis of many possible variables that
might be suitable as a basis for forecasting the expenditure for payroll and
other items. This analysis revealed a high correlation between the advance
sales orders received in a month and those expenditures in the next month.
The following relationships useful for cash forecasting have been identified:

$(N$ = the forecast month)

1.   Collections on account

$C_N = .9S_{N-1} + .1S_{N-2}$; where S = sales

2.   Disbursements for raw material purchases

$D_N = R_{N-1}$; where R = raw material purchases

3.   Monthly fixed obligations

$F_N = \$400,000$

4.   Payroll and other expenditures

$P_N = .25A_{N-1} + 70,000$; where A = advance sales orders

Coefficient of correlation	= .96
Standard error of the estimate	= 10,000
Standard error of the regression coefficient of the independent variable	= .0013
t-statistic for 95% confidence interval	= 2.07

Required

A.   Estimate the change in the cash balance for July 19_5 using
the relationships specified above and the following data:

	Sales (S)	Raw Material Purchases (R)	Advance Sales Orders (A)
April	$1,300,000	$300,000	$1,225,000
May	1,200,000	400,000	1,050,000
June	1,000,000	350,000	1,400,000

B.   Revise your estimate of the change in cash to recognize the uncertainty associated with the payroll and other expenditures.

C.   How could management use this information to study alternative plans to reduce the short-term borrowing costs?

IV—Q7. Least-Squares Time Regression Technique; Exponential Smoothing (CPA)

The Martin Corporation, which operates seven days a week, orders Product B from the Whiting Company each morning. Product B, which arrives soon after the order is placed, spoils if it is not sold at the end of the day.

   The president of Martin has been using his executive judgment to determine how much of Product B to order each morning. You, as Martin's controller, have noticed that a number of costly forecasting errors have been made by the president and wish to show him that the use of a more sophisticated method of determining the order quantity of Product B would save money for the company. As part of the preparation for your presentation of the use of various forecasting techniques, you have compiled the following data regarding the past eleven days of orders of and demand for Product B.

X	Y Number of Units Ordered	Z Demand in Units	Y–Z Number of Units Spoiled (Short)
January 1, 19_3	21	16	5
January 2, 19_3	19	18	1
January 3, 19_3	17	21	(4)
January 4, 19_3	19	22	(3)
January 5, 19_3	23	20	3
January 6, 19_3	23	20	3
January 7, 19_3	22	21	1
January 8, 19_3	19	22	(3)
January 9, 19_3	20	22	(2)
January 10, 19_3	21	20	1
January 11, 19_3	20	18	2
Total	224	220	4

In answering each of the following items, round all calculations to the next highest whole number.

1. Using the least-squares time regression technique* for forecasting and based on the data for the first eleven days of January, the number of units that Martin will order on January 16, 19_3, is
    a.   23
    b.   20
    c.   21
    d.   22

2. Had Martin's president based his January 2, 19_3 order on the exponential smoothing technique of forecasting using an alpha of 0.2 and a base of 21 units, the number of units ordered on January 2 would have been
    a.   20
    b.   23
    c.   19
    d.   22

3. After your presentation, the president favors the use of the exponential smoothing technique of forecasting, but he points out that during each month there is a single day in which demand will increase to 40 or 50 units and he desires to minimize the effect of this occurrence on the forecast. Martin should
    a.   Use the exponential smoothing technique with a large alpha factor
    b.   Use the exponential smoothing technique with a small alpha factor
    c.   Use the least-squares time regression technique rather than the exponential smoothing technique
    d.   Use a moving average technique rather than the exponential smoothing technique

4. The president mentions that he expects demand to jump to approximately 35 units per day and stay at that level. He desires to use the exponential smoothing technique of forecasting but wants it to respond as quickly as possible to this expected increase. Martin should
    a.   Use a moving average technique rather than the exponential smoothing technique

---

* See the editors' note attached at the end of the problem.

b. Use the exponential smoothing technique with a large alpha factor
c. Use the exponential smoothing technique with a small alpha factor
d. Use the least-squares time regression technique rather than the exponential smoothing technique

* Editors' Note: The Least-Squares Time Regression Technique

Where sales is a function of the period or year, we have a time series problem. Time series is an example of an extrapolation technique. See the first page of the introductory discussion for Part IV.

For the least-squares method, the values of a and b in the equation $Y = a + bX$ may be calculated by solving the two simultaneous equations below. Note that Σ = sum and n = number of observations.

$$(1) \quad \Sigma Y = na + b(\Sigma X)$$
$$(2) \quad \Sigma XY = a(\Sigma X) + b(\Sigma X^2)$$

For a least-squares time regression problem, the year (i.e., the independent variable X) can be given a number value so that the $\Sigma X = 0$. If an odd number of years is involved, 19_1 through 19_5, then 19_3 (the middle year) is assigned a zero value, and years before 19_3 are assigned numbers -1 and -2 and after 19_3 $+1$ and $+2$, so that the sum of X equals zero. If there is an even number of years, 19_1 through 19_6, then the 2 years 19_3 and 19_4 are given the numbers -1 and $+1$ respectively and 2 would be added to the number each time rather than 1 as in the previous example; this is explained as part of the discussion below.

Odd Number of Years		Even Number of Years	
19_1	-2	19_1	-5
19_2	-1	19_2	-3
19_3	0	19_3	-1
19_4	$+1$	19_4	$+1$
19_5	$+2$	19_5	$+3$
$\Sigma X =$	0	19_6	$+5$
		$\Sigma X =$	0

The equations to be solved, using (1) and (2) above but with $\Sigma X = 0$, would be $Y = na$ and $\Sigma XY = b(\Sigma X^2)$ or

$$a = \frac{\Sigma Y}{n} \text{ and } b = \frac{\Sigma XY}{(\Sigma X^2)}.$$

Assume we want to predict sales (Y) for the odd number of years case (i.e., we have 5 years of observed values for sales) using time series and the formula $Yc = a + bX$. Where $\Sigma X = 0$, we would determine the a and b values from the equations above. Assume we determine $a = 85$ and $b = 10.3$. The origin is July 1, 19_3, and in the equation for a straight-line trend (odd number of years case) $X =$ one year. If it is desired to estimate sales for 19_6, then the regression equation would be $85 + 10.3(X)$ or $85 + 10.3(3)$. Note that $+3$ is the X value for 19_6 (i.e., $+2$ is the value for 19_5 and 1 is added each year for the odd number of years case). Sales for 19_7 would be estimated as $85 + 10.3(4)$.

Assume the information given above (i.e., $a = 85$, $b = 10.3$ and sum of X equals zero) is for the even number of years case. The origin for the six years case is 19_3 − 19_4 (the end of year 3 or the beginning of year 4) or January 1, 19_4, and in the equation for a straight line (even number of years case) $X = 6$ months. We assign each six-month interval a value of 1 and we designate values for the middle years of the series 19_3 and 19_4 (each at July 1) as −1 and +1 respectively. Note that the 19_5 value for X is $+3$ because there are two six-month periods since 19_4. The prediction of sales for 19_7 would be $85 + 10.3(X)$ or $85 + 10.3(7)$. Note that $+7$ is the X value for 19_7 (i.e., $+3$ is the value for 19_5 and 2 is added each year for the even number of years case).

Given a least-squares time regression problem with Y values of 3, 4, 5, 7, and 9, the determination of the ΣX, ΣY, ΣX^2 and ΣXY is shown below.

Year	X	Y	X²	XY
19_1	−2	3	4	−6
19_2	−1	4	1	−4
19_3	0	5	0	0
19_4	+1	7	1	7
19_5	+2	9	4	18
Σ	0	28	10	15

The a and b values are determined from:

$$a = \frac{\Sigma Y}{n}$$

$$b = \frac{\Sigma XY}{\Sigma X^2}$$

Determine Yc for 19_6. Solution: $Yc = 5.6 + 1.5(3) = 10.1$

The calculation of a regression equation and correlation coefficient (dependent variable against time) is part of the discussion in an article by Tim Coldicutt, "Forecasting in the Long Term," *Accountancy*, October 1973, pp. 23–32. For additional information about time series and time series research, see the discussion and bibliography in an article by George Foster, "Quarterly Accounting Data: Time-Series Properties and Predictive-Ability Results," *The Accounting Review*, January 1977, pp. 1–21.

IV—Q8. Simple Regression—Portions of a Computer Printout Included

The following is from a computer printout for a simple linear regression analysis problem. For the problem, 12 observations of X and Y were entered into a computer. Note that $E - 01$ on the printout means the decimal is moved 1 place to the left, $E + 00$ means the decimal is not moved and $E + 01$ means it is moved 1 place to the right.

VARIABLE	MEAN	VARIANCE	STD DEVIATION
X	5.48333E + 01	2.19472E + 02	1.48146E + 01
Y	3.15000E + 01	2.60833E + 01	5.10718E + 00

INDEX (R ↑ 2)*	EXPL VAR	UNEXPL VAR	STD ERROR
9.45837E–01	2.46706E + 01	1.41275E + 00	1.18859E + 00

PARAMETER	VALUE	95% CONFIDENCE LIMITS	
A	1.31158E + 01	9.89771E + 00	1.63339E + 01
B	3.35274E – 01	2.78617E – 01	3.91931E – 01

Required

A. From the printout, determine (1) the coefficient of determination, (2) the standard error of estimate and (3) the values of a and b.

B. What use might be made of the standard error of estimate for the problem?

C. What does the coefficient of determination indicate for this problem?

D. Describe how the 95% confidence limits for the regression coefficient are determined. (See the editors' note to IV—Q5.)

E. For each of the original observations, the printout shows estimated values of Y and confidence limits. For one of the years, the listing shows:

X-ACTUAL	Y-ACTUAL	Y-CALC	95% CONFIDENCE LIMITS	
4.0000E + 01	2.7000E + 01	2.6527E + 01	2.3386E + 01	2.9668E + 01

(1) Show the calculation of Yc using the values of a and b listed on the printout.
(2) How can the 95% confidence interval be determined?

---

* R^2

F.   A simple linear regression equation may be used to forecast values for the dependent variable and the method especially might be used if it is easier to forecast values for X than it is to forecast Y by using some other means. (1) What other methods might be used to forecast Y if it is assumed Y represents sales? Answer the question assuming Y represents overhead cost. (2) How can Y be determined beyond the original observation periods by using the least-squares method? What pitfalls or problems might be involved in such a forecast?

G.   Given the following values for Y and X, use the computer to perform a simple linear regression.

Y Values:
  34, 31, 38, 40, 41, 39, 42, 44, 50, 47
X Values:
  41, 46, 49, 54, 57, 59, 64, 68, 76, 79

Assume Y represents overhead cost in thousands of dollars. What might X represent? Explain whether or not you would use the regression equation coefficients that appear on the printout to forecast overhead cost.

IV—Q9. Multiple Regression Analysis Computer Printout

A.   Refer to Exhibit A in answering the following questions:

1.   Which step of the computer printout (Exhibit A) gives the best model for estimating Y?
2.   State the criteria used to select a particular step.
3.   Interpret the model you have selected, i.e., give the equation from the computer printout and explain it.
4.   How many dependent variables are there in the model described in Step 8?
   a.   9
   b.   8
   c.   1
   d.   7
   e.   None of the above
5.   Is the model described in Step 8 a significant model that can be used in the real world? Explain.
6.   The a value for the model in Step 7 is −6.595852?
   a.   True
   b.   False

7. The R squared value of the model in Step 7 is .99998079.
    a. True
    b. False
8. In the model in Step 7 there is a 99% chance that the
    actual value will be within the range of + or − .00379816
    of the estimated value.
    a. True
    b. False
9. In the model in Step 7 the most efficient variable is:
    a. 1
    b. 5
    c. The intercept
    d. 8
    e. None of the above

B. Assume that for a firm, overhead cost is estimated as a function
    of machine hours, what other independent variables might be
    considered for estimating the cost if it is determined that the
    r^2 for the problem is not sufficiently high? If management
    wants to estimate the overhead cost by using direct labor
    hours and machine hours, could there be a problem of
    multicollinearity? Explain.

STEP 7   Exhibit A

VARIABLE ENTERED   3
SUM OF SQUARES REDUCED IN THIS STEP 00096673
PROPORTION OF VARIANCE OF Y REDUCED 00085828
CUMULATIVE SUM OF SQUARES REDUCED 1.12631901
CUMULATIVE PROPORTION REDUCED 99996158
FOR 7 VARIABLES ENTERED
    MULTIPLE CORRELATION COEFFICIENT 99998079
    F-VALUE FOR ANALYSIS OF VARIANCE 44614.54719257
    STANDARD ERROR OF ESTIMATE 00189908

VARIABLE NO.	REG. COEFF.
1	−3.000486E−01
8	2.708816E−01
5	4.021762E−01
7	2.988566E−01
4	3.069396E−01
2	1.028038E−01
3	3.025392E−02
INTERCEPT	−6.595852E−04

DO YOU WISH TO GO TO THE NEXT STEP (YES OR NO)?   YES

STEP 8

VARIABLE ENTERED   9
SUM OF SQUARES REDUCED IN THIS STEP 00000085
PROPORTION OF VARIANCE OF Y REDUCED 00000076
CUMULATIVE SUM OF SQUARES REDUCED 1.12631986
CUMULATIVE PROPORTION REDUCED 99996234
FOR 8 VARIABLES ENTERED
   MULTIPLE CORRELATION COEFFICIENT 99998117
   F-VALUE FOR ANALYSIS OF VARIANCE 36504.82796669
   STANDARD ERROR OF ESTIMATE 00196386

VARIABLE NO.	REG. COEFF.
1	−2.999619E−01
8	2.711753E−01
5	4.019881E−01
7	2.991453E−01
4	3.041260E−01
2	1.026940E−01
3	3.006039E−02
9	3.261629E−03
INTERCEPT	−6.591181E−04

**IV—Q10. Multiple Regression Analysis—Computer Printout Included
[Prepared by Yow-Min R. Lee]**

The following data are given for a multiple regression analysis problem.

Required

    A.   1.   Using the data for years 2 through 16, develop a
             regression equation for cost of goods sold. As possible
             independent variables, use sales, labor cost, number of
             employees, and expenses. Note: A stepwise multiple
             regression computer printout that includes each of these
             variables is presented below. From the printout,
             determine the independent variable(s) to be used in a
             regression equation and explain why you would include
             the variable(s) selected.
          2.   Is there a problem with using both labor costs and
             number of employees as independent variables? Explain.

Data Used in Constructing the YM Company's Operating Budget Model to Forecast Sales, Cost of Goods Sold, and Expenses for the 17th Year

Year	Sales	Disposable Personal Income	Housing Starts Last Year	Selling and Advertising Expenses	Research and Development	Cost of Goods Sold	Labor Costs	Pension Expenses	Number of Employees	Expenses
1	238.000	206.900	—	18.610	3.100	141.980	81.300	2.030	18.100	40.290
2	244.700	226.600	1,091	20.270	3.520	152.660	98.200	3.000	18.200	45.400
3	252.600	238.300	1,127	22.160	3.820	158.830	104.000	3.180	18.400	48.810
4	253.200	252.600	1,104	22.960	4.010	165.580	106.200	3.610	17.900	47.210
5	284.700	257.400	1,220	24.930	4.790	178.550	116.800	3.800	18.600	51.680
6	310.400	275.300	1,329	27.080	5.540	195.690	127.500	3.970	19.400	56.630
7	308.300	293.200	1,118	28.440	5.990	204.410	130.900	5.950	19.400	59.830
8	331.700	308.500	1,042	27.760	6.380	216.640	135.700	5.500	18.300	58.900
9	377.600	318.800	1,209	32.030	6.490	240.070	145.900	5.710	20.000	67.150
10	356.200	337.300	1,379	33.830	7.500	242.830	146.300	6.120	20.200	58.100
11	377.800	350.000	1,296	35.990	8.290	256.930	150.300	6.160	20.300	60.780
12	392.300	364.400	1,365	35.340	6.290	265.700	151.900	6.100	19.700	63.060
13	414.900	385.300	1,492	37.370	5.620	281.200	159.200	6.350	19.900	61.880
14	458.900	404.600	1,642	39.640	7.250	313.740	176.000	6.960	20.600	68.150
15	480.200	438.100	1,561	41.810	7.420	327.270	184.800	7.420	21.200	69.410
16	512.500	473.200	1,510	44.120	7.470	344.720	189.600	7.140	21.500	73.120

Note: Disposable personal income is measured in billions of dollars. Housing starts and numbers of employees are measured in thousands. Other items are measured in millions of dollars. DPI and housing starts are external data. The problem assumes a large construction business.

How do these two variables affect the regression equation you selected?

Note: A statistical package of computer programs which includes a correlation matrix can help an analyst with the problem of multicollinearity. See the brief discussion of the correlation matrix at the end of the solution note to VI—Q17.

B.   Using a stepwise multiple regression computer program, develop an equation to forecast sales.

The computer printout for Part A follows:

```
TYPE NO. OF VARIABLES AND OBSERVATIONS 5, 15
WILL INPUT DATA BE BY TERMINAL OR DISK FILE? TERMINAL
INPUT DATA IN FORM XX.X,XX.X,XX.X, . . . XX.X (RET)
152.66, 158.83, 165.58, 178.55, 195.69, 204.41, 216.64, 240.07, 242.83
256.93, 265.70, 281.20, 313.74, 327.27, 344.72
98.20, 104.00, 106.20, 116.80, 127.50, 130.90, 135.70, 145.90, 146.30
150.30, 151.90, 159.20, 176.00, 184.80, 189.60
18.20, 18.40, 17.90, 18.60, 19.40, 19.40, 18.30, 20.00, 20.20, 20.30, 19.70
19.90, 20.60, 21.20, 21.50
45.40, 48.81, 47.21, 51.68, 56.63, 59.83, 58.90, 67.15, 58.10, 60.78, 63.06
61.88, 68.15, 69.41, 73.12
244.70, 252.60, 253.20, 284.70, 310.40, 308.30, 331.70, 377.60, 356.20
377.80, 392.30, 414.90, 458.90, 480.20, 512.50
DO YOU WISH TRANSFORMATIONS OF DATA? NO
LISTING?    (YES OR NO)?    YES
VARIABLE
```

OBS.	1	2	3	4	5
1	152.6600	98.2000	18.2000	45.4000	244.7000
2	158.8300	104.0000	18.4000	48.8100	252.6000
3	165.5800	106.2000	17.9000	47.2100	253.2000
4	178.5500	116.8000	18.6000	51.6800	284.7000
5	195.6900	127.5000	19.4000	56.6300	310.4000
6	204.4100	130.9000	19.4000	59.8300	308.3000
7	216.6400	135.7000	18.3000	58.9000	331.7000
8	240.0700	145.9000	20.0000	67.1500	377.6000
9	242.8300	146.3000	20.2000	58.1000	356.2000
10	256.9300	150.3000	20.3000	60.7800	377.8000
11	265.7000	151.9000	19.7000	63.0600	392.3000
12	281.2000	159.2000	19.9000	61.8800	414.9000
13	313.7400	176.0000	20.6000	68.1500	458.9000
14	327.2700	184.8000	21.2000	69.4100	480.2000
15	344.7200	189.6000	21.5000	73.1200	512.5000

DO YOU WISH TO SAVE THIS DATA ON A DISK FILE? NO

SPECIFY THE DEPENDENT VARIABLE IN THE FORM XX [RET] 01
IF YOU WISH TO DELETE VARIABLES, SPECIFY THE TOTAL NUMBER OF VARIABLES
TO BE DELETED IN THE FORM XX [RET] OTHERWISE TYPE 0 [RET] 00

STEP 1

VARIABLE ENTERED 5
SUM OF SQUARES REDUCED IN THIS STEP 53400.065
PROPORTION OF VARIANCE OF Y REDUCED 993
CUMULATIVE SUM OF SQUARES REDUCED 53400.065
CUMULATIVE PROPORTION REDUCED . . . .   .993 OF 53776.496
FOR 1 VARIABLES ENTERED
  MULTIPLE CORRELATION COEFFICIENT 996
  F-VALUE FOR ANALYSIS OF VARIANCE 1844.163
  STANDARD ERROR OF ESTIMATE 5.381
            VARIABLE NO.   REG. COEFF.
              5   7.311415E − 01
          INTERCEPT   −2.474492E + 01
DO YOU WISH TO GO TO THE NEXT STEP? YES

STEP 2

VARIABLE ENTERED 2
SUM OF SQUARES REDUCED IN THIS STEP 81.445
PROPORTION OF VARIANCE OF Y REDUCED 002
CUMULATIVE SUM OF SQUARES REDUCED 53481.510
CUMULATIVE PROPORTION REDUCED . . . .   .995 OF 53776.496
FOR 2 VARIABLES ENTERED
  MULTIPLE CORRELATION COEFFICIENT 997
  F-VALUE FOR ANALYSIS OF VARIANCE 1087.809
  STANDARD ERROR OF ESTIMATE 4.958
            VARIABLE NO.   REG. COEFF.
              5   4.767992E − 01
              2   7.576495E − 01
          INTERCEPT   −4.117557E + 01
DO YOU WISH TO GO TO THE NEXT STEP? YES

APPENDIX B

STEP 3

VARIABLE ENTERED 4
SUM OF SQUARES REDUCED IN THIS STEP 143.248
PROPORTION OF VARIANCE OF Y REDUCED 003
CUMULATIVE SUM OF SQUARES REDUCED 53624.758
CUMULATIVE PROPORTION REDUCED . . . .   .997 OF 53776.496
FOR 3 VARIABLES ENTERED
   MULTIPLE CORRELATION COEFFICIENT 999
   F-VALUE FOR ANALYSIS OF VARIANCE 1295.812
   STANDARD ERROR OF ESTIMATE 3.714
            VARIABLE NO.   REG. COEFF.
                  5   4.681056E – 01
                  2   1.142754E + 00
                  4   –1.289336E + 00
            INTERCEPT   –1.607419E + 01
DO YOU WISH TO GO TO THE NEXT STEP? YES

STEP 4

VARIABLE ENTERED 3
SUM OF SQUARES REDUCED IN THIS STEP 1.167
PROPORTION OF VARIANCE OF Y REDUCED 000
CUMULATIVE SUM OF SQUARES REDUCED 53625.924
CUMULATIVE PROPORTION REDUCED . . . .   .997 OF 53776.496
FOR 4 VARIABLES ENTERED
   MULTIPLE CORRELATION COEFFICIENT 999
   F-VALUE FOR ANALYSIS OF VARIANCE 890.373
   STANDARD ERROR OF ESTIMATE 3.880
            VARIABLE NO.   REG. COEFF.
                  5   4.680053E – 01
                  2   1.166517E + 00
                  4   –1.278208E + 00
                  3   –7.296275E – 01
            INTERCEPT   –5.781215E + 00

ALL VARIABLES ARE ENTERED.

IV—Q11. Learning Curve (CPA)

1.   The Green Company's new process will be carried out in one
     department. The production process has an expected learning
     curve of 80%. The costs subject to the learning effect for the
     first batch produced by the process were $10,000. Using the
     simplest form of the learning function, the cumulative average

cost per batch subject to the learning effect after the 16th batch has been produced may be estimated as

a. $3,276.80
b. $4,096.00
c. $8,000.00
d. $10,000.00

2. The learning function's mathematical form, enabling it to be plotted as a straight line on log-log graph paper, is

a. Trigonometric
b. Cyclical
c. Linear
d. Exponential

IV—Q12. Learning Curve (CPA)

The average number of minutes required to assemble trivets is predictable, based upon an 80 percent learning curve. That is, whenever cumulative production doubles, cumulative average time per unit becomes 80 percent of what it was at the previous doubling point. The trivets are produced in lots of 300 units and 60 minutes of labor are required to assemble each first lot.

Using the concept of the learning curve and the letters listed below, select the best answer for each of questions 1 through 5:

Let TT = Total time
MT = Marginal time for the xth lot
M = Marginal time for the first lot
X = Lots produced
b = Exponent expressing the improvement;
b has the range $-1 < b \leq 0$

1. A normal graph, i.e., not a log or log-log graph, of average minutes per lot of production, where cumulative lots are represented by the x-axis and average minutes per lot are represented by the y-axis, would produce a

a. Linear function sloping downward to the right
b. Linear function sloping upward to the right
c. Curvilinear function sloping upward to the right at an increasing rate
d. Curvilinear function sloping downward to the right at a decreasing rate

2. A log-log graph of average minutes per lot of production, where cumulative lots are represented by the x-axis and average minutes per lot are represented by the y-axis, would produce a
   a. Linear function sloping downward to the right
   b. Linear function sloping upward to the right
   c. Curvilinear function sloping upward to the right at a decreasing rate
   d. Curvilinear function sloping downward to the right at a decreasing rate

3. The average number of minutes required per lot to complete four lots is approximately
   a. 60.0
   b. 48.5
   c. 38.4
   d. 30.7

4. Average time to produce X lots of trivets could be expressed
   a. MX^{b+1}
   b. MX^{b}
   c. MT^{b+1}
   d. MX^{b-1}

5. Assuming that $b = -.322$, the average number of minutes required to produce X lots of trivets could be expressed
   a. $40.08X^{.673}$
   b. $40.08X$
   c. $60X^{-.322}$
   d. $60X^{1.322}$

PART FIVE QUESTIONS

PERFORMANCE EVALUATION AND CONTROL

V—Q1. Responsibility Accounting (CMA)

An important concept in management accounting is that of "responsibility accounting."

Required

A. Define the term "responsibility accounting."

B. What are the conditions that must exist for there to be effective "responsibility accounting?"

C. What benefits are said to result from "responsibility accounting?"

D. Listed below are three charges found on the monthly report of a division which manufactures and sells products primarily to outside companies. Division performance is evaluated by the use of Return on Investment. You are to state which, if any, of the following charges are consistent with the "responsibility accounting" concept. Support each answer with a brief explanation.

    1. A charge for general corporation administration at 10% of division sales.

    2. A charge for the use of the corporate computer facility. The charge is determined by taking actual annual

computer department costs and allocating an amount to each user on the ratio of its use to total corporation use.
3.   A charge for goods purchased from another division. The charge is based upon the competitive market price for the goods. (See Article 29.)

V—Q2. ROI

In judging the performance of a division manager, a controllable income or contribution margin may be divided by controllable investment. In judging the performance of a division (rather than the manager) for purposes of investment in the division or investment center, the net income of the division may be divided by the total investment in the division. Thus,

$$\frac{\text{Net Income of a Division}}{\text{Invested Capital of a Division}}$$

equals return on investment for the division and this also can be determined from capital turnover times profit margin on sales, i.e.,

$$\frac{\text{Sales}}{\text{Invested Capital}} \times \frac{\text{Net Income}}{\text{Sales}}.$$

Evaluate the usefulness of return on investment as a planning target and measure of divisional performance.

V—Q3. Imputed Interest, ROI, Residual Income

Where "imputed" interest on the assets used by an investment center is deducted from the operating income of the investment center, the remainder has been called residual income. (a) Discuss the determination of "imputed" interest for residual income purposes. (b) Evaluate ROI versus residual income for the measurement and control of divisional performance.

V—Q4. Effectiveness of a Budget Procedure for Planning and Controlling Operations; Use of Return on Assets to Evaluate Performance; Effect of the Performance Measurement System on the Behavior of Managers (CMA)

Clarkson Company is a large multidivision firm with several plants in each division. A comprehensive budgeting system is used for planning operations and measuring performance. The annual budgeting process commences in August, five months prior to the beginning of the fiscal year. At this time the division managers submit proposed budgets for sales, production and inventory levels, and expenses. Capital expenditure requests also are formalized at this time. The expense budgets include direct labor and all overhead items which are separated into fixed and variable components. Direct materials are budgeted separately in developing the production and inventory schedules.

The expense budgets for each division are developed from its plants' results, as measured by the percent variation from an adjusted budget in the first six months of the current year, and a target expense reduction percentage established by the corporation.

To determine plant percentages, the plant budget for the just completed half-year period is revised to recognize changes in operating procedures and costs outside the control of plant management (e.g., labor wage rate changes, product style changes, etc.). The difference between this revised budget and the actual expenses is the controllable variance, and is expressed as a percentage of the actual expenses. This percentage is added (if unfavorable) to the corporate target expense reduction percentage. A favorable plant variance percentage is subtracted from the corporate target. If a plant had a 2 percent unfavorable controllable variance and the corporate target reduction was 4 percent, the plant's budget for next year should reflect costs approximately 6 percent below this year's actual costs.

Next year's final budgets for the corporation, the divisions, and the plants are adopted after corporate analysis of the proposed budgets and a careful review with each division manager of the changes made by corporate management. Division profit budgets include allocated corporate costs, and plant profit budgets include allocated division and corporate costs.

Return on assets is used to measure the performance of divisions and plants. The asset base for a division consists of all assets assigned to the division, including its working capital, and an allocated share of corporate assets. For plants the asset base includes the assets assigned to the plant plus an allocated portion of the division and corporate assets. Recommendations for promotions and salary increases for the executives of the divisions and plants are influenced by how well the actual return on assets compares with the budgeted return on assets.

The plant managers exercise control only over the cost portion of the plant profit budget because the divisions are responsible for sales. Only limited control over the plant assets is exercised at the plant level.

The manager of the Dexter Plant, a major plant in the Huron division, carefully controls his costs during the first six months so that any improvement appears after the target reduction of expenses is established. He accomplishes this by careful planning and timing of his discretionary expenditures.

During 19_3, the property adjacent to the Dexter Plant was purchased by Clarkson Company. This expenditure was not included in the 19_3 capital expenditure budget. Corporate management decided to divert funds from a project at another plant since the property appeared to be a better long-term investment.

Also during 19_3 Clarkson Company experienced depressed sales. In an attempt to achieve budgeted profit, corporate management announced in August that all plants were to cut their annual expenses by 6 percent. In order to accomplish this expense reduction, the Dexter Plant manager reduced preventive maintenance and postponed needed major repairs. Employees who quit were not replaced unless absolutely necessary. Employee training was postponed whenever possible. The raw materials, supplies and finished goods inventories were reduced below normal levels.

Required

A. Evaluate the budget procedure of Clarkson Company with respect to its effectiveness for planning and controlling operations.

B. Is the Clarkson Company's use of return on assets to evaluate the performance of the Dexter Plant appropriate? Explain your answer.

C. Analyze and explain the Dexter Plant manager's behavior during 19_3.

V—Q5. Appraisal of the Performance of a Division Manager; Contribution Return on Division Net Investment (CMA)

George Johnson was hired on July 1, 19_1 as assistant general manager of the Botel Division of Staple, Inc. It was understood that he would be elevated to general manager of the division on January 1, 19_3, when the then current general manager retired and this was duly done. In addition to becoming acquainted with the division and the general manager's duties, Mr. Johnson was specifically charged with the responsibility for development of the 19_2 and 19_3 budgets. As general manager in 19_3, he was, obviously, responsible for the 19_4 budget.

The Staple Company is a multiproduct company which is highly decentralized. Each division is quite autonomous. The corporation staff approves division prepared operating budgets but seldom makes major changes in them. The corporate staff actively participates in decisions requiring capital investment (for expansion or replacement) and makes the final decisions. The division management is responsible for implementing the capital program. The major method used by the Staple Corporation to measure division performance is Contribution Return on Division Net Investment. The budgets presented below were approved by the corporation. Revision of the 19_4 budget is not considered necessary even though 19_3 actual departed from the approved 19_3 budget.

Botel Division (000 Omitted)

Accounts	Actual			Budget	
	19_1	19_2	19_3	19_3	19_4
Sales	1,000	1,500	1,800	2,000	2,400
Less Division Variable Costs:					
Material and Labor	250	375	450	500	600
Repairs	50	75	50	100	120
Supplies	20	30	36	40	48
Less Division Managed Costs:					
Employee Training	30	35	25	40	45
Maintenance	50	55	40	60	70
Less Division Committed Costs:					
Depreciation	120	160	160	200	200
Rent	80	100	110	140	140
Total	600	830	871	1,080	1,223
Division Net Contribution	400	670	929	920	1,177
Division Investment:					
Accounts Receivable	100	150	180	200	240
Inventory	200	300	270	400	480
Fixed Assets	1,590	2,565	2,800	3,380	4,000
Less: Accounts and Wages Payable	(150)	(225)	(350)	(300)	(360)
Net Investment	1,740	2,790	2,900	3,680	4,360
Contribution Return on Net Investment	23%	24%	32%	25%	27%

Required

A. Identify Mr. Johnson's responsibilities under the management and measurement program described above.

B. Appraise the performance of Mr. Johnson in 19_3.

C. Recommend to the president any changes in the responsibilities assigned to managers or in the measurement methods used to evaluate division management based upon your analysis.

V—Q6. Comparing Costs of Operating a Department with Budgeted Costs Under a Responsibility Accounting System (CMA)

The Argon County Hospital is located in the county seat. Argon county is a well-known summer resort area. The county population doubles during the vacation months (May–August) and hospital activity more than doubles during these months. The hospital is organized into several departments. Although it is a relatively small hospital, its pleasant surroundings have attracted a well-trained and competent medical staff.

An administrator was hired a year ago to improve the business activities of the hospital. Among the new ideas he has introduced is responsibility accounting. This program was announced along with quarterly cost reports supplied to department heads. Previously cost data was presented to department heads infrequently. Excerpts from the announcement and the report received by the laundry supervisor are presented below.

The annual budget for 19_3 was constructed by the new administrator. Quarterly budgets were computed as one-fourth of the annual budget. The administrator compiled the budget from analysis of the prior three years' costs. The analysis showed that all costs increased each year with more rapid increases between the second and third year. He considered establishing the budget at an average of the prior three years' costs, hoping that the installation of the system would reduce costs to this level. However, in view of the rapidly increasing prices, he finally chose 19_2 costs less 3 percent for the 19_3 budget. The activity level measured by patient days and pounds of laundry processed was set at 19_2 volume which was approximately equal to the volume of each of the past three years.

> The hospital has adopted a "responsibility accounting system." From now on you will receive quarterly reports comparing the costs of operating your department with budgeted costs. The reports will highlight the differences (variations) so you can zero in on the departure from budgeted costs (This is called "management by exception"). Responsibility accounting means you are accountable for keeping the costs in your department within the budget. The variations from the budget will help you identify what costs are out of line and the size of the variation will indicate which ones are the most important. Your first such report accompanies this announcement.

Required

A. Comment on the method used to construct the budget.

B. What information should be communicated by variations from budgets?

C. Does the report effectively communicate the level of efficiency of this department? Give reasons for your answer.

Argon County Hospital
Performance Report—Laundry Department
July–September 19_3

	Budget	Actual	(Over) Under Budget	Percent (Over) Under Budget
Patient Days	9,500	11,900	(2,400)	(25)
Pounds Processed—Laundry	125,000	156,000	(31,000)	(25)
Costs				
Laundry Labor	$ 9,000	$12,500	$(3,500)	(39)
Supplies	1,100	1,875	(775)	(70)
Water, Water Heating & Softening	1,700	2,500	(800)	(47)
Maintenance	1,400	2,200	(800)	(57)
Supervisor's Salary	3,150	3,750	(600)	(19)
Allocated Administration Costs	4,000	5,000	(1,000)	(25)
Equipment Depreciation	1,200	1,250	(50)	(4)
	$21,550	$29,075	$(7,525)	(35)

Administrator's Comments: Costs are significantly above budget for the quarter. Particular attention needs to be paid to labor, supplies and maintenance.

V—Q7. Standards and Motivation (CMA)

Harden Company has experienced increased production costs. The primary area of concern identified by management is direct labor. The company is considering adopting a standard cost system to help control labor and other costs. Useful historical data are not available because detailed production records have not been maintained.

Harden Company has retained Finch & Associates, an engineering consulting firm, to establish labor standards. After a complete study of the work process, the engineers recommended a labor standard of one unit of production every 30 minutes or 16 units per day for each worker. Finch further advised that Harden's wage rates were below the prevailing rate of $3 per hour.

Harden's production vice-president thought this labor standard was too tight and the employees would be unable to attain it. From his experience with the labor force, he believed a labor standard of 40 minutes per unit or 12 units per day for each worker would be more reasonable.

The president of Harden Company believed the standard should be set at a high level to motivate the workers, but he also recognized the standard should be set at a level to provide adequate information for control and reasonable cost comparisons. After much discussion, the management decided to use a dual standard. The labor standard recommended by the engineering firm of one unit every 30 minutes would be employed in the plant as a motivation device, and a cost standard of 40 minutes per unit would be used in reporting. Management also concluded that the workers would not be informed of the cost standard used for reporting purposes. The production vice-president conducted several sessions prior to implementation in the plant informing the workers of the new standard cost system and answering questions. The new standards were not related to incentive pay but were introduced at the time wages were increased to $3 per hour.

The new standard cost system was implemented on January 1, 19_4. At the end of six months of operation, the following statistics on labor performance were presented to top management:

	Jan.	Feb.	Mar.	Apr.	May	June
Production (units)	5100	5000	4700	4500	4300	4400
Direct Labor Hours	3000	2900	2900	3000	3000	3100
Variance from Labor Standard	$1350U	$1200U	$1650U	$2250U	$2550U	$2700U
Variance from Cost Standard	$1200F	$1300F	$ 700F	$ -0-	$ 400U	$ 500U

Raw material quality, labor mix, and plant facilities and conditions have not changed to any great extent during the six-month period.

Required

A. Discuss the impact of different types of standards on motivation, and specifically discuss the effect on motivation in Harden Company's plant of adopting the labor standard recommended by the engineering firm.

B. Evaluate Harden Company's decision to employ dual standards in their standard cost system.

V—Q8. Quantitative Techniques for Performance Evaluation and Control

A. Discuss how to apply a statistical model in determining if a variance from budget and/or standard should be investigated.

B. How would a model based on Bayesian statistics affect your discussion for part A?

V—Q9. Performance Evaluation and Probability, Whether Corrective Action Should Be Taken (CPA)

Items 1 through 4 are based on the following information: The Folding Department foreman must decide each week whether his department will operate normally during the following week. He may order a corrective action if he feels the Folding Department will operate inefficiently; otherwise he does nothing. The foreman receives a weekly Folding Department efficiency-variance report from the Accounting Department. A week in which the Folding Department operates inefficiently is usually preceded by a large efficiency variance. The graph below gives the probability that the Folding Department will operate normally in the following week as a function of the magnitude of the current week's variance reported to the foreman:

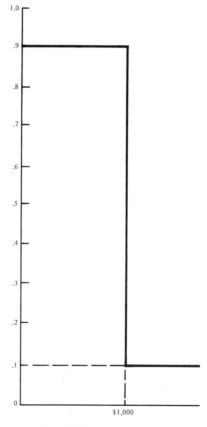

Probability of Folding Department Operating Normally Next Week

$1,000

Magnitude of Folding Department Efficiency Variance

658   APPENDIX B

1. An efficiency variance of $1,500 this week means the probability of operating normally the following week is
   a.   0%
   b.   10%
   c.   90%
   d.   100%

2. What are the possible relationships between the current efficiency variance and next week's operations?
   a.   Large variance followed by normal operation, large variance followed by inefficient operation, small variance followed by normal operation, and small variance followed by inefficient operation.
   b.   Large variance followed by normal operation, small variance followed by inefficient operation, and small variance followed by normal operation.
   c.   Large variance followed by inefficient operation, small variance followed by normal operation, and small variance followed by inefficient operation.
   d.   Large variance followed by 90% of normal operation, small variance followed by 10% of normal operation, large variance followed by inefficient operation, and small variance followed by inefficient operation.

3. If the foreman can determine for certain whether the Folding Department will operate normally next week, and the cost of corrective action is less than the extra cost of operating the Folding Department inefficiently, then the best decision rule for the foreman to follow is
   a.   If normal operations are predicted, do not take corrective action; if inefficient operations are predicted, take corrective action.
   b.   Regardless of the current variance, do not take corrective action.
   c.   If normal operations are predicted, take corrective action; if inefficient operations are predicted, do not take corrective action.
   d.   Regardless of the current variance, take corrective action.

4. The following cost information is relevant to the Folding-Department foreman in deciding whether corrective action is warranted:

   $500   =   cost of corrective action which will assure normal operation of Folding Department for the following week.
   $3,000   =   excess cost of operating Folding Department inefficiently for one week.

The foreman receives a report that the Folding Department efficiency variance is $600. The expected cost of not taking corrective action is

a. $0
b. $300
c. $2,700
d. $3,000

V—Q10. Transfer Prices (CPA)

1.   In a decentralized company in which divisions may buy goods from one another, the transfer-pricing system should be designed primarily to
a.   Increase the consolidated value of inventory
b.   Allow division managers to buy from outsiders
c.   Minimize the degree of autonomy of division managers
d.   Aid in the appraisal and motivation of managerial performance

2.   In order to evaluate the performance of individual departments, interdepartmental transfers of a product preferably should be made at prices
a.   Equal to the market price of the product
b.   Set by the receiving department
c.   Equal to fully-allocated costs to the producing department
d.   Equal to variable costs to the producing department

3.   Mar Company has two decentralized divisions, X and Y. Division X has always purchased certain units from Division Y at $75 per unit. Because Division Y plans to raise the price to $100 per unit, Division X desires to purchase these units from outside suppliers for $75 per unit. Division Y's costs follow:

Y's variable costs per unit	$70
Y's annual fixed costs	$15,000
Y's annual production of these units for X	1,000 units

If Division X buys from an outside supplier, the facilities Division Y uses to manufacture these units would remain idle. What would be the result if Mar enforces a transfer price of $100 per unit between Divisions X and Y?

a.   It would be suboptimization for the company because X should buy from outside suppliers at $75 per unit.

b.   It would provide lower overall company net income than a transfer price of $75 per unit.
c.   It would provide higher overall company net income than a transfer price of $75 per unit.
d.   It would be more profitable for the company than allowing X to buy from outside suppliers at $75 per unit.

V—Q11. Setting an Intracompany Selling Price (CMA)

The Ajax division of Gunnco, operating at capacity, has been asked by the Defco division of Gunnco Corp. to supply it with Electrical Fitting number 1726. Ajax sells this part to its regular customers for $7.50 each. Defco, which is operating at 50% capacity, is willing to pay $5.00 each for the fitting. Defco will put the fitting into a brake unit which it is manufacturing on essentially a cost plus basis for a commercial airplane manufacturer.

Ajax has a variable cost of producing fitting number 1726 of $4.25. The cost of the brake unit as being built by Defco is as follows:

Purchased parts—Outside vendors	$22.50
Ajax fitting—1726	5.00
Other variable costs	14.00
Fixed overhead and administration	8.00
	$49.50

Defco believes the price concession is necessary to get the job.

The company uses return on investment and dollar profits in the measurement of division and division manager performance.

Required

A.   Consider that you are the division controller of Ajax. Would you recommend that Ajax supply fitting 1726 to Defco? (Ignore any income tax issues.) Why or why not?

B.   Would it be to the short-run economic advantage of the Gunnco Corporation for the Ajax division to supply Defco division with fitting 1726 at $5 each? (Ignore any income tax issues.) Explain your answer.

C.   Discuss the organizational and manager behavior difficulties, if any, inherent in this situation. As the Gunnco Controller what would you advise the Gunnco Corporation President do in this situation?

V—Q12. Transfer Pricing; Profit Centers for Divisional Operations (CMA)—(Answer Included for the Profit Center Concept—Part C)

A. R. Oma, Inc. manufactures a line of men's perfumes and after-shaving lotions. The manufacturing process is basically a series of mixing operations with the addition of certain aromatic and coloring ingredients; the finished product is packaged in a company-produced glass bottle and packed in cases containing 6 bottles.

A. R. Oma feels that the sale of its product is heavily influenced by the appearance and appeal of the bottle and has, therefore, devoted considerable managerial effort to the bottle production process. This has resulted in the development of certain unique bottle production processes in which management takes considerable pride.

The two areas (i.e., perfume production and bottle manufacture) have evolved over the years in an almost independent manner; in fact, a rivalry has developed between management personnel as to "which division is the more important" to A. R. Oma. This attitude is probably intensified because the bottle manufacturing plant was purchased intact 10 years ago, and no real interchange of management personnel or ideas (except at the top corporate level) has taken place.

Since the acquisition, all bottle production has been absorbed by the perfume manufacturing plant. Each area is considered a separate profit center and evaluated as such. As the new corporate controller you are responsible for the definition of a proper transfer value to use in crediting the bottle production profit center and in debiting the packaging profit center.

At your request, the Bottle Division General Manager has asked certain other bottle manufacturers to quote a price for the quantity and sizes demanded by the perfume division. These competitive prices are:

Volume	Total Price	Price Per Case
2,000,000 eq. cases*	$ 4,000,000	$2.00
4,000,000	$ 7,000,000	$1.75
6,000,000	$10,000,000	$1.67

*An "equivalent case" represents 6 bottles each.

A cost analysis of the internal bottle plant indicates that they can produce bottles at these costs.

Volume	Total Price	Cost Per Case
2,000,000 eq. cases	$3,200,000	$1.60
4,000,000	$5,200,000	$1.30
6,000,000	$7,200,000	$1.20

(Your cost analysts point out that these costs represent fixed costs of $1,200,000 and variable costs of $1.00 per equivalent case.)

These figures have given rise to considerable corporate discussion as to the proper value to use in the transfer of bottles to the perfume division. This interest is heightened because a significant portion of a division manager's income is an incentive bonus based on profit center results.

The perfume production division has the following costs in addition to the bottle costs:

Volume	Total Cost	Cost Per Case
2,000,000 cases	$16,400,000	$8.20
4,000,000	$32,400,000	$8.10
6,000,000	$48,400,000	$8.07

After considerable analysis, the marketing research department has furnished you with the following price-demand relationship for the finished product:

Sales Volume	Total Sales Revenue	Sales Price Per Case
2,000,000 cases	$25,000,000	$12.50
4,000,000	$45,600,000	$11.40
6,000,000	$63,900,000	$10.65

Required

A. The A. R. Oma Company has used market price transfer prices in the past. Using the current market prices and costs, and assuming a volume of 6,000,000 cases, calculate the income for:
1. The bottle division.
2. The perfume division.
3. The corporation.

B. Is this production and sales level the most profitable volume for:
1. The bottle division?
2. The perfume division?
3. The corporation?
Explain your answer.

C. The A. R. Oma Company uses the profit center concept for divisional operation.
1. Define a "profit center."
2. What conditions should exist for a profit center to be established?
3. Should the two divisions of the A. R. Oma Company be organized as profit centers?

Answer for Part C

C. 1. A segment of a business that is responsible for both revenues and expenses and whose performance is measured by profits.

2. Some of the conditions that should exist are:
    a. Proper organization attitudes for decentralized operations.
    b. The division level (or segment) must have freedom and independence so that it can buy outside the company when it is to its advantage to do so.
    c. Other sources that are willing to quote a price for the quantity and sizes demanded.
    d. Freedom to sell to outside parties.
    e. Revenues and costs of the segment must be distinguishable from revenues and costs of other segments.

3. The bottle division should not be organized as a profit center. The bottle division makes special bottles for the perfume division and, therefore, it does not have an opportunity to sell to outside parties.

    The perfume division could be treated as a profit center. There are other manufacturers that are willing to quote a price for the quantity and sizes demanded by the perfume division and the perfume division sells to the outside.

PART SIX QUESTIONS

ADDITIONAL APPLICATIONS OF QUANTITATIVE
        TECHNIQUES: LINEAR PROGRAMMING,
        INVENTORY CONTROL, PERT/COST
        RESOURCE ALLOCATION, MATRIX
        APPLICATIONS, OPTIMIZATION AND
        DIFFERENTIAL CALCULUS

VI—Q1. Linear Programming—Formulation of the Objective Function and the Constraint Functions, Graphic Solution of a Linear Programming Problem (CMA)

Part A

The Witchell Corporation manufactures and sells three grades, A, B, and C, of a single wood product. Each grade must be processed through three phases—cutting, fitting, and finishing—before it is sold.
    The following unit information is provided:

	A	B	C
Selling Price	$10.00	$15.00	$20.00
Direct Labor	5.00	6.00	9.00
Direct Materials	.70	.70	1.00
Variable Overhead	1.00	1.20	1.80
Fixed Overhead	.60	.72	1.08
Materials Requirements in Board Feet	7	7	10
Labor Requirements in Hours			
Cutting	3/6	3/6	4/6
Fitting	1/6	1/6	2/6
Finishing	1/6	2/6	3/6

Only 5,000 board feet per week can be obtained.
    The cutting department has 180 hours of labor available each week. The fitting and finishing departments each have 120 hours of labor available each week. No overtime is allowed.
    Contract commitments require the company to make 50 units of A per week. In addition, company policy is to produce at least 50 additional units

of A and 50 units of B and 50 units of C each week to actively remain in each of the three markets. Because of competition only 130 units of C can be sold each week.

Required

Formulate and label the linear objective function and the constraint functions necessary to maximize the contribution margin.

Part B

The graph provided presents the constraint functions for a chair manufacturing company whose production problem can be solved by linear programming. The company earns $8 for each kitchen chair sold and $5 for each office chair sold.

Required

1. What is the profit maximizing production schedule?

2. How did you select this production schedule?

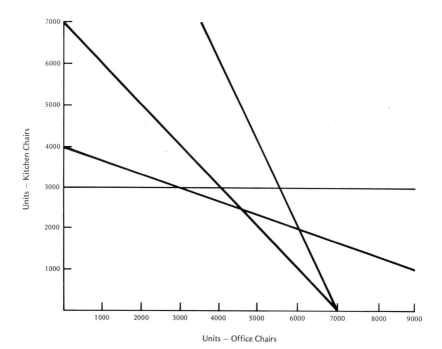

Units — Office Chairs

VI—Q2. Linear Programming—Constraints and Objective Function (CPA)

Items 1, 2, and 3 are based on the following information:

The Random Company manufactures two products, Zeta and Beta. Each product must pass through two processing operations. All materials are introduced at the start of Process No. 1. There are no work-in-process inventories. Random may produce either one product exclusively or various combinations of both products subject to the following constraints:

	Process No. 1	Process No. 2	Contribution Margin Per Unit
Hours required to produce one unit of:			
Zeta	1 hour	1 hour	$4.00
Beta	2 hours	3 hours	5.25
Total capacity in hours per day	1,000 hours	1,275 hours	

A shortage of technical labor has limited Beta production to 400 units per day. There are no constraints on the production of Zeta other than the hour constraints in the above schedule. Assume that all relationships between capacity and production are linear, and that all of the above data and relationships are deterministic rather than probabilistic.

1. Given the objective to maximize total contribution margin, what is the production constraint for Process No. 1?
   a. Zeta + Beta ≤ 1,000
   b. Zeta + 2Beta ≤ 1,000
   c. Zeta + Beta ≥ 1,000
   d. Zeta + 2Beta ≥ 1,000

2. Given the objective to maximize total contribution margin, what is the labor constraint for production of Beta?
   a. Beta ≤ 400
   b. Beta ≥ 400
   c. Beta ≤ 425
   d. Beta ≥ 425

3. What is the objective function of the data presented?
   a. Zeta + 2Beta = $9.25
   b. $4.00 Zeta + 3($5.25) Beta = Total Contribution Margin
   c. $4.00 Zeta + $5.25 Beta = Total Contribution Margin
   d. 2($4.00) Zeta + 3($5.25) Beta = Total Contribution Margin

4. Patsy, Inc., manufactures two products, X and Y. Each product must be processed in each of three departments: machining,

assembling, and finishing. The hours needed to produce one unit of product per department and the maximum possible hours per department follow:

Department	Production Hours Per Unit X	Y	Maximum Capacity In Hours
Machining	2	1	420
Assembling	2	2	500
Finishing	2	3	600

Other restrictions follow:

$X \geqslant 50$
$Y \geqslant 50$

The objective function is to maximize profits where profit = $4X + $2Y. Given the objective and constraints, what is the most profitable number of units of X and Y, respectively, to manufacture?

a. 150 and 100
b. 165 and 90
c. 170 and 80
d. 200 and 50

5. In a linear programming maximization problem for business problem solving, the coefficients of the objective function usually are
   a. Marginal contributions per unit
   b. Variable costs
   c. Profit based upon allocations of overhead and all indirect costs
   d. Usage rates for scarce resources
   e. None of the above

6. The constraints in a linear programming problem usually model
   a. Profits
   b. Restrictions
   c. Dependent variables
   d. Goals
   e. None of the above

7. If there are four activity variables and two constraints in a linear programming problem, the most products that would be included in the optimal solution would be
   a. 6
   b. 4
   c. 2
   d. 0
   e. None of the above

8.   Linear programming is used most commonly to determine
     a.   That mix of variables which will result in the largest quantity
     b.   The best use of scarce resources
     c.   The most advantageous prices
     d.   The fastest timing
     e.   None of the above

9.   Assume the following data for the two products produced by Wagner Company:

	Product A	Product B
Raw material requirements (units)		
X	3	4
Y	7	2
Contribution margin per unit	$10	$4

If 300 units of raw material X and 400 units of raw material Y are available, the set of relationships appropriate for maximization of revenue using linear programming would be

a. $3A + 4B \geqslant 300$
     $7A + 2B \geqslant 400$
     $10A + 4B$ MAX
b. $3A + 7B \geqslant 300$
     $4A + 2B \geqslant 400$
     $10A + 4B$ MAX
c. $3A + 7B \leqslant 300$
     $4A + 2B \leqslant 400$
     $10A + 4B$ MAX
d. $3A + 4B \leqslant 300$
     $7A + 2B \leqslant 400$
     $10A + 4B$ MAX
e.   None of the above

10. The following schedule provides data for product A, which is processed through processes 1 and 2, and product B, which is processed through process 1 only:

	Product A	Product B
Raw material cost per gallon	$ 4	$ 9
Process 1 (500 gallon input capacity per hour):		
Processing cost per hour	$60	$60
Loss in processing	30%	20%
Process 2 (300 gallon input capacity per hour):		
Processing cost per hour	$50	
Loss in processing	10%	
Selling price per gallon	$20	$40

If the objective is to maximize profit per eight-hour day, the objective function of a profit-maximizing linear programming problem would be

a. $20A + 40B - 4A - 4B$

b. $20A + 40B - 4A - 4B - 60(A + B) - 50A$

c. $20(.63A) + 40(.80B) - 4(.63A) - 9(.8B)$

$$- 60 \left(\frac{A + B}{500} \right) - 50 \left(\frac{.7A}{300} \right)$$

d. $20(.63A) + 40(.80B) - 4A - 9B$

$$-60 \left(\frac{A}{500} + \frac{B}{500} \right) \quad 50 \left(\frac{.7A}{300} \right)$$

e.   None of the above

11. Assuming the same facts as in item 10, a constraint of the problem would be

a. $.63A \leqslant 2,400$

b. $.8A \leqslant 2,400$

c. $.7A + .8B \leqslant 4,000$

d. $.9A \leqslant 4,000$

e.   None of the above

12. A linear programming model is being used to determine for two products having different profitabilities per unit, the quantities of each to produce to maximize profit over a one-year period. One component of cost is raw materials. If both products use the same amount of the same raw material,

a.   This cost may be ignored because it is the same for each product.

b.   This cost must be ignored because it is the same for each product.

c.   This cost must be included in the objective function since it varies with the independent variables in the model.

d.   More information about the products and the other components of the objective function is needed to determine whether to include this cost.

e.   None of the above

VI—Q3. Various Linear Programming Questions—Simplex Method (CPA Adapted)

Beekley, Inc. manufactures widgets, gadgets, and trinkets and has asked for advice in determining the best production mix for its three products. Demand for the company's products is excellent, and management finds that it is unable to meet potential sales with existing plant capacity.

Each product goes through three operations: milling, grinding, and painting. The effective weekly departmental capacities in minutes are: milling—10,000, grinding—14,000 and painting—10,000.

The following data is available on the three products:

	Selling Price per Unit	Variable Cost per Unit	Per Unit Production Time (in Minutes)		
			Milling	Grinding	Painting
Widgets	$5.25	$4.45	4	8	4
Gadgets	5.00	3.90	10	4	2
Trinkets	4.50	3.30	4	8	2

1. The quantitative technique most useful in determining the best product mix would be
    a. Least-squares analysis
    b. Queuing theory
    c. Linear regression
    d. Linear programming

2. The objective function for this problem using the simplex method might be expressed
    a. $f \min = 4.45X_1 + 3.90X_2 + 3.30X_3 + 0X_4 + 0X_5 + 0X_6$
    b. $f \max = 5.25X_1 + 5.00X_2 + 4.50X_3 + X_4 + X_5 + X_6$
    c. $f \max = .80X_1 + 1.10X_2 + 1.20X_3 + X_4 + X_5 + X_6$
    d. $f \max = .80X_1 + 1.10X_2 + 1.20X_3 + 0X_4 + 0X_5 + 0X_6$

3. The requirement that total production time in the painting department may not exceed 10,000 minutes per week might be expressed
    a. $4X_1 + 2X_2 + 2X_3 \geqslant 10,000$
    b. $4X_1 + 2X_2 + 2X_3 > 10,000$
    c. $4X_1 + 2X_2 + 2X_3 \leqslant 10,000$
    d. $4X_1 + 2X_2 + 2X_3 < 10,000$

4. The variables X_4, X_5, and X_6 included in the answers to item 2 are referred to as
    a. Artificial variables
    b. Primary variables
    c. Stochastic variables
    d. Slack variables

5. The variables X_1, X_2, and X_3 included in the answers to item 2 are referred to as
    a. Artificial variables
    b. Primary variables
    c. Stochastic variables
    d. Slack variables

6. The coefficients for X_1, X_2, and X_3 included in the answers to item 2 are
    a. The coefficients of the objective function in the problem
    b. The coefficients of the artificial variables in the problem
    c. The coefficients of the constraints in the problem and represent the contribution margin for each project
    d. The shadow prices of the stochastic variables in the problem

7. If Beekley were willing to pay $.12 for every minute of additional grinding time which might be made available, this may be called
    a. A primal restraint
    b. A slack variable
    c. A shadow price
    d. An artificial variable

8. A significant advantage of applying the simplex method to certain problems having four or more variables of a single class is that solutions may be arrived at quickly using
    a. Graphic analysis
    b. Electronic computer routines
    c. Simple algebraic methods
    d. Set theory

Interpretation of a Simplex Tableau. (For questions 9 through 11, see the discussion about computer solution of linear programming problems in Article 30. For question 12, see the editors' note about the solution. Also see the sensitivity analysis discussion in Article 30.)

9. A final tableau for a linear programming profit maximization problem is shown below:

	X_1	X_2	X_3	S_1	S_2	
X_1	1	0	4	3	-7	50
X_2	0	1	-2	-6	2	60
	0	0	5	1	9	1,200

If X_1, X_2 and X_3 represent products, S_1 refers to square feet (in thousands) of warehouse capacity and S_2 refers to labor hours (in hundreds); the number of X_1 that should be produced to maximize profit would be
   a. 60
   b. 50
   c. 1
   d. 0
   e. None of the above

10. Assuming the same facts as in item 9, the contribution to profit of an additional 100 hours of labor would be
   a. 9
   b. 2
   c. 1
   d. -7
   e. None of the above

11. Assuming the same facts as in item 9, an additional 1,000 square feet of warehouse space would
   a. Increase X_1 by 3 units and decrease X_2 by 6 units
   b. Decrease X_2 by 6 units and increase X_1 by 2 units
   c. Decrease X_1 by 7 units and increase X_2 by 2 units
   d. Increase X_1 by 3 units and decrease X_2 by 7 units
   e. Do none of the above.

12. The following is the final tableau of a linear programming profit maximization problem:

	X_1	X_2	S_1	S_2	
X_1	1	0	-5	3	125
X_2	0	1	1	-1	70
	0	0	5	7	500

The marginal contribution to profit of 5 for each added resource unit S_1 can be maintained if the added resource units do not exceed*

   a.   125

   b.   100

   c.   70

   d.   25

   e.   None of the above

---

   *Answer: 25 (This is explained by Case 2 in the sensitivity analysis section of Article 30 and is discussed below.)

   Editor's Note: Determination of the upper limit of the range for the amount of a resource such that the shadow price of 5 is applicable (part 12 of VI—Q3).

   In addition to obtaining an optimal solution, we may want sensitivity analysis information about the effect on the solution of changes in constraints or objective function coefficients. Article 30 contains a section about the interpretation of simplex tableaus (computer solution of linear programming problems). Working with the optimal solution tableau printout, it is usually possible to determine the effect of changes without working the problem over again. In the final tableau, the substitution rates represented by the various coefficients are applicable only as long as the basis does not change. Therefore, we would like to determine the range over which some of the more important factors can change without changing the basis (see sensitivity analysis in Article 30). Article 30 shows the determination and use of right-hand side (RHS) and profit ranges for sensitivity analysis purposes.

   After obtaining the optimal solution tableau for part 12 of this problem, we are informed that the available amount of a resource has changed. As long as the optimal basis remains feasible, we do not have to calculate a new solution, but can determine the increase or decrease in profit associated with the change in this resource by using the value of the shadow price associated with the slack variable for the resource.

   The section of Article 30 concerned with changes in RHS values shows how to find the permissible range for the amount of a given resource such that the shadow price is applicable. The article shows two cases (1) a resource which is not fully utilized, and (2) a resource which is fully utilized (see part 12 of VI—Q3). The maximum allowable increase or decrease in the available amount of a resource can be identified as Δ^+ and Δ^- respectively. Also in the optimal tableau let b_i = RHS value in row i, c_j = objective function coefficient in column j, a_{ij} = row i coefficient in column j.

   See the paragraph headed Case 2 in the sensitivity analysis section of Article 30. For Case 2, a resource is fully utilized (as in part 12 of problem VI—Q3) so the associated slack variable = 0. For Δ^- we use the smallest test ratio b_i/a_{ij}, where j is the column in which the associated slack variable appears. Only positive a_{ij} values are used. For Δ^+ we choose the smallest b_i/a_{ij}, but we only consider negative a_{ij}. Refer to the lathe time resource in the optimal tableau in Article 30. The associated slack variable $S_1 = 0$. It appears in column 3, i.e., j = 3. Rows 1 and 3 have negative coefficients and the coefficients are positive in row 2. Thus, $\Delta^- = b_2/a_{23} = 300/2 = 150$, Δ^+ = the minimum of b_1/a_{13}, b_3/a_{33} or $[\,|300/-2|, |50/-1|\,] = 50$. Therefore, the shadow price range is 600 to 800 hours, i.e., (750 − 150) to (750 + 50).

   For part 12 of VI—Q3, we are asked for Δ^+. The appropriate slack variable S_1 appears in column 3. The slack variable equals zero; the resource is fully utilized. For Δ^+ where a resource is fully utilized, we use only negative a_{ij} values as discussed above and choose the test ratio b_i/a_{ij} which has the smallest absolute value. The coefficient a_{13} is negative in row 1 only. Since there is only one negative value, the test ratio b_1/a_{13} would be the smallest. Therefore, $\Delta^+ = 125/-5 = 25$.

VI—Q4. Linear Programming—Product Mix (CPA Adapted)

The Marcia Company, your client, has asked your assistance in determining an economical sales and production mix of their products for 19_4. The company manufactures a line of dolls and a doll dress sewing kit.

The company's sales department provides the following data:

Doll's Name	Estimated Demand for 19_4 (Units)	Established Net Price (Units)
Laurie	50,000	$5.20
Debbie	42,000	2.40
Sarah	35,000	8.50
Kathy	40,000	4.00
Sewing kit	325,000	3.00

To promote sales of the sewing kit there is a 15% reduction in the established net price for a kit purchased at the same time that a Marcia Company doll is purchased.

From accounting records you develop the following data:

1. The production standards per unit:

Item	Material	Labor
Laurie	$1.40	$ .80
Debbie	.70	.50
Sarah	2.69	1.40
Kathy	1.00	1.00
Sewing kit	.60	.40

2. The labor rate of $2 per hour is expected to continue without change in 19_4. The plant has an effective capacity of 130,000 labor hours per year on a single-shift basis. Present equipment can produce all of the products.

3. The total fixed costs for 19_4 will be $100,000. Variable costs will be equivalent to 50% of direct labor cost.

4. The company has a small inventory of its products that can be ignored.

Required

A. Prepare a schedule computing the contribution to profit of a unit of each product.

B. Prepare a schedule computing the contribution to profit of a unit of each product per labor dollar expended on the product.

C. Prepare a schedule computing the total labor hours required to produce the estimated sales units for 19_4. Indicate the item and number of units that you would recommend be increased (or decreased) in production to attain the company's effective productive capacity.

D. Without regard to your answer in "C," assume that the estimated sales units for 19_4 would require 12,000 labor hours in excess of the company's effective productive capacity. Discuss the possible methods of providing the missing capacity. Include in your discussion all factors that must be taken into consideration in evaluating the methods of providing the missing capacity.

E. Assume the plant has an effective capacity of 62,000 labor hours per year on a single-shift basis and that the company manufactures and sells just the line of dolls (i.e., the company does not produce or sell a sewing kit). Prepare the problem for solution by the simplex method of linear programming with the aid of a computer.

Answer to Part E

The selling price for the Laurie doll is $5.20. The production costs for Laurie are material $1.40, labor $.80, and variable overhead $.40. Subtracting the variable costs of $1.40 + $.80 + $.40 or $2.60 from the selling price of $5.20 equals a contribution margin of $2.60, and this becomes part of the objective function. The other contribution margins are Debbie $.95, Sarah $3.71, and Kathy $1.50. The contribution margin figures are used in the objective function and the firm should attempt to maximize:

$$\$2.60L + \$.95D + \$3.71S + \$1.50K$$

The constraints for the problem are labor hours and demand. The labor hours constraint can be shown as:

$$.40L + .25D + .70S + .50K \leqslant 62,000$$

The coefficient of .40 for the labor hours constraint for the Laurie doll can be determined as $.80 (the labor cost for a Laurie doll) divided by the labor rate per hour of $2. The other coefficients for the labor hours constraint can be determined by the same procedure as for the Laurie doll. The total labor hours available for the production of dolls must be less than or equal to ($\leq$) 62,000, which we have given above as the plant's effective capacity of labor hours on a single shift basis.

The demand constraints given in units are $\leq$ inequalities and are entered as 50000, 42000, 35000, 40000 for L, D, S, K respectively. Part E of the problem assumes the company sells dolls only, and not the sewing kit.

The computer printout identifies Laurie, Debbie, Sarah, and Kathy as variables 1 through 4 respectively. Variable 9 represents slack. For the problem, the slack variable is 26,000 units. This is the difference between the total demand for the Kathy doll (variable 4) of 40,000 units and the 14,000 units listed for that doll on the printout for the product mix that maximizes the objective function with the given problem constraints. The problem has 5 constraints or restrictions. The particular computer program used for this problem requires that the constraints for the problem be entered in the following order:

> "less than" inequalities
> "equalities"
> "greater than" inequalities

In the problem, all the restrictions (labor hours and demand for the different dolls) are "less than" inequalities. The solution for this problem using a linear programming and sensitivity analysis (LPS) computer program is given below.

```
ENTER THE NUMBER OF RESTRICTION EQUATIONS — ? 5
ENTER THE NUMBER OF VARIABLES — ? 4
HOW MANY RESTRICTIVE EQUATIONS WITH THE LESS THAN SYMBOL — ? 5
HOW MANY RESTRICTIVE EQUATIONS WITH THE EQUALS SYMBOL —
? 0
HOW MANY RESTRICTIVE EQUATIONS WITH GREATER THAN SYMBOLS — ? 0

ENTER 4 VALUES FOR RESTRICTION EQUATION # 1    (LEFT-HAND SIDE OF LABOR
.40,.25,.70,.50                                 HOURS)
ENTER 4 VALUES FOR RESTRICTION EQUATION # 2    (LEFT-HAND SIDE OF L DEMAND)
1,0,0,0
ENTER 4 VALUES FOR RESTRICTION EQUATION # 3    (LEFT-HAND SIDE OF D DEMAND)
0,1,0,0
ENTER 4 VALUES FOR RESTRICTION EQUATION # 4    (LEFT-HAND SIDE OF S DEMAND)
0,0,1,0
ENTER 4 VALUES FOR RESTRICTION EQUATION # 5    (LEFT-HAND SIDE OF K DEMAND)
0,0,0,1
ENTER THE 5 RESTRICTION VALUES FOR THE 5 EQUATIONS   (RIGHT-HAND SIDE OF
62000,50000,42000,35000,40000                         RESTRICTIONS)
```

ENTER THE COEFFICIENTS OF THE OBJECTIVE FUNCTION
THE CONTRIBUTION MARGIN OF EACH OF THE PRODUCTS
ENTER 4 FUNCTION VALUES:
2.60,.95,3.71,1.50

COLUMN STATISTICS:
YOUR VARIABLES 1 THROUGH 4
SLACK VARIABLES 5 THROUGH 9

ANSWERS:

VARIABLE	VALUE
4	14000
1	50000
2	42000
3	35000
9	26000

OBJECTIVE FUNCTION VALUE   320750

DUAL VARIABLES:

COLUMN	VALUE
5	3
6	1.4
7	.2
8	1.61
9	0

The solution shows the company's mix should be Laurie 50,000 units, Debbie 42,000 units, Sarah 35,000 units, and Kathy 14,000 units. The value for the objective function, listed in the printout as $320,750, is the total contribution margin and results from $2.60(50,000) + $.95(42,000) + $3.71(35,000) + $1.50(14,000).

The initial tableau (tableau after 0 iterations) supplied by the LPS computer program, and the optimal tableau (tableau after 4 iterations) are shown below.

DATA TABLE

TABLEAU AFTER 0 ITERATIONS [INITIAL TABLEAU]

.4	.25	.7	.5	1	0	0	0	0	62000
1	0	0	0	0	1	0	0	0	50000
0	1	0	0	0	0	1	0	0	42000
0	0	1	0	0	0	0	1	0	35000
0	0	0	1	0	0	0	0	1	40000
−2.6	−.95	−3.71	−1.5	0	0	0	0	0	0

BASIS BEFORE ITERATION 1

VARIABLE	VALUE
5	62000
6	50000
7	42000
8	35000
9	40000

OBJECTIVE FUNCTION VALUE 0

TABLEAU AFTER 4 ITERATIONS [OPTIMAL TABLEAU]

0	0	0	1	2	-.8	-.5	-1.4	0	14000
1	0	0	0	0	1	0	0	0	50000
0	1	0	0	0	0	1	0	0	42000
0	0	1	0	0	0	0	1	0	35000
0	0	0	0	-2	.8	.5	1.4	1	26000
0	0	0	0	3	1.4	.2	1.61	0	320750

DO YOU WISH TO DO SENSITIVITY ANALYSIS Y/N ? N

(For sensitivity analysis see VI—Q16.)

See Article 30 for an interpretation of tableaus (computer solution of linear programming problems). Article 30 also discusses shadow prices and the use of tableaus in determining the effect on the optimal solution if constraints or objective function coefficients change (sensitivity analysis). As stated in Article 30, substitution rates represented by the various coefficients in a final tableau are applicable as long as the basis does not change. Therefore, one of the first things we would like to determine is the range over which some of the more important factors can change without changing the basis. Article 30 shows the use of a tableau in (1) the determination of ranges for right-hand side (RHS) values, and (2) profit ranging for sensitivity analysis purposes. For questions concerned with the interpretation of a tableau and involving sensitivity analysis, see VI—Q3 parts 9 through 12. Also see the problem about optimal solutions and sensitivity analysis at the end of Article 30.

VI—Q5. Inventory Control (CPA)

Inventories usually are an important asset for both manufacturing and merchandising firms. A proper balance of inventory quantities is desirable from several standpoints. Maintaining such a balance is dependent upon a number of factors including ordering at the proper time and in the correct lot size. Serious penalties may attend both overstocking and stockout situations.

Required

A.   In connection with inventory ordering and control, certain terms are basic. Explain the meaning of each of the following:
1.   Economic order quantity.
2.   Reorder point.
3.   Lead time.
4.   Safety stock.

B.   1.   What are the costs of carrying inventories? Explain.
2.   How does overstocking add to the cost of carrying inventories?

C.   1.   What are the consequences of maintaining minimal or inadequate inventory levels?
2.   What are the difficulties of measuring precisely the costs associated with understocking?

D.   Discuss the propriety of including carrying costs (of normal inventory, overstocking and understocking) in the inventory cost:
1.   For external reporting.
2.   For internal decision making.

VI—Q6. Economic Order Quantity, Reorder Point, Cost of a Stockout (CPA)—Problem for Study (Answer Included)

You have been engaged to install an accounting system for the Kaufman Corporation. Among the inventory control features Kaufman desires as a part of the system are indicators of "how much" to order "when." The following information is furnished for one item, called a komtronic, which is carried in inventory:

1.   Komtronics are sold by the gross (twelve dozen) at a list price of $800 per gross F.O.B. shipper. Kaufman receives a 40 percent trade discount off list price on purchases in gross lots.

2.   Freight cost is $20 per gross from the shipping point to Kaufman's plant.

3.   Kaufman uses about 5,000 komtronics during a 259-day production year and must purchase a total of 36 gross per year to allow for normal breakage. Minimum and maximum usages are 12 and 28 komtronics per day, respectively.

4. Normal delivery time to receive an order is 20 working days from the date a purchase request is initiated. A rush order in full gross lots can be received by air freight in five working days at an extra cost of $52 per gross. A stockout (complete exhaustion of the inventory) of komtronics would stop production, and Kaufman would purchase komtronics locally at list price rather than shut down.

5. The cost of placing an order is $10; the cost of receiving an order is $20.

6. Space storage cost is $12 per year per gross stored.

7. Insurance and taxes are approximately 12 percent of the net delivered cost of average inventory and Kaufman expects a return of at least 8 percent on its average investment (ignore return on order and carrying cost for simplicity).

Required

A. Prepare a schedule computing the total annual cost of komtronics based on uniform order lot sizes of one, two, three, four, five and six gross of komtronics. (The schedule should show the total annual cost according to each lot size.) Indicate the economic order quantity (economic lot size to order).

B. Prepare a schedule computing the minimum stock reorder point for komtronics. This is the point below which the komtronics inventory should not fall without reordering so as to guard against a stockout. Factors to be considered include average lead-period usage and safety stock requirements.

C. Prepare a schedule computing the cost of a stockout of komtronics. Factors to be considered include the excess costs for local purchases and for rush orders.

Answer

A.

Computation of Economic Order Quantity for Komtronics

Gross Ordered	Orders Per Year	Net Cost Per Order (1)	Freight Per Order	Net Delivered Cost Per Order	Average Inventory (2)	Annual Carrying Cost (3)	Annual Storage Cost	Annual Order Placing and Receiving Cost (4)	Total Annual Cost (5)
1	36	$ 480	$ 20	$ 500	$ 250	$ 50	$12	$1,080	$19,142
2	18	960	40	1,000	500	100	24	540	18,664
3	12	1,440	60	1,500	750	150	36	360	18,546
4	9	1,920	80	2,000	1,000	200	48	270	18,518*
5	7.2	2,400	100	2,500	1,250	250	60	216	18,526
6	6	2,880	120	3,000	1,500	300	72	180	18,552

Notes:

(1) List price per gross $800
    Less 40% trade discount   320
    Net cost per gross $480

(2) Average inventory = $\dfrac{\text{Beginning} + \text{ending inventory}}{2}$

(3) Insurance and taxes   12%
    Imputed interest   8%
    Total   20% × average inventory

(4) Order cost $10
    Receiving cost 20
    Total $30 × orders per year
    _____

(5) Orders per year × net delivered cost per order =
    $18,000 + annual carrying cost + annual storage
    cost + annual order placing and receiving cost

Proof by formula (not required):

Let $Q = \sqrt{\dfrac{2UO}{C}}$

where   Q = economic order quantity
         U = annual quantity required
         O = cost of placing and receiving an order
         C = cost of carrying one unit in stock for one year

therefore $Q = \sqrt{\dfrac{2(36)(\$10 + \$20)}{(.08 + .12)(\$480 + \$20) + \$12}} = 4.4$ gross

round down to 4 gross

*Economic order quantity is at point of least total annual cost (this is also the point where annual carrying and storage costs are approximately equal to annual order placing and receiving costs).

B.

Kaufman Corporation
Computation of Minimum Stock Reorder Point for Komtronics

Average daily usage = $\dfrac{5{,}184 \text{ annual usage}}{259 \text{ working days}}$ = 20 per day.

Normal lead time = 20 working days

Average lead-period usage: 20 × 20 =	400 units	(A)
Maximum daily usage	28 per day	
Less average daily usage	20	
Excess above average	8 per day	
Normal lead time	20 days	
Safety stock	160 units	(B)
Average lead-period usage	400 units	(A)
Safety stock	160 units	(B)
Minimum stock order point (based on reasonable maximum usage prior to receipt of newly-ordered stock)	560 units	

C.

Computation of Cost of a Stockout of Komtronics

Excess cost for local purchase of one gross (Note A):		
List price locally per gross	$800	
Kaufman's net delivered cost per gross ($480 + $20)	500	
Excess cost for one gross	300	
Order and receiving cost	30	
Total cost first five days of stockout		$330
Extra cost for rush orders:		
Extra freight and order costs for each order	52	
Order and receiving cost	30	
Extra cost per order each additional five days	82	
Number of potential extra orders (Note B)	× 3	
Total extra cost for rush order		246
Total potential cost of stockout		$576

Note A: One gross purchased on a local basis will be sufficient as rush order will be received in five working days and maximum usage in a five-day period is 140 units (5 × 28).

Note B: 28 units × 20 days = 560 ÷ 144 = 3.9 gross maximum requirement during the 20-day period which must elapse before normal delivery of a regular order can be received. However, since 1 gross must be purchased locally, only 2.9 gross need be ordered by air freight, but the order must be rounded up to 3 gross because only full gross lots are obtainable.

Not required:

Cost of carrying ample stock to prevent stockout is $62* × 4 gross = $248.

*Annual carrying cost of $50 per gross plus storage cost of $12 per gross.

VI—Q7. Economic Order Quantity, Reorder Point, Problems in Applying EOQ (CMA)

The Robney Company is a restaurant supplier which sells a number of products to various restaurants in the area. One of their products is a special meat cutter with a disposable blade.

The blades are sold in packages of 12 blades for $20 per package. After a number of years, it has been determined that the demand for the replacement blades is at a constant rate of 2,000 packages per month. The packages cost the Robney Company $10 each from the manufacturer and require a three-day lead time from date of order to date of delivery. The ordering cost is $1.20 per order and the carrying cost is 10% per annum.

Robney is going to use the economic order quantity formula:

$$EOQ = \sqrt{\frac{2 \text{ (Annual Requirements) (Cost per Order)}}{\text{(Price per Unit) (Carrying Cost)}}}$$

Required

A.   Calculate:
   1.   The economic order quantity.
   2.   The number of orders needed per year.
   3.   The total cost of buying and carrying blades for the year.

B.   Assuming there is no reserve (e.g., safety stock), and that the present inventory level is 200 packages, when should the next order be placed? (Use 360 days equals one year.)

C.   Discuss the problems that most firms would have in attempting to apply this formula to their inventory problems.

VI—Q8. Inventory Control (CPA)

1.   A company places orders for inventory with its suppliers for a certain item for which the order size is determined in advance as:

$$\frac{\text{Order}}{\text{Size}} = \sqrt{\frac{2 \times \frac{\text{Cost to Place}}{\text{One Order}} \times \frac{\text{Demand per}}{\text{Period}}}{\frac{\text{Cost to Hold One Unit}}{\text{for One Period}}}}$$

All orders are the same size. When the policy is implemented, demand per period is only one-half what was expected when order size was computed. Consequently, actual total inventory cost will be

a. Larger than if the expected demand per period had occurred, and larger than if the actual demand per period had been used to calculate order size.
b. Larger than if the expected demand per period had occurred, and smaller than if the actual demand per period had been used to calculate order size.
c. Smaller than if the expected demand per period had occurred, and larger than if the actual demand per period had been used to calculate order size.
d. Smaller than if the expected demand per period had occurred, and smaller than if the actual demand per period had been used to calculate order size.

2. The following data refer to various annual costs relating to the inventory of a single-product company:

	Cost Per Unit
Transportation-in on purchases	$.20
Storage	.12
Insurance	.10

	Total Per Year
Interest that could have been earned on alternate investment of funds	$800
Units required	10,000

What is the annual carrying cost per unit?
a. $.22
b. $.30
c. $.42
d. $.50

3. A business determines its inventory policy using the economic-order-quantity model that allows a finite stockout cost per period and back ordering. Which one of the following statements accurately describes that stockout cost?

a. The stockout cost will have to be accumulated in a special account for comparison with expected stockout cost.
b. The smaller the stockout cost, the more often stockout will occur.
c. The larger the stockout cost, the more often stockout will occur.
d. The smaller the stockout cost, the larger will be the average amount of inventory on hand.

Items 4 and 5 are based on the following information: Expected annual usage of a particular raw material is 2,000,000 units, and the standard order size is 10,000 units. The invoice cost of each unit is $500, and the cost to place one purchase order is $80.

4.   The average inventory is
    a.   1,000,000 units
    b.   5,000 units
    c.   10,000 units
    d.   7,500 units

5.   The estimated annual order cost is
    a. $16,000
    b. $100,000
    c. $32,000
    d. $50,000

VI—Q9. PERT and Critical Path (CPA Adapted)*

A construction company has contracted to complete a new building and has asked for assistance in analyzing the project. Using the Program Evaluation Review Technique (PERT), the following network has been developed:

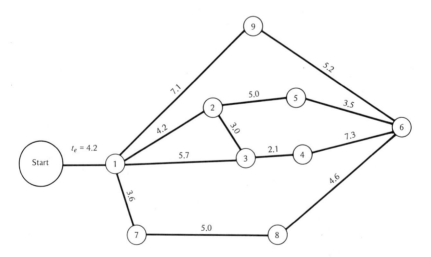

All paths from the start point to the finish point, event 6, represent activities or processes that must be completed before the entire project, the

---

* See the PERT(PERT/Time) editors' note, p. 495.

building, will be completed. The numbers above the paths or line segments represent expected completion times for the activities or processes. The expected time is based upon the commonly used, 1-4-1, three-estimate method. For example, the three-estimate method gives an estimated time of 4.2 to complete event 1.

1. The critical path (the path requiring the greatest amount of time) is
   a.   1-2-5-6
   b.   1-2-3-4-6
   c.   1-3-4-6
   d.   1-7-8-6
   e.   1-9-6

2. Slack time on path 1-9-6 equals
   a.   4.3
   b.   2.8
   c.   .9
   d.   .4
   e.   0

3. The latest time for reaching event 6 via path 1-2-5-6 is
   a.   20.8
   b.   19.3
   c.   17.4
   d.   16.5
   e.   12.7

4. The earliest time for reaching event 6 via path 1-2-5-6 is
   a.   20.8
   b.   16.9
   c.   16.5
   d.   12.7
   e.   3.5

5. If all other paths are operating on schedule, but path segment 7-8 has an unfavorable time variance of 1.9
   a.   The critical path will be shortened
   b.   The critical path will be eliminated
   c.   The critical path will be unaffected
   d.   Another path will become the critical path
   e.   The critical path will have an increased time of 1.9

6. Discuss the dimensions added to the PERT technique by the PERT/Cost resource allocation procedure (Articles 32 and 33).

VI—Q10. Matrix Operations (CPA)

1. Assume the following per unit raw material and labor requirements for the production of products A and B.

	Product A	Product B
Pounds of lead	5	7
Hours of labor	3	4

    Assuming that 13,400 pounds of lead and 7,800 hours of labor are available, the production of products A and B required to use all of the available lead and labor hours is shown in the following final Gaussian tableau.

    $$\begin{array}{cc|cc|c} 1 & 0 & -4 & 7 & 1{,}000 \\ 0 & 1 & 3 & -5 & 1{,}200 \end{array}$$

    If the available amounts were increased to 15,000 pounds of lead and 8,800 hours of labor, the matrix operation to determine the production schedule which would fully utilize these resources is

    a. $\begin{pmatrix} 5 & 7 \\ 3 & 4 \end{pmatrix} \begin{pmatrix} 15{,}000 \\ 8{,}800 \end{pmatrix}$

    b. $\begin{pmatrix} 15{,}000 \\ 8{,}800 \end{pmatrix} \begin{pmatrix} -4 & 7 \\ 3 & -5 \end{pmatrix}$

    c. $\begin{pmatrix} -4 & 7 \\ 3 & -5 \end{pmatrix} \begin{pmatrix} 1{,}000 \\ 1{,}200 \end{pmatrix}$

    d. $\begin{pmatrix} -4 & 7 \\ 3 & -5 \end{pmatrix} \begin{pmatrix} 15{,}000 \\ 8{,}800 \end{pmatrix}$

    e. None of the above

2. Dancy, Inc. is going to begin producing a new chemical cleaner. It will be produced by combining alcohol, peroxide and enzyme. Each quart of the new cleaner will require $\frac{1}{2}$ quart of alcohol, one quart of peroxide and $\frac{1}{3}$ quart of enzyme. The costs per quart are 40¢ for alcohol, 60¢ for peroxide and 20¢ for enzyme. The matrix operation to determine the cost of producing one quart of cleaner is

    a. $(\frac{1}{2},\ 1,\ \frac{1}{3}) \begin{pmatrix} .40 \\ .60 \\ .20 \end{pmatrix}$

    b. $\begin{pmatrix} \frac{1}{2} \\ 1 \\ \frac{1}{3} \end{pmatrix} \begin{pmatrix} .40 \\ .60 \\ .20 \end{pmatrix}$

    c. $(\frac{1}{2},\ 1,\ \frac{1}{3})\ (.40,\ .60,\ .20)$

    d. $\begin{pmatrix} .40 \\ .60 \\ .20 \end{pmatrix} (\frac{1}{2},\ 1,\ \frac{1}{3})$

    e. None of the above

VI—Q11.

Given the following $A \mid I \mid b = \begin{pmatrix} 4 & 2 & 1 & 0 & 20 \\ 6 & 8 & 0 & 1 & 60 \end{pmatrix}$ determine the inverse matrix or A^{-1} and the solution values.

VI—Q12. An Application of Matrix Algebra for Full Costing Purposes— Cost Allocation of Service Department Costs (CPA)

A manufacturer's plant has two service departments (designated below as S_1 and S_2) and three production departments (designated below as P_1, P_2, and P_3) and wishes to allocate all factory overhead to production departments. A primary distribution of overhead to all departments has already been made and is indicated below. The company makes the secondary distribution of overhead from service departments to production departments on a reciprocal basis, recognizing the fact that services of one service department are utilized by another. Data regarding costs and allocation percentages are as follows:

SERVICE DEPARTMENT OVERHEAD COST ALLOCATION

Service Department	Percentages to Be Allocated to Departments				
	S_1	S_2	P_1	P_2	P_3
S_1	0%	10%	20%	40%	30%
S_2	20	0	50	10	20
	Primary Overhead to be Allocated				
	$98,000	$117,600	$1,400,000	$2,100,000	$640,000

Matrix algebra is to be used in the secondary allocation process. The amount of overhead to be allocated to the service departments you express in two simultaneous equations as:

$$S_1 = 98,000 + .20S_2 \text{ or } S_1 - .20S_2 = \$ 98,000$$
$$S_2 = 117,600 + .10S_1 \text{ or } S_2 - .10S_1 = \$117,600$$

1. The system of simultaneous equations above may be stated in matrix form as

a.
$$\begin{array}{ccc} A & S & b \\ \begin{bmatrix} 1 & -.20 \\ -.10 & 1 \end{bmatrix} & \begin{bmatrix} S_1 \\ S_2 \end{bmatrix} = & \begin{bmatrix} \$ \ 98,000 \\ \$117,600 \end{bmatrix} \end{array}$$

b.
$$\begin{array}{ccc} A & S & b \\ \begin{bmatrix} 1 & \$ \ 98,000 \\ -.20 & \$117,600 \end{bmatrix} & \begin{bmatrix} 1 \\ -.10 \end{bmatrix} \begin{bmatrix} S_1 \\ S_2 \end{bmatrix} = & \begin{bmatrix} \$ \ 98,000 \\ \$117,600 \end{bmatrix} \end{array}$$

c.

$$\begin{array}{cc} & A \\ \begin{bmatrix} 1 \\ -.20 \end{bmatrix} & \begin{matrix} S_1 \\ S_2 \end{matrix} \end{array} \begin{bmatrix} 1 \\ -.10 \end{bmatrix} \begin{bmatrix} S_1 \\ S_2 \end{bmatrix} = \begin{array}{c} b \\ \begin{bmatrix} \$\ 98,000 \\ \$117,600 \end{bmatrix} \end{array}$$

d.

$$\begin{array}{cc} & A \\ \begin{bmatrix} 1 \\ -.20 \end{bmatrix} & \begin{matrix} 1 \\ -.10 \end{matrix} \begin{matrix} S_1 \\ S_2 \end{matrix} \end{array} \begin{bmatrix} S_1 \\ S_2 \end{bmatrix} = \begin{array}{c} b \\ \begin{bmatrix} \$\ 98,000 \\ \$117,600 \end{bmatrix} \end{array}$$

2. For the correct matrix A in item 1, there exists a unique inverse matrix A^{-1}. Multiplication of the matrix A^{-1} by the matrix A will produce
    a. The matrix A
    b. Another inverse matrix
    c. The correct solution to the system
    d. An identity matrix

3. Without prejudice to your previous answers, assume that the correct matrix form in item 1 was:

$$\begin{array}{cc} A \\ \begin{bmatrix} 1 & -.20 \\ -.10 & 1 \end{bmatrix} \end{array} \begin{bmatrix} S_1 \\ S_2 \end{bmatrix} = \begin{array}{c} b \\ \begin{bmatrix} \$\ 98,000 \\ \$117,600 \end{bmatrix} \end{array} .$$

    Then the correct inverse matrix A^{-1} is

    a. $\begin{bmatrix} \dfrac{1}{.98} & \dfrac{.20}{.98} \\ \dfrac{.10}{.98} & \dfrac{1}{.98} \end{bmatrix}$

    b. $\begin{bmatrix} \dfrac{1}{.98} & \dfrac{1}{.98} \\ \dfrac{.20}{.98} & \dfrac{.10}{.98} \end{bmatrix}$

    c. $\begin{bmatrix} \dfrac{1}{.30} & \dfrac{.20}{.30} \\ \dfrac{.10}{.30} & \dfrac{1}{.30} \end{bmatrix}$

    d. $\begin{bmatrix} \dfrac{1}{.98} & -\dfrac{1}{.98} \\ -\dfrac{.20}{.98} & \dfrac{.10}{.98} \end{bmatrix}$

4. The total amount of overhead allocated to department S_1 after receiving the allocation from department S_2 is
    a. $141,779
    b. $124,000
    c. $121,520
    d. $117,600

5.   The total amount of overhead allocated to department S_2 after receiving the allocation from department S_1 is
   a. $392,000
   b. $220,000
   c. $130,000
   d. $127,400

6.   Without prejudice to your previous answers, assume that the answer to item 4 is $100,000 and to item 5 is $150,000; then the total amount of overhead allocated to production department P_1 would be
   a. $1,508,104
   b. $1,495,000
   c. $1,489,800
   d. $108,104

VI—Q13. Application of First and Second Derivatives for a Profit Maximization Problem (CPA)

MacKenzie Park sells its trivets for $.25 per unit, and during 19_9 reported net sales of $500,000 and net income of $35,000. Production capacity is limited to 15,000 trivets per day and trivets are produced 300 days each year. Variable costs are $.10 per trivet.

The company does not maintain an inspection system, but has an agreement to reimburse the wholesaler $.50 for each defective unit the wholesaler finds. The wholesaler uses a method of inspection which detects all defective units. The number of defective units in each lot of 300 units is equal to the daily unit production rate divided by 200.

Letting X = daily production in units, select the best answer for each of questions 1 through 5.

1.   The number of defective units per day could be expressed
   a. $\dfrac{X}{60,000}$
   b. $\left(\dfrac{200}{X}\right)\left(\dfrac{X}{300}\right)$
   c. $\dfrac{X}{500}$
   d. $\dfrac{X^2}{60,000}$

2.   The equation to compute the maximum daily contribution to profit, including the reimbursement to the wholesaler for defective units, could be expressed

a. $.25X - .10X - .50 \left(\dfrac{X}{60,000} \right)$

b. $.25X - .10X - .50 \left(\dfrac{X^2}{60,000} \right)$

c. $.25X - .10X - \dfrac{X^2}{60,000} - \dfrac{125,000}{300}$

d. $.25X - .10X - \dfrac{X}{60,000} - 125,000$

3.   The first derivative of the equation to determine the number of units to maximize daily profits could be expressed

a. $.25 - .10 - \dfrac{X}{60,000}$

b. $.10 - .25 - \dfrac{X^2}{60,000}$

c. $\dfrac{X^2}{60,000}$

d. $\dfrac{X}{(200)\,(300)}$

4.   The second derivative of the equation to determine the number of units to be produced daily to maximize profits would be

a. $\dfrac{1}{(200)\,(300)}$

b. $\$.25 - \$.10 - \dfrac{1}{60,000} - \$125,000$

c. $\dfrac{\$125,000}{60,000}$

d. $- \dfrac{1}{60,000}$

5.   To maximize profits, the results of the equation to determine the daily contribution margin of MacKenzie Park Co. should yield
a.   Negative first derivative and a positive second derivative
b.   Positive first derivative and a negative second derivative
c.   Negative first and second derivatives
d.   Positive first and second derivatives

VI—Q14. Second Derivative Test; Integral (CPA)

1. A second derivative that is positive and large at a critical point indicates
    a.   An important maximum
    b.   An unimportant maximum
    c.   An important minimum
    d.   An unimportant minimum
    e.   None of the above

2. The integral of a marginal cost function is a function for
    a.   Average cost
    b.   Marginal cost
    c.   Total cost
    d.   Fixed cost
    e.   None of the above

VI—Q15. Derivatives and Optimal Quantity of Goods to Produce Per Production Run to Minimize Production and Inventory Carrying Costs (CPA)

A manufacturer expects to produce 200,000 widgets during the year ending June 30, 19_2 to supply a demand which is uniform throughout the year. The setup cost for each production run of widgets is $144 and the variable cost of producing each widget is $5. The cost of carrying one widget in inventory is $.20 per year. After a batch of widgets is produced and placed in inventory, it is sold at a uniform rate, and inventory is exhausted when the next batch of widgets is completed.

Management wishes an equation to describe the above situation and determine the optimal quantity of widgets to produce in each run in order to minimize total production and inventory carrying costs.

Let c = Total annual cost of producing and carrying widgets in inventory.

X = Number of widgets to be produced in each production run.

1. The number of production runs to be made in fiscal year 19_2
    could be expressed as
    a.   200,000 + 144X
    b.   200,000 + X
    c.   200,000
    d. $\dfrac{200,000}{X}$
    e. $\dfrac{X}{200,000}$

2. Total setup costs for fiscal year 19_2 could be expressed as
    a. $\$144\left(\dfrac{200,000}{X}\right)$
    b. $\dfrac{\$200,000}{X}$
    c. $\$144X$
    d. $\dfrac{\$144X}{200,000}$
    e. $\dfrac{\$144}{200,000} - \$X$

3. Total cost of carrying inventory during fiscal year 19_2 could
    be expressed as
    a. $\$.20\ (\$144X)$
    b. $\$.20X$
    c. $\$.20\left(\dfrac{200,000}{X}\right)$
    d. $\$.20\left(\dfrac{X}{2}\right)$
    e. $\$.20\left(\dfrac{\$144X}{200,000}\right)$

4. The derivative, $\dfrac{dc}{dx}$, of the equation to determine the optimal
    quantity of widgets which should be produced during each
    production run in fiscal year 19_2 is
    a. $-28,800,000\ X^{-2} + \dfrac{.20}{2}$
    b. $-144(200,000)\ X^{-1} + \dfrac{.20}{2}$
    c. $-28,800,000\ X^2 + 1,000,000 + \dfrac{.20}{2}$
    d. $-28,800,000\ X + \dfrac{.20}{2}$
    e. $-28,800,000\ X$

5. The quantity of widgets (to the nearest whole number) which should be produced in each run in fiscal year 19_2 to minimize total costs is
    a. 19,000
    b. 17,000
    c. 16,000
    d. 12,480
    e. 12,000

VI—Q16. Linear Programming and the Computer

The solution of the following simple product-mix problem for the Tri-Product Company demonstrates the use of linear programming, sensitivity analysis, and the computer. As simple as this problem may seem, realize that it would be extremely difficult to solve by trial and error methods.

The Tri-Product Company is presently producing three products, X, Y, and Z. The company is small and can sell all of any product it produces without affecting the sales price; the volume of its purchases will not affect the cost prices. The relevant factors or limitations are as follows:

1. *Sales price.* X = $30, Y = $20, Z = $11. The objective is to find a combination of X, Y, and Z that will maximize profit and remain within the limiting factors.

2. *Production time.* The company employs ten men who each work 40 hours a week. This means the maximum labor time is 400 hours a week. The time required to produce a finished product is: X = 2 hours, Y = 1 hour, Z = ½ hour.

3. *Storage space.* The plant has 1,500 square feet of storage space for raw materials and completed goods inventories. Due to trade custom, purchase and sales shipments are made weekly; therefore, goods are normally on hand for one week from the time received as raw material until shipped out as completed goods. The products require the same amount of storage space in the raw material state as they do when completed. Space required per unit is: X = 5 square feet, Y = 2 square feet, Z = 10 square feet.

4. *Cost and financing.* The financial situation of the company limits the direct cost outlay to $1,650 per week. The direct cost per product is: X = $7, Y = $4, Z = $3.

Required

A.   Prepare the objective function and the constraints.

B.   Determine the solution which will provide the maximum profit contribution. (See Exhibit 1 for the linear programming solution.) The solution printout shows the firm should produce 400 units of variable 2 (variable Y), and zero units of variables X and Z, to realize a profit of $6,400. This is the largest profit contribution that can be realized within the restrictions specified. It also indicates that the storage required will be 700 square feet less than the limit (slack variable 5 equals 700) and that the cost outlay will be $50 less than the limit (slack variable 6 equals 50). However, the production time is used to the maximum (slack variable 4 equals zero) and is the only restriction factor which is limiting the profits.
    We can verify these conclusions by substituting the solution in the restrictive equations as follows:

1. $2X$ $+$ $1Y$ $+$ $.5Z$ $= 400$
        $(2*0)$ $+ (1*400)$ $+$ $(.5*0)$ $= 400$ hours

2. $5X$ $+$ $2Y$ $+$ $10Z$ $= 1500$ sq. ft.
        $(5*0)$ $+ (2*400)$ $+$ $(10*0)$ $\leqslant$ 800
                                     Slack $=$ 700

3. $7X$ $+$ $4Y$ $+$ $3Z$ $\leqslant \$1650$
        $(7*0)$ $+ (4*400)$ $+$ $(3*0)$ $=$ 1600
                                     Slack $=$ $\$50$

4. $23X$ $+$ $16Y$ $+$ $8Z$ $=$ Profit contribution
        $(23*0)$ $+ (16*400)$ $+$ $(8*0)$ $=$ $\$6400$

C.   Sensitivity Analysis. (See Exhibit 2.) Determine the effect of the following possible prediction errors.
    1.   The cost of variable Y increases by 10% from $4.00 to $4.40
    2.   The production time of Y increases by 10%
    3.   The price of variable X increases from $30 to $37 or the cost is reduced by $7
    4.   The cost of Y increases by $.20 or the price decreases by $.20
    5.   The profit contribution of variable Z is increased to $10 from $8
    Exhibit 2 presents an example of the effect on the solution of varying the profit contribution of variable Y—question 1 above.

Shadow Prices. (See Exhibit 3.) In this problem, the restrictions on the production process are the 400 direct labor hours, the 1,500 square feet, and the $1,650. Shadow prices are measures of the profit lost because of these bottlenecks in the production process. In our first solution (see Exhibit 1), we had 700 square feet of storage and $50 unused. The bottleneck was the production time; we used all of the 400 hours (ten employees working 40 hours per week). Thus, our profit contribution is restricted by the limited number of direct labor hours available. If we had one more direct labor hour, we could produce one more unit of Y and increase our profit contribution by $16.

The shadow price of the direct labor hour restriction is $16. The shadow price represents the value per unit of an increment in each of the resources that is scarce in the solution to the problem. In this case, it would appear desirable to increase the number of direct labor hours available, if possible, to realize an increased profit.

Exhibit 3 verifies the above conclusion and demonstrates the use of a computer program (LPS) to determine the shadow prices of restricted resources and to evaluate the desirability of easing a particular bottleneck in the production process.

The job of the manager is to allocate scarce resources to the best possible uses. Linear programming with sensitivity analysis aids the manager in performing this function of optimizing decisions to provide the maximum profit contribution from the available resources.

Exhibit 1. The Linear Programming Solution

```
RUN LPS[10,9]
LINEAR PROGRAMMING AND SENSITIVITY ANALYSIS

DO YOU WANT INSTRUCTIONS? NO

ENTER THE NUMBER OF RESTRICTION EQUATIONS — ? 3
ENTER THE NUMBER OF VARIABLES — ? 3
HOW MANY RESTRICTIVE EQUATIONS WITH THE LESS THAN SYMBOL — ? 3
HOW MANY RESTRICTIVE EQUATIONS WITH THE EQUALS SYMBOL —
? 0
HOW MANY RESTRICTIVE EQUATIONS WITH GREATER THAN SYMBOLS — ? 0
```

ENTER 3 VALUES FOR RESTRICTION EQUATION # 1 (LEFT-HAND SIDE OF THE
2,1,.5   EQUATION)
ENTER 3 VALUES FOR RESTRICTION EQUATION # 2 (LEFT-HAND SIDE OF THE
5,2,10   EQUATION)
ENTER 3 VALUES FOR RESTRICTION EQUATION # 3 (LEFT-HAND SIDE OF THE
7,4,3   EQUATION)

ENTER THE 3 RESTRICTION VALUES FOR THE 3 EQUATIONS
400,1500,1650   (RIGHT-HAND SIDE OF THE EQUATION)

APPENDIX B

ENTER THE COEFFICIENTS OF THE OBJECTIVE FUNCTION
ENTER 3 FUNCTION VALUES:
23,16,8

COLUMN STATISTICS:
YOUR VARIABLES 1 THROUGH 3
SLACK VARIABLES 4 THROUGH 6

ANSWERS:

VARIABLE	VALUE
2	400
5	700
6	50

Conclusion: The optimum solution is to produce 400 units of variable 2 (Y) with a resulting profit contribution of $6400.

OBJECTIVE FUNCTION VALUE   6400

DUAL VARIABLES:

COLUMN	VALUE
4	16
5	0
6	0

Tableau Printout for the Problem

The initial tableau (tableau after 0 iterations) supplied by the LPS computer program, and the optimal tableau (tableau after 2 iterations) are shown below. Compare the optimal tableau printout with the solutions (answers) printout above.

DATA TABLE

TABLEAU AFTER 0 ITERATIONS

2	1	.5	1	0	0	400
5	2	10	0	1	0	1500
7	4	3	0	0	1	1650
-23	-16	-8	0	0	0	0

BASIS BEFORE ITERATION 1

VARIABLE	VALUE
4	400
5	1500
6	1650

OBJECTIVE FUNCTION VALUE   0

TABLEAU AFTER 2 ITERATIONS

2	1	.5	1	0	0	400
1	0	9	-2	1	0	700
-1	0	1	-4	0	1	50
9	0	0	16	0	0	6400

Exhibit 2. Sensitivity Analysis

Sensitivity analysis allows the user to change a variable and determine how sensitive the solution is to this change. It allows the user to ask questions of the type: "What if?" For example, what if the actual direct manufacturing cost of product Y was $4.40 instead of $4, would the solution still be the same? In other words, how accurate must our estimation of the direct manufacturing cost be for the solution to remain the same?

For linear programming to be useful in a practical sense, we must determine the effect on the solution of any minor change in any of the variables. Sensitivity analysis allows us to determine which estimates of the relevant factors are most important and require our best efforts.

After our initial solution to the problem, as presented in Exhibit 1, the program we call LPS will ask the user: "Do you wish to do sensitivity analysis (Y/N)?" If we answer yes (Y), the program will display all the variables indicating the row and column of a matrix in which the variable is stored. The program will then allow the user to change any variable, by entering the row, column, and new amount of the variable, to determine a new solution to the problem. The user may change one variable or more, and the program will present a new solution to the problem.

The printout below presents an example of the effect on the solution of varying the profit contribution of variable Y. (Part C, question 1.)

DO YOU WISH TO DO SENSITIVITY ANALYSIS Y/N? Y

ROW	COLUMN	AMOUNT
0	1	2
0	2	1
0	3	.5
0	4	1
0	7	400
1	1	5
1	2	2
1	3	10
1	5	1
1	7	1500
2	1	7
2	2	4
2	3	3
2	6	1
2	7	1650
3	1	-23
3	2	-16
3	3	-8

Row 0 refers to constraint equation 1; the row 0 column amounts 2, 1, .5, 1 and 400 refer respectively to the coefficients for X, Y, Z, slack, and to the amount on the right-hand side of the equation. Note that constraint equation 1 is really an inequality, i.e., ≤ 400 hours and adding the slack variable turns it into an equality used in obtaining an algebraic or a computer solution; the slack variable coefficient is 1. Rows 1 and 2 and the column amounts for those rows refer to constraint equations 2 and 3 respectively. The column amounts for row 3 refer to the coefficients of the objective function. Note that the computer routine results in placing a minus sign in front of the objective function coefficients of 23, 16 and 8. The minus sign results from the fact that the objective function is converted into an equation by adding a value for total contribution. Therefore, $-23X - 16Y - 8Z + V = 0$ (objective function).

ENTER THE ROW, COLUMN, AMOUNT OF THE VARIABLE YOU WISH TO CHANGE
? 3,2,–15.60

ANSWERS:

Conclusion: If the cost of variable Y increases by
10% (from $4.00 to $4.40), or if the price of
variable Y decreases by 2% (from $20 to $19.60),
the profit contribution of Y will be $15.60 and
the optimum solution will be to produce 375
units of Y and 50 units of Z with a resulting profit
of $6250. Thus, the solution is very sensitive to a
small change in cost or price of variable Y.

VARIABLE	VALUE
2	375
5	250
3	50

OBJECTIVE FUNCTION VALUE   6250

DUAL VARIABLES:

COLUMN	VALUE
4	14.8
5	0
6	.2

Exhibit 3. Shadow Prices

DO YOU WISH TO DO SENSITIVITY ANALYSIS Y/N? Y

ROW	COLUMN	AMOUNT
0	1	2
0	2	1
0	3	.5
0	4	1
0	7	400
1	1	5
1	2	2
1	3	10
1	5	1
1	7	1500
2	1	7
2	2	4
2	3	3
2	6	1
2	7	1650
3	1	–23
3	2	–16
3	3	–8

ENTER THE ROW, COLUMN, AMOUNT OF THE VARIABLE YOU WISH TO CHANGE
? 0,7,401

ANSWERS:

VARIABLE	VALUE
2	401
5	698
6	46

OBJECTIVE FUNCTION VALUE   6416

DUAL VARIABLES:

COLUMN	VALUE
4	16
5	0
6	0

Conclusion: The production resource that is restricting the profits of the company is the production time. The company employs ten men, who each work forty hours a week, a total of 400 production hours are available. If the production time is increased 1 hour to 401 hours, the profits will increase from $6400 to $6416. Thus, the loss in potential profits by not having that one additional hour of production time is $16. The shadow price of the production time restriction is $16 per hour (dual variables column 4).

Therefore, it would appear desirable to hire an additional employee or have employees work overtime to provide additional production time and to increase profits. This may be done until we meet the limits of the second most important restriction, the cost outlay of $1650. Since there is a slack of $46 in the cost outlay, and production requires $4 per unit of Y, we could produce 11 more units of Y with 11 more hours of production time and increase our profits $176.

VI—Q17. Comprehensive Problem Requiring the Use of a Computer—Review Problem in Planning Involving Linear Programming and Regression Analysis (Accounting Review Supplement to Vol. XLVI, pp. 229–231)

BAYVIEW MANUFACTURING COMPANY*

In November, 19_9, the Bayview Manufacturing Company was in the process of preparing its budget for the next year. As the first step, it prepared a pro forma income statement for 19_9 based on the first 10 months' operations and revised plans for the last two months. This income statement, in condensed form, was as follows:

*From the "Report of Committee on the Measurement Methods Content of the Accounting Curriculum." This problem is a considerably modified version of a problem originated by Professor Carl Nelson.

Sales		$3,000,000
Materials	$1,182,000	
Labor	310,000	
Factory overhead	775,000	
Selling and administrative	450,000	2,717,000
Net income before taxes		283,000

These results were better than were expected and operations were close to capacity, but Bayview's management was not convinced that demand would remain at present levels and hence had not planned any increase in plant capacity. Its equipment was specialized and made to its order; over a year's lead time was necessary on all plant additions.

Bayview produces three products; sales have been broken down by product, as follows:

100,000 of Product A @ $20.00	$2,000,000
40,000 of Product B @ 10.00	400,000
20,000 of Product C @ 30.00	600,000
	$3,000,000

Management has ordered a profit analysis for each product and has available the following information:

	A	B	C
Material	$ 7.00	$ 3.75	$16.60
Labor	2.00	1.00	3.50
Factory overhead	5.00	2.50	8.75
Selling and administrative	3.00	1.50	4.50
Total costs	$17.00	$ 8.75	$33.35
Selling price	20.00	10.00	30.00
Profit	$ 3.00	$ 1.25	($−3.35)

Factory overhead has been applied on the basis of direct labor costs at a rate of 250%; and management asserts that approximately 20% of the overhead is variable and does vary with labor costs. Selling and administrative costs have been allocated on the basis of sales at the rate of 15%; approximately one-half of this is variable and does vary with sales in dollars. All of the labor expense is considered to be variable.

As the first step in the planning process, the sales department has been asked to make estimates of what it could sell; these estimates have been reviewed by the firm's consulting economist and by top management. They are as follows:

A	130,000 units
B	50,000 units
C	50,000 units

Production of these quantities was immediately recognized as being impossible. Estimated cost data for the three products, each of which requires activity of both departments, were based on the following production rates:

| | Product | | |
	A	B	C
Department 1	2 per hour	4 per hour	3 per hour
Department 2	4 per hour	8 per hour	4/3 per hour

Practical capacity in Department 1 is 67,000 hours and in Department 2, 63,000 hours, and the industrial engineering department has concluded that this cannot be increased without the purchase of additional equipment. Thus, while last year Department 1 operated at 99% of its capacity, and Department 2 at 71% of capacity, anticipated sales would require operating both Department 1 and 2 at more than 100% capacity.

These solutions to the limited production problem have been rejected: (1) subcontracting the production out to other firms is considered to be unprofitable because of problems of maintaining quality; (2) operating a second shift is impossible because of shortage of labor; (3) operating overtime would create problems because a large number of employees are "moonlighting" and would therefore refuse to work more than the normal 40-hour week. Price increases have also been rejected; although they would result in higher profits this year, the long-run competitive position of the firm would be weakened resulting in lower profits in the future.

The treasurer then suggested that the Product C has been carried at a loss too long and that now was the time to eliminate it from the product line. If all facilities are used to produce A and B, profits would be increased.

The sales manager objected to this solution because of the need to carry a full line. In addition, he maintains that there is a group of customers who have provided and will continue to provide a solid base for the firm's activities, and these customers' needs must be met. He provided a list of these customers and their estimated purchases (in units) which total as follows:

A	80,000
B	32,000
C	12,000

It was impossible to verify these contentions, but they appeared to be reasonable and they served to narrow the bounds of the problem so that the president concurred.

The treasurer reluctantly acquiesced, but maintained that the remaining capacity should be used to produce A and B. Because A produced 2.4 times as much profit as B, he suggested that the production of A (in excess of the 80,000 minimum set by the sales manager) be 2.4 times that of B (in excess of the 32,000 minimum set by the sales manager).

The production manager made some quick calculations and said that this would result in budgeted production and sales of:

A	104,828
B	42,344
C	12,000

The treasurer then made a calculation of what profits would be as follows:

A	104,828 @ $3.00	$314,484
B	42,344 @ $1.25	52,930
C	12,000 @ ($−3.35)	(−40,200)
		$327,214

As this would represent an increase of almost 15% over the current year, there was a general feeling of self-satisfaction. Before final approval was given, however, the president said that he would like to have his new assistant check over the figures. Somewhat piqued, the treasurer agreed and at that point the group adjourned.

The next day the above information was submitted to you as your first assignment on your new job as the president's assistant. Prepare an analysis showing the president what he should do.

Exhibits A and B contain information that you are able to obtain from the accounting system.

Exhibit A

Department	Direct Labor Expense (000)			Overhead Expense (000)		
Year	1	2	Total	1	2	Total
19_9	$140	$170	$310	$341	$434	$775
19_8	135	150	285	340	421	762*
19_7	140	160	300	342	428	770
19_6	130	150	280	339	422	761
19_5	130	155	285	338	425	763
19_4	125	140	265	337	414	751
19_3	120	150	270	335	420	755
19_2	115	140	255	334	413	747
19_1	120	140	260	336	414	750
19_0	115	135	250	335	410	745

* rounding error

Exhibit B

Year	Prod. A	Prod. B	Sales (000) Prod. C	Total	Selling and Administrative Expense (000)
19_9	$2,000	$400	$600	$3,000	$450
19_8	1,940	430	610	2,980	445
19_7	1,950	380	630	2,960	445
19_6	1,860	460	620	2,940	438
19_5	1,820	390	640	2,850	433
19_4	1,860	440	580	2,880	437
19_3	1,880	420	570	2,870	438
19_2	1,850	380	580	2,810	434
19_1	1,810	390	580	2,780	430
19_0	1,770	290	610	2,670	425

Note: The following (trials 1–4) refer to the variable profit schedules shown in the problem solution.

Different variable profit (contribution margin) schedules can be determined for this problem.

Trial 1. Management's estimates of fixed and variable costs can be accepted and used in contribution margin determination. To aid us in determining whether management's estimates are correct (variable overhead is 50% of direct labor expenses in each department), we can use a simple linear regression analysis and determine an equation for overhead as a function of total direct labor dollars. The results of the analysis will indicate that management's estimates are in total accurate. Prepare the contribution margin schedules for each product.

Trial 2. You can consider the differing overhead experience in each department, and a regression analysis can be carried out for each of the departments using overhead for a department as the dependent variable and direct labor expenses for a department as the independent variable. Your analysis should result in departmental rates of 29% and 70% and these should be used in determining the variable overhead per product and new contribution margin schedules should be prepared.

Trial 3. The previous trials assumed that 50% of the selling and administration expenses were variable and that this percentage was the same for each product. Test this assumption by using simple regression analysis with total selling and administrative expenses as the dependent variable and total sales as the independent variable. This will indicate that slightly less than 50% of the selling and administrative expenses are variable. Then try a multiple regression analysis with total selling and administrative expenses as the dependent variable and total sales for each of the products as the independent variables. You should then evaluate the usefulness of this multiple regression equation for the problem; because the individual variables of the equation are needed in determining contribution margins, a check for multicollinearity should be made. For this purpose, a correlation matrix computer program can be used.* For the contribution margin schedules in trial 3, use management's estimate for variable overhead (from trial 1) and the results of the multiple regression (trial 3) for variable selling and administrative expenses. The selling price of each product is multiplied by the appropriate b from the regression equation to determine the variable selling and administrative expense for a product.

Trial 4. Use the variable overhead, as determined by the regression in trial 2, and the variable selling and administrative expenses, as determined by the multiple regression in trial 3, for the preparation of the contribution margin schedule for each product.

For each of the trials listed above, use a computer to obtain the linear programming solutions; determine the production plan to use and explain why that plan was selected. The treasurer had a plan so you could have five production plans to consider. However, the treasurer did not apply a legitimate optimization technique and for this reason the plan can be rejected.

---

* The correlation matrix shows:

VAR	1	2	3
1	1.000	.415	.087
2	.415	1.000	−.135
3	.087	−.135	1.000

The independent variables 1, 2, 3 represent total sales for products A, B and C respectively. The correlation coefficients of the independent variables are:

Product A vs. Product B = .41
Product A vs. Product C = .09
Product B vs. Product C = .14

The correlation coefficients are small enough so that multicollinearity is not a problem.

READING REFERENCES FOR QUESTION SOLUTION

Part I — Project Profit Planning (Articles 1-6 and Parts of Articles 9 and 11)
Introductory Discussion for Part I, pp. 2-4.

I-Q1 Articles 1 and 2
I-Q2 Articles 1 and 2
I-Q3 Articles 1 and 2
I-Q4 Contribution margin statement — Article 2, also see Article 1; Breakeven analysis — Article 9 (pp. 124-128), also see Article 11.
I-Q5 Article 1 (pp. 15-17)
I-Q6 Article 3 (pp 31-36) for the traditional cost accounting approach to the make or buy decision; the article applies linear programming to a make or buy decision, pp. 36-41.
I-Q7 Article 1 (pp. 17-18) for the decision without considering the time value of money. Part III questions include time value considerations.
I-Q8 Direct costing for inventory valuation — Article 9 (pp. 128-131); Variable cost pricing — Article 1 (pp. 7-12), Article 2 (p. 22), and Article 9 (pp. 128-131).
I-Q9 Articles 1 and 2 for Part 1; Part 2, pp. 133, 265-266, 305-306; Part 3, Article 5, also pp. 165-168 and payoff table to I-Q10.
I-Q10 Article 5, also Article 12 (pp. 165-168).
I-Q11 Contribution margin statements and dropping a product — Article 2; Adding a product that increases fixed cost, breakeven computation — Article 9 (p. 127), Article 11 (pp. 159-162).
I-Q12 Articles 1 and 2
I-Q13 Article 4
I-Q14 Article 6

Part II — Period Profit Planning (Articles 7-13)
Introductory Discussion for Part II, pp. 76-80

II-Q1 Part A — A solution is attached to the problem
Part B — Articles 7, 9, pp. 132-135, pp. 265-266, also see Article 8
II-Q2 Article 8
II-Q3 See the references for V-Q4
II-Q4 Article 7
II-Q5 Article 7 and Article 9 (p. 116 for background). A partial solution is attached to the problem. For the cash budget, Article 10 (pp. 132-138)
II-Q6 Article 9
II-Q7 Articles 7, 9
II-Q8 Article 9
II-Q9 Article 9, p. 385, pp. 7-12
II-Q10 pp. 7-12, Article 9
II-Q11 Article 10
II-Q12 Article 10
II-Q13 Article 9 (pp. 124-128), Article 11
II-Q14 Article 11 and the editors' note, pp. 593-594
II-Q15 Article 9 (pp. 124-128) Article 11
II-Q16 Part A — see the reference for II-Q15 and the solution for A.1 (pp. 596-597) as a guide to the solutions
Parts B and C — probability Article 5 and pp. 165-168; also see the solution to I-Q10, pp. 566-568
II-Q17 See the references for parts B and C of II-Q16
II-Q18 Same as for II-Q17
II-Q19 Probability — see the references for Parts B and C of II-Q16
Present value (part D of the problem) — see the present value discussion in Article 14, also see the editors' note to III-Q7, p. 616

II-Q20 Article 13
II-Q21 Article 10, also see p. 87 for an illustration of manufacturing relationships for cost of goods sold determination

Part III — Capital Budgeting (Articles 14-18)
  Introductory Discussion for Part III, pp. 193-195

III-Q1 Article 14
III-Q2 Article 14
III-Q3 A solution is attached to the problem, Article 14
III-Q4 See the solution to III-Q3
III-Q5 Article 14
III-Q6 A. Article 15
  B. Articles 16-18
III-Q7 Articles 4, 14 and the editors' note, p. 416
III-Q8 A solution is attached to the problem.
  A cost of capital computation is shown; see cost of capital pp. 194, 195n, 208, and computation 355-357, 620

Part IV — Forecasting (Articles 19-23)
  Introductory Discussion for Part IV, pp. 265-271

IV-Q1 Part A — A solution is attached to the problem
  Parts B and C — pp. 265-271, Article 20 (pp. 289-292)
IV-Q2 Article 20 (pp. 289-292)
IV-Q3 Article 20 (pp. 292-301)
IV-Q4 High-Low Method, Article 9 (pp. 119-120)
  Scattergraph and linear regression, Article 20
IV-Q5 Regression analysis and prediction — see the tests of the regression equation Article 20 (pp. 292-296), and see the editors' note for the problem, pp. 630-633
IV-Q6 Article 20 (pp. 292-296) and editors' note to IV-Q5 (pp. 630-633)
IV-Q7 Part 1 — see the editors' note to the problem pp. 637-638
  Parts 2-4, Article 19 (pp. 273-276)
IV-Q8 Article 20 and editors' note to IV-Q5
IV-Q9 Article 21 for a discussion of multiple regression applications and Article 22 for an explanation of the computer printout.
IV-Q10 Article 21 background, Article 22 for the computer printout explaination. Also see the explanation of a correlation matrix, p. 706
IV-Q11 pp. 270-272, Article 23 (pp. 332-335)
IV-Q12 See the references given for IV-Q11; for a discussion of the — .322 learning expression for an 80% learning rate see pp. 336, 340.

Part V — Performances Evaluation and Control (Articles 24-29)
  Introductory Discussion for Part V, pp. 345-350

V-Q1 Article 25, Article 2 (pp. 23-30)
V-Q2 Article 24
V-Q3 Article 24
V-Q4 pp. 115-116, Articles 24, 25, 8, pp. 372-375
V-Q5 Article 24
V-Q6 Article 8 (especially see pp. 98-99), pp. 9-10, 115-116, 123-124, Article 7, Article 25 (pp. 372-375), Article 26 (pp. 377-382)
V-Q7 p. 346, Article 25 (especially pp. 372-375), Article 26
V-Q8 Articles 27 and 28
V-Q9 Articles 27 and 28

SUBJECT INDEX – TEXT

SUBJECT INDEX – TEXT

SUBJECT INDEX – TEXT

SUBJECT INDEX – TEXT

SUBJECT INDEX – TEXT

SUBJECT INDEX - TEXT